P9-DTE-225

Stage Makeup

Widely referred to as the "bible of stage makeup," the timely revision of this classic text addresses principles and techniques in the use of makeup for the contemporary performer.

This extensive exploration of the application and use of stage makeup and makeup for a variety of performance venues covers all aspects in detail and contains over 1,000 photographs, drawings, and diagrams demonstrating step-by-step procedures. Thoroughly updated and revised, this classic text remains accurate and comprehensive, providing information from which all readers—whether students to the field or seasoned, professional makeup artists—will benefit.

New to this edition:

- Updated full-color photography throughout;
- Expanded information on makeup design and application;
- 48 new step-by-step instructions in color;
- Expanded chapter on modeling with highlights and shadows;
- New chapter on cross-gender makeup;
- New instruction on making dentures, noses, and face casting;
- New instructions for creating zombies, animals, aging effects, and trauma;
- Expanded information on makeup for television and film;
- Up-to-date information on Special Effects Makeup;
- Up-to-date information on prosthetic makeup;
- Updated chapters on facial hair and wigs;
- Updated resources for products, advanced training, and health and safety.

Richard Corson (late) was the author of several fashion and makeup books. He taught courses in theatrical makeup in several colleges across the United States. In 1972 he received the Founders Award (International Thespian Society) "in recognition of distinguished contributions to theatre and youth." His name is perhaps the most well-recognized in the industry.

James Glavan is the Professor of Costume Technology and Makeup at the University of Texas at Austin. He has worked at many of the great opera, ballet, and theater companies in the US, including the Santa Fe Opera, Seattle Opera, Minnesota Opera, Boston Opera, the Gunthrie Theatre, Hartford Stage, and the Hartford Ballet. For many years he worked as a puppet builder at Jim Henson Productions, Inc. in New York City. Internationally, he has taught costume, makeup, and animatronics in Taipei, Taiwan; Hong Kong; San Jose, Costa Rica; Shanghai, China; Medellin, Colombia; and Moscow, Russia.

Beverly Gore Norcross received her MFA in Costume Design from California State University, Fullerton. She freelanced in Los Angeles with IATSE Locals 705 and 768. Her academic posts have included Purdue University, San Joaquin Delta College and California State University, Fullerton. She has won a Daytime Emmy Certificate, American College Theatre Festival Award, and an Elly Award. Beverly is currently at Western Nevada College, IATSE Local 363, and her studio BelleVue Designs.

Stage Makeup

Eleventh Edition

Richard Corson
James Glavan
Beverly Gore Norcross

NEW YORK AND LONDON

Eleventh edition published 2019
by Routledge
52 Vanderbilt Avenue, New York, NY 10017

and by Routledge
2 Park Square, Milton Park, Abingdon, Oxon, OX14 4RN

Routledge is an imprint of the Taylor & Francis Group, an informa business

First edition published by Pearson Education, Inc 1942
Tenth edition published by Routledge 2016

Library of Congress Cataloging-in-Publication Data
A catalog record has been requested for this book

ISBN: 978-1-138-23258-7 (hbk)
ISBN: 978-0-367-18332-5 (pbk)
ISBN: 978-1-315-31221-7 (ebk)

Typeset in GillSans Std-Light
by Newgen Publishing UK

It is not often that avocation and vocation come together. Richard Carson was one of those fortunates who achieved that happy state while still a student.

A Phi Beta Kappa student at DePauw and Louisiana State Universities, he chose his interest in makeup as the subject of his Master's thesis. This innovative work became the first edition of his first book, *Stage Makeup.*

Immediately in demand as a teacher, Corson used classwork to hone his techniques. He became fascinated with new products and experimented with them, and the new techniques he devised led to subsequent editions.

Because hairstyle and wigs, beards, and mustaches were integral to a complete makeup, Corson created an appendix of sketches of hairstyles through the years to guide the actor. The sketches caught the eye of the distinguished British publishing house, Peter Owen Ltd, which commissioned an expanded version, a handbook to accompany *Stage Makeup.* The handbook, *Fashions in Hair: The First Five Thousand Years*, became a tome, the bible of hairdressers, stylists, and designers throughout the industry. Further explorations led to *Fashions in Eyeglasses*, which has been published in Japanese as well as English.

Corson's writing, however, never superseded teaching. Regular classwork gave way to seminars, workshops, and periodic engagements at major universities, always stressing in his thesis that a makeup should not be simply a painted mask but rather an integral part of an actor's performance.

Although Corson rarely worked as a makeup artist *per se*, he occasionally designed a production and supervised its execution. His credits include *The Passion of Joseph D.* with Peter Falk as Stalin, Tony Richardson's production of *Arturo Ui*, starring Christopher Plummer, and Stella Adler's production of *Johnny Johnson.* Individual actors frequently consulted him about specific makeup problems.

Throughout his career, Corson remained steadfast in his belief in the individuality of the actor and his performance: that there be no one Hamlet, Shylock, or Cyrano "look" and performance. He maintained that each actor should be as original in his appearance as in his characterization, thus making for an ever richer and more rewarding theater experience.

Richard Corson died on January 13, 1999. This eleventh edition of *Stage Makeup*—respectfully updated—will stand as a memorial to his career and his many accomplishments.

Mitchell Ericson

CONTENTS

ILLUSTRATIONS

FOREWORD

My love for makeup started in 1963 when I was seven years old. I used to watch old Universal Monster movies on television and it became a staple in my life. My brothers bought a copy of the book *Do-It-Yourself Monster Make-up Hand Book* by Dick Smith in 1966 for me and it became my go-to reference magazine until the fall of 1971 when my drama and English teacher introduced me to the fourth edition of *Stage Makeup* by Richard Corson. That book became my bible of makeup, my Holy Grail. In the book there were photos of the prosthetic makeup on Hal Holbrook as Mark Twain by my hero, the great Dick Smith. I was enthralled by the way he had made his molds, created the prosthetic appliances, and the application of the foam latex pieces. I was sold and knew then and there I wanted to become a professional makeup artist. That fourth edition of *Stage Makeup* is still in my library today, although it's a bit worse for wear now.

Cut to 1999, I received a call from Jim Glavan who was introduced to me by my mentor and teacher, Joe Blasco. Jim wanted to know if I would be interested in contributing to a book he was working on at the time. It just happened to be the ninth edition of *Stage Makeup*. I immediately said yes and was so excited that I would have a little part in the book that introduced me to the art of makeup. For the book, I created a gelatin prosthetic old age makeup. I began by making a face cast, then sculpted the character, made all the molds and then completed the final application.

I am so proud to be participating in this new, exciting all-color edition of *Stage Makeup*. I know there are many people out there like me who reminisce about which edition they learned from and were inspired by. My greatest hope is that this edition will be an introduction and provide encouragement to a new generation of young and talented makeup artists who will one day look back at this eleventh edition of *Stage Makeup* and remember it as the book that inspired them to enter this wonderful world of makeup.

Matthew W. Mungle

PREFACE

Stage Makeup is intended to be used as a text and as a reference by actors, and by anyone who might in some way be involved with the makeup, whether as a designer, a director, a makeup artist, or a teacher.

As a textbook, it can be used by individuals learning either on their own or in a workshop. Both methods have their advantages. In learning by yourself, it's possible to work at your own convenience and at your own speed, and to experiment with your own ideas and develop your own techniques. In a workshop that is not always possible. But a workshop does provide the advantage of not only having the guidance of a teacher but of seeing other students' work and learning from their successes and failures. If you are, or intend to be, an actor, it is important that you work on your own face rather than on someone else's. Only if you are planning to be a makeup artist or a teacher is it really useful to work on faces other than your own.

Whether you are working alone or in a group, taking photographs of your makeups will enable you to look at your work objectively. Students seriously interested in makeup as a profession would do well to take courses in freehand drawing and to spend some time in art museums, studying paintings and observing how different artists have achieved their effects. They should also train themselves to observe people wherever they go—not just casually, but analytically, noting color and texture of the skin and hair, conformation of the wrinkles, and size, shape, color, texture, and location of any blemishes. Students should also make note of any indications of a possible profession or type of work and general lifestyle.

Students would do well, if they have any talent for it at all, to take a course in acting to help them understand the actor's problems. And unless the student has the patience of a saint, the compassion of a doting mother, and the meticulous fingers of a jeweler, he or she might do well to consider choosing another profession.

R.C.

ACKNOWLEDGMENTS

We are extremely grateful to our new publisher, Focal Press, for their support of this completely updated full-color edition of *Stage Makeup*. Their enthusiasm to distribute color images throughout the book allowed us the opportunity to expand upon the many artistic and technical processes already located in the various chapters and the freedom to create many new step-by-step lessons using contemporary products and techniques. Our goals were to expand the scope of the book to include detailed lessons on makeup design and application, a new chapter on cross-gender makeup, expanded information on makeup for film and television, updated lessons on facial hair and wigs, and contemporary techniques and products used for nonrealistic, special effects and prosthetic character makeup.

Although the responsibility to keep this wonderful book current has been passed on to the next generation of artist/ teachers, it is our intention that the book retain Richard Corson's makeup techniques, theoretical approach, his spirit, and his voice. In an effort to maintain the high standard of quality instruction this book has enjoyed, we invited a number of individuals, including professional makeup artists, wig designers, performers, teachers, cosmetic company executives, world-class photographers, and theater companies, both national and international, to participate in the revision process. The level of enthusiasm was overwhelming. So many were thrilled and honored to share their expertise with the next generation of makeup students, teachers, and professionals. There was a unanimous expression of pride in the opportunity to give back to a book that had been their guide and inspiration for their own careers.

We are grateful to all of you: the actors—Chanel, Vanessa J. Lopez, Cristofer Jean, Jamie Ann Romero, and Britney Simpson for their kindness in permitting numerous photographs to be taken as they worked on their makeup for their current productions; Kelly Bland, Andrew Carlson, Jennifer Ekoki, John Haas, Joseph Harrington III, Tyler Hollin, Marika Klein, Connor Sullivan, and YuJung Shen for serving as models in demonstrations of makeup products and techniques; the makeup artists—Tara Cooper, Caleena Horn, Serret Jensen, Allison Lowery, and Jasmin Walsh for their time and enormous talent in providing live, in-studio makeup demonstrations; and Lisa Berczel, Megan Brantley, Raul Cuadra, Joe Dulude II, Nathan Jones, Olga Masurev, Rebecca Morgan, Alison Rainey, and Marie-Laurence Tessier for their generous contributions of photographs of their brilliant makeup designs; Dana Nye of Ben Nye Cosmetic Company and Claudia Longo of Kryolan Professional Makeup for their generous contributions of makeup products and support; to the theater companies and production companies that granted us permissions to use images from their productions—the Glyndebourne Festival, Stratford Festival, Oregon Shakespeare Festival, The Fugard Theatre of Cape Town, Pickled Image Limited of the UK, The Victoria Theatre of Victoria, Texas, Warner Bros. Distributing, Inc., Disney Enterprises, Feld Entertainment, and Paramount Pictures.

A special thanks to the following artists: the world-class photographs by Jenny Anderson, Barbara Bordnick, Peter Casolino, Jesse Kramer, Joan Marcus, Matthew Murphy, Christopher Nelson, Marcio del Nero, and the late Martha Swope; the estate of Brian Bedford; to the brilliant Glenn Close for personally gifting us images from the film, *Albert Nobbs*; Jinkx Monsoon; and to the brilliant Stephan Tessier, Special Makeup Effects Artist and Head of the Makeup Department at CBC (Canadian Broadcast Corporation), for generously sharing photographs from his vast archive and his valuable technical information. A whole-hearted thank you to my colleagues and students in the Department of Theatre and Dance at The University of Texas, Austin for their continued support and patience.

I want to personally thank three remarkable makeup artists for their generous contributions to this edition:

- Academy Award-winning Special Makeup Effects Artist, Matthew Mungle, for the many step-by-step in-studio makeup demonstrations of his contemporary practice for special effects and prosthetic character makeups.

- Michael Meyer, Director of the Wig and Hair Design at the Academy of Makeup Arts, for his complete re-write of Chapters 12 and 13 on Beards and Mustaches, and Wigs.
- Tara Cooper, for her insight and contribution of contemporary practice in film and television makeup.

Their enthusiasm, dedication, and passionate support for maintaining Richard Corson's *Stage Makeup* as the "Bible" of makeup books will inspire actors, young makeup artists, and their teachers for generations.

Thank you to Beverly Norcross for her enthusiastic participation, wisdom, and tireless editing of the manuscript, and to Ashley Lords and the talented staff (a big shout out to Ben Rittenhouse) and students at the Academy of Makeup Arts in Nashville, Tennessee for allowing us to observe classes and interview their brilliant professional educators.

I would like to acknowledge the generations of students who have been inspired by this book and who have gone on to advance the art form through their passion, skill, and ingenuity.

Thank you Richard Corson, for sharing with us your passion for *Stage Makeup*.

Finally, I would like to dedicate this edition of *Stage Makeup*, in loving memory, to Broadway legend and musical comedy star, Carol Channing (1921–2019). "Good-bye, Dolly."

James Glavan

INTRODUCTION

The actor's dream is to play a wide range of characters, to explore many facets of life in roles that encompass all humanity. To fulfill this dream, the actor requires not only talent and training, but an unstinting devotion to the art.

In many areas of this endeavor, actors are assisted by the artistry and technical skills of brilliant craftspeople. From the original script to the set, lighting, and costumes, every effort is made to achieve perfection. Curiously, in the field of makeup, actors are left quite to their own devices. Except for the rare production so exotic or stylized that a specialist is necessary, actors must design and execute their own makeup.

It is therefore of considerable concern that many young professionals in the theater are unfamiliar with even so elementary a problem as projection of the actors' features, essential to the fullest communication of the characters' inner lives. Even on the rare occasions when a professional makeup artist is available, it is still the actors who are more aware than anyone else of the special problems posed by their own features and by the characters they are playing. Thus, it is the responsibility of each to learn the craft of makeup, that final dressing of the character that will enable him or her to perform the role as fully and as effectively as possible.

In addition to such fundamentals as the assimilation and projection of the character in terms of age, environment, and health, there is an area of psychological support that makeup can give actors, comparable only to the assistance of a perfect costume. Just as robes or rags can give actors the "feel" of a character, so also can makeup. The visual image reflected in their dressing-room mirrors can be as important to the actors as it will later become to the audience.

The authority of the arch of brow or the sweep of a profile can be as compelling as Lear's crown and scepter. The psychological effect of shadows and pallor or glowing health can be as conductive to mood and manner on stage as in life, while an important tilt to a nose or the simple graying of the hair will inevitably make more specific the delineation of character. The most detailed characterization can be performed only with full freedom and authority when the actors know that visual image supports and defines their work.

Actors untrained in makeup are deprived of an invaluable aid to their art—and little is done to remedy the situation. Large universities may give courses in makeup intermittently, or not at all. Drama schools often merely glance at the problem or train in outmoded techniques.

It is therefore most exciting and encouraging to all actors when a book such as this comes to our rescue. Richard Corson's approach to makeup is meticulous and eminently practical. Perhaps even more important is his stress on the creative aspects of makeup and the avoidance of stereotypes and formulae. The insistence on supporting technical skill with imagination and individuality reflects a positive and rewarding approach. With fullest exploitation of the mind and the senses, an unsuspected range of roles exists for each of us. It is through the assistance of the art and craft of makeup presented in this book that we can hope for a more complete realization of our goals in acting.

Uta Hagen

CHAPTER 1

FACIAL ANATOMY

The first step in preparing to study makeup is to examine the structure of bone, muscle, and cartilage that lies beneath the skin. In remodeling a face to fit a particular character, you should know how the face is constructed. Even when you are applying a corrective makeup on yourself, you need to be aware of which features you wish to emphasize and those you wish to minimize. Actors, or makeup artists, should familiarize themselves not only with the basic structure of a human face, but also with the particular structure of any face they make up, whether it be their own or someone else's.

BONES OF THE FACE

Anatomy is a complex subject and memorizing an exhaustive list of the technical names for all of the bones and muscles of the face is not essential for an actor or makeup artist. There is, for example, no particular virtue in referring to the *zygomatic arch* when the term *cheekbone* is simpler and more generally understood. In a few instances, however, when the precise location of shadows and highlights is to be discussed, it is advantageous to be able to refer to the exact area. The term *forehead* is useful only if we really mean the entire forehead. And in makeup we seldom do. There are two separate and distinct eminences, the *frontal* and the *superciliary*, which must ordinarily be considered separately when highlighting. In some individuals these are clearly defined, especially when the source of light is directly overhead, forming a slight shadow between the two. In other individuals the whole forehead may be smoothly rounded with no hint of a depression. In this case then, the technical terms are useful.

Familiarity with the bones of the face becomes increasingly important when applying age makeup, and when sculpting facial features for prosthetics. When a character's age is advancing, the muscles show a loss of tone and begin to sag. Sometimes, in extreme old age, the face can take on the effect of a skull draped with skin.

The *cheekbone* or *zygomatic arch* is one of the most important bones of the face for the makeup artist, and familiarity with its location and shape is essential for accurate modeling. Some people have prominent cheekbones that are easily observed, but with others the flesh may need to be prodded with the fingers to find them. In studying the bones of your own face, you should locate them by feel as well as by sight. To feel the cheekbone, prod the flesh along the entire length, beginning in front of the ear, until you know its exact shape. Start with the top of the bone, then feel how it curves around underneath. Keep prodding along the bottom until you reach the enlargement of the bone under the eye. Familiarize yourself with the general shape and exact location of the bone. Observe the angle of the cheekbone as it slopes gently down from the ear toward the center of the face.

Then there are the hollows in the skull. The *orbital hollows* (or eye sockets) are clear-cut and easy to feel with your finger. The *temporal* hollows are normally referred to as the *temples*. These are not deep, but there is a slight depression that tends to show up increasingly with age. The *infratemporal* hollows you will have already found in the process of prodding the cheekbone. The lack of bony support here allows the flesh to sink in underneath the cheekbone, resulting in the familiar hollow-cheeked effect. In extreme old age or starvation this sinking-in can be considerable.

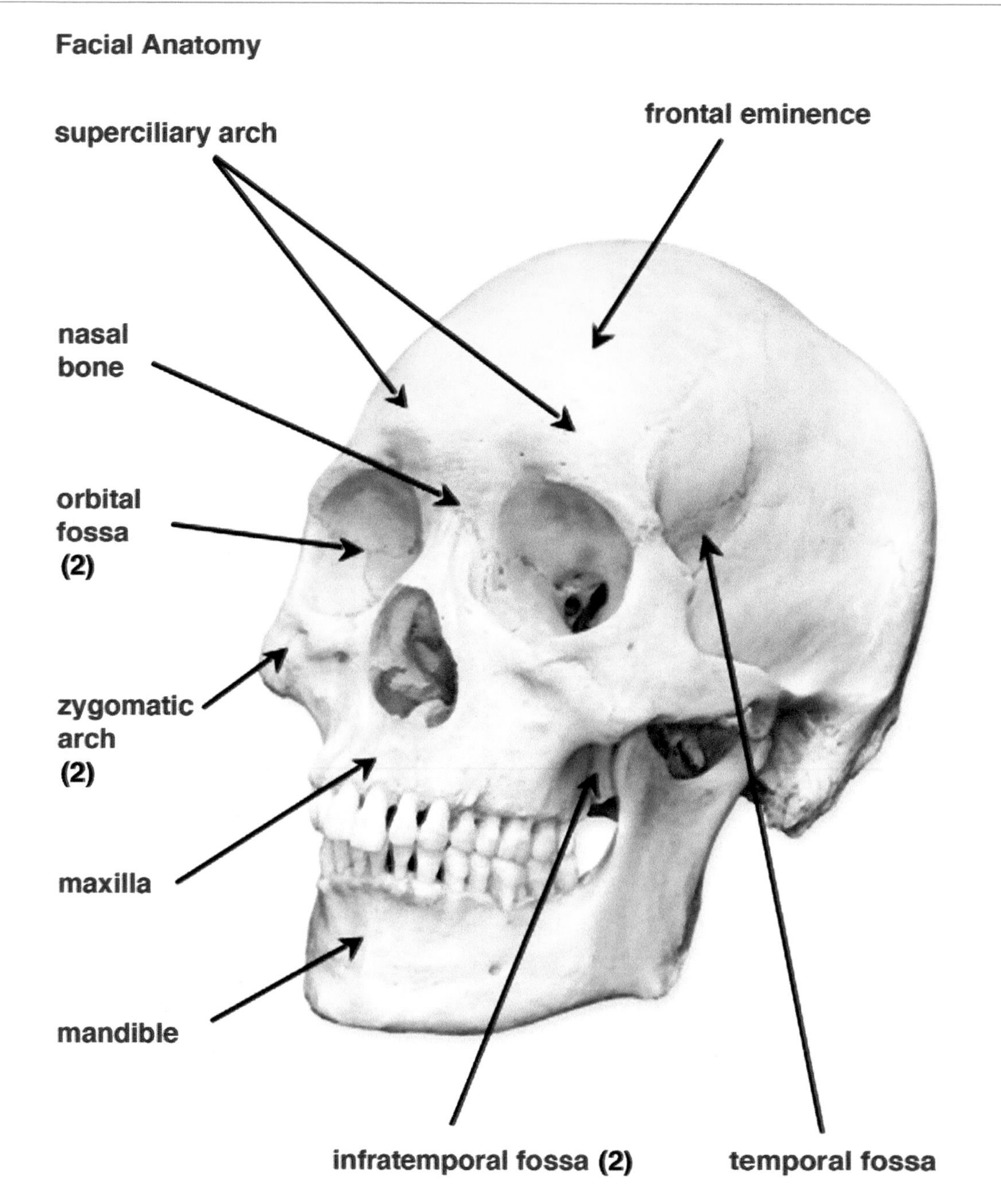

FIGURE 1.1 *A diagram of the bones of the skull and hollows (or fossae). The maxilla and the mandible are the upper and lower jaws, and the nasal bone is simply the bony part of the nose. The upper section of the nose is part of the nose and part of the bony structure of the skull. The lower, more movable part is constructed of cartilage attached to the nasal bone.*

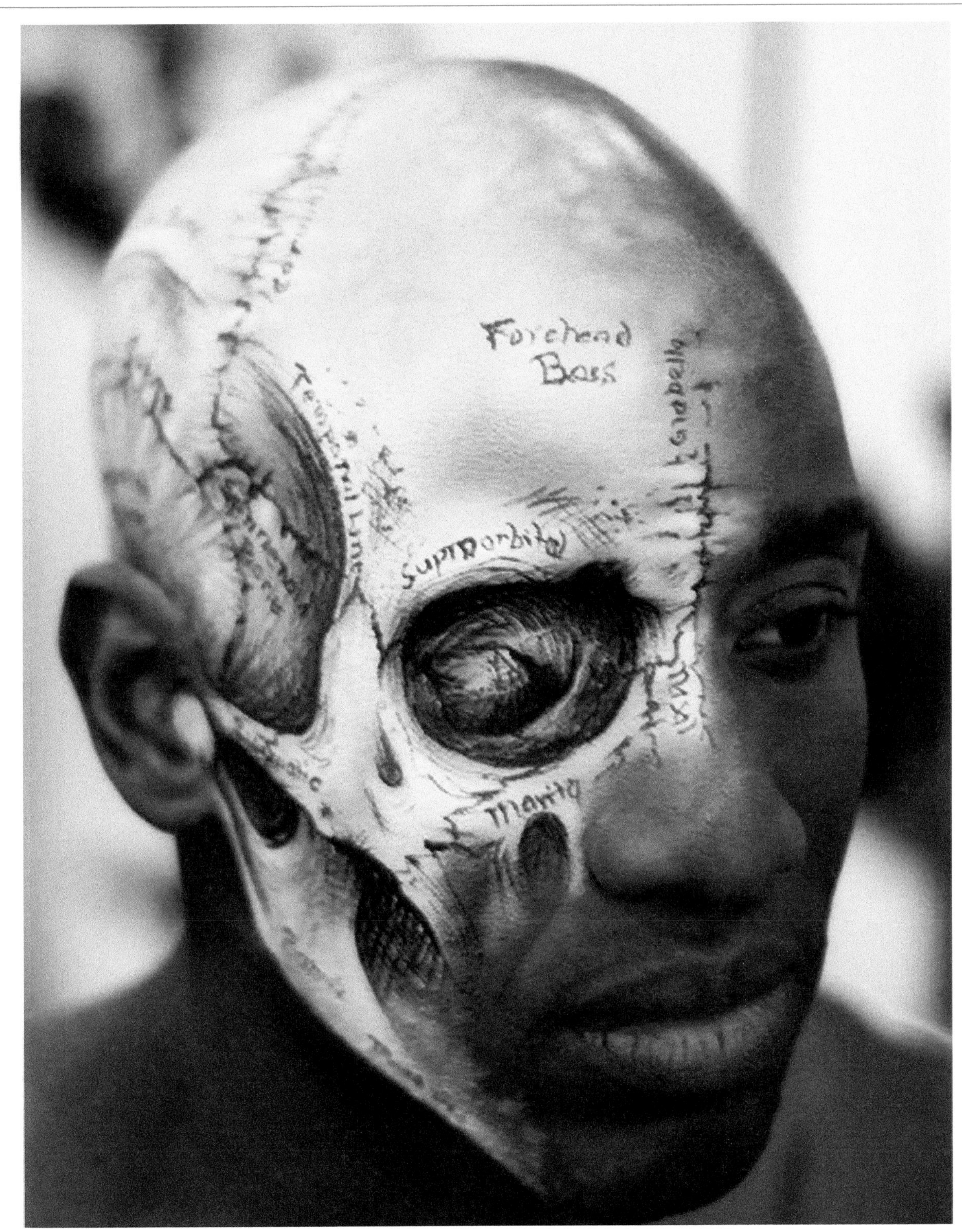

FIGURE 1.2 *A skull makeup inspired by Gray's Anatomy. Makeup artist, Lisa Berczel.*

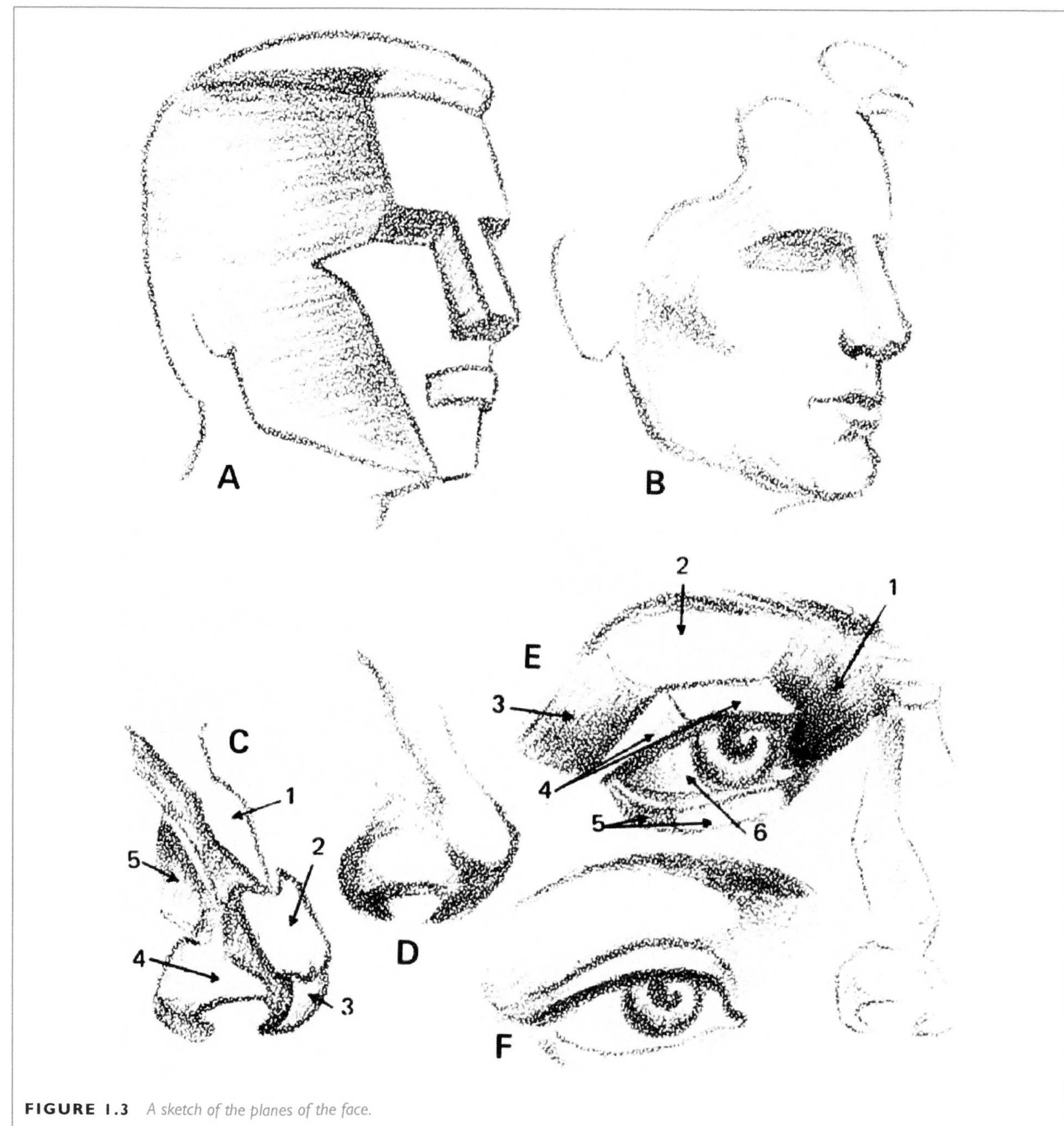

FIGURE 1.3 *A sketch of the planes of the face.*

FACIAL PLANES

If you were to divide anyone's face in half vertically and lay the halves on top of one another, you would most likely observe some remarkable differences between the two sides. Most faces have some degree of asymmetry and we subliminally form judgments about beauty based on the amount of symmetry in the facial features.

Another way to divide the face and check out the degree of symmetry is to divide it into three horizontal sections. The first division begins at the hairline/top of the forehead and ends at the top of the eye socket, the second picks up there and stops at the bottom of the nose, and the third division starts there and finishes at the bottom of the chin. The width of each of these sections is usually close to equal. Sometimes there will be a noticeable portion that is larger or smaller. Once again, the symmetry, or asymmetry, of the face can be noted and incorporated into the plan for the makeup.

HEAD AND NECK: STRUCTURE

The *neck* is included in all makeups, even if it is only to note that the base will be blended just over the jawline. A complete character makeup includes all exposed areas that can help convey the "look" of that character. The muscles of the neck are attached to the base of the skull, with some attached to the sternum, and others that run from the jaw to the clavicle. These muscles facilitate the acts of speaking and swallowing. The cervical region of the spine is located in the neck with what are called the cervical vertebrae (C-1 to C-7). In the throat area, there is a "floating bone" called the hyoid that anchors the tongue and throat. The larynx is also in this area of the throat; it is part of the respiratory system, and can be referred to as the "Adam's Apple" in male physiology.

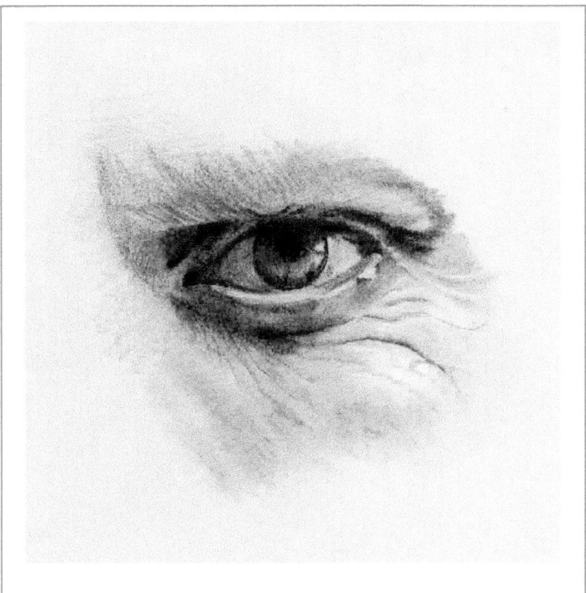

FIGURE 1.4 *Sketch of the eye.*

Eyes

The *eyes* (in Figure 1.3 E) are the sense organ for vision that react to light and pressure. They are fused into a two-piece unit that includes the anterior segment (cornea, iris, lens) and the posterior segment (vitreous, retina, choroid, sclera) (Figure 1.3 E6). When the artist is designing a makeup, they should observe not only the shape and planes of the lids (Figure 1.3 E4), with the size and color of the eyes, but also the condition of the eye area. For instance, this area can appear bright and vital, or tired and irritated with puffiness and discoloration. The depth and size of the eye can be altered by how planes 1,2, 3, and 5 are sculpted with makeup.

FIGURE 1.5 *Sketch of the mouth and chin.*

Mouth

The primary function of the *mouth* (with the teeth, lips, and tongue) is to act as the beginning of the digestive system and for communication. Although the throat provides the primary aspects of speech, the tongue and lips are necessary to produce sounds. The appearance and shape of the lips is a focal point of the face along with the eyes. The condition of the teeth can be an important trait of a character, especially if that person is from a time and/or place where dental hygiene was not practiced. There are four types of teeth: incisors, canines, premolars, and molars, and they all have specific functions. There are 32 permanent adult teeth with half (16) in the upper/*maxilla* area of the mouth and the other half (16) in the lower/*mandible* area. Teeth can be temporarily colored, or covered with a set of custom-made teeth, as part of a makeup design.

Nose

The nose (Figure 1.3) is composed of the ethmoid bone or bridge and the dorsum or nasal ridge (plane 1), the supratip lobule or tip (plane 2), the columella (plane 3), and the nasal alas or nostrils (plane 4). As part of the respiratory system, the nose is lined with mucous membrane and fine hairs that act as a natural filtration system. Changing the shape of the nose can have a dramatic effect on the appearance and proportion of the face.

FIGURE 1.6 *Sketch of the ear.*

Ear

Ears are the organ used for hearing and balance. Although there are three sections that compose the outer, middle, and inner ear, only the outer portion is visible. The pinna (or auricle) is the external part of the ear structure and it is made of one piece of elastic cartilage. The earlobe is the fleshy portion at the bottom of the ear and its shape and size can be a very distinctive character trait. The ear has two sets of muscles (intrinsic and extrinsic), which can adjust the position of the ear in some animals.

Research

The anatomy of the specific human face that you are going to apply a makeup on is the foundation for planning and executing a successful look. The makeup design can be for corrective, beauty, character, age, trauma, creature, alien, monster, or any fantasy being from your imagination—the process must begin with knowledge and analysis of facial structure. The skull is, as you know, covered with various muscles, which operate the mandible (the only movable part of the skull) and the mouth,

FIGURE 1.7 *Half skull makeup. Makeup artist, Marie-Laurence Tessier.*

eyelids, and eyebrows. A search of internet sources using key words like "anatomy" can begin the research process and provide some reference images. However, whenever you are using the internet be aware of the IP (Internet Protocol) address and the intentions for that website. An excellent primary source for anatomy images are the textbooks used for courses in the medical professions.

The popularity of television shows that deal with crime scene investigation, forensic science, surgery, and emergency rooms in both fictional and real formats has given a large audience an introduction into the human anatomy and its reaction to trauma. The real world of forensic science employs some computer software that can produce facial reconstruction approximation. The artists in this field can also use sketches and sculptures based on the skull and tissue depth markers for specific age, sex, and ethnicity. Creating the face that once covered a skull is still considered subjective and cannot be used as legal evidence proving identity. These forensic tools are additional resources for facial anatomy research. Thorough research into the bones and muscles will guide the design of the makeup and provide a foundation of realism to any character.

Sources

Kopf-Maier, P. Dr. (ed.), *Wolf-Heidegger: The Color Atlas of Human Anatomy*, Karger AG, Basel, Paperback edition 2006 by Sterling Publishing Co., Inc. Sterling

Wikipedia. Ear Anatomy. Retrieved from http://en.wikipedia.org/wiki/Ear_anatomy

Wikipedia. Eye Anatomy. Retrieved from http://en.wikipedia.org/wiki/Eye_anatomy

Wikipedia. Facial Anatomy. Retrieved from http://en.wikipedia.org/wiki/Facial_anatomy

Wikipedia. Mouth Anatomy. Retrieved from http://en.wikipedia.org/wiki/Mouth_anatomy

Wikipedia. Nose Anatomy. Retrieved from http://en.wikipedia.org/wiki/Nose_anatomy

CHAPTER 2

COLOR THEORY

Color theory from the artist's point of view is based on *subtractive* color perception. The full-color spectrum that is present in white light will reveal one color on a surface while all the others are absorbed—thus subtracting all the colors not present on the surface that we are viewing. "Red" lips, for example, absorb all light rays except the red ones, which they reflect, making the lips appear red. A clown's white face reflects all of the component rays of "white" light and therefore appears white. Black eyelashes, on the other hand, absorb all of the component rays in white light and therefore appear black. Mixing colors to create another specific color is the *additive* version of color perception. Even though makeup products are available in just about any color imaginable, the makeup artist will be dealing with the size of their kit, their budget, unforeseen circumstances, unique design characteristics, and many other situations that may require a customized color to be mixed. The knowledge, and confidence, that are acquired from practicing color-mixing exercises are essential for every artist (see Color Theory chart, Figure 2.5).

BACKGROUND ON COLOR THEORY

The English mathematician and physicist Sir Isaac Newton is well known for his laws of motion and gravity. He also observed the subtractive properties of white light and the color spectrum. His book on the subject, *Opticks*, was published in 1704. The book included a study of light refraction along with color mixtures in the spectrum and he organized his findings into a color wheel. Johann Wolfgang von Goethe was known for his poetry, and his theater critiques. Goethe observed the color spectrum produced by light and wrote an essay detailing his approach to color theory. His treatise, with a color wheel, was published in 1810. Goethe focused on an intuitive exploration of the psychology of color. The new science of psychology, in addition to the use of the intuitive approach, inspired many of the early abstract painters in the twentieth century. Wassily Kandinsky was one of the artists who was interested in the psychological effects of color. There are many works published on this subject. When theater artists are going through the design process they can consciously employ the psychological impact of colors. There has been a wide range of studies of the psychology of color, but it is difficult to find information that is directly related to scientific fact. The majority of the studies were funded by corporations attempting to predict marketing strategy pertaining to color choices. Swiss psychologist Carl Jung (1875–1961) is perhaps the most notable person to use a study of color as a tool in his practice. He felt that art could be used as an option in therapy. His patients would create works of art, sometimes based on images from dreams, as a part of their analysis. The use of color in expressing emotion was integral to inner exploration through its symbolism. One exact formula, or template, for interpreting color does not exist; research may depend upon generalizations and specific production requirements.

More recently, there has been a standardized color-matching system developed that is used in the printing, paint, fabric/fashion, and plastics industries. This system was created by Pantone, Inc., a corporation headquartered in New Jersey. The colors have reference numbers and the swatches can be purchased in a "fan deck" that is updated every year. Pantone began featuring a color of the year in 2000 as a result of secret

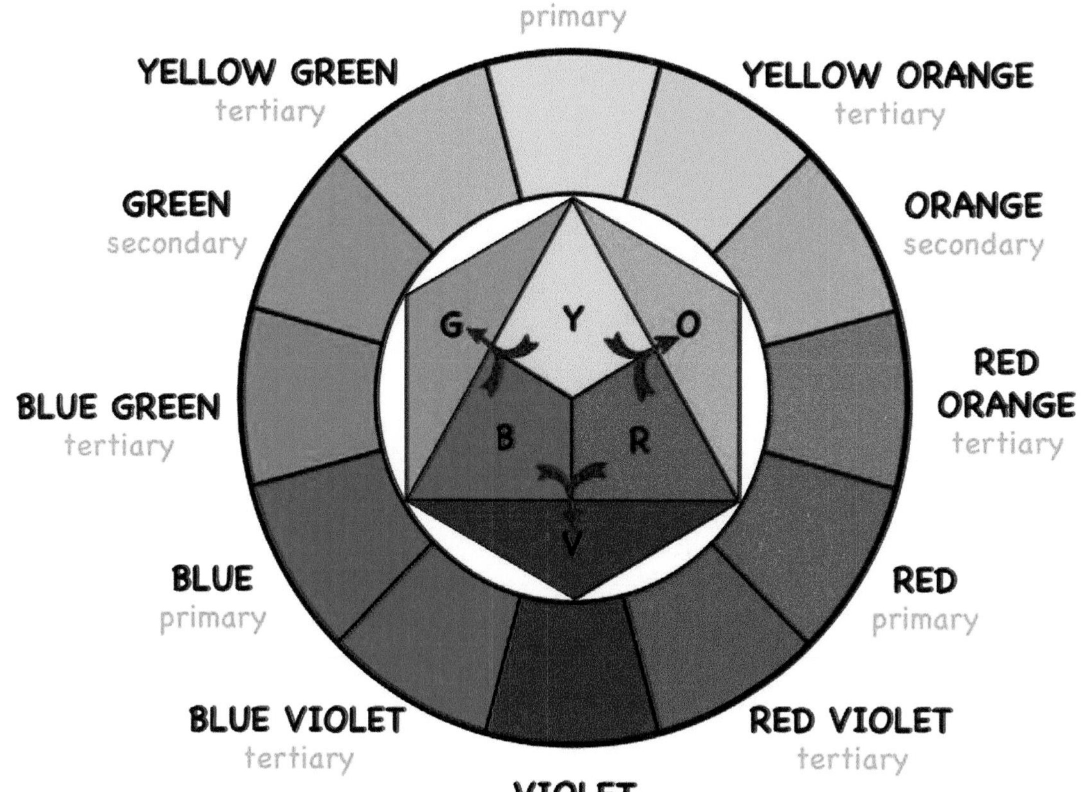

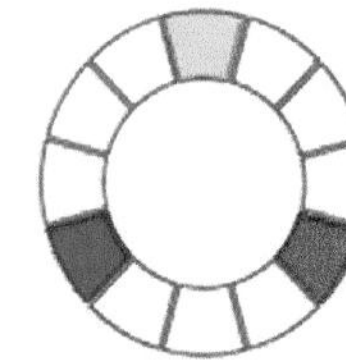

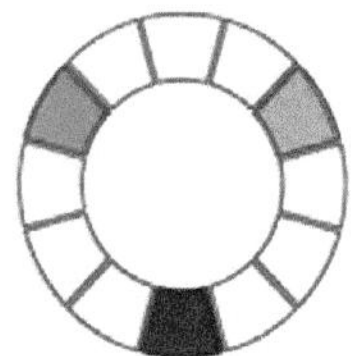

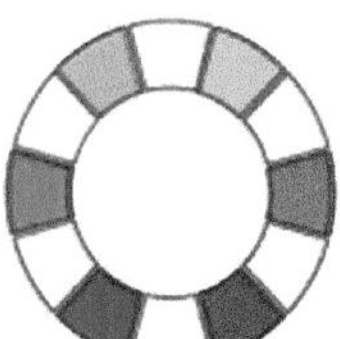

FIGURE 2.1 *Color theory illustration.*

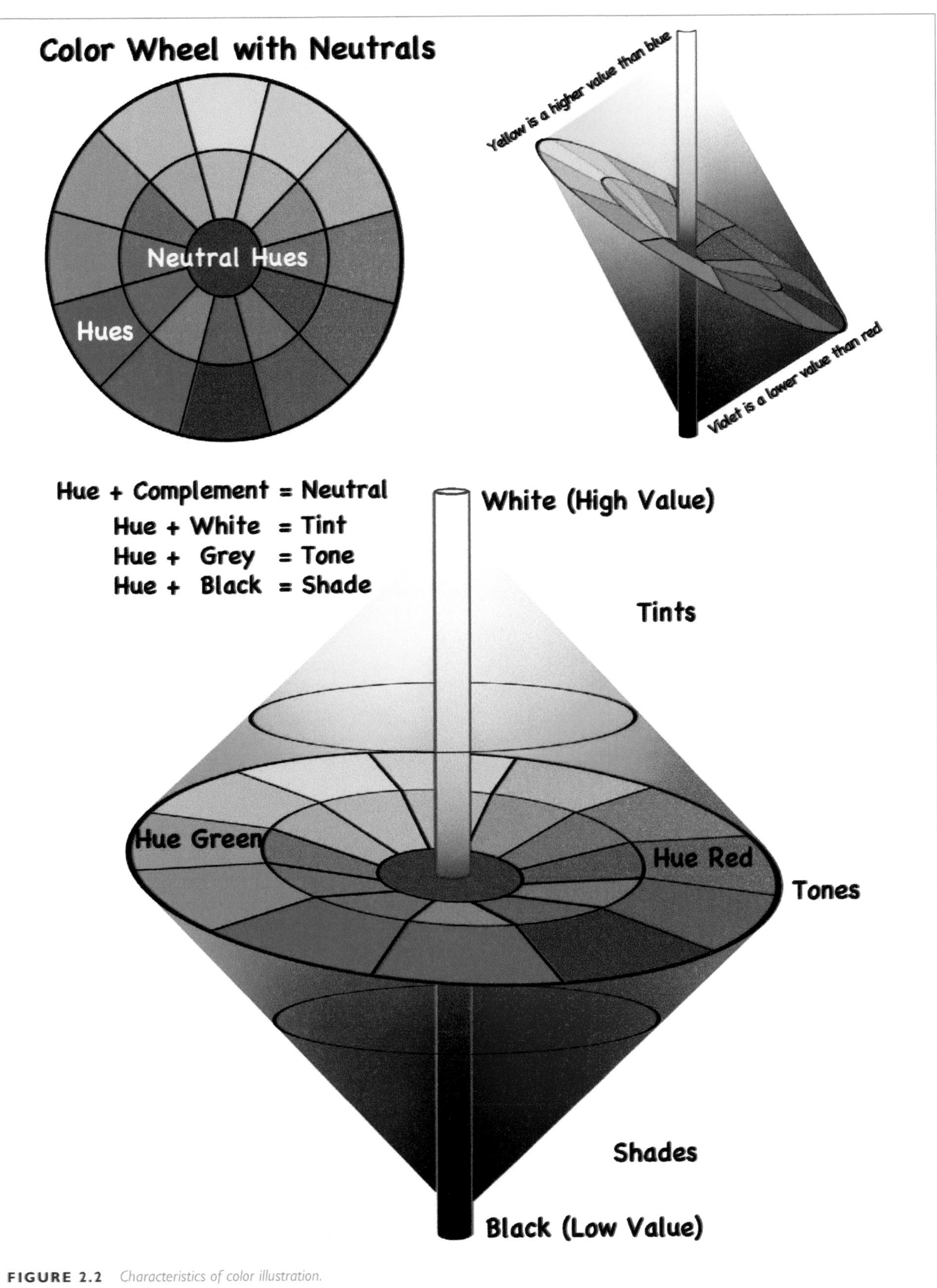

FIGURE 2.2 *Characteristics of color illustration.*

meetings with color standards groups from various nations. The two-day meetings are held in a European capital city where, after presentations and debates, the color of the following year is chosen. These annual colors are used to highlight fashion collections and makeup color palettes. Munsell is another company that specializes in color systems. Their website has a gray scale available as a "fan deck" that is useful for finding the specific *value* of a color. Gray scales begin with black at value 1 and finish with white at value 10. Their website has educational options and a blog with posts that address a wide variety of topics related to color. Becoming familiar with color theory, especially color mixing, makes the artist comfortable integrating any of the color trends that may be requested by a director, client, or their own choice of palette. When researching for a specific historical period, color trends can be integral in conveying the styles that defined that time.

FIGURE 2.3A *Cool makeup color palette of blues, purples, white, and a touch of pink. Makeup by Marie-Laurence Tessier.*

FIGURE 2.3B *Warm makeup color palette of orange, copper, banana yellow, mustard, espresso, black and white, and a touch of pink. Makeup by Olga Mesurev.*

CHARACTERISTICS OF COLOR

In order to be able to talk intelligently about color and to approach the problem in an organized way, it is convenient to know the terms usually used to designate the characteristics of color—*hue*, *intensity*, and *value*.

Hue—The hue of a color is simply the name by which we know it—red or green or blue or yellow. Pink and maroon are both variations of the basic red hue; brown is a deep, grayed orange; orchid is a tint of violet.

If we take samples of all of the major hues with which we are familiar and drop them at random on a table, the result, of course, is chaos. But as we place hues next to each other that are somewhat similar, we begin to see a progression that by its very nature becomes circular—in other words, a color wheel. That is the traditional form of hue arrangement and for our purposes the most practical one.

Since, however, the progression from one hue to another is a steady one, the circle could contain an unlimited number of hues, depending only on one's threshold of perception—the point at which two hues become so nearly alike as to be indistinguishable to the naked eye and, for all practical purposes, identical. But since a wheel containing hundreds of colors would be impractical, certain hues are selected at regular intervals around the circumference.

Note with color wheel illustration (Figure 2.1): There is usually an indication on standardized color wheels that separates the warm colors from the cool ones. These terms use the characteristics of nature—the yellow sun and the blue water, for example. This separation can also be divided into dynamic (warm) or receding (cool) colors, terms that can be related to the psychological, or intuitive, view of color. Therefore, the choices for designing with a warm color palette (Figure 2.3a) or a cool color palette (Figure 2.3b) can be based on practical, emotional, historical accuracy, and even the science of optic perception.

Intensity—Thus far we have been speaking only of bright, saturated colors. But more often than not we shall be using colors of less than maximum brightness. A gray-blue is still blue, but it is different from the blue at the outer edge of the color wheel. Although of the same hue, it is lower in intensity. This color would be shown as being nearer the center of the wheel—more gray, in other words. Colors on the periphery are of maximum brilliance. Colors nearer the center are less brilliant (of lower intensity) and are commonly referred to as *tones*.

Value—In addition to being blue and low in intensity, a specific color may also be light or dark—light gray-blue, medium gray-blue, dark gray-blue. This darkness or lightness of a color is called its *value* (see Figure 2.2). A light color has a high value, a dark color has a low value. Pink is a high value of red; orchid is a high value of violet; midnight blue is a low value of blue. Since the color wheel is only two-dimensional, it obviously cannot be used to demonstrate values, the third color dimension. A "color tree," or dimensional color scale, has been developed using computer imaging. Websites for companies that deal with color systems have accurate illustrations of these color systems. As mentioned previously, using a gray scale can aid in determining the value of a color.

COLOR MIXING AND COLOR SCHEMES

If you don't have the exact color you need, you can, provided you have the three primary colors to work with, mix virtually any color you want. The three primary hues for paint (and for our purposes) are *red*, *yellow*, and *blue*. These *primary* hues can be mixed to achieve the three *secondary* hues—*orange*, *green*, and *violet*—as well as an infinite number of intermediate hues. The *tertiary* colors can be made by mixing a primary color with a secondary color; for instance using red mixed with orange. These hues will have less intensity, or be less brilliant, than the hues compounded directly from their sources in nature. Mixed colors always lose some *intensity*.

When you want to change the value (lighter or darker), *and* change the intensity (brilliance), you can add white, black, or gray to the hue. For example, starting with the primary color red and adding white will result in a *tint* of red: pink. Adding black to red will create a *shade* of red: maroon/burgundy. For a less brilliant, less intense version of red, add gray and you will have a *tone*, or a mauve color.

The importance of color in design stems from the significance of color to the human mind. Color in specific combinations expresses both subtle and not so subtle messages, sparks interest from the viewer, and inspires emotional connections. When an artist chooses a palette of colors, it is done so in a thoughtful manner and with purpose (see Figure 2.4). There is a particular message and the message should be clearly articulated. When one singular color and its tints, tones, and shades are at the center of a color scheme, that is referred to as *monochromatic*. Colors falling opposite each other on the color wheel are called *complements* and when they are mixed will produce *neutral* hues of gray or brown. *Achromatics* or neutrals are located toward the center of the color wheel. The complementary colors blue and orange, for example, can be mixed to produce a gray-brown. However, if only a little blue is added to the orange, the result is a burnt orange. Slowly adding more blue will give varying intensities of brown. Black, white, gray, and sometimes brown and beige are considered neutral colors. They can be used to mix other colors, as described previously, or they can be a focal point in a color palette, and also used to balance a color scheme.

A *split complementary* mixture uses a color and the two colors on each side of its complementary color. For example, blue is the color you select, and yellow-orange along with red-orange are on either side of its complementary color of orange. *Analogous* colors are next to each other on the color wheel, like blue and green with all the variations of blue-green and green-blue. When the color theme uses analogous colors, that creates a harmonious palette. If a palette is created using a selection of analogous colors as the main theme, then the artist can add some of the complementary colors for accents. A *triad* color scheme includes three hues equidistant from one another on the wheel, creating a triangle of hues, and a *tetradic* scheme is colors chosen in a square or rectangular pattern on the wheel. There are commercially made color wheels that can be used to help with mixing colors and creating color palettes. They usually have all of the color theory vocabulary printed in the center of the wheel.

The makeup artist will find that becoming familiar with mixing colors to match skin tones, to create suitable highlight and lowlight colors, adjusting one color with its complementary color to neutralize, and covering tattoos are a few of the related skills. These practical applications are covered in Chapters 6, 7, 8, and 9. Extending your studies to other visual arts (life drawing, painting, sculpting) will serve to enhance your makeup skills as well.

FIGURE 2.4 *Color scheme examples.*

Color Theory Homework

Painting tints, tones, shades, and color wheel with neutrals.

Tint: Color plus White

Hue	Value 2	Value 3	Value 4	Hue+ 50%White	Value 6	Value 7	Value 8	100%White

Tone: Color plus Gray

Hue	Value 2	Value 3	Value 4	Hue+ 50%Gray	Value 6	Value 7	Value 8	100%Gray

Shade: Color plus Black

Hue	Value 2	Value 3	Value 4	Hue+ 50%Black	Value 6	Value 7	Value 8	100%Black

Color Wheel with Neutrals

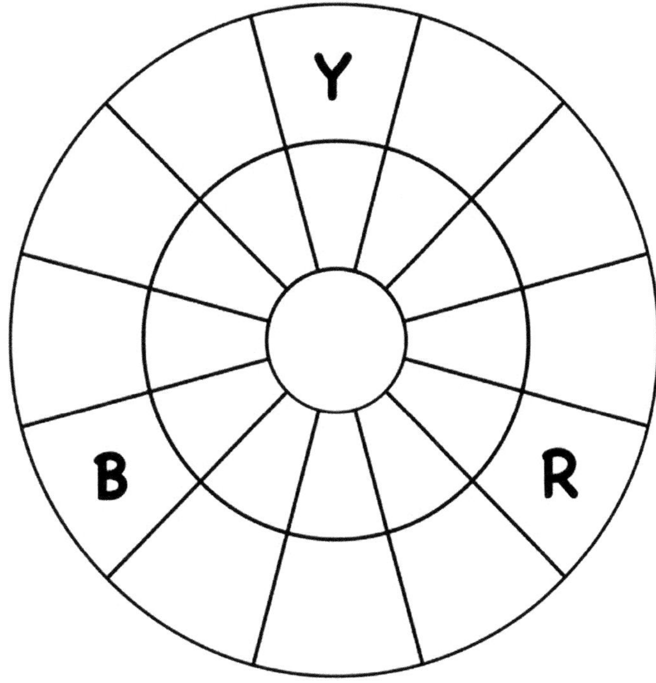

FIGURE 2.5 *Color theory chart.*

Source: Illustrations in the figures created by Yu-Jung Shen.

SOURCES

Munsell Color System: https://munsell.com
Pantone: www.pantone.com
The Color Wheel Company: www.colorwheelco.com
Wikipedia. Carl Jung. Retrieved from https://en.wikipedia.org/wiki/Carl_Jung
Wikipedia. Color psychology. Retrieved from https://en.wikipedia.org/wiki/Color_psychology
Wikipedia. Color theory. Retrieved from https://en.wikipedia.org/wiki/Color_theory
Wikipedia. Sir Isaac Newton. Retrieved from https://en.wikipedia.org/wiki/Isaac_Newton
Wikipedia. Johann Wolfgang von Goethe. Retrieved from https://en.wikipedia.org/wiki/Johann_Wolfgang_von_Goethe

CHAPTER 3

THE STUDIO CLASSROOM

In most instances, the classroom that serves as the makeup studio was not specifically designed for that purpose. If the class is being taught at a college, or university, then it is more than likely in a dressing room. The majority of foundational makeup courses are offered as a part of a theater program and address the needs of the actor and the technical/design students. The typical classroom usually has makeup mirrors with lighting and, hopefully, a sink nearby for clean-up. This chapter will compare the studio classrooms at the Academy of Make Up Arts (AMUA) in Nashville, Tennessee and California State University, Fullerton (CSUF). In addition to general space usage, the lighting, storage, tools, and supplies, equipment, wig and hair accommodations, and health and safety concerns in the classroom will be covered. Wherever makeup classes are being taught, at a professional ("trade") school or as part of a university curriculum, there is a range of adaptations, solutions, and safety procedures that can enhance the classes and the teaching space.

FIGURE 3.1 *AMUA beauty makeup classroom.*

FIGURE 3.2 *CSUF makeup classroom.*

FIGURE 3.3 *AMUA demonstration area in the beauty studio.*

SPACE USAGE

AMUA leases its space in an office complex, so there was a certain amount of choice involved when deciding on the location initially. CSUF had an opportunity in the late 1990s to add on to the existing Performing Arts building, and a new makeup studio was part of that addition. Budgets for both of these schools are dependent upon various factors, and that directly affects the choices made, both initially and with ongoing needs.

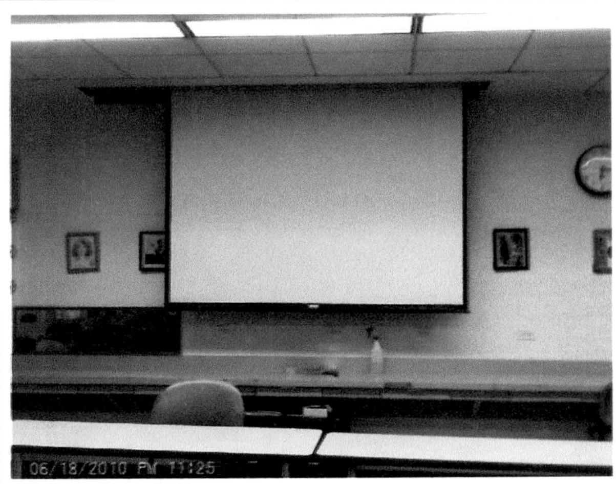

FIGURE 3.4 *California State University, Fullerton makeup classroom with automatic retractable projection screen.*

The AMUA requires enough space to house their educational administration along with the instructional areas:

Main space (6,000 square feet): office, restrooms, break room with computers and a library, storage area, beauty lab, wig/hair studio, photography area, and a professional makeup store.

Second space (1,500 square feet): lobby, office, restroom, storage areas, and a special effects lab.

The beauty, special effects, and hair/wig programs accommodate maximum class enrollment of 12 students per semester. In each of the classrooms the student has about 3 feet of working counter space. All of the teaching areas have monitors for visual presentations. Demonstration models are provided for occasional course content and portfolio photography.

CSUF has a theater arts and dance program with two theaters, offices, scene shop, prop room, lighting lab, costume shop, various storage areas, classrooms, and a makeup studio.

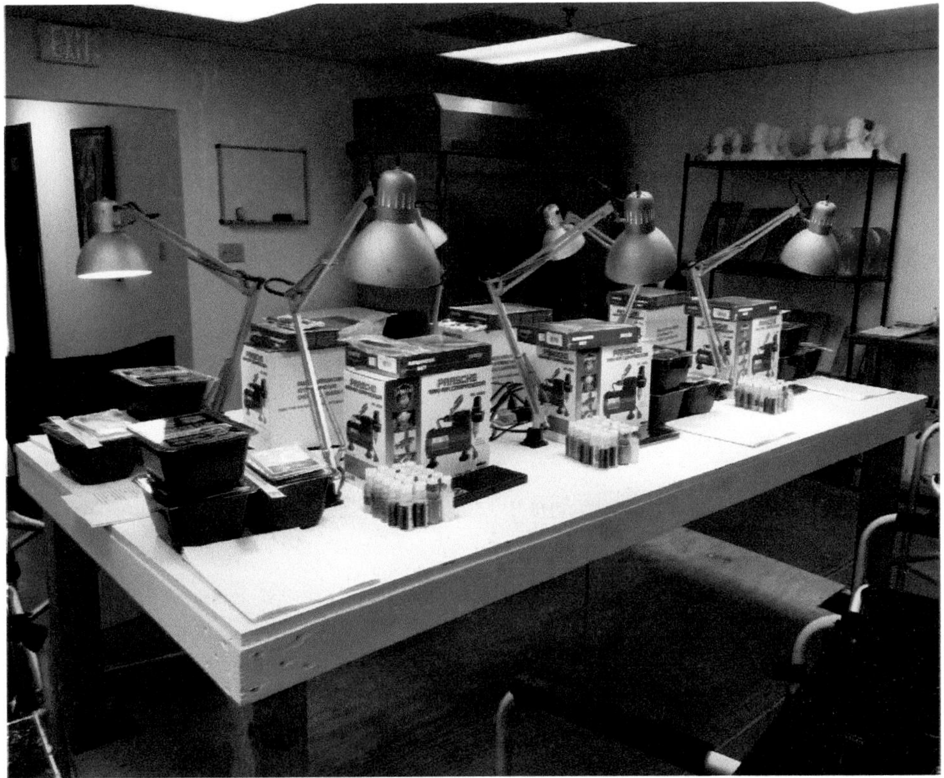

FIGURE 3.5 *AMUA FX lab student work stations with a walk-in foam latex oven.*

FIGURE 3.6 *AMUA FX lab work station.*

FIGURE 3.7 *CSUF storage room adjoining classroom.*

The 1,000 square foot makeup classroom has an attached 200 square foot storage room. Connecting doors provide access from the room with the costume shop and crafts room that is useful during show production periods. There is a projection screen recessed into the ceiling. Digital projectors attached to mobile media carts are brought into the classroom for visual presentations. The classroom has makeup mirrors, for a maximum of 26 students with 2.5 feet of counter space at each station.

Ideally, the counter space should allow each student to set up their supplies for the day and there should be some accommodation for their kit boxes, backpacks, purses, and outerwear to be stored out of the way. Arranging for a demonstration model that is not a member of the class itself can streamline the teaching process. Having a monitor or projection screen for showing film clips, research images, finished class makeups, and PowerPoint presentations is very helpful for augmenting discussions and lectures. The students at the AMUA have photos taken of their work, view the results on the monitor, and select the image that they will use for their web page and portfolio.

Lighting

There are very few facilities with windows in the makeup area, especially if the theater is in the same building. If natural light is not available, some lighting that simulates it should be provided if at all possible. Art supply companies offer a range of lamps that reveal true color for the artist. A search of "lighting for makeup" internet sites will give a range of options and cost. The OttLitte Technologies Inc. carries a variety of choices and the Reveal bulb manufactured by GE is not only energy efficient, its enhanced spectrum mimics natural light. There are also vanity, wall-mounted, and portable mirrors with LED lighting. Both spaces at the AMUA have banks of windows for front walls that allow some ambient, natural light into the classroom areas. The overhead lighting at both schools is fluorescent. Mirrors with LED lighting are used in the beauty lab at the AMUA and CSUF has incandescent bulbs (GE 38 watt, white) around the makeup mirrors. The incandescent bulbs produce heat, making the room very warm, and they would like to replace these with LED eventually. LED desk lamps are used at work stations for special effects and wig/hair students at the AMUA. The teaching demonstration area at CSUF has a warm light focused on it for the model's face. This light is a halogen lamp and is in a recessed ceiling fixture with a dimmer control. If classrooms can be lit for observing accurate colors, another useful feature would be lighting instruments with changeable color media to offer the students a preview of what their makeup looks like onstage or on camera. Using a digital camera along with the lighting instruments, then showing the results on the monitor, is a useful tool as well.

Storage

If the studio classroom is also where production work takes place then adequate room for storage becomes even more essential. Using the space for both instruction and actualizing designs for a show means whoever is working in the room at the time needs the space to be cleared for their work to proceed. Organized, clean storage options for makeup supplies, equipment, wig/hair supplies and equipment, and finished wigs and hairpieces are essential for success. Flammable/hazardous substances need their own safe storage area and the MSDS (Material Safety Data Sheet) should be kept with these supplies.

FIGURE 3.8 *AMUA storage in the wig and hair studio..*

The 200-square foot storage room at CSUF holds most of the supplies and equipment for both classes and productions. There are shelves above the makeup stations that are used to store some of the wigs and masks. Cabinets under the sink area are used for some supplies, while the equipment and materials for the special effects class are kept in a closet in another part of the Performing Arts building.

At the AMUA, the students have lockers in the break room for personal items. Larger supplies are kept in the small rooms adjacent to class space. The wig/hair and special effects areas have shelving for various materials, along with a few cabinets. The beauty lab instructor uses a rolling tool chest for personal and class makeup items.

VENTILATION

The majority of makeup spaces have no special accommodations for airborne particles and fumes beyond the standard air-exchange system present in all buildings. In some cases, there may be a spray booth with an exhaust fan often located in the scene shop. Unfortunately, going outside with sprays is the most common option for avoiding inhalation. Fumes from spirit gum, acetone, alcohol, hair spray, latex with ammonia, and many other products, including setting powders, used frequently in the makeup room can be a source of physical reaction by those present in that space. The mist produced by airbrushes has not been subjected to a thorough study of long-term, unventilated exposure. A larger working space will offer a healthier advantage as far as dispersing fumes and particles with the usual ventilation system. The only choice that many studio classrooms may have is to either move to an alternate, larger space for some of their work or remove course topics that use these products. In some situations, standing fans may be the only option for times when moving the work to another location is not possible.

MAKEUP SUPPLIES AND HYGIENE PROCEDURES

The CSFU students purchase pre-packaged makeup kits, and the AMUA student supplies are provided by the school as part of their initial enrollment fees. Aside from that, there are instructional demonstration and communal items that are a part of the studio class. When starting to orient students to the makeup work space the instructor needs to explain the required hygiene, safety procedures, and etiquette that create a healthy environment. The care and cleaning of the face, hands and nails, brushes, sponges, kits, makeup products, tools, equipment, counters, and the makeup room itself are absolutely necessary as the foundation for working with makeup and hair. Communal supplies should be properly labeled, organized, properly stored, and some will require noting the purchase dates so that they may be replaced when they have reached their expiration date. Products like mascara, liners, and liquid eyeliner have a shelf life of three months, and students should understand the risks involved if eye products are shared (i.e. eye infections like conjunctivitis). Cream shadow, lipstick, and lip gloss are limited to a six-month usage. The mouth can absorb substances that are then carried into the bloodstream. Students need to be aware of viruses found in cold sores, along with bacteria and E. coli that can survive in communal makeup products. A cream blush should be used for 18 months, while powder shadows and lip pencils can be kept for two years. Taking the class time to discuss issues like cross-contamination and the need to establish a checklist for maintaining the health and safety of everyone in the makeup room is an essential preventative procedure. Storing supplies away from heat and moisture is important. Looking for damaged packaging, and liquids that have separated, should be part of the regular inventory checklist. If you are using a commercially produced makeup product there is an online service (checkfresh.com) that will provide the manufacturing date if you have the brand name and batch number.

Part of the introduction to working in the makeup studio is also providing the correct sanitizing products and instructing everyone about how and when to use them. Brush cleaners, soaps, alcohol wipes for metal tools, sprays for jars, tubes, and containers, along with disposable wands, brushes, and sponges should be readily available. Kits can be emptied and wiped down with 70% alcohol periodically. It is also advisable to sterilize any pump dispensers on a regular basis. Additional cleaning routines can include sharpening pencils with a sterilized sharpener, changing-out brushes frequently while applying a makeup, and working with clean sponges. When using fabric towels of any kind they should be machine-washed after each use. Wipes with disinfectant are a good way to clean the makeup counters and surfaces around the room. When setting up makeup products for the performers in a show, assigning that person their own items, and keeping them in a bag with their name on it, is a good way to organize and streamline setting up the room. Using plastic scoops and metal spatulas to transfer contents from the makeup container to a palette work well when there is a makeup product that is going to be shared and/or mixed with another product. The metal spatulas can be sterilized with 99% alcohol, while the plastic can be cleansed with hot water and soap. Disposable paper palettes can be purchased in quantities, and metal, hard plastic, and glass (including mirrors and ceramic tile) all with smooth, finished edges are viable options as palettes.

Personal hygiene is a necessary, and sometimes sensitive, subject for class discussion. The judicious use of personal hygiene products is mandatory, especially when working in the close proximity of the makeup room and applying makeup on someone else's face. Some people, most often singers, are very sensitive to perfumes and scented products and it is a safe practice to forego using anything that may be an issue. It is also advisable to approach these subjects with the person who is going to be sitting in the makeup chair.

The person applying the makeup should get in the habit of having cleansing products available, noticing the condition of the performer's skin, asking about allergies and if they wear contact lenses. The makeup artist should have clean hands and fingernails and a generally neat appearance. The makeup space should be complete with the basic tools, appropriate makeup, and cleansing supplies. The artist should provide hand sanitizer, breath mints, hair fasteners, and a makeup cape to protect the performer's costume.

CONCLUSION

CSUF and the AMUA have makeup studio classrooms that answer their educational needs with creative use of the space and budget. The physical characteristics of each facility are contributing factors for the types of spatial solutions that are unique to their programs. There are many makeup education situations that may have less choice for adapting the classroom. These two examples are presented with the intention of not only illustrating specific elements, but to also serve as a starting point for developing the best possible makeup education environment. Establishing health and safety priorities, proposing budgets that accommodate current standards, and keeping a vigilant eye out for current health and safety information are a few of the steps that lead this process. Students that graduate from a conscientiously run program with professional habits are the goal of every educational institution. (For additional health and safety information refer to Appendix C.)

Hygiene Procedures

At the beginning of each class:

- Set up the materials you will be using for that day's makeup neatly on your counter.
- Hang up your overlay and/or mood board for that makeup.
- Clean your hands.
- Remove any street makeup that you have been wearing before class, cleanse your face, apply astringent, and moisturize. Apply any additional skin preparations and moisturize your lips. Put on a protective cape, smock, apron, etc. Secure your hair out of the way.

Products and supplies:

- Make a note of the dates that you begin using your products and keep track of when they will expire:
    - mascara, liners, and liquid eyeliners—3 months
    - cream shadow, lipstick, lip gloss—6 months
    - cream blush—18 months
    - powder shadow and lip pencils—2 years
- Never share eye products like mascara and eyeliners.
- If you have a cold sore, eye infection, or skin lesion, where makeup is going to be applied, avoid that area to prevent transferring a virus or bacteria.
- If a package has been damaged, liquids have separated, there is an odor, or anything else that seems off about the product, discard it.

Sanitizing:

- Clean brushes with brush cleaner or soap and water after every makeup application.
- Use brush cleaner every time you are going to use that brush with a different product.

- Use alcohol wipes for metal tools, eyelash curlers, tweezers, scissors, and pencil sharpeners.
- Sanitizing sprays can be used for jars, tubes, and containers.
- Use disinfectant wipes for the counters, surfaces, and pump dispensers.
- Clean natural sponges with warm water and soap. Discard used latex sponges.
- Periodically clean the inside of your kit with 70% alcohol.
- Use disposable mascara wands, and eye-makeup applicators.
- Machine-wash fabric towels after each use.
- Change-out brushes and sponges frequently during an application.
- Use plastic scoops and/or metal spatulas to transfer makeup products from containers onto a palette. (This is a generally healthy practice especially for mixing products.)
- During production use individually assigned bags of products for each performer.

Hygiene:

- Personal
    - Avoid personal products that have a strong scent.
    - Clean your hands frequently, keep your nails clean and your breath fresh.
    - Wear appropriate attire and keep a generally neat appearance.
- Models (be attentive to your model)
    - Take notice of any skin conditions that may affect the application. Ask about allergies and if they are wearing contact lenses.
    - Secure their hair out of the way and use a protective cape.
    - Check on how they are doing periodically.
    - Keep a supply of hand sanitizer and breath products for your models.

CONTRIBUTORS

Ashley Driver, Executive Director, Academy of Make Up Arts
Karen Weller, Faculty, California State University, Fullerton
Katie Wilson, Faculty, California State University, Fullerton

CITATIONS

www.fda.gov
www.osha.gov
Chris Koseluk, *Makeup Artist Magazine* (June/July 2016).

CHAPTER 4

RELATING MAKEUP TO THE CHARACTER

One of the basic purposes of most makeup is to assist the actor in the development of a character by making suitable changes (when necessary) in the actor's physical appearance. It seems reasonable, therefore, that our study of makeup should begin with an examination of the principles of character analysis.

CHARACTER ANALYSIS

The first step in arriving at a suitable image for the character is to study the play. Directly through the dialogue and stage directions, you come to know the character. You become acquainted not only with the character's physical appearance, but also with his or her background, environment, personality, age, and relationships with other characters in the play. Although this probing into the character is essential for the actor, it is also essential preparation for the makeup. It is important to be able to translate the information into visual terms.

Take, for example, the nose of Cyrano de Bergerac (see Chapter 11, Figure 11.50). This would appear at first glance to be the basis for Cyrano's makeup. But is it sufficient to simply attach a large nose to the actor's face? Without it there is no Cyrano, but to what extent is the nose comic and to what extent tragic? What elements of nobility and courage and kindness should appear in the visual impression aside from the one exaggerated feature? And from a purely practical point of view, what effect will any given shape of nose have on the particular actor's face?

Such questions as these should be asked about any character you are analyzing. And, in answering each question, there is a choice to be made. You may not always make the right choice, but you should make a definite one. A fine makeup, like a fine painting or a fine performance, is a product of thorough preparation, intelligent selection, and meticulous execution.

When you are reading the script and it mentions a character's state of health with specific details, that will be one of the aspects of the makeup. If Fontine in Victor Hugo's *Les Misérables*, and more recently in the musical of the same name by Alain Boublil and Claude-Michel Schönberg, plays her death scene with rosy cheeks and a bloom of health, the credulity of the audience is going to be severely strained. Or if a pale, sallow-complexioned actor is supposed to be playing a villainous rogue, the more alert members of the audience may suspect a sinister twist of the plot. Therefore, it is essential, at the very least, to provide the minimum requirements of the physical appearance so as to correlate what the audience sees with what it hears. But beyond this you have an obligation to use the resources of makeup creatively to solve more subtle problems.

It is, for example, not only possible but commonplace to find members of the same family who have similar backgrounds and similar environments, as well as a family resemblance, but who are still very different. The differences between the sisters Goneril and Cordelia in *King Lear*, for example, are crucial to the play. It will surely help both the actors and the audience if these differences can be reflected in the makeup. This requires an analysis to determine what each character should look like.

Such an analysis can be simplified by classifying the determinants of physical appearance into six categories: heredity, ethnicity, environment, temperament, health, and age. These are not, of course, mutually exclusive. Ethnicity, for example, is merely a subdivision of heredity and may be a basic consideration in such a

FIGURE 4.1 *Angela Lansbury as Mrs. Lovett in Sweeney Todd: The Demon Barber of Fleet Street.*

Source: Photograph by Barbara Bordnick, with permission from Angela Lansbury.

play as August Wilson's *Fences*, and of no significance at all in a play like *The Iceman Cometh*, which was, in fact, performed on Broadway with both white and black casts. Temperament is obviously a more important consideration than environment in studying the character of Lady Macbeth, whereas with Blanche in *A Streetcar Named Desire*, both environment and temperament are basic to an understanding of the character and the play. In any character analysis, therefore, it works well to concentrate one's attention on those groups which are of most significance to the character. It is not important to know which group any specific feature or character trait belongs in. The divisions are laid out merely as a practical aid in organizing the research for the character.

HEREDITY

Generally speaking, this group includes those characteristics, physical and mental, with which a person is born. The red hair of all the boys in *Seven Brides for Seven Brothers* and in *Life with Father* is obviously hereditary. Since it is required by the play, there is no choice to be made. But in most instances you must decide such things as the color of the hair, the shape of the nose, and the line of the eyebrow, and you must base your decision on knowledge of the relationship between physical features and character and personality. In the character analysis, it is a challenge to choose exactly the kind of feature that will tell the audience most about the character and that will best support the character portrait the actor is trying to present.

ETHNICITY

In realistic plays written to chronicle specific human experience, ethnicity is always a factor to be considered, whether it is mentioned in the play or not. Contemporary history plays such as August Wilson's *Gem of the Ocean*, Octavio Solis' *Se Llama Christina*, and David Henry Hwang's *Chinglish* paint a picture of American history fashioned out of unique cultural experiences. Demands of each script require specific cultural images to advance the dramatic action. Members of the same family should appear to be of the same ethnicity—unless there are adopted children of other ethnic backgrounds, a fact that would surely be brought out in the dialogue. Historical characters should appear to be of whatever ethnicity or combination of ethnicities they actually were—unless the playwright or director has decided to disregard the historical facts (i.e. the Broadway production of *Hamilton*).

ENVIRONMENT

In addition to ethnicity and other hereditary factors, environment is of considerable importance in determining the color and texture of the skin. A construction worker and a computer programmer are likely to have different colors and textures of skin, and a color which is right for one would probably look incongruous on the other.

One must take into consideration not only the general climatic conditions of the part of the world in which the character lives, but also the character's physical work conditions and leisure-time activities. Offices, mines, fields, foundries, night clubs, and country estates all have different effects upon the people who work or live in them. But remember that a character may have had a variety of environments. Monsieur Madeleine in Victor Hugo's *Les Misérables* may be a wealthy and highly respected mayor, but his physical appearance will still bear the marks of his years of imprisonment as the convict Jean Valjean. If environment is to be construed as referring to all external forces and situations affecting the individual, then custom or fashion may logically be considered a part of the environmental influences, and a very important one. Influences arising from social customs and attitudes have throughout the centuries brought about superficial and self-imposed changes in appearance.

During most of the first half of the twentieth century it was assumed that men's hair would be short and that women's hair would be longer. A man might have been capable of growing long hair and might even have preferred long hair, but social pressures were at work to discourage him. During other periods of history, however, customs were different, and men wore their hair long and in some periods wore wigs. Research into the historical period that the character is from should include finding accurate visual images like paintings from that time.

Similarly, the wearing of makeup off stage has varied throughout the centuries. If an eighteenth-century fop appears to be wearing makeup, no harm is done because he might very well have done so, but if any of the men in a realistic mid-twentieth-century play are obviously made up, they immediately become less believable. Furthermore, styles in street makeup vary. The plucked eyebrows, brilliant rouge, and bizarre lips of the late 1920s would seem anachronistic in most other periods. Similar eccentricities such as the heavy, stylized eye makeup of the ancient Egyptians can be found in other periods in history.

Remember that, on the stage, makeup should look like makeup only when the character would normally be wearing it. That means that your character must be analyzed in the light of the social customs to determine not only possible hairstyles, but also the accepted usage in regard to makeup. Sally Bowles, a nightclub singer at the Kit Kat Klub in the musical *Cabaret*, was considered a "Weimar Girl" or New Woman, a movement that began at the end of WWI in Weimar, Germany when women were granted suffrage and equality. It was a time when gender roles were in question and women began expressing their new freedoms. *Cabaret* was set in 1931. The look at that time included bobbed hair, pale foundation, thinly painted, arched brows, rosy, flushed cheeks (evening color), deep purple eyeshadow (or blue), shiny eyelids, and a lip shape wider than the 1920s but with a similar over-painted bow in a dark red-plum color (see Figure 4.2). For every character that you make up, always analyze the skin color, hairstyle, and street makeup in terms of environmental influences.

FIGURE 4.2 *Claire Taylor as Sally Bowles in the musical, Cabaret, at The Fugard Theatre, Johannesburg, South Africa.*

Source: Photograph by Jesse Kate Kramer.

FIGURE 4.3 *Charl-Johan Lingenfelder as the Emcee in the musical, Cabaret, at The Fugard Theatre in Cape Town, South Africa. The Emcee represents sexual freedom and makes extreme sexuality appealing (Scott Miller).*

***Source:** Photograph by Jesse Kate Kramer.*

TEMPERAMENT

An individual's temperament, which can be interpreted as including personality, disposition, and personal habits, affects physical appearance in many ways (see Figure 4.4). The adventurer and the scholar, the Bohemian artist and the shrewd business person, the prizefighter and the cross-dresser, all are widely different in temperament, and these differences are to a greater or lesser degree apparent in the physical appearance. The convivial Sir Toby Belch and the melancholy Sir Andrew Aguecheek in Shakespeare's *Twelfth Night*, for example, are, aside from all other differences, widely contrasting in temperament and could not conceivably look alike.

FIGURE 4.4 *Character makeups on the same actor showing differences in age and temperament. Actor Colm Fiore in the film, Storm of the Century. Makeup effects by Maestro Studios F/X, Inc. Quebec, Canada.*

The March sisters in *Little Women* are products of the same environment and the same heredity. Temperamental differences make them strongly individual, and their individuality should be reflected in the makeup.

Agnes Gooch, the shy, dowdy secretary in the movie *Auntie Mame* (and musical, *Mame*) would certainly not be wearing false eyelashes and it is most unlikely that she would be wearing green eyeshadow. Yet green eyeshadow might be quite right for a dissolute, aging actress in Tennessee Williams' *Sweet Bird of Youth*.

The hair is an even more striking and obvious reflection of personality. One would expect the mature and socially correct Lady Bracknell in *The Importance of Being Ernest* to have her hair beautifully done, not a hair out of place, perhaps not in the latest fashion but in one considered proper for a woman of her years and of her elevated social station (see Figure 14.2).

The Cockney flower girl Eliza Doolittle in *My Fair Lady (Pygmalion)*, on the other hand, might be expected to give her hair no attention at all, except, perhaps, to push it out of her

FIGURE 4.5 *Michelle Lee as Madame Morrible, the wicked Headmistress of Crage Hall at Shiz University in the Broadway musical, Wicked. Strong contrasts between the white foundation and hair color and the severe red lipstick, dark eyes, dark, arched brows support the antagonist temperament of this character. Makeup design by Joe Dulude II.*

Source: Photograph by Joan Marcus.

eyes. When she is transformed into a "lady," her hair, as well as everything else about her, must reflect the change.

There are fewer opportunities for men to express their personality in this way, but the ones which exist must not be overlooked. When a beard or a mustache is to be worn, it offers an opportunity to reflect personality. First of all, there is the choice of whether to wear facial hair at all. And the choice is always related to fashion. In other words, it would take as much courage not to wear a mustache or beard in 1870 as it would to wear one in, say, 1940. In 1960 it would take less courage than in 1940, but the mere fact of wearing a beard would still be significant and a clear reflection of personality.

Second, once the decision to wear the beard has been made, there is the equally important decision as to what kind of beard to wear. You must know first of all what type of beards were being worn in the period. If fashions were very limiting, there is less freedom of choice: if the character departs from the fashion (and there are always those who do), it is doubly significant. But there are several periods in history, especially in the late nineteenth century and early twenty-first century, for example, when facial hair was the rule and the style was limited only by the imagination, taste, and hair-growing capability of the individual. In such periods there is an extraordinary opportunity to express personality through conscious choice of style in facial hair.

The same principles apply, as well, to hair on the head. There are often limitations on styles for men, but even during periods when convention was very restrictive, as in the second quarter of the twentieth century, there was still some variation in length, in wave or absence of it, in the location of the part, and in color.

An interesting case of temperamental differences resulting in both conscious and unconscious physical changes is found in Jean Giraudoux's *Madwoman of Chaillot*. There are, in fact, four madwomen, each completely different from the others temperamentally, each showing that difference in her face. Countess Aurelia, the Madwoman of Chaillot, is calm, compassionate, clever, rather tragic, and completely charming. Mme. Constance, the Madwoman of Passy, is garrulous, argumentative, bad-tempered, flighty, and quick to take offense. Mlle. Gabrielle, the Madwoman of St. Sulpice, is shy, retiring, and easily hurt. And Mme. Josephine, the Madwoman of La Concorde, is forthright, practical, and very businesslike. A makeup that would be appropriate for one of the madwomen would be completely wrong for any of the others.

These are not problems to be faced only with certain striking characters, like the madwomen or Sir Toby Belch, or on special occasions when circumstances demand it. They should be considered and solved for every character.

An actress of 25 who is playing a contemporary character of 25 must not assume that her hairstyle or her way of making up her eyebrows or her lips will automatically be suitable for the character. The problem becomes particularly acute in repertory theater or summer stock when an actor is playing a different role every week or even every night, sometimes with very little variations in age. It is then more important than ever that ways of distinguishing among the characters be found. This means finding the most revealing ways in which character might be expressed and using these to help develop individuality in the makeup.

HEALTH

In most cases a character's state of health has nothing to do with the play. But sometimes, as with Mimi in RENT and Mimi in the opera *La Bohème*, there are noticeable changes that are important to the characterization or the plot. At other

FIGURE 4.6 *Jamie Ann Romero as Viola and Thomas Kent (respectively) in the 2017 Oregon Shakespeare Festival production of Shakespeare in Love. Ms. Romero changed between these two characters throughout the play using a wig change and facial hair to distinguish one character from the other.*

times, as with Laura in *The Glass Menagerie*, there is no specific illness, just a state of delicate health. A character may also be undernourished and must give physical evidence of this. By contrast, there are those who are over-nourished and suffer from gout. And there are others who are bursting with health and should show it in their faces.

Even when a specific illness is not indicated, it is seldom necessary, therefore, to try to reproduce medically accurate physical symptoms. Any physical suggestions of the illness can usually be confined to changes in the skin color, the eyes, and perhaps the hair. Addiction to drugs or alcohol, often a debilitating illness, must be presented carefully. Not all addictions appear the same because each character deals with their addiction differently. Leading characters in Andrew Lippa's *The Wild Party*, and John LaChuisa's *See What I Wanna See* are living and dealing with drug addictions. Even though they have the same addiction, during the design process they should be considered differently. Mental illness is also a complicated medical condition covering multiple behaviors. Anxiety, for example, experienced by the character Deb singing "Calm" in *Ordinary Days* is quite different from the depression of the character singing "Anyway" from *Tales from the Bad Years*. As always, it is better to do too little than too much. Above all, avoid attributing specific physical symptoms to certain illnesses that are inaccurate and that will be spotted immediately by medical professionals in the audience. In certain areas of makeup it is best to curb the imagination and rely strictly on factual information (Maddy McClouskey, newmusicaltheatre.com).

AGE

Since age invariably affects all people in physical terms, it is an essential consideration in every makeup, but not necessarily the most important one. How old is Falstaff, for example, or Lady Macbeth? Is it important to know this information precisely? Are there not more important facts to know about those particular characters? Before beginning the makeup, there must be some definite decision made about the age, and that decision will rest with the actor and the director. But in makeup we are interested in the apparent, not the actual, age, and this depends on the kind of life the character has led and how the character feels about it.

Thus, the environment may have affected the character's apparent age, but so has his or her mental attitude. Is it positive or negative? Is he or she cheerful or morose? Does the character feel sorry for himself or herself, or is he or she glad to be alive? Do they look forward or backward? And how old do they think they are? Are they conscious of getting older each year or does time seem to have stopped? Do they really want to remain young?

Remember also that apparent age is related to nutrition and thus involves health, which depends on both nutrition and mental attitudes. As you can see, the various factors affecting the appearance are in many cases interrelated and cannot always be considered separately. For example, Mrs Lovett in *Sweeney Todd: The Demon Barber of Fleet Street* (see Figure 4.1), is characterized in the lyrics (by Stephen Sondheim and Hugh Wheeler) as "a vigorous, slatternly woman in her forties, is flicking flies off the trays of pies with a dirty rag as she sings or hums." Through her ragged, dirty looks, bug-infested bake shop, and the fact that she "hasn't had a customer in weeks," we can assume she is impoverished and a bit disorganized.

Discussing specific effects of age can be only general and indicate the kind of changes that may take place. The conventional divisions of youth, middle age, and old age are serviceable for this discussion.

Youth (see Figure 7.10): There is an unfortunate custom in the theatre of referring to any youthful makeup as a straight makeup. This means simply that you do nothing but heighten the color and project the features. Designating a makeup as "straight" can lead to neglect of essential work. Conceivably, the term has a certain validity in the event that a specific role is cast so that the actor's features are exactly right, with not a hair to be changed. If makeup is required that will change the actor to fit the character being played, this is called a character makeup (Figure 8.5 Ebenezer Scrooge).

Now, there are instances when there is no clearly defined character, or perhaps no character at all. Sometimes in the chorus of a play, musical, or opera, or as an extra in a film, it is expected that the actors appear as themselves, but it is rare to find an actor who cannot profit by some facial improvement. And a straight makeup does not improve; it merely projects. When we wish to improve an actor's face without relating it to a specific character, we use *corrective makeup* (see Figure 7.10).

Makeup for youth, except when actors are appearing as themselves, requires a character analysis. The physical attributes of youthfulness are usually smooth skin; a good deal of color in the face; soft, full lips; smooth brows following the shape of the eye; an abundance of hair, and so on. Those are, of course, generalized characteristics. Heredity, environment, temperament, and health may counteract the normal effects of youth, as in the case of Richard III. Despite the fact that Richard is a young man at the time of the play, he is hardly an average, normal one. Although there may be little in his face to suggest age, it will probably not seem particularly youthful. Temperament and environment will have had strong influences on his physical appearance.

Ophelia in *Hamlet* is a young girl, but her profound unhappiness and confusion, which finally result in a complete

FIGURE 4.7 *Soprano Beverly Sills as Queen Elizabeth I in the New York City Opera production of Giacomo Donizetti's, Roberto Devereux. Queen Elizabeth I is known to have worn a type of white makeup that contained lead and vinegar called Ceruse. This product quickly caused severe dryness and premature aging to the skin. It is also known to have caused pock marks and other skin conditions. Plucked hairlines, high arching brows, and black kohl eyeliner were also fashionable. In the 1970s, when this photograph was taken, makeup for the opera stage was quite dramatic. Notice the dark arching eyelid crease, black and white lines surrounding the eyes, dark lines defining the nasalabial folds, strong lip liner, and highly contoured nose, cheeks, jawline, and neck. Contemporary opera makeup practice has become more realistic in style. In the era of the high-definition (HD) camera, opera is often broadcast worldwide and projected on large format screens in movie theaters and at outdoor venues.*

Source:* *Photograph by Jack Mitchell (licensed by Getty Images).

FIGURE 4.8 *Soprano Sondra Radvanovky as Queen Elizabeth I in the 2017 Metropolitan Opera's production of Donizetti's Roberto Devereux. Ms. Radvanovsky's interpretation of this queen is realistic in nature, and in the final moments of the story reveals her emotional and physical breakdown at the death of her lover, Roberto Devereux. At that moment she removes the façade and finery of her court gown revealing a broken old woman. In this photograph the makeup artist is creating a realistic makeup showing the high forehead, pale skin color with a severe skin condition, and subtle aging effects (notice the neck wrinkles) without the dramatic highlight and shadow effects once common in opera stage makeup.*

Source: Photograph by Ken Howard.

mental breakdown and suicide, must certainly, along with other elements in her personality, be reflected in some way, however subtly, in the makeup.

Middle Age: This is an indefinite period somewhere in the middle of life. It reaches its climax perhaps in the fifties or even the sixties, depending on the individual. For purposes of this discussion it can be considered as including all ages between 40 and 65. But remember that in earlier historical times middle age came much sooner. In any case, it is the apparent rather than the actual age that is important in makeup.

Age can, and often does, bring with it changes in the color of the skin and the hair—sagging muscles, graying and thinning hair, an increased thinning in the lips, deeper creases and wrinkles in the skin, and the hollowing of the cheeks—but the exact nature of these changes will depend on factors other than age. So it is important in every case to determine how seriously and in what ways age has affected appearance. And remember that the effects of age are modified radically by health, environment, temperament, and mental habits.

Old Age: As a person advances beyond middle life, the skull structure usually becomes more prominent especially if the person is thin. A large person will have a greater tendency toward flabbiness, with pouches and puffs and double chins. Along with a general sagging of the flesh, the tip of the nose may droop, hair may fall out, eyebrows may become bushy or scraggly, lips almost invariably become thinner, teeth may discolor and possibly fall out, skin and hair color will probably change, the skin on the neck may droop, the hands may become bony, and the face may be a mass of wrinkles. It is up to you to decide which of these effects apply to your character. Again, changes will be affected by health, environment, temperament, and mental attitudes.

The creative aspect of makeup lies in the mind of the artist and stems directly from the artist's understanding of the character. Following such a plan of character analysis means, of course, that all consideration of makeup cannot be left until the night of dress rehearsal. It is something that should be planned as carefully as the sets and the costumes. If, before you sit down at your dressing table, you have intelligently planned the physical changes you wish to make, you will have mastered the creative part of your problem and will have left only the technical task of executing your ideas.

PHYSIOGNOMY

Since the beginning of the human race people must have observed other people and drawn conclusions from their appearances as to their probable behavior. Through trial and error, certain correlations have been found that seem to hold up with reasonable consistency. Just as people draw these conclusions consciously or unconsciously in daily life, so they continue to do so when they see characters on the stage in the theater. The actor may choose to turn this into an advantage by becoming consciously aware of the correlations of physical appearance with character and personality traits. If not, the actor is taking the risk of assuming physical characteristics that could mislead the audience and detract from the believability of the character. (See image of Richard III, played by actress, Seana McKenna, Figure 14.8.)

The practice of relating physical appearance to character and personality traits is defined by the dictionary as physiognomy. A familiarity with some of the principles of physiognomy can be enormously helpful in designing a face for the actor's character.

Much of this you already do unconsciously. Look, for example, at the faces in Figure 5.4. Study each character sketch and ask yourself why it suits the character. Is it a strong face or a weak one? Does it look optimistic or pessimistic? Sensitive or crude? Aggressive or timid? Determined or vacillating? Intelligent or not?

Whether your response to the face is intuitive or analytical, it comes under the heading of physiognomy, and it is essentially what the audience does in relation to every character on the stage. Actors would do well to be aware of the ways in which an audience may relate physical appearance to personality and character traits.

In making changes in the face, remember that you are dealing with a whole face, not just a single feature, and those changes you do make will inevitably be affected by other areas of the face.

Eyes: Perhaps no other feature betrays the inner person so clearly as the eyes. In general, prominent eyes are found on dreamers and aesthetes who live largely through their senses, whereas deep-set eyes are more likely to be an indication of an observant, analytical mind. We might say that one is the eye of a Romeo, the other of a Cassius. Many eyes will be neither strongly one nor the other, and thus the individuality might be expected to include characteristics of both types.

The eyes and the mouth often change markedly during one's lifetime. These changes are usually associated with the aging process, but the kind of changes that take place will depend upon the sort of mental, emotional, and physical life one leads. The kind of wrinkles which develop through frequent laughter, for example, quite logically suggest a happy, kindly disposition.

Eyebrows: One of the most expressive and easily changed features of all. Even a slight change in the eyebrow can affect the entire face. Eyebrows vary in placement, line, thickness, color, length, and direction of the hairs. They can reveal mental or physical energy (Figure 4.10a), suggest weakness or lack of concentration (Figure 4.9, Brad and Janet), and define a practical, intelligent personality from a simple, erratic one (Figures 4.10c and 4.10e). If you want to suggest treachery or cunning, put a curve in the brow and angle it upwards (Figures 4.9 and 4.10b, Frank N. Furter). This would also be an appropriate brow for Iago and Richard III and is, in fact, the brow of Henry VIII.

Nose: These can be classified as to size and shape (in profile). They can also be described in definitive terms such

FIGURE 4.9 *The Rocky Horror Show. Jenny Stead as Janet; Brendan van Rhyn as Frank N. Furter; and Paul du Toit as Brad. The emotional states of each of these characters are clearly revealed through their expressions and makeup design.*

Source: Photograph by Jesse Kate Kramer.

FIGURE 4.10 *Five character makeups on the same actor. As an exercise, develop a story around each of these characters using the principles presented in this chapter.*

Source: Makeup by Richard Corson.

as Grecian or straight nose, Aquiline or Roman, and retroussé (slightly turned up); and with descriptive words such as strong, refined, aristocratic, cute, and inquisitive.

The nose is the bony feature that is relatively easy to remodel in three dimensions. A very little added to or subtracted from the nose can, like a change in the eyebrows, alter the entire face. And since the change is so dramatic, it is important that the right kind of change be made. Once the decision to change the shape of the nose is made, questions such as what qualities would be appropriate for the character must be asked. Should it be straight or crooked, long or short, convex or concave, narrow or wide? Imagine, if you can, a Lady Macbeth with a small, delicate, turned-up nose or a Snow White with a large Roman one. Researching a variety of profiles and choosing one that seems appropriate is an invaluable next step. How it will look on the actor's face is a simple matter of experimentation.

Mouth: The size and shape of the mouth and the thickness and color of the lips affect the overall impression of character. The mouth can be large and expansive or small and contracted. It can curve upward or downward, be held loosely or tightly closed. Lips can be thin and straight or full and shapely. They can reveal a social personality or an introverted one. They can indicate warmth or reserve, a serious nature or one full of humor. The mouth is a good indicator of age, becoming thinner, more angular, and losing color as one becomes older.

The suggestions in this chapter are to be used only as guides. Use these brief suggestions with discretion and try always to correlate the features and not rely on only one to suggest the character. You will rarely be able to make all of the changes you consider ideal, but the purpose of character analysis is to discover the determining factors in the character's behavior and then to visualize the final look.

CHAPTER 5

DESIGNING THE MAKEUP

Once you have decided what you want the character to look like, the next step is to put your ideas into concrete form—an experimental makeup, a sketch, or a computer rendering showing what you have in mind. Which you do will probably depend to some extent on whether you are an actor or a makeup designer. In either case, making a visual representation of the makeup can be extremely helpful. For a makeup designer, professional or nonprofessional, it is almost essential.

FIGURE 5.1 *Scene from the Broadway musical, Anastasia (at Hartford Stage)—Mary Beth Piel as the Dowager Empress and Christy Altomare as Anya. Makeup design by Joe Dulude II.*

Source: Photograph by Peter Casolino: Special to the Hartford Courant.

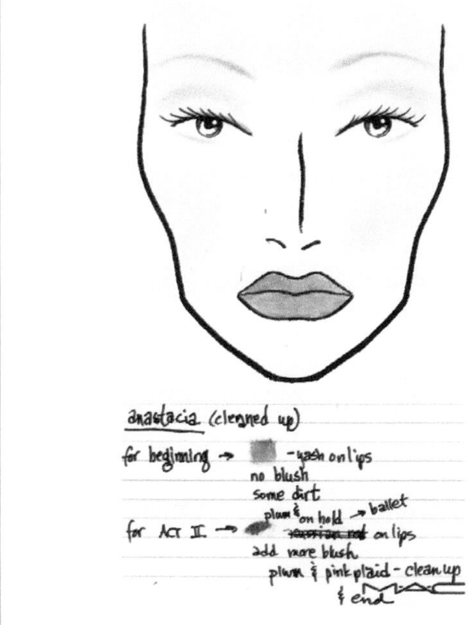

FIGURE 5.2 Makeup face chart for the character, Anastasia. A very simple classic beauty look. This did change over time. We added blush and took away the dirt. Makeup designer, Joe Dulude II.
(Act I. Eyes:
Vanilla on lid (from lash line to brow)
Crease—Sushi Flower (pinky-coral)
Top liner—Espresso (muted golden-brown)
Bottom liner—Quarry (soft plum-brown)
Natural brows
Blush—Mocha (plum-pink)
Lipstick—Pink Plaid with a sheer red over
Lip Liner—Plum
Act II. Add a smokier eye using Espresso and Carbon
Blush—Whole Lotta Love (flush pinky-rose)
Lipstick—for Begin act—Full Fuchsia lipstick, then change to Make Up For Ever 401 lipstick for last look and ballet. All the previous items are from MAC Cosmetics. #7 lashes for Act II.)

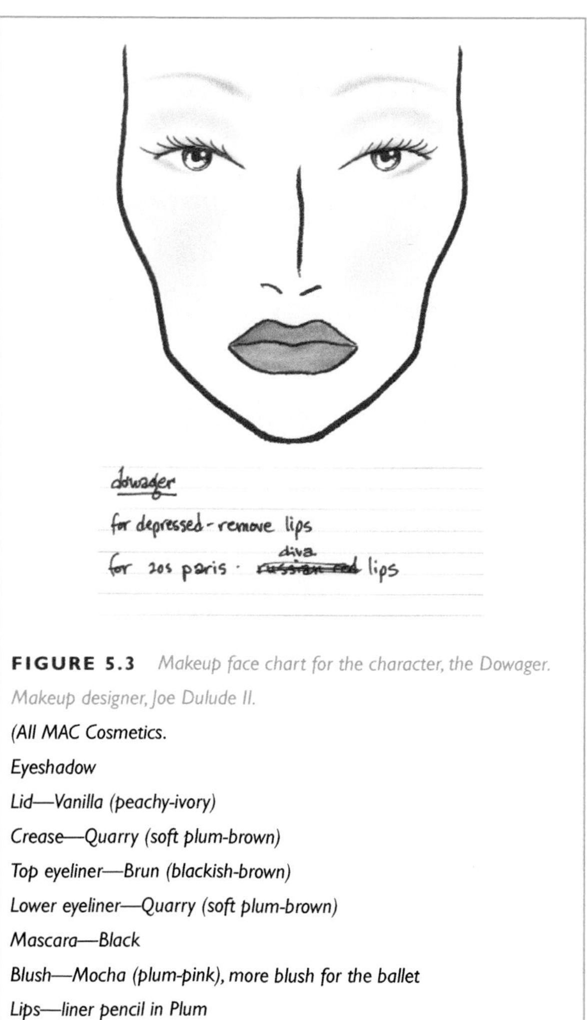

FIGURE 5.3 Makeup face chart for the character, the Dowager. Makeup designer, Joe Dulude II.
(All MAC Cosmetics.
Eyeshadow
Lid—Vanilla (peachy-ivory)
Crease—Quarry (soft plum-brown)
Top eyeliner—Brun (blackish-brown)
Lower eyeliner—Quarry (soft plum-brown)
Mascara—Black
Blush—Mocha (plum-pink), more blush for the ballet
Lips—liner pencil in Plum
Lipstick—Peach Blossom (peachy-pink satin)
Diva for the ballet.)

THE MAKEUP DESIGNER

If all of the makeups are being designed by one person, he or she will first study the play, then consult with the director, the costume designer, and, ideally, with the actors before designing the makeups and will also obtain photographs of the actors before making the sketches. Then, after the sketches have been approved by the director, the designer should make certain that the actors can do the makeup. If not, it is the responsibility of the makeup designer to teach the actors to do it, making sure they understand the instructions on the makeup charts (see Figure 5.12). And if the time for applying the makeup is going to be limited (as with quick changes or with the actors playing more than one part), it is the makeup designer's responsibility to make certain that the makeup, as designed, can be done by the actors (or the makeup artist) in the time available. Unless the makeups are unusually simple, all of this should be taken care of before the first dress rehearsal. The makeup designer should be present at the first dress rehearsal with lighting in order to see the makeup in action on the stage. He or she can then consult with the director if necessary and suggest to the actors any changes that need to be made. Only when the designer is completely satisfied that the makeups are being executed satisfactorily should the actors be left on their own. In the case of a long run, the designer should check the makeups regularly. This, of course, is completely dependent upon the contract the designer has with the producing organization. On Broadway, for example, the makeup designer is brought on board by the costume designer, but the terms of the contract—design development, budget, and contact time with the cast before and after the opening of the show—is determined by the producers.

In television and film, on Broadway, in opera, and some regional theaters, the makeup designer is a professional makeup artist. In other theaters and dance companies the makeup design is often the responsibility of the actor or the costume designer and is executed by the actor. On occasion, a makeup artist will be contracted for special makeup effects. In academic theater the designer may be the makeup teacher, the costumer, or one of the more advanced makeup students, who should, when competent to do so, be given the opportunity to design the makeups for public productions.

Many professional productions, especially musicals, use makeup artists to assist the actors. *The Lion King* productions (Broadway and the touring shows) employ full-time makeup artists who assist the performers on a daily basis. The musicals *Beautiful* and *Anastasia*, on the other hand, require the performers to apply their own makeup. Other companies, professional or not, usually do not have the budget to retain makeup artists for the show, but the designer responsible for the makeup can schedule training sessions with the actors before dress rehearsals begin. The ultimate goal for both situations is to achieve the desired look and make sure the actor is confident and at ease.

When the makeup is finished, photographing it with a cell phone or digital camera can be very helpful and may, in fact, lead to further work on the makeup. When the actors are satisfied with the makeup, they then learn—with the help of the makeup artist, if necessary—to do the makeup themselves, using drawings and photographs as a guide. The actors should also keep the photographs on a dressing table until they are secure in doing the makeup without them (see Britney Simpson's makeup application for her performance as Madame De La Grande Bouche in Disney's Beauty and the Beast in Chapter 6).

THE ACTOR AS DESIGNER

If there is no makeup designer for the production and no makeup artist is called in to help individual actors, the actors then become their own makeup designers. As such, they have the advantage of knowing, better than anyone else, the character as they want to portray it. They also have the opportunity to experiment with the makeup over a period of time until they achieve the results they want. A "selfie" taken with a cell phone can provide the means for actors to look at the makeup objectively. They can then make any changes or corrections that seem desirable.

In designing their own makeup, actors must consult with the other cast members to agree on a makeup style that suits the production's design concept and makeup style (realistic, futuristic, high fashion, or stylized). They can begin by sketching their ideas on paper, as a makeup designer does, or by experimenting directly with makeup on their own faces. They should, of course, choose whichever method works better for them and make notes as they develop the look.

The actor can show their sketches, or a "selfie," of the design to the costume designer for approval or suggestions. Or they may prefer to show the director concept photographs (mood boards) of makeup ideas they have in mind. Although none of these will be expected, they can be useful in avoiding basic disagreements about the makeup the first time the director sees it at a dress rehearsal.

COSTUME DESIGNER'S INFLUENCE ON THE MAKEUP DESIGN

The first images to appear when developing the look of any character will, more often than not, originate from the costume designer. After spending months in collaboration with the director, scene designer, and lighting designer, the costume designer will produce sketches or renderings of each character in the production. These sketches are based on thorough research of the period in history in which the production is placed, on a thorough examination of each character, on the designer's intuition and aesthetic, and on a thorough understanding of the meaning and intentions of the story being told. The sketches are intended to represent the "look" of the production. They provide visual information about the character to the director, to the actor, to the costume shop, to the milliner (when appropriate), and to the hair and makeup departments. Some designers' sketches are to be interpreted literally and are such detailed and precise representations that fabric design, shoe styles, and even eyeshadow and lipstick colors can be perfectly matched (see Figure 5.17). Other designers provide sketches that allow for greater interpretation.

Costume designers' renderings can often be used as character sketches, revealing not only the costume, but also the personality of the character through physical appearance. The sketches in Figure 5.4 have been selected from full costume renderings to illustrate the costume designer's insight into the character and how that might influence the makeup design.

FIGURE 5.4 *Costume designer renderings used as character sketches. A. Marley by Sheila Hargett from A Christmas Carol. Southwest Texas State University. B. Francis Flute by Martin Pakledinaz from A Midsummer Night's Dream. Pacific Northwest Ballet. C. Scrooge by Esther Marquis from Charles Dickens' Christmas Carol, A Ghost Story of Christmas. The Alley Theatre. D. Antonio by Sheila Hargett from The Tempest. Southwest Texas State University. E. Amelia by Susan Tsu from Lost Electra. Asolo Theatre Company. F. Dr. Watson by Robert Morgan from Sherlock's Last Case. G. Kate Hardcastle by Susan Tsu from She Stoops to Conquer. Theatre Virginia. H. King Arthur by Desmond Heeley from Camelot. National Tour with Richard Burton. I. Dona Elvira by Robert Morgan from Don Juan. The Huntington Theatre. J. Trinculo by Sheila Hargett from The Tempest. Southwest Texas State University. K. Salome by Martin Pakledinaz from Salome. Santa Fe Opera. L. Dracula by Susan Tsu from Dracula, A Musical Nightmare. The Alley Theatre.*

SKETCHES AND DRAWINGS

Two kinds of sketches or drawings can be used in designing makeups—*character* (those which present a visual conception of the character, as in Figure 5.5) and *makeup* (those which show the character conception adapted to the actor's face, as in Figures 5.7, 5.8, and 5.9). Whether they are called *sketches* or *drawings* depends largely on the relative degree of spontaneity with which they are executed. A sketch (Figure 5.9) is the more spontaneous and is usually done more quickly than a drawing (Figure 5.16). It is the makeup drawings, rather than the character sketches, that show what the actor can really be expected to look like when the makeup is finished.

Preliminary Sketches: These can be done in any medium you choose—pencil, charcoal (or charcoal pencil) and chalk, pen and ink, pastel, conté crayon, or makeup. They will usually be in black and white or sepia but can, of course, be in color if you wish. If you are inexperienced at sketching, it may be easier for you to use an outline of a head (front view and profile), such as those shown on the worksheet in Figure 5.13.

ADAPTING THE MAKEUP TO THE ACTOR

One of the simplest—and certainly most reliable—methods of adapting the ideal concept of the character to the face of the actor who is to play the part is to work from photographs—front and profile—of the actor, making sure, of course, that the photographs are recent enough so that the face will not have significantly aged. Place a sheet of tracing paper over the photograph (Figure 5.8a) and sketch the character in pencil, being very careful not to change the actor's face in any way in which it cannot actually be changed with makeup. The drawings in Figure 5.9 were sketched from the photographs in Figures 5.10a and b. Figures 5.10c and d show the final makeup. Note the close resemblance between the drawing and the makeup—a result of working directly from a photograph of the actor.

If you have not previously worked from photographs in this way, you may prefer to begin by making a drawing of the actor's own face. This is the procedure:

FIGURE 5.5 *Character rendering of Sir Toby Belch in* Twelfth Night *by Romanian costume designer, Miruna Boruzescu (produced at the Guthrie Theatre).*

FIGURE 5.6 *Costume rendering of Count Dracula for the Alley Theatre production of* Dracula, A Musical Nightmare *by costume designer Susan Tsu.*

FIGURE 5.7 *Makeup worksheets for The Wedding Singer by makeup designer Joe Dulude II. The designs follow the makeup quick changes of actor Adinah Alexander through one performance of the production of the Broadway musical (set in the 1980s). Ms. Alexander played Angie, Julia's mother, and was a member of the ensemble. This performer is "tracked" through the show playing a variety of different characters with lines that required the designer to create some dramatic changes so she would be less recognizable to the audience. The design concept was to start simple, build to a more dramatic look, then remove the makeup and start over, simple to more dramatic.*

a. Look 1—The opening of the show as a wedding guest.

b. Look 2 and 3—Begins as Angie, the Mom, then changes lip color to be a bridesmaid at the wedding.

c. Look 4—simpler makeup using more neutrals as the "weight-challenged down-on-her-luck lady."

d. Look 5—Faye, complete change of eye makeup with green shadow and liner completely around the eye.

Look 6—NYC nightclub goer, add dark purple lip liner for a more goth look.

e. Look 7—Opening of Act II as a stock trader. More simple with neutrals. The entire cast changed from club makeup to office makeup for Act II.

f. Look 8—Angie's Mom again. More dramatic.

g. Look 9—Angie for the wedding was even more dramatic.

h. Look 10—Change of lipstick color to play an Airline agent who was an Annie Lennox celebrity look-a-like. With little time to change makeup she wore a pair of sunglasses to completely change her look.

1. Place a large glossy photograph of the actor under a sheet of tracing paper. You can tape both the photograph and the tracing paper to a drawing board, or if you prefer to use a pad of tracing paper, you can simply insert the photograph under the top sheet.
2. Using a sharp pencil with a medium (B) lead, trace the outline of the face and the features and fill in lips, eyebrows, eyes, and shadows. Paper stumps can be used for blending small areas, and the fingers for larger ones.
3. The hair should be sketched in but need not be done in great detail.
4. Remove the photograph and add finishing details to the drawing.

In making a drawing of the character from a photograph of the actor, follow the same procedure, but instead of copying the actor's features exactly, change those you wish to alter for the character, as illustrated in Figure 5.8.

QUICK CHANGES

If there are quick changes to be made or if your facilities or your time for making complicated prosthetic pieces are limited, then you should make sure that the requirements for the makeup are reasonable. If they are not, you will need to modify your design to meet practical considerations. Performers playing more than one character throughout a performance must plan their makeup changes carefully, especially if they change back and forth more than one time (see Figure 4.6). The designer can be helpful to the performer by planning the changes in a way that provides a smooth transition between characters.

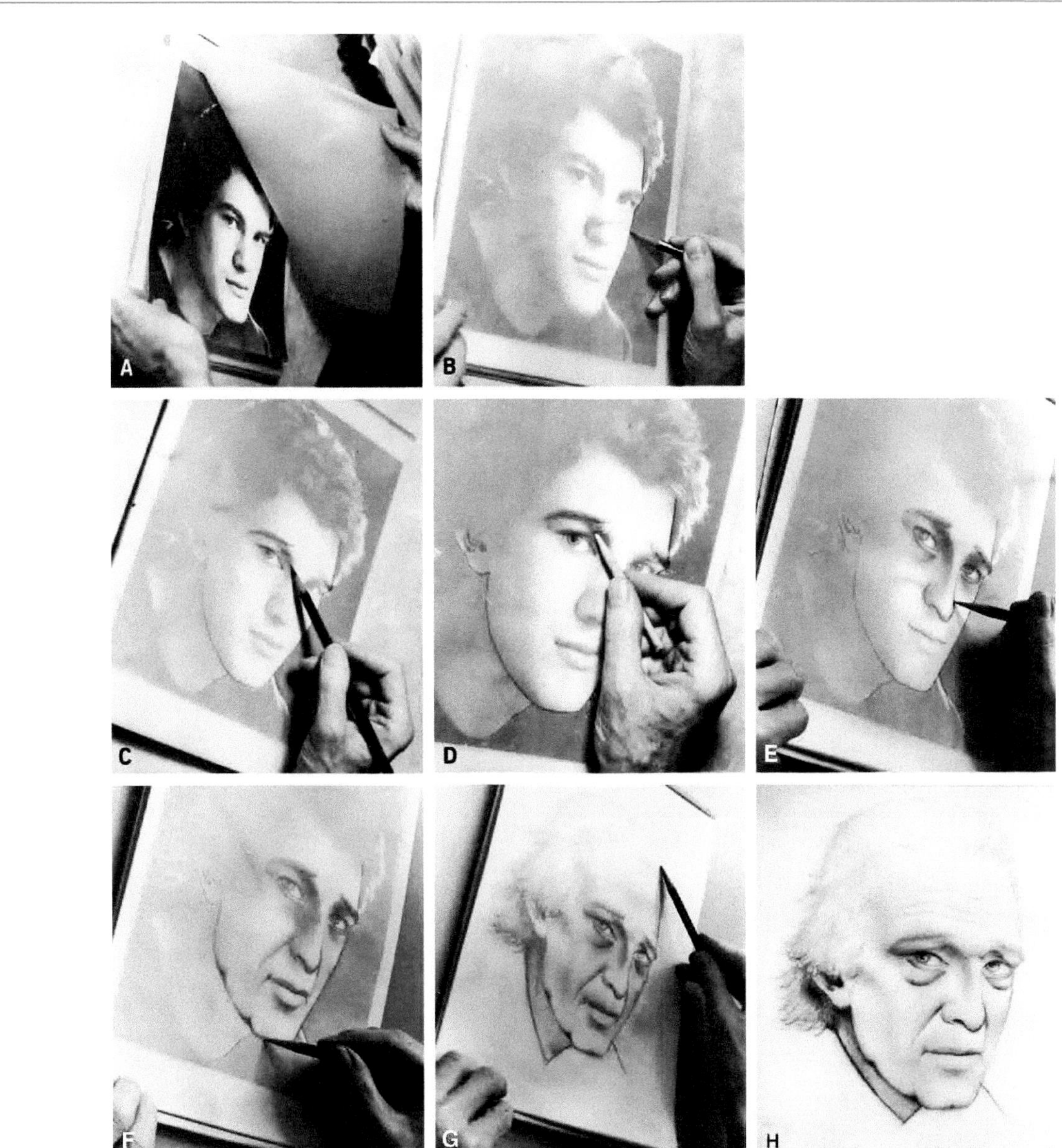

FIGURE 5.8 *Making a character drawing from a photograph. A. Placing photograph of the actor under a sheet of tracing paper. B. Outlining the face with a drawing pencil. C. Shadows in the eye area being laid in with a pencil. D. Shadows being blended with a paper stump. E. Nose being reshaped. F. Jawline being aged. G. The character's hair being sketched in after the photograph has been removed. H. Finished drawing.*

FIGURE 5.9 *Pencil drawings by Costume Designer, Esther Marquis for Ebenezer Scrooge in Charles Dickens' Christmas Carol, A Ghost Story of Christmas at the Alley Theatre.*

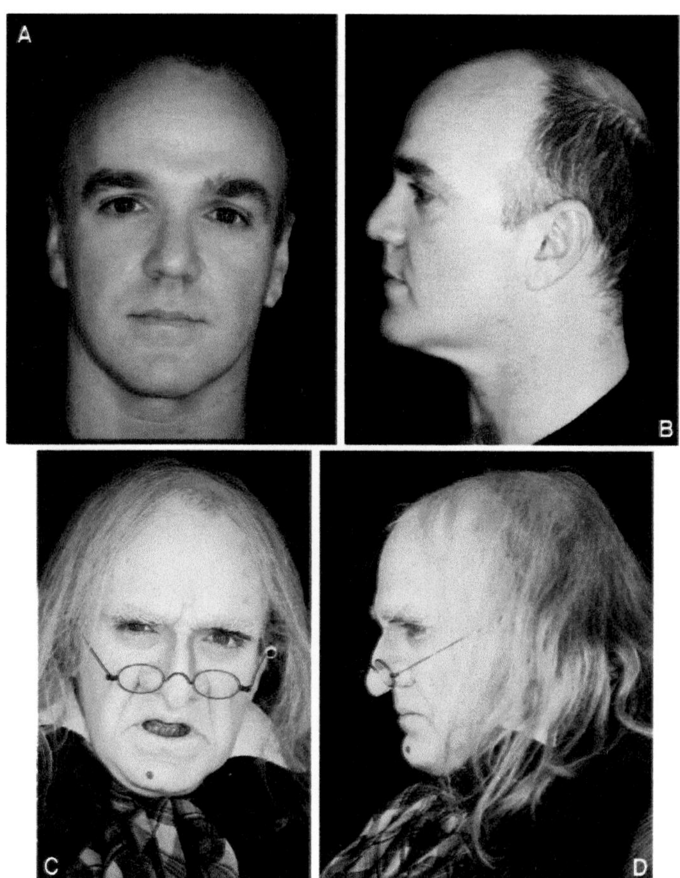

FIGURE 5.10 *Scrooge in Charles Dickens' Christmas Carol, A Ghost Story of Christmas. A. and B. Actor James Black. C. and D. Final makeup based on sketches in Figure 5.9.*

FIGURE 5.11 *Deborah Cox as Lucy in the Broadway production of Jekyll and Hyde. Makeup designer Joe Dulude II.*

Source: Photograph by Chris Bennion.

Deborah Cox as Lucy
Step 1 - Orb pressed shadow over the entire lid from lash to brow
Step 2 - Add Naked Lunch pressed powder on the inner corner
Step 3 - Add Amber Lights on the center and outer lid
Step 4 - Apply Carbon in the crease and use as a smudge liner on top and bottom lashline
Step 5 - Apply Smolder eye kohl around the entire lashline to darken
Step 6 - Apply blach mascara and full lashes
Step 7 - Raizin blush as a contour under the cheek bones
Step 8 - Apply Full Fuschia pressed blush as a blush to the cheek bones
Step 9 - Chestnut lip liner to define the lips and Ruby Woo lipstick

FIGURE 5.12 *Makeup sketch by Joe Dulude II for Deborah Cox as Lucy in Jekyll and Hyde.*

(Eyeshadow: MAC Orb over the entire lid from lash line to brows
MAC Naked Lunch on the inner corner of the eye
MAC Amber lights on the center and outer lid
MAC Carbon in the crease as a smudged liner on top and bottom lash line
MAC Eye kohl around the entire lash line to darken liner
Black mascara and lashes
Contour: MAC Raizin blush
Blush: MAC Full Fuchsia
Lip liner: Chestnut pencil
Lipstick: MAC Ruby Woo.)

MAKEUP CHARTS

Makeup charts should be provided for the actor or the makeup artist to follow in doing the makeup. They can be in the form of drawings (such as the makeup drawings previously described or the ones used on the worksheets in Figure 5.7), with indications of changes to be made. The outline of a face, front and profile, shown on the worksheet in Figures 5.9 and 5.13 could be used for the diagrams. Instructions for the makeup could then be connected to various parts of the diagram with arrows. However, since the drawings show approximately what the makeup will actually look like, whereas the diagrams do not, the drawings are much to be preferred. If you particularly want to relate your written instructions for the makeup to very specific areas of the face by means of arrows, that can be done as well with drawings as with a diagram.

The charts or drawings (or photocopies of them) should be made available to the actor to mount on or near a makeup mirror.

For makeup charts, the most common practice is to use the actual *makeup products* to illustrate the design (see Figures 5.7, 5.12, and 5.16). An alternate method is to use colored pencils. It's a good idea to protect all such drawings with acetate or transparent plastic sheets.

WORKSHEETS

When the final sketch for a makeup has been approved (if approval is required), you should then prepare a makeup worksheet to be followed in doing the makeup. If you have not already done a finished drawing of the makeup, it can be

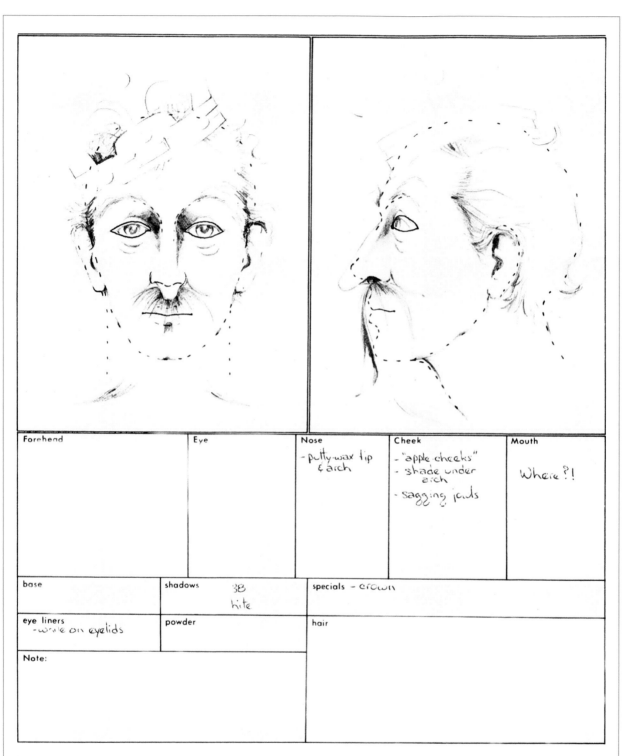

Forehead	Eye	Nose	Cheek	Mouth
		- putty-wax tip & arch	- "apple cheeks" - shade under arch - sagging jowls	Where?!

base	shadows	specials
	38 hite	- crown

eye liners	powder	hair
- white on eyelids		

Note:

FIGURE 5.13 *Makeup worksheet for King Pellinore.*

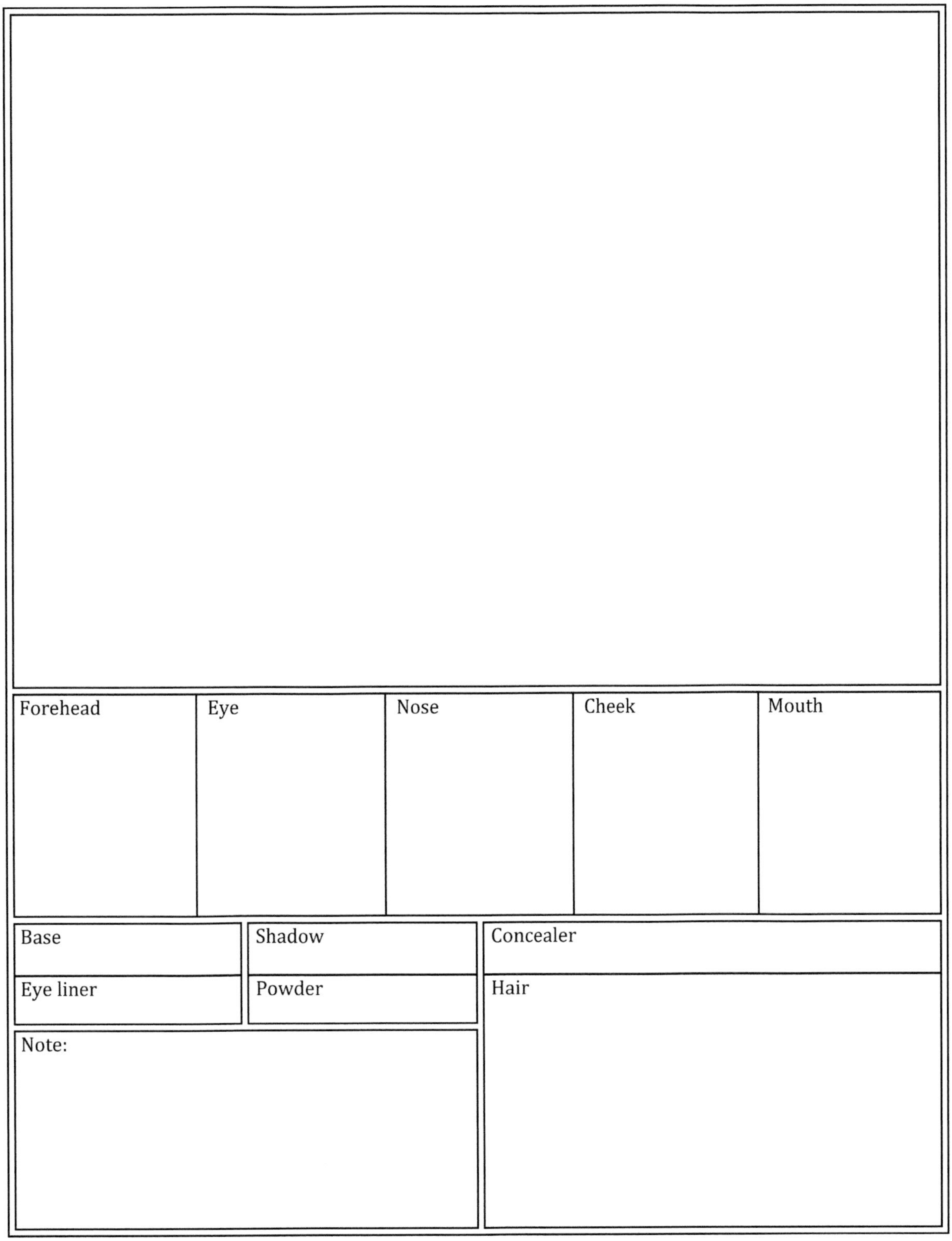

Forehead	Eye	Nose	Cheek	Mouth

Base

Shadow

Concealer

Eye liner

Powder

Hair

Note:

FIGURE 5.14 *Blank makeup worksheet.*

FIGURE 5.15 *Meryl Streep (in a makeup design in the style of the 1920s) and Christopher Lloyd in a scene from the Chelsea Theatre Center's production of the musical, Happy End, 1977.*

Source: Photograph by Martha Swope. Copyright Billy Rose Theatre Division. Courtesy of The New York Public Library for the Performing Arts.

FIGURE 5.16 *Makeup Worksheet for a 1920s makeup design (worksheet by The Face Chart). This worksheet was painted with makeup, makeup brushes, brow and lip pencils, and liquid eyeliner by the author.*

FIGURE 5.17 *Original costume and makeup design by Martin Pakledinaz for the Tango Woman from the ballet, "Zirkus Weill" at the Pacific Northwest Ballet.*

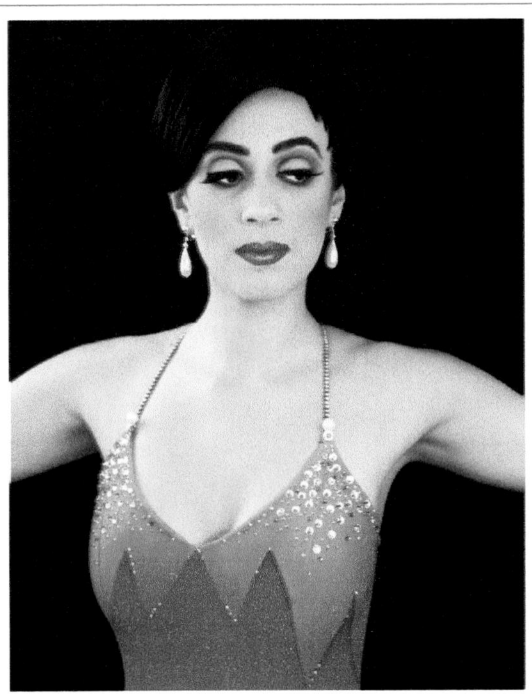

FIGURE 5.18 *The makeup for the Tango Woman from the ballet "Zirkus Weill" designed by costume designer, Martin Pakledinaz for the Pacific Northwest Ballet, This recreation by makeup artist Serret Jenson. Model, Claire Davis.*

Complexion Primer: Optical Illusion by Urban Decay (allow to settle onto the skin before applying foundation)
Foundation: Matte Foundation Palette by Ben Nye—RCE-3 Cine Light Beige
Setting powder: Ben Nye. Color: Fair
Eyeshadow: Pale Blue-gray
Eyeliner: Black kohl liner pencil
Dark iridescent pressed shadow used to smudge the black
Cheek color: Ben Nye—Tangerine Flame Red
Eyelid glitter: Dark iridescent loose glitter. Glitter Glue by Ben Nye
False lashes applied with Duo Lash adhesive
Mascara: Ben Nye—Black
Lip Liner: Ben Nye lip pencil: Cherry Pop
Lipstick: Velvetines Matte Liquid by Lime Crime—Red Velvet
Lip highlighter: Metallic Velvetines by Lime Crime. Color-Siren (sunset/peach/gold).)

drawn front view and profile on the worksheet, following the dotted lines or departing from them, using drawing pens or pencils (black or colored), water colors, watercolor pencils, conté crayon (black or sepia), or the makeup itself. When using pencils or conté crayon, the wrinkles and shadows can be blended with a paper stump or cotton-tipped applicator. When using a black lead pencil, it's possible to run your fingers lightly over the entire drawing to gray all the white areas, then to pick out the highlights carefully with an eraser. When using makeup, simply place the makeup on the page and blend.

Precise information on makeup colors to be used, special techniques of application, hairstyles, and any three-dimensional additions to the face, including beards and mustaches, can be entered in the appropriate spaces on the chart. Additional detailed sketches or diagrams can be included when necessary.

Figure 5.12 shows a completed makeup chart/worksheet used to assist and train the actor to complete her own makeup. If possible, a photograph of the final makeup (Figure 5.11) should be attached to the chart.

CHAPTER 6

APPLYING THE MAKEUP

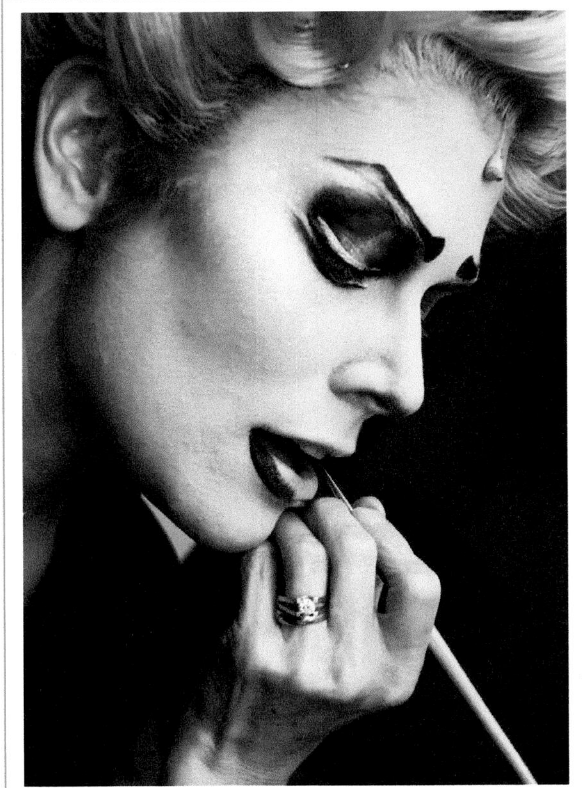

FIGURE 6.1 *Heidi Blickenstaff backstage applying her makeup as Ursula in The Little Mermaid, from the Disney Theatrical Productions Broadway production. Makeup designer, Angelina Avellone.*

Source: Photograph by Jenny Anderson.

Choosing the appropriate makeup, applicators, and application techniques for the various types of makeups can be a challenging process. Which type of makeup you choose will likely depend on one of the following:

1. Performance medium: television, film, theater, opera, dance;
2. Skin type: dry, normal, oily;
3. Surface to be painted: skin, latex, foam latex, silicone, gelatin;
4. Personal preference.

Once the makeup has been acquired, choosing the appropriate applicator for each type of makeup or makeup product will assist you in applying that product successfully. A full range of sponge applicators and makeup brushes is available for applying specific products to specific parts of the face and body. It is not necessary to acquire every product on the market, but professional makeup artists will argue that an assortment of quality brushes is a necessity. Good quality brushes are made with natural fibers (sable, squirrel, and camel) as well as from synthetic fibers (usually nylon) and come in a variety of shapes and sizes (Figures 6.4 and 6.5). Sponge applicators are available in foam rubber and polyurethane in a variety of densities and textures (Figure 6.6).

FOUNDATIONS

This type of makeup is available in liquid, cream, cake, and airbrush formulas and can be used in all performance venues. The amount of coverage, surface texture, and sheen required will determine how it is used and which formulation is chosen.

FIGURE 6.2 *Foundations. (left to right) Celebré HD Pro by Mehron; TV Paint Stick by Kryolan; Ben Nye MediaPro Sheer Foundation Palette; MAC Full Coverage; Interface; Make Up For Ever Pro-Finish Multi-Use Powder Foundation; Ben Nye Creme Foundation.*

FIGURE 6.3 *Wolfe Face Art & FX palette (monster).*

Liquid foundations in satin or matte formulas can be used on both the face and the body and applied with a sponge, a brush, an airbrush, or your fingers. They can be used on their own (do not need setting powder) or in combination with cream foundations for greater coverage (cream or airbrush applied over liquid).

Liquid foundations move well over the skin and are formulated to cover a greater surface area of the body evenly and with relative speed. They come in full-coverage, long-wear, sheer coverage, and high-definition (HD) formulas. The foundations dry quickly and are often water resistant. Choose a brand that does not rub off on clothing (find a brand that works for your situation). Cream and dry contour and accent colors can be used over liquid foundations.

Cream foundations are applied to the face with a brush or foam sponge. They can be purchased in a flat container or in stick form, in satin or matte finish. Cream foundations are manufactured in formulas ranging from highly pigmented, full-coverage products to the sheerest HD formulas, using only enough to even out the skin tone and conceal minor blemishes. When using the stick form of cream makeup, performers often apply it directly with the stick, then blend it out with a Beauty Blender sponge. If you need to mix colors in order to obtain the desired hue, that can be done by transferring the foundation from the container to a mixing palette using a metal or plastic palette knife. Cream foundations usually require a setting powder; however, cream-to-powder formulas do not.

Cream formula highlights and shadows, rouge, eye and cheek makeup used to contour and shape the face should be applied with a flat brush, foam sponge, or with the fingers over the cream foundation *before* it has been powdered. Dry or pressed formulas should be applied with brushes in a variety of sizes and shapes, *after* the foundation has been set with setting powder.

Cake makeups used for the face and body are available in a full rainbow of colors. Decorative and fantastical designs can be seen in theater and dance performances, makeup competitions, public festivals, and in commercial advertisements. They can be mixed with water or setting liquids to produce a smudge-proof, waterproof surface that is easily removed with soap and water. They can also be applied with a sponge or brush.

PROFESSIONAL BRUSHES

Makeup Brushes (See Figure 6.4):

1. Liner—Small, round, tapered brush for creating fine lines, and veining.
2. Glue/PAX brush—For applying adhesives, contour and cheek colors, PAX colors, and aquacolors.
3. Lip—Beveled sides allow for accurate application of lip color.
4. Brow—Angled brush for shaping the eyebrows.
5. Small pointed crease—For creating soft lines around the eye.

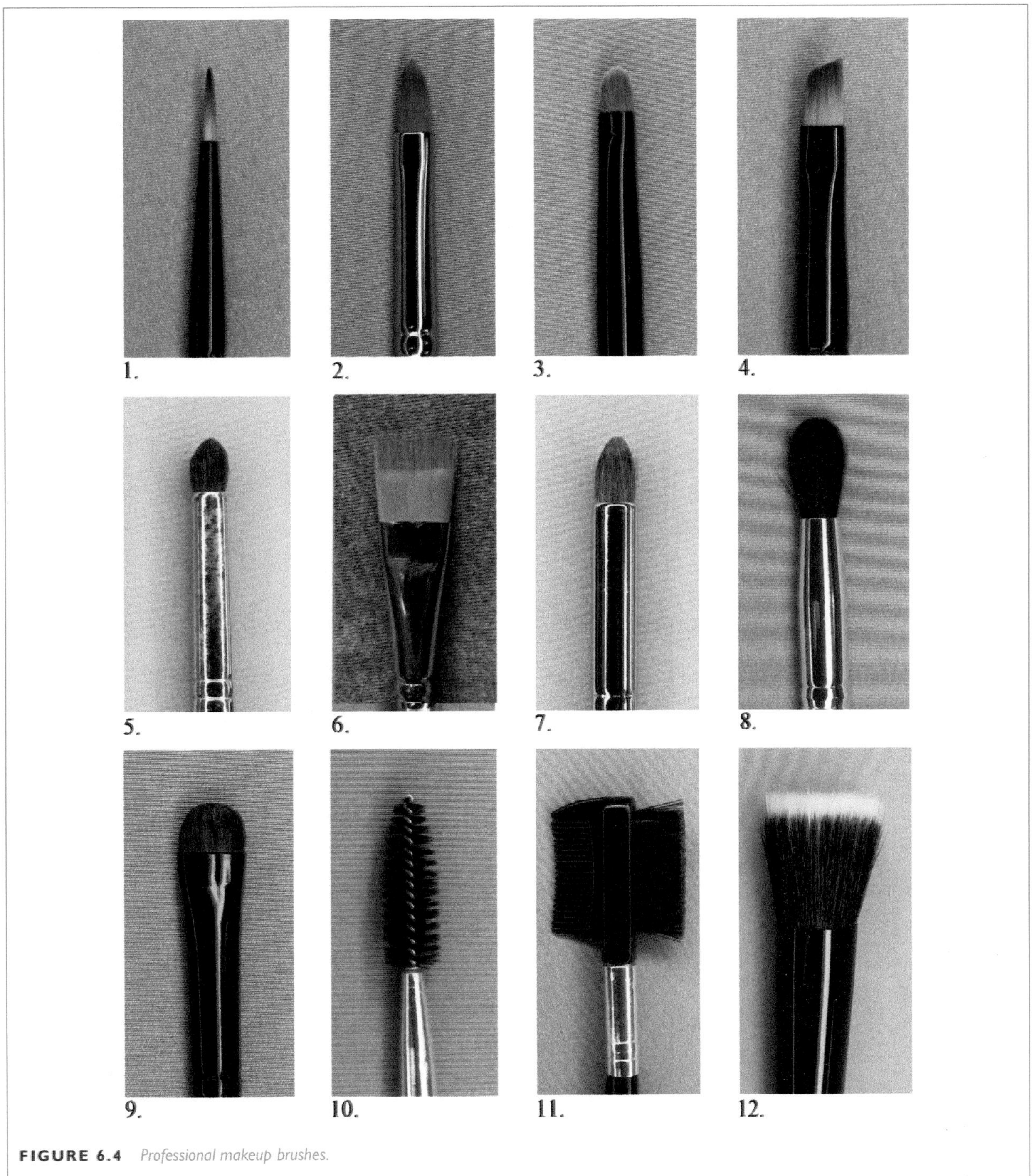

FIGURE 6.4 *Professional makeup brushes.*

6. Rake brush —For creating delicate hair-like strokes (see Figure 15.27.5).
7. Medium pointed crease—For creating soft lines around the eye.
8. Soft shadow—Soft and fluffy eyeshadow or used as a small powder brush.
9. Firm shadow—For applying eyeshadow.
10. Lash—Spiral lash brush or wand for applying mascara.
11. Eyelash comb and brow brush.
12. Flat Kabuki Foundation Blender.

FIGURE 6.5 *Professional makeup brushes.*

The following brushes can be seen in Figure 6.5:

1. Stipple brushes—For adding texture.
2. Foundation, camouflage, and concealer brushes—For applying dense foundations and coverups.
3. Fan brushes—For blending.
4. Powder/blush domes and angled blush—For applying powders, contour, and cheek colors.
5. Flat liners—For creating sharp edges, and the application of adhesives for beard laying.
6. Tapered contour kabuki brush—For applying foundation and powders.
7. Angled round—For applying medical adhesive and Prosaide.

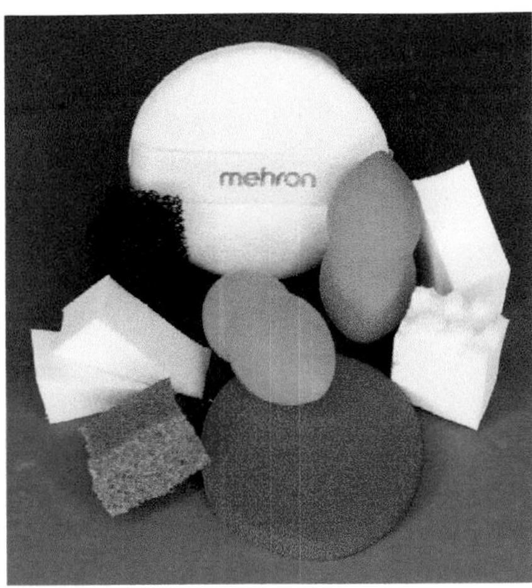

FIGURE 6.6 *Sponge applicators. (Clockwise from the left) Orange stipple sponge; white latex wedges; black stipple sponge; powder puff; orange and pink blenders; white foam sponge made into a texture sponge; round red cream makeup applicator.*

FIGURE 6.7 *Hand-painted Pierrot-style clown makeup by makeup artist Marie-Laurente Tessier (Snazaroo Face Paint Palette).*

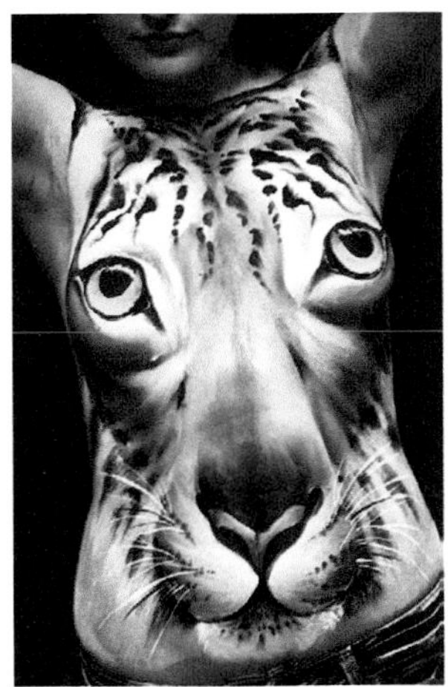

FIGURE 6.8 *Snow leopard body art by makeup artist Olga Masurev.*
(TAG Pearl Black
Cameleon Strong Black
Paradise White
Wolfe FX White
TAG Regular Teal
Cameleon Victorious
Paradise Storm Cloud
Paradise Coral
Loew Cornell 795 series round brush #4
Loew Cornell 795 series round brush #8
Paradise wide chisel brush
Paradise small chisel brush
Cameleon big blending brush
Wolfe FX yellow sponge.)

Cake makeup is a highly pigmented, pressed formula for the face and body. It is manufactured in two types: dry and moist. The dry formula such as Ben Nye Color Cake Foundation and Mehron's StarBlend, and the moist formula such as Kryolan's Aquacolor and Graftobian's ProPaint are both activated with water or other liquids (i.e. LiquiSet or Final Seal by Ben Nye for a longer-lasting application). The moist formulas are glycerin-based and can also be used as eyeliner and for defining the eyebrow. A pointed, round brush dipped in water and stroked across the surface is very useful in accomplishing this technique.

For large areas these products are best applied using a natural silk sea sponge or the round synthetic Hydra Sponge (used by ceramic artists). Smaller areas can be applied using large- and medium-sized, domed foundation brushes for general

FIGURE 6.9 *Corset body paint by Liza Berczel (battledress.deviantart.com).*

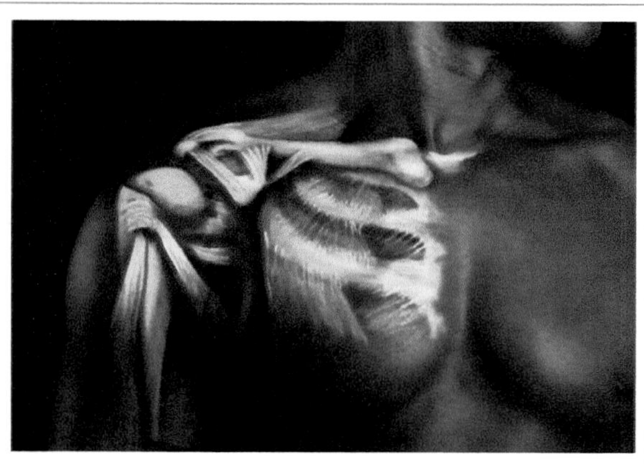

FIGURE 6.10 *Shoulder and chest anatomy body paint by Liza Berczel (modelmayhem.com).*

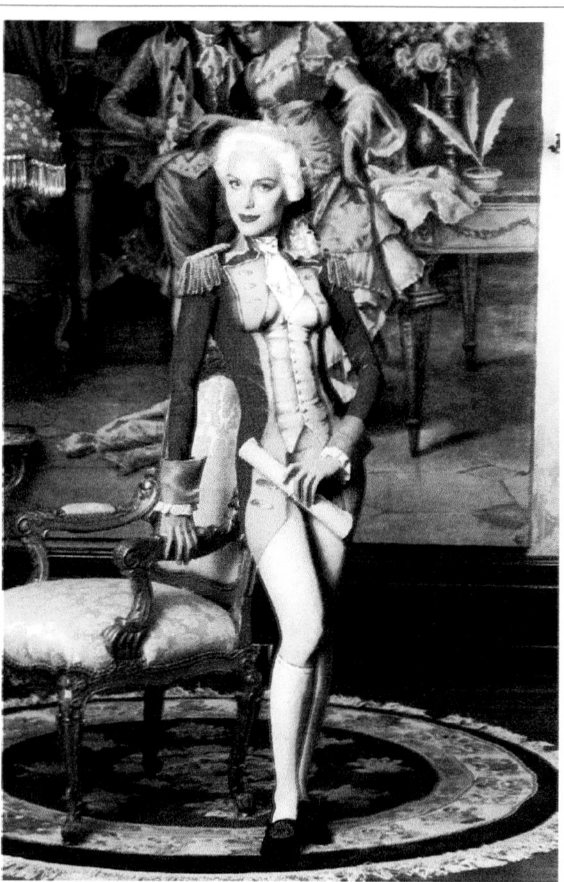

FIGURE 6.11 *Body painting for commercial advertising. Hand-painted with Ben Nye's MagiCake Aqua Paint.*

Source: Photograph courtesy of Ben Nye Company, Inc.

application and the smaller round brushes for drawing details. Some artists prefer natural-hair brushes, arguing that they hold the watery pigments better than synthetic brushes, but others promote the use of synthetic sable watercolor brushes for the same reasoning. This argument proves that every artist should experiment with a variety of products until they find those with which they can be most successful.

Face and body paints such as Wolfe, Cameleon, Snazaroo, ProPaint (moist formula by Graftobian) and Paradise (Mehron) are each dry formula, water-based paints applied to the skin with a damp sponge and/or a brush.

After the makeup has been taken up on the sponge, stroke the sponge lightly across the face until the whole area is covered

FIGURE 6.12 *Kryolan Aquacolor.*

FIGURE 6.13 *Setting powders. Loose powders by Ben Nye, Kryolan, MAC, and Joe Blasco. Pressed Finishing Powder by Make Up For Ever. Face powders come in no color (transparent), translucent, and pigmented.*

FIGURE 6.14 *No-color/colorless face powder. Neutral Set Colorless Face Powder by Ben Nye, No-Color Powder by RCMA, MAC Prep +Prime.*

smoothly with a thin film of color. Cake makeup requires no powder. Performers with dry skin and mature performers should avoid cake makeups, choosing instead a cream formula foundation to help the skin retain moisture.

FACE POWDER

Face powder is generally used to set makeup (to keep it from moving) and to remove any undesirable shine. Face powders are manufactured in pigmented, translucent, and transparent (no-color) formulas, and in matte, semi-matte, and shimmer surface textures. They are available as foundations, setting powders, and translucent finishing powders. They come in two forms: pressed and loose. *Pressed powder*, which looks similar to cake makeup, is applied with a puff and/or a large, soft brush and pressed into, not wiped onto, the makeup. It can be denser than loose powder and care must be taken to avoid a heavy application. Although appropriate shades of face powder may, on occasion, serve as a foundation color for "natural" makeup applications in the theater, the look is often too heavy and powdery for film.

Loose powder can be applied with either a puff or a large powder brush. When applying loose powder with a puff, first distribute a small amount onto the surface of the puff, fold the puff in half, and rub the powder into the fibers, then open the puff and tap off any excess powder. When using a puff, you should first fold it in half around the forefinger (powder side out) and press it firmly into the makeup with a rolling motion.

To apply powder with a brush, gently dip the brush into the powder, tap off excess powder and lightly tap onto the surface of the face. Excess powder is removed with a very soft powder brush or sometimes—especially for small areas—with a clean rouge brush. Experience and personal preference will help determine when to use which type (see Chapter 9 for further information).

Brush-On Eyeshadow/Eye Color. These come in smaller cakes and palettes in both cream and dry formulas. They are manufactured in an almost endless color range in matte, shimmery, and sparkle textures. Eyeshadows can be applied with a series of small, domed shadow and blender brushes. They can also be applied and blended with cotton-tipped applicators. Natural bristled brushes tend to hold more pigment than synthetic brushes, therefore delivering more product to the face. The choice to use a natural or synthetic brush will be determined by the desired effect and by personal preference. There are excellent quality brushes in both categories from which to choose. Any eyeshadow colors suitable for general shadowing can, of course, be used for that purpose. Eyebrows can also be defined using cake shadows and a small, angled brow brush.

Dry Rouge/Cheek Color/Bronzers: Dry (or pressed powder) accent colors, rouge, cheek colors, contours and highlights, and bronzers are best applied with a medium-sized round, domed, or angled blush brush. Dry rouge can be applied over cake makeup, liquid makeup, or any cream makeup that has been set with powder.

FIGURE 6.15 *Heidi Blickenstaff backstage in makeup as Ursula from The Little Mermaid, the Disney Theatrical Productions Broadway production. Makeup designer, Angelina Avellone.*

Source: Photograph by Jenny Anderson.

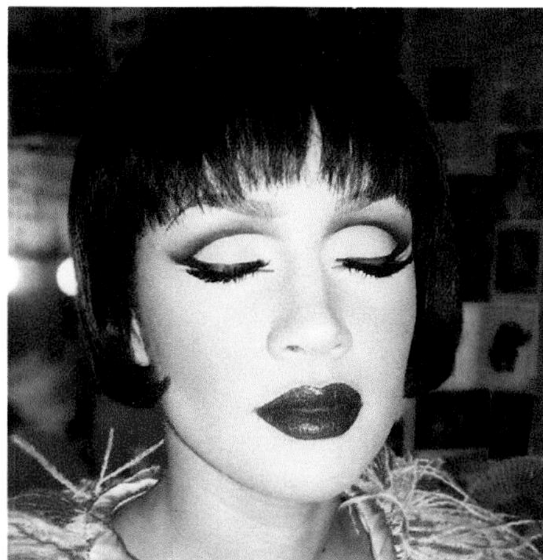

FIGURE 6.16 *Vanessa Williams' makeup from Kiss of the Spider Woman, the Broadway production of the musical. Makeup by Kate Best.*

Concealer:	*RCMA Chinese I and II (light yellow tone) under eyes and on T-section.*
Foundation:	*Laura Mercier SC 4 (center of the face) & SC 6 (around the edges).*
Cream blush:	*William Tuttle Blusher, a pinky-peach tone on apple of cheeks, forehead and temple.*
Powder:	*LeClerc Banana at center of face, LeClerc Bronze along the rest of face and outer edges. Blend well.*
Eyeshadow:	*MAC Black cream liner in crease (blend edges with orange-toned blush). MAC Vanilla and Gesso under the brow.*
Eyeliner:	*MAC Black cream liner. White pencil along lower rim.*
Blush:	*MAC Cheek (warm orange/gold tone).*
Contour:	*Pinkish/brown tone to add warmth into the edges of the face and to shape and shade nose.*
Brows:	*MAC Black cream liner with a light application near the center.*
Lip pencil:	*MAC Spice liner, MAC Brun fill-in.*
Lipstick:	*MAC Viva Glam to cover.*

Source: Makeup and photograph courtesy of Kate Best.

EYELINER

Eyeliners are available in liquid, pressed powder, gel, and pencil styles. They come in a full range of colors from white to black. Liquid and gel liners in waterproof formulas are applied using a fine-tipped brush and produce a defined line that does not smudge easily. Pencil liners and pressed powder create a soft, natural lash line but are less permanent and can begin to fade after several hours of wear. Pencils and pressed powders can be carefully applied to simply knit the lash roots together to create a perfectly natural look or easily blended to create a smoky period style. Eyeliners can be used to make the eyes larger and wider by extending the lash line (the cat eye), and raising the crease line to a more perceptible arch. Liners can be applied to both the upper and lower lash line and to dramatic effect on the waterline (the area between the lash line and the eyeball).

MASCARA

Mascara comes in two basic formats: the cake variety applied with a dampened brush and the tube style with a wand applicator. While the tube and wand variety are convenient and readily available at any cosmetic counter, it must be noted that they are not easily cleaned and sterilized and that their use should be limited to personal, rather than group, makeup kits. Mascara also comes in regular and waterproof, and in thickening and lengthening formulas. Waterproof mascara is recommended for performance, but not for daily wear since it tends to dry out the lashes. The lengthening formulas apply more evenly and go on more smoothly than the thickening formula. Try applying several thin coats rather than one thick one. Mascaras come in a variety of colors.

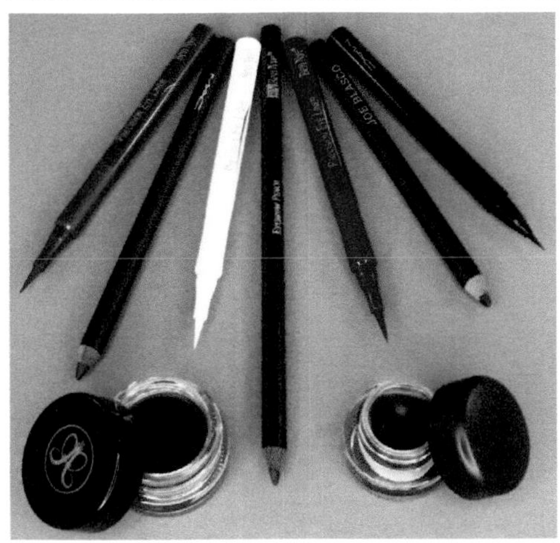

FIGURE 6.17 *Eyeliners by Ben Nye (liquid and pencil), MAC (liquid, pencil and gel), Joe Blasco (pencil), and Anastasia of Beverly Hills (gel).*

FIGURE 6.18 *Mascara. Ben Nye Black Mascara; Revlon Grow Luscious; Ben Nye Clear Gel Mascara; Kryolan Hair Mascara; mascara wands.*

EYELASHES

Women's lashes are nearly always curled and darkened with mascara. Black is the preferred color although brown may be used on blonde lashes and for a more gentle, soft, natural look.

Before applying the mascara, gently curl the lashes, then hold the wand parallel to the eye and stroke from the roots to the tips of the lashes upward on the lower side of the upper lashes and downward on the upper side of the lower lashes (Figure 6.21.31). Avoid clumps and keep the lashes separated for a natural effect. If men's eyelashes are very light or very sparse, brown or black mascara will be helpful in defining the eye; otherwise clear mascara is suggested. Be extremely careful to avoid getting mascara into the eyes, as it can be painful. If you get smudges of mascara on the skin around the eye, they should be carefully removed with a cotton swab dampened with water or, for waterproof mascara, with mascara remover. *Caution*: Never share your mascara or your mascara wand with anyone else!

Women often wear false eyelashes on the upper lid, less often on the lower. If the lashes are too full, snip out some of the hairs with small pointed scissors—*before* applying the lashes to the eyelid. Using excessively long or heavy lashes may at times be fashionable but does not necessarily make the eyes more attractive.

False eyelashes (see Figure 6.19), in both full top and bottom or as individual and cluster, are relatively easy to apply. Full false lashes add immediate length and fullness to the entire lash line. Single and cluster lashes add a more natural look by filling in sparse areas and to add a dramatic frame to the eye. When using single or cluster lashes try mixing short, medium, and long together, locating short lashes toward the inner end, medium on the outer end, and long in the middle. To achieve a "doe-eyed" effect attach the longer lashes to the outer end.

A better integration of the false eyelash with the natural lash line can be achieved by first applying a soft, narrow dark line of color to the base of the lashes. This allows the lash band to disappear *into* the liner rather than just sit *on* the skin. Use a gel liner or wet/dry pigment shadow rather than a cream formula for better adhesion. False eyelashes can also be made more delicate and natural-looking by lightly sanding them with an emory board. Place the lash onto a wooden or plastic dowel and lightly draw the emory board across the surface in the direction of the hair growth. Using a small, flat, angled brush, press the dry pigment into the lash line to knit the lashes together. False eyelashes are attached with a special eyelash adhesive (Duo Eyelash adhesive) (see Appendix A). The adhesive is placed on the tip of an applicator (end of a brush, tooth pick, or small wooden stick), then applied to the eyelash strip (avoid applying the adhesive to the lash strip directly from the tube) (Figure 6.21.32), which is set in place along the lash line then secured by pressing carefully and gently with your fingers (Figure 6.21.33), a cotton-tipped applicator (Figure 7.13.30), or the end of a makeup brush. Avoid any space between the false lashes and the natural lash line. *Never use any sharp-pointed instrument near the eye!* If the eyes are to be made to seem farther apart, the lashes can be extended beyond the corner of the eye. Apply false eyelashes and mascara only after the makeup has been powdered.

FIGURE 6.19 *Eyelashes.*

LIP COLOR

This product comes in a variety of formats: traditional tube lipsticks, color palettes, individual flat containers, lip color pencils, lip liners, and wand applicator styles. The lip color genre includes lip gloss, lip stains, lip paints, tinted lip balm, long-lasting, matte finish, and those containing sunblock. Lip colors can be applied directly to the mouth by using a traditional lipstick, by drawing them on with a lip pencil, and by painting them on with a brush or a wand. When using long-lasting or matte formulas (which tend to dry out the lips) or for actors with dry, cracked lips, hydrate the lips first (at the beginning of the makeup application) with a thin layer of moisturizer, lip balm, or petroleum jelly.

For a longer-lasting lip color try one of the following techniques: (1) apply lip color, powder, then apply a second layer; (2) apply lip color, blot using a single-ply tissue (kiss the tissue rather than pressing it between your lips), then apply a second layer; (3) outline and then fill in entire lip with a lip pencil, then apply lip color with a brush to the edge of the lip line; (4) or use a combination of these three methods.

FIGURE 6.20 *Lip color. (from the top, l–r) Ben Nye lipstick, Cailyn Extreme Matte Tint lip paint, MAC lipgloss, Ben Nye Lip Palette, Ben Nye lip pencils.*

1. Makeup application by actress—Britney Simpson for her role as Madame De La Grande Bouche in the Oregon Shakespeare Festival production of Disney's Beauty and the Beast.
   Skin preparation: Rose Water cleaning, LORAC Eye Primer (Figure 6.21).
2. Shaping eyebrow with an angled brow brush using Anastasia Dipbrow Pomade (dark brown).
3. NYX Above & Beyond Full Coverage Concealer (Ivory).
4. Apply NYX Above & Beyond Full Coverage Concealer (Ivory) above and below the eyebrow using a small, domed shadow brush and blend into the surrounding skin.
5. Spraying the face with rose water prep.
6. Create a crease line using "Unafraid" from the LORAC Unzipped Gold Palette as a starting point.
7. Place LORAC "Undressed" on the brow bone (under the brow).
8. Then, from the Urban Decay Vice Palette 2 add "Dope" as a sheen for brow bone.

9, 10, & 11. From the LORAC Palette, use "Unlimited" & "Unleashed" to create an ombre effect from the crease up toward the brow.

12. HARD CANDY Glamoflauge Heavy duty concealer (Ultra Light).
13. Place a small dot of concealer on the back of the hand.
14. Brush Glamaflauge concealer on lid to the crease line.

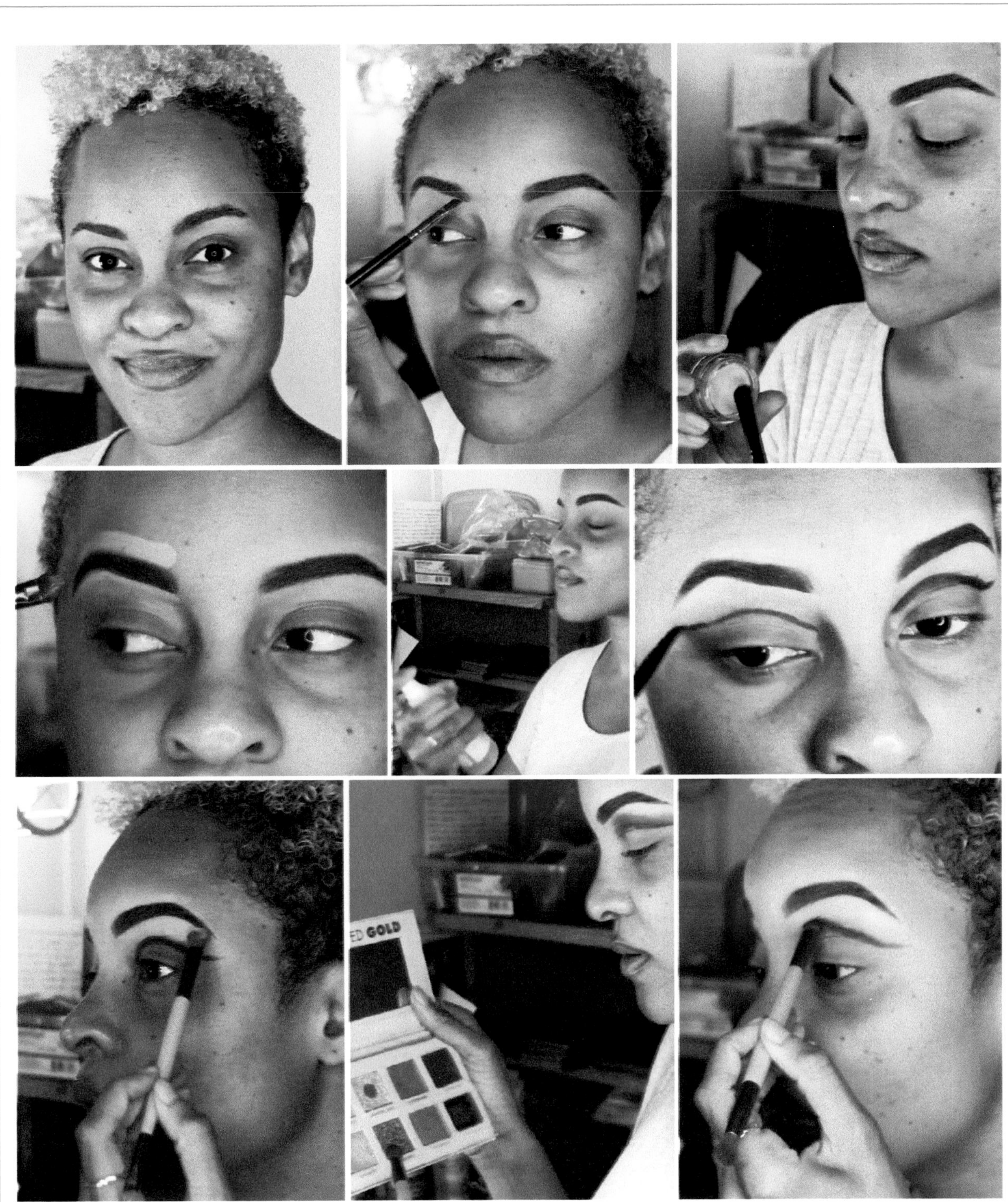

FIGURE 6.21 *Britney Simson. Makeup application for her role in Beauty and the Beast as Madame de la Grande Bouche in the Oregon Shakespeare Festival 2017 production. Costume design by Ana Kuznetsov.*

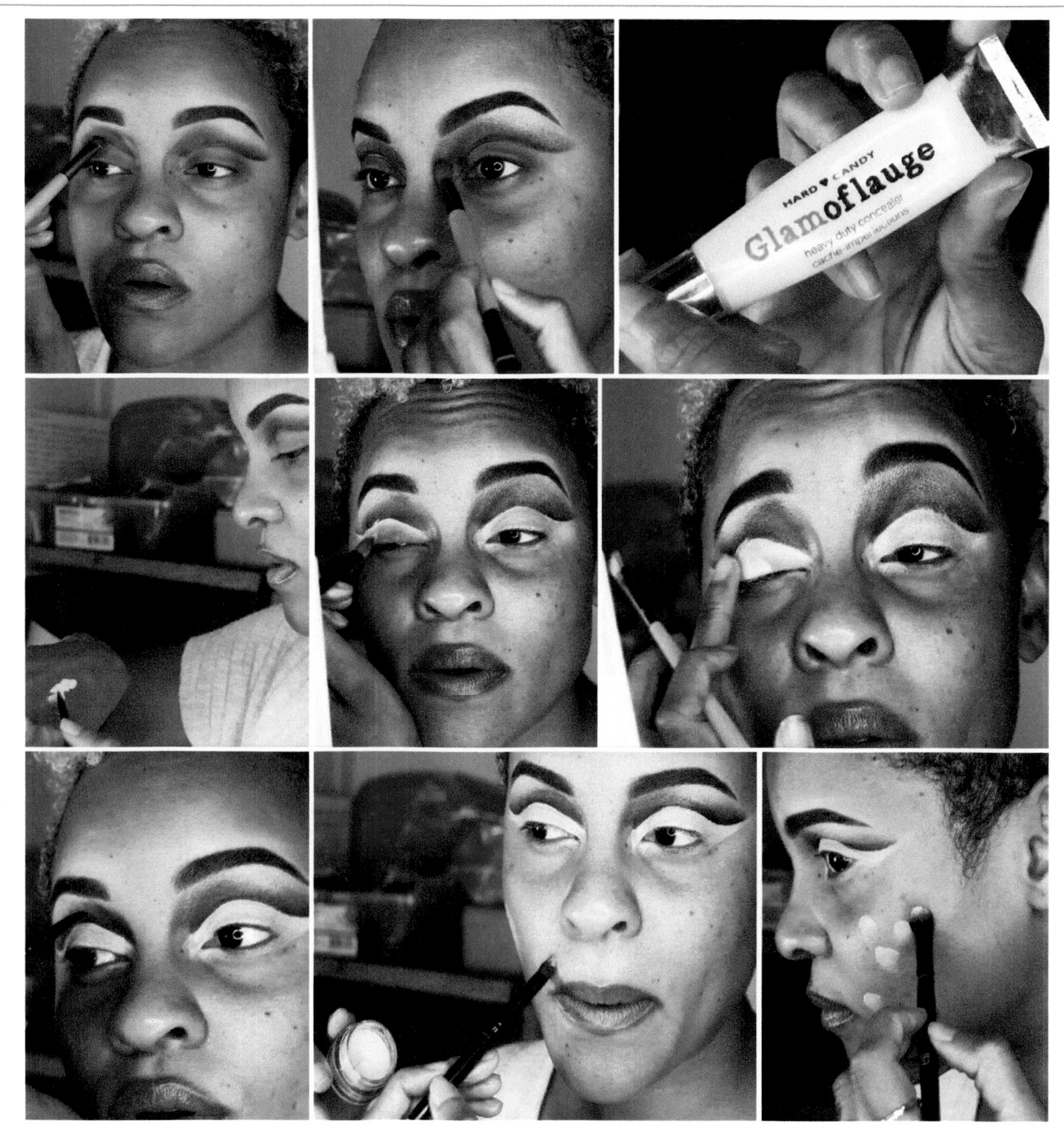

FIGURE 6.21 *(continued)*

FIGURE 6.21 *(continued)*

FIGURE 6.21 *(continued)*

FIGURE 6.21 *(continued)*

FIGURE 6.21 *(continued)*

15. Place LORAC "Unlocked" over the concealer onto the lid using a small shadow brush and finger (if needed). Also, add Urban Decay "Shellshock" to the inner eye and tear duct as a highlight.

16. Use Urban Decay "Smokeout" to emphasize the darkness of cut crease.

17 & 18. Neutralize any redness by applying NYX Above & Beyond Full Coverage Concealer (Green). Apply only to red area and spots. Blend lightly.

19. Cover/neutralize any darkness under the eye with NYX Dark Circle Concealer Correcteur (Orange/Dark peach). Lightly blend.

20. Squeeze a small amount of Tarte Amazonian Clay 12-hour liquid foundation (SPF 15), "Tan-Honey" to the round end of a Beauty Blender sponge (lightly mist the sponge before applying the foundation to it).

21. & 22. Apply the liquid foundation to the entire face using the Beauty Blender sponge. Use a light tapping motion until it is smooth and perfectly blended. Avoid wiping the foundation onto the skin.

23. Apply highlight under the eyes, to the bridge of the nose, the center of the forehead, under the nose, and onto the chin using HARD CANDY Glamoflauge Heavy duty concealer (Ultra Light).

24. Blend using a slightly dampened Beauty Blender sponge.

25 Lightly powder with a no-color setting powder.

26. Using a white liner pencil, draw on a highlight along the waterline.

27. & 28. Add a shadow under the lower lashes using a combination of LORAC "Unlimited" & "Unleashed." Then, place a silver highlight at the inner eye at the tear duct area (Urban Decay Vice Palette 2 "Shellshock" silver highlight or Ben Nye's Silver Shimmer Crayon).

29. Add black eyeliner to the upper lash line only. Extend the line as shown using Sephora collection Wink-It, felt-tip liner waterproof (01 Little Black Dress). (Note: Outline a small triangle at the outer edge of the eye, then fill in with the waterproof eyeliner.)

30. Paint on four lower lashes under each eye with the Sephora felt-tip liner. Add a short highlight to the lower side of each painted lash using the Urban Decay "Shellshock" silvery shadow.

31. Using the Urban Decay Perversion mascara cover the lashes starting at the root.

32. Before applying the false eyelashes, apply Duo Striplash adhesive along the lash band. Squeeze a dot of adhesive onto a palette, pick up a small amount with the tip of an applicator stick and apply along the lash band. Add a little extra to each end.

33. Gently place the false lashes onto the lash line.

34. Adjust and finish the application using a pair of tweezers.

35. & 36. Using the ColourPop Cosmetics Contour (Cream) Stix in the color "Easy Peasy," draw contour lines under the cheekbone and onto the apple of the cheek, shadow the sides and tip of the nose, then create a spiral on the chin.

37. Finished shadow contour lines.

38. Using a pointed blender brush, add Urban Decay Vice Palette 2 "Smokeout" to darken and slightly widen the contour line.

39. Blend and soften the shadow/contour with a large soft blending brush.

40. Apply shadow along the jawline and blend onto the neck.

41. Ben Nye Lumiere Luxe Powder, "Sun Yellow."

42. Using an angled blush brush apply Lumiere Luxe Powder to the cheeks, forehead, nose, upper lip, chin, and along the jawline.

43. Using a small, domed shadow brush, apply Urban Decay Vice Palette 2 "Shellshock" silver highlight details.

44. Reshaping the lip with lip liner pencil, ColourPop Cosmetics lip liner, "Ellaire."

45. Filling in the lip with NYX Professional Makeup Turnt Up! Lipstick, "Rock Star."

46. Add lip highlights with Lime Crime Diamond Crushers, "Lit."

47. Adding a beauty mark using the Sephora waterproof felt-tip liner.

48. Finished makeup.

49. Britney Simpson in wig and costume.

CONCEALERS, NEUTRALIZERS, AND TATTOO COVERS

Also called cover-up or camouflage, concealers are used to hide or minimize unwanted facial discoloration, blemishes, birthmarks, beard shadow, and tattoos. They are manufactured in highly pigmented opaque creams, liquid, and in alcohol-based formulas. Nearly every makeup manufacturer produces some form of concealer. Tattoos, blemishes, and birthmarks are generally the three most requested skin discolorations makeup artists are asked to cover up. Every artist has his/her own technique, utilizing some combination of opaque cream, liquid, or alcohol-based concealer along with a highly pigmented setting powder. Some artists will first use a *neutralizer* to counter the effect of the dominant discoloration. The neutralizing effect is accomplished when an unwanted discoloration is covered with a concealer containing the complementary color to the discoloration. Many tattoos, for example, tend to appear in the blue/black color range. Applying a neutralizer containing orange pigment (the complement of blue) will, theoretically, neutralize the dominant tattoo coloration. This is how it works: when light hits the skin, it reveals the bluish cast of the tattoo. When the blue reflects back through the orange-toned concealer it is neutralized and appears skin-toned. Dark circles under the eyes, often appearing purple in color, are neutralized with a golden or orangey-peach-toned formula. Cream concealer

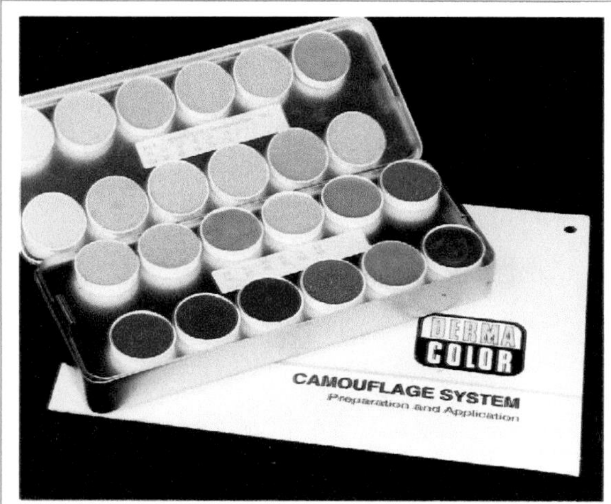

FIGURE 6.22 *Kryolan Dermacolor Camouflage System.*

FIGURE 6.23 *Neutralizers, color correctors, and concealers. (top) Make Up For Ever HD Ultra Concealer; Tarte shape tape concealer. (middle) Make Up For Ever Redness Correcting Primer; Smashbox Color-Correcting Sticks; LancômeHigh Coverage Corrector. (bottom) Make Up For Ever Camouflage Cream Palette.*

formulations must be powdered with translucent, no-color, or lightly pigmented powders. Carefully brush away excess powder.

The highly pigmented opaque cream formula concealers and the new airbrush concealers were developed to color-correct by means of camouflaging or completely covering skin imperfections such as acne blemishes and scars, scars caused by injury, birthmarks, tattoos, and extremely dark circles under the eyes. After choosing or mixing a color one or two shades lighter than the skin tone, apply to the skin with a brush or finger until the discoloration is no longer visible. Careful blending into the surrounding skin is essential. If the covered area appears slightly grayer than the surrounding skin, warm it up a little with a blush, foundation, or cheek color that matches the skin's undertone (red, orange, or yellow).

Moist or cream colors can be blended into the concealer, then powdered in order to set the makeup and remove the shine. Dry colors cannot be applied until the makeup has been powdered.

TATTOOS

Should the script call for the addition rather than the elimination of a tattoo for a given character, one of the following techniques can be used:

1. Using a fine-pointed, ⅛-inch round sable brush, paint the tattoo design directly onto the skin surface using REEL Creation's Body Art Inks, TEMPTU's Body Art paints or Inkbox Semi-permanent Tattoos (transfer or freehand liquids). The products, available in liquid and solid formulas, use 70% isopropyl rubbing alcohol as the solvent.
2. Place temporary tattoo paper transfers available from the same manufacturers against the skin, then paint with alcohol (or water depending on the manufacturer) to reveal a smudge-proof, water-resistant tattoo. After adding the appropriate colors, simply set the design with talcum

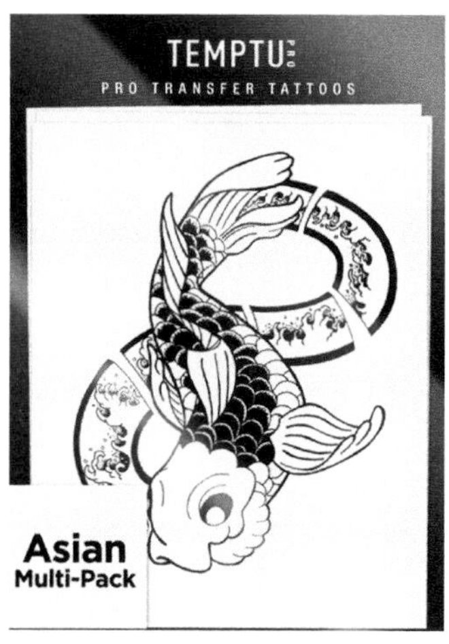

FIGURE 6.24 *TEMPTU: Pro Transfer Tattoos.*

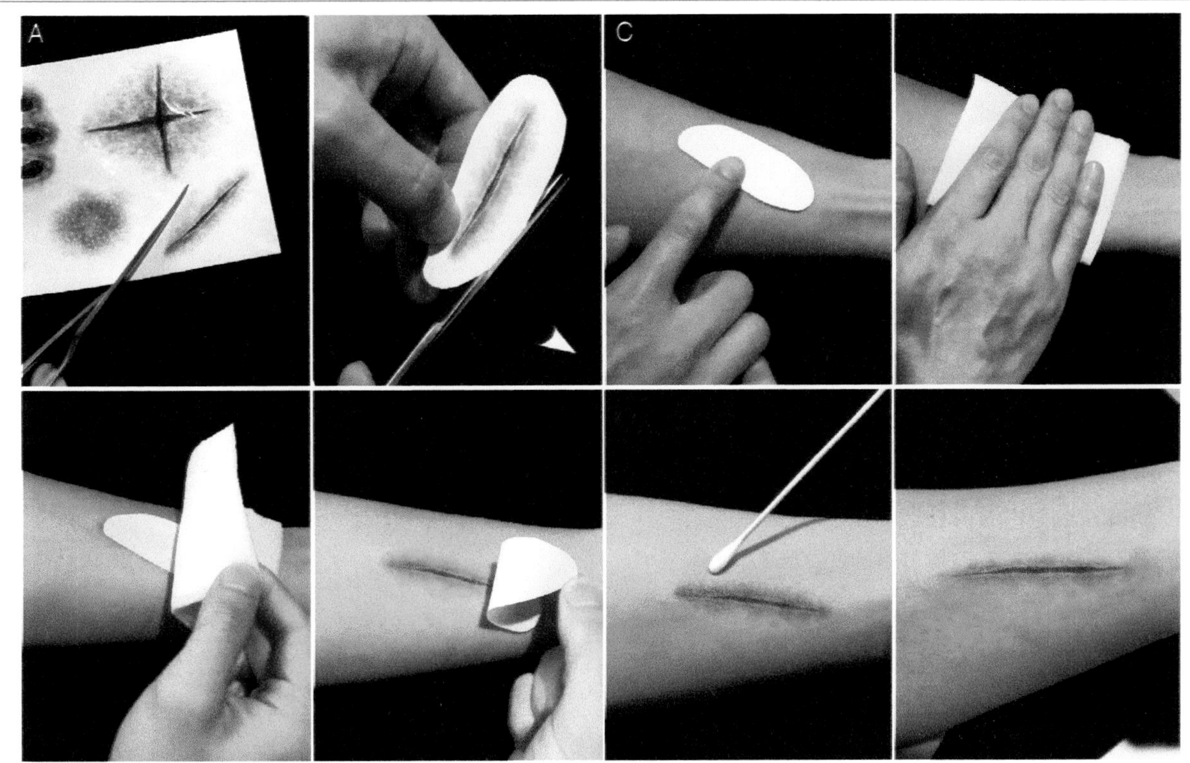

FIGURE 6.25 *Tattoo sticker transfers by JIRO. A. Choose the transfer tattoo from the sheet of tattoo designs. B. Cut out the tattoo sticker. C. Place on the body, tattoo side against the skin. D. Place a damp cloth on the tattoo paper and press until the water is completely absorbed by the transfer paper. E. Remove the damp cloth. F. Carefully peel away the transfer paper. G. Blend the edges and remove some of the sheen from the tattoo sticker with 99% alcohol and a cotton-tipped applicator. Apply a small amount of cream foundation to the edges and powder. H. Finished tattoo transfer.*

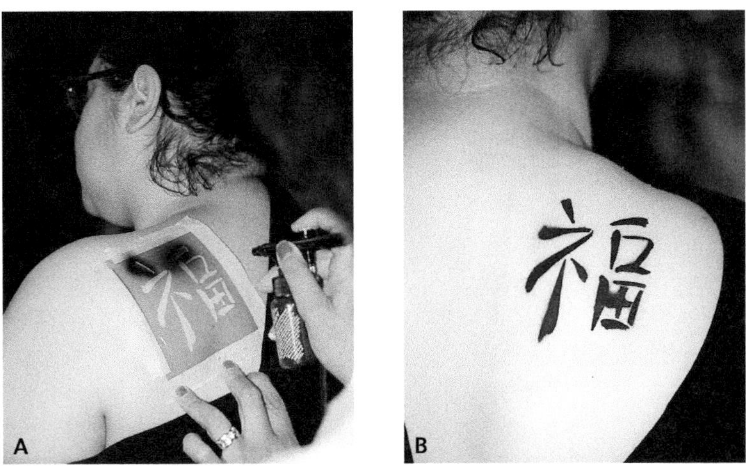

FIGURE 6.26 *Temporary airbrush tattoo. A. Airbrushing over an acetate stencil. B. Temporary tattoo using the Dinair Airbrush Makeup System.*

powder. (Some manufacturers will reproduce your original design on their transfer paper.)

3. Have the design sculpted into a rubber stamp. Using a brayer, transfer fabric paint evenly onto the surface of the stamp. Press the stamp onto the skin. Using fabric paint or makeup, paint in additional colors, then stipple with skin-toned foundation for a more natural appearance and powder.
4. Design the tattoo on a sheet of clear acetate. Cut out the design with a utility knife. Tape the stencil onto the skin and stipple with fabric paint or spray with airbrush cosmetics. Remove the stencil (Figure 6.26).

APPLIANCE MAKEUP

Rubber Mask Greasepaint (RMGP): This is a castor oil-base makeup used primarily over latex (regular and foamed), though it can be used over other three-dimensional makeup, such as derma wax, nose putty, and gelatin. The castor oil in the formula allows the makeup to lie on the surface of the appliance rather than absorbing into the surface like regular foundations. RMGP, also sold as Appliance Foundations by RCMA (Research Council of Makeup Artists), and RMG from Kryolan, applies easily and smoothly to the surface, blends well, and retains its color. Unlike regular makeup, it is usually stippled on with a red-rubber sponge. It is never powdered by rubbing or brushing the puff across the surface of the paint but always by pressing a heavily powdered puff into the makeup. Excess powder is removed by brushing lightly with a soft powder brush. If the RMGP makeup is to be stippled with various colors, that should be done after it has been set with face powder.

PAX Paint: This combination of Prosaide medical adhesive and Liquitex acrylic paint was created to color foam latex appliances. It is applied with either a brush or a texture sponge (a sturdy polyurethane foam sponge textured on one side by removing bits of foam with your fingers). (See Chapters 10 and 11.)

AIRBRUSH COSMETICS

Airbrush-grade cosmetics provide an extremely light coverage with a seamless application that balances the natural skin tones. The speed of application is surprising, leaving a natural, sheer, smudge-proof, matte, or dewey finish. Sprayed on in light layers, this cosmetic can cover imperfections, broken blood vessels, dark circles, blemishes, age spots, and tattoos. When used for glamour makeup it takes no more than 5 to 15 drops of base, blush, and eyeshadow to complete the entire makeup. Airbrush cosmetic can also be used as body makeup (Figure 6.41); as a concealer; to diminish the effects of thinning hair; with stencils for face and body painting (Figure 6.39); for making temporary tattoos (Figure 6.26); and for covering foam latex and gelatin prosthetic appliances.

Airbrushing tools include the airbrush, an air compressor, an air pressure gauge, liquid airbrush cleaner, and an airbrush cleaning brush set (see Figure 6.34). As the airbrush and cosmetics need only 3–6 lbs per square inch (psi) of air pressure to distribute the cosmetic evenly across the skin, the smallest air compressors are quite sufficient. Pressurized canisters and battery-operated units allow for mobility on a set and for location work and can be stored in a canvas set bag.

The airbrush comes in several styles: gravity-feed (seen in Figure 6.30 by Iwata); Syphon-feed (Figure 6.31 also by Iwata); external-mixing (Figure 6.32 by Paasche), and the "pod" style

FIGURE 6.27 *Kett Cosmetics Pro-Kit Airbrush.*

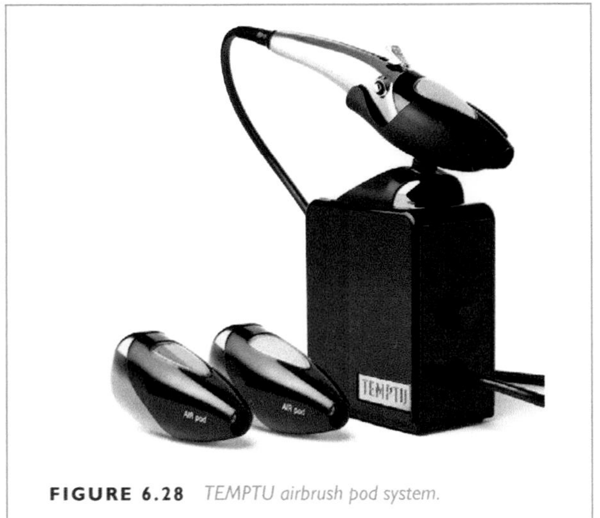

FIGURE 6.28 *TEMPTU airbrush pod system.*

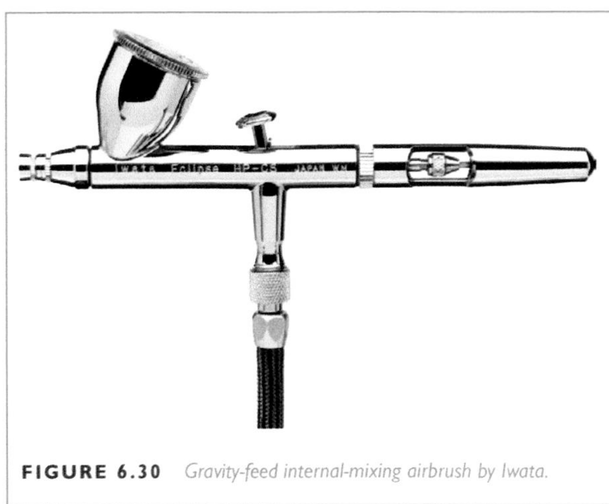

FIGURE 6.30 *Gravity-feed internal-mixing airbrush by Iwata.*

FIGURE 6.29 *Airbrush compressor.*

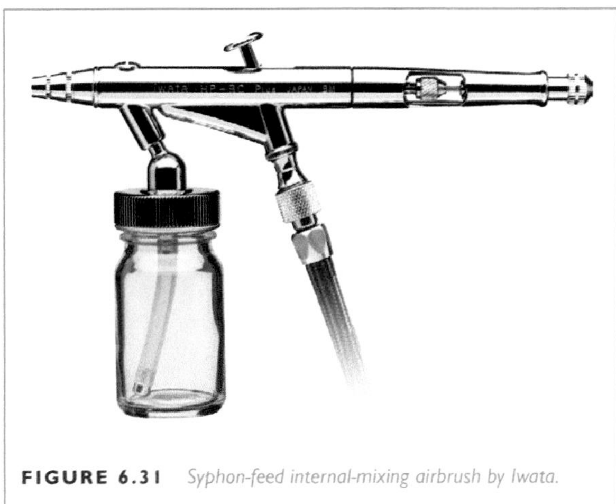

FIGURE 6.31 *Syphon-feed internal-mixing airbrush by Iwata.*

(Figure 6.28 by TEMPTU). Airbrush cosmetics are transferred to the gravity-feed airbrush by squeezing just a few drops from the plastic makeup containers into the cup attached to the top of the brush. The makeup flows into the brush and the release of air pushes it through the nozzle tip onto the skin. This is referred to as an *internal-mixing* airbrush. The meeting of air and paint is called *atomization*. For the syphon-feed type, a cup or jar of makeup is attached to the bottom or side of the brush. When air is released into the brush it flows over the hole of the tube, creating a kind of suction that draws the liquid into the brush (internal mixing) and then out again through the nozzle tip. The Paasche is a syphon-feed, external-mixing airbrush. When the air is released through the brush it syphons the liquid to the tip where it mixes with the air outside the brush. The pod-style airbrush, developed by TEMPTU, places the airbrush makeup inside a container (pod) that can be easily changed from one color to another quickly without having to cleaning the brush between color changes.

Airbrushes can be purchased as dual action or single action brushes. Dual action brushes allow the artist the ability to control both the flow of air and the flow of the makeup by pushing down and pulling back on the *trigger level*. A single action airbrush allows for the variable control of the air by pressing down on the trigger level. The trigger lever will not pull back, it will only move up and down. The flow of makeup is controlled by adjusting the *spring housing* dial near the back of the airbrush. The spring housing dial controls the position of the needle in relation to the nozzle tip. It allows for a consistent, rather than variable, flow of makeup through the tip.

Airbrushes are usually connected to an external air supply: an air compressor (Figure 6.29) or an air canister of compressed air. Some compact designs have small compressors built into the housing of the unit. The compressor usually has

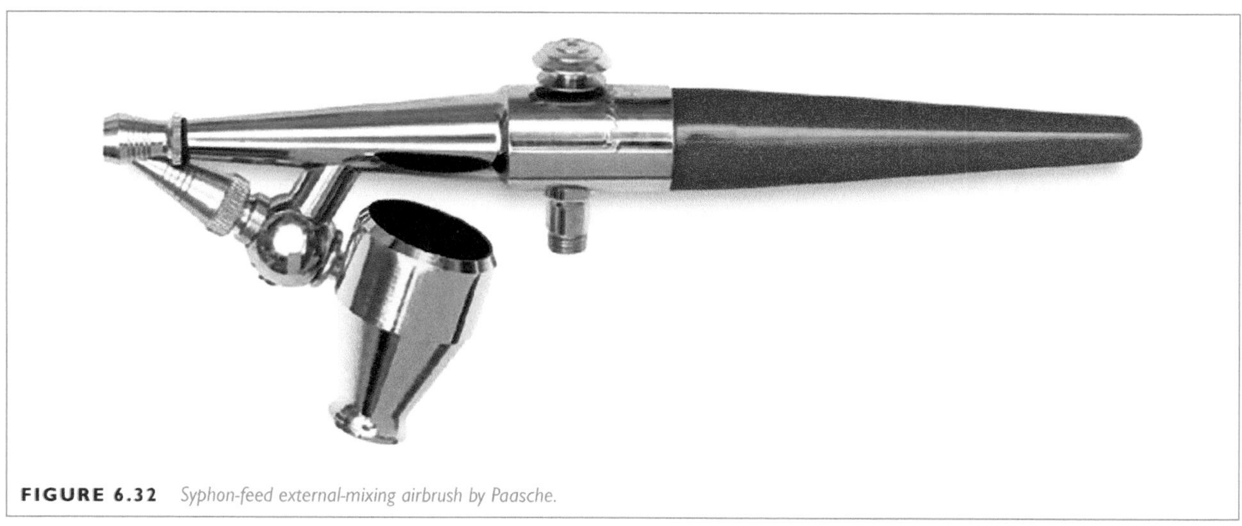

FIGURE 6.32 *Syphon-feed external-mixing airbrush by Paasche.*

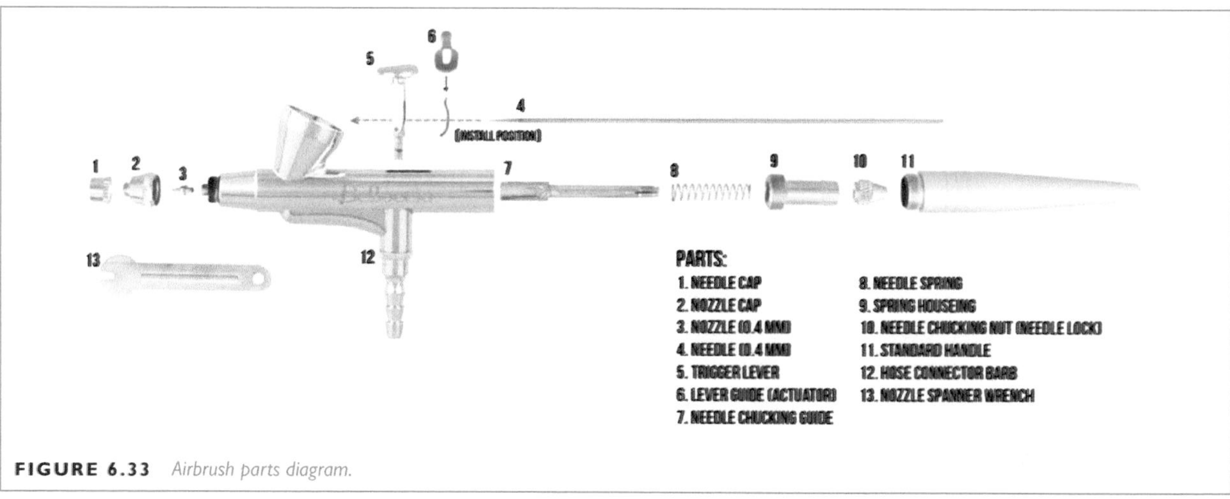

FIGURE 6.33 *Airbrush parts diagram.*

an air pressure gauge to adjust the psi. The ability to adjust the air pressure allows the artist to use a variety of liquid makeups with varying viscosities.

Most airbrushes have 13 parts (not counting the main cylinder). The parts are assembled as instructed in Figure 6.33. It is always useful when first purchasing the airbrush to assemble and disassemble the brush several times to familiarize yourself with the assembly process. It is recommended to place all the parts on a small plate, tray, or on a towel in the order shown (Figure 6.33) until you are confident you can assemble it with ease. The parts are quite small and can easily be lost.

The airbrush must be handled with care. There are two particularly delicate parts: the nozzle and the needle. The two are usually sold as a pair because the tip of the needle and the opening in the nozzle must be compatible. Figure 6.33 shows a .4 mm needle tip and a .4 mm nozzle opening. They are available

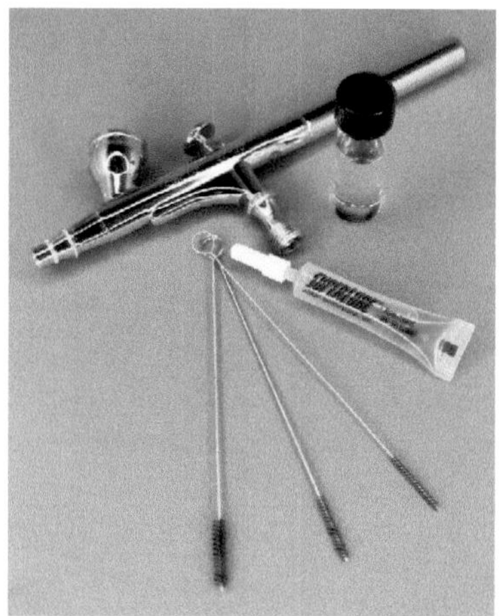

FIGURE 6.34 *Basic airbrush cleaning kit includes cleaning fluid, several tiny brushes, and lubricating fluid.*

FIGURE 6.35 *Airbrush cleaning pot by MakeBake. The cleaning pot is used to contain the excess liquid spray droplets expelled during the cleaning process.*

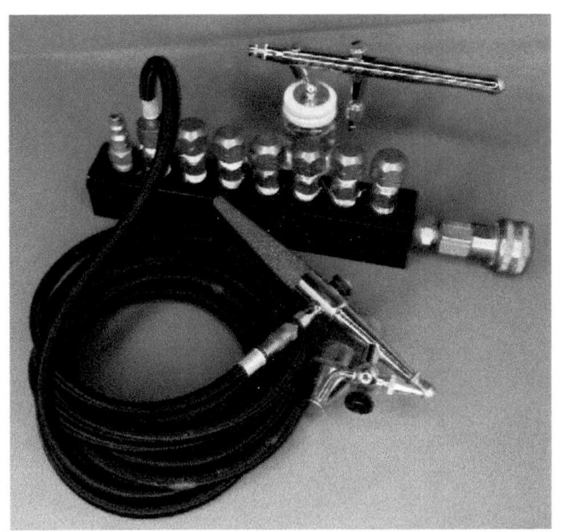

FIGURE 6.36 *Airbrush manifold. The manifold is used for attaching multiple brushes when different colors are used and for allowing multiple users to work at the same time.*

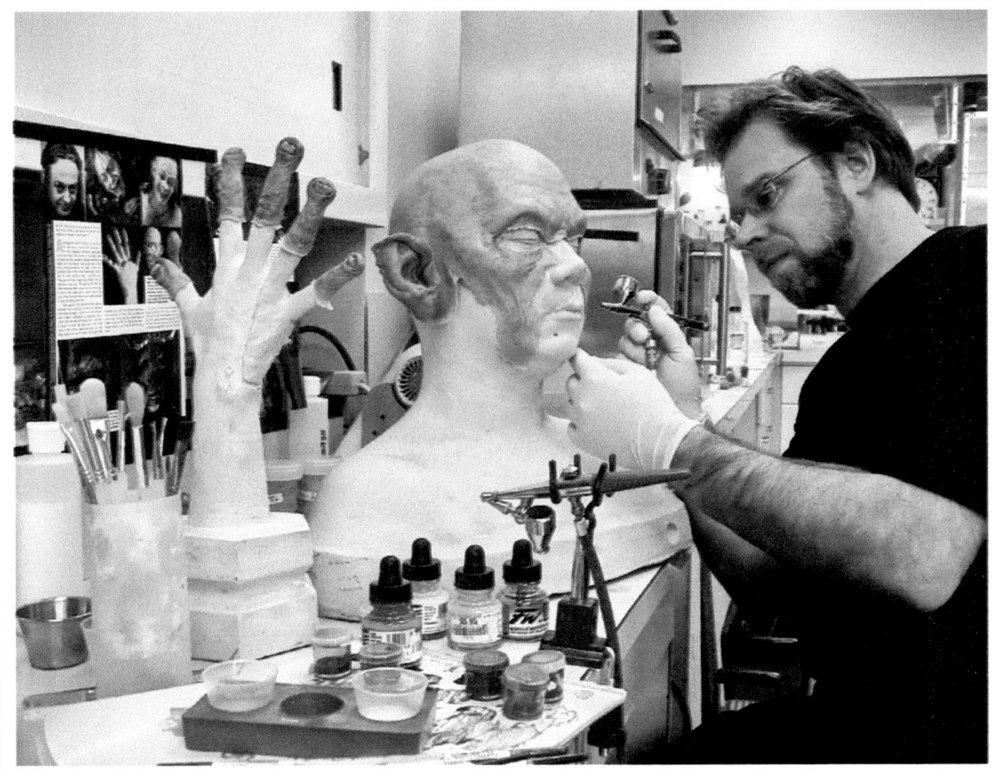

FIGURE 6.37 *Makeup artist Stephan Tessier using a gravity-feed, internal-mixing airbrush to paint a prosthetic facial appliance and finger tips. (Notice the Paasche syphon-feed, external-mixing airbrush resting in the airbrush holder attached to the table.)*

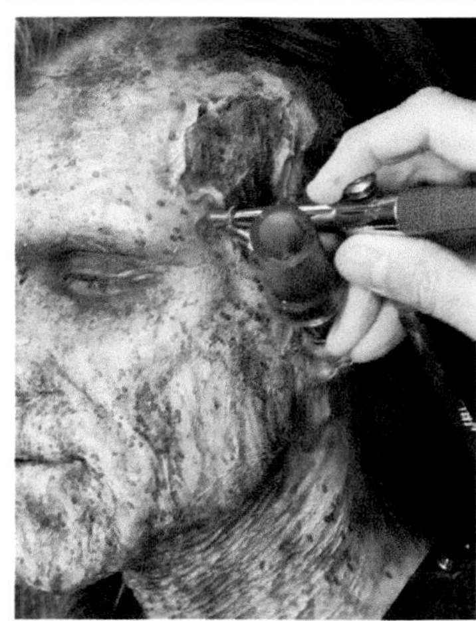

FIGURE 6.38 *Makeup artist Matthew Mungle using a Paasche syphon-feed, external-mixing airbrush to paint the final details of a zombie character makeup.*

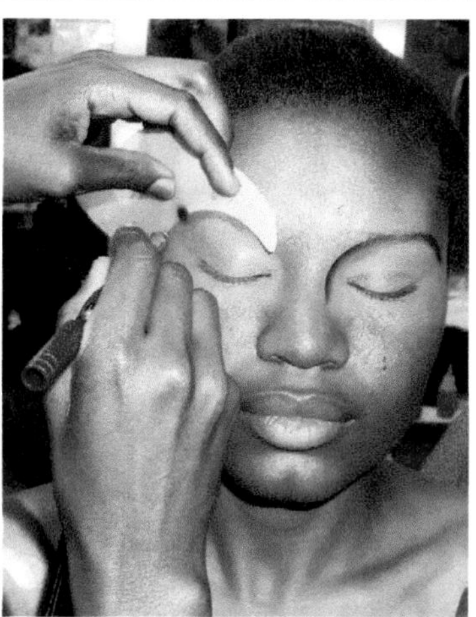

FIGURE 6.39 *Makeup artist using a curved plastic stencil to create the eyebrows.*

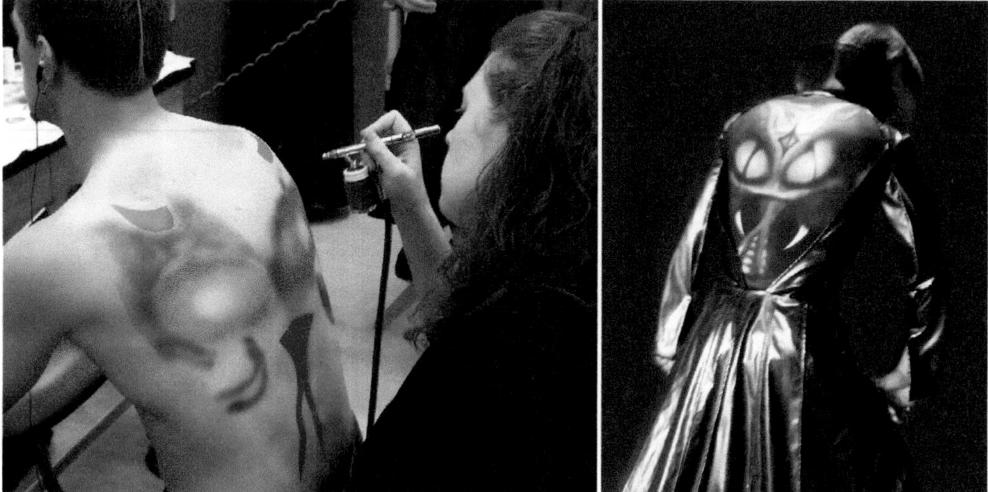

FIGURE 6.40 *Airbrush body painting by artist Stacey Bridges.*

in sizes from .1 mm to .5 mm. It is a general rule that the smaller the needle/nozzle size, the finer the details of the work. The needle and the needle tip are very delicate and can be easily bent. The slightest bend in the needle shank and/or the needle tip can compromise the way the tip enters the nozzle, causing problems with how air and paint flow through the airbrush.

The nozzle spanner wrench has one function and that is to release and tighten the nozzle before and after the cleaning process. The nozzle is quite soft and can easily be snapped if too much pressure is used when replacing it. If it happens to snap, the threaded end will stay in the tool and will have to be removed before a replacement part can be attached.

Cleaning the airbrush after each use with airbrush cleaner and airbrush brushes is a simple operation. Once you are finished with your work, replace the paint in the vessel (the cup or jar) with water and spray until all the color has been washed out of the brush, then pour into the vessel a small amount of airbrush cleaner and repeat the spraying process until the brush runs clear. Spraying into a cleaning pot wash

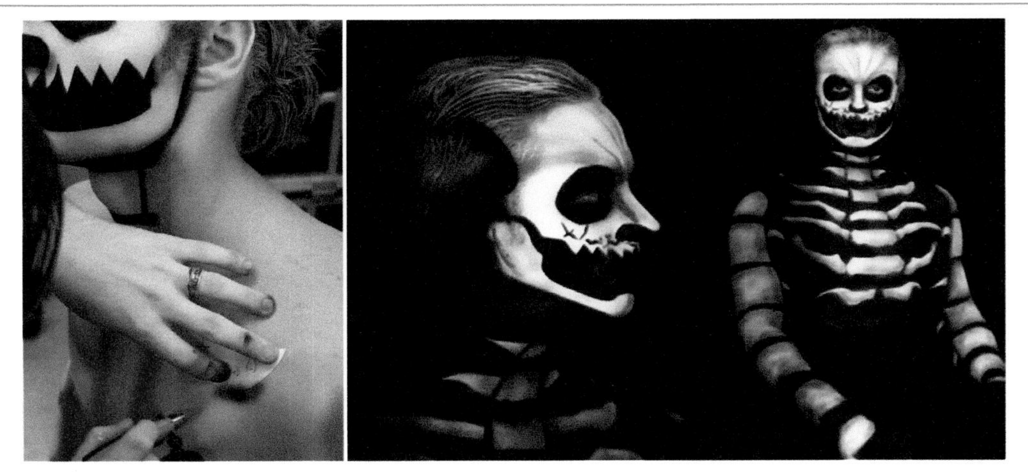

FIGURE 6.41 *Airbrush body painting by artist Cody Sadler.*

station (see Figure 6.35) rather than into the room airspace will keep the air in your studio or makeup room free of airborne particulates. Disassemble the brush and place all the parts in front of you. Each part can be cleaned separately. Use the various sized brushes to clean the interior of the parts and a cotton-tipped applicator to clean out the nozzle and needle caps, and the interior of the makeup vessel. When the airbrush is completely clean and all the parts are dry, lubricate the needle with a light coating of petroleum jelly (wipe off excess petroleum jelly with a tissue or clean cloth).

There is one thing to know about airbrush makeup when applying realistic makeup for fashion, bridal, and basic stage makeup: as soon as you can see the makeup on the skin, you have already applied too much. Airbrush makeup is intended to look invisible, natural, and smooth. The airbrush applies millions of tiny dots to the skin which allows the natural color of the skin to show through. It also allows the skin to breathe. However, it does not take long for the makeup to look like a mask, turning the model into a doll or mannequin. It will take practice to know when the application is complete.

CHAPTER 7

CORRECTIVE MAKEUP

The purpose of corrective makeup is to help actors look their best. This may involve only minor adjustments, such as changing the curve of the eyebrows, or it may involve making the actor look younger. And, for the stage, it may involve adjusting the color of the skin.

THE FOUNDATION

In corrective makeup the purpose of the foundation is to provide a skin color that will enhance the actor's appearance under the stage lighting used for a particular performance. Since a skin coloring that looks normal and healthy off stage may look pale and washed out under stage lights, some additional color may be needed. If the skin does not need to be changed in color, the actor may not need to use a foundation. However, some product should be present for light to reflect off the surface, even if it is only to even out the skin tone without changing the color or shape of the face. In this chapter, however, we shall assume that a foundation is needed.

Perhaps the easiest way to choose a suitable foundation (or base) color is to simply match the skin color of the performer. This is never an easy choice since how we perceive color of skin is not always how we perceive color in a foundation container. Matching a skin's hue to a foundation is a learned exercise and must, at first, be accomplished through careful observation and a little trial and error. First, what do we know about a skin hue by direct observation? Is it high value, low value, or somewhere in the middle? Is it pinkish, olive, golden, or the color of caramel, espresso, or ebony? Could the color of the skin be characterized as slightly cool or slightly warm? Or neutral? A cool or warm skin tone can be determined through observing the skin's undertones. Every skin color, whether light or dark, almond or ebony, has its unique undertone. Here are some determiners for cool undertones:

- When looking at the inside of the arm, if the veins appear slightly blue or purple.
- There is a pink, cool red, or bluish cast to the skin. Also, look for some olive tones.
- Naturally dry or slightly ashy skin.
- Blue, blue/green, blue with gold flecks, light and dark brown eyes.
- The skin has a tendency to burn easily or turn pink when out in the sun.
- Hair colors: light blonde, ash blonde, ginger, medium brown, dark brown, blue (cool) black, burgundy highlights, silver gray.
- The skin looks best against silver jewelry.

Some determiners for warm undertones:

- When looking at the inside of the arm, if the veins appear slightly green (blue veins reflected through yellow skin tone).
- There is a natural color to the skin: light creamy-yellow, golden, yellow-brown, golden-brown, pale peach, golden-peach. Also, look for copper (golden-orange with a little red).
- Freckles.

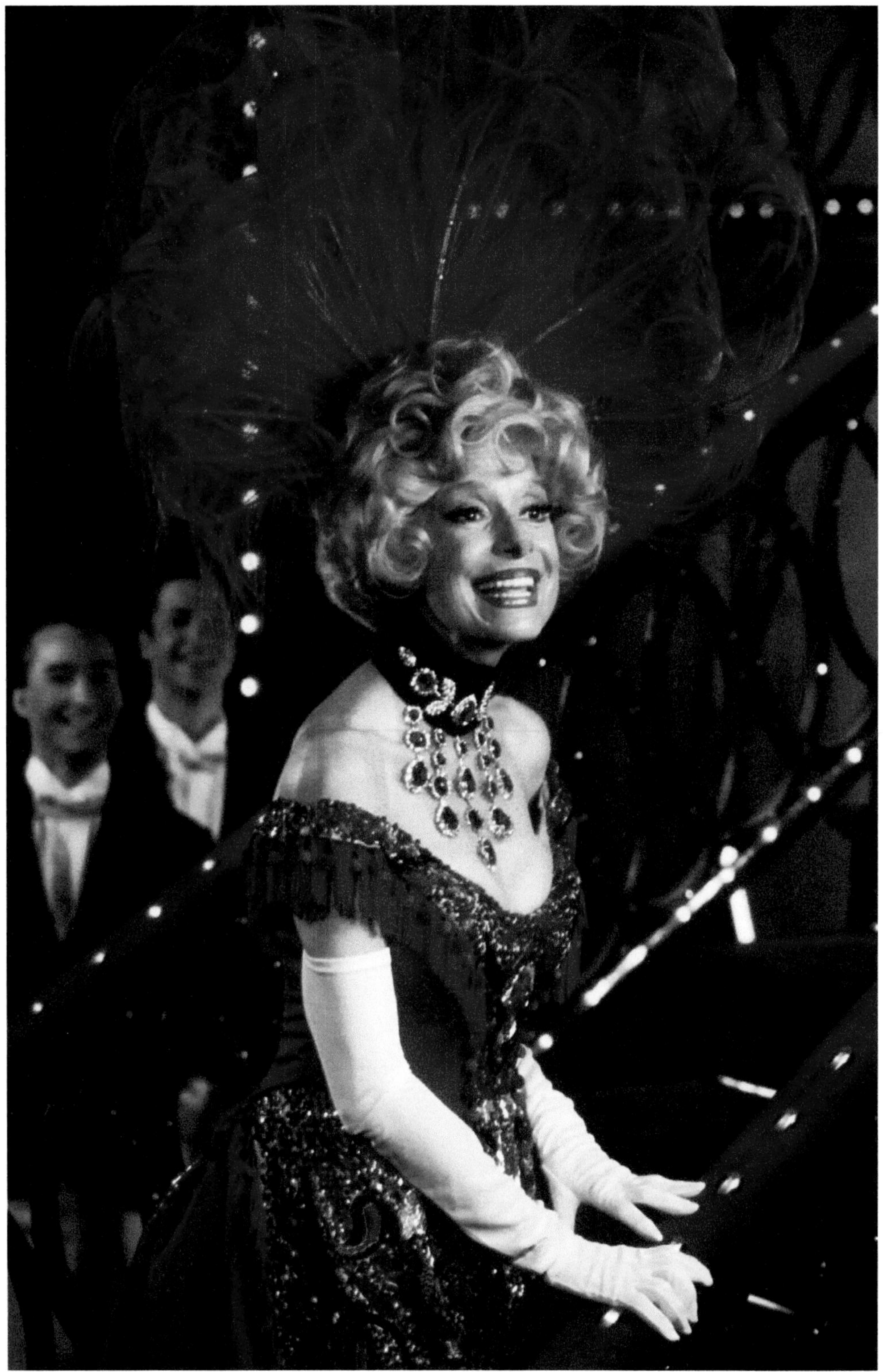

FIGURE 7.1 *Carol Channing as Dolly Levi in Hello Dolly, the Broadway production.*

Source: Photograph by Joan Marcus.

FIGURE 7.2 *Actress Chita Rivera in the Broadway musical Chicago.*

Concealer:	MAC C-2 (light yellow tone) under the eyes and on the T-section.
Foundation:	MAC C-3 (slightly yellow).
Powder:	N-2 adds a bit of pink to the foundation. One shade lighter than foundation.
Eyeshadow:	MAC Vanilla all over (lash line to brows), MAC Chill as highlight, MAC Stencil (pale apricot) on lid and crease, MAC Ocre in crease, blend up and out with MAC Rule (bright orange) adds the effect of bright skin color.
Eyeliner:	MAC Black cream liner, blend and soften the edges with Rule. White pencil along lower rim.
Blush:	MAC Cheek (pinkish/peach), blend into the surrounding skin tone with MAC Rule (golden/orange), add a bit of MAC Melba (irridescent).
Contour:	MAC Buff (pinkish/peachy and slightly brown) below cheek.
Brows:	Taupe pencil with a lighter application near the center.
Lip pencil:	MAC Spice (scarlet).
Lipstick:	MAC Russian Red.

Source: Makeup and photograph courtesy of Kate Best.

- When in the sun, the skin tans easily.
- Golden blonde, ginger, orange-red, auburn, brown with red or gold highlights, deep brown, taupe-gray, or gray-brown hair color.
- The skin looks best against gold jewelry.

A neutral undertone can have characteristics of both warm and cool, pink, blue, green, and yellow.

When choosing a foundation it is important to remember that skin tone is directly related to the foundation color. For a light to medium olive-brown skin tone, a light to medium olive-brown foundation should be chosen. The foundation must, however, contain a small amount of undertone color to perfectly match the skin. When looking for a foundation that matches the skin tone of the performer it is useful to research as many choices as possible. The Ben Nye Matte Foundation Palette II for Film, Print and Fashion (Figure 7.3) contains a full range of possible foundation colors to match most skin tones. The palette is organized in rows from high to low values, and in color series with names such as (top to bottom on the chart) Shinsei, Ciné, Natural Olive, Beige Natura, Olive Beige, Sahara, Soft Beige and International. These color series indicate a clear understanding of how skin undertones influence foundation hues. With the foundation colors side-by-side it becomes clearly visible that the Shinsei (the Japanese word for "New Life") Series is warmer (more yellow) than the cooler Beige Natura Series (which is more pink), a few rows below. The foundation named "Soleil" is more pink than "Chinois," and "Sumatra" is more golden than "Mocha."

Another way to determine a cool or warm undertone is to drape the performer in white, then beige. If they look better in white, they have a cool undertone; if they look better in beige, they have a warm undertone. While this could seem a rather subjective choice, other color choices in the cool and warm ranges can be draped on the performer as a tool to determine undertones.

There are no hard-and-fast rules about what color an actor may or may not use. The actor, along with the makeup artist (if available), should choose one that matches their skin tone and looks attractive in the lighting in which he or she will be seen. A good rule of thumb is to first match the skin tone of the performer, check the color under the lighting in the performance space, then, if needed, raise or lower the color value and/or temperature (cool or warm) to meet your needs. Considerations for choosing the right foundation color can come from character analysis, costume color palette, wig color, set and lighting color choices.

SKIN TYPES AND CONDITIONS

Before choosing makeup products, a makeup artist should have a basic understanding of skin types and basic routines that work with each skin type.

There are three basic types of skin: dry, oily, and combination. Dry skin lacks a natural sheen, looks dull, is prone to developing lines and wrinkles, and tends to age prematurely. This type of skin has small pores, is lacking moisture, and has under-active sebaceous glands (produces sebum, the skin's natural oil). Recommendations for skin care include cleansing

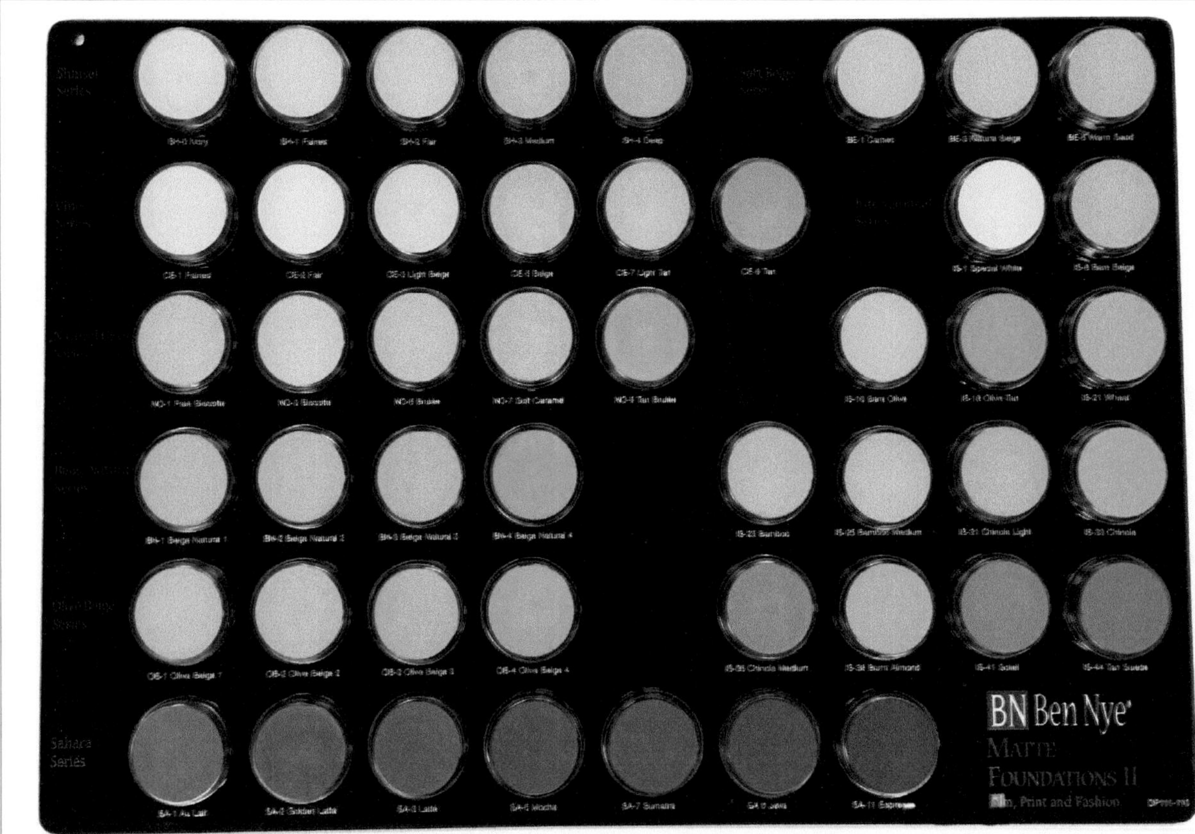

FIGURE 7.3 *Ben Nye Matte Foundation Palette II.*

FIGURE 7.4 *Makeup design and application by artist David Arevalo for a Billie Holiday look-a-like makeup.*

creams, cleansing lotions, and moisturizers (day and night) formulated for dry skin. Moisturizers should be applied under cream-style foundations, blushes, eye color, and lipsticks.

Oily skin appears shiny and is greasy to the touch. This type of skin has active sebaceous glands and is generally characterized by the appearance of large pores. This type of skin is slightly thicker than other types and is susceptible to pimples and impurities under the surface. To prepare for makeup application, clean the skin twice a day using a facial soap (not body soap) followed by a facial cleanser, both formulated for oily skin. Clean the skin gently; excessive scrubbing with a wash cloth may only cause the skin to produce more oil. On a weekly basis, apply a cleansing mask (specifically for oily skin) to remove impurities left behind from daily cleaning. The drying action will absorb excess oils and give the skin a smoother appearance. Apply an oil-free moisturizer for daily wear, but avoid nightly applications and products called "night creams." They tend to aggravate oily skin. Many actors with oily skin recommend regular exfoliation with an alpha hydroxy acid. This product helps promote soft, smooth, younger looking skin by slowly removing dry skin cells without the damaging effects of other more abrasive cleansers.

In general, the darker the skin, the more shiny it will appear. Mattifying creams (that dry to a matte finish) and oil-control lotions can be applied under oil-free foundations to help stop excessive shine. When applying foundation on very oily skin, dampen the sponge in very warm water before applying foundation (if cream based); this technique helps to absorb some of the excess oils from the skin. However, it is best to use a long-lasting liquid foundation instead of a cream-based one which tends to be oilier. Lancôme's Teint Idol or Revlon's Color Stay are good examples of liquid makeup with excellent staying power. These makeups dry very quickly because of the volatile silicone oils, so it is best to work on small areas of the face and blend quickly instead of applying all over the face at the same time. When these foundations dry they become very difficult to remove. Once set, apply a setting powder with a puff. Rule of thumb on oily skin: always powder the foundation. If you are having trouble with powders, use a no-color powder first to set the foundation, buff off the excess, then use a pressed powder about two shades lighter than the actor's complexion and apply a small amount to remove any residual from the no-color powder.

Antishine products such as MAC's Matte, Smashbox's Mattifying Primer, Lancôme's Pure Focus T-Zone Mattifier, Mehron's Touchup, Peter Thomas Roth's Max Anti-Shine Mattifying Gel, Benefit Cosmetics Dr Feelgood, and Origins Zero Oil (deep pore cleanser) can also be used but must be applied sparingly. They can be applied before or after the foundation. Test each product before the initial application as some of them may turn gray or ashy on dark skin.

The most common skin type is combination skin. This type of skin usually has an oily T-zone (across the forehead and down the center of the face from forehead to chin) and normal to dry areas surrounding the zone. Each area has different needs and must be cared for separately.

Skin Conditions: *Hyperpigmentation* is marked discoloration recognized by unevenness in the skin color where some areas of the skin look darker than others, including black spots on the face usually from the incorrect extraction of impurities from the skin. Heavy darkness under the eyes or on the lids, cheek area, around the mouth, and neck are areas where hyperpigmentation might be noticeable. Hormonal changes during pregnancy can also contribute to this condition. (Note: darkness under the eyes may also be due to allergies or might be genetic.)

It is very difficult to cover these discolorations with a lighter foundation because it will simply become a lighter dark spot. It is best to neutralize these discolorations with an orange-colored base product, and then stipple with a foundation that matches the skin tone. Blend the foundation and the neutralizer together, eliminating all edges. Powder and apply accent colors as usual. Realize that you might not be able to completely eliminate all of the discoloration but this technique will soften and diffuse the area so that the naked eye is not drawn directly to it.

Pseudofolliculitis is the medical name for the inflammation of the follicle or ingrown hair. Many men with overly curly hair suffer from this condition. It can cause infection and lead to scarring. Products such as Tend Skin and Bump Stop can be used before and after shaving to help prevent this condition. Facial massage and regular exfoliation with a gritty facial scrub before shaving are also recommended. Some men who have problems shaving use depilatories such as Magic to remove facial hair. Depilatories are rather strong chemicals that dissolve the hair but must be monitored carefully to avoid burning the skin. Use minimum makeup to cover this condition as the makeup can be unsightly and focus attention on the problem.

Vitiligo is a condition characterized by the loss of pigment on areas of the skin. Opaque camouflage systems such as Kryolan's Dermacolor, Mehron's Tattoo Cover, Dermablend, and Fashion Fair Cover Tone Concealing Cream products can successfully add color back into these areas.

Technique for covering vitiligo:

1. Stipple light areas with one of the above foundations that match closely to the darker skin color.
2. Blend edges properly.
3. Lightly powder with setting powder.
4. Cover entire face with another foundation that matches the darker area of the pigmentation. Blend properly and powder to set.
5. Apply colors as usual.

Keloids are large dark scars caused by injury to the skin or by infection. People predisposed to keloids should see a skin

FIGURE 7.5 *Keyloid scars. (Prosthetic transfer makeup by Stephan Tessier.)*

care specialist before considering cosmetic procedures such as ear piercing.

FACIAL ANALYSIS

Before corrective makeup is applied, the actor's face should be analyzed to determine how it can be made more attractive. If the two sides of the face are sufficiently different to appear obviously asymmetrical, the less pleasing side can be made up to match, as nearly as possible, the more pleasing one. Which side is to be corrected can usually be judged by covering first one half of the face with a sheet of paper, then the other. An even more effective technique is to take a full-face photograph, then make a reverse print. Both the normal print and the reverse one can be cut vertically in half and the halves switched and pasted together. You will then have two photographs of the face with both sides matching, but one will be based on the right side, the other on the left. The less appealing face will indicate the side that is to be corrected. It is essential, of course, that the photograph be taken straight on if the technique is to work properly.

Decisions as to what is to be corrected will be based on personal taste, which may, in turn, be affected by current fashions. More often than not, individual features—such as eyebrows and lips—rather than overall proportions will be corrected. But there are certain classic features and classic proportions that seem to transcend fashion and personal taste.

The classically proportioned face can be divided horizontally into three equal parts:

1. from the hairline to the eyebrows,
2. from the eyebrows to the bottom of the nose, and
3. from the bottom of the nose to the tip of the chin.

If these three sections are not equal, they can be made to appear equal—or more nearly so—in various ways. But since a face not having classical proportions may sometimes be more interesting on stage than a classically proportioned one, making such a change is not necessarily advantageous.

If you decide that you do want to change the proportions of the face, the following suggestions can be used as a guide.

Forehead

If you want to create the illusion of a lower forehead, darken the area next to the hairline with a foundation color two to three shades darker than the rest of the face. This color can be blended downward very gradually so that it disappears imperceptibly into the foundation. That makes the forehead appear lower because light colors reflect light and attract the eye, whereas dark colors absorb light and attract less attention. Following the same principle, a low forehead can be made to look higher by using a color two to three shades lighter than the base and applying it at the hairline as before. That will attract the eye upward, emphasizing the height of the forehead.

The forehead can be made to seem narrower by shadowing the temples and blending the shadow onto the front plane of the forehead, apparently decreasing the actual width of the front plane. Or it can seemingly be widened by highlighting the temples, carrying the highlight to the hairline. This will counteract the natural shadow that results from the receding of the temple areas and will appear to bring them forward. It will also seem to extend the front plane of the forehead horizontally. As always, there should be a difference of only two or three shades between the shadows and the base since deeper shadows at the temples tend to age the face. If the front lobes are too prominent, tone them down with a darker foundation color, and bring forward the depression between the frontal lobes and the superciliary arch with a highlight. If the temples are normally sunken, they can be brought out with a highlight.

Nose

If you want the nose shorter, apply a deeper color under the tip and blend it up over the tip. That will tone down the natural highlight and take the attention away from the tip. If a short highlight is placed on the upper part of the nose, it will attract the eye to that area and help to give the illusion of a shorter nose. If you want the nose longer, you can carry a highlight down over and under the tip, pulling the viewer's eye downward and apparently lengthening the nose.

If you want to widen the nose, run a broad highlight down the center and blend carefully. That will appear to widen the front plane of the nose—not the entire nose. You might also highlight the nares, giving an illusion of still greater width.

If you want to narrow the nose, reverse the procedure by shadowing the nares and the sides of the nose and running a very narrow highlight down the center. Then blend the edges. That will give the illusion of a sharp and narrow bone and cartilage.

To flatten the nose, reverse the usual modeling by shadowing the front and highlighting the sides. Blend all edges carefully.

If the tip of the nose is fuller than you want it to be, shadow it slightly on either side of the painted highlight to tone down part of the natural highlight.

If the nose is crooked, run a fairly narrow highlight down the nose, then shadow it on either side wherever there is a natural highlight that reveals the crookedness. Blend the highlight and the shadows. The highlight may be straight, or it may bend slightly in the opposite direction from the real bend. Use whichever method proves the more effective (see Figures 8.20 and 8.21).

In general, then, decide where you want to attract the eye of the viewer, and place the highlights in that area, shadowing areas that you want to recede or to seem smaller or less conspicuous.

Normally, in corrective makeup, highlights and shadows are about three shades lighter and darker than the base. But in making up the nose it is often necessary to take a more subtle approach. This applies particularly when you are using shadows to counteract strong natural highlights.

The corrective techniques just described, though effective from the front, have practically no effect on the nose in profile. That requires a three-dimensional addition (see Chapters 10 and 11).

Jawline and Chin

If the jawline is too square or too prominent, shadow the part that needs to be rounded off or toned down, carrying the shadow both under and over the jawbone, and blend carefully into the foundation. If you want to make the jawline more firm and youthful, add some highlight along the jawbone, softening the lower edge and blending the top edge imperceptibly into the foundation. A section of shadow can be run along under the bone and both edges blended.

If the chin is too prominent—that is, if it juts forward too much—darken the whole chin with a light shadow. If it is too long in proportion to the rest of the face, it can be shortened by shadowing the lower part. Make sure that the edge of the shadow is thoroughly blended. If you want the chin longer, highlight the lower part, and if you want it more prominent, highlight the whole chin. If it's too square, round off the corners with shadows. If it's too pointed, flatten the point with a square shadow. A double chin can be minimized by shadowing the fullness to make it less noticeable.

Wrinkles

Wrinkles can seldom be blotted out completely, but they can be minimized by carefully brushing in highlights where you find the natural shadows and subtly shadowing the prominent part of each wrinkle where you find a natural highlight. This applies also to circles or bags under the eyes.

Eyes

In making up the eyes, keep in mind that ideally the space or distance between the eyes should be the width of one eye. If the space is less than that, you can make the eyes appear to be farther apart than they actually are. For corrective makeup it is seldom that eyes seem to be brought closer together, though that may be done for certain character makeups. Either of these changes can easily be brought about by making use of an optical illusion.

If the eyes and the eyebrows are made up as in Figures 7.6a and 7.6f, they will seem closer together. If they are made up as in Figure 7.6b, they will seem farther apart. For women, false eyelashes can be worn along with eyeliner and eyeshadow to make the eyes look farther apart. The lashes should be trimmed so that they are fuller at the outer corners, and they can be shortened and placed away from the inner corners of the eye so that they actually extend over only the outer two-thirds of the upper lids.

Eyeshadow

Eyeshadow for a corrective makeup application for women should consist of three color values: a highlighter and a medium and dark shadow. Choose natural colors that are harmonious with the actor's skin tone and that blend well into one another (i.e. bone, taupe, and charcoal/brown). Generally, the lightest color is placed on the lid, the darkest in the crease, the mid-tone between the crease and the brow, and a highlight under the brow in order to make the eyes more prominent. Avoid using brighter colors unless they are slightly grayed and truly complement the eyes. Whenever possible, choose an eyeshadow that is not the same color as the eyes. The color should complement the actor's eyes, not compete with them.

Cream eyeshadows tend to migrate and gather in the creases of the eye if they are not promptly set with powder. Once powdered they will stay looking smooth and natural. There are primers made specifically for the eyelids to help the eyeshadow stay in place. These primers are applied to the eyelid before the makeup is added.

Eyeliner (also see Chapters 6 and 9): The eyes can be accented by lining them, using a small brush or an eyeliner pencil. The brush can be used with cake, gel, or liquid eyeliner. With either the brush or the pencil, draw a line along the upper lash line. This line should start about two-thirds of the way in

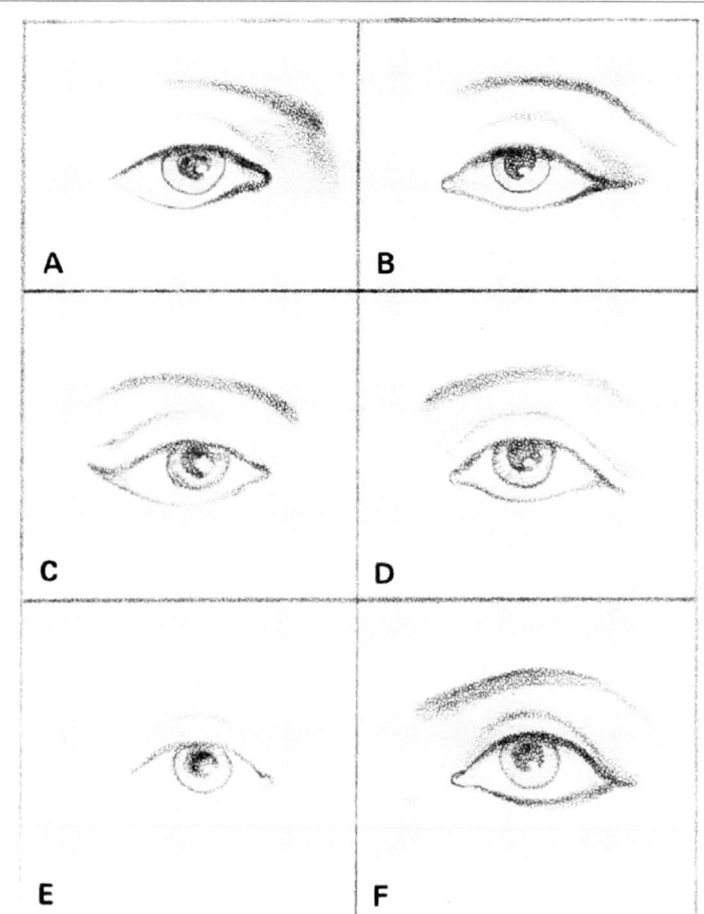

FIGURE 7.6 *Eye illusions. A. Shading the eye area and penciling the eyebrow to make the eye appear closer to the nose. Used on both eyes, it will give the illusion of the eyes being closer together. B. Shading the eye area and penciling the eyebrow to make the eye appear farther from the nose. Used on both eyes, it will give the illusion of the eyes being farther apart. C. Shading to turn the eye up at the corner. D. Shading to droop the eye at the outer corner. E. Highlighting (or absence of shading) around the eye to make it smaller. F. Shading the eye and darkening it and extending the brow to make the eye appear larger.*

toward the nose or may even begin close to the tear duct. The line follows the lashes and extends about a quarter of an inch beyond the outer corner of the eye. It should end in a slight curve, and when a natural effect is desired, it should fade out, not end abruptly. It can line the entire eye or be applied only partially.

For some performance venues and on some faces it may be necessary to line the lower lash line (see Figure 7.7). Starting at the outer edge of the lash line draw a soft line nearly the length of the lashes. This lower line should fade out about two-thirds of the way toward the tear duct. Liner can be applied to the lash line from above and/or below the lashes and depends on the effect that is being created. The upper and lower lines may be softened and blended together where they meet at the outer edge by going over them with a narrow, flat shading brush. The purpose of eyeliner is to enlarge the eye slightly as well as to emphasize it. For a natural corrective makeup, eyeliner should not completely surround the eye.

Sometimes a small amount of white is brushed or penciled in at the outer edge of the eye (see Figure 7.2) in order to help enlarge the eye. White can also be applied along the inside rim of the lower eyelid. This technique of adding white to the lower rim does tend to make the eyes appear larger, but may cause serious injury to the eye.

If the eyes are to be made to appear farther apart, the accents should be strongest at the outer ends and carried

FIGURE 7.7 *Glenn Close in the Broadway production of Sunset Boulevard. Ms. Close uses a technique of placing the eyeliner below the natural lash line to create the illusion of a larger eye. The line carefully tapers to a fine point at either end.*

Source: Photograph by Joan Marcus.

farther beyond the corner of the eye than usual. If the eyes are to be closer together, the accents are shifted to the inner corners and should not extend to the outer corners at all.

Men should avoid lining the eyes when a natural effect is required. A bit of brown or clear mascara may be all that is needed. In large performance venues such as opera, ballet, outdoor theater, and houses with over 800 seats, eyeliner is quite appropriate. A technique for enlarging the eye in large venues is to draw the lower lash line below the natural lash line. The space created between the two lines can be highlighted.

Performers with extremely dark circles, bagging or puffiness, or excessive wrinkles under the eye should avoid blending the liner below the lash line since it tends to draw attention to that area of the face.

Eyebrows

For corrective makeup, men's eyebrows should always look natural, whereas women's may or may not. That does not mean that changes should never be made in a male actor's eyebrows, but it does mean that they should not look made up. Unkempt, scraggly, or excessively heavy brows can be improved or controlled in a number of ways:

- by combing or brushing with a small amount of hair spray;
- by judicious plucking or waxing to remove hairs between the brows;
- by carefully clipping unruly hair with a pair of small, sharp scissors;
- by plucking or waxing to create an attractive arch.

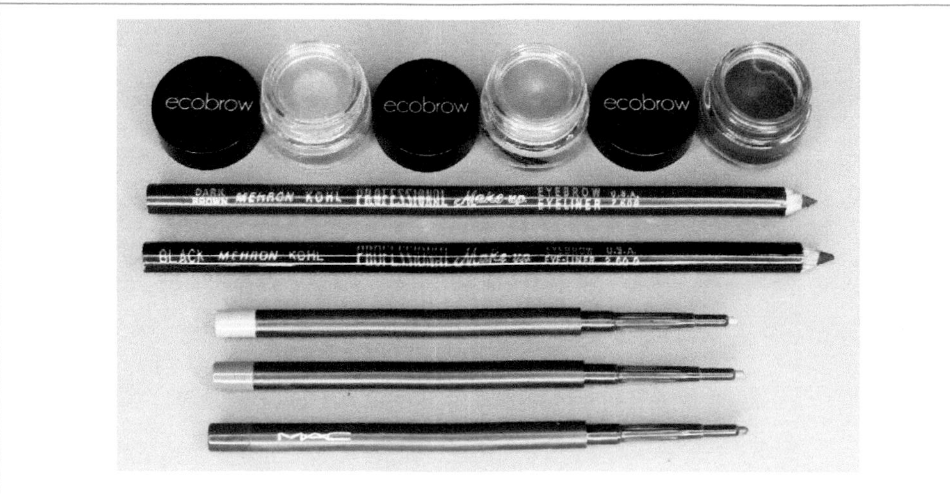

FIGURE 7.8 *Eyebrow products. (top to bottom) Ecobrow Defining Wax; pencils by Mehron; MAC Brow Liners.*

If you're planning to pluck more than a few hairs, it would be wise to experiment with blocking out the portions of the brow to be plucked in order to make sure you're improving the brows, not mutilating them.

If the brow is well formed and well placed there is no need to add any color. For purposes of projection they may need filling in and can simply be darkened using pencil, pressed eyeshadow, brow wax (by Ecobrow) or mascara. With pencils (they should be sharpened), use short, quick, light strokes following the direction of the hair. For a more natural-looking eyebrow transfer some pigment from the tip of the pencil to a stiff bristled eyebrow brush (it is often combined with an eyelash comb) and brush onto the eyebrows. Remember that the intention is to darken the hairs, not the skin underneath—except when the natural brow needs filling out. Using a slightly lighter shade of pencil than the brow color will also aid in achieving a more natural look.

If there is not much space between the eyebrow and the eye, it may be advantageous to open up the eye area by lifting the outer end of the eyebrow. This can be done by brushing the hair upward, removing excess hairs from below the brow and reshaping the outer end slightly with a pencil, giving more of a lift to the brow and thus to the entire face.

For women's corrective makeup, as for men's, it is not necessary to make the eyebrows fit one single pattern—rather, they should be as flattering as possible to the individual eye and to the face in general.

Cheeks

Cheeks should appear naturally soft and rounded. Subtle contour should be placed below the bone on an angle starting near the ear and softly blended forward toward the apple of the cheek. Cheek color, or blush, should be placed on the bone above the contour and a subtle highlight on top of the bone. The edges of the three colors should be softly blended and should look completely natural. Cheek color should not be placed too near the eye or the nose. If the face is narrow, blush should be kept even farther from the nose and placed nearer the ears in order to increase the apparent width of the face. If the face is wide, keep the blush away from the ears and apply it in a pattern more nearly vertical than horizontal. For corrective makeup it should never be applied in a round spot, and it should always be carefully blended.

Cheek Color: Cream blush should be blended into the cream foundation before it is set with powder. Powder or dry blush is applied over the foundation (after it has been set) with a large powder brush or angled blush brush. Gel blush is extremely sheer and can be used directly on the skin without foundation for a more natural look.

Rouge or blush is usually applied after the modeling is done, though it is sometimes used as a shadow in modeling the cheeks. For men, if called for, a soft, natural shade of bronzer can be used. The placement should be on areas of the face where the sun naturally colors the skin: the bridge of the nose, the brow bone, the cheekbones, and the chin. Whenever foundation is being used, the face should be powdered before using bronzer powder. This will ensure a smooth, even application and will avoid discoloration of the bronzer on oily skin, which tends to turn it a bit orange. Above all, it ought to look as natural as possible. In case of doubt, use none.

For women, the shade of blush chosen will depend on skin color, fashion, costume, and personal preference. For a natural look, mix a small amount of true red with the chosen

FIGURE 7.9 *Makeup Lesson by Kate Best on actress Julia Sweeney for God Said "Ha!" at the Lyceum Theatre. New York makeup artist Kate Best has been successful in a variety of performance mediums, including Broadway, film, and fashion photography. While her personal choice in makeup includes many products from the MAC line of cosmetics, she is quick to point out that it is simply a product line with which she is most familiar. In many instances she has included a color description of the product along with its name (MAC Buff, for example, is a slightly brown, pinkish-peach tone used as a contour below the cheekbone). This artist stresses the importance for making appropriate color choices from the product line or lines that best suit your performance needs. Many of the makeups have been designed for the bright lights of the Broadway stage and can be modified for other venues by varying the intensity of the effect.*

Step 1 Concealer: Apply concealer under the eye area, along the T-section of the face and over any discolorations. Use Kryolan's Dermacolor #D1.5 and #D2.

Step 2 Foundation: Apply L'Oréal Hydra Perfecte Nude Beige foundation with a sponge over the entire face. Blend well toward the neck and hairline.

Step 3 Powder: Set foundation with LeClerc loose powder—Camille, with a sponge or puff.

Step 4 Eyeshadow: Apply Il Makiage pressed eyeshadow—Banana, over the entire eyelid up to the brows and at the inner edge of the eye.

Step 5 Highlight the brow bone and the inner edge of the lower lid with Vanilla shadow by MAC. For extra highlight on brow bone and in a half-moon shape on the upper lid close to the lashes use Chill shadow by MAC (use MAC brush #29).

Step 6 Apply MAC's Omega shadow as a contour in the crease of the eye. Begin at the outer edge, brushing it three-quarters of the way across the lid, leaving the inner edge of the eye open. Using a blending brush, blend "up and out" with Coffee by Il Makiage to soften.

Step 7 Apply Coffee lightly to the lower lid at the lash line and blend with Omega for balance.

Step 8 Eyeliner: Apply Ebony pencil to the back of the hand. Pick up a small amount with an eyeliner brush and with the tip of the brush apply short, controlled, even strokes as close to the lashes as possible. Blend with a small blending brush (clean this brush constantly!).

Step 9 Repeat #8 along the lower lid beginning at the center and blending toward the outside corner. * Use Maybelline Black mascara.

Step 10 Blush: To contour, apply Coffee on the temples and below cheekbone with a blush brush. Add Peach dry blush by Shu Uemura on the apple of the cheeks, the temples, the tip of the nose, and along the jawline.

Step 11 Lips: The lips are lined with Maybelline's Light Brown lip pencil and filled in with Retro by MAC set with powder.

Step 12 Brows: Carefully line the brows with Maybelline's Blonde pencil. Starting at the center, draw a light line at the lower edge of the brow up to the arch. Finish the tail of the brow on the top line. Straighten the top line of the brow with the Blonde pencil. Fill in most of the brow with whatever remains on the ***Omega*** brush. (Note: Leave the inner edge of the brow SOFT! Do not add color to this area.) (Shu Uemura #60B can also be used for eyebrows.)

Source: Makeup and photograph courtesy of Kate Best.

foundation. This will at least give you a close approximation of a suitable color. While you should never match eyeshadow to eye color, it is an appropriate technique to match blush color to lip color.

Lips

There are various ways of reshaping lips. Thin lips can usually be corrected for women by over-painting—that is, by first drawing on with a lip pencil new lips of the shape and size wanted. Then fill in with lip color (see Figures 8.28 and 8.29). This over-painting should never be done for men. It is usually best to make the lower lip lighter than the upper. A thin highlight over the edge of the upper lip may help to define it. Regular or tinted lip balm may be all that is needed on the male performer.

If a man's lips are too full, it is usually best to leave them the natural color. If they are already too red, the lower one can be lightened. For women the fullness can be minimized by covering the lips with the foundation, then using the lip color only toward the inside of the lips and fading it outward into the foundation color. Deep colors should be avoided.

For too-wide lips, keep the lip color toward the center of the lips and cover the outer corners with the foundation color. The upper lip may be left slightly wider than the lower. If the mouth is too narrow, carry the lip color out to the extreme corners, particularly on the upper lip. It is seldom possible to carry the color beyond the natural corners of the mouth with any degree of success. The artifice becomes apparent as soon as the mouth is opened.

In the case of a turned-down mouth with a heavy upper lip and a thin lower one, the solution is to over-paint the lower lip to match the upper one and, if possible, to turn up the corners with paint. Or, if the outline of the upper lip is not too definite, it can be partially blocked out with foundation color and the lower one filled in to match. That much correction may not be possible for men.

For a mouth with a thin upper lip, the upper lip can—for women, at least—be over-painted to match the lower.

Lip coloring can best be applied with a narrow flat brush and blotted with tissue. The color should usually not be carried to the extreme corners of the mouth unless you wish to widen it. It is frequently helpful to define the lips by outlining them with a lip pencil, using the same or slightly darker shade than the lip color. The outline should then be blended inward with your brush. Now apply the lip color with a brush or directly with the lipstick.

For men, especially when no lip rouge is used at all, the outline of the lips can be defined very subtly with a brown makeup pencil, then blended. Further definition may be possible by deepening the natural shadow immediately below the center of the lower lip. If there is a natural shadow there, this will, of course, not be necessary, but if the natural shadow is slight, it may be helpful. It should, however, be done with great care so as to look completely natural. Observe the shadows under the lips in Figure 7.10[9].

Lip Color. Lip coloring should be compatible with the rouge. And like rouge it will depend—for women—on the color of the skin, hair, costume, and perhaps on colors fashionable at the time. Lips and eyes should be kept in balance with each other. If accentuating the eye area, keep the lip soft and vice versa. Bizarre fashions (such as white lipstick) should obviously be avoided in corrective makeup. For men a natural color is safest. Often it is best not to color the lower lip at all.

Neck

If the neck shows signs of age, it can be camouflaged somewhat by shadowing the prominent muscles and highlighting the depressions. Even a sagging neckline can be minimized, at least for the front view, by shadowing. The shadow should be strongest just under the jawline and should blend gradually into the foundation, which can be darker on the neck than on the face. The neck shadow must never be allowed to come up over the jawline. The jawline itself can be defined with a shadow. That will tend to strengthen it and take the attention away from the neck.

Teeth

Dark or discolored teeth can be lightened with professional whitening and/or bleaching techniques used by dentists. It is highly effective and relatively inexpensive. More serious deficiencies, such as broken, missing, or extremely irregular teeth, require the services of a dentist or orthodontist. This can be expensive, but for professional actors it is important to have attractive teeth.

Hair

The actor's usual hairstyle should be considered carefully in relation to the shape of the face. If it can be made more becoming, it should be restyled. That can often be done merely by recombing in various ways and checking in the mirror, though it is sometimes better to consult a hairdresser whose work you know and can depend on.

If you want to make the face seem shorter and broader, avoid placing the bulk of the hairdo high on the head. Try, instead, to keep it flat on top and wider at the sides. If you want the face longer and narrower, the reverse will apply. If the face is too round, avoid a round hairdo that follows the shape of the face, since that would only emphasize the roundness. But a round hairdo could be helpful for a face that is too square or too angular. If the features are sharp, the hairdo should be soft around the face, not sleek—unless, of course, you have chosen deliberately to emphasize the sharpness.

If a man's hairline is receding slightly, it may be possible to restyle hair to conceal the fact. Or the hairline can sometimes be corrected by using eyebrow pencil of the appropriate color on the scalp. In doing this, never draw a hard, horizontal line; instead, use short strokes of the pencil following the direction of the hair. These strokes should be softened and blurred with the finger so that there is no definite line, and they should also be powdered to avoid shine. Darkening the base color at the hairline will also help. Makeup to match the hair color can be applied to small bald spots and can also be used with some success on the hairline. If the hair has receded beyond the point at which it can be corrected with paint, the actor should procure a toupee or a wig. The best ones are handmade and are expensive, but good inexpensive ones made with synthetic hair are also available. No matter what you pay for a wig or a hairpiece, be sure to have it skillfully styled.

Stage Makeup for Young Male (see Figure 7.10):

1. Testing four foundation colors from the Kryolan Ultra Foundation 24 Palette on the model: (from right to left) Alabaster, Ruddy Beige, Nutmeg, Mauby.
2. Apply lip balm to the model's lips before starting the makeup application. This will ensure the lips are soft and smooth by the time the makeup is complete.
3. Apply the Alibaster Ultra Foundation using the end of a triangular sponge. Note how the sponge is prepared by pinching off small pieces around the four corners. This eliminates the possibility of impressing lines into the surface of the foundation.
4. Apply the foundation evenly to all areas of the face. The foundation is being applied carefully under the eye.
5. Apply foundation to the ears.
6. Add contour colors (Nutmeg and Mauby) to the temples, under the cheekbone, along the sides of the nose and into the eye socket, and at the edge of the eyelids. Subtle application of color creates a more realistic "no makeup" look for men onstage.
7. Blend the contour colors with a small triangular sponge. Prepare the sponge as in step 3.

8. & 9. Add highlights (Kryolan TV White) on the cheekbones, the center of the forehead, the bone above the temple, the jawline slightly below the ear, on the center of the chin, and on the bridge of the nose (notice that the tip is left natural).

10. Blend with a clean, prepared white sponge applicator. In most cases it is better to *light tap* the makeup to blend it than drag the applicator over the makeup with a wiping motion. Wiping tends to remove the makeup, drags it into places it was not intended, and often causes streaking.
11. Lightly powder the makeup using a medium, domed powder/blush brush. Kryolan Derma Color Fixing Powder was used in this exercise.
12. Shape the brows first with a clean mascara wand. Use a soft brown colored cream, dry cake, or pencil. Here a medium brown cream is applied with a small brush.
13. Apply another layer of lip balm with a small lip brush. Finished makeup.

CHOOSING MAKEUP FOR DARKER SKIN TONES

Foundation

When choosing a suitable foundation, look for formulas containing a mixture of yellow, red, and yellow-green tones with the brown pigment. Check the color for clarity by smearing a sample onto a white piece of paper. Are the added tones clearly visible in the foundation or does the foundation simply appear muddy? If any of the foundation samples appears to have a white cast to them, they will not be appropriate for dark skin. These foundations may contain talc or titanium dioxide and will leave an ashy or gray cast on the skin. These additives are used to create an opaque formula to enhance coverage. Manufacturers who produce a broad range of foundations and accent colors appropriate for darker skin tones include: Fenty Beauty by Rhianna, Black Opal, Fashion Fair, Iman, Bobbi Brown, MAC, William Tuttle, RCMA, Mehron, Kryolan, Ben Nye, Joe Blasco, Makeup Forever, Maybelline, and Cover Girl (to name a few). Additional foundations available include mineral-based powder foundations such as Colorscience, airbrush foundations such as TEMPTU and Kett and Dinair, and Classified Cosmetics Era spray-on foundation.

After selecting the basic color palette in a light to medium or medium to dark range, include a few "mixing colors" or "blending colors," such as foundations that are highly pigmented with yellow, yellow-green, red, or orange-red. These mixing colors are indispensable in any makeup kit and are used to adjust the undertones in the basic brown foundations. Some examples of useful mixing or blending colors are MAC cream color in orange and red, William Tuttles' Chocolate Cream and Toasted Almond, Fashion Fair's Copper Glo and Tawny Glo, RCMA's Shinto Series, Visiora's 101 and 102, and Black Opal's Truly Topaz.

As mentioned in previous chapters, foundations are used to give the skin an even texture, to enhance skin tone, and to provide a smooth canvas for color and dimension. The following techniques provide you with the ability to begin building dimension into the face with the initial foundation application.

FIGURE 7.10 *Corrective makeup for male youth. Makeup by Michael Meyer. Model, Tyler Hollins.*

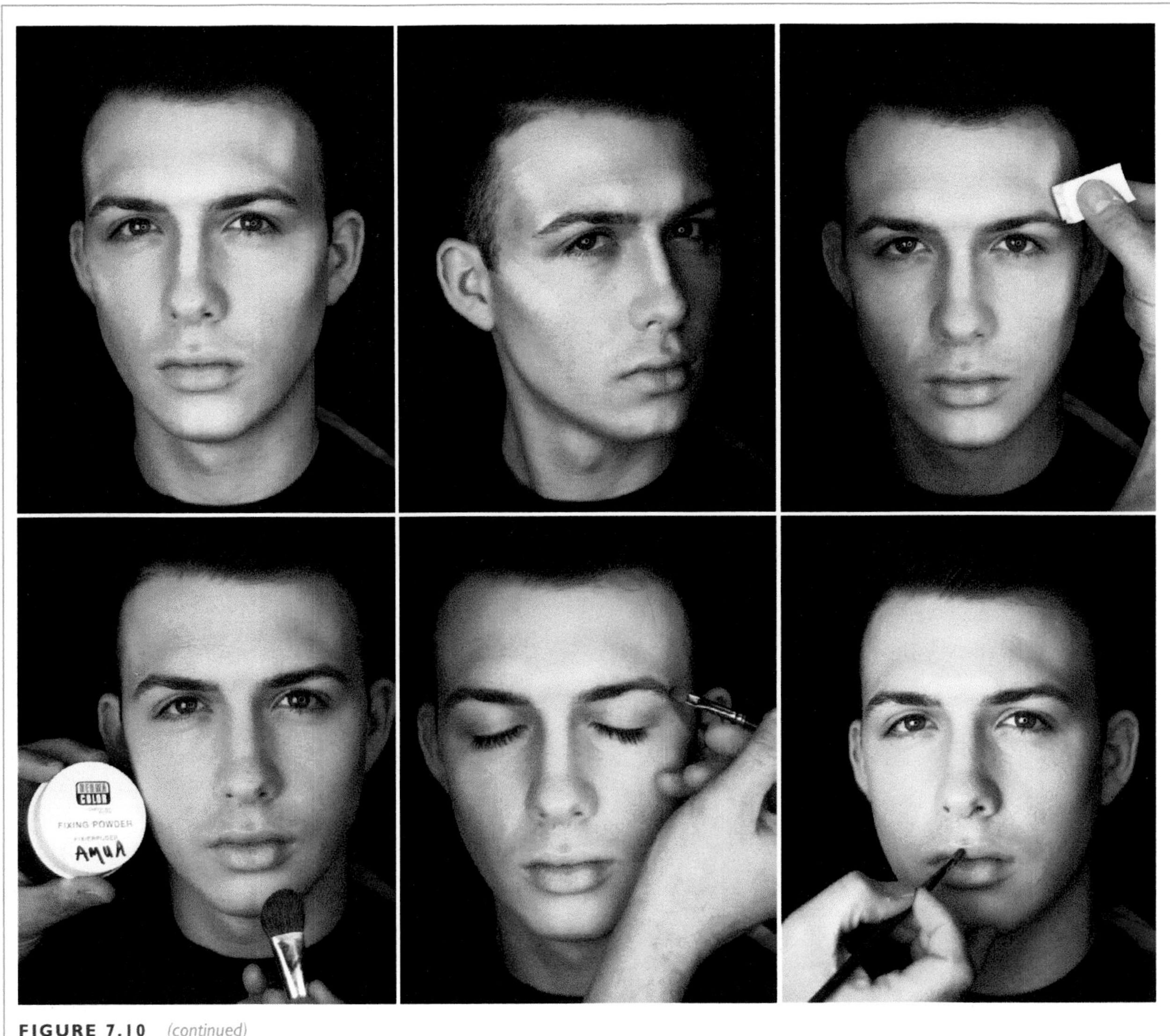

FIGURE 7.10 *(continued)*

Technique A—Use the Face as its own Palette

Many people have unevenness in the skin; that is the forehead, chin, and outer areas of the face may be darker, and the cheek areas lighter.

1. Choose two foundations—one that closely matches the outer areas of the face and a second that closely matches the cheek areas or inner areas of the face.

2. Contrary to what most people think, apply the darker foundation to the darker areas and the lighter foundation to the lighter areas then blend together on the face. The face will appear even in color when applied like this. (Note: if you blend the colors together you will not receive the same effect, sometimes this causes the subject to look gray. Also if you apply the darker foundation to the lighter area, it darkens that area and that is not going to be flattering to your subject; you want to keep that area of the face light. If you apply the lighter to the darker, it might cause the darker area to look gray and ashy. *Rule of thumb*: you cannot make dark skin light; it does not work.)

3. For concealer, use foundation shades that are in the orange family such as the Fashion Fair colors. These colors tend to neutralize darkness under eyes and blend better without creating an ashy look. With practice you will soon see that orange shades tend to blend better into the skin. Ben Nye Beard Covers, MAC Pure Orange Color Corrector and Makeup Forever Camouflage Cream work well as concealers or neutralizers on darker skin tones. Yellow shades tend to go very ashy and sit on top of the skin.

FIGURE 7.11 *The Shirelles from the Broadway production of "Beautiful" (close-up). The 1960s inspired makeup design included pink eyeshadow, a strong black eyeliner with short angled extension (cat eye) and pink lip color. Although lip liner was not used in the 1960s, in an effort to see a distinction between the pink lip color and the surrounding skin from the audience, the makeup designer added the dark lip liner. Makeup by Joe Dulude II.*

Source: Photograph by Joan Marcus.

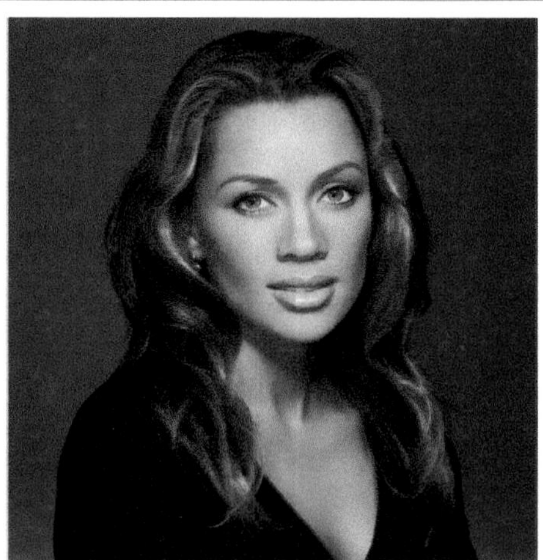

FIGURE 7.12 *Vanessa Williams. Print makeup and styling by Kate Best.*

Source: Photograph by Michael Zeppatello.

Concealer :	Laura Mercier #4 (higher value than #6).
Foundation:	Laura Mercier #6.
Powder:	LeClerc Banana on center of face. LeClerc Bronze around the outer areas. Il Makiage Banana in a half moon under each eye.
Eyeshadow:	Ben Nye Fireworks Cream Fantasy Wheel in Gold, Copper, Diamond Ice.
Eyeliner:	MAC Black Cream.
Blush:	MAC Cheek (warm orange/gold tone).
Contour:	Pinky-brown tone on the cheeks, temple, sides of nose.
Brows:	Maybelline Blonde Pencil.
Lip pencil:	MAC Spice.
Lipstick:	MAC Twig.
Mascara:	Maybelline Great Lash.

4. Use loose powder to set the foundation. Powders should be two to three shades lighter, preferably translucent. No-color powders work great; they can be blended with darker powders such as Ben Nye's Banana, Topaz or Chestnut, Fashion Fair's powders or BLK/OPL (Black Opal) True Color Finishing Powders, to set concealers/neutralizers. Laura Mercier Secret Brightening Powder # 2 also works quite well.

Technique B—Apply Foundation Only Where Needed

Apply foundation only in the areas where needed. For example if the forehead is smooth and even and does not need coverage, apply under the eyes and the rest of the face where necessary. Blend, then powder to set the application. The powder will help to even out the entire face and make it look smooth and flawless.

Concealers, Highlighters, and Neutralizers

Concealers and neutralizers for dark skin are used much the same way as for other skin tones: to cover imperfections such as scars, blemishes, discolorations, and under-eye circles (see Chapter 6 and Chapter 9, Concealers). For medium to very dark complexions, it is important to use concealers and neutralizers in the orange to orange-red family such as Ben Nye's Beard Covers, Fashion Fair's Copper Glo and Tawny Glo, MAC Orange or Red cream colors. These products work well to neutralize or eliminate dark spots on the face, especially for those suffering from hyperpigmentation (see Figure 7.13). Concealers are not always distinguished as a particular product, but are a function of any product that provides the appropriate coverage, enough to diminish the effects of unwanted discolorations.

Unlike concealers and neutralizers, highlighters are used to exaggerate and project bone structure and facial features. Use highlighters in the gold to orange, orange-red family of colors such as Black Opal's Golden Glow, MAC Cream Color base in

Gold or Bronze. Foundation colors one to two shades lighter than the primary foundation are also recommended for under the eye and for other areas of discoloration or uneven skin tone. Highlighting under the eye may not even be necessary since natural discolorations do not contrast as much against darker skin.

Contouring

The same theoretical approach and techniques discussed earlier in this chapter can be used when contouring light to medium skin tones. Contouring or shadowing with darker colors on dark to very dark skin, however, can be impractical and often unflattering. When the skin is very dark it is best to simply highlight the features and allow the color of the skin to act as its own contour. This works for the eyes, cheeks, nose, jawline, forehead, and temples.

For those occasions when your director (film, video, or theater) insists on more contouring, small amounts of black can be blended into the foundation color. While some makeup artists believe contouring very dark skin does not work under any circumstances, others will do what is necessary to successfully achieve the desired effect.

Powder

When the skin's natural oils mix with the foundation and the powder, the powder will darken by two to three shades; so it is better to use finely milled pigmented powders that are two to three shades lighter than the foundation. Use a loose powder to set foundation and pressed powder (close to skin color) for touch-ups. For a truly matte finish use a velour powder puff. For lighter coverage, apply powder with a large powder brush. To remove any powdery residue, use a clean, large powder brush to buff the face in a circular motion. Avoid powders containing too much talc or titanium dioxide because they may appear dusty or may leave a powdery residue on the surface of the skin which could look gray and ashy. Many manufacturers including Black Opal, Bobbi Brown, Ben Nye, Fashion Fair, MAC, Clinique, and Prescriptives provide pigmented powders to complement darker foundations. The availability of mineral powder foundations provides additional choices for makeup artists as well as actors of color. Also available are true no-color powders such as Ben Nye's Neutral Set, RCMA No-Color, and Makeup Forever's High-Definition Powder. All of these powders can be used on anyone. (Needs to be used sparingly.) In addition, pigmented powders in the yellow-orange color range can be used as highlights and accent colors on cheekbones, the forehead, under the eye, and on the nose and chin. These yellow-orange hues can be mixed with other powders in the orange-brown, yellow-brown, or red-brown color range to complement all skin tones.

Blush

The primary concern when choosing a blush or cheek color is to avoid those products that appear ashy (a dusty gray color) on the skin. This is a concern consistent with most cosmetic products for people of color. For application techniques, refer to Chapters 6 & 9. For added dimension, use cream blushes (no muted colors) or cheek tints to create a radiant look. When using cream products remember to apply after foundation and before powder; then enhance cream application with a light dusting of a powder blush. It is important to remember that darker skin tones do not "blush" as lighter skin tones do. Keep this in mind when creating a natural look.

Suggestions for choosing accent colors for specific skin tones and color palettes are: For cool skin palettes choose—blue-reds, deep reds, purple, fuscia, violet, raspberry, and magenta. For warm palettes choose—peach, apricot, salmon, orange-red, and reddish-brown.

Eyeshadow

To create long-lasting eyeshadow use an eyeshadow primer, such as Fashion Fair's Cover Stick, or apply the foundation over the eyes, blend thoroughly, then powder with Laura Mercier's Secret Brightening Powder # 2. This technique removes excess oil and provides a smooth, dry canvas for eyeshadows to adhere. Powdered eyeshadow provides a softer, more even consistency and will also help absorb the natural oils from the eyelids. Apply eyeshadow with a cotton swab applicator for a soft look, a sponge-tipped applicator to create a smooth and even texture, and with your fingers for heavier coverage. Choose deep, natural tones such as sable, coffee, and espresso, or vibrant jewel tones such as blue-green, purple, and wine, or shades of gray, navy blue, and muted green. Highlight the lid and below the brow with bone, matte yellow, pink, light coral, or beige in warm or cool tones. With dark skin often providing its own shadow, contouring the crease may not be necessary.

Lip Color

Lip color can be custom blended by mixing equal amounts of primary or true red with the foundation color. While this is not necessarily a rule it will guide you toward a family of colors appropriate for a given skin tone. This method, along with the correct undertone palette of colors, will assist you in making appropriate choices for any skin tone in a variety of performance venues.

The following suggestions are intended to assist you in developing techniques for proper lip color application:

1. *Uneven Lip Color:* If there is a certain amount of discoloration on the lips, it is found most often in the lower lip which tends to be pink toward the center. Even out the color by applying a base color with brown pencil over the entire lower lip. Set the pencil with a light dusting of translucent powder and blend off with a damp sponge. Then apply the lip color over both lips. This will produce a more accurate and long-lasting lip color. Using the same pencil technique for men, apply a lip conditioner over both lips, replacing the lip color and powder. You can also use Fashion Fair's Lip Balancer which balances and color-corrects this discoloration.
2. *Full Lips:* Full lips cannot be made smaller, but you can create the illusion of smaller size. To downplay the size of full lips, simply use soft, natural tones. Bright colors and colors of high value will only draw more attention. Remember, colors of high value and intensity project while low value, low intensity colors recede. Another method is to first line the lips just inside the natural lip line with a lip pencil in a color matching the skin tone before filling in with a soft, natural color.
3. *Skin tone and lip color:* As a general rule, the darker the skin tone, the darker the lip color. For performers working in large venues, however, choosing a color that assists in projecting the facial features far outweighs the need to follow the latest fashion trends. Contouring the lower lip with highlights of vanilla, gold, or bronze will help to add shape and dimension.

Adhesives

On very dark skin, some adhesives such as spirit gum tend to crystallize in extreme weather conditions. To remedy this, apply a small amount of foundation over the lace and crystallization with a small, stiff brush until it blends into the skin or simply remove the lace pieces during the earliest break, clean, and reapply.

Lighting

Working under intense bright lights is not usually a problem for actors of color. Unlike their lighter-skinned co-workers, bright lights do not "wash out" the skin tone and therefore require less makeup adjustments. Warm lighting colors are often more flattering to darker skin tones because they accentuate the yellow-red undertones already present in the skin. The challenge comes as the inescapable cool blue shades of evening light wash across the stage. Skin tones and facial features in the cool palette often become darker and bluer which reduces much of their definition. This problem is compounded when the wardrobe is also in the same cool palette. From a professional standpoint, it is your responsibility as a makeup artist to develop strong and meaningful collaborative relationships with the costume designer, lighting director, lighting designer, or director of photography, because they play an integral role in having your makeup appear as you intended it to be. Forming these professional relationships with your colleagues will also help develop your confidence and respect as an artist as well as open the door to proper communication with these departments. Remember, makeup is only flattered or enhanced by the quality of light that it is seen under, as well as the costume color reflecting onto the face.

1. Makeup demonstration for the character Carmen in the Broadway musical, The Life (Figure 7.13). Model/Performer—Jennifer Ekoki (Skin Primer used is Maybelline "Baby Skin").
2. Foundation palette colors. Graftobian HD Crème Super Palette.
3. Foundation color testing on the performer's natural skin. (from l–r):
   - Warm Umber blended with Hazelnut
   - Chestnut
   - Warm Umber
   - Warm Umber blended with Hazelnut plus a dot of Hidden Magic
   - Hazelnut.
4. Graftobian Foundation:
   - Center of face: Forehead/nose/chin—Chestnut
   - Upper lip/jawline/forehead sides—Warm Umber
   - Cheekbones/sides of nose—Warm Umber+Hazelnut+Hidden Magic.
5. Under-eye highlight—Joe Blasco: Dark Skin Highlight.
6. Blend with a foundation brush.
7. Apply Ben Nye Cream Liner—Yellow on the forehead/nose/sides of mouth/chin and Joe Blasco: Dark Skin Highlight (this has a slight peachy color) to the cheekbones and jawline.

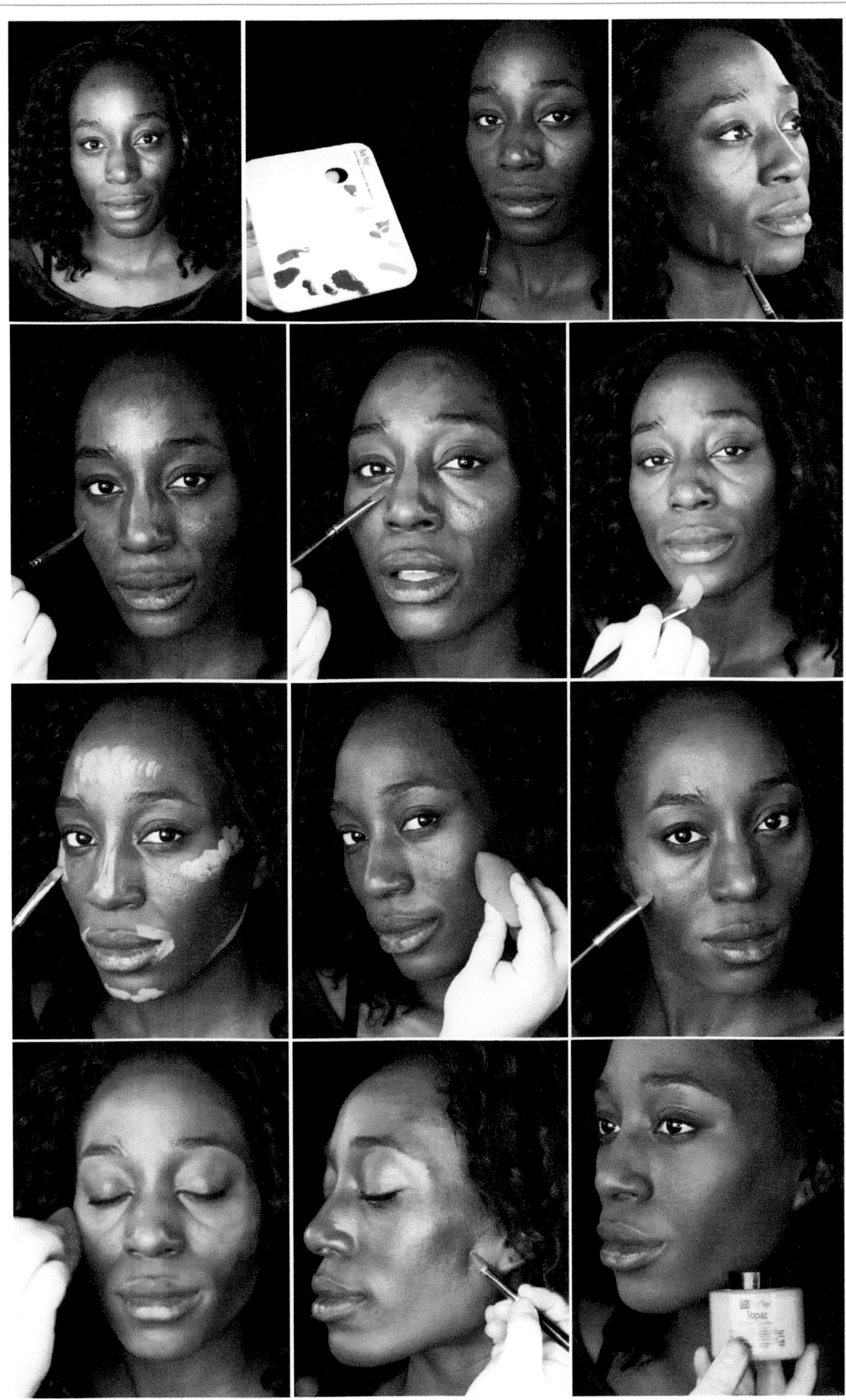

FIGURE 7.13 *Makeup application for the character Carmen in the Broadway production of the musical The Life. Costume design by Martin Pakledinaz. Original makeup design by Kathy Pomerantz. (This makeup application has been recreated specifically for this edition by Allison Lowery.)*

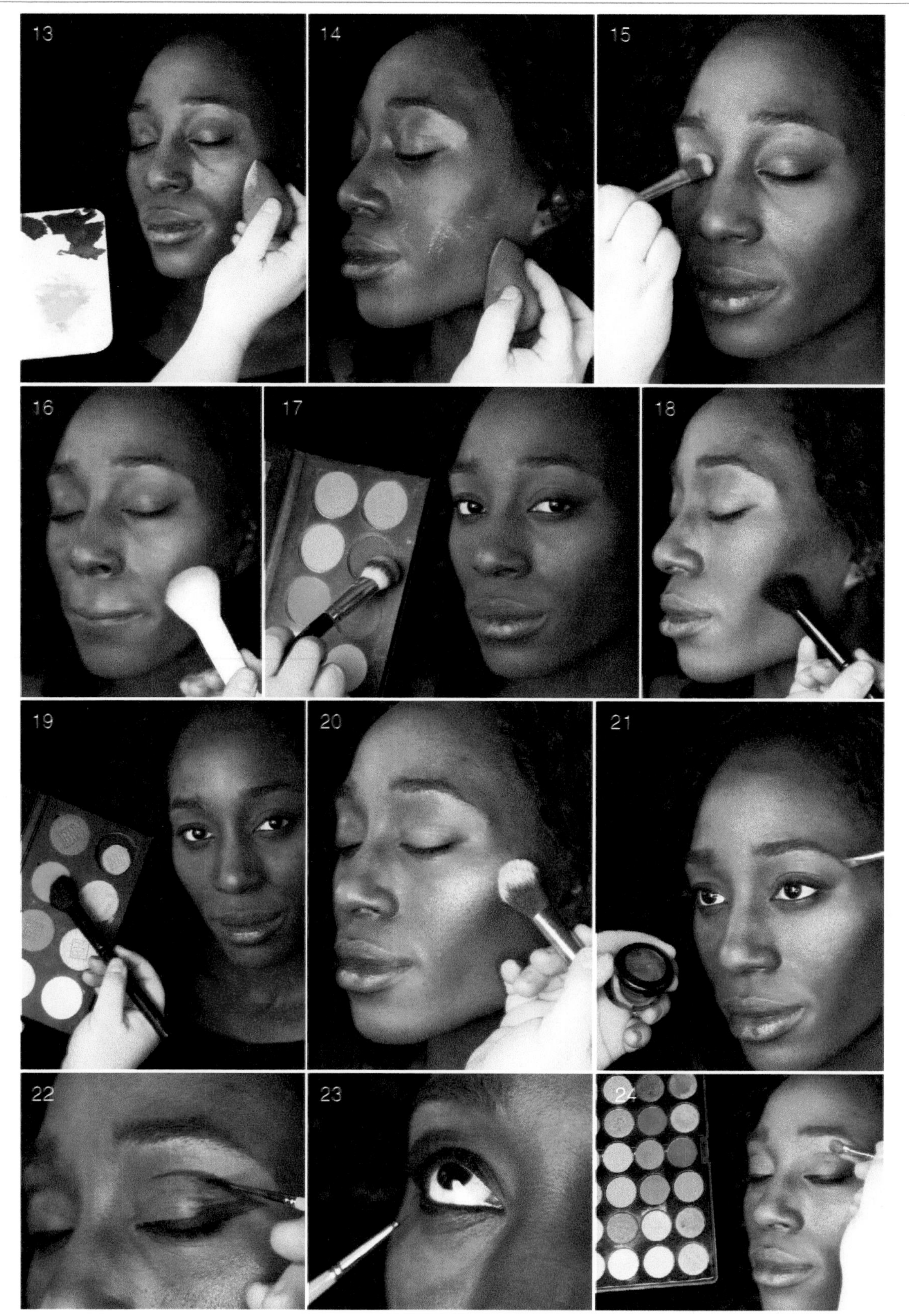

FIGURE 7.13 *(continued)*

FIGURE 7.13 *(continued)*

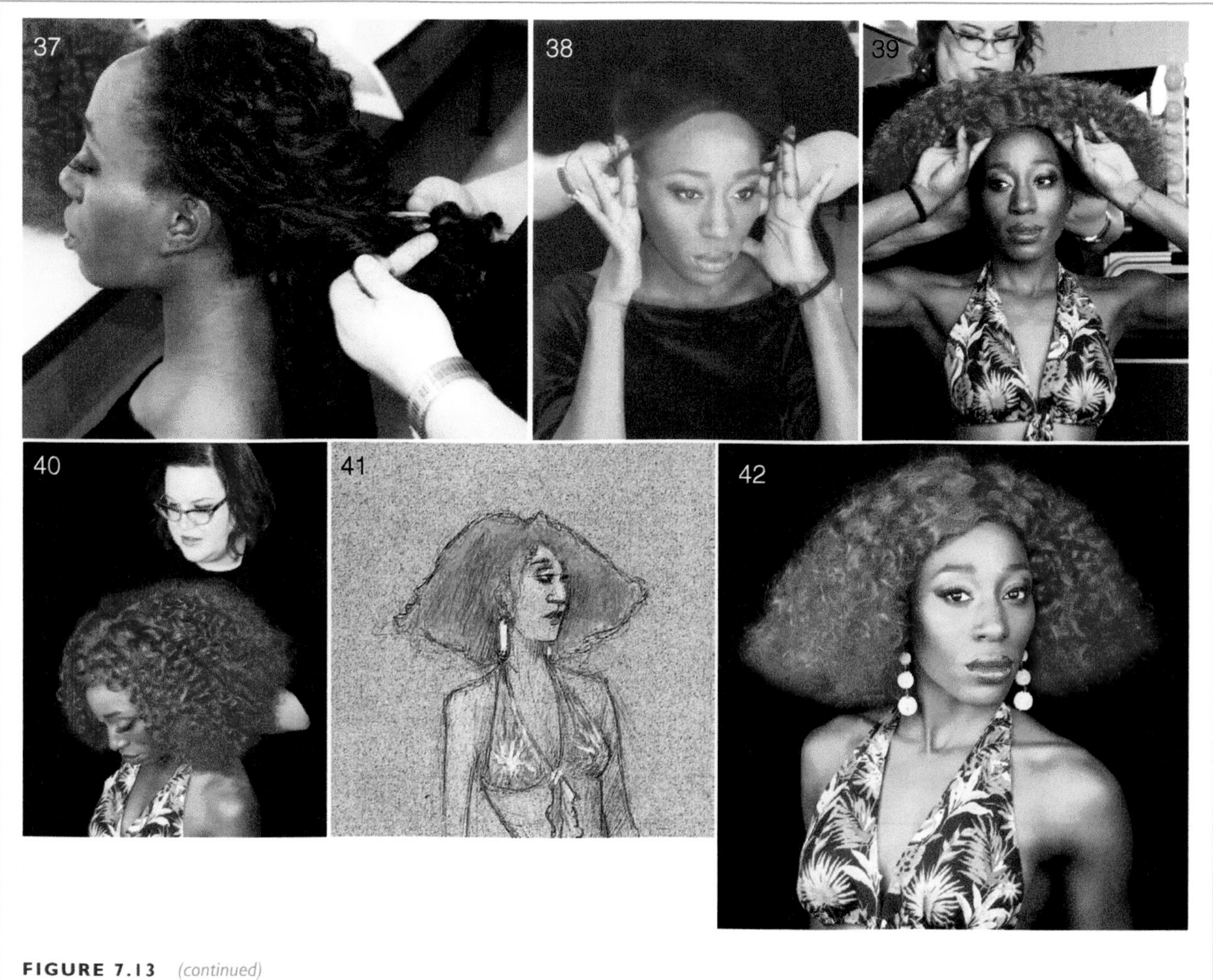

FIGURE 7.13 *(continued)*

8. Blend using a damp, shaped Beauty Blender-type makeup sponge. Use a tapping motion, rather than long strokes, to achieve a smooth, blended surface.
9. Apply cream cheek color using a small foundation brush. NYX Vivid Brights: Cyber Pop (color name).
10. Blend.
11. Apply cream contour color and blend. Graftobian HD Glamour Super Palette: Nightfall.
12. Setting powder by Ben Nye Luxury Powder: Topaz (powder color).

13. & 14. Apply setting powder with a Beauty Blender-type makeup sponge.

15. Apply Topaz setting powder to the eyelids using a large soft blender brush.
16. Remove excess powder using a large powder brush.
17. Contour powder: Ben Nye—Espresso.
18. Apply contour powder just below the cheekbone.
19. Cheek color (pressed: Ben Nye—Flamed Red).
20. Apply cheek color just above the contour. Then place this highlight on the cheekbone. The highlight is the Ben Nye Lumiere: Golden Apricot (color name) pressed powder. Apply cheek colors, contours, and highlight using an angled, flat, or domed blush brush.
21. Using a small, angled brow brush, shape the brow with MAC eyeshadow: Concrete. The pressed powder shadow is applied to the brow with a wet brush.
22. Eyeliner and the crease line are painted with Kryolan Aquacolor: Black.

23. Apply eyeliner along the lower lash line. Use Kryolan Aquacolor: Black.
24. Apply highlight on the brow bone under the brow with a small, domed shadow brush. Ben Nye Lumiere pressed shadow: Iced Gold. Blend.
25. Apply same Golden Apricot Lumiere color to the lids.
26. Choose the copper shimmer color from the Crown—Smoke It Out, Too Eyeshadow Palette. (The colors in this palette are not labeled.)
27. Apply this copper color to the crease and along the lower lash line using a very small crease brush.
28. Squeeze a small drop of Duo adhesive from the tube to the tip of a brush handle, then apply it to the lash strip. Allow the adhesive to get tacky on the lash before applying it to the lash line of the performer.
29. Carefully position the false lash on the lash line.
30. Secure the strip lash to the lash line by gently pressing it against the lid using a cotton-tipped applicator.

31. & 32. Incorporate the human lashes into the false lashes by applying mascara and eyeliner.

33. Close-up of the eye makeup.
34. Strengthen the eyeshadow at the corner of the lid using Crown Brush 35 Color Metal palette. Choose a dark brown color (the colors in this palette are not named).
35. Apply and blend the eyeshadow (Crown Brush 35 Color Metal palette) into the lower lash line with a small, domed shadow brush.
36. Apply lip color with a small domes lip brush. A mix of Color Pop: Clique (color name) and MAC: Diva.
37. Braid the hair to fit under the wig cap.
38. Applying the wig cap.
39. Applying the wig.
40. Makeup and wig artist, Allison Lowery, secures the wig.
41. Costume rendering, by Martin Pakledinaz, of the character, Carmen, for the Broadway musical "The Life."
42. Jennifer Ekoki as Carmen in "The Life" (this makeup was created for this publication).

CHAPTER 8

MODELING WITH HIGHLIGHTS AND SHADOWS

LIGHT AND SHADE

Although some three-dimensional changes can be made in creating makeup for the stage, more often than not we create the illusion of three-dimensional changes, using the principles of light and shade.

This is essentially what the painter does. But instead of a painter's flat, white canvas, the makeup artist—or the actor—begins with a three-dimensional face—a face that will reflect, as the actor moves his head onstage, a continually changing relationship between the face and the source of light.

In spite of these differences between the painter and the makeup artist, the principles of their art remain the same. Both observe in life what happens when light falls on an object. Both see the patterns of light and shade that reveal to the eye the real shape of an object. Then, with colored paints of varying degrees of lightness and darkness, of brightness and grayness, both recreate those patterns. Only in *trompe l'oeil* paintings is it the aim of the painter to imitate reality so closely that viewers are fooled into believing they are actually seeing the real thing rather than a painted representation of it (see Figure 8.1). But in creating a realistic makeup, the makeup artist *must* aim to convince the audience that they are seeing the real thing.

FIGURE 8.1 *Principles of trompe l'oeil drawing used to create the illusion of a three-dimensional head. Faber Castell Drawing Pencils. Artist: YuJung Shen.*

FIGURE 8.2 *Portrait illustrating the principles of chiaroscuro. Charcoal. Artist: YuJung Shen.*

FLAT AND CURVED SURFACES

Since the basis of actual makeup technique lies, then, in understanding and applying the principles of *chiaroscuro* (or *light and shade*) as demonstrated in Figure 8.2, that have been used by artists for centuries, our next step is to study these principles in theory, to observe them in life.

What, then, is *chiaroscuro*?

Perhaps the simplest way to approach it is to imagine the two forms in Figure 8.3 in total darkness. This would result, of course, in their appearing completely black. In other words, there is a total absence of light; and light, after all, provides the only means of our seeing these or any other objects. But if we turn on a light in the position of the arrow E, on the right, the light hits the objects and is reflected from them to our eyes, enabling us to see them. Observe, however, that the light does not illuminate the entire object in either case. Only those surfaces upon which the rays of light fall directly are fully visible because only they receive light rays to reflect to the eye. Surfaces that are situated away from the light source remain in darkness. That enables us to determine the direction in which the surface planes of an object lie and whether they are flat, curved, or irregular. In other words, it tells us the shape of the object.

HARD AND SOFT EDGES

In both of the forms in Figure 8.3, part of the form is lighted, and part remains in darkness. But the shift from the lighted plane to the shadowed plane is entirely different in the two. In one there is a gradual shift from light through semi-light (or gray) to dark. In the other the shift is sudden and sharp. Thus, we know that one object has a rounded surface and that the other has flat, angular surfaces. The sharp division between the two flat surfaces is known as a *hard edge*, and the gradual change between planes on the curved surface, though technically not an edge at all, is known as a *soft edge*. That is a principle basic to all character makeup.

Look, for example, at the two largest wrinkles in the face—the nasolabial folds, which extend from the nose to the lips. In a nasolabial fold, especially if it is well developed, as are the ones in Figure 8.25, there is a definite crease in the flesh—and in drawing or painting, the effect of a crease is created by means of a hard edge, with the darkest dark next to the lightest light. The puffy part of the fold is somewhat like a half cylinder, with a gradual transition from the dark at the crease to a soft-edged highlight along the most prominent part of the fold and fading away into a soft-edged shadow (Figure 8.24).

This effect occurs—and can be reproduced with makeup—in various areas of the face, neck, and hands. Forehead wrinkles, eye pouches, sagging jowls, prominent veins in the hands—the illusion of all of these can be created with highlights and shadows, provided one understands the principles of hard and soft edges and learns to apply those principles meticulously in doing character makeups.

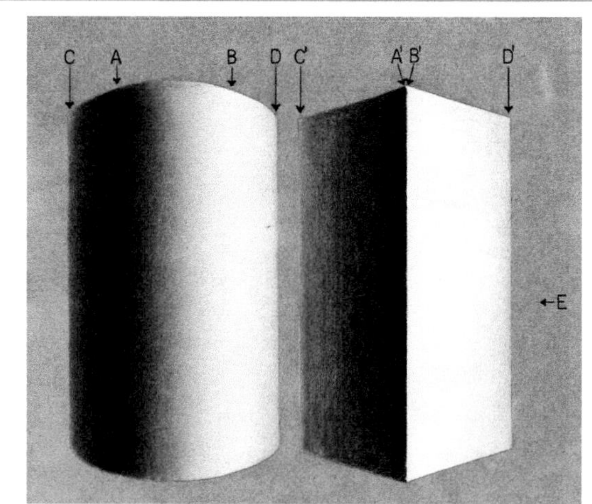

FIGURE 8.3 *Modeling curved and angular surfaces. Note the combination of hard and soft edges.*

DRAWING WITH HIGHLIGHTS AND SHADOWS

In order to make sure that you understand the principle and can apply it, draw some simple, three-dimensional objects, such as a cylinder and a box, with charcoal and chalk on gray charcoal paper. These will serve to demonstrate the principles of light and shade you will use in makeup.

Perhaps the simplest way to begin is to do a drawing similar to the one in Figure 8.3. Before beginning your drawing, pay particular attention to the areas indicated by the arrows. Arrow A designates the darkest area on the cylinder and B designates the lightest. You will observe that neither of these areas is precisely at the edge of the cylinder. The edge of the dark side (C) is slightly less dark than the darkest part, whereas the light edge (D) is not quite so light as the highlight (B). The reason for this is simply that on the dark side a small amount of reflected light is always seen at the extreme edge, and on the light side the surface of the edge is curving away from us so abruptly that it seems to be less brightly lighted. If you were to draw a cylinder with maximum light and dark areas at the extreme edges, the cylinder would seem to stop abruptly at the edges instead of continuing around to complete itself.

The source of light in the drawing in Figure 8.3 has been arbitrarily placed in the position of the arrow E. Thus, the right side of the cylinder is in direct light, resulting in a strong highlight and a gradual diminution of light from this highlight to the darkest part of the lowlight, or shadow, on the opposite side of the cylinder. No matter from which direction the light is coming, it will create a highlight on the part of the object on which it falls and leave a lowlight on the opposite side—a natural phenomenon that must be carefully observed in doing makeup.

In drawing such an object, there is an additional principle—that of aerial perspective—to be taken into consideration. According to that principle, first observed—or at least first applied—by the painter Uccello in the fourteenth century, the centralization of value (the relative brightness or darkness of a color) and of intensity (the relative brilliance or dullness of a color) is inversely proportional to the nearness of the color to the eye. In relation to *chiaroscuro*, this means simply that, with distance, both black and white become more gray—in other words, less strongly differentiated. You have undoubtedly observed this effect in distant mountains or tall buildings or even in cars or houses at a considerable distance. This is known as *atmospheric perspective*. Thus, the near edge of the rectangle is made to appear closer by increasing the intensity, no matter what the value may be. The far edges are made to recede by means of a decrease in intensity and a centralization of value. In makeup, this principle can be applied in highlighting the chin, for example, or the superciliary bone of the forehead in order to make them seem more prominent—in other words, closer to the viewer. Conversely, either one could be made to seem less prominent—farther from the viewer—by decreasing the strength of the highlight or perhaps even using a lowlight instead.

The term *lowlight* is sometimes used to refer to shadows used in makeup and to differentiate them from *cast* shadows. When non-directional light falls upon an object, it not only leaves part of the object itself in shadow, but it also casts a shadow of the object on any area around it from which the light is cut off. In other words, when an object intercepts the light, it casts a shadow. This shadow is known as a *cast* shadow. A cast shadow always has a hard edge, it follows the shape of an object upon which it falls, and it is darkest at the outer edge. Cast shadows are not normally used in makeup because of the continual movement of the actor and the resultant directional changes in light. Probably the only makeup for which they might be used would be one in which both actor and light source were immobile, as in a tableau or for a photograph.

In doing your own drawings, you might begin with the flat-sided box. Start with your lightest light at what is to be the hard edge, and blend it gradually out toward the outer edge, allowing it to become slightly less light as you go. This can be done by applying the chalk directly along the vertical line, as carefully as you can, then blending with the fingers or with a paper stump to achieve smooth transitions. The precise technique you use is of little importance as long as you achieve the results you want. When the light side is completed, do the dark side in the same way, starting with a heavy application of charcoal at the hard edge next to the white.

In the cylinder there is a gradual transition from light to dark. Both the light and the dark can be applied in either horizontal or vertical strokes, then blended, leaving the gray paper to serve as the middle tone between the light and the dark.

Figure 8.4 illustrates the principle of modeling a third basic shape—the sphere—and the application of that principle to makeup. Notice how the same principle is used in painting the

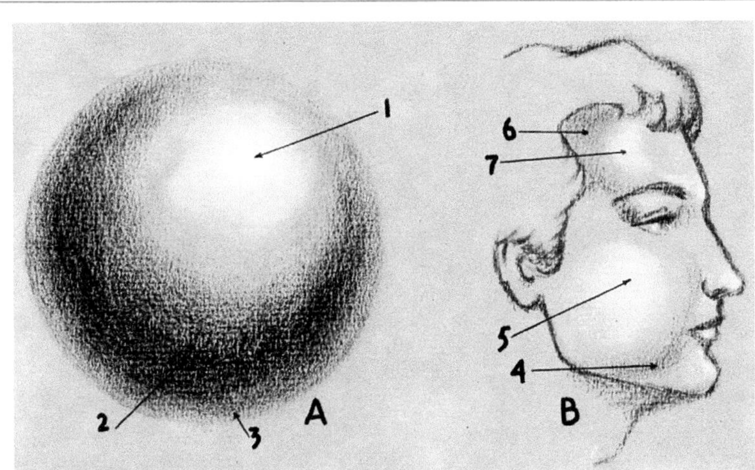

FIGURE 8.4 *Drawing a sphere with highlights and shadows. Relating the drawing of a sphere to the roundness of the human cheek.*

apple cheeks. In the sphere, all shadows and highlights fall in a circular pattern.

Remember that whenever a single light falls on a three-dimensional object, those parts of the object not in the direct line of light will remain in shadow. Whenever there is a lowlight, or shadow, there is a corresponding highlight. When the surface changes direction abruptly, the shadow and the highlight are immediately adjacent. But when the surface changes direction gradually, shadow and highlight are separated by a gradation of intermediate shades.

MODELING THE FACE WITH HIGHLIGHTS AND SHADOWS

You have already studied the general structure of the face. The next step is to learn to modify the appearance of this structure through the use of highlights and shadows. Although the illusion created may involve making cheeks rounder, chins more pointed, or noses crooked, more often than not, it will include some aging.

In youth, firm muscles and elastic skin fill out the hollows and smooth over the bumps in the bony structure of the skull. But with age and the accompanying sagging of muscles and loss of elasticity of the skin, this bony structure becomes increasingly evident. Therefore, the first thing to do in learning to age the face is to visualize the bones of the skull and to locate them by prodding with the fingers.

The solution to most challenges concerning realistic modeling in makeup can be found simply by asking three questions:

1. What is the exact shape of the structure (a cheekbone, for example, or a wrinkle) that is to be represented?
2. Where is the light coming from? (On the stage it will normally be from above rather than from below.)
3. What happens, in terms of light and shadow, when a light from that direction falls on a structure of that shape?

The answers to these questions will make it clear where the structure (wrinkle or cheekbone) would be light and where an absence of light would make it appear dark. These light and dark areas can then be painted onto the face, creating for the observer the illusion of prominent bones and wrinkles where they do not actually exist.

For a natural age/character makeup all highlights and shadows should look natural. Remember, the actor with age/character makeup will be interacting on stage with those actors who may be wearing a more age-appropriate makeup, a corrective makeup, or possibly no makeup at all. The amount of makeup used to create this type of makeup should then remain as minimal as possible. If the design is highly stylized (i.e. The Addams Family [musical]) then all of the makeups in the production including the age/character will be stylized to maintain a design continuity throughout the production.

In order to make sure that the final makeup will fit the actor's face, you should always be aware of how every highlight and every shadow relates to the structure of the face, including bone, cartilage, muscle, fatty tissue, and skin. To demonstrate this, the following makeup application for the character Scrooge in the Alley Theatre's production of *A Christmas Carol* uses highlights and shadows to bring out the bone structure and to create the effect of sagging muscles and skin.

Begin by lightly applying a cream foundation color that matches the model's skin tone. Then, using a pale cream or ivory color, highlight areas of the face as they might look in middle or old age, with bones becoming more prominent and flesh sagging. (See Figure 8.38, which can be used as a guide but should be adapted to your own face rather than copied exactly.) For this exercise make the highlights *very strong,* but soften the edges except when creating the effect of creases. Subtle modeling effects can be introduced after you have a thorough understanding of the basic concepts and have practiced the techniques. The following information provides a series of steps for laying in a foundation of highlights and shadows.

Apply highlights to the areas of the face indicated with an H and shadows with an S (Figure 8.5). These include:

H1—The frontal bone of the forehead. The frontal area spans the width of the brow and is defined left to right by the temporal bone.

H2—The prominent brow bone or supercilliary arch (brow ridge) above the inner eye. If you look at your forehead in profile, you may find a horizontal break or a change in direction of the planes about halfway up. If you do, this break will represent the top limit of the highlight area.

H3—The zygomatic process above the outer corner of the brow nearly always catches the light, highlight it, softening the edges. Do not highlight the glabella (the indentation between the eyebrows). You may also wish to highlight the lid itself, though if you were creating a very deep-set eye, it would be shadowed instead.

H4—Along the ridge of the nose, highlight the bone and the cartilage that form the top or front of the nose since these invariably catch the light strongly. Keep the highlight off the sides.

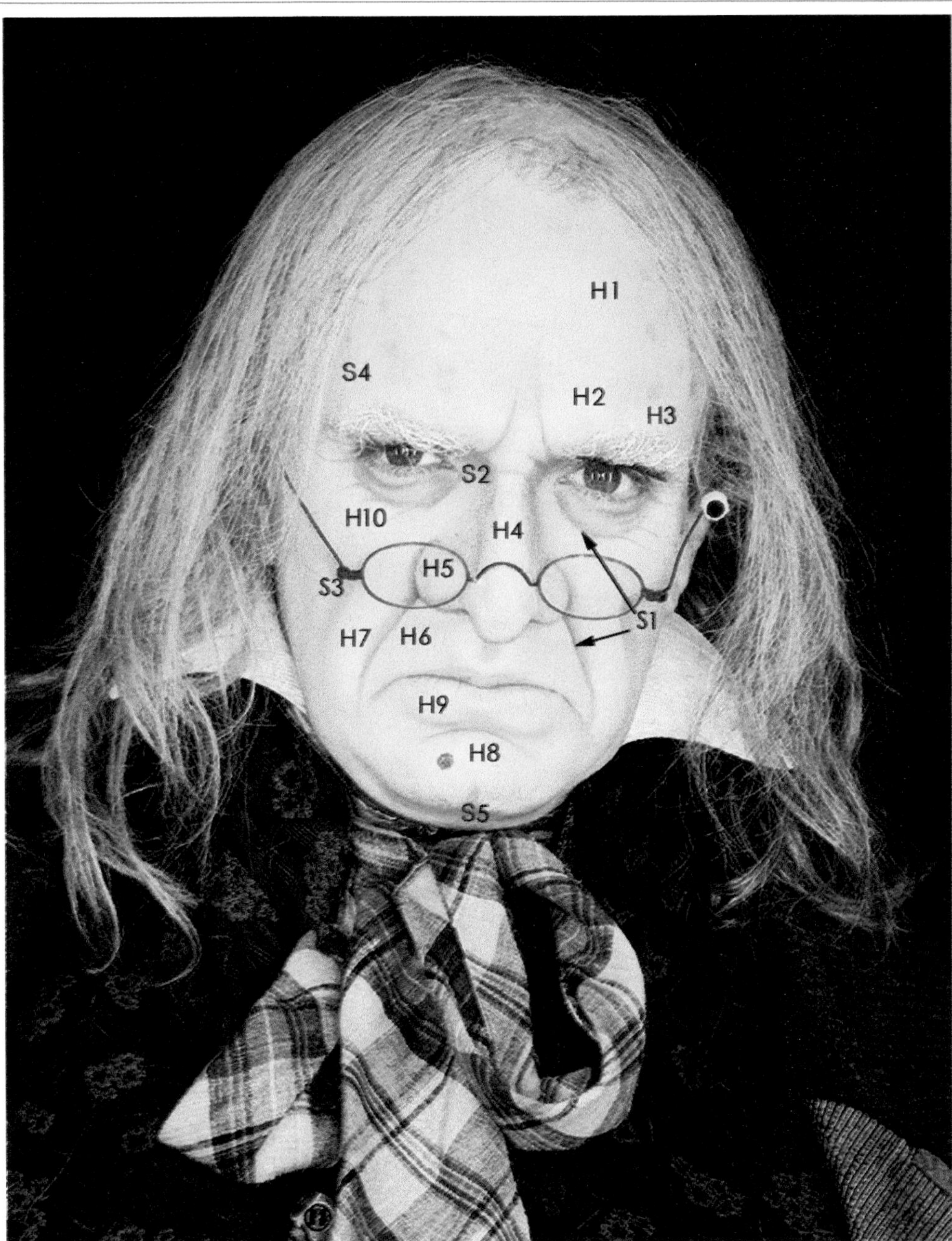

FIGURE 8.5 *Actor James Black as Scrooge in A Christmas Carol, A Ghost Story of Christmas, the Alley Theatre's production. (This exercise is designed to begin the modeling process by highlighting the prominent areas of the face. It is equally as valid an exercise to begin with the shadows.)*

H5—Add a soft highlight on the top of the nares.

H6—The upper lip, all the way from the nose to the mouth, catches light, especially at the crease of the nasolabial fold. With a wide or an extra-wide brush, start your highlight at the nose, making a very sharp, clean edge along the crease, then fade it out as it moves toward the center of the lip.

H7—This is the top of the nasolabial fold. It may not always be this pronounced, but the area is nearly always prominent in age. It catches a strong highlight with soft edges. Be sure not to carry the highlight all the way to the crease. To the outside of the crease is an area (S1) that folds under and away from the light and therefore should not be highlighted.

H8—Highlight the chin (not too strongly since it picks up a significant amount of light by virtue of its position on the face) with a wide or a medium-wide brush. Be sure to keep the highlight below the break between the lip and the chin, making it strongest right at the break where there will be a fairly hard edge in the very center. This edge softens as it moves away to the right and to the left.

H9—Now you can begin to use sagging muscles and flesh along with the bone structure in placing your highlights. The flesh at the corners of the mouth may puff out or sag with age, catching the light. Shadows are placed at the ends of the mouth in a downward slope to help create this downward sagging of the skin. Highlight this area (H9) with a medium or a wide brush.

H10—Using a wide brush, add a highlight along the *top* of the cheekbone and along the arching curves of the zygomatic (malar) bone that creates the eye socket and cheekbone, draw a semi-circle following this bone, starting at the inner eye and working outward. Soften both edges of the highlight.

S1—If you want a pouch under the eye, continue the cheekbone highlight to the pouch, letting it stop with a hard edge along the lower boundary of the pouch and making it strongest at the very edge of the pouch. Adding an eye bag or a hollow-eye look, place a shadow above the highlight that forms the arch following the orbital bone. Beginning under the tear duct, extend the curved line to the outer eye where it will dissipate. The darkest part of the line will be the place at the deepest part of the curve. With a clean brush, blend the shadow upward, but only slightly. Clean the brush frequently when softening edges of a shadow line. A hard edge will be formed where the highlight and shadow meet.

Using the same color and a medium-narrow flat brush (¼ inch to ½ inch), merely suggest a shadow beginning at the root of the nasolabial fold just above S1. The edge of the shadow along the crease should be hard; the edge toward the cheek should be soft.

S2—The aging process will often cause the eyes to recess into the orbital socket. Apply the shadow under the brow ridge, blending it onto the sides of the nose. This shadow continues up underneath the inside edge of the brow bone and fades into the crease of the eye. It may also continue down onto either side of the nose, blending and fading as it nears the tip. The soft edges of this shadow should not be blended onto the front plane of the face or onto the ridge of the nose (H4). Unless the eyes are to appear sunken in, avoid the eyelid. Frown lines and nose wrinkles can be created at this time. These crease lines naturally originate from the shadow and terminate to a finely tapered point.

S3—This shadow will contribute to the sagging skin of the aged face by creating a hollow located under the cheekbone. The shadow helps this area recede while creating a visual prominence to the cheekbone above it and the soft fleshy column of skin alongside the nasolabial fold.

S4—The hollow behind the temporal bone and along the side plane of the forehead area often becomes more pronounced with age. Highlight the bone where the forehead and side plane meet. Then add a soft shadow to the depression or temple area. The shadow will be slightly darker next to the highlight and will fade completely as you blend it toward the hairline.

S5—In this image, the actor added a narrow shadow directly under the chin to define and shorten his face to appear slightly rounder. The shadow is applied nearly straight across the chin to help separate the chin from the neck. A strong highlight is placed below the shadow to accentuate or create the appearance of a double chin.

Adding highlights and shadows to contour the face should be done with care. The face should not look unnaturally light or dark, but should stay within the natural tones of the performer's skin color. If you have been using cream makeup, it should now be powdered. Press translucent powder into the makeup, and remove the excess with a powder brush. (Be sure to choose a translucent powder that does not darken the highlights too much.)

Now, observe yourself in a spotlight at some distance from the mirror. If you have done your highlighting skillfully, your skull structure should be more apparent, and your flesh, in some areas, should have begun to seem more puffy and perhaps to sag.

Modeling Hard and Soft Edges

Choose a medium flesh tone for the cream foundation, a medium dark color for the shadows, and a very light color for the highlights. Use a wide or an extra-wide flat brush. With a metal or plastic makeup spatula, take up a small amount of makeup and transfer it to a makeup palette. This enables you to control the amount of paint on your brush much more effectively than when you work directly from the container of makeup. This is also a more hygienic practice. If you are using paint from a palette box (see Appendix A), you can use the inside cover of the box as your palette for mixing colors.

The following procedures for modeling hard and soft edges concentrate on the nasolabial fold (smile lines) and the eye bags. The wrinkles running from either side of the nose downward to the mouth are the *nasolabial folds*. These folds vary considerably in form and development. Each one has one hard edge and one soft edge. Wherever there is a crease in the flesh, as there is in the nasolabial fold, a hard edge is automatically formed. This technique is presented by makeup artist and teacher Richard Corson, the original author of *Stage Makeup* (Figure 8.6).

1. After the foundation is applied (do not powder a cream foundation until later in the process), the nasolabial fold and eye bag are defined with highlight as shown in Figure 8.6. Use a flat ⅜-inch brush to apply a high value such as Mehron's Celebré Pro-HD Cream Foundations in Light 1, 2, 3, 4, Ben Nye's Ultralite and Natural Lite, Joe Blasco's TV White, or Kryolan's TV White. The highlight should be strongest at the edge of the crease. With a clean brush, the highlight is blended away from the crease line. This creates a hard edge and a soft edge.
2. A fleshy rose color is applied above the highlight on the nasolabial fold using a flat ¼-inch brush. Blend away from the crease line with a clean brush. Use a cream accent color such as Ben Nye Auguste, Mehron Pink Coral, or MAC Shell.
3. Using a sharp red pencil, apply a line defining the nasolobial fold. This color should be used sparingly. The line should start at the top of the fold near the nare and end at approximately two-thirds of the length of the crease. This color should not be placed on the highlight, but next to it. (Note: If this hue of red is too intense for some skin tones, try a deep, warm coral color.)
4. Blend the red pencil line with a clean ¼-inch brush in a direction away from the crease and toward the cheek. Clean the brush regularly to avoid spreading the color too far. It should remain within the narrow column of the shadow side of the nasolabial fold.
5. Define the fold by drawing a thin line with a sharpened dark brown pencil. Press the pencil lightly onto the crease line. (Note: This color may be too intense for some skin tones. A higher value of brown/brown-gray may be used. Remember a darker color will create a deeper shadow.)
6. Soften the upper edge of the brown shadow line.
7. Blend the edge of the shadow using a small, clean, flat brush.
8. Define the lower edge of the eye bag using the same sharpened red pencil. Blend the upper edge of the red with a clean brush.
9. Deepen the bottom of the eye pouch shadow with a dark brown pencil. Blend the edge toward the lower lid with a clean brush.
10. After adding a small highlight above the eye bag to complete the three-dimensional shaping, outline the eye with red to age and weaken it.
11. Model the jaw area by first pulling your chin in and back. Turning slightly to the left, then to the right, stipple the tops of the wrinkles with the highlight color.
12. Keeping the same position, deepen the creases with a shadow color using a ¼-inch brush. Blend the line up toward the face as before.
13. Stipple the neck wrinkles using a stipple sponge with a dark shadow color to create texture.
14. Add rouge to the apple of the cheek with a ⅜-inch brush. In an effort to find the apple of the cheek, simply smile. Apply a red or natural rose blush to the under side of the cheek and blend.
15. Add a shadow to the under side of the apple of the cheek. Allow some of the rouge to show above the darker shadow. Blend the shadow with a clean brush.
16. Clean up the hard edge of the highlight at the nasolabial fold. Here, Corson is using a white pencil, but any natural highlight, pencil, or cream can be used. (Note: the entire upper lip is not necessarily part of this highlight, only the edge of the crease needs to be highlighted.)
17. Close-up of the modeled apple cheek and eye area. (Note: Liver spots on forehead and temple area.)
18. Completed age/character makeup.

STIPPLING

Stippling is a technique used to add texture to the surface of the face. As a person ages there are more textures that appear in the skin. Along with wrinkles, discolorations, age spots, broken capillaries, and creping can appear. Stippling is often applied with a textured stipple sponge, the point of a fine brush, the flick of

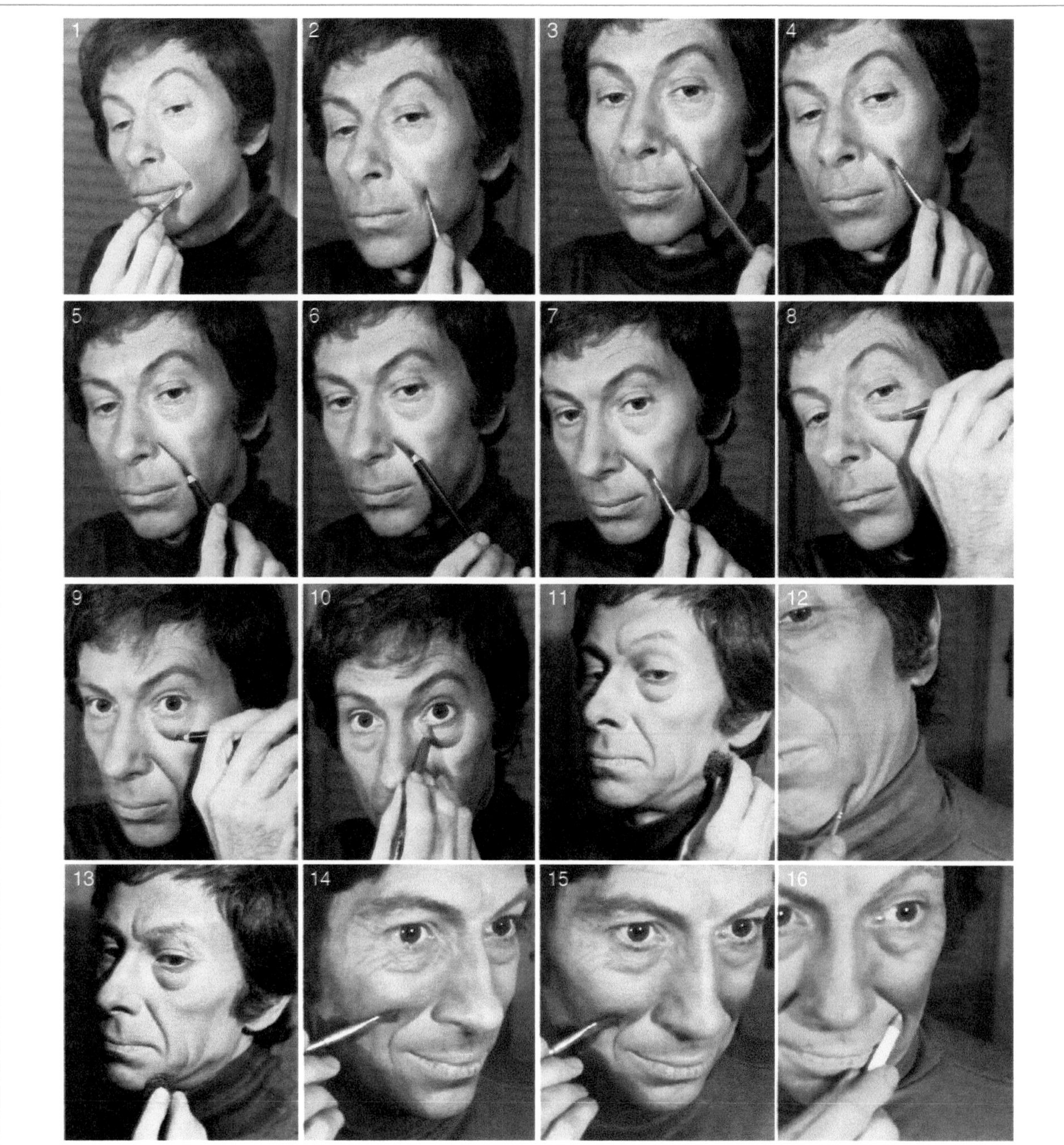

FIGURE 8.6 *Modeling soft and hard edges to create a character age makeup. Makeup artist and model, Richard Corson.*

the bristles of a toothbrush, or with an airbrush. Colors darker than the highlight and lighter than the deep shadow are usually the best choices for stippling. Use your base color, if you like, or for a pinker effect either use a pinker color or add a stipple of red to simulate broken capillaries. This is a good opportunity to experiment with different colors of stipple. In any case, stipple gently, barely touching the sponge to the face, so as to give added texture to the skin. Keep examining the results in the mirror as you go, and observe that, as you tone down the highlights, the makeup begins to lose its three-dimensional quality. It is important, therefore, to avoid over-stippling. (For more detailed instructions in stippling, see Chapters 10 and 11.)

FIGURE 8.6 *(continued)*

AGING THE YOUNG FACE (FIGURE 8.9)

Aging the youthful face takes great care, precise application of highlights and shadows, and of course well-placed lighting. Advanced aging techniques on the young face can best be accomplished with the application of prosthetic makeup (see Chapter 11 Prosthetic Makeup, Dustin Hoffman in *Little Big Man*, Figure 11.21). However, some amount of aging can be accomplished by two-dimensional painting techniques. The following makeup application demonstrates how highlights and shadows can effectively and subtly add several decades of age to the young performer, especially when age-appropriate casting is not available (see Figure 8.7). The actor must also be a committed participant in the aging process by studying the physicality, vocal production, and idiosyncratic movements of the aged character.

1. Products as shown in Figure 8.9: Kryolan Supracolor Ultra Foundation Palette and Kryolan ColorVision Palette (Stage). RCMA Setting Powder, a variety of brushes; white applicator sponges, waxed paper mixing palette, metal spatula.
2. The foundation Alabaster was applied with a small white sponge. Alabaster is the fourth foundation color sample located on the model's cheek (from the left).
3. The first of many age lines are applied using Kryolan 046 (warm brown). The nasolabial fold lines are applied with a ⅛-inch flat brush.
4. All age lines and shadows are applied with the same ⅛-inch brush. Shadows are placed at the temples, under the cheekbone, at the inner corner of the eyes, along the sides of the nose and in the crease of the nostrils.
5. Age lines are blended using a clean ¼-inch flat, domed brush. The nasolabial fold lines are brushed up toward the cheek. This creates a hard lower edge and a soft upper edge.
6. All of the age lines are blended. Notice how the edges are blended and where the hard and soft edges are located.
7. Using Kryolan "TV White" and a ¼-inch flat brush, apply highlights on the length of the nose (but not in a continuous line), along the nasolabial folds, at the corners of the mouth, the top of the chin, along the forehead bone above the temple shadow, under the eyes, next to the crow's feet, at the fleshy part of the eyelid below the brow, and on the bony protuberance above the inner corner of the brow.
8. Blend the highlights. Use a small flat brush and a white sponge. The left half of the face has been blended.
9. A heavy eyelid is created by first drawing a curved crease line (as shown). Blend the upper edge of this shadow. Add a highlight to the fleshy part of the lid and blend toward the shadow.
10. Apply Kryolan "075" (a warm rusty/brick color) in the shadow/contour areas, as shown (apply at the top of the nasolabial fold, under the lower lip, above the temple shadow, above the cheekbone, a light brush stroke above the brow wrinkles, a light touch below the outer corner of the brow).
11. Blend this warm rust-cream color with a prepared white triangular sponge. To prepare this sponge, simply pinch off small pieces from around the edges. This will help to eliminate the hard lines on the makeup often caused by the sharp edges of the sponge.
12. Make a textured sponge to lightly stipple texture onto the cheeks, nose, forehead, and temples. Use Kryolan "101" (blackish-brown).
13. Using a clean texture sponge, lightly stipple the cheeks, nostrils, and forehead with Kryolan "Lake" (burgundy wine color) to create texture, discoloration, and broken capillaries.
14. Add the look of graying eyebrows by lightly painting them with TV White.
15. Gray a few lashes by painting them with TV White.
16. Lightly powder the face with a "no-color" setting powder and a small soft powder brush.
17. Add a few age spots using a small, round pointed brush using Kryolan 043/101. Final age makeup.

FIGURE 8.7 *Aging a young face. A. Opera student Tracey Staver. B. Tracey Staver as Judge Turpin in the musical, Sweeney Todd, at the Cincinnati Conservatory of Music. This age makeup includes the reshaping of the eyebrows, shadowing the inner corner of the eye socket, adding a highlight to the brow bone under the enhanced brows, creating eye bags and a few wrinkles. The nares are highlighted and a shadow placed in the crease is extended creating the nasolabial folds. The nostrils are enlarged, the cheeks are shaded to simulate a longer more narrow face, the lower lip is reshaped with a highlight along the lower lip edge and a dark shadow below, and the jawline is shadowed to create jowls. Notice the two curved forehead wrinkles that assist in the appearance of a raise brow. Mustache and beard (mixture of human and yak) applied over clean skin for secure adhesion. Makeup by Lenna Kaleva.*

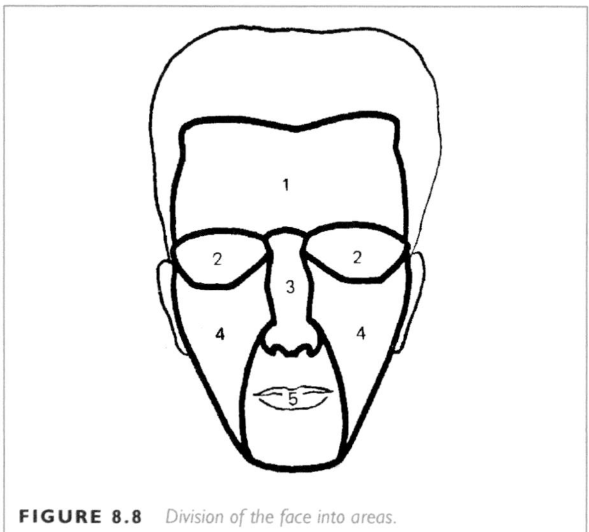

FIGURE 8.8 *Division of the face into areas.*

Now that you have experimented with highlights and shadows in restructuring the face as a whole and considered the problem of choosing colors for specific characters, the face will be divided into areas so that you can examine in detail the modeling of these areas. The five area divisions—forehead, eyes, nose, cheekbones and jawlines—are diagrammed in Figure 8.9. Each area will then be subdivided into planes for more detailed analysis. The discussion of each area will indicate the various possible treatments of that area.

FOREHEAD

The forehead is divided into five planes, as shown in Figure 8.10. Planes A and C are the frontal and the superciliary bones; D, the temporal hollows; and B, the slight depression between the two prominences.

A simple method of aging the forehead is to highlight and shadow these planes. The two prominences, A and C, catch the light and should, therefore, be highlighted. The depression, B, falling between them, may be slightly shadowed. Be careful, however, in doing a realistic makeup, not to emphasize the transverse shadow too strongly.

The highlighting can be done with a brush, a sponge, or the fingers. Figure 8.11 illustrates the technique that can be used with a brush. A wide or an extra-wide brush should be used. If you have only narrow brushes, then use your fingers for cream makeup or a sponge for cake.

For a prominent overhanging brow, carry a strong highlight all across the front plane of the superciliary arch, rather than just over the eyebrows, and shadow deeply across the bridge of the nose to sink it in.

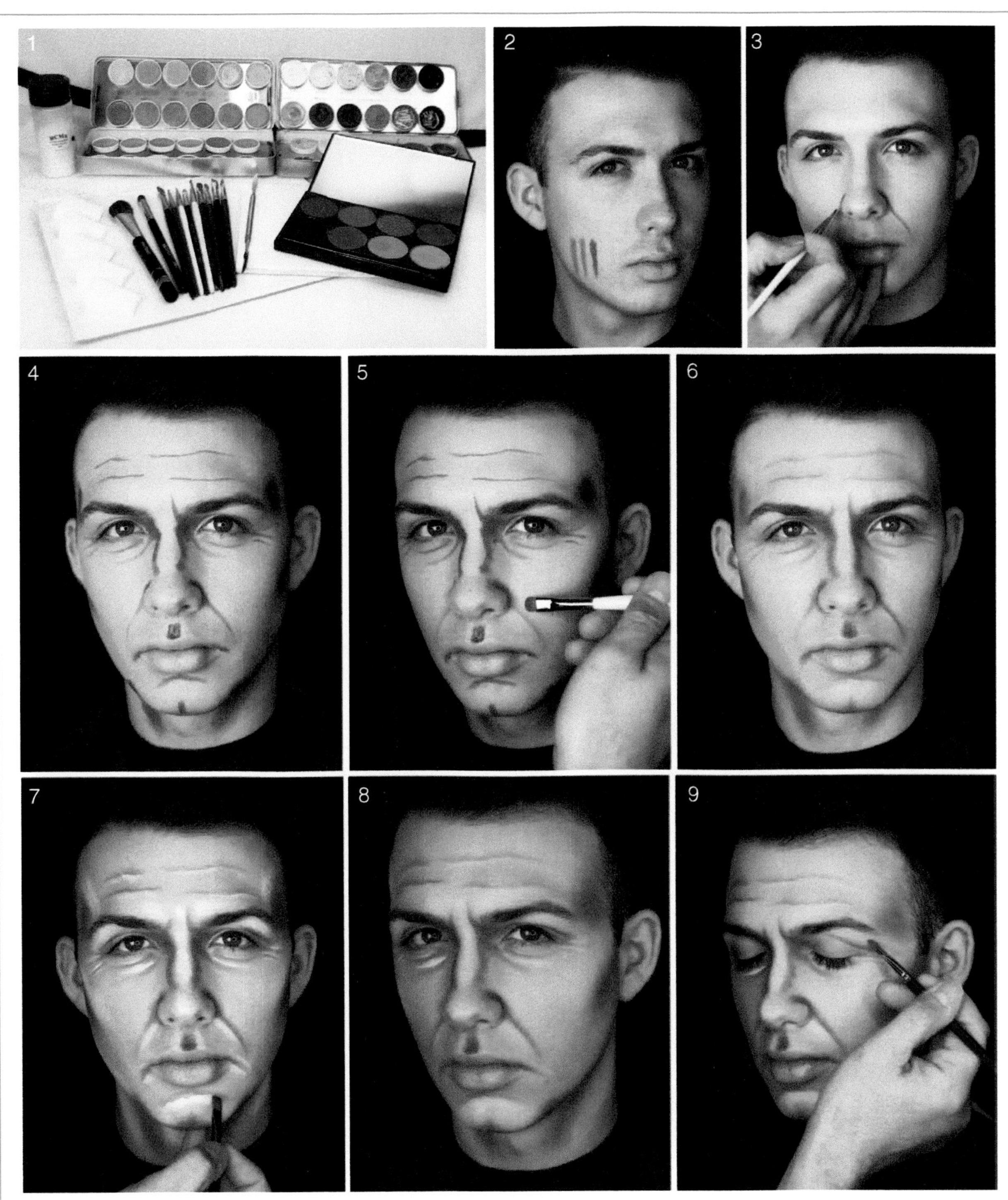

FIGURE 8.9 *Aging a young face. Makeup artist, Michael Meyer. Model, Tyler Hollin. (This makeup is being applied onto the basic male youth makeup application located in Chapter 7.)*

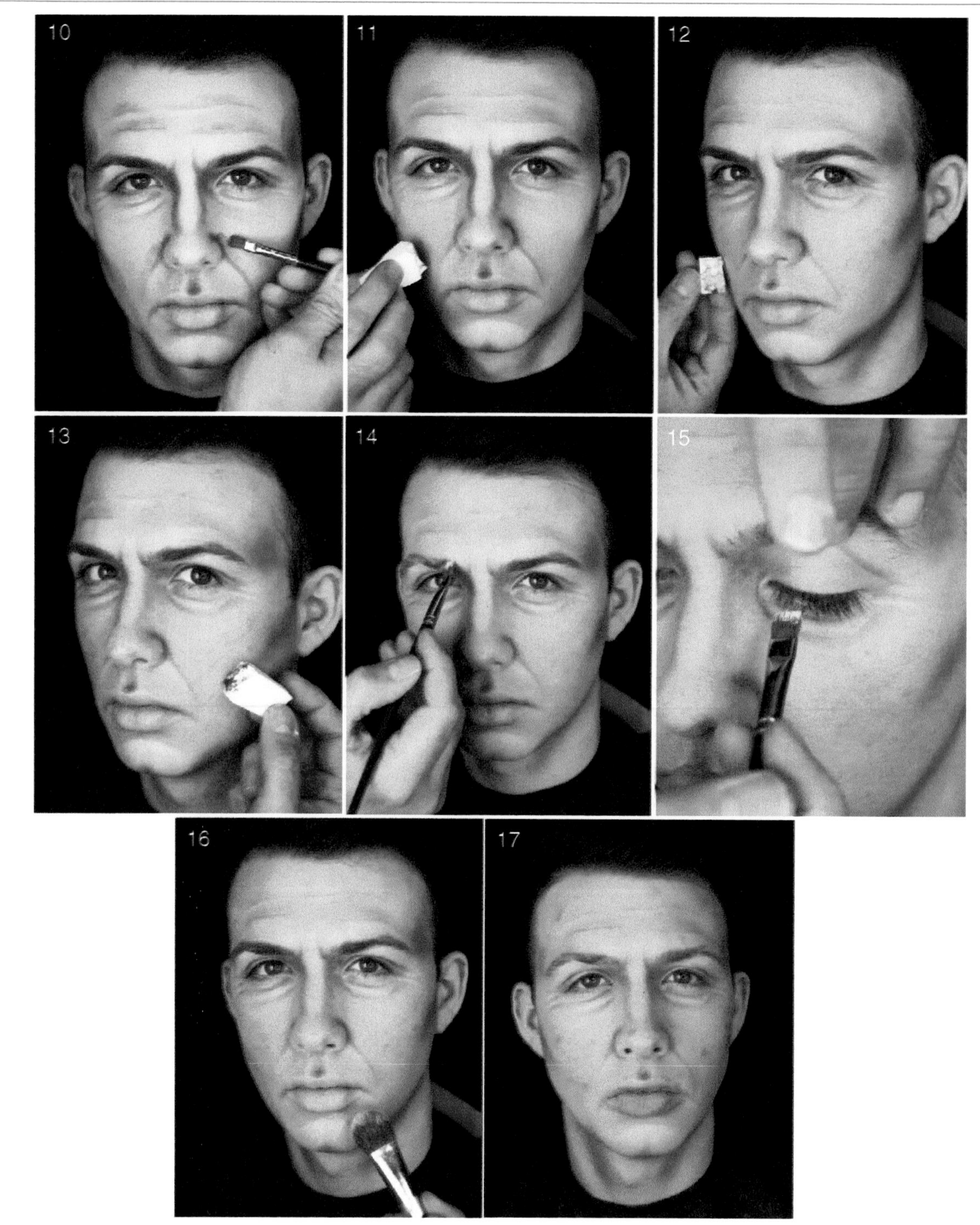

FIGURE 8.9 *(continued)*

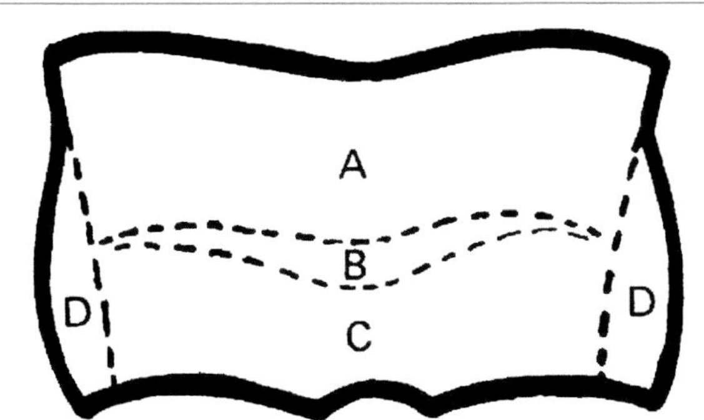

FIGURE 8.10 *Forehead. A and C indicate prominences that are normally highlighted for age; B, a slight depression that may or may not be lightly shadowed; and D, a depression that is usually shadowed for age.*

The temples are nearly always shadowed for age. These shadows may be barely perceptible in middle age but are usually quite pronounced in later years. The shadows tend to be more intense at the inner edge and to lighten as they approach the hair.

In placing the highlights, keep in mind the light source on the stage. With light coming from above, a strong light will fall on the upper part of the frontal bone. If there is a horizontal division approximately in the middle of your forehead (most clearly observable in profile), the area coming forward below this division will catch another strong highlight, and the area immediately above the division will be less strongly lighted. This is the area where you may or may not wish to use a very slight shadow. When there are no wrinkles to crease the skin, all edges of highlights and shadows will be soft. If you want to make the forehead more rounded or bulging, apply the highlights and shadows in a curved pattern.

Wrinkles: If you want to give the effect of a wrinkled forehead, make sure that you model the wrinkles meticulously and that you follow the natural wrinkles—otherwise, you will have a double set of wrinkles when the forehead is raised. Young people who have not yet developed any natural creases and cannot form any by raising the forehead may wish to use photographs of wrinkled foreheads as a guide.

Before beginning to model forehead wrinkles, observe your own or someone else's natural wrinkles, and with your light source from above, note where the wrinkles catch the light. Is it above or below the crease? Carefully examine photographs in your morgue and those in this and other chapters (especially Figure 8.12) to see exactly how the light pattern falls, giving the effect of a series of half cylinders. Much like the nasolabial fold, the dark crease (or shadow) is established, then blended up and away from the crease line with a clean brush. The highlight is placed at the top of the fold where light would naturally fall, then blended downward into the shadow color. This technique is repeated for each fold.

EYES

No feature is more important in suggesting character than the eyes, and none can be changed in a greater variety of ways. Figure 8.13 illustrates a few of the changes that can be made in a single eye. For photographs of youthful eyes and eyebrows, see Figure 8.14; and for aged ones, Figure 8.15. In studying these photographs, always determine the light source in the photograph and make the necessary adjustments for stage lighting.

EYEBROWS

Changing the eyebrows for corrective makeup has been dealt with in Chapter 7. But besides having the potential for making the face more attractive, eyebrows provide a particularly useful means of characterization. Figure 8.13 illustrates a few such changes that can be made with an eyebrow pencil, paint, and an eyebrow brush in order to age the eye as well as to suggest character.

Using the eyebrows to suggest character can be just as important in makeups for youth as for age. In determining what you want to do with the eyebrows for characters of any age, it's a good idea to manipulate the natural eyebrows with your fingers, in order to help determine the effect on the face of different eyebrow shapes and positions. Unless your eyebrows (or those of your subject) are unusually adaptable, you might do well to add hair to them (see Character Makeup Application, Chapter 10), cover them completely with additional hair, or block them out by one of the methods suggested in Chapter 14.

Aging the Eyebrows: In aging the eyebrows, first decide exactly what effect you want, then determine how that can best be achieved. The brows may take a variety of forms. They may be sparse (Figure 8.14e and k), irregular (Figure 8.15), bushy (Figure 8.15e), or overhanging (Figure 8.15l). They may be wide (Figure 8.14d), narrow (Figure 8.14m), thick (Figure 8.14d), or thin (Figure 8.14k). But in suggesting age they should never look plucked unless that is really appropriate for the character.

Eyebrows can be aged quickly, when that is necessary, by running a white stick liner, white cream stick, or hair whitener through them against the direction of hair growth (Figure 8.18, 8.37). This can also be done with clown white, cake makeup, or white mascara.

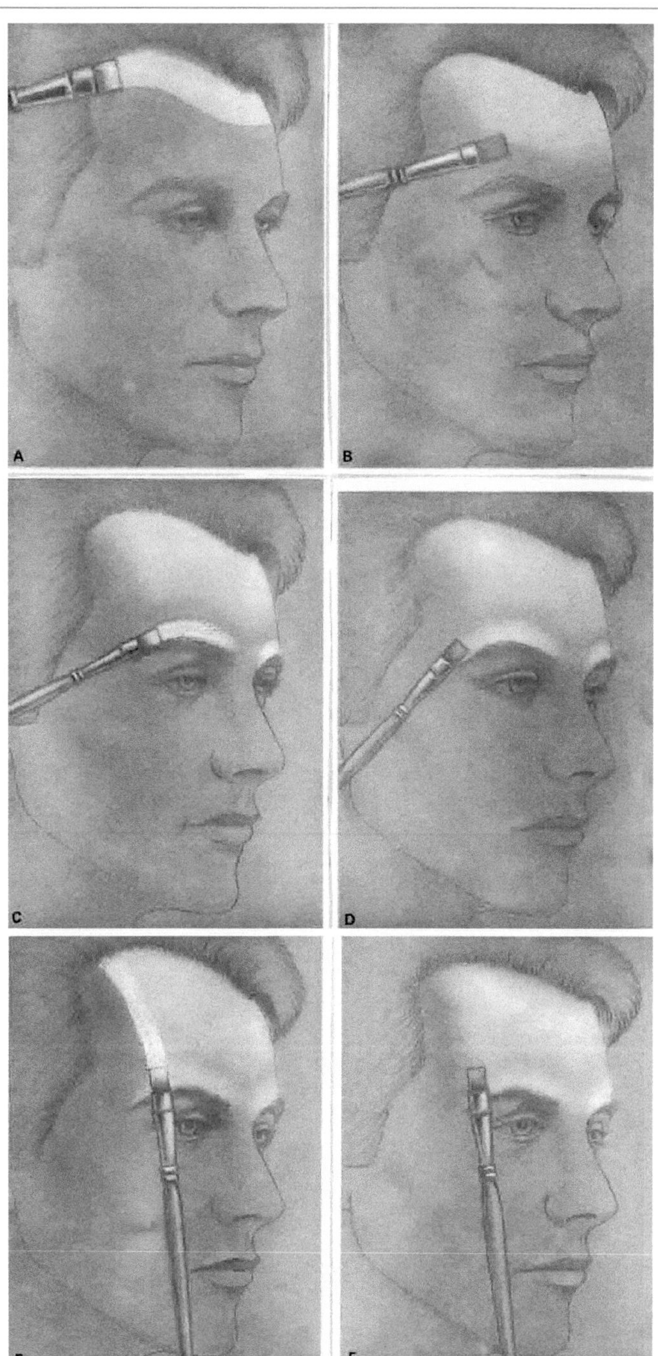

FIGURE 8.11 *Highlighting the forehead. A. Highlighting the frontal bone with an extra-wide brush. B. Blending the lower edge of the highlight. C. Highlighting the superciliary bone with a medium-wide brush. D. Blending the superciliary bone highlight with a clean brush. E. Highlighting the vertical edge of the frontal bone with a wide brush. F. Blending the edge of the highlight with a clean brush.*

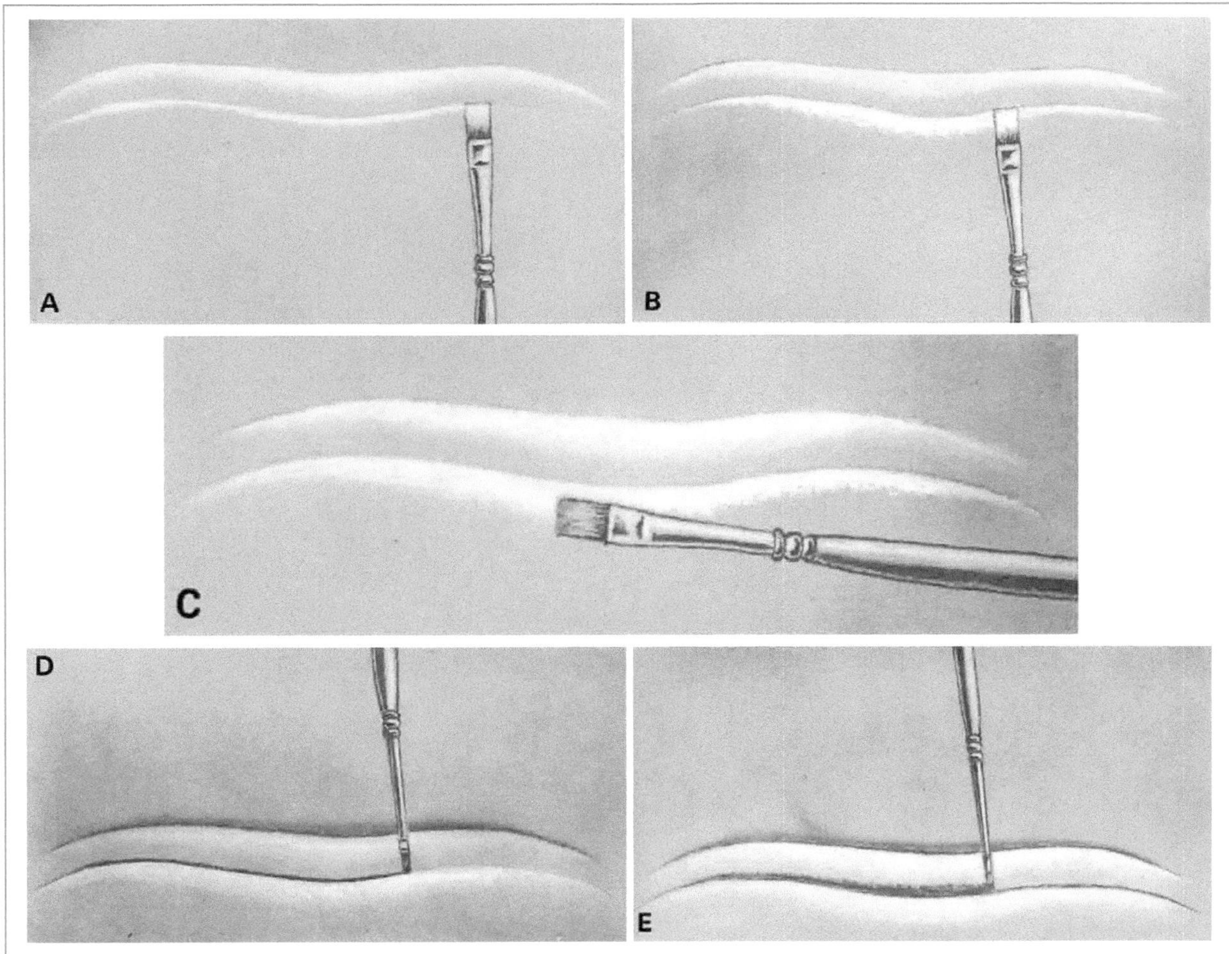

FIGURE 8.12 *Modeling forehead wrinkles with paint. A, B. Highlighting the wrinkle. C. Blending the highlight. D. Shadowing wrinkle. E. Blending shadow.*

NOSE

If the nose tends to flatten out under lights or if it is to be altered in appearance for either corrective or character requirements, it will need a certain amount of remodeling. The nose area has seven planes (Figure 8.19).

Plane A is the very small depression usually found, except in the classic nose, between the superciliary arch and the nose. It is shadowed for age and usually contains one to three vertical wrinkles (Figures 8.15d and 8.15i). The two appearing at the inner ends of the eyebrows have their inception in plane A of the eye socket and usually become narrower as they continue upward (Figure 8.38). The center wrinkle may be narrow at both ends and wider in the middle. These are the frowning wrinkles and if made rather deep, they will lend severity to the facial expression. Like all facial wrinkles, they should follow the actor's natural ones if there are any. Painted wrinkles must never conflict with an actor's natural wrinkles—including those that appear when the actor smiles or frowns.

Plane B is the prominent part of the nose and is highlighted both in indicating age and in sharpening and narrowing the nose. If the nose is too long, the lower end of the plane can be left the base color or lightly shadowed (Figure 8.20b) as indicated for corrective makeup. The width of the highlight will largely determine the apparent width of the nose (see Figure 8.20a). If the nose is too sharp and needs to be broadened or flattened, plane B can be left the base color or lightly shadowed. If the nose is too short, a highlight can be added to the full length of the nose to even past the tip (Figure 8.20c).

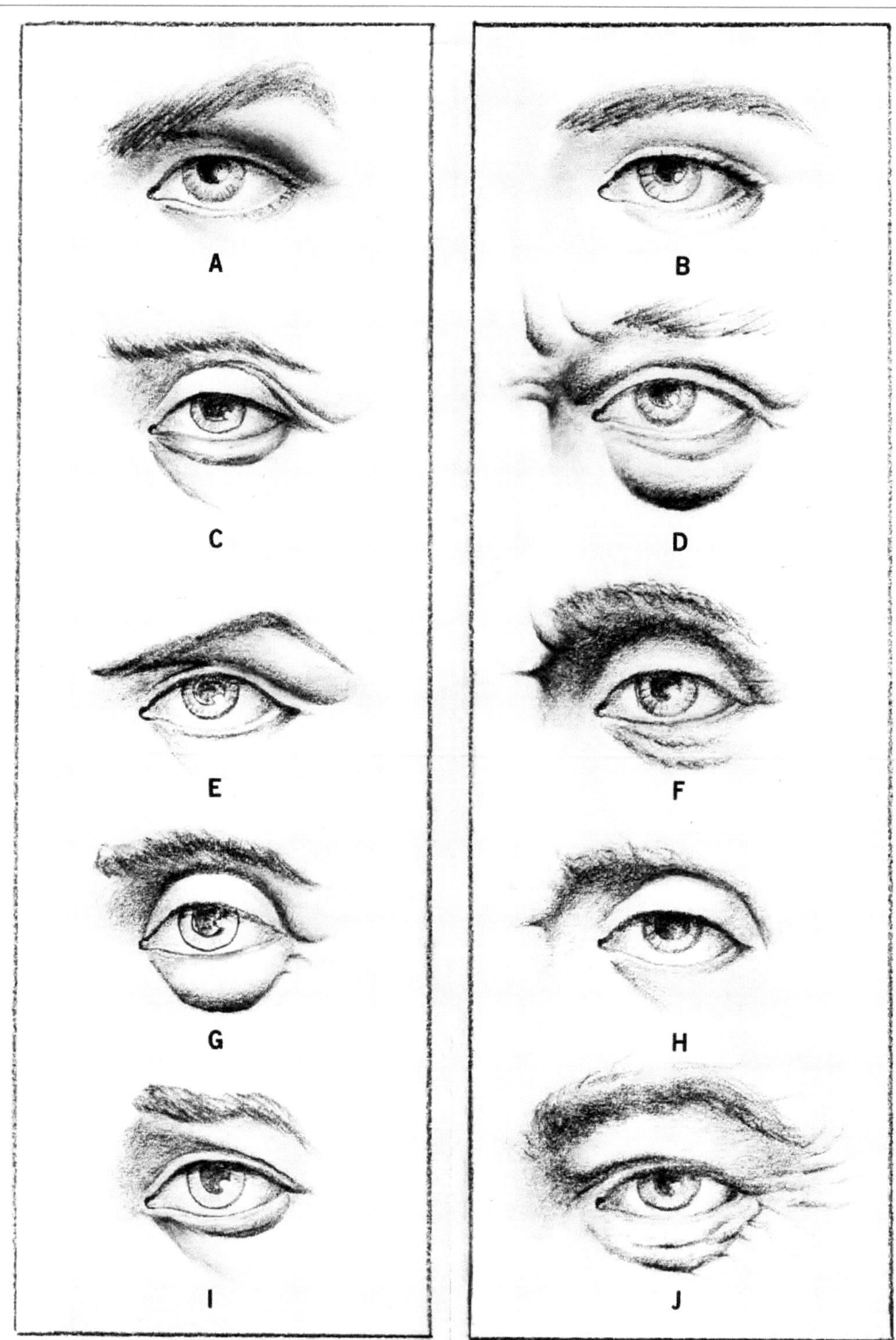

FIGURE 8.13 *Changing the eye. Ten sketches for the possible makeups for the same eye. All of the changes can be made by blocking out all or part of the eyebrow and creating a new brow and by modeling with highlights and shadows.*

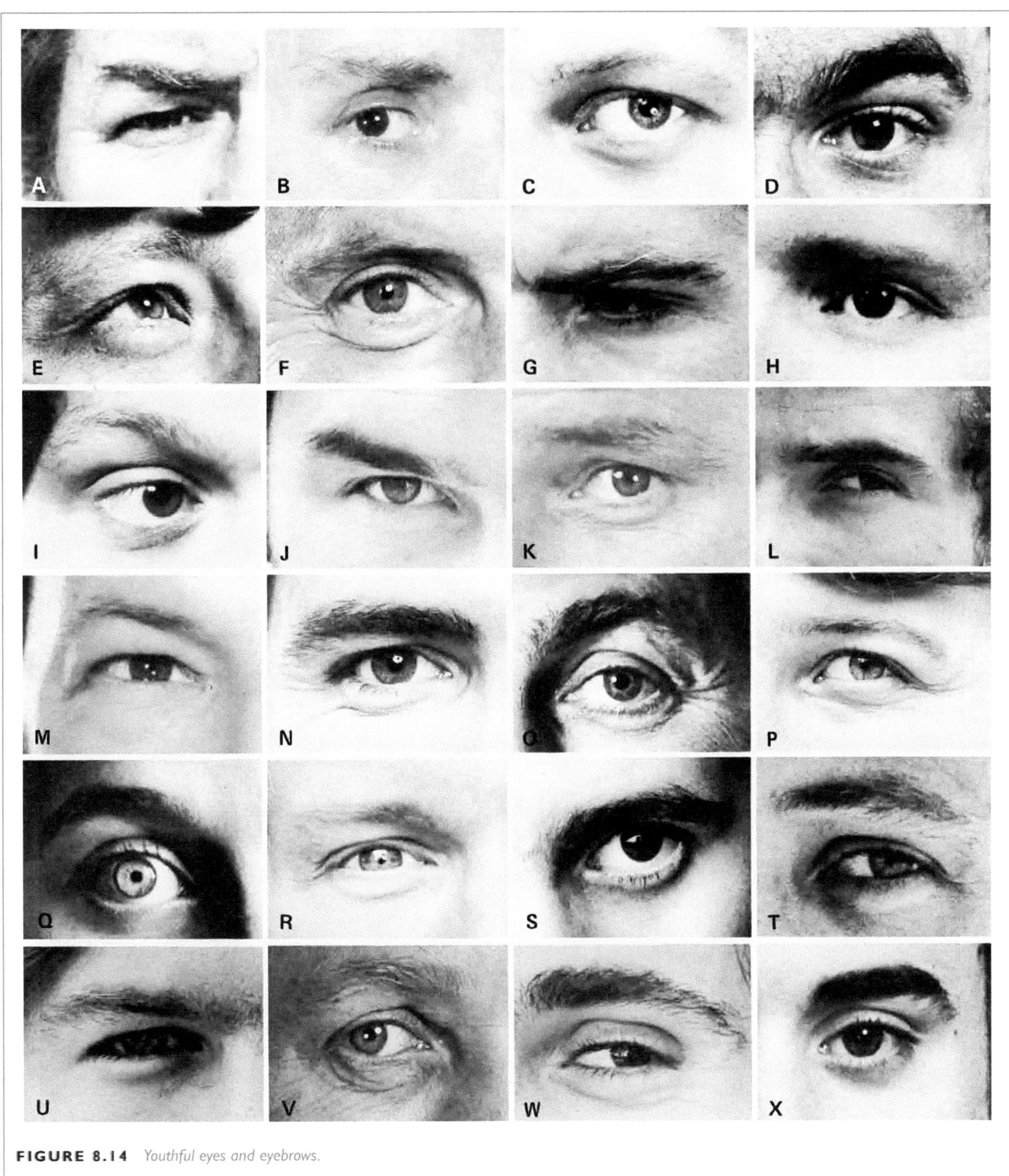

FIGURE 8.14 *Youthful eyes and eyebrows.*

The effect of a broken nose can be achieved by giving the illusion of a crook or a curve in plane B (see Figures 8.20d, 8.21). This is done by using not only a crooked or a curved highlight to reshape plane B, but also shadows to counteract the natural highlights on those parts of plane B which should not be prominent on the crooked or broken nose. In Figure 8.21, for example, A represents a normal nose, and B, C, and D show three possible shapes that could be created by the application of highlights and shadows to the nose in A.

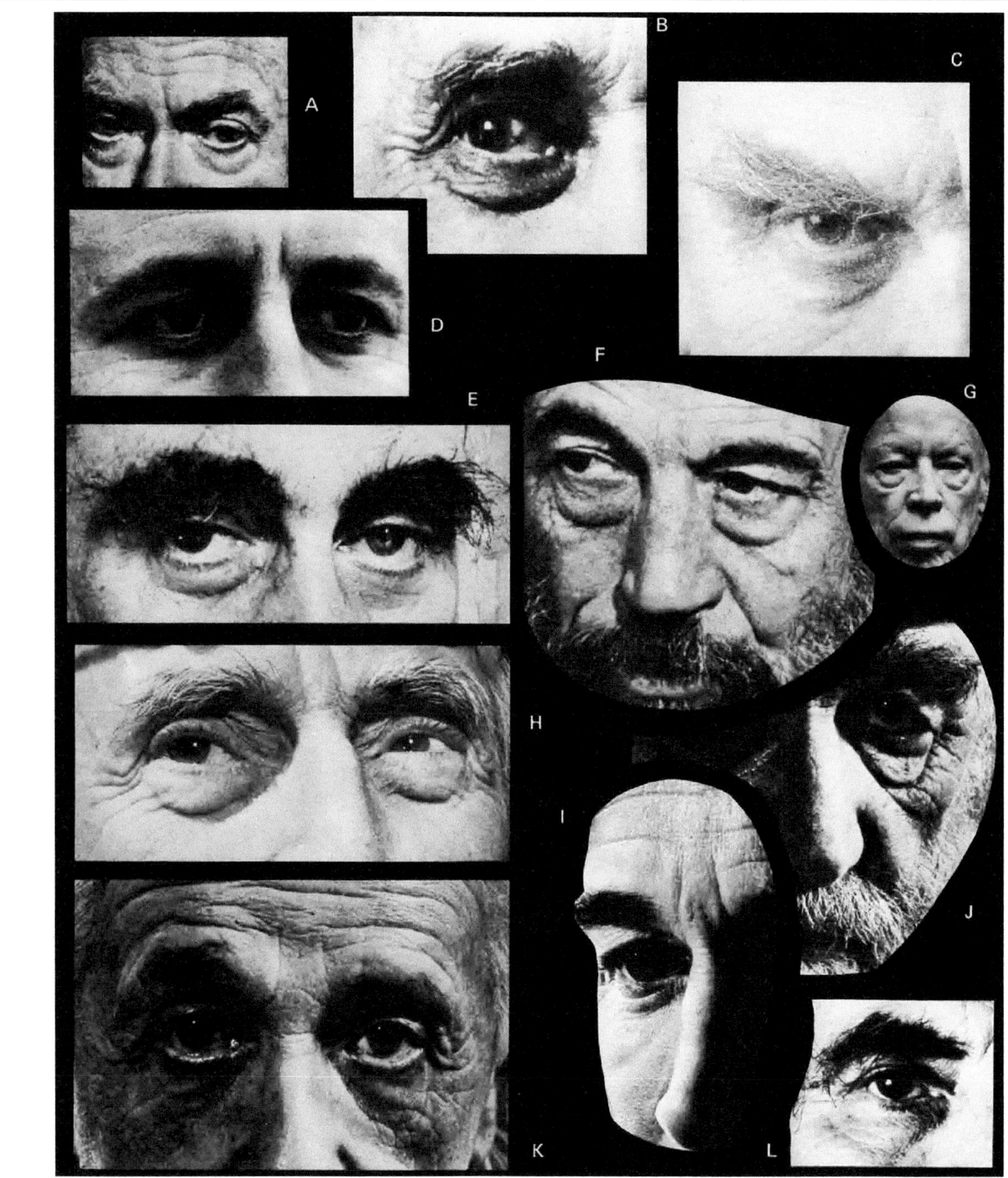

FIGURE 8.15 *Aging male eyes and eyebrows.*

CHEEKBONES

As you have already discovered in the study of facial anatomy, the cheekbone (Figure 8.23) is rounded, so that when light is coming from above (the usual assumption in makeup for the stage), the upper part of the bone receives strong light, whereas the lower part, which curves downward and inward, does not receive direct light and therefore appears considerably darker. This means that in modeling the cheeks for age or to achieve the effect of prominent cheekbones in youth or for character makeup, the cheekbone should be highlighted and the hollow below it shadowed (see Figures 8.24 and 8.38.)

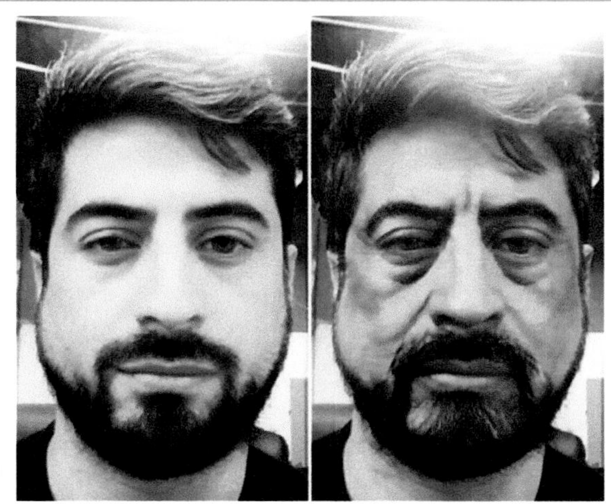

FIGURE 8.16 *Before and after age makeup. Makeup artist and model, Raul Cuadra (Chile). This makeup design was created in Adobe Photoshop as a pre-visualization or concept drawing for a film.*

FIGURE 8.18 *Aging the brows and facial hair. Notice the well-placed shadows at the temple, under the cheekbone, along the nose and eye socket, and the defined nasolabial fold and forehead wrinkles. The eye bags and crow's feet are subtle additions to this effective age makeup.*

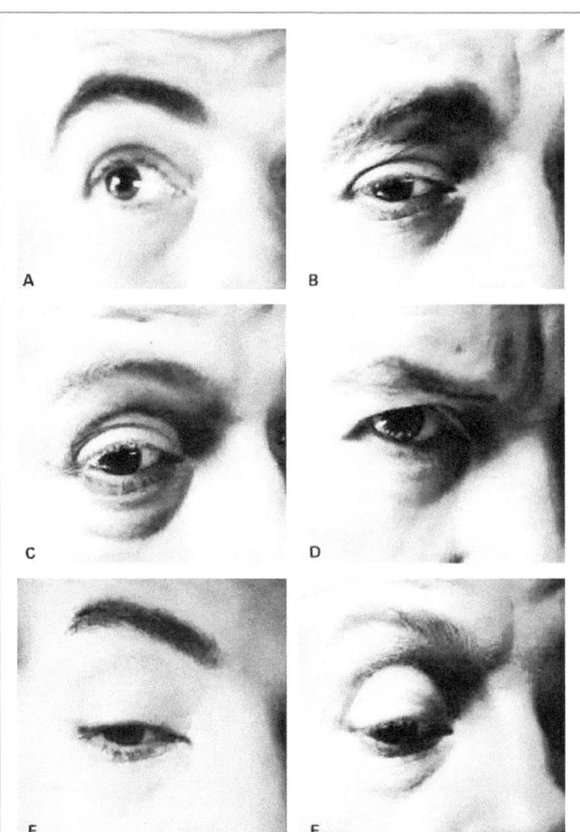

FIGURE 8.17 *Changing the eye with makeup. All makeups are on the same eye. The brow in E was partially blocked out using spirit gum adhesive, a sealer and powder. Makeup by Richard Corson.*

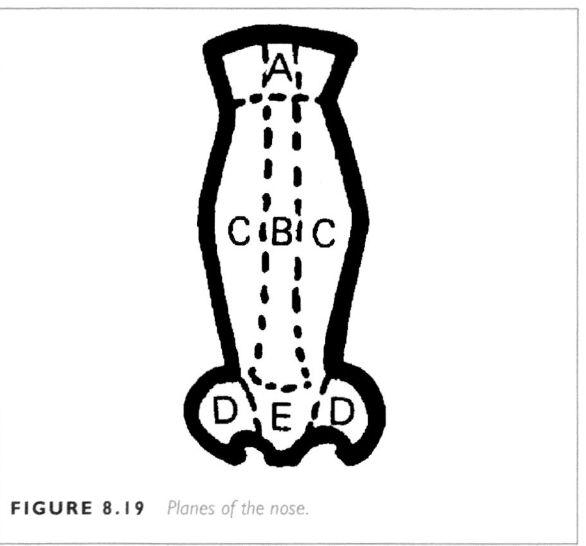

FIGURE 8.19 *Planes of the nose.*

How much the cheek sinks in and how prominent the bone is will depend on the intensity of the highlight and the shadow. For youthful makeups the contrast may be fairly subtle. For age makeups it may be relatively strong.

JAWLINE

One of the most effective ways of adding age to the youthful face is to create the illusion of sagging jowls. The correct placement of the jowls can usually be determined by gently squeezing the flesh of the jaw between the fingers to see where it creases naturally or by pulling back the chin and turning the head in various ways until creases or bulges appear. It is also possible to estimate the usual position from photographs in Figure 8.25.

The point at which the front and back areas of sagging flesh meet can nearly always be located by pressing the thumb or a finger upward somewhat beyond the middle of the jaw until you locate an indentation in the bone. This will be the correct point for ending the front sag and beginning the back one.

There are too many possible variations in jaws and sagging muscles at the jawline for us to give precise instructions for modeling that will fit every case, but general principles can be adapted and applied to individual faces. In any case, Figure 8.26 demonstrates the procedure for modeling one particular kind of jowl.

MOUTH

This area includes seven planes (Figure 8.27). When there are well-developed nasolabial folds, the outer edge of plane A is always hard (Figures 8.5, 8.6, and 8.24). The highlight decreases in intensity as it approaches plane B, which may or may not be shadowed.

Depending on the natural formation of the actor's upper lip, it is sometimes possible to model the plane B, in such a way B appears to curve inward and plane A outward, and then area C will naturally sink in. This can be done by modeling the planes like a horizontal cylinder—strongly highlighting the upper part of plane A, then letting the highlight fade into a medium shadow on B and into a deep shadow on plane C.

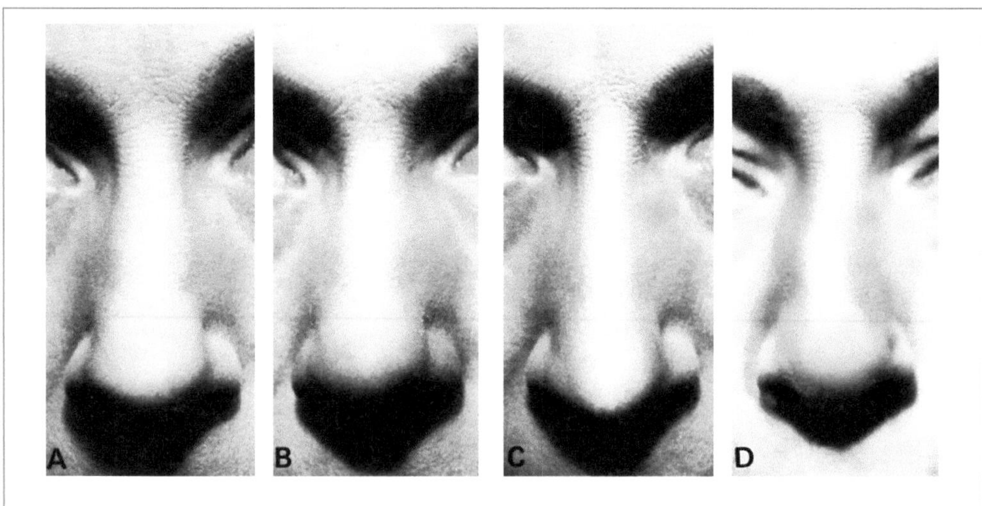

FIGURE 8.20 *Remodeling the nose with paint. A. Wide. B. Shortened. C. Lengthened. D. Crooked.*

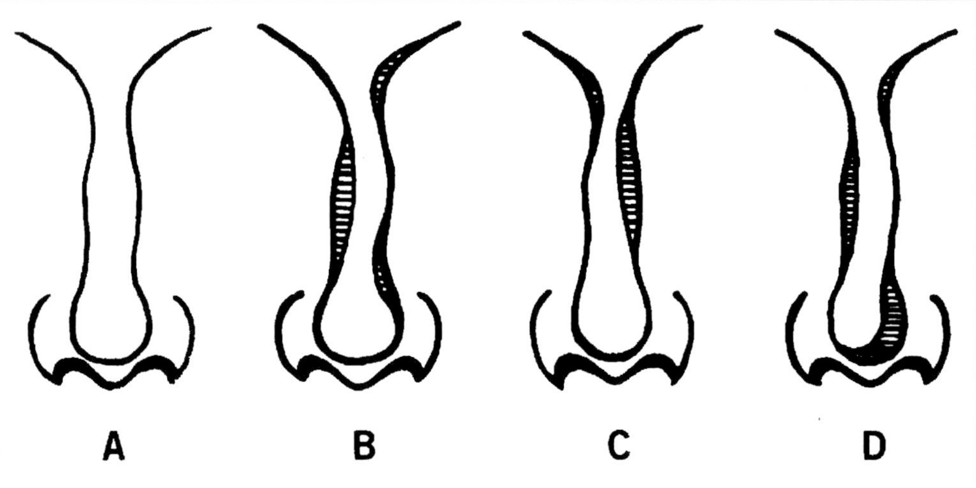

FIGURE 8.21 *Placement of highlights and shadows for crooked noses. A. Normal nose. B, C, and D. Crooked noses. The shaded areas show the placement of shadows: the unshaded areas would be highlighted.*

Size of Lips: The size of the lips (both width and thickness) will depend to some extent on the actor's own lips and how much they can be changed. For a realistic makeup, a very narrow mouth, for example, cannot successfully be made into a very wide one, but a wide one can sometimes be narrowed. A stylized lip design can be enlarged to suit the character, the performer, or the whims of the designer. The techniques for changing the apparent size of the lips begin with the drawing of the new lip line with a nude or darker pencil. The pencil is then blended onto the lip with a lip brush. The lip color is then applied with a lip brush or wand (see Figures 8.28 and 8.29).

Lip Texture: Variations in lip texture has to do largely with age, environment, and health. In youth the texture is usually smooth, but later in life, depending on the condition of the skin generally, the lips may be rough, cracked, or wrinkled. It is, therefore, important in aging youthful faces that the lips be aged as well (see Figure 8.9). This caution is based on observation of too many makeups in which youthful lips in a wrinkled face have destroyed the believability of an otherwise effective makeup. Suggestions for aging the lips are given below.

Aging the Lips: In addition to causing changes in texture, aging and changes inside the mouth (loss of teeth or wearing of false ones) can bring about changes in shape, size, and general conformation of the mouth. Lips are likely to become thinner (Figure 8.25), and they may be cut by numerous vertical wrinkles, as in Figures 8.31 and 8.40.

If the mouth is to be wrinkled, it is helpful to make it smaller and, if possible, thinner—unless, of course, it is already small and thin. Thinner lips can be accomplished by first applying foundation to both lips along with the rest of the face, then powder. Shape the lips by lining them with a natural lip tone on the bottom and a slightly darker shade on the top. After filling in the lips, blot with a tissue to remove any excess oil (if cream foundation is used). The lips should now be pursed tightly and gently stippled with a natural highlight. When the lips are relaxed the wrinkle effect will appear.

Painted-on wrinkles can be accomplished with a narrow brush, modeling the wrinkles carefully and using strong highlights with very narrow, deep shadows to form deep creases. Be sure that each highlight has one hard edge and that the hard edge is very sharp and clean (see Figure 8.31). If the wrinkles are too strong, they can be toned down by stippling. The important thing is to make them *subtle* and convincingly three-dimensional.

CHIN

The chin itself changes relatively little with age, except for the changes in the texture of the skin, which can be achieved with stippling. What is usually called a double chin is actually a sagging neckline, resulting from a relaxing of the muscles of the jaw and neck area. It begins just behind the chin and cannot be effectively simulated with paint unless the actor already has the beginnings of one that can be highlighted. Lowering the head slightly and pulling it back will help to emphasize whatever fullness is already there (see Figure 8.5).

A crease may develop, with age, between areas E and F (see Figure 8.27). Or there may be a rather abrupt change of plane without an actual crease. In either case, the top of the chin should be more strongly highlighted than it would be in youth in order to emphasize the increased angularity (see Figures 8.5, 8.22, 8.38, and 8.40).

NECK

The neck, of course, ages along with the face and sometimes even more rapidly (see Figure 8.25). A youthful neck, like youthful lips, can destroy the believability of an otherwise effective age makeup. For juveniles, nothing needs to be done, but for age, the neck requires modeling.

There are four prominences in the neck and two at the jawline that are important in makeup. They are labeled A–F in Figure 8.32. A is the sternocleidomastoid (sternal head), B is the trapezius, C is the levator scapulae, D is the thyroid cartilage, E is the superficial masseter muscle, and F is the depressor anguli oris. Because these muscles, along with the top of the larynx and parts of the tracheal column, catch the light, they should be highlighted. All of these, being roughly cylindrical in shape, should be modeled like cylinders, with the highlight fading around to a shadow. The hollow at the breastbone, where the sternocleidomastoid muscles almost meet, is usually in shadow. In old age there may be two folds of flesh starting above the larynx and hanging down like wattles from under the chin (Figure 8.25). Small ones can be effectively painted on for a front view (Figure 8.33) but are, of course, ineffective in profile.

It is also possible to model the wrinkles that form around the neck and diagonally upward toward the ears. To determine the correct placement of the wrinkles, it is usually necessary to twist and turn the head until natural wrinkles are formed. These can be carefully modeled with highlights and shadows. For aging plumper characters, these transverse wrinkles should nearly always be used, but they should be wider and fewer in number.

HANDS

In representing youth, the hands should always be made up to go with the color of the face. The extent of modeling

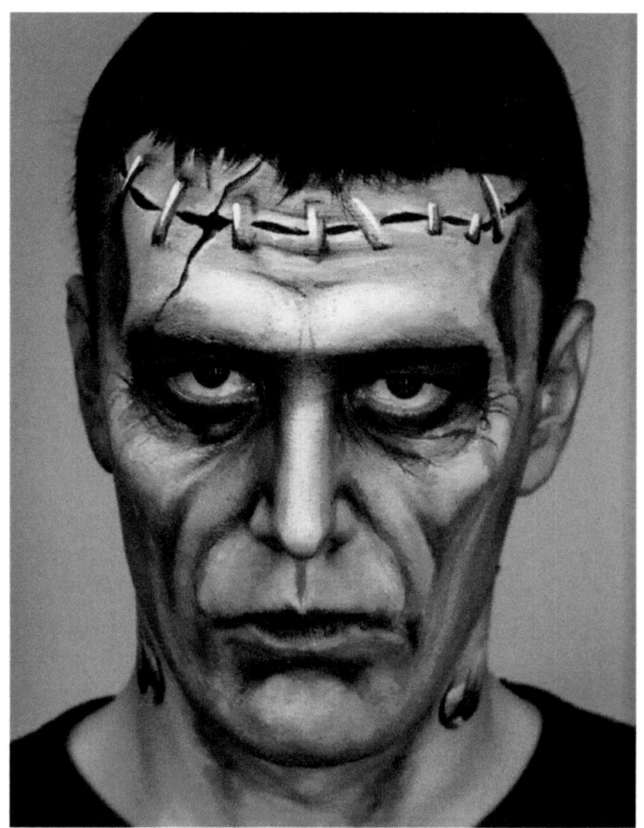

FIGURE 8.22 *Frankenstein character makeup. Makeup artist, Olga Murasev. The carefully placed highlights and shadows in this stylized makeup of the Frankenstein monster show a clear understanding of how a two-dimensional painting technique can restructure the face by manipulating how the eye interprets low-value hues (receding colors) and high-value hues (advancing colors). Notice the wide, lengthened nose and shaped nares, the strong prominent square brow, deep-set eyes, the recessed temples, the high cheekbones, and full, round chin shaped by a strong highlight and deep, arching shadow below the lower lip (the shading resembles the sphere mentioned earlier in this chapter). The eyes bags appear three-dimensional and the wrinkles are delicately applied using a variety of line weights and brush sizes (thick and thin lines). The mouth has been reshaped and the added trompe l'oeil neck bolts complete the effect. The color choices include the following face and body paints:*
TAG Bronze Green; Paradise Lime; Paradise Light Green; Cameleon Clover Green; TAG Silver; TAG Earth Brown; TAG Pearl Black; Wolfe FX White; Paradise White; Cameleon Strong Black; Mehron Bruise Wheel (Red and Dark Red colors); Wolfe FX yellow sponge; Loew Cornell 795 series round brush #6; Loew Cornell 795 series round brush #3; Loew Cornell 7500 series filbert brush #10; Cameleon big blending brush; Cameleon small blending brush.

needed for bone, knuckles, and veins of the hands will depend on both age and the care that the hands have been given. Usually, unless the character tends to be quite pudgy, the bones of the hands, in age, tend to become more prominent and the veins begin to stand out (Figure 8.35). The bones, both in the back of the hand and in the fingers, should be modeled like cylinders, with highlights along the top and shadows along the sides. The joints may sometimes swell and often, with light skins, redden. A little rouge will give the color. The swelling can be suggested by rounded highlights on top of the joint and narrow, crescent-shaped shadows around them.

A dark-skinned actor who wants to create the effect with makeup can make his hand into a fist and cover the

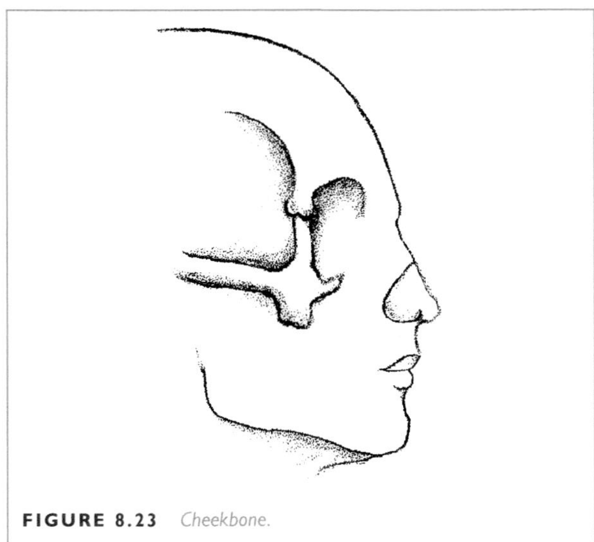

FIGURE 8.23 *Cheekbone.*

FIGURE 8.24 *Character makeup. Dramatic application of highlights and shadows to change the basic structure of the human face. Where there is a strong highlight, there is a strong shadow next to it. When a soft highlight is used a soft shadow follows.*

joints with very dark brown makeup. The hand can then be straightened out and the dark brown makeup wiped off the surface of the joint, which can be shadowed, slightly highlighted, and powdered. This technique will leave natural-looking dark ridges in the deepest part of the wrinkles on the joints.

The veins, if at all prominent, should appear three-dimensional, not flat, which means that there should be a highlight along one side of every vein and a shadow along the other (see Figure 8.35). Decide arbitrarily which way the light is coming from. Veins should be treated as elongated cylinders. Their roundness will be particularly pronounced as they cross over bones. They are nearly always irregular, often forking out and meandering across the hand. If the actor's natural veins are visible, and prominent, they should be followed. Otherwise, it is possible to place the veins wherever they appear to be most effective. Be careful, however, not to use too many. A few veins carefully placed and convincingly painted will be far more effective than a complicated network.

The color of veins will depend on the type and color of the hand. A pale, delicate, fine-skinned hand will naturally reveal much more blue in the veins than a deeply tanned or a black or a brown one, on which the veins may not appear blue at all and can be modeled with the normal highlight and shadow colors. Often veins that are not extremely prominent are a light greenish blue, in which case a very pale tint of blue-green can be used for highlighting. Very prominent veins under a delicate white skin are likely to be a much deeper blue, with no green cast, and would be expected to have blue-gray shadows. Observe the coloration in elderly hands—of the skin as well as the veins.

The brown spots so often found on older hands can be painted on with a yellowish brown—about the same color as freckles. They should be of various sizes and unevenly distributed. If the hand is to be rough textured, it should be stippled or given a three-dimensional skin texture (see Chapters 10 and 11).

Fingernails: In aging the hands, always make sure that the nails are aged in harmony with the rest of the hand. The aging may involve filing or cutting the nails (either real or artificial) to a length and shape appropriate for the character, and it may also require changing the color and the apparent texture of the nails, both of which can be done with makeup pencils, used with latex, sealer, flexible Collodion, or spirit gum.

When the nails have been appropriately colored, they should be coated with a spray sealer (Final Seal by Ben Nye, Green Marble SeLr by Premiere Products, Inc., Fixative "A" by Mehron). No matter which one you use, it should be powdered when it has dried in order to remove the shine and give a duller finish to the nail. An alternative method of aging the nails is to coat them with spirit gum, then, with one finger, to tap the gum until it becomes tacky, at which point you can press white or neutral face powder into the gum. That gives a dull whitish effect suitable for some aged characters.

If dirt under and around the nails is appropriate, gray or gray-brown cream or cake makeup can be applied with a small brush (see Figure 8.36).

Colored nail polish can be applied to help create aged nails. Red, black, brown, yellow, cream, frosted or any other color can

FIGURE 8.25 *Jawlines.*

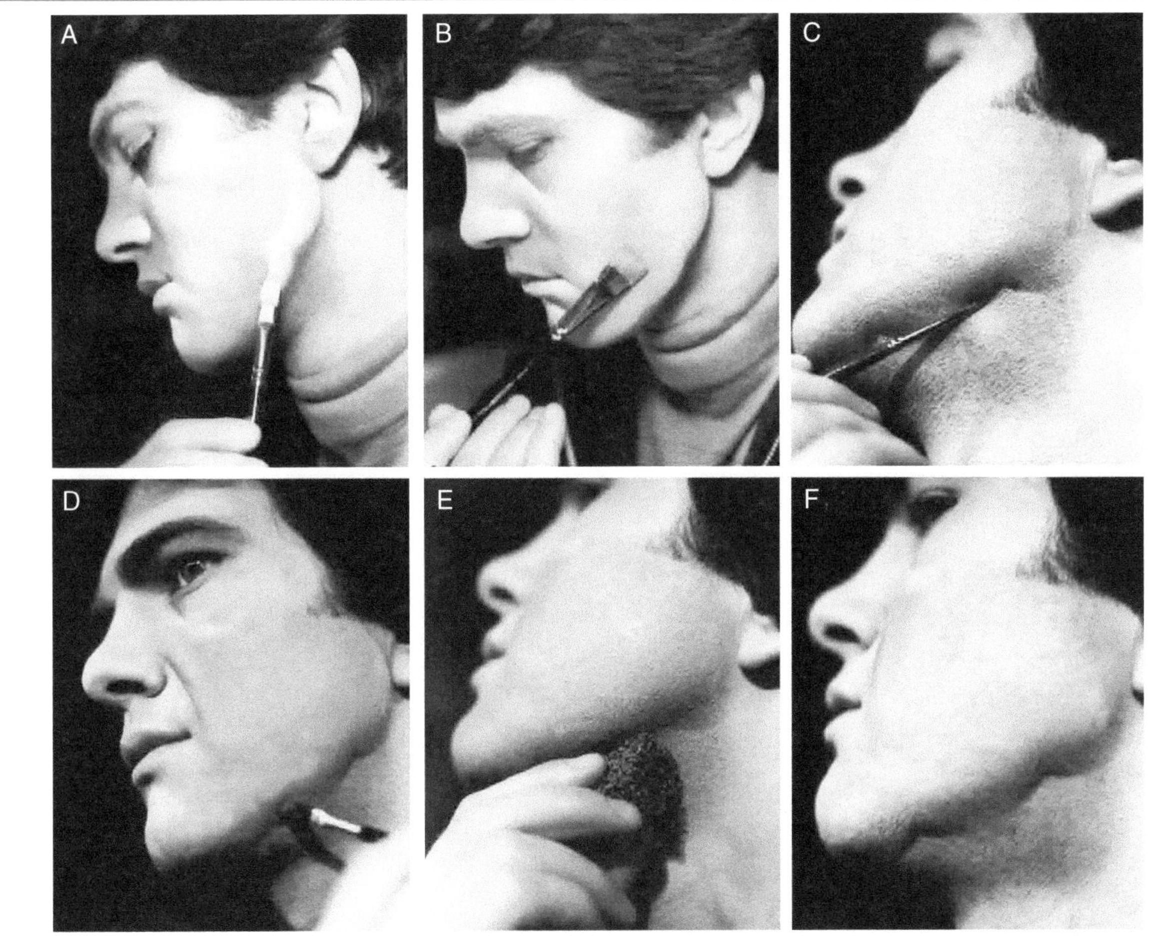

FIGURE 8.26 *Modeling sagging jowls. (Actor Eugene Bicknell.) A. Highlighting the jawbone with a wide brush. B. Blending the upper edge of the highlight. C. Applying a medium-toned shadow color along the lower edge of the highlight to strengthen the crease caused by sagging skin. Blend the shadow down slightly onto the neck with a clean brush. D. Adding dry rouge with a soft eyeshadow brush. E. Stippling the highlights and shadows. F. Completed jawline.*

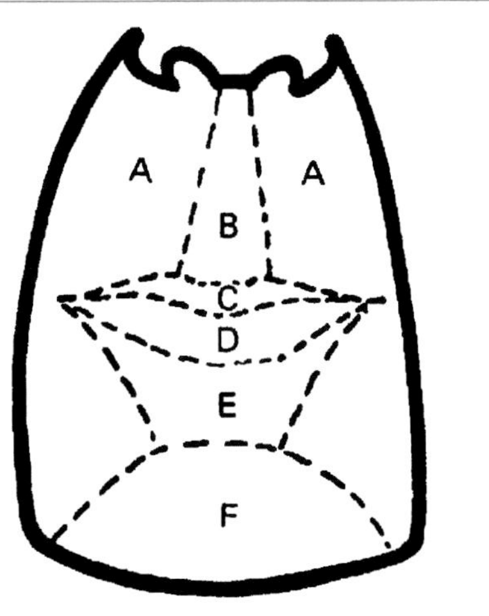

FIGURE 8.27 *Planes of the upper and lower jaws.*

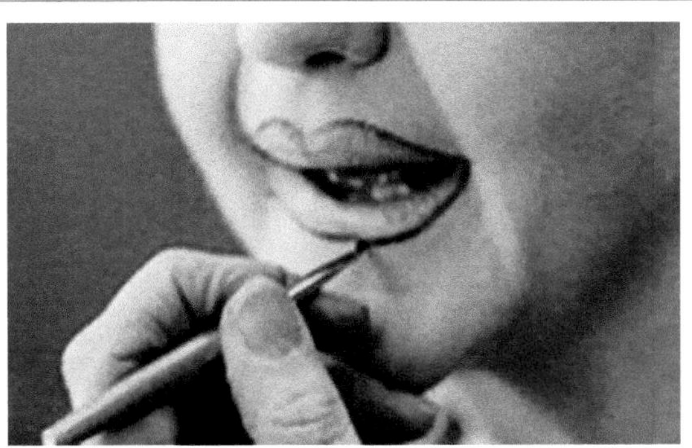

FIGURE 8.28 *Changing the size of the lips by drawing a new lip line with a nude or darker pencil outside the normal lip line.*

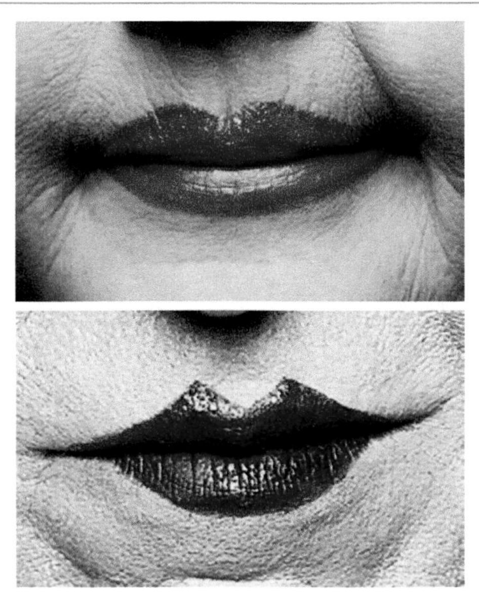

FIGURE 8.29 *Example of lips made larger with lip liner and lip color.*

FIGURE 8.30 *Creating natural aging on the lips. James Black as Scrooge has first applied a slightly darker foundation to his lips, then powdered with a no-color setting powder. To create the wrinkled texture, he pursed his lips tightly and lightly tapped highlight on the lips with a small wedge sponge. When the lips are relaxed the creases will appear.*

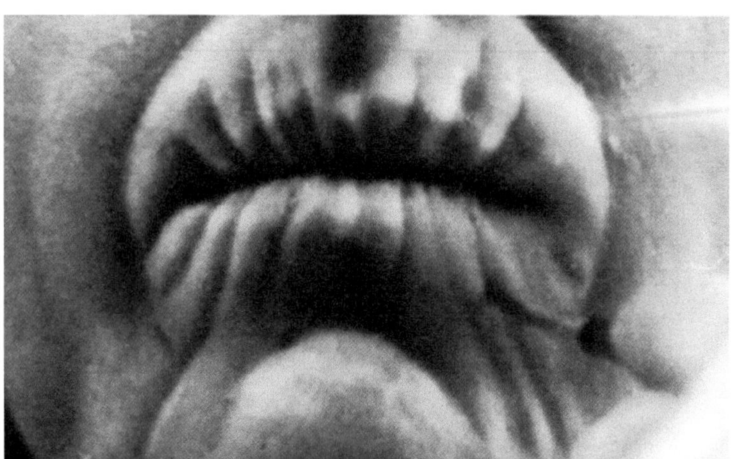

FIGURE 8.31 *Aging the mouth. Painting on wrinkles with highlights and shadows, which will then be stippled. Makeup by Barbara Murray.*

be dulled and textured with powders, cornmeal, or any number of materials. For removing nail polish, makeup, and pencils, spray sealers, spirit gum, or any other creatively useful product from the nails, use 99% alcohol, polish remover, spirit gum remover, or soap and water. A good nail brush should also be part of your makeup kit when trying to restore the nails back to their natural state.

TEETH

Teeth, if too white and even for the character, can be darkened with an appropriate shade of non-toxic temporary tooth enamel available in shades such as Black, White, Nicotine, Decay, and Zombie Rot (Mehron, Kryolan, and Ben Nye) (see Figure 8.37). The effect of chipped or missing teeth

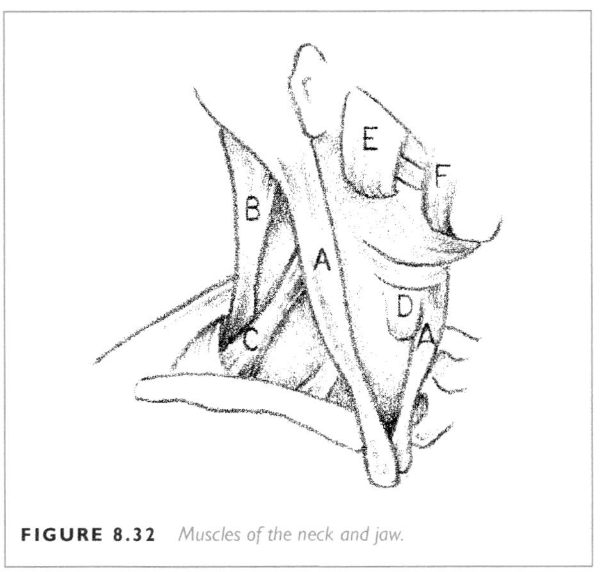

FIGURE 8.32 *Muscles of the neck and jaw.*

FIGURE 8.33 *Neck aged with cake makeup. Makeup by Richard Corson.*

FIGURE 8.34 *Aging hands.*

can be created with black tooth enamel or black wax. Black eyebrow pencil can also be used, but it may require touching up during the performance. The teeth should always be dried with a tissue before being blocked out.

Black tooth enamel can also be used to make the edges of the teeth uneven.

RESHAPING THE FACE

There are times when, in addition to working with individual features, you may wish to think in terms of reshaping the face—making it more square, long, wide, round, or oval—in order to make it more appropriate for a particular character. This can be done—at least to some degree—by means of highlights and shadows and beards, mustaches, hair, and eyebrows (see Chapter 12).

The Long Face: A face can be made to look longer by increasing the apparent height of the forehead and the apparent length of the nose and the chin by highlighting. Narrowing the face by subtly shading the sides of the forehead and the cheeks will also make it seem longer, as will a high, narrow hairstyle or one that covers the sides of the face. A pointed goatee or a long, narrow beard will have the same effect (Figures 12.11h and 12.21d). A long nose and long nasolabial folds (Figure 8.38) will also contribute to the illusion.

To make a long face look less long, follow the suggestions below for the wide face.

The Wide Face: To make a face look wider, you can do just the reverse of lengthening—lower the forehead (which can be done with the hairstyle, as well as with the makeup) and shorten the chin (if doing so would not be inappropriate for the character), highlight rather than shadow the sides of the forehead and the cheeks, shorten the nose, flatten and widen the hairstyle, and dress any facial hair horizontally (Figures 12.6 and 12.21a) rather than vertically. Making the eyebrows farther apart will also help, as will avoiding long nasolabial folds and making apple cheeks instead. In order to decrease the apparent width of a wide face, follow any of the suggestions for the long face that seem appropriate.

The Square Face: To make a face more square, the forehead should be vertical at the temples, giving a squared-off effect, and should usually be made to look as broad as possible. This can be done by highlighting the temples and even blocking out the hairline, if necessary, to take it farther back at the sides. The top

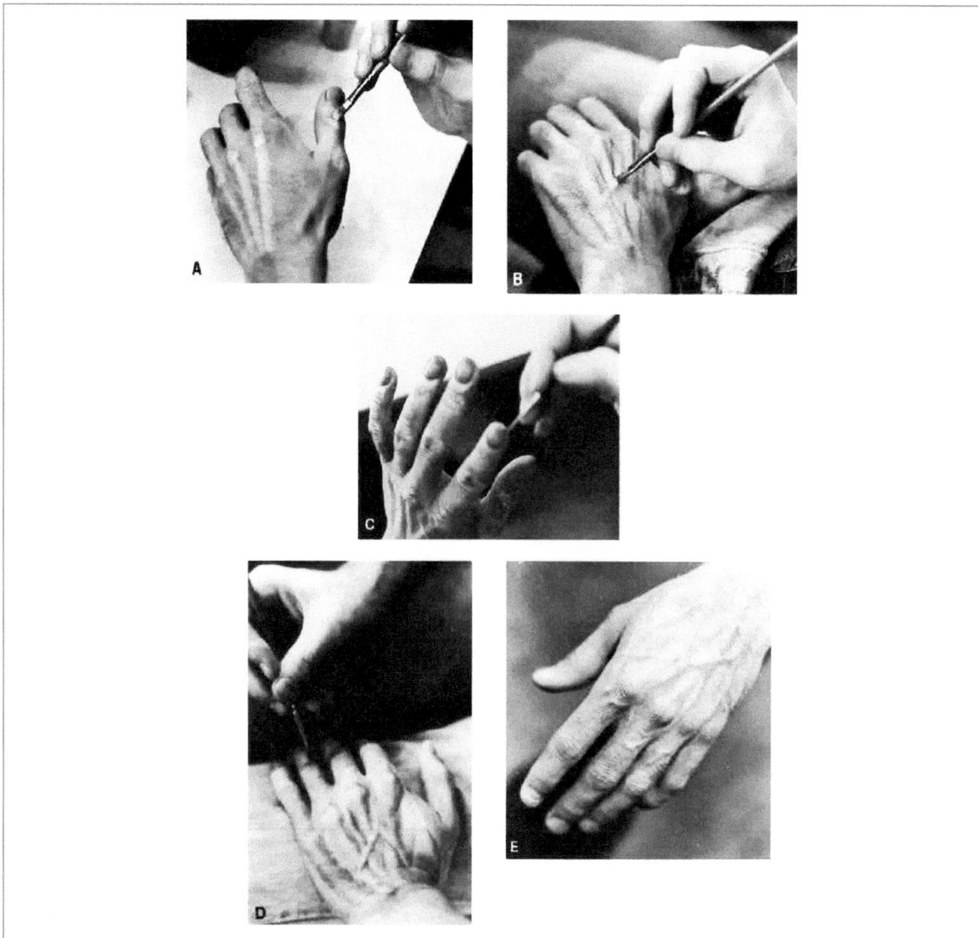

FIGURE 8.35 *Aging a male hand. A. Highlighting the bones of the hand. B. Shadowing between the bones. C. Adding an aging effect to the fingernails. D. Adding details. E. Finished makeup after powdering.*

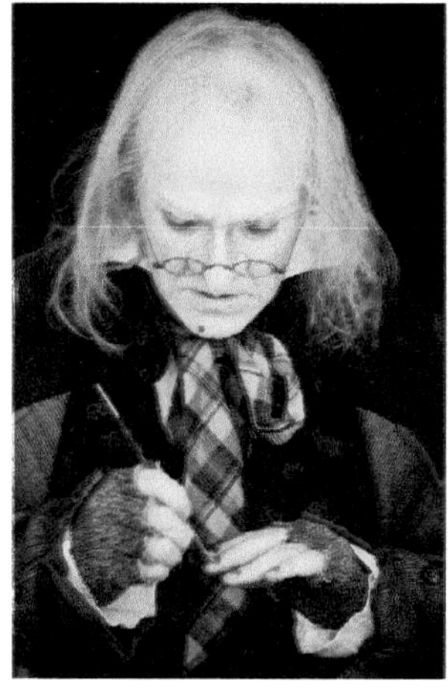

FIGURE 8.36 *James Black as Scrooge painting his fingernails.*

FIGURE 8.37 *Discoloring the teeth. Actor James Black rubbing "Nicotine" tooth color by Ben Nye on his teeth in preparation for the role of Scrooge, in the Alley Theatre production of Charles Dickens' Christmas Carol, A Ghost Story of Christmas.*

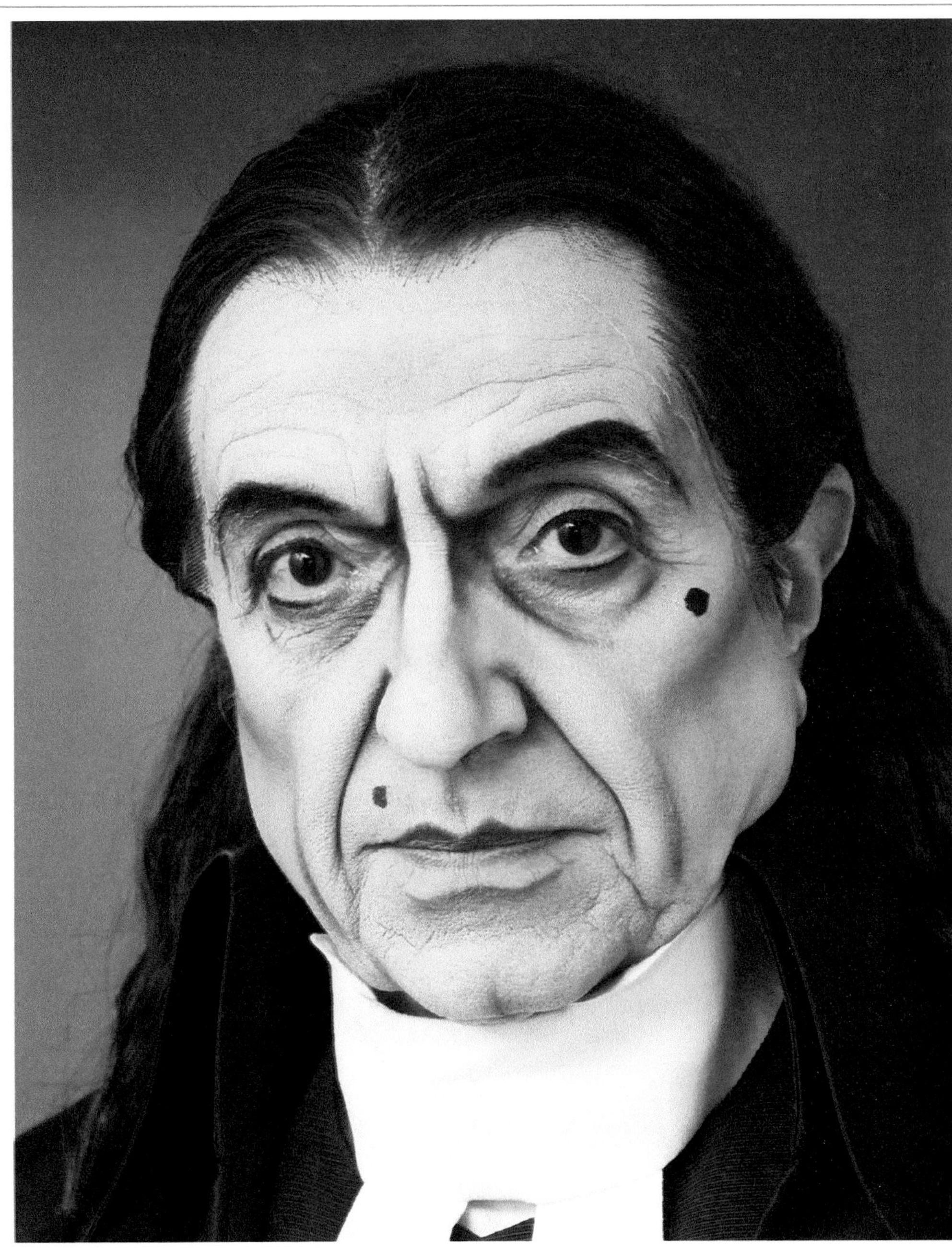

FIGURE 8.38 *Painted character makeup. Opera singer (bass-baritone) Ruggero Raimondi as Don Basilio in Rossini's The Barber of Seville. Makeup artist and photographer, Kevin Rawlings. (Kevin Rawlings recently retired from the Metropolitan Opera after for 25 years as Principal Makeup Artist.)*

Source: Photograph courtesy of Kevin Rawlings.

FIGURE 8.39 *Creating a Joker fantasy makeup using the principles of highlight and shadow to transform the features of the face. Makeup artist Marie-Laurence using Snazaroo water-based face and body paint. A. After a foundation of white is applied, the style lines are laid in with black. B. The yellowish teeth are added and outlined with black paint. The lips are roughly applied in red and the brows are drawn in black. C. The teeth are touched up with a pale yellow and then shaded with black to add dimension. D. The makeup is completed by intensifying the black lines, strengthening the red around the mouth and eyes, and adding the green wig.*

hairline should be fairly straight across. If much hair needs to be blocked out, it would usually be better to wear a wig that will cover the natural hairline and provide a hairline more suitable for the character.

The jaw can be highlighted at the sides, if necessary, to make it look wider, and the chin can sometimes be squared off a bit. A square-cut beard can be very helpful (see Figure 12.12i). Straight eyebrows will also contribute to the illusion (Figure 8.13b and 8.14w).

If the face is noticeably longer than it is wide, follow the instructions for the wide face in order to give a squarer look.

A square face can be made to look less square by rounding off the forehead, the jaw, and the chin, wearing a longer and more rounded beard, and giving the face an illusion of greater length.

The Oval Face: A face—unless it is already too round—can be made to look more oval by rounding off the upper corners of the forehead either by shadowing or by changing the hairline and doing the same to the jaw with shading or with a beard, creating a sweeping curve down to a rounded chin. A round face can be made to look less round by shadowing the sides of the cheeks, curving the shadow gently downward at an angle towards the chin.

The Round Face: To round a youthful face and keep it youthful, follow the principles used in modeling a sphere, as illustrated in Figure 8.4, in which drawing A illustrates the

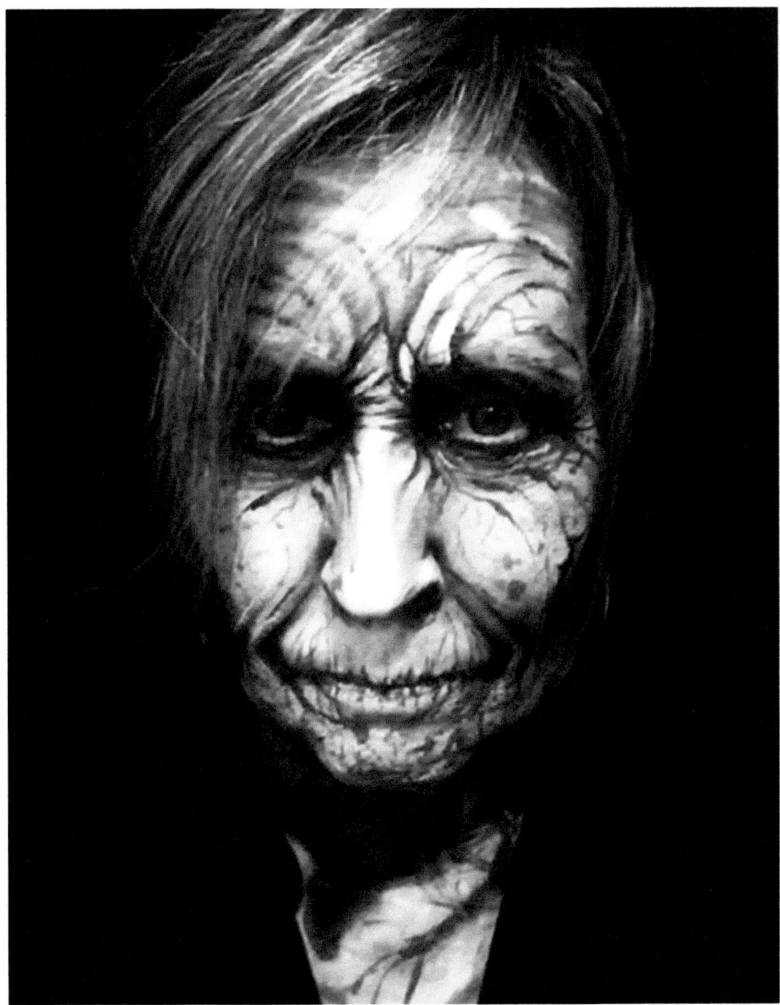

FIGURE 8.40 *Extreme painted old age. Painted with Cameleon Face and Body Paint. Makeup artist, Jasmin Walsh (Brazil). This makeup was created by first modeling (under-painting) the face with layers of highlights and shadows of various hues: Pure White, Almond, Macchiato, then the wrinkle lines and wrinkle contours were applied using a mixture of Macchiato, Coffee Brown, and Black Velvet.*

shading and highlighting for a sphere and drawing B, the outline of a youthful face. The effect of the roundness is achieved with a highlight at B5 made in a round pattern in about the center of the cheek, and a thin, crescent-shaped shadow drawn in an arc from close to the eye, past the nostrils and the mouth, and around to the back of the jaw, as shown in B4. All edges should be soft and the shadow very subtle. Although some faces cannot be made to look round without the use of three-dimensional makeup, an *effect* of roundness can usually be achieved by rounding various features or areas of the face, as illustrated in Figure 8.4b. Rouging the face in a round pattern can also be helpful. An effect of roundness can also be achieved by rounding individual features rather than the face as a whole.

In addition, whatever effect of roundness you have achieved with makeup can often be enhanced with the hairstyle and facial hair. A rounded collar in the costume may also help.

CHAPTER 9

NATURAL MAKEUP FOR FILM AND TELEVISION

Film and television makeup allow for as many variations in character as does the stage makeup process. The full range of techniques used for straight makeup, corrective makeup, modeling with highlights and shadows, and three-dimensional makeup can be translated for film and television. The major differences between theater and film and television include the following:

- Actors normally do not have to do their own makeup (unless it is a low-budget film).
- Makeup must look good in the trailer, meaning it must appear completely natural when the actor is standing next to you. Minute details are easily seen in film and television.
- Contouring with highlights and shadows that enhance facial features for the stage will read as unnatural for the camera.
- Weather, set and location characteristics, and time constraints greatly affect film makeups.
- Maintaining accurate continuity records is essential when doing makeup in film and television. This is especially useful when the production is "block shooting" (the filming of sequences out of consecutive order to accommodate the schedule of particular actors).
- There are seldom any quick changes in film.

HIGH-DEFINITION DIGITAL TECHNOLOGY

The high-definition (hi-def, HD) and 4K cameras produce images in almost three-dimensional detail and more areas in shots can be in focus at one time. HD and 4K cameras can film in low-light levels and still get ultra-clear images. There are occasions when filtration, softening the light, or diffusing the image can be used to make the appearance less defined. The fact that every imperfection, unevenness, and change in skin texture shows on camera has led to some creative challenges for contemporary makeup artists. Technology for HD cameras changes quickly, so what worked for one set of circumstances may not be applicable for the next project. Testing makeups, referred to as the makeup test (screen tests are generally for actors), is used to consider whether the makeup color, amount, and surface finish are acceptable on camera beforehand and is the best way to check for problems.

Sponges and brushes are still viable for applying makeup but the final look has to be seamless and subtle. Airbrushing a foundation on its own or over a sponged or brushed makeup can help blend the look and create an even more flawless, natural makeup. Because of the attention to minute details a "natural" makeup may take longer to achieve. Prosthetics, wig lace, and anything with an edge will present a need for extra time to adjust. The shine from glues, the texture of wig lace, and the reflective nature of some cosmetics present another consideration. Professional makeup artists keep up with the new developments in the chemical makeups of cosmetic products. Many of these new technologies help to combat some of the problems attributed to shooting with HD. Continued practice and experimentation are key to developing successful makeup applications in the HD era.

As a makeup artist what you see in the studio, or more often the trailer, and what an audience will view on the screen cannot always be determined beforehand. The camera, monitor,

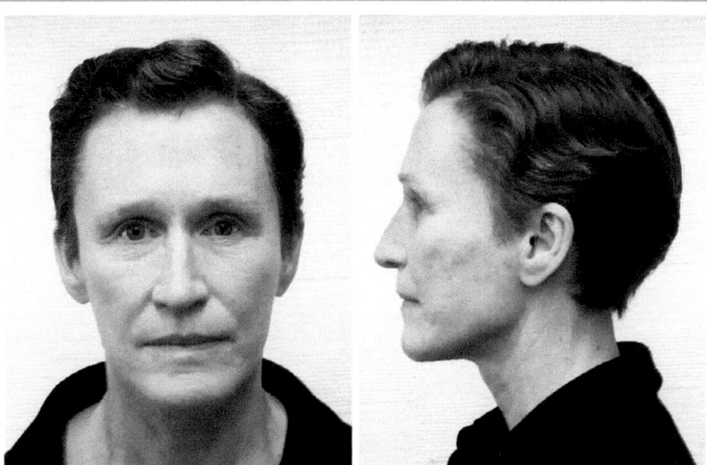

FIGURE 9.1 *Glenn Close makeup and hair test for Albert Nobbs in the 2011 Rodrigo Garcia film, Albert Nobbs. Makeup by Matthew Mungle, Lynn Johnson; wig created by Martial Corneville.*

FIGURE 9.2 *Glenn Close as Albert Nobbs. The makeup artist added silicone earlobes and nose tip. She is not wearing makeup in this film.*

Source: Image provided by Glenn Close.

FIGURE 9.3 *Liquid foundations. (left to right) Black Opal oil-free True Color, Revlon ColorStay, Make Up For Ever Ultra HD, MAC Pro Longwear, Estée Lauder Double Wear.*

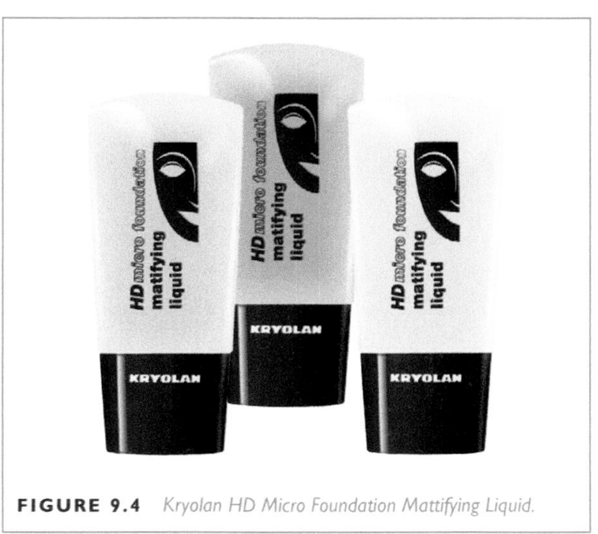

FIGURE 9.4 *Kryolan HD Micro Foundation Mattifying Liquid.*

FIGURE 9.6 *Mehron's Celebré HD Pro Foundation.*

FIGURE 9.5 *Ben Nye Media Pro HD Foundation Palette.*

broadcast quality, and the individual screen all contribute variations to the look of the face. With television, the way information is sent from the studio and received from the cable company, or satellite, and sent into homes is programmed by a manufacturer. The size of the viewing screen from a smart phone to an IMAX movie screen will require the makeup artists to adjust their design plan to meet the variations in scale and clarity. As a makeup artist, knowing the medium that your work will be broadcasted through is the first step in knowing how to tackle any makeup design. Even technical variations like greenscreens and small banner advertisements online will affect the choices you make. Professional makeup artists through training and experience understand how the camera captures the image of an actor's face, how lighting influences surface texture and color, and choose products that achieve the most natural look.

Skin care and preparation are more important than ever in film and television, and careful choices in facial cleansers, moisturizers, and exfoliants combine to create a skin surface that with minimal cosmetic application will create an effect that the camera reads as completely natural. The cosmetic industry has responded to the technological advancements in HD cameras, HD projectors, and HD monitors (including televisions and other visual recording devices) by developing complete lines of HD products, including primers, foundations, micro setting and finishing powders, eyeshadows, cheek and lip colors. It is vital now, more than ever, for performing artists to properly care for and maintain smooth, healthy skin. This begins with the performer having a personal understanding of his/her skin type and condition. Is the skin mostly oily or mostly dry? Or a combination of both? Is the skin sensitive to new products, prone to acne breakouts, uneven skin tone, sun damage, dark circles, large pores, ingrown hairs, or rough texture? It is always a good idea to seek professional assistance from a licensed aesthetician or dermatologist before purchasing products that may not be correct for a performer's skin type and condition.

Working in film and television is a collaboration just as it is in the theater. For the best results, lines of communication must be kept open with all of your artistic colleagues. Building relationships with the producers, directors, AD (Assistant Director), the DP (Director of Photography/Cinematographer), production designers, and lighting director (to be more accurate, the "gaffer") is, what most working makeup artists will tell you, one of the most important things you can do to develop a long and successful career. Lighting will be crucial to the makeup, as well as how it is being filmed with the camera. Learning the difference between wide, medium, and close-up shots, as well as listening in on what types of lenses the DP will be using are also good things to learn and listen for while on set. In production meetings, discuss any potential needs with these team members. Look as closely at the performer's face as the camera will allow. Once a realistic look is achieved, good makeup artists place themselves in front of a monitor, watching carefully for touch-ups and for continuity. "Last looks," which is something called out by a member of the AD team, is your final chance to go in for last-minute touch-ups before shooting. Generally, you will be checking that your makeup is matching *continuity*, and that the actors aren't shiny, sweaty, their lipstick is on, no liner runs, etc. There are times when you will need to look at your actor between every shot. A few examples of these times are: when the location or set is in hot weather conditions or locations making your actors sweaty; during kissing and make-out scenes for lipstick touch-ups; or when the actor has been tearing up in the dramatic shot and you need to run in with tissues and reset the makeup to look like it did at the top of the crying scene.

FIGURE 9.7 *Skin care products (left to right). Neutrogena Face Scrub for men, Kiehl's Original Formula Eye Cream, Kiehl's Exfoliating Cleanser, Kiehl's Facial Fuel Eye De-Puffer, Kiehl's Blue Astringent, Rosewater Face Cream by Lovett Sundires, Kiehl's Midnight Recovery Concentrate, Kiehl's Facial Fuel Energizing Moisture Treatment for Men, Kiehl's Deep Pour Daily Cleanser, Keihl's Super Multi-Corrective Cream.*

Continuity in makeup is defined as the maintenance and consistency of all visual details. For the makeup artist, it is simply being aware of every detail and reproducing those details the exact same way each day. The makeup artist is expected to keep a detailed written and visual account of the makeup design, products, and application techniques used on each performer to maintain continuity on set. Continuity involves taking pictures to document every aspect of your makeup, and then organizing it by script day, scene number, episode, and any other pertinent information that will make it easier to use when asked to recreate the specified look in the future.

For principal actors, make sure to take close-up pictures of their full face, front and sides. One can also take pictures of eyelids, tattoo alterations, nail applications, or body makeup coverage. Be sure that the lighting in your pictures is even, so you can actually see the makeups that you will be replicating. If sharing your continuity books with the hair department, then be sure to also get photographs of all the principal actors' hairlines. Continuity does not just involve principal actors, photographs also need to be taken of background artists and actors. When there are a lot of background extras for the day, collaging pictures before printing is helpful and cost-effective. Pictures from the monitors of the entire scenes are also essential for proper continuity. They help you fill in the gaps of your continuity if you accidentally miss something or your photographs of something specific are not very helpful. These records should be detailed to the point where another artist could look at them and replicate the makeup from your notes.

FIGURE 9.8 *SyncOnSet—a digital continuity and collaboration tool that helps manage script breakdown, continuity photos, inventory, approvals, and meeting and repair notes.*

Continuity pictures are often taken with your phone, tablet, or camera with wireless capabilities, and then printed out on photo printers. Most professional artists have photo printers on their trailers and print out the continuity photos almost daily. Some artists still use Polaroids, while others use digital applications, like SyncOnSet, to organize their photos into appropriate categories.

For hair and makeup artists much of the time it's beneficial to have hard copies of the main establishing images. Traditionally, the labeled continuity pictures are organized in thick binders and can be separated out in a number of ways—by episodes, principal and background actors, establishing shots for episodes or scenes, or whatever works best for the particular production. At the end of the shoot, all of the finished continuity binders are returned to the production office and can be used later for possible re-shoots, additional principal photography needs, and sequel and additional season references.

It is important for makeup artists, like professionals in other fields, to remain current with industry standards and innovations. Many makeup schools, unions, professional organizations, trade shows, and makeup suppliers offer seminars in the techniques for working professionals, students, and those just starting out, with the latest technology, techniques, and career development strategies (for example, IMATS [the International Make-up Artist Trade Show], offers to the amateur and professional hundreds of vendors, and access to workshops and demonstrations on contemporary practice).

Weather can often have a bigger effect on the makeup than lighting. Heat and humidity, dryness, differing

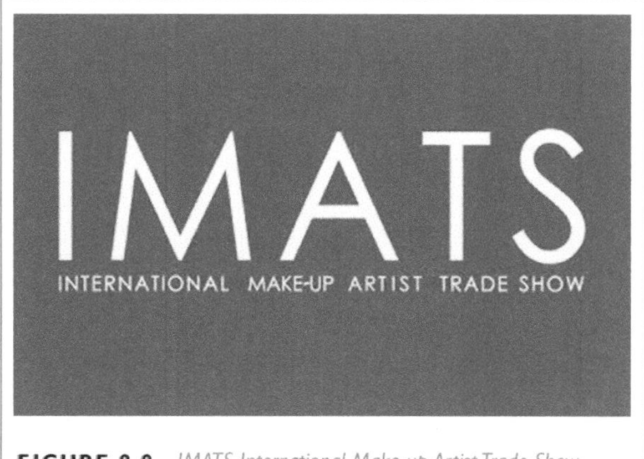

FIGURE 9.9 *IMATS International Make-up Artist Trade Show.*

temperatures, skin adjusting to changing climates and altitudes, and sun are just some of the aspects that keep a makeup artist's job challenging. Heat causes sweating and shininess to pop up on an actor's skin in a moment's notice. Heat also causes eye makeups to run and foundations to slip. Using heavier primers can help combat this, but knowing when it's a good time to use a blotter versus a powder is also good. If you are shooting outside in the sun with no shade, you will want to switch your primer out for a strong matte face primer with SPF (and a separate one for the lips).

You will also want to make sure that you are covering any exposed skin with a strong sunscreen. Test the sunscreens before you use them on set; sometimes they can leave a whitish residue when the actors start sweating. Tanning and sunburns can really mess up continuity in between shooting days. Background artists and extras also need adequate amounts of sunscreen. This falls under the makeup budget to have that supply on hand. Also, when shooting in the sun, be sure that the actors have umbrellas over them when not shooting and remember to reapply sunscreen throughout the day. (Side note: In extreme weather, you may need specialized set bags that are actually more like coolers, so the makeups won't melt in the heat.)

In dry weather, adequate amounts of moisturizer applied to the skin and lips is a necessity. Dry skin is very difficult to counteract, so staying on top of the flakiness is key. If flaking does start to occur, Eucerin, Homeoplasmine, and Aquaphor© are good products to use, as well as a light exfoliator, every so often.

When shooting in locations that differ greatly from the actor's normal environment (see Figure 9.10), their skin may break out or become unstable due to the change. In this situation, a professional artist needs to be prepared to deal with and combat these changes. Have things on hand like zinc to help

FIGURE 9.10 *Makeup artist Stephan Tessier on location for the Decouverte 2017 program Occupation Du Territoire, produced by the SRC (Saskatchewan Research Council).*

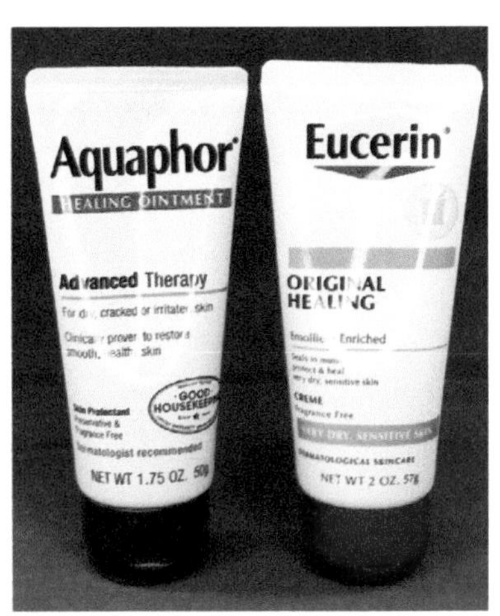

FIGURE 9.11 *Healing ointments: Aquaphor and Eucerin.*

shrink blemishes, homeoplasmine for dry spots, moisturizers, and oil absorbers. Also, suggest any additional skin care requirements to the actor, so they can help remedy any problems while at home.

CHOOSING THE PRODUCTS

As an actor, be careful not to use too many retinol, AHBA (Alpha Beta Hydroxy Acid), or exfoliating products in your regimen. These products interact with the makeups and sometimes cause rolling up of the foundations and concealers, peeling of the skin, and chemical interactions with primers and sunscreens. Wait at least 48 hours after you have exfoliated before arriving at the makeup trailer. This will give your skin a chance to heal, and any redness fade.

Primers

Makeup primer is a base for foundation or face makeup that allows it to go on smoother and last longer. Primers are manufactured in a variety of formulas: oil-free, moisturizing, mattifying, SPF, tinted, and color-correcting. They are an important tool for any makeup artists working in HD mediums. Makeup artists use this product after moisturizing the skin and before applying the foundation. Moisturizer should always be allowed to absorb into the skin before any other product application. The skin should feel soft and dry. If it feels at all

FIGURE 9.12 *Primers (left to right). Make Up For Ever Mattifying Primer, Urban Decay Complexion Primer, Becca Illuminating Primer, MICA Bella Primer, Laura Mercier Tinted Moisturizer, Crown HD Under-Eye Primer, Urban Decay Eyeshadow Primer.*

greasy, then you are either using too much moisturizer or the moisturizer is the wrong formulation for your skin type. You do not want your foundation to slip, move, or become shiny due to improper use of the moisturizer. Apply the primer to the center of your face and use gentle, circular motions to blend it outward. The motion should be similar to the one you use when applying your moisturizer. Work the product evenly into your skin so you get smooth, even coverage. Make sure you blend it up to your hairline and over your neck as well.

Foundation

Since it is sometimes difficult to dictate exactly how the makeup will read on screen, a professional makeup artist should make educated decisions on what types of makeups they utilize in their work on different productions. HD technology can enhance the properties found in varying types of foundations. Pressed powder, cream, and liquid formulas are all available and useful for the desired effect. A natural, no-makeup look on film may require the lightest touch when choosing and applying a foundation. In this case a pressed powder foundation, that can often appear dry and a little heavy, might not be the best choice. The natural look might be best accomplished by using a liquid or cream HD formula. A natural look may only require a light application of moisturizer, tinted moisturizer, or a combination of moisturizer and a tinted primer. Here are some product combinations that might be used to create a natural look:

- Clear or tinted moisturizer and a light setting powder
- Moisturizer, HD primer, and a light HD setting powder
- Moisturizer, HD face and eye primer, HD cream or liquid foundation, HD setting powder
- Moisturizer, HD face and eye primer, color corrector, HD cream or liquid foundation, HD setting powder, HD finishing powder
- Moisturizer, HD face and eye primer, color corrector, concealer, HD cream or liquid foundation, HD setting powder, HD finishing powder

No matter which combination works, always avoid ingredients that alter the natural look of the skin unless it's called for in the character's makeup design. Use a foundation with a texture appropriate to the period and needs of the production, such as matte, dewy, powdery, and airbrushed. In locations with harsh weather conditions a "color stay" foundation with a high SPF might work the best, or if you are doing a film based in the 1990s you may want to try a more dry matte-looking foundation to create a more period look.

Once you are ready to apply the foundation, try mixing two to three different shades together in order to better mimic the natural colorations of a particular skin tone. Sculpt the face as you would with any corrective makeup using foundation brushes, non-latex makeup sponges, or Beauty Blenders, making sure that your *edges* are completely blended and that there are no signs of heavy contour. Edges do not necessarily refer only to the edges of the face, but to the edges of each product and color application. For example, the edges of each blush and contour color application to the cheek must be completely

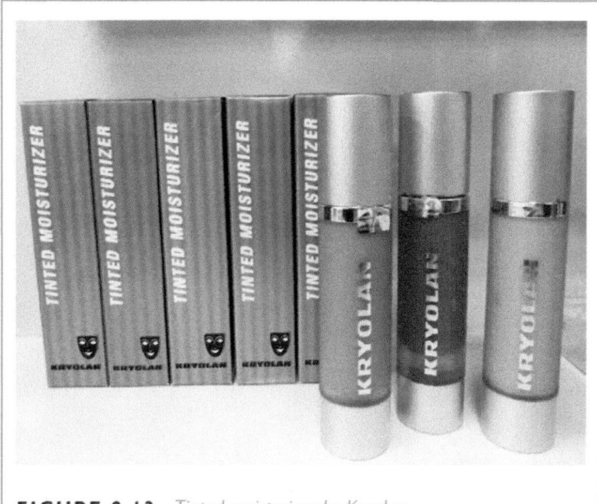

FIGURE 9.13 *Tinted moisturizer by Kryolan.*

blended or buffed into the surrounding foundation. There are many specially formulated HD foundations that work well. A combination of sponge, brush, and airbrush can be effective. Most importantly, you should use whatever you can to create the most natural look.

NATURAL MAKEUP FOR THE FEMALE PERFORMER

Cream foundations should be applied with foundation brushes, fine polyurethane foam sponges, or Beauty Blenders. Pick up a small amount of color from the container, placing it on your makeup palette if you are using a single foundation on multiple actors, and apply it as thinly as possible, giving the skin as little coverage as needed. Building up a little more coverage around the nostrils or any areas of discoloration with a brush is fine as well. After covering a small area of the face, check the color for a correct match. Color must always be matched on the face, specifically the neckline, not from the container or on the back of the hand. The base should be blended carefully at the hairline, leaving no traces of makeup color on the hair, eyebrows, or lashes. Color should be blended to the lash line on both the upper and lower lids and to just under the jawline where it meets the neck. The area under the jawline is a good blending-off point for two reasons: (1) it is high enough to avoid rubbing off on the wardrobe; and (2) it is usually in the shadows from overhead lighting or daylight. Continue the foundation on the neck back toward the hairline, and if the ears are slightly redder than the face, then also onto the top surfaces of the ears. Remember that a subtle shift in color to the naked eye may become far more noticeable to the digital camera.

The specially formulated airbrush foundations should be applied in even light layers until the desired coverage is achieved. These foundations can stand up to moisture and resist being rubbed off. They can be applied over other makeup and used to blend and/or add a fine, natural texture. Airbrush foundations are also a great option for quickly covering tattoos.

FIGURE 9.14 *Ben Nye Lux Loose Powders.*

Powder

There are a lot of options when choosing which HD powder is right for your project. There are powder foundations, setting powders, finishing powders, and blotting powders. All HD powders are manufactured as pressed powder and loose powder. They can be pigmented, translucent, or transparent. They come in matte, semi-matte, and shimmer finishes. Pressed powders tend to be slightly more dense than loose powders due to the emollients used to hold the particles together during the pressing process, and range from full-coverage foundations to extremely light, no-color blotting powders (used to mattify the skin and absorb oils). They are known as a "buildable" product, where successive light layers can be applied until the desired coverage is achieved. Pressed powders are choice items to use on film sets. They do not blow away due to wind, air conditioning, or breathing, make less of a mess on wardrobe, and are smaller and more compact to fit better in the actor's set bag.

It is also much easier to control the amount of powder that is used on an actor when it is in the pressed form. Since some that are highly pigmented are buildable, it is important to alternate using light setting powders and blotters when trying to control shine on an actor's face. Loose powders tend to be lighter in feel, and take a very light application to create a natural look. They are much more difficult to use on set due to their light and loose nature, and it is generally recommended to keep their usage to the trailer.

Technically, all cosmetic powders have an ingredient list that includes talc and/or silica.* Both talc and silica are used in cosmetics for the following reasons:

- They absorb oil and sweat, so your makeup lasts longer and helps your makeup adhere to your face better.
- They thicken the consistency of a cream or lotion.
- They help foundations spread onto your skin more easily.
- They improve even distribution of pigments in cosmetics, preventing them from settling in makeup.
- They are used as fillers, meaning they fill in uneven areas of the skin (pores) to create a smoother surface.

- Talc has a slight texture and tends to make a product more opaque.
- Silica has an extremely smooth texture and helps products with transparency.

Powder foundations in loose form (i.e. Bare Minerals) or pressed form (i.e. MAC Studio Fix Powder, Laura Mercier Smooth Finish Foundation) are applied over moisturizer, will add coverage, smooth out skin tone, and create a soft matte finish. They are generally not recommended for mature or acne-prone skin and should not be used in place of setting powders over cream or liquid foundations. *Setting powders*, whether pressed or loose, are formulated to successfully set cream and liquid foundations and concealers so they will not move, crease, or appear oily throughout a day of shooting. Touch-ups on the set should be only on those areas that are shiny. Powders should be used sparingly throughout a day of shooting to avoid creating a "cakey" makeup look on set. Remember less is more with HD technology. While it is recommended to use a no-color powder for natural looks, pigmented powders might be useful for some skin tones and effects. For example, the Ben Nye Luxury Powder in the color Banana has become popular with some celebrities and is most effective on medium to dark olive skin tones. When using pigmented powders, choose a color one to two shades lighter than the actor's skin tone, since some pigmented powders darken slightly when they contact the cream foundation.

FIGURE 9.15 *Make Up For Ever Pressed Finishing Powder.*

HD finishing powders are the most recent cosmetic product line specifically intended for use with HD technologies. They are formulated to be applied over setting powders. They are not intended to be used as a setting powder since they do not contain the proper ingredients. They are often made from pure silica that creates an ultra-smooth, natural skin surface under film, studio, and even theatrical lighting. Finishing powders are not intended for use for all occasions. Silica particles tend to reflect light back to the camera under direct flash photograph (called "flashback"). This reflection causes the appearance of a white powdery color on the surface of the skin (in the photograph) that is not apparent under other lighting environments. It is the responsibility of the makeup artist to know the conditions under which their client/actor will be viewed/filmed/photographed and to plan accordingly.

Remember, one makeup style is not always functional for all occasions. For those occasions where flash photography is used, it is a better strategy to design the makeup using products that contain talc rather than silica. Silica, or silicon dioxide, is part of a family of oxides used as ingredients in cosmetics and many other products. They function as thickeners, lubricants, and

FIGURE 9.16 *MAC Pressed Blot Powder.*

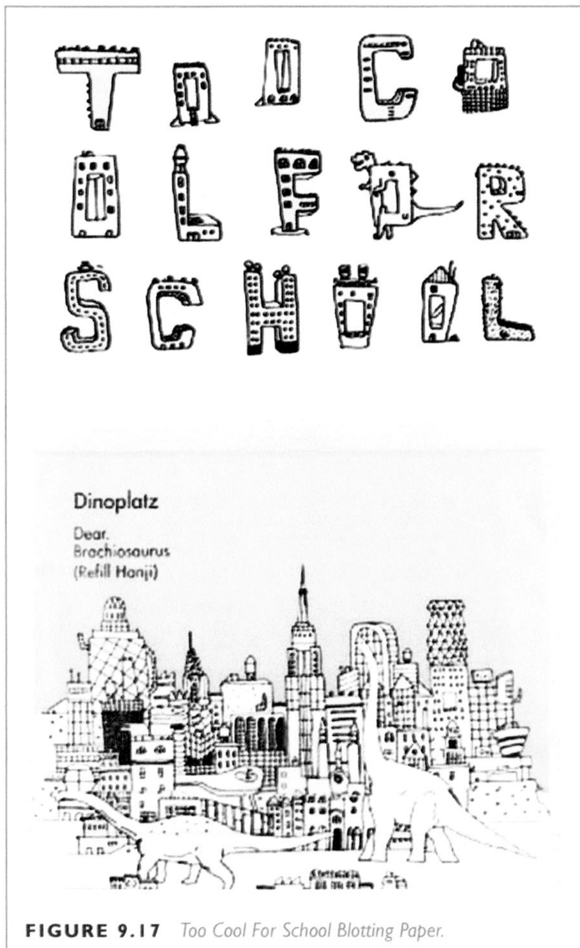

FIGURE 9.17 *Too Cool For School Blotting Paper.*

colorants. Iron oxide, for example, is used as a colorant (yellow, orange, red, rust, brown, gray, and black) and titanium dioxide, a pure white powder, is also a colorant and opacifier. They all have an inherent reflective property that must be considered when planning a project.

Blotting powders are extremely sheer powders used specifically for spot absorption of oily or shiny spots on the face. When used lightly this lightweight pressed powder is completely transparent and will not become "cakey" on the skin (examples are MAC Blot Powder, Too Cool for School Blotting Paper).

The following are suggestions for the successful use of powders:

- Apply powder foundations over moisturizer and primer with a large round powder brush or Kabuki Face Brush. Avoid using a powder puff or sponge. Powder puffs hold too much product and will cause a "cakey" appearance. Sponges often cause streaking.
- Do not use powder foundation as a setting powder. Powder foundations are highly pigmented on their own and will cause a "cakey" unnatural appearance if used over another foundation.
- Do not use setting powder as a foundation. It will not provide the same coverage as a foundation powder.
- Do not use finishing powder as a setting powder. It will not "set" your foundation. Your foundation will still move and crease throughout the day.
- Use finishing powders over setting powders sparingly. This class of powders is transparent to the eye, so uneven buildup will not be noticeable until, of course, a photographer snaps a flash photograph of you or your client. You will clearly notice the white "flashback" in the photograph. To avoid this unwanted phenomenon, change the finishing powder to a talc-based rather than silica-based powder.
- Choose a setting powder that flatters the skin tone and foundation. This might be a no-color powder or a pigmented translucent powder. Pigmented powder should be one or two shades lighter than the foundation as some powders darken slightly when applied to cream or liquid foundations.
- Do not use powder foundations on mature or acne-prone skin. Use cream or liquid foundations instead. These products go on smoother and add a slightly dewy youthful appearance to the skin. They also smooth out wrinkles and other skin texture.
- The feel of the powder should be smooth, almost liquid, with no grit. The goal is a face that is neither too shiny nor too matte, but has a natural, fresh look.

*The authors/publisher of this book suggest that readers do their own research as to the safety of talc and silica in cosmetics.

Concealer

Concealers are most often used to cover dark circles under the eyes and to eliminate redness and other skin discolorations on the face. They are available in a variety of formulas, ranging from sheer neutralizers to opaque camouflage systems. There are many choices for concealer products available at the drug store and makeup counter, as well as most of the professional makeup lines. Choose one that is slightly lighter (one to two shades) than the foundation and is slightly warm (golden) in color. It may be necessary on some performers (actors, dancers, broadcasters) to first correct any skin discoloration before applying foundation and concealer. Discolorations such as rosacea, (a reddening of the face at the cheek area), hyperpigmentation, sunburn, darkness around the eye, acne, sallow complexions, and heavy beard shadow may need to be

FIGURE 9.18 *Concealer (left to right). Derma Color by Kryolan, Dermablend Leg and Body Makeup, Kat Von D Lock It Full Coverage Matte, MAC Full Coverage Foundations, Ben Nye Tattoo Cover.*

color-corrected using a "neutralizer" before the makeup application begins. *Neutralizers* are a translucent crème-based product used to diminish the appearance of facial discoloration by employing color theory; specifically the use of complementary colors. Complementary colors, when mixed together, produce a neutral tone, a shade of brown. By applying the complementary color over a skin discoloration, that discoloration should be neutralized. It is most often applied under the foundation. A foundation can also be adjusted by mixing it with a complementary color from an adjustor palette for an overall shift in the tint, or tone. The following list is a helpful guide for using color correctors or neutralizers:

- a subtle yellow, soft orange, or peach tint to counter the common purple undertones found around the eye;
- a subtle green tint to counter red discolorations;
- a subtle orange tint to balance the blue areas caused by large veining, heavy beard shadow, and tattoos;
- a subtle lavender tint to balance yellow or sallow skin color;
- avoid using white and very light-colored concealers. They can appear chalky on the skin and create a raccoon effect around the eyes.

For under-eye concealer to be effective, proper placement is of utmost importance. Apply the concealer with a concealer brush under the eye from just outside the edge of the socket up to the lower lashes and on the inner most corner of the eye (often the darkest area). It should be used mainly on the discolored area and blended carefully toward the natural highlights. If the concealer is used outside the discolored area it may increase the effect of the "bags" and cause other areas to appear puffy. Smooth and blend with a light patting motion with your concealer brush or slightly dampened Beauty Blender (latex sponges easily absorb cream foundation and should be avoided) for an even application and greater coverage. Do not over blend. Lightly powder the area with a translucent setting powder or with one that is slightly lighter than the concealer.

Should concealer be applied before or after the foundation? Many makeup artists believe that a practical method for determining the amount of concealer to be used is dependent upon the amount of visible discoloration appearing through the foundation after it has been applied to the face. Too much concealer applied too soon may indeed be just as unattractive or cause just as much focus as the original discoloration. After all, the purpose of the concealer/foundation combination is to leave the skin looking smooth and natural. Therefore, apply the concealer around the eyes after the foundation, apply the concealer around the rest of the face (where needed) after putting on the foundation, then set with setting powder after all of the concealer has been applied to ensure it stays in place.

Products used in Figure 9.19

Skin prep—Burt's Bees natural acne gel face cleanser
Cetaphil lotion
Concealer—Maybelline cover stick concealer
Foundation—Maybelline *Fit Me* matte foundation (Natural Ivory)
Setting Powder—Covergirl *Tru Blend* minerals powder (Meadow)
Covergirl *Tru Blend* powder makeup, for contour (Soft Honey)
Blush—e.l.f. Powder Blush Palette (Light)
Eyeshadow—Urban Decay Eyeshadow Primer, Maybelline, the *Nudes* collection all over lid
Beauty Control eyeshadow palette (Sandstone)
Eyeshadow highlight—Sephora eyeshadow (Tahitian pearl)
Eyeliner—Maybelline EyeStudio Master Precise Liquid Liner (Black)
Mascara—Maybelline, Volum' Express *The Falsies* Waterproof Mascara.

Process (Figure 9.19)

1. Wash face.
2. Apply Cetaphil lotion and lip balm.
3. Concealer on the eyelids, blend.
4. Eyeshadow primer on lids.

FIGURE 9.19 *Megan Brantley—TV News Anchor, CBS affiliate, WHNT News, Huntsville, AL.*

5. Nude eyeshadow on lid, mocha brown in crease, and black/brown shadow at the corner of the eye and under lower lashes as a liner.
6. Blend all three eyeshadow colors, and end with adding Tahitian pearl white at the inner corner.
7. Fill in the eyebrows with eyebrow pencil; add Tahitian pearl white under the arch of the brow.
8. Apply liquid eyeliner on the top lid at the lash line.
9. Black mascara on the upper and lower lashes.

(Tip: Apply eye makeup before starting the face makeup to avoid eyeshadow particles falling into face makeup.)

10. Concealer under the eyes, blend.
11. Light coverage foundation on the face.
12. Use concealer stick as a highlight on the tip of the nose, create a fan on the forehead, bow of the lips, and the chin.
13. Use a darker cream foundation as the contour on the jawline, outer edges of the nose, hairline, and under the cheekbones.
14. Blend with a Beauty Blender type makeup sponge.
15. Mix three colors of e.l.f. Blush Palette and add that to the apples of the cheeks.
16. Use Tahitian pearl white from the temples onto the cheeks.
17. Finish with a lip liner, lipstick, and gloss.

Cheek Color and Blush

Cheek color adds a natural healthy glow to the skin. Whether you choose an airbrush liquid, cream, gel, or pressed dry formula, finding the proper color can be confusing. One method for developing an appropriate color is to mix together equal amounts of foundation and a primary red. This is an excellent reference point from which to choose cheek colors. Be sure to integrate cream and gel formulas into the foundation *before* the setting powder is applied. Choose colors that complement the lips and provide a matte finish. The colors should not be too bright, dark, shimmery, or frosted.

Avoid using any intense levels of red, magenta, and pink, unless the character's design calls for something more unnatural.

Cheek color is applied on the cheekbone with a sponge, or a foundation brush (cream and gels), a blush brush (cake and powders), or the airbrush and should not be used to attempt contouring or shadowing under the cheekbone. It should appear and act as a soft, natural glowing highlight. Begin applying the cheek color at the middle apple of the cheek and blend toward the hairline (avoid tinting the hair, especially blonde hair). Blend carefully to avoid creating a horizontal line. All traces of color should blend away approximately one inch from the hairline. Unless a fuller "apple cheek" effect is desired, keep cheek color off the front plane of the face. Contour colors, placed slightly below the cheekbone, should start near the hairline and end before the outside of the apples of the cheeks.

Eyeshadows

Dry pressed eyeshadows in three harmonious shades (light for highlighting under the brow, medium for the upper lid, and dark along the lash line) should be used to naturally accent the eye. These shades should blend together invisibly. While cream formulas are easily applied and blend smoothly, they tend to migrate into the creases of the eye, necessitating regular attention to maintain a consistent appearance throughout

FIGURE 9.20 *Makeup artist Stephan Tessier on the television news set at the Canadian Broadcast Corporation (CBC).*

filming. Eyeshadow primers lightly applied to the lid with a concealer brush from the lash line to just above the crease will keep shadows from migrating to the creases, eyeliners staying on much longer, and allow for longer-lasting true color.

The area of the eyelid between the lashes and the crease should be highlighted with a color two to three shades lighter than the foundation. This can be accomplished with a cream foundation, or concealer, set with a high-value matte or semi-matte, no-color, or pigmented powder or eyeshadow. The highlight is strongest over the highest projection of the eyelid and should then be blended away from the center in all directions. The area of the brow bone directly under the arch of the brow should also be lightly highlighted. Using the same color, apply a small amount to the outer half of the brow, blending out and down toward the crease. Sometimes, you can also highlight with a slightly lighter shade of a concealer as well for a very natural look.

For a natural makeup application on light to medium skin tones use a brown, gray-brown, taupe, warm peachy-brown, or cocoa shadow. For darker skin tones use dark browns, brown blacks, rich eggplants, and dark pewters or bronzes. Apply the shadow with a pointed crease or a small fluffy shadow brush. Starting at the outer edge of the upper lash line, follow the crease to approximately two-thirds of the way toward the inner eye. The shadow can be applied into or slightly above the crease. Using a firm shadow brush, blend upward toward the brow. Blend the shadow from dark to light before reaching the highlighted area under the brow. The darkest shade is used as an eyeliner (see the following section on eyeliner).

Eyeshadow in a natural makeup should always have a matte or semi-matte finish. Avoid opalescent or pearlized colors. Remember that subtlety in application and blending is key to a successful film or television makeup. It should appear so subtle that one should wonder if there was any makeup at all.

Also note that "natural" makeup can be slightly varied for each production. For example, a "natural" look in a period Western film is most definitely going to be very different from a "natural" look in a modern comedy. Your script will generally dictate the production's needs, and bring up any questions about what directions you should go with the makeups in production meetings.

Eyeliner

The purpose of eyeliner in a natural makeup is to enhance and darken the lash root line, and therefore must be similar to or darker than the hair color. Four types of eyeliner should be considered: pencil, pressed powder, gel, and liquid. The *pencil* liner (choose a long-wearing formula) can be easily blended, creating a soft, natural eyelash line, but the waxy color is affected by body heat and can smudge during a long shooting schedule, so it is important to choose a long-wearing waterproof formula and utilize shadow primers. Using a dark *eyeshadow* along the lash line creates an even softer line than the pencil and is quite easy to control, but can come off quite quickly. Although *gel* and *liquid* liners require a bit more skill to apply, they have the advantage of drying and do not smudge as easily. Gel and liquid liners can be left with a hard edge or blended with a damp brush, a synthetic-haired shadow brush, or a cotton-tipped applicator, and need to be first placed on a makeup palette in order to avoid cross-contamination in between actors. They are very versatile, normally waterproof, and can even be used to create subtle, natural-looking smoky looks.

For performers with blonde hair and light skin, a blonde, light brown, sable, or slate-colored liner should be used. Performers with red hair can choose light brown or auburn liner colors based on skin and hair coloration. Light brown hair with light skin tones should use a medium brown, cocoa, or charcoal eyeliner. Those with medium to dark brown to black hair colors and medium to darker skin tones should use a dark brown, mahogany, charcoal, and/or black eyeliner.

The width of the eyeliner at the inner edge of the upper lash line (towards the nose) should be quite thin and then widen as it moves away from the center of the face, ending at the last lash. If liner is needed on the lower lashes, use one a shade or two lighter on the bottom to avoid closing up the eye from a distance. Great care should be given to making these lines thin and blended. The goal is to frame and enhance the eye.

Deciding on which type of liner will be most useful for your situation is based on the final look you are creating. You will also have to make a judgment as to whether you choose a drug store or luxury brand in a waterproof formula. It is important to choose one that is safe and long-wearing especially for use on the waterline (the edge of the lower lid above the lash line).

Pencil Eyeliner

Pencil eyeliners are the most standard type of eyeliner and come in different sizes and ranges of colors. They are easy to use, easy to fix mistakes, and great for the novice makeup artists. Here are the pros and cons to using a pencil:

Pros	*Cons*
Can provide a natural look	Unable to provide a shiny, saturated look
Can be easily smudged for a smoky look	Not as good for fine, clean line
Works best on waterlines	Needs regular sharpening
Easy to apply (do not need a steady hand)	
Easy to fix mistakes	
Dries quickly	

Liquid eyeliner provides a precise line definition along the lash line, usually dispensed with a fine-tipped round brush or a felt-tipped applicator:

Pros	*Cons*
Can create precise clean-edged lines	Not safe for waterlines
Can easily achieve a dark saturation	Sometimes hard to put on evenly
Good for creating a cat-eye and winged look	Difficult to create a natural look
Can achieve a shiny, wet look	Must use with a palette for good hygiene
Is often waterproof	
No sharpening required	

Gel Eyeliner

Gel eyeliner is a highly pigmented gel medium that goes on wet and dries to a rich matte finish. It is a long-lasting versatile eyeliner and can be applied with a fine-point round brush, a small, fine, domed brush or a small, thin, flat angled brush. Any number of useful looks can be created, from a thin lash line enhancer to a soft, smoky look to a dramatic, winged effect. It is the most versatile type of eyeliner. It is typically sold in a small round container.

Pros	*Cons*
Creamy consistency allows for a smooth application	Matte finish
Good for a natural lash line enhancer	Needs practice for a successful effect
Good for a soft smoky-eye look	Must use with a palette for good hygiene
Good for cat eye	Some brands set too quickly
Good for dramatic wing effect	
No sharpening required	

Eyebrows

The eyebrow should look well-groomed and defined and be of a color the same or slightly darker than the hair. A well-groomed eyebrow may actually allow you to use less makeup. The shape should follow the natural brow line and can be tweezed, waxed, threaded, trimmed, or shaved to remove excess hairs. Be aware that small bumps can appear after waxing caused by ingrown hairs that can be painful, unsightly, and are very difficult to naturally cover with makeup. They can be avoided by first cleaning the brow with a toner before the waxing process and then exfoliating the area regularly with a gentle cleansing scrub, as well as not waxing the brows within 24 hours of a schedule shooting day. (Applying a drop of Benzoin Peroxide to the area once a day for several days after waxing will also prevent this problem.) When tweezing, first pluck any hairs between the brows above the bridge of the nose, then carefully remove stray hairs from below the brow. The highest point of the arch should be created at approximately two-thirds of the distance along the brow from the inner edge (see Figures 9.19a and 9.24.15).

The thickness of the brow is not as important as its shape. The brow should be thickest near the center of the face, gradually become thinner at the arch, and then taper into a fine point. If the natural brow does not follow this direction, light strokes in the same direction of the hair growth with an appropriately colored pencil can be used to alter the shape. Picking up a small amount of pressed powder with a slightly dampened brush can also be used to fill in and shape the brow.

Adding color to the eyebrow will help to frame the face. It is important to add enough color to fill in the brow without creating a painted-on look. Brow color can be applied with a sharpened pencil or thin, flat angled brush. Products such as pressed eyeshadow, pencils, and brow wax are used in a color one shade lighter than the hair color (for example: for blonde or auburn hair use a blonde or taupe with a red undertone or a light auburn/blonde pencil). Should the brows look too dark or artificial after using a pencil, try applying dry eyeshadow or a pigmented brow wax with a small, flat brush angled at the tip. For thin and short brows, fill in the sparse areas using short hair-like strokes in the direction of the hair growth, then brush over the entire brow with a brow brush or clean mascara wand.

(Note: If you are too heavy-handed with a pencil, try rubbing the small angled brush over the pencil lead, then with the brush, apply color to the brow with the same short strokes.)

Some suggestions for adding color to eyebrow:

- Use a color one shade lighter than the hair color.
- Whether using a pencil or a brush always begin applying color ¼ inch from the front edge of the brow, also called the "medial edge," to avoid too heavy an application. Then lightly fill it in afterwards.
- If using a shadow, you can use a matte or semi-matte natural shade.
- If your actor is a heavy sweater, then you will probably want to go with a waxed-based pencil or brow pomade for longer wear.
- If your actor has sparse light brows or has very invisible blonde hairs, try using a very light auburn or taupe shadow and very, very lightly fill in the brows with strokes in the same direction as the hair growth would be.
- For performers with alopecia or lacking brows completely, there are ventilated brows available as well as stencils in different shapes that make it easier to create more natural-looking brows.
- For rogue hairs underneath the natural brow that you don't have time to shape or you encounter a client with unkempt brows, you can sometimes camouflage them with a makeup primer and a heavier coverage concealer and concealer brush.
- Attending to the brows goes for both men and women.

Mascara

Black or brown mascara should be used for nearly every makeup application when trying to achieve a natural look. Brown appears most natural, produces a gentle soft-looking lash, and can be used on those occasions when no makeup is required. Blonde lashes look best with a reddish-brown colored mascara for film work and black mascara for television (the intense lighting will wash out lighter colors). For those performers with extremely dark hair or for darker-skinned performers, black mascara is always preferred. Clear mascaras are also good for performers or children that do not need to add length to their lashes, but more of a glisten. Clear (non-pigmented) mascara is also good to separate individual lashes and enhance the lashes' natural color. It can also be used to control and shape brow hair as a clear brow gel.

While waterproof mascaras are not recommended for daily wear (they tend to dry out the lashes), their durability can be useful for television production. Holding the wand parallel to the floor, apply a lengthening formula mascara (thickening formulas tend to clump on the lashes) to the underside of the top lashes and to the upper side of the lower lashes. Apply two to three thin layers, letting the mascara dry between coats. Here are a few mascara tips:

1. Always curl eyelashes before applying mascara.
2. Avoid pointing the tip of the wand towards your eye.
3. Mascara on the lower lid may accentuate discoloration and puffiness, so a gentle touch over lashes just to add a hint of product is most of the time sufficient.
4. For a fresher, cleaner look apply mascara only to the upper lash.
5. Avoid bright-colored mascara.
6. Always use less mascara on the lower lashes.
7. For reasons of keeping good hygienic practices, each actor should have her own mascara, curlers, and wand.

Lip Color

The purpose of lip color in a natural makeup is to heighten the color of the lip, even out the skin tone, and add definition to the lip line. Without it, the camera may confuse the often soft or broken edges between the lip and the surrounding skin. HD will exaggerate any dry or flaky texture on the lips, so it is important to exfoliate and condition the lips as you would the face, before adding color. The color should be similar to the performer's natural color, which can then be toned and contoured with either brown or ivory. The upper lip, usually in a natural shadow, can be slightly darker in color while the lower lip is slightly lighter or brighter and often highlighted to create a fuller appearance. One method to accomplish a natural-looking lip is to first create a defined edge using a brush or pencil and then blend the color softly out onto the lip. This method does not require coloring in the entire lip area. Another method is to first cover the entire lip with a natural-colored lip pencil, then apply lip color with a brush. This method ensures longer-lasting coverage and assists the makeup artist when reshaping the lip is necessary. Once again, avoid using intense levels of red, magenta, and pink. Lip gloss can "move" and reflect too much light on camera and is not often used. The matte, or satin, look is the most natural. Things to remember:

FIGURE 9.21 *Makeup artist Stephan Tessier in the makeup room applying lip color while preparing French politician Marine Le Pen for a television interview. CBC Television (Canada).*

1. Find a lip color that is easy to apply.
2. Use a long-lasting lip color (sheer matte or semi-matte colors work well).
3. Regular and colored lip balms are great for male actors.
4. Use lip sunscreen for outdoor scenes.
5. Avoid high shine lipsticks and glosses.
6. Lip color is something that is normally in need of constant touch-ups, so be sure to always have the actors' lipsticks and chapsticks on set with you, preferably in their actors' bags.
7. Avoid using lipsticks that appear too dramatic and "makeup-y" for natural looks; the lips should look comfortable with the rest of the face, not stand out too much.

The following demonstration is an example of a makeup application for broadcast television (Figure 9.24).

1. Vanessa J. Lopez—Performer.
2. Apply Kiehl's Ultra Facial Moisturizer to the entire face. Allow to absorb into the skin for at least 15 minutes before applying primer of foundation.
3. Apply moisturizer to the lip.
4. Make Up Forever Mattifying Primer (for oily skin).

5., 6., & 7. Apply primer to the cheeks, forehead, and nose (can also use a triangular sponge).

8. Urban Decay Eyeshadow Primer.

9. & 10. Apply a small amount of eyeshadow primer with a small brush and blend into the skin.

11. Crown HD Effect Under-Eye Primer.
12. Squeeze a small "dot" onto the back of the hand.
13. Apply primer to the under-eye area and blend.
14. Brush eyebrows up and out with a clean mascara wand.
15. Use an eyebrow pencil, Anastasia Beverly Hills Perfect Brow Pencil: Dark Brown, to shape and lightly fill in the brows.
16. Concealer—Tarte Amazonian Clay Waterproof 12-hour: Tan.
17. Define the brow by applying concealer above and below with a small angled brow brush.
18. Blend concealer into the surrounding skin with a small egg-shaped sponge.

- Eyeshadows used for this makeup application are from the Two-Faced—Chocolate Bar Eyeshadow Palette.

19. & 20. Apply a high-value base color to the entire lid with a small, soft, domed eyeshadow brush: White Chocolate (color).
21. & 22. Apply medium-value shadows, one to the crease: Salted Caramel (color) the other to the lid: Semi Sweet (color).
23. & 24. Apply a lower value reddish-brown into the crease using a pointed blender: Cherry Cordial (color).
25. & 26. Apply a low value dark brown to the outer corner of the lid using a very small blender brush: Black Forest Truffle (color).
27. Carefully blend all of the edges of the eyeshadow colors with a clean soft blender brush.
28. Apply liquid eyeliner to the upper lash line—Kat Von D Tattoo Liner: Trooper (color). Create a short wing extension by first drawing a straight line at a slight upward angle from the end of the lash line. From the end of that line draw another straight line towards the center of the eyelid. This will create a small narrow triangle. To complete the eyeliner, fill in the triangle with liquid liner.
29. Completed eyeliner.
30. Apply "red" neutralizer to any red discolorations on the face (it will be green in color). (Note: The neutralizer must be applied only to the specific area that needs correction. Do not place it on the surrounding skin.)
31. Apply a "Purple-blue" neutralizer to any discoloration under the eyes (it will be a peach-orange color).
32. Gently blend the neutralizers using a small egg-shaped Beauty Blender sponge.
33. & 34. Apply foundation (Tarte Amazonian Clay Full-Coverage: Light Medium Honey).
35. Blend the foundation using a large egg-shaped sponge.
36. Apply concealer (Makeup For Ever Ultra HD Invisible Cover: R40-Apricot Beige) to the lower forehead, the bridge of the nose, the center of the upper lip, the center of the chin, and under each eye (as shown) and blend.
37. & 38. Lightly powder the entire face with Ben Nye Luxury Powder: Banana. Use an angled or domed blush brush.
39. Kat Van D Shade and Light Contour Palette: Shadow Play (this is a dry pressed powder palette).
40., 41., & 42. Apply contour color (Shadow Play) under the cheekbone, along the hairline, and along the jawline (as shown) using a large angled blush brush.
43. Narrow and straighten the nose by applying contour (Shadow Play) along the sides of the nasal ridge.
44. Apply cheek color along the cheekbone above the contour. Cheek color by MAC Sheertone Shimmer Blush: Plum Foolery. Use a large, domed blush brush.
45. Using a large soft powder brush, apply "Finishing" powder to the entire face. Finishing powder is a colorless powder used to give the surface of the face a cohesive finish.
46. Lightly apply a highlight above the blush. Amazonian Clay highlighter: Exposed Highlight by Tarte is applied with a fan brush.
47. Apply a small amount of shadow along the lower lash line. Shadow by Two-Faced Chocolate Bar Shadow Palette: Cherry Cordial. This shadow color should be applied from the outer edge of the lash to about three-quarters of the way toward the inner eye (see example). Use a small pointed round eyeshadow brush.
48. Use a tiny clean, domed eyeshadow blender to soften the lower lash line.
49. Curl the eyelashes.
50. & 51. Apply mascara to the upper and lower lashes. Mascara by Benefit: Black.

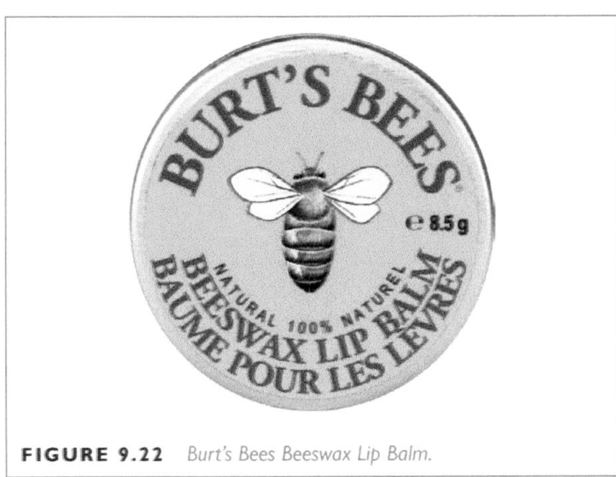

FIGURE 9.22 *Burt's Bees Beeswax Lip Balm.*

FIGURE 9.23 *Burt's Bees Tinted Lip Balm.*

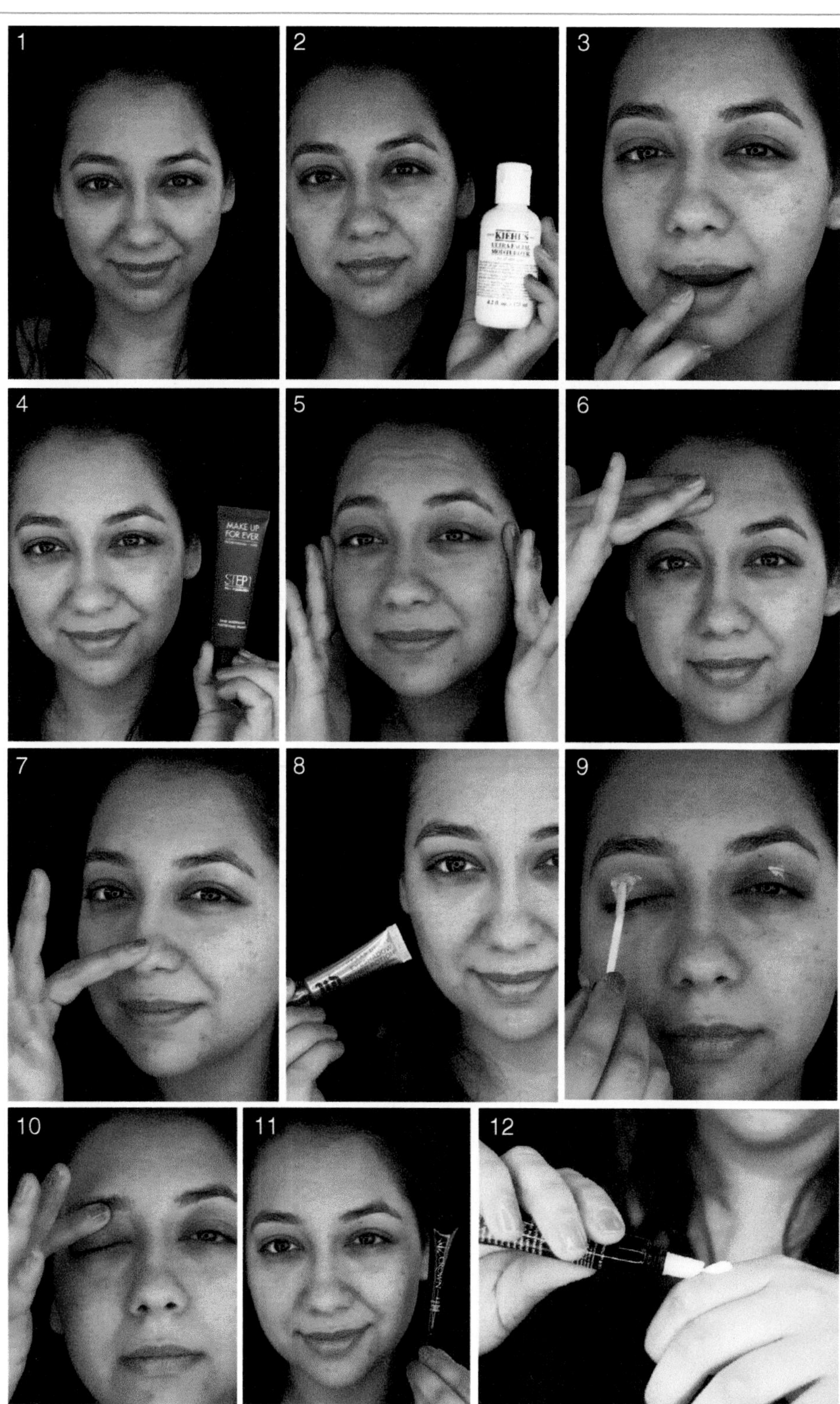

FIGURE 9.24 *Makeup application for broadcast television. Makeup artist and model, Vanessa J Lopez.*

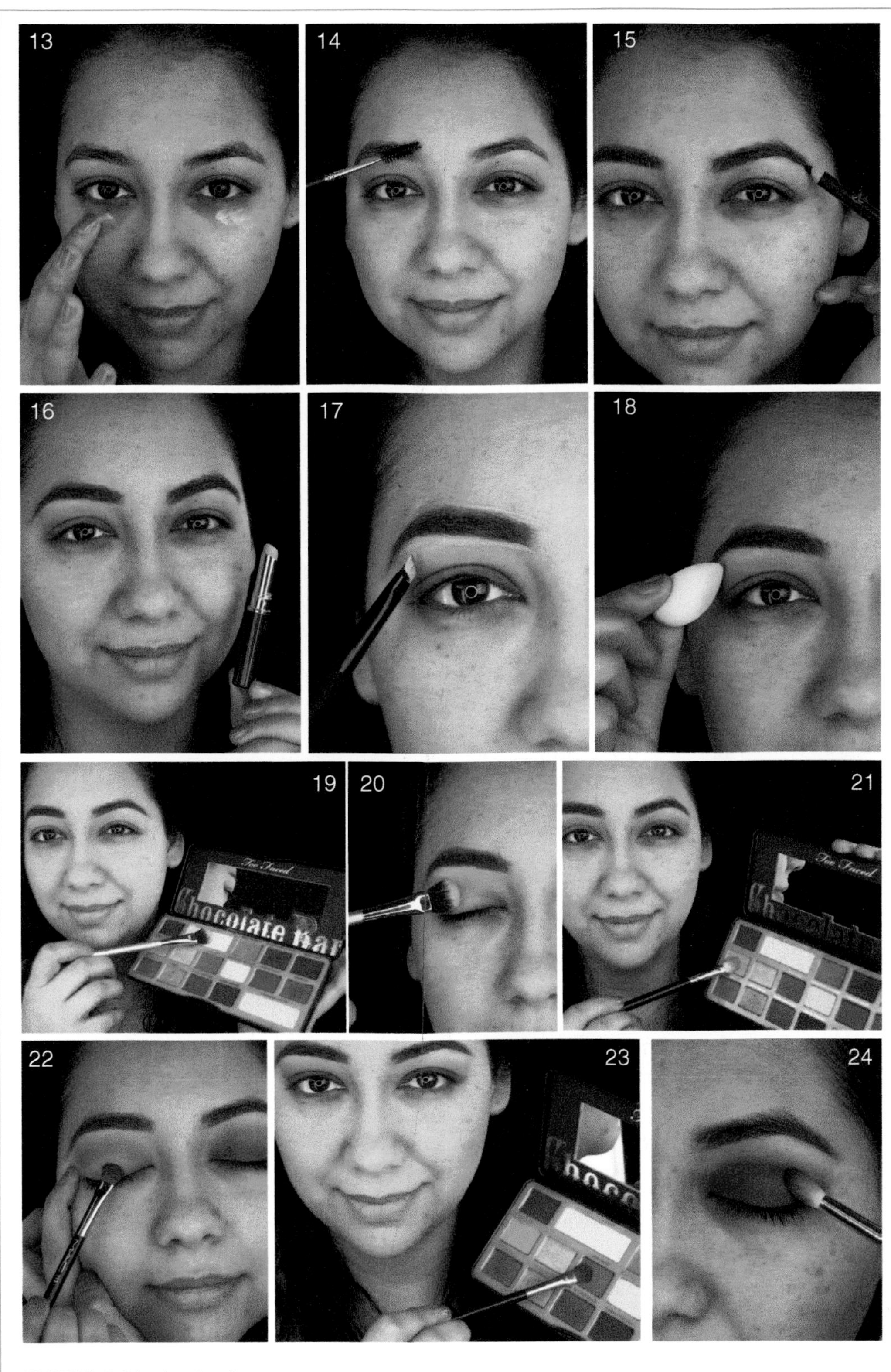

FIGURE 9.24 *(continued)*

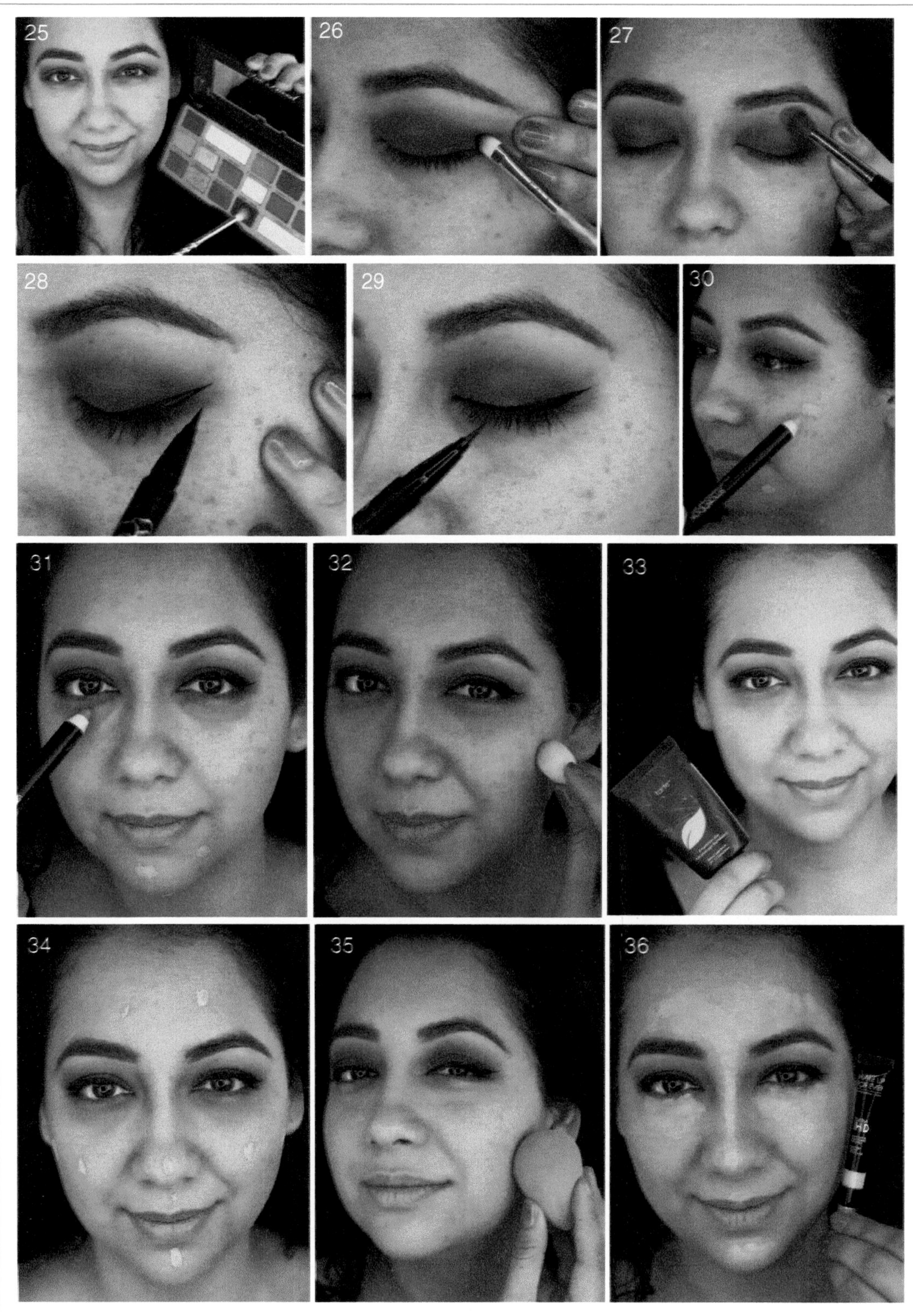

FIGURE 9.24 *(continued)*

FIGURE 9.24 *(continued)*

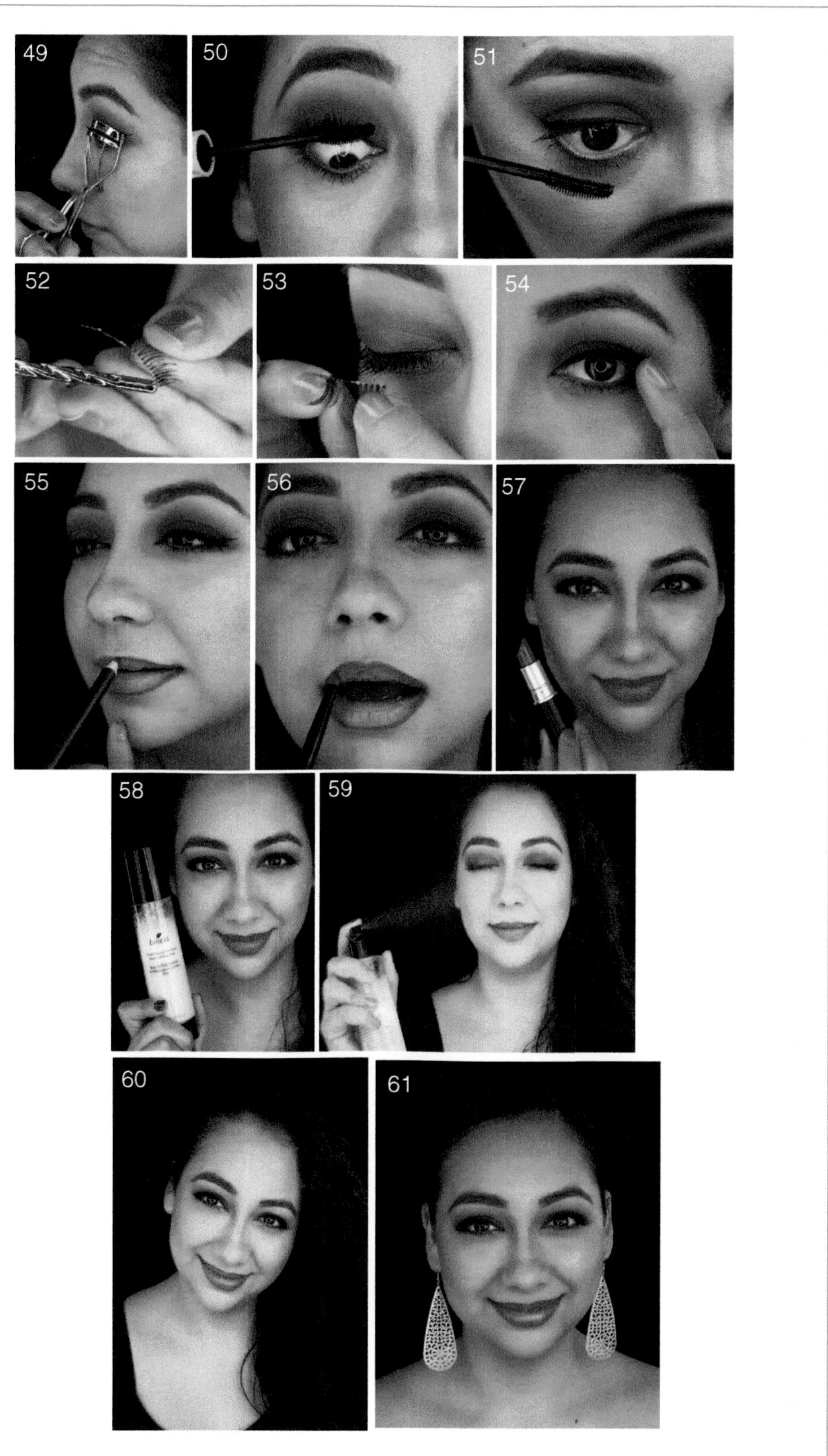

FIGURE 9.24 *(continued)*

52. Apply eyelash glue to the false lashes. Use the end of a brush or other applicator to transfer the glue to the lash. (Note: Avoid applying glue to false lashes directly from the container.)
53. Apply the lashes.
54. To avoid droopy lashes, press up on the end of the lash to help set the direction.
55. Define the edge of the lip line using a lip pencil. Lining the lips first with a pencil will keep the lipstick from migrating and will help it stay on longer. Lip liner pencil by MAC: Plum.
56. Blend the pencil line onto the lip using a small, domed lip brush.
57. Apply lip color. Lipstick by MAC: Twig.

58. & 59. Setting spray is used to help keep the makeup in place. Setting spray by Boscia: White Charcoal Mattifying Setting Spray. To apply—hold the spray bottle about 18 inches from the face. Depress the pump and create a light mist in the air. Bring the face to the mist, turning the head to the left and right. Repeat a couple of times. Spraying directly onto the face from too close a distance may cause an unnatural surface finish; either too wet, too shiny, blotchy water marks, or too plastic-looking.

60. Final look with hair down.
61. Final look with hair up and earrings.

MAKEUP FOR THE MALE PERFORMER

The approach to makeup for men working in film and television has changed dramatically in recent years. The way contemporary film stock captures the human face requires the performer to wear far less makeup than in the past. As mentioned previously, makeup will be seen more naturally on film than in any other medium and must be used sparingly or sometimes not at all. Most men on television—actors, reporters, news anchors, sports personalities, and politicians—use makeup to even out their skin tones and give themselves a healthier look on screen. Depending on the quality of the performer's skin, and the intensity of the lighting, more or less coverage will be needed on a personal basis. The amount of coverage will depend on what the camera picks up on the monitor. Particular attention must be paid to shaving, beard trimming, length of sideburns, nose and ear hair, and eyebrow maintenance (yes, even eyebrows must be shaped exactly the same each time an actor is in front of the camera) in an effort to properly maintain continuity from day-to-day, shot-to-shot or scene-to-scene. For men who are prone to developing ingrown hairs after shaving, products like Tend Skin are used by many makeup artists to quickly remedy this problem.

Foundation

Male actors, like their female counterparts, should also develop a skin and hair care regiment that includes cleansing, exfoliation, and moisturizing. It is more likely that healthy skin will look better on camera, foregoing the need for foundation. There are a number of products formulated specifically for men with names like Facial Fuel, Men Pure-Formance, and Skin Hydrator and Nourishing Beard Grooming Oil. Foundation, if needed, should be applied lightly over a cleanly shaven face. For most men, eliminating the beard shadow is not required, for the appearance of some shadow will help to maintain a natural masculine image. As beard stubble has become fashionable for some men in television and on film, applying foundation has become less and less necessary.

As a general rule, the foundation should match the skin tone (the face, neck, and ears) of the performer. Remember, the skin on the ears is quite thin and can often appear redder than the rest of the face. A careful observation of the entire face will maintain a balanced look. At all cost, avoid the man-in-makeup look. In summary:

1. The foundation, if needed, should match the skin tone.
2. Avoid eliminating the beard shadow and never try to apply foundation to stubble.
3. Remember to consider the ears in an effort to keep the entire face balanced.
4. Use foundation primer under foundations and concealers. If the skin is particularly dry use a clear or tinted moisturizer before the primer. Allow the moisturizer to settle into the skin (at least 10 minutes) before applying the primer and foundation.
5. Tinted moisturizers can be used on their own to create a more natural look.
6. For bald men and men with larger pores, it is recommended to use a heavy primer application and a light application of powder.
7. There are many cases in which foundations are not needed. In this case, you can use a tinted primer or moisturizer, or simply a sheer pressed powder.

Powder

When capturing an image on film, the foundation, if applied sparingly, may not need to be powdered immediately. A slight sheen is natural and gives the skin a healthy appearance. When natural skin oils begin to appear through the makeup, apply powder touch-ups to remove the shine. If the temperature is hot on location or if you have a naturally shiny actor, then you may want to consider alternating using powder and shine blotters when you go in for touch-ups in between takes. Also note that you do not need to re-powder or blot the entire face every time you touch up, just the areas that are shiny. When blotting, use a stippling versus a wiping motion in order to keep the makeup in place. Blotters come in many different varieties, ranging from rice paper to ultra-absorbent paper towels that have been cut up into thirds or fourths. Men should always be minimally shiny unless the action in the scene calls for them to look exerted. Men should pay particular attention to maintaining a matte finish on bald spots and receding hairlines (see Figures 9.14, 9.15, 9.16, 9.17 for various types of powder).

Eyeliner

Except in cases where the lashes are blond or extremely faint, eyeliner is rarely used on men. Should it be necessary, either apply a soft, faint line at the root of the eyelash with a sharp pencil or shadow brush and blend with a clean brush until the line disappears, or apply a light coating of brown mascara to the lashes. For an even more natural look, use liners or powders that are a shade or two lighter than the lashes. For a men's natural makeup look, gel and liquid liners would *never* be used under any circumstance. Any sign of eyeliner on a man's lash line will tend to look feminine.

Concealer

In video production, under-eye cover is generally used in the same manner or slightly lighter in saturation than as on women. Be mindful to blend the color evenly into the surrounding skin to create a natural look. In all makeup types, it is paramount to avoid creating the raccoon eye. Any concealer must be blended perfectly into the surrounding foundation and set in order to avoid creasing.

Cheek Color

The flattening out of natural facial colors and contours created by the application of foundation is usually not as problematic for men as it is for women. A stronger bone structure and the slight beard shadow tend to minimize the effects of the foundation. If cheek color is to be used, a bronzer placed on the areas of the face that are naturally warmed by the sun can help to create a natural outdoor ruddiness. Avoid using shades of red (pink, rose, wine, burgundy) on the cheeks and cheekbones unless a specific character makeup is being requested.

Lip Color

Lip color is hardly ever used in natural makeups for men. Lip balms, such as Chapstick, Burt's Bees, Carmex, and Nivea Moisture Lip Care, and healing ointments, such as Aquaphor©, are, however, must-haves on set and in the studio to help male performers maintain healthy lip care. In cases where your locations are mainly outside during the day, be sure to use a lip SPF and exfoliate the lips if any dryness or peeling occurs.

TATTOOS

In recent years, tattoo cover, application, alteration, and manufacture have become a much larger part of a makeup artist's job. Tattoos have become more a part of everyday life, and trademarking by the original artist has become more of a common practice. For this reason the necessity to cover tattoos is not only appropriate to the script but legally practical.

Unless the actor has a release form from the tattoo's artist, then the tattoo has to be covered.

Covering tattoos is the most common practice many makeup artists are required to carry out while in production. Covering a tattoo can be accomplished in two different ways: the direct application of concealer method; and the color-correction method. Tattoos can be directly covered with a foundation or an airbrush with the correct color of foundation, and by the color-correcting method using a complementary color to neutralize the colored areas of the tattoo then covering the entire area with foundation.

Most of the time, tattoo covers need to be waterproof, so that it is more long-wearing during shooting and requires less touch-ups throughout the day. Some tattoo covers are more like waterproof foundations. Dermablend has been a popular waterproof full-coverage foundation to cover tattoo and other skin discolorations for decades. In conjunction with a setting powder, it lasts most of the day with minimal touch-ups. Alcohol-based foundations have increasingly become more and more popular throughout the last few years. They can only be applied and removed with 99% isopropyl alcohol, requiring almost no touching up throughout the day. They dry extremely quickly, require no setting powders, and can be used in a palette form or as an airbrush paint. Premiere product Skin Illustrator has become an industry standard in terms of tattoo cover and comes in a wide variety of colors. The following examples illustrate techniques for covering tattoos:

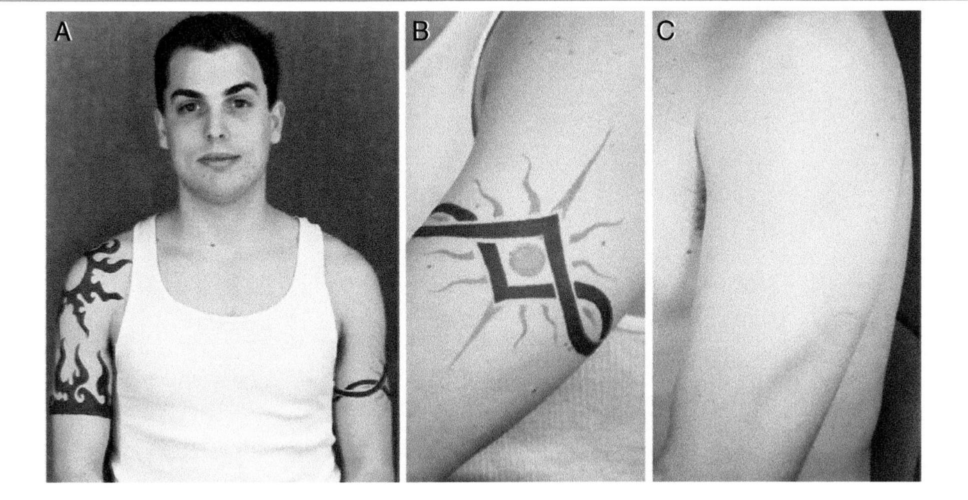

FIGURE 9.25 *Tattoo cover.*

A. Actor Gilford Adams with tattoos (Figure 9.25).
B. Close-up of tattoo.
C. Tattoo cover process: apply Joe Blasco Red and Blue Neutralizers; lightly powder with no-color powder; apply Mehron Tattoo Cover TC-1 and TC-3; lightly powder with Ben Nye Buff Visage Poudre; apply Ben Nye Cream Foundation P-121 Lite Japanese and stipple (use fingers) with P-12 Japanese; powder with Ben Nye Neutral Set Translucent Face Powder.

A. Model Cole Noble (Figure 9.26).
B. Apply Ben Nye Red Neutralizer over discolorations using a foam sponge. Mehron ProColoRing Concealer in Soft Sandalwood and Honey Glaze are being stippled with a brush over the Port Wine Stain; lightly powder with Ben Nye Visage Poudre Buff. Apply Joe Blasco's Warm Beige cream foundation. Contour with Ben Nye Cinnamon. Powder with Ben Nye BV-71 Beige Suede. Add a bit of color with Blasco's Warm Cocoa dry blush.
C. Finished makeup application.

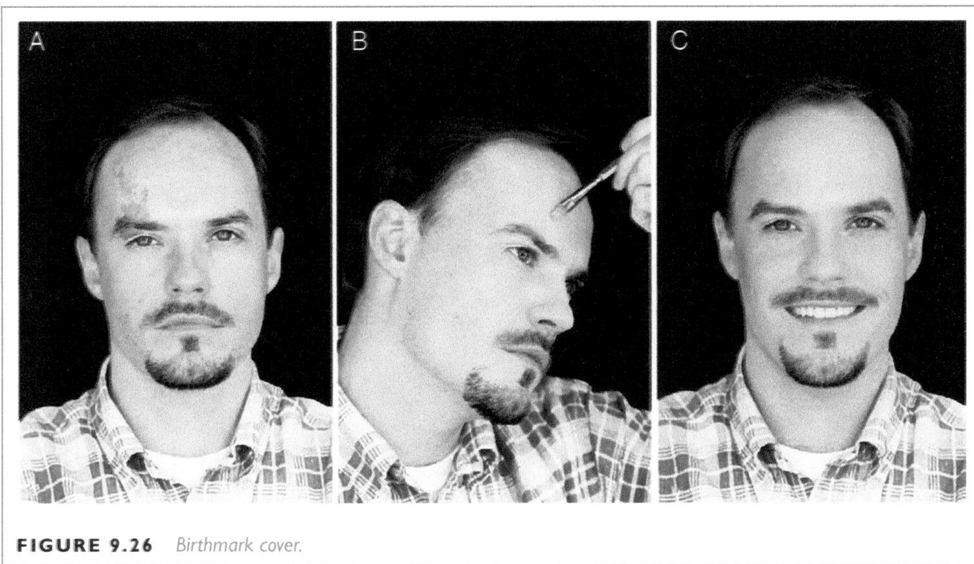

FIGURE 9.26 *Birthmark cover.*

THE MAKEUP DEPARTMENT

There are six classifications in the makeup category: Department Head Makeup; Key Makeup Artist, Assistant Makeup Artist, or "Second"; sometimes Body Makeup Artists; Special Effects Makeup Artist; Department Head Hairdresser, Key or Assistant Hairdresser; and Makeup and Hair Stylist Additional Artists. The Makeup Category is responsible for all makeup, hairdressing, wigs, beards, mustaches, body makeup, nails, prosthetic appliances, and Special Effects Makeup.

The duties of this department can be summarized as follows:

During the span of time allotted for pre-production activities, the department heads will study or *break down* the script to determine the makeup and hairdressing requirements, estimate if the budget that they were given will match the needs of the production, and raise questions and concerns. This will include the type and number of characters, and the number of performers and extras that will need attention. At this point, some artists will do preliminary research of what they think these characters should look like. They will then work with the director to design believable characters based on the director's and production's wants, the makeup department's abilities, and realities of the production budget. The makeup department might also do a few hair and makeup tests with camera and lighting during pre-production to see if their makeup will read in the anticipated lighting for the shoot. Finally, a preliminary makeup schedule and makeup charts or makeup style sheets (composed of inspirational images and ideas for the general look) for each performer will be prepared. The makeup charts/style sheets are distinguished by character and scene number and contain a complete list of all items and products used for each character. Included is a detailed schedule of how long each performer is expected to be in the makeup chair (i.e. men—15 minutes, kids—7 minutes, women—30 minutes, and, well, much longer for special effects, etc.). This information is discussed with the AD (Assistant Director) department, which is in charge of creating the overall schedule for the production, daily call sheets for all principle actors, day players, and background artists.

As production begins the Department Head Makeup Artist will instruct the Key/Assistant Makeup Artist(s) and hair stylists on the design and requirements of the production. He or she will also schedule and assign category artists (additional makeup artists and/or hair stylists) to specific actors and/or extras. On a daily basis throughout the entire shooting schedule, department heads will do a run down over the call sheet with their department to ensure that their team knows the full expectations throughout the day. This is important since most days in film are not identical and require different daily preparations. After being given the full aspects of their days, the makeup department is ready to apply all required makeup and hairstyles. Sometimes "keys" take care of actors on set while department heads take care of actors in the trailer. Makeup department heads are almost always in charge of the principle actors in a production. Other responsibilities include makeup touch-ups between takes and developing and maintaining complete and accurate continuity records during filming. Accurate continuity records will ensure that an actor with a black eye, for example, will appear with the same black eye, on the same eye, painted in the proper way to show healing throughout a shoot, over the course of successive shooting days. Careful attention to makeup continuity during filming is of the utmost importance and will also be of great assistance during the editing process.

Professional makeup artists are trained to pay attention to every detail. They notice when the back light is picking up flyaway hairs or creating a hole in a hairstyle; they make sure that lipstick is not feathering, that the nose and forehead are not shiny, there is no broccoli in the teeth, and that hands are the same color as the face. In short, they make sure the performer is camera ready at all times throughout the entire shooting schedule.

WORKING WITH A MAKEUP ARTIST

Having a working knowledge of theatrical makeup is crucial for stage performers. Actors working in live theater are, with few exceptions, responsible for applying their own makeup. Film and television projects, however, will nearly always have a makeup artist on set who is solely responsible for applying the actor's makeup and how it appears on camera. For some actors, it may at first seem awkward, for others it will be a great relief. The professional actor about to make the transition from stage to screen should become familiar with the organization and responsibilities of the makeup department. The actor must also become familiar with what is expected of him or her by the makeup department to ensure a professional, appropriate, and expedient makeup application.

RESPONSIBILITIES OF THE PERFORMER

The following is a list of Makeup Do's and Don'ts, compiled from interviews with professional makeup artists, to assist the performer making his or her first appearance in the makeup trailer or on set. While actors do not normally bring their own makeup supplies, it is important that any personal needs, such as allergies or special requirements, be addressed before the production begins.

Makeup Dos and Don'ts for the Actor:

Do …

- arrive on time to get into makeup
- if others are already in the hair and makeup trailer, loudly say "Stepping" *before* heading up the steps of the trailer
- eat before you arrive at the hair and makeup trailer
- arrive *completely* barefaced (no makeup, no liner, no mascara)
- arrive with your face clean and moisturized
- sit quietly in the makeup chair
- ask the makeup artist any questions or requests before the makeup application begins
- try to stay away from overly salty or spicy foods (including onions and garlic) and alcohol for a few days before shooting to avoid puffiness
- be sure to take everything with you that you came in with—i.e. coffee cups, water bottles, coats, etc.

Don't …

- bring food, coffee, breakfast, etc. to the makeup chair
- study your lines during makeup, unless it is unavoidable
- use your cell phone while sitting in the makeup chair
- touch makeup items unless you ask
- get facials (including exfoliation with or waxing) done within 48 hours of coming to the trailer to avoid irritations and breakouts
- change your makeup. If you have concerns, ask politely if changes are possible
- touch your face after makeup!

When working on a low-budget project, it may be appropriate for an actor or performer to bring a small personal makeup bag with a few essential items. Although it is not appropriate to insist that the makeup artist, if there is one, use an actor's makeup (all makeup artists have professional products that work for the given performance medium), it is an option if the actor has contracted a skin contagion or if the actor notices a lack of hygiene in and around the artist's kit. This makeup bag or kit should include the following:

- a few new professional sponge wedges or a Beauty Blender
- a new powder puff
- one foundation blended to your skin tone
- concealer
- a set of professional brushes—liner, blush, brow, two shadow brushes, a lip brush
- black mascara
- blush
- lip pencil and lipstick in shades to flatter your complexion and meet the needs of the character.

As a final suggestion to any performer anticipating a long day of filming, here is a list of items to bring with you to make you more comfortable: a good medicated lip balm; toothbrush, toothpaste, floss, and mouthwash; a nailbrush and hand cream; body lotion (with SPF if working outdoors); eye drops, lens solutions, contact case, and glasses; feminine products; and breath mints or chewing gum.

While techniques and materials may vary to accommodate their respective technologies, makeup for film, TV, and the stage are very similar: foundations must be applied and facial features must be defined. Character makeups are remarkably alike throughout all performance mediums. What does distinguish the mediums from one another is how they are viewed by the audience: fixed seating and distance in the theater or flexible vantage points and enlarged, hyper-real images on film and TV. The proximity of the viewer to the performer is the primary factor in determining the intensity of the makeup application. It is not, however, the only consideration. Attention must be paid to variations in lighting, types of camera technology, location of the work, and the post-production process. The density, color, and texture of any makeup effect will be influenced by one or more of these variables.

Basic Film Makeup Kit for the Young Professional:

- A basic set of cream foundations in the spectrum of colors, perhaps in a palette form
- A basic set of concealers in the spectrum of colors, perhaps in a palette form
- Light, medium, dark blot powders

- Foundation primers
- Neutral setting powder
- Brown and black waterproof mascaras
- Disposable mascara wands
- Brown and black eye pencils
- Neutral lip pencils—one that's good for lighter skin tones and another for darker skin tones
- Neutral lipsticks—one that's good for lighter skin tones and another for darker skin tones
- Chapstick or Burt's Bees
- Clear lip gloss
- Eyeshadow palette filled with an array of matte and semi-matte natural toned colors—ranging from light bone shades to dark ebony or black
- Blush palette with a set of natural blushes that will cover light to dark skin tones
- Bronzer
- Brushes
    - Multiple powder brushes
    - Blush brush
    - Lip brush
    - Multiple shadow brushes, sized large to small
    - Thin angled brow/liner brush
    - Multiple foundation brushes, sized large to small
    - Concealer brush
    - Various synthetic-haired craft brushes are good to have as well
    - Fan brush.
- Non-latex makeup sponges
- Brush-off brush cleaner or another brush cleaner and sanitizer
- Isopropyl alcohol in a small spray bottle
- A palette
- A palette knife
- Pencil sharpener
- Tweezers
- Small set of shears
- Cape
- Hand sanitizer or wet wipes
- Tissues
- Paper towels.

Additional Items to Get When you Become More Advanced:

- Skin Illustrator palette or Dermablend for tattoo cover
- 99% isopropyl alcohol in a spray bottle
- Beard trimmer
- Face shavers
- Clippercide
- Canned air
- Small bottle of fake blood
- A small spray bottle of Evian or glycerin for sweat effects
- A menthol blower or menthol tear stick for tears
- Nail clippers
- Fingernail polish remover.

Additional Items for Set Bags:

- Teeth flossers
- Sunscreen
- Mints
- Eye drops
- Small boxes of tissues
- Actors' bags—small labeled bags with pockets that keep small makeup kits separated for each actor to carry to set in your set bag
- Travel hand sanitizer.

USEFUL FILM TERMINOLOGY

Assistant Director—Person who acts as a liaison between the director and the rest of the crew to ensure that everything runs smoothly and on time. These crew members can often be identified by their headsets and baseball caps. If you need to know what scene you're shooting, when lunch is, or when we are "wrapping," these are the people you should ask.
Background—"Extras" used in a scene to create a sense of realism. When filming a crowd scene, after you hear "Rolling," and "Action," you will hear the director or

AD call out "background," which is the cue for the *extras* or *background performers* to begin their movement or action. Once "Cut" is called, you will hear someone say, "Back to ones," or "Reset," which means go back to your starting places for the shot.

Body cast—A body cast can be a full or partial cast of the performer's body.

Boom—The large fuzzy microphone on the end of a pole that floats above the actors.

Broken lunch—Under FAA (Film Artistes Association) agreement it is an additional payment if you are not given a meal break within a set time.

Call in—"We will email your details the night before you work. If you can't pick up email, please call our office the night before you work to find out your Call Time and Location."

Call sheet—A daily report normally produced by the second AD. Given to the crew so they know what is being filmed that day.

Call time—The time you must report to your given location. You must be on time.

Change page—"Change Pages" are handed out on set if a script is altered while filming is underway. They are normally a different color from the original script.

Clapper or slate—A board displaying key information about the scene being filmed (scene number, take number, film name), filmed by the camera before each take. On top (or bottom) is a piece of wood on a hinge (traditionally painted in black and white stripes), which claps down to the board, allowing for audio-visual synchronization. Also known as "clapboard."

Clean speech—A take in which there were no errors with dialogue recording.

Continuity report—A list specifying everything that happened when a scene was filmed, including weather conditions and camera settings. This is meant to prevent continuity errors creeping in between takes or during re-shoots. Also known as the "continuity script."

Costume fitting—You may need to have a costume fitted before filming. You may also be asked to go to a wig or prosthetics fitting if they are going to change your appearance.

Craft service—Nickname: *Crafty.* 1) The area or table where all kinds of food and drink are served on a continual basis all day long for everyone in the cast and crew. You can generally find crew members who aren't currently busy grazing in this area. 2) The person on set who has industrial first aid training for any accidents or injuries that might occur, and who prepares and serves foods and snacks to the crew throughout the working day. Also may be shown on the call sheet as FACS, CSFA, or Craft Service/First Aid.

Cut—This is your cue to stop. You will then often be asked to return to your first positions.

Dailies—The prints of footage shot the previous day, often viewed by the director and producers at the end of each day to monitor progress. Also known as "rushes." Can cause side-effects ranging from nervous breakdowns to over-confidence back at the studio.

Dope sheet—A list of scenes that have already been filmed, usually compiled by the assistant cameraperson.

Double—A person used when the actor is not available. Usually from long distance or from behind, or for a part of the body such as hands and feet.

Dress—To decorate and arrange items such as furniture, drapes, and artwork on a set. When you hear someone say "That's going to be a *full dress*," they mean taking a blank space and completely creating the look of the set or location.

Gaffer—Head electrician.

Gel—Something that covers a light to create different effects.

Greenscreen—A technique where actors perform in front of a stark, monochromatic background, usually bright green or blue. This is then replaced with a background image, often with CGI (computer-generated imagery). Also known as "bluescreen" or "chromakeying."

Grips—Crew members involved in building platforms, laying tracks, or helping out blacking out for night shoots.

Hair and makeup ready—To arrive with your hair and makeup done ready to go as per instruction.

Hero—A prop, car, location, or element that is the featured item during shooting. For example, while shooting a toy commercial, many toys may be used throughout the day, but only one is the *hero toy*, or the one that is polished and perfect for filming purposes.

Hero shot—Head shot or close-up.

Hold the red—Another take is about to happen.

Holding area—Similar to crowd base, a place where a group of you will be waiting before being called onto set.

Honeywagons—A Portaloo or portable toilet.

IATSE—(International Alliance of Theatrical Stage Employees) Local union organization that covers art directors, Costume Designers (local 892), Makeup Artists and Hair Stylists Guild (local 706), studio lighting technicians, set painters.

Insert—A close-up, often filmed by the second unit, usually of an object.

Long shot—Full-length shot with some of the background captured in the shot.

Magic hour—The "golden hour" is a period of time shortly after sunrise or before sunset when light levels change dramatically and very quickly. Daylight is redder and softer and great for

photography and cinematography. The shots will look "very Terrence Malick." See the opening shot of *Hot Fuzz* or virtually any Michael Bay movie.
Master shot—Wide shot that covers the main action throughout.
Mid shot—Shot of the top half of the body.
Multi-episodic—An additional payment paid under some contract agreements if more than one episode of a production is recorded in one day.
Nightshoot—Filming through the night. No set hours but could start as early as 4 pm and finish as late as 7 am.
Pick-ups—Footage filmed after shooting wraps, usually of minor shots. In the case of something like *The Lord of the Rings*, however, pick-ups were major and essential. Peter Jackson even went so far as to film a few pick-ups for the extended edition of *Return of the King*, after the film won 11 Oscars.
Print—Along with "Check the gate!" "Print it!" is a fun but antiquated catchphrase on film sets. It means that the latest take of a scene was good, that everyone's happy they have the shot needed, and that it should be developed.
Rainbow script—The first draft of a script is always on white paper. As each revision is done prior to and during shooting, new script changes are added to the existing script in different colors each step along the way. By the time the script is in its final form it often has all of the colors of the rainbow in it.
Red light and bell—A red light and bell will be sounded (usually in a studio) before filming is about to happen. Also, *Save the red*, marked by two bells, means filming has stopped.
Re-shoots—Footage filmed after shooting wraps, re-doing scenes from the film rather than adding additional scenes or minor reaction shots etc. The existence of re-shoots is often seen as evidence that a film is in trouble, so filmmakers will go out of their way to describe re-shoots as pick-ups.
Rhubarb—Background conversation by extras. So-called because extras were often asked to mutter the word "rhubarb" to produce the effect of genuine conversation, with their mouths moving convincingly. Also known as "walla."
Rushes (also known as *Dailies*)—A first look at unedited footage shot during the making of a film.
Shot list—A planned list of the scenes and angles to be shot that day, including details such as location, and which actors and departments are involved.
Sides—The call sheet and script for the day condensed.
Squib—A small explosive charge that is planted and camouflaged on an area where a gunshot is supposed to hit. A *squib* is generally wired or connected to a remote control device and then discharged at the appropriate time by the special effects crew.
Stills photographer—An official photographer who will snap on-set pics while scenes are being rehearsed or shot, for use in promoting the film.
Tech survey (*Technical survey*)—Once all of the locations have been selected and "locked in" for a production, a survey is attended by the department heads to assess each individual location's requirements and restrictions. Shooting usually starts one to three days after the tech survey.
Under-five (also known as an under-5 or a U/5)—A SAG-AFTRA (Stage Actors Guild-American Federation of Television and Radio Artists) contract term for an American television or film actor whose character has fewer than five lines of dialogue. An under-five role falls between an *extra* (a nonspeaking role) and a *day player* (a full part). Per SAG-AFTRA, for an under-five the total number of words in the five lines or less must be below 50. Exceeding this reclassifies the role as a full part, which constitutes a substantial rise in pay.
Walk on—A step up from a supporting artiste, someone the viewer is more likely to identify as an individual, who may have a few words to say.
Window Shot or *Martini Shot*—The last shot of the day. One of the happiest things you can hear after a 15-hour day. "O.K. everybody, this is the *window shot* so let's concentrate." The meaning goes back to the early days of filmmaking when everyone on the crew was paid in cash daily. After the last shot was completed they went to the *window* to get their payment.
Wrap—End of shooting. As in, "That's a ..."

(Selected terms from *A to Z Guide to Film Terms*, 5th edition by Tim Moshansky.)

CHAPTER 10

SPECIAL EFFECTS MAKEUP

In modeling with paint, there was no attempt to make actual changes in the natural shape of the actor's features but merely to give the impression that such changes had been made. Three-dimensional makeup involves actually building up parts of the body—usually the face, neck, or hands—with various materials, such as nose putty, derma wax, silicone gels, cotton, cleansing tissues, latex, gelatin, and liquid plastic. *Molded prosthetic makeup* will be discussed in the next chapter.

NOSE PUTTY

Nose putty is used primarily for changing the shape of the nose (see Figures 10.1 and 10.2), though it does have other uses. An actor who settles for his or her own nose instead of the nose of the character is failing to take advantage of a particularly useful and relatively simple means of physical characterization.

The use of nose putty need not be restricted to fantastic noses or even to large ones. There are minor changes that can easily be made in order to give the actor a nose more suited to the character. Whether the changes are major or minor, the less putty you need to use, the easier the shaping and the blending will be.

Building Up the Nose: The first step in building up the nose—the easiest feature to change three-dimensionally—should be to make a profile sketch of the shape you want, bearing in mind that no matter what the shape or size of the addition, it must appear to be an integral, living part of the face. This means that whatever additions you make to the nose must give the impression of being supported by bone and cartilage and must be so carefully blended into the natural skin that it is impossible to tell where the real nose leaves off and the false one begins.

Once you have completed your research (see Figure 10.4 for various nose shapes), a clear plan firmly in mind and know exactly what you intend to do, applying and shaping the nose putty is not difficult, but it does require patience. This is the procedure:

1. Keep your sketch in front of you and use two mirrors to give you a profile view of the nose as you work.
2. Make sure the skin is free from all grease and makeup before applying the putty. Use 70% or 99% alcohol sparingly on an absorbent cotton swab to cleanse the skin.

FIGURE 10.1 *Nose putty/scar wax products.*

3. Separate a small piece of putty from the mass and knead it with your fingers until it is very pliable. If the putty is too stiff and the heat of the hand does not soften it sufficiently, immerse it in hot water for a few minutes or in a microwave oven for a few seconds.

4. Stick the softened ball of putty on the part of the nose that is to be built up the most, pressing it into the skin for good adhesion. If it does not seem to be securely attached, remove it, then paint the nose with spirit gum and let it dry before reapplying the putty. To assist you in smoothing out the surface, coat your fingers lightly with K-Y Lubricating Jelly (not petroleum jelly) to keep the putty from sticking to them.

5. When the blending is finished, you can make final adjustments in the shape. Use your sketch as a guide and two mirrors to check the nose from all angles. A final light massaging with lubricating jelly will help to eliminate unintentional cracks and bumps and give a completely smooth surface.

6. When the surface of the putty is smooth, the edges perfectly blended, and the lubricating jelly dried, stipple the putty with your black stipple sponge or a texture pad to give skin texture. Then, if the putty is lighter or less red than the skin, stipple it with rouge—dry rouge (applied with a damp sponge) or cream rouge (applied with an orange stipple sponge). If cream rouge is used, powder it well, then brush off the excess powder.

7. Powder the nose, pressing gently with the puff. Remove excess powder with a powder brush.

8. Stipple the foundation color (preferably cream or RMGP-Rubber Mask Greasepaint) over the entire nose, using a natural sponge for cake makeup and a white textured triangular sponge for cream or RMGP, making sure to blend the edges of the makeup thoroughly into the skin, then powder. If this does not adequately cover the putty area, powder, then stipple on more of the foundation color.

Removing the Putty: A thread can be used to remove the putty. Starting at either the base or the bridge of the nose, run the thread along the nose under the putty pulling the thread tight with both hands. This does *not* preserve the putty nose intact for future use—it is simply a more efficient way of removing the putty than pulling it off with the fingers. Any bits of putty remaining on the nose after the bulk of it has been detached with the thread can be removed by massaging with makeup remover until the putty is soft enough to be wiped off with tissues. If spirit gum and cotton were used as a base they can be removed using spirit gum remover or RJS Gel Adhesive Remover. Always do this gently in order to avoid irritation.

Building Up the Chin: On this part of the face where there is a great deal of movement of the muscles of the mouth, chin, and jaw it is seldom practical to use any other product except a molded flexible prosthetic attached with a medical-grade adhesive (Prosaide adhesive, Telesis adhesive). Prosthetics made from foam latex, silicone, and 300 Bloom Gelatin are lightweight, flexible, can resemble the translucency of skin (especially silicone and gelatin), and are easily secured using one of the adhesives mentioned above.

DERMA WAX

Derma wax (see Appendix A) is softer than nose putty. It can be shaped and blended more easily, but it is also more easily damaged when touched than is nose putty and can loosen and fall off unless it is very firmly attached to the skin. Experiment with a variety of waxes from the different manufacturers. (Naturo Plasto Mortician's Wax, from Alcone, Frends Beauty, and Namie's, has been used quite successfully.) Like nose putty, it should be confined to bony parts of the face. For close work you may wish to blend the edges of the wax into the skin with alcohol and a soft brush.

Cotton Under Derma Wax/Nose Putty: For still greater security, cotton fibers can be added to the undercoat of spirit gum before applying the derma wax.

(Figure 10.2) A. Applying spirit gum to the nose. B. Tapping the spirit gum to make it tacky. C. Applying the cotton. D. Pulling excess cotton off the nose after the spirit gum is dry. E. Cotton foundation for the derma wax. F. First application of derma wax. A small amount of wax is pressed into the cotton, then blended into the skin. G. Second application of derma wax. A ball of derma wax is pressed onto the nose at what is to be the most prominent part. H. Blending the derma wax with lubricating jelly. I. Applying Rubber Mask Grease paint foundation with a red-rubber sponge. J. Powdering the nose. K. Pressing the wax with a stipple sponge to add skin texture. The entire nose is then stippled with cream rouge and a dark and light cream makeup for additional texture effect. L. Completed nose. M. Removing the derma wax with tissue.

Makeup can be applied directly over the derma wax or the wax can be coated first with sealer (see Appendix A). If cake makeup is to be used, apply it directly to the wax with no coating of sealer. The makeup for the nose is completed in the usual manner.

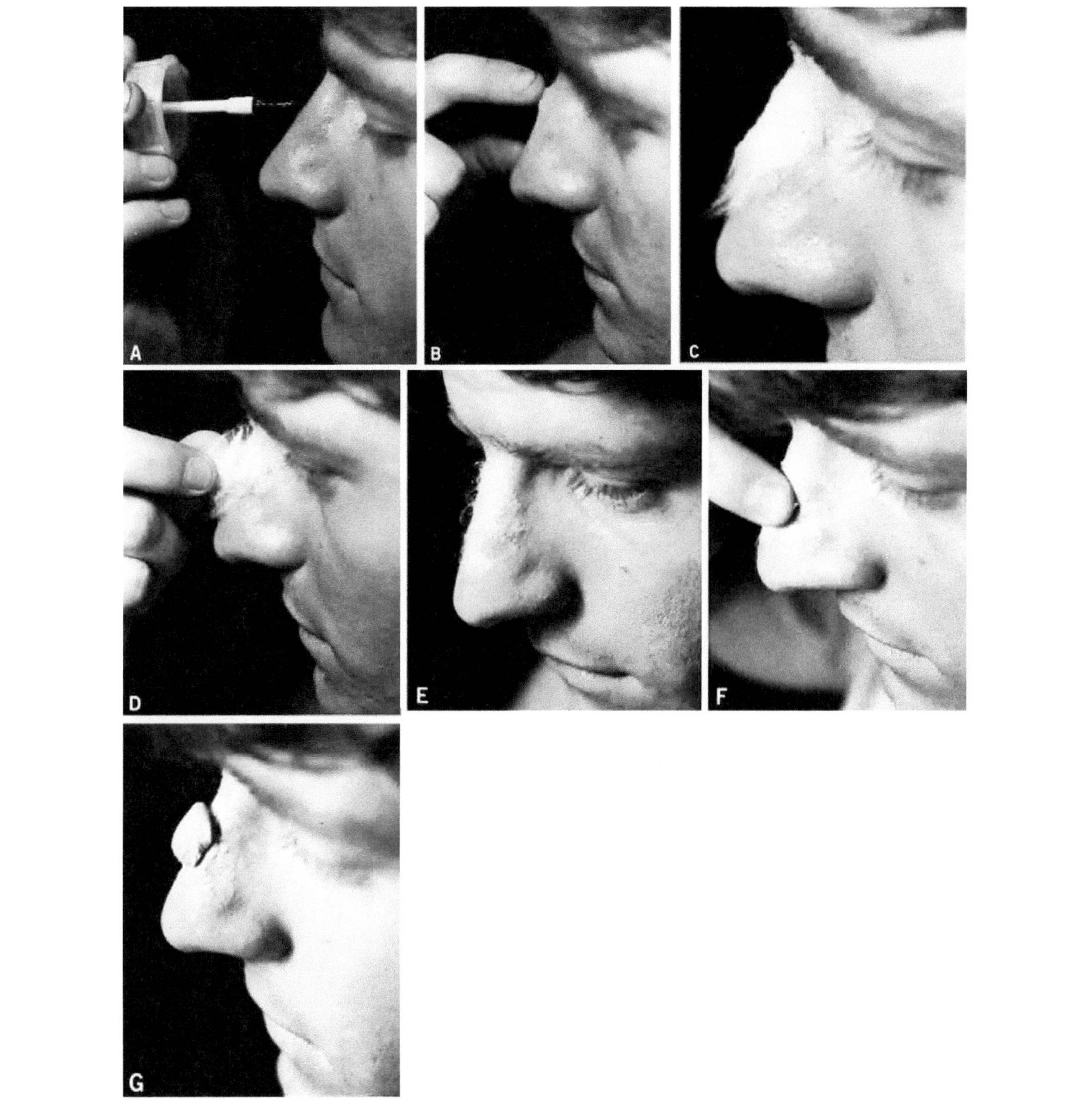

FIGURE 10.2 *Building up the nose with derma wax over cotton.*

PUTTY WAX

A half-and-half mixture of nose putty and derma wax combines to some extent the advantages of each—the greater adhesives of the nose putty and the ease of blending of the derma wax. The mixture can be made up to an ounce or so at a time by melting the two together in the microwave (do not allow this mixture to boil). The mixture can then be poured into a container, cooled, and used as needed.

GELATIN

A highly refined, colorless, tasteless water-soluble protein made from collagen, often produced in sheets, granules, and powder is used in food products such as gummy bears, marshmallows, Jell-O, medicine capsules, and desserts. Can be used for certain types of quick three-dimensional skin additions. It is also used for manufacturing gelatin appliances for makeup effects. It is produced in "bloom values" (or jelly strength) ranging from 30,

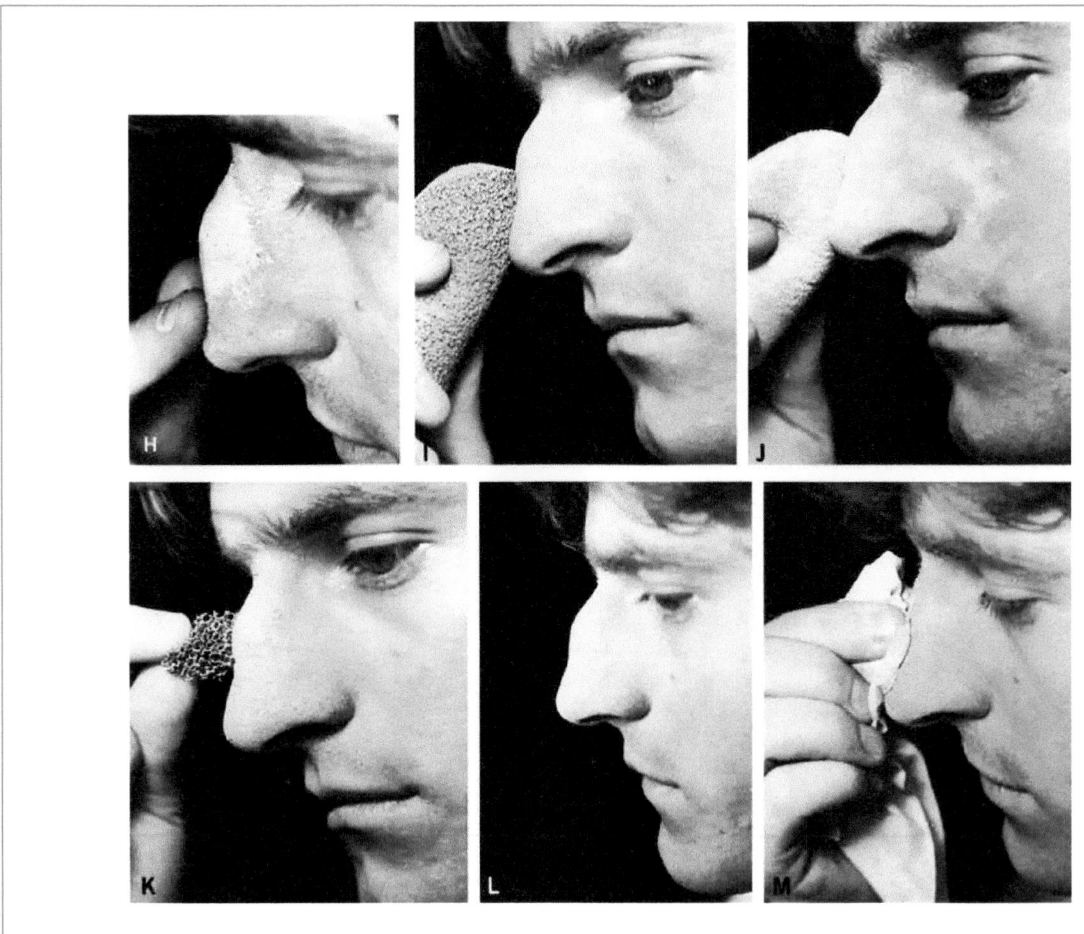

FIGURE 10.2 *(continued)*

FIGURE 10.3 *Kryolan Rubber Mask Grease Paint Palette.*

the most soft, to 300, the most firm (and resilient). An industrial quality called 300 Bloom gelatin is recommended. This gelatin is often mixed with glycerin, sorbitol, and zinc oxide to form a substance to create flexible, resilient, and translucent skin-like appliances. Also sold in ready-to-use cubes. The recipe, application procedure, and coloring techniques for prosthetic gelatin are discussed in Chapter 11.

LIQUID LATEX

Natural rubber latex is the sap harvested from the rubber tree. Ammonia, the smell with which it is commonly associated, is added as a preservative to help keep it from decomposing and coagulating. There are different types of latex developed for different purposes. Natural, prevulcanized latex without any fillers is often called pure gum latex or balloon rubber. This type makes thin translucent products such as balloons, rubber gloves, and condoms. It is not recommended for brushing or slushing

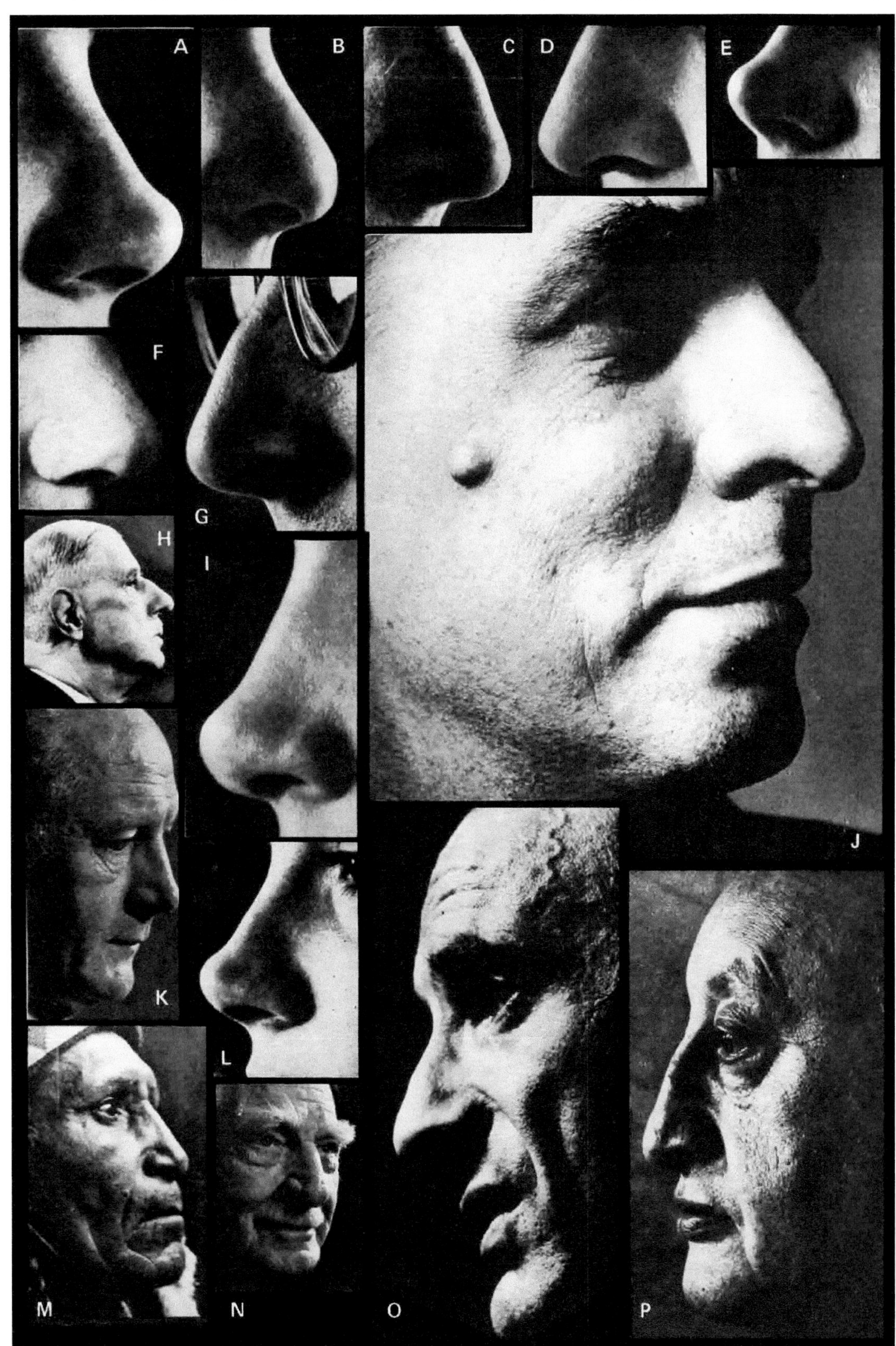

FIGURE 10.4 *Noses.*

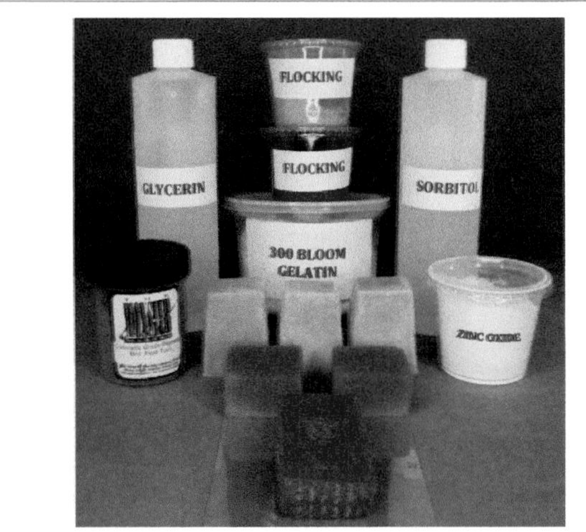

FIGURE 10.5 *Products used to make gelatin.*

into molds. Other prevulcanized latexes contain a variety of thickeners and fillers designed to either build up layers inside a mold or to be painted on in heavy layers to form thick rubber molds. When purchasing latex, be sure to describe exactly what kind of product and process you are planning in order to receive the appropriate one.

Adding color to latex, whether it be bright colors or fleshtones, will assist you in applying makeup or color to the finished piece. Latex, in a color that closely matches the final skin or surface tone, will require less makeup and provide a more even coverage. Sold in tubes and purchased from your local paint or hardware store, universal colorants or tinting colors are generally used to color interior and exterior house paints. They can be thinned with distilled water (regular water may upset the pH balance and cause some gelation of the rubber) and used to color the latex. The best colorants are pigment dispersions, specifically manufactured to color latex. (See Appendix A, *Latex*.) Latex can also be tinted with a few drops of food coloring (use mostly yellow, some red, and a tiny bit of blue). When coloring liquid latex, remember that it turns darker when it dries.

You could also choose to simply use pre-tinted latex from the manufacturer in order to provide a foundation color. When using tinted latex, remember that it turns much darker after it dries.

Liquid latex (see Appendix A) can be used for casting in plaster molds (see Figure 11.11) and for painting on flat, smooth surfaces (glass, for example) in order to create pieces, such as welts and scars, that can be transferred to the skin after the latex has dried; and for applying directly to the skin to create three-dimensional wrinkles and skin texture. When using latex on the skin, use only the type that is intended for that purpose. Because latex can be irritating to some skins, it is advisable to test the skin first for allergic reactions. If latex causes irritation or feels as if it is burning the skin, *don't use it*, or try another brand or try applying a skin barrier like Barrier Spray by Mehron, Final Seal by Ben Nye, Aquacream by ADM Tronics, and Top Guard by Premiere Products, Inc. (see Appendix B).

One method of using latex for a subtle aging effect is to apply clear latex directly to the skin. Working on one area of the face at a time, pull the skin tight with the fingers and, using either a red-rubber or a foam latex sponge, stipple the latex over the completed makeup. When each area is dry, dust it with powder, then release the skin, which should form wrinkles (see Figure 10.7). If you want deeper wrinkles, apply additional coats of latex in the same way. When the entire face has been covered, the makeup can be touched up with Rubber Mask Greasepaint (RMGP), or PAX (see Chapter 11 and Appendix A). When using makeup other than RMGP, the latex must be stippled with a light coating of castor oil to protect it from the cosmetic oils.

Latex can also be used to age the hands. But if the hands are hairy, either shave the hair first or make absolutely certain that the hairs are protected from becoming embedded in the latex, for that would almost certainly result in a good many of them being removed with the latex after the performance. To protect the hairs, coat hairy parts of the hand with spirit gum first, making sure that all of the hairs are embedded in the spirit gum, which should then be allowed to dry before the latex is applied.

Before applying the latex, stretch the skin tightly by making a fist. Then the latex can be applied, allowed to dry, and powdered. When the hand is relaxed, wrinkles will form. For deeper wrinkles, use several coats of latex, making sure that each coat is dry before applying the next. Drying time can be shortened by using a hairdryer.

Before applying latex to the faces of women and girls or boys of pre-shaving age, it is important to consider the fact that facial fuzz will become embedded in the latex, which will cause considerable discomfort and irritation on removal. Unfortunately, applying a barrier such as petroleum jelly or a light coating of cream makeup will cause the latex to eventually separate from the skin, defeating the purpose. If shaving is out of the question, try coating the hair with spirit gum as mentioned above.

OLD AGE STIPPLE

Dick Smith has created a remarkably effective latex stipple for aging the skin (read Dick Smith's bio in Chapter 11). This is the formula:

1. Place 90 grams of foam latex base in an 8-oz. paper cup.
2. In another paper cup mix together 10 grams of talc U.S.P., 6 grams of pulverized cake makeup of whatever shade

you want for the makeup, and one teaspoon of plain Knox gelatin.

3. Stir three tablespoons of hot distilled water into the powders, one at a time, until they are dissolved.
4. Stir the solution slowly into the latex, then pour the mixture into glass jars.
5. Place the open jars into hot water for 10 minutes, and stir occasionally.
6. Cap the jars and keep them refrigerated until needed.
7. To prepare the mixture for use, heat a jar of the mixture in hot water until the contents become liquified.
8. To use the latex mixture, stipple it over the stretched skin, and keep the skin stretched until it is dry and has been powdered.

Old Age Stipple (Kryolan, RCMA), Wrinkle Stipple (Ben Nye), and Old Skin Plast (Kryolan) and Green Marble Aging Concentrate (Premiere Products, Inc.) are available in a variety of skin tones. It can also be painted with sheer layers of RMGP (also called appliance makeup), cream and cake foundations (cake and cream foundations may be mixed with castor oil or GP-20 for a smooth, sheer application of color), and alcohol-based foundation color palettes (Skin Illustrator by PPI, REEL Color by REEL Creations, Stacolor by W.M. Creations). Apply as usual: stretch the skin; stipple latex onto the skin; dry thoroughly; powder, then release, and apply makeup. (See Character Makeup Application, Figure 10.7.)

Another recipe for Old Age Stipple combines the water-based adhesive Prosaide with Liquitex Matte Medium in equal portions. Mix thoroughly and add a high grade of cosmetic talc to help bulk up the recipe and assist you in building up layers. Stretch the skin and stipple as recommended in the previous paragraphs. Thinner solutions will produce finer wrinkles; slightly thicker solutions will produce larger and deeper wrinkles. This formula is nearly transparent, will dry with a slight shine, and will remain tacky to the touch. It should be lightly powdered. Because of this natural transparency, it can be applied over a powdered foundation for a natural-looking aging technique.

The technique for applying any of the Old Age Stipple products is the same as for the liquid latex. Clean the skin with 99% alcohol, stretch the skin with one hand (you can ask the model to assist you), apply the product with a texture sponge, thoroughly dry the product with a hairdryer, powder, then slowly release the skin to create the wrinkles. There is no need to use tissue with this product. It is intended to produce realistic-looking aging effects.

FIGURE 10.6 *Gelatin prosthetic age makeup for Sissy Spacek in the film, Blast from the Past, with age stipple around the eyes. Makeup by special makeup effects artist Matthew Mungle.*

CHARACTER MAKEUP APPLICATION (FIGURE 10.7)

1. Makeup set-up materials: witch hazel, Beta Bond adhesive, brushes, small metal spatula, large sponge cutting scissors, cotton-tipped applicators, CC measuring cups for witch hazel—Beta Bond and 99% alcohol, hair-cutting scissors, tweezers, comb, W.M. Spirit Gum, brush holders, RCMA No-Color Powder, 99% alcohol, W.M. Soft Sealer, Bondo, powder puffs, hair gel, tissues, gelatin nose appliance, Ben Nye FX Wheel, Bondo eye bags, black nylon stocking, W.M. Old Age Stipple B or C, dentures, torn and cut white foam sponges, torn orange stipple sponges, W.M. Creations Stacolor Kits* (Character & Full Color), curling iron and wig (not pictured: hair, hackle). A mixture of 1-part castor oil and 5-parts 70% alcohol will also be needed.

*(*This product is activated with 99% alcohol)*

Preparing Sponges

2. Cut a solid white foam latex sponge into three pieces with sponge scissors.
3. Tear one piece of cut sponge in half.
4. Tear into the end of the torn sponge, piece by piece, to create a rough stipple sponge.
5. Cut the second piece of sponge in half.
6. Tear into the sponge, leaving flat areas to create liver/old age spots.

FIGURE 10.7 *Character makeup with old age stipple. Actor, Andrew Carlson. Makeup by Matthew Mungle.*

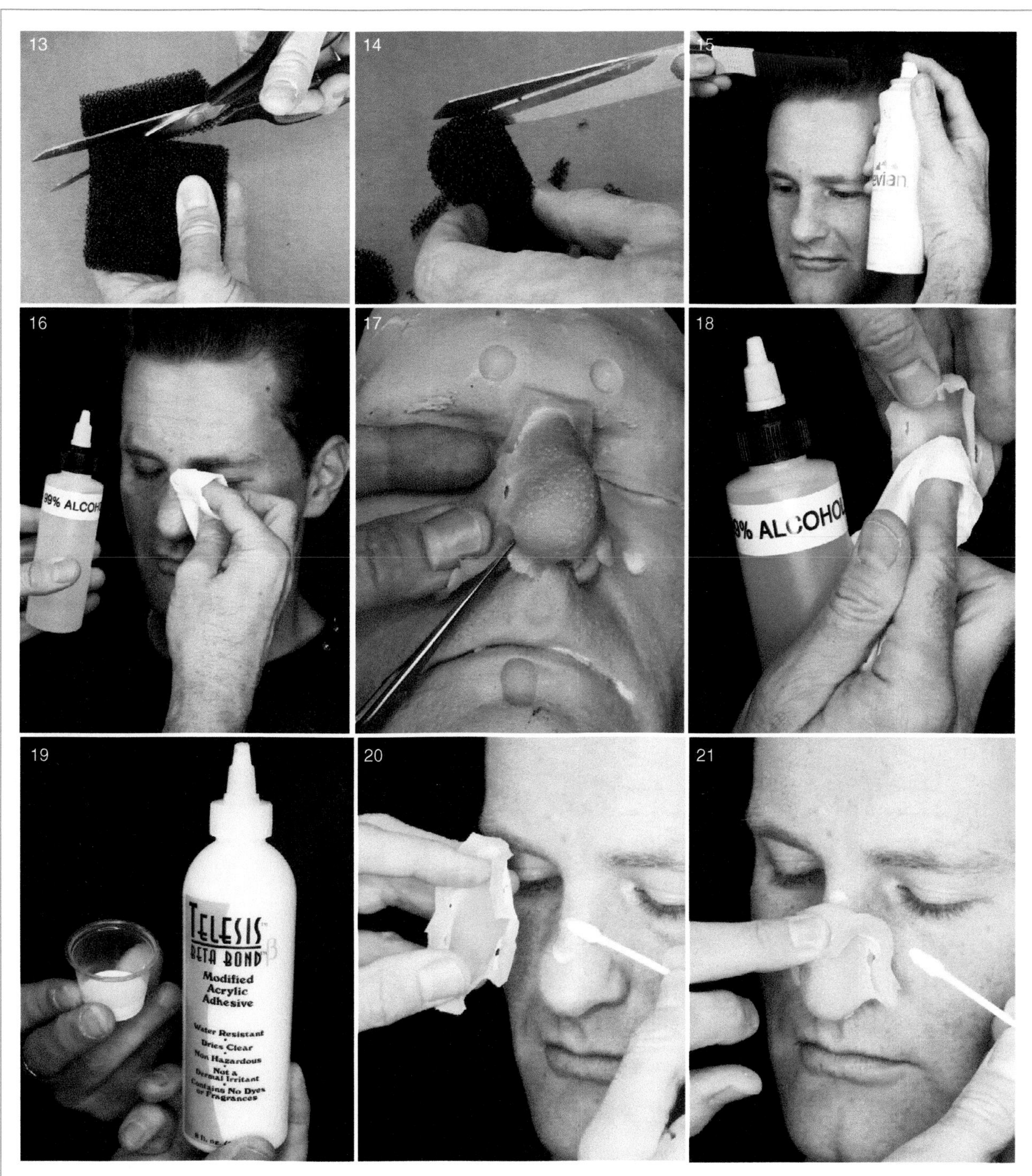

FIGURE 10.7 *(continued)*

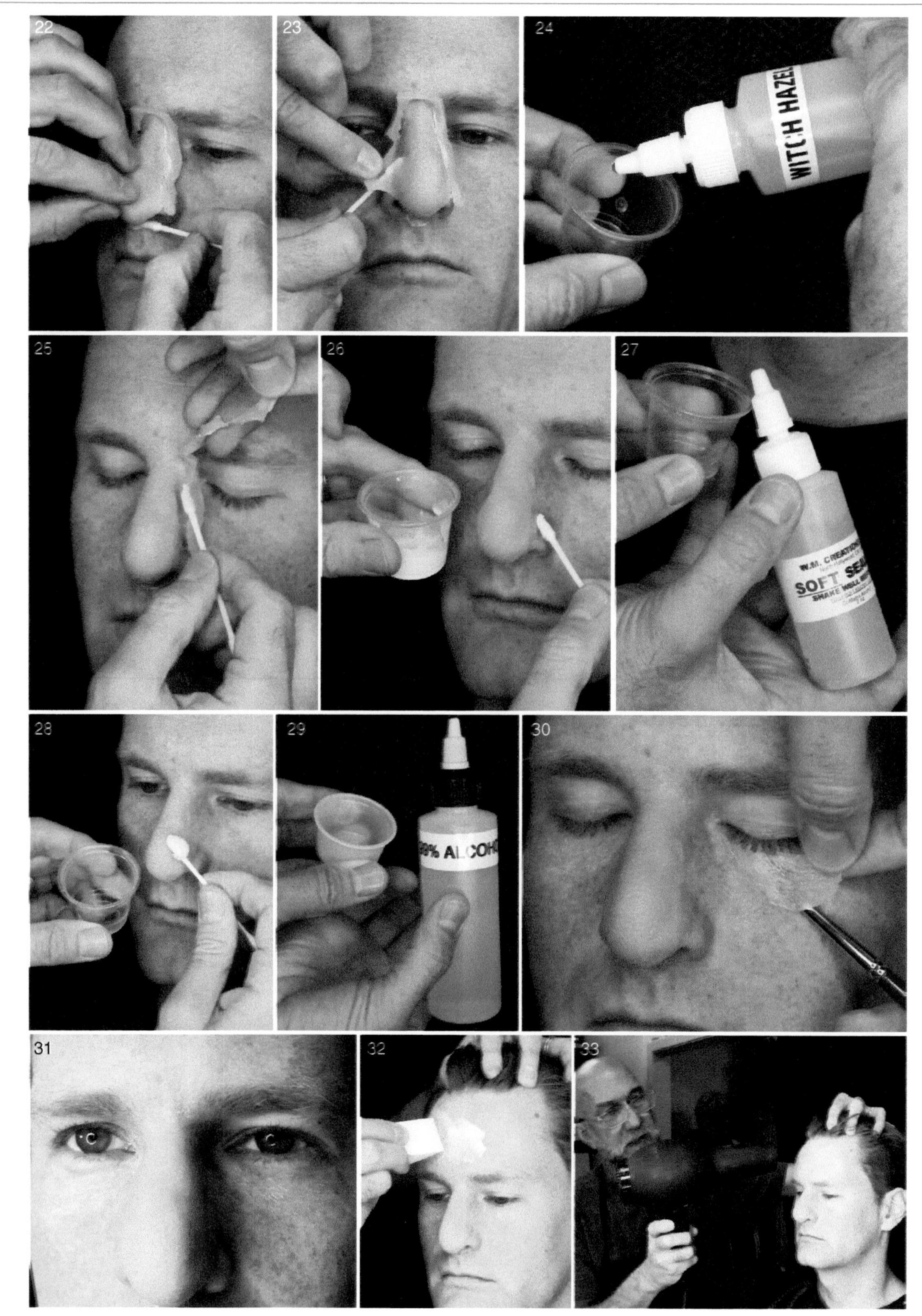

FIGURE 10.7 *(continued)*

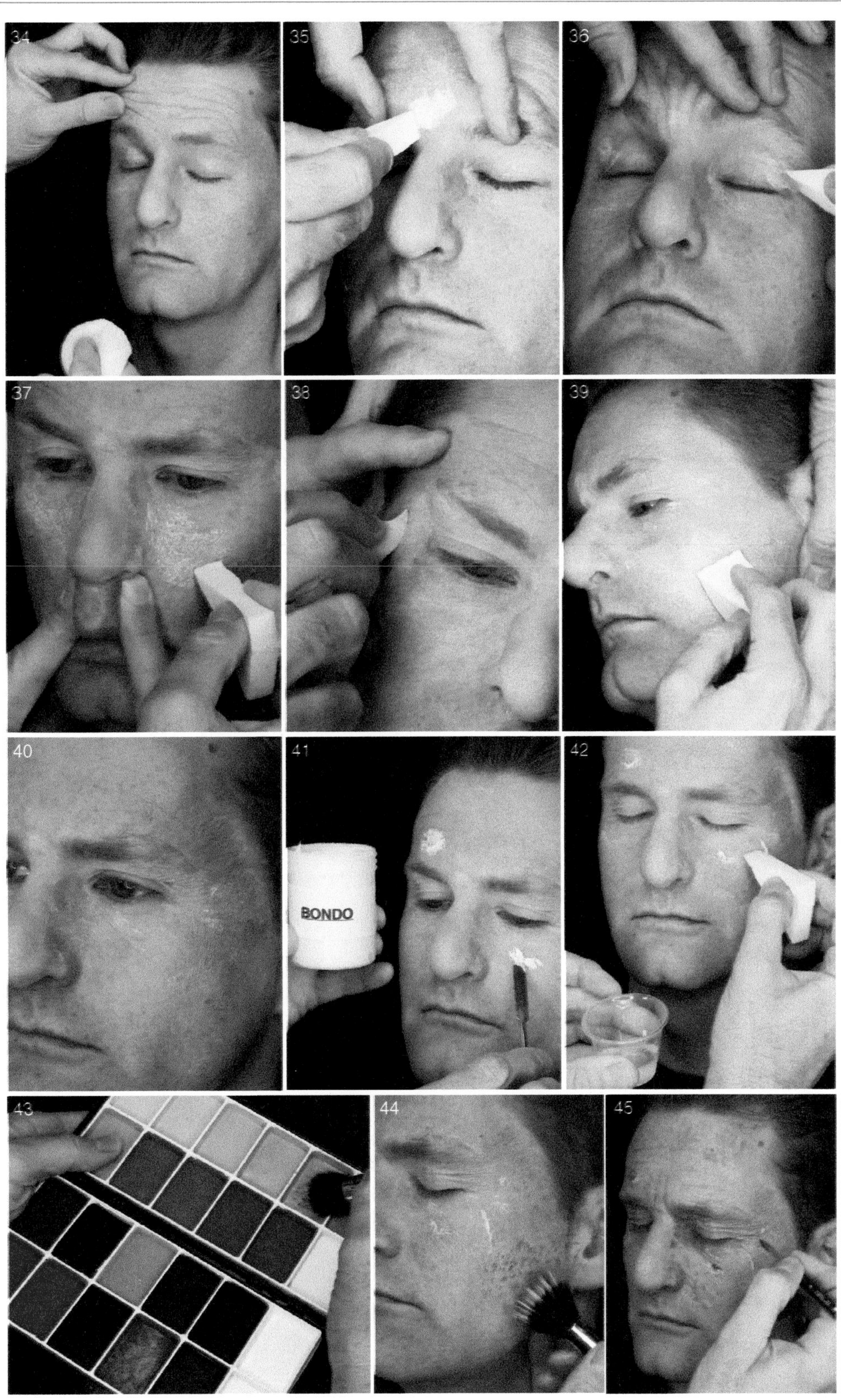

FIGURE 10.7 *(continued)*

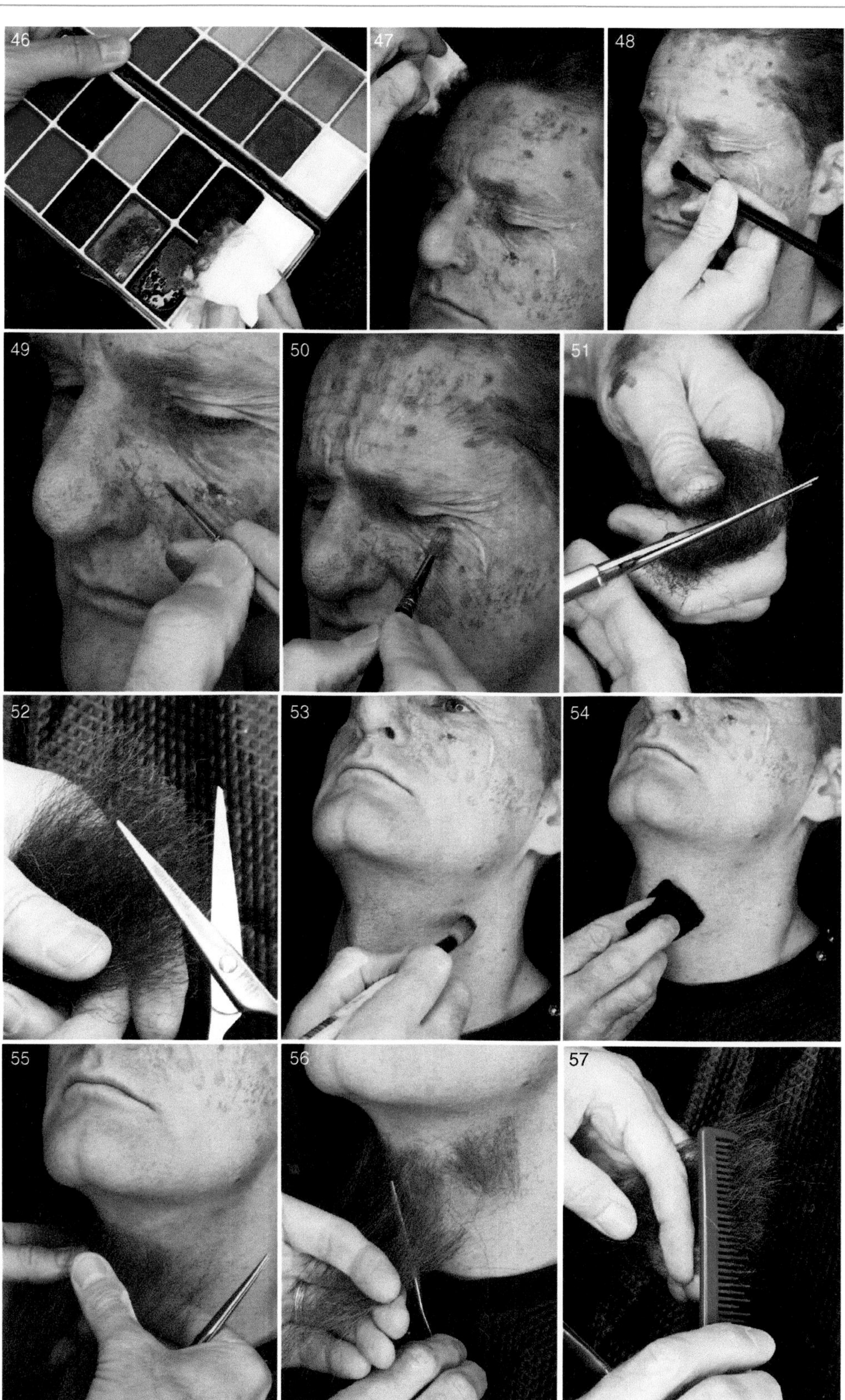

FIGURE 10.7 *(continued)*

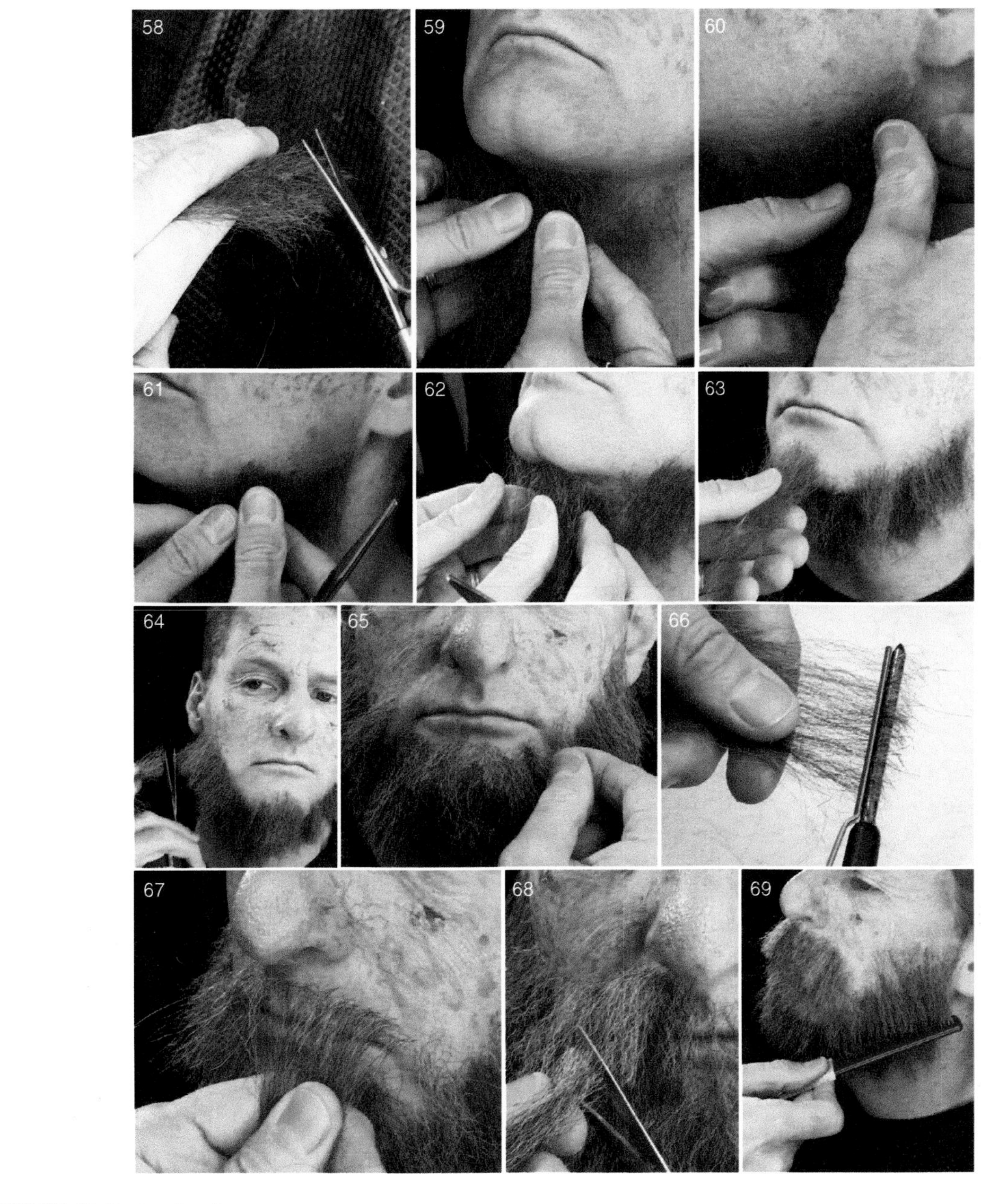

FIGURE 10.7 *(continued)*

7. Finished liver/old age spot sponge.
8. Finished sponges.
9. Cut an orange stipple sponge in half.
10. Tear into the end of the sponge, piece by piece, to create a rough stipple sponge.
11. Tear a wedge of white foam sponge off the brick of sponges.
12. Cut a few wedges in half for use in small areas of the face.
13. Cut a piece of beard stipple sponge off.
14. Round the end of the beard stipple sponge off with scissors.

Character Makeup

15. Spray water into the actor's hair and comb through it.
16. Clean the actor's nose with 99% alcohol and a tissue.

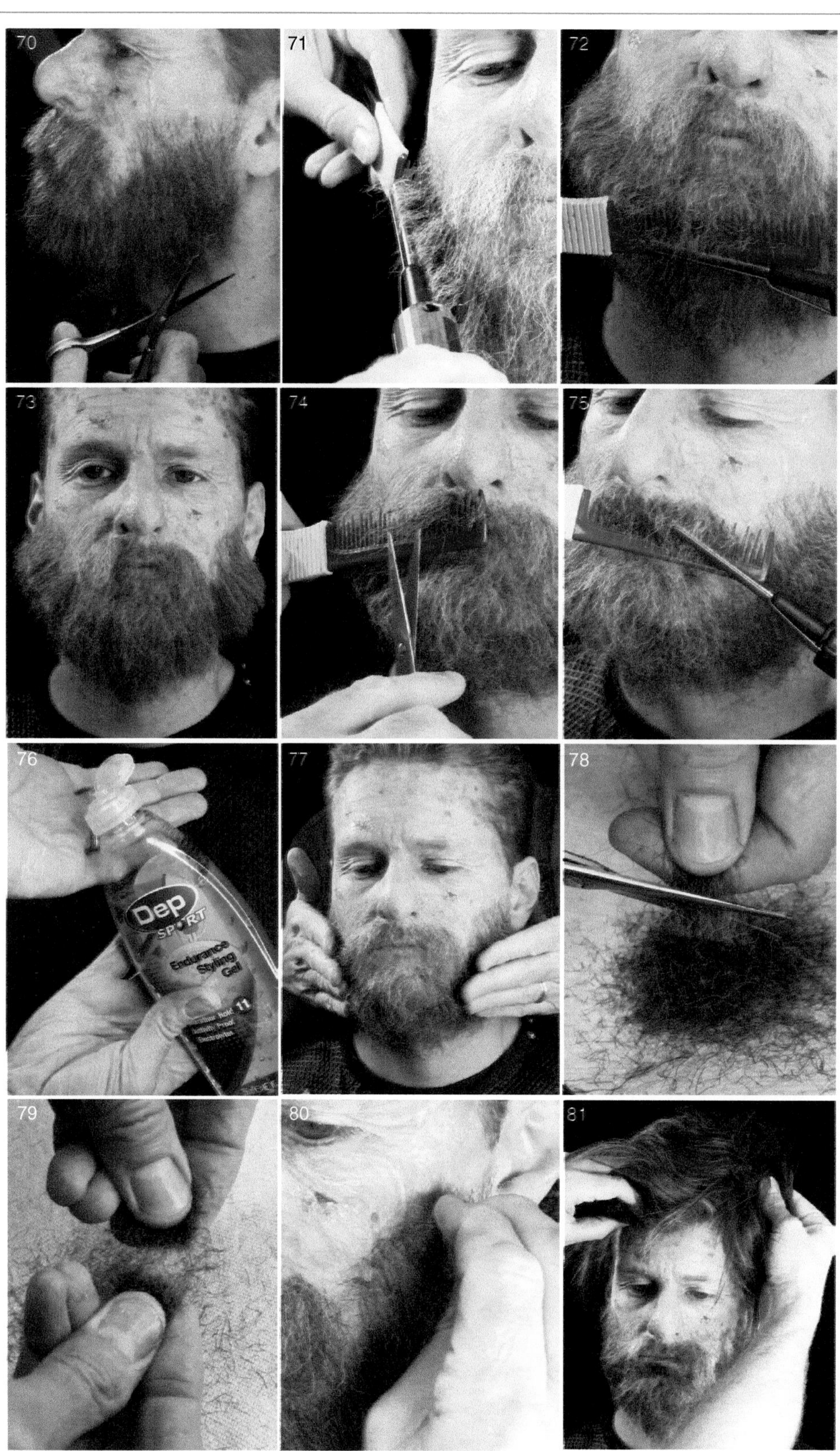

FIGURE 10.7 *(continued)*

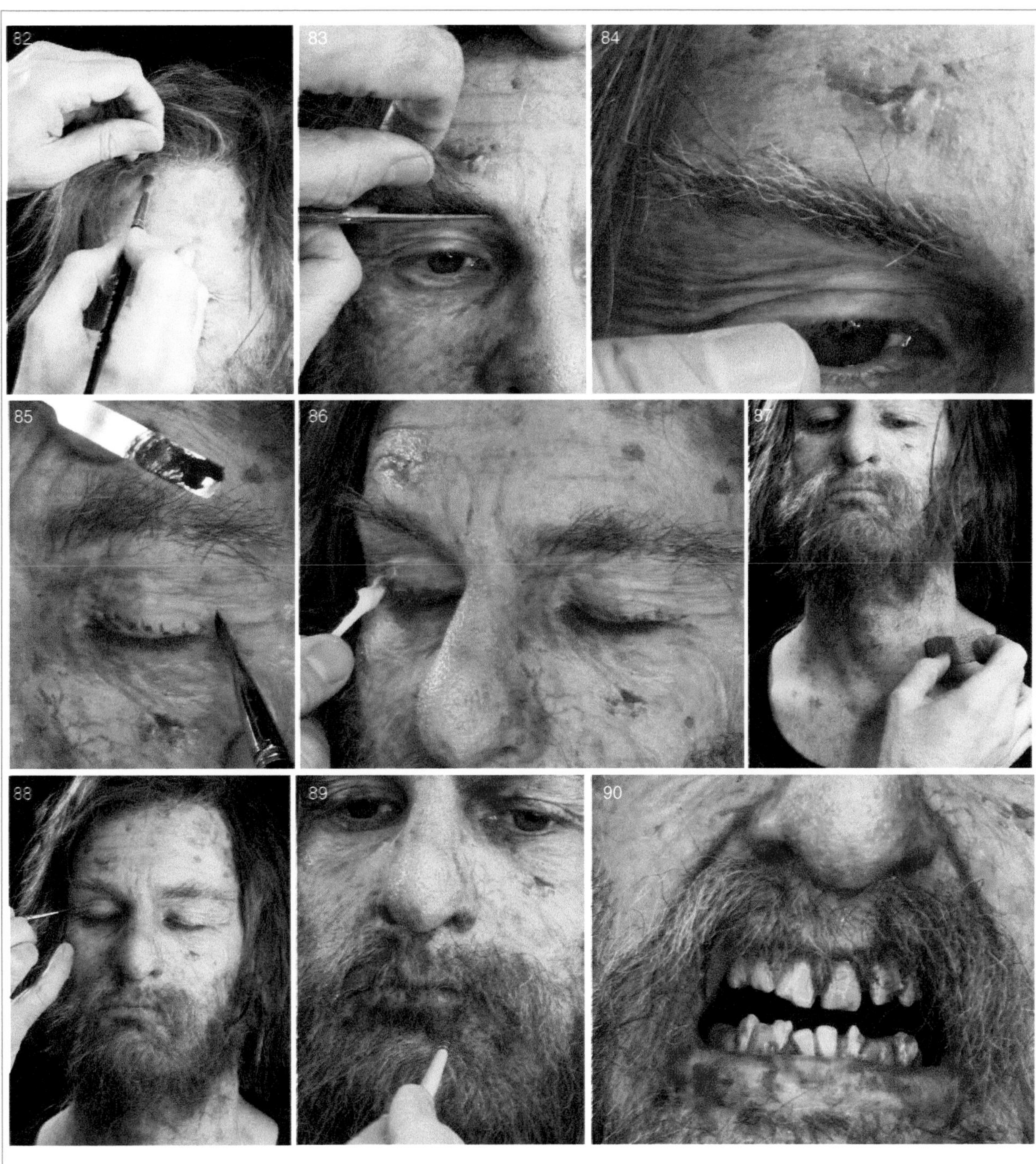

FIGURE 10.7 *(continued)*

FIGURE 10.7 *(continued)*

17. Cut out the nostril area of the gelatin nose with small scissors.
18. Clean the entire gelatin nose with 99% alcohol, inside and out.
19. Pour out a small amount of Beta Bond Adhesive into a CC measuring cup.
20. Apply a small amount of Beta Bond with a cotton-tipped applicator onto the bridge of the nose. This will anchor the appliance while completing the prosthetic application.
21. Place the gelatin appliance onto the actor's nose exactly where it was sculpted and continue the gluing process.
22. Continue to glue the gelatin nose down with a cotton-tipped applicator and Beta Bond.
23. When the gelatin is glued down correctly the thin edges will appear transparent.
24. Decant a small amount of witch hazel into a CC measuring cup.
25. Melt down edges of the gelatin appliance, blending it into the actor's skin, with a cotton-tipped applicator and witch hazel.
26. Tap a small amount of Beta Bond with a cotton-tipped applicator onto the blended edge of the gelatin appliance.
27. Pour out a small amount of Soft Sealer into a CC measuring cup.

28. Apply a light wash of Soft Sealer onto the entire nose, extending ⅛ inch past the edge of the appliance.
29. Decant a small amount of 99% alcohol into a CC measuring cup.
30. After placing the Bondo eye bag appliance under the eye, run a pointed brush dipped in 99% alcohol between the skin and the appliance. The appliance will dissolve into the skin. Repeat the process under the other eye.
31. Eye bags applied.
32. Stretch the forehead up and stipple a light coat of W.M. Old Age Stipple B or C with a large white foam sponge wedge. Be careful not to get the stipple into the actor's eyebrows or hair.
33. Dry the stipple using a hair dryer while still pulling up the forehead. Stipple two more coats within the perimeter of the first layer. Dry each coat between applications.
34. Powder the last dry coat of stipple with RCMA No-Color Powder and a powder puff. Pinch forehead wrinkles together while the stipple is fresh to encourage deeper furrows. Additional layers of stipple may be added if more intense wrinkles are desired.
35. Stretch the skin between the eyebrows and stipple three light coats of Old Age Stipple onto the skin. Dry each layer then powder the final layer.
36. Stretch the skin above the eyelids up and stipple three light coats of Old Age Stipple onto the skin. Dry and powder.
37. Have the actor stretch the skin around the nasolabial fold down and inward and stipple three layers of Old Age Stipple under the eyes to create wrinkles. Dry and powder.
38. Using the thumb and forefinger, stretch the outside of the eyes up and down and stipple three layers Old Age Stipple to create crow's feet wrinkles. Dry and powder.
39. Stretch the cheek back toward the ears and stipple the skin with Old Age Stipple. Three to four coats should be sufficient. Dry and powder.
40. Finished stippled skin.
41. Apply Bondo (Cab-O-Sil Thickened Prosaide) to the skin in selected areas to create three-dimensional cuts, scars, and skin dermatitis.
42. Apply the castor oil/alcohol mixture (1-part castor oil to 5-parts 70% alcohol) to the stippled area with a cut white foam sponge wedge to remove the powdery look of the Old Age Stipple, returning a natural sheen to the skin.
43. From the Stacolor palette colors, mix the brown, lip, and light flesh tone colors together using a stipple brush.
44. Apply the Stacolor with the stipple brush to selected areas on the forehead, cheeks, and nose. This will break up the coloration of the face and create a realistic skin texture.
45. Apply a reddish-brown Stacolor with a round pointed brush into the creases of the wrinkles in the stippled areas.

46. & 47. Using the liver/old age spot white foam sponge, apply a reddish-brown Stacolor to the forehead and outer edges of the face.

48. Apply a flesh tone Stacolor, matching the actor's skin tone, to the pink gelatin nose appliance.
49. Apply red Stacolor with a small pointed round brush to create broken capillaries around the nose.
50. Having the actor squint, apply a light flesh tone Stacolor onto the raised areas of the wrinkles around the eyes to create highlights.

Hand Laying a Beard

51. (Refer to Figure 12.1 – "Prepping Crepe Human Hair", for the preparation of hair used to lay this beard.) Cut a small hank of 10-inch-long darker hair in half with hair scissors.
52. Bevel the back side of one 5-inch length hank of the pre-cut darker hair with hair scissors at a 45-degree angle.
53. Apply spirit gum to the neck area with a large round brush.
54. Tap the spirit gum with the black nylon stocking before applying the hair. This process should be repeated each time a layer of hair is applied.
55. Press the beveled hair directly into the spirit gum. Do not flatten the hair onto the skin. The hair should look like it is growing out of the skin.
56. Cut the laid hair with hair scissors from underneath the hairs at a slight angle. This cut makes the finished hair beveled rather than straight cut.
57. Comb through the end of the other side of the hair cut (in step #51).
58. Bevel the back of the hair (as in step #52). All the hair laid for the rest of the beard will be treated this way.
59. Apply spirit gum to the skin above the last layer of hair laid and lay the next row of hair. Hair should not be laid in flat rows. They should be soft and airy.
60. Continue combing, cutting, and layering the hair on the jawline. Graduate to a lighter colored hair as the hair is laid further up the face.

61. Hair laid on the jowl area.
62. Hair laid under the chin.
63. Hair laid over the chin.
64. Repeat hair laying on the opposite side of the face.
65. Alternate medium and lighter colored hair as the hair is laid further up the face. Small patches of hair can be laid on the high points of the beard. Lighter hair should be continually used to lay the remaining beard. Never use dark hair on the upper edge of the beard.
66. Prepare a hank of medium-colored hair for the mustache by slightly curling the ends of the hairs using the electric curling iron.
67. Apply spirit gum and lay the first row of curled hair slightly above the lip line.
68. Lay a lighter hair color for the top row of the mustache, trim.
69. Gently comb through the beard hairs with a wide-spaced comb to remove any loose hairs and to organize the hairs.
70. Cut the beard hairs to the desired length. Be careful not to make any straight cuts on the hairs.
71. Insert the wide-spaced comb through the hairs and *carefully* curl the hairs. To protect the actor's skin, keep the comb between the hot curling iron and the skin.
72. Continue curling the beard with the comb in between the skin and the hot curling iron.
73. Left side curled, right side not curled.
74. Trim the mustache by placing the comb into the hairs and clipping the hairs vertically, not horizontally.
75. Carefully curl the mustache with the comb inserted into the hairs.
76. Squeeze out a quarter-sized dollop of hair gel into one hand and rub into the palm of the other hand.
77. Gently press the hair gel onto the beard and mustache, shaping the hairs with the fingers.
78. Cut the lightest colored hair into a small pile of ¼-inch lengths.
79. Pick up a ball of the hair and pull it in half.
80. Press the ends of the hairs into a spirit-gummed area above both sides of the beard and under the bottom lip.
81. Place the wig onto the actor's head.
82. Glue the edges of the wig down with spirit gum and secure the wig with bobby pins.
83. Lay 1-inch lengths of the lightest hair color into the eyebrow area after the application of spirit gum. Trim to desired length.
84. Finished eyebrows.
85. With a small amount of dark red color lining color from the Ben Nye FX Color Wheel, on a small spatula, apply onto the upper and lower eyelids with a round brush.
86. Tap and slightly blend the dark red lining color out with a cotton-tipped applicator.
87. Apply a brown Stacolor on the neck with a torn orange stipple sponge to resemble dirt.
88. Finish any detailing with a small round brush and color of choice.
89. Finish the lips with irregular color application to create aged, dry, sore lips.
90. Dentures added. (See Making Dentures, Figure 10.33 later in this chapter.)
91. Finished makeup.
92. Finished makeup.
93. As the beard was being removed a new character was discovered.
94. Actor, Andrew Carlson. His character makeup was removed in the following manner:
    a. Spirit gum can be removed with RJS Adhesive Gel Remover, after pulling the hair off the face.
    b. Remove the stipple by massaging a liquid hand soap onto the latex and laying a warm, wet towel over the face. Repeat this process until the latex rolls off the skin. *Do not* use any oil-based makeup remover on the latex.
    c. Remove any residual makeup with Isopropyl Myristate.

LATEX, SPIRIT GUM, COTTON, AND TISSUE

The following example (Figure 10.8) for creating a zombie makeup utilizes a combination of techniques for aging the skin and creating skin texture. These techniques involve the use of spirit gum and cotton fiber, and liquid latex and cleansing tissue. It is usually best to cover the whole face with tissue and/or cotton in order to avoid unnatural contrasts in texture between the tissue/cotton-covered wrinkles and the relatively smooth skin. For some applications, spirit gum will be applied first, then the cotton, then the liquid latex directly over the cotton. For this procedure, the tissue will be added as the final layer. To begin:

1. Be sure the skin is clean and dry. Then use a non-irritating liquid latex to paint the area to be wrinkled. *Avoid getting latex into the hair, eyebrows, eyelashes, or beard.* If the eyebrows are to be covered, block them out first by one of the methods suggested in Chapter 14 so that there are no free hairs. Then they can be safely covered with latex. If there is fuzz on the face, either shave first, use a skin barrier, or cover with a light coat of spirit gum.
2. Tear (do not cut) a single thickness of tissue to the approximate size and shape of the area to be covered, pull the skin tight with one hand, and with the other apply the tissue to the wet latex. For the area around the mouth, a broad smile will probably stretch the skin sufficiently. For best results, work on only a small area at a time.
3. Paint another layer of latex over the tissue and let it dry or force-dry it with a hairdryer.
4. Release the skin and powder the latex. Wrinkles will form.
5. When all of the latex work is finished, color the surface by using one of the following methods: (1) stipple (do not rub) the surface with RMGP; (2) paint a very thin layer of castor oil onto the surface, then stipple with regular cream foundation; (3) stipple with PAX Paint (see Chapters 10 and 11). If you have used a fairly dark latex, apply a lighter foundation color, catching only the tops of the wrinkles, leaving the darker latex showing through in the creases or tiny depressions. That will emphasize the texture as well as the wrinkles that have formed. Stippling with various colors of paint will produce a more natural effect.
6. Complete the makeup as usual with highlights, shadows, and powder. Use brushes, sponges, and/or an airbrush. In order to take advantage of the texture, keep the shading subtle.

The latex can be peeled off quite easily after the performance.

If you want to build up parts of the face when using this technique, it can be done with either derma wax, nose putty, or Bondo. It is best to keep the additions small, and care should be taken to blend the products smoothly into the skin.

ZOMBIE MAKEUP APPLICATION (FIGURE 10.8)

1. Makeup set-up materials:

Paper towel	Latex	Cotton
Brushes	Cotton-tipped applicators	CC, deli cups & deli lids
Powder puffs	99% alcohol	RCMA No-Color Powder
Water	Tweezers	Comb
Spirit gum	Tissues	Tissues pulled apart to 1-ply
Olive-Yellow PAX	Raw Umber Liquitex Acrylic Paint	
Torn & cut white foam sponges	Torn orange stipple sponges	
Stacolor palettes (Character & Full Color)	Ben Nye FX Wheel	
Telesis 8 adhesive & thinner	Holder	
Cheeks & forehead brow appliances (store bought)		

NOT Pictured:

Prosaide Bondo	Hairdryer	GAF Quat
Lubricating jelly	Instant coffee	Drying blood
1-inch disposable chip brush		
Zombie dentures (store bought or custom made)		
Contact lenses—*must* be prescribed and purchased from an optometrist		

Olive-Yellow PAX Formula

38 grams—Titanium White
10 grams—Raw Sienna
2 grams—Burnt Umber
0.5 gram—Red Oxide
1 gram—Yellow Oxide
51 grams—Prosaide

2. For best adhesion of prosthetics and latex aging techniques, clean the skin using a cotton swab dipped in 99% alcohol. Wet the hair with spray water in the temple area, comb it back and apply a small amount of Gaf Quat.

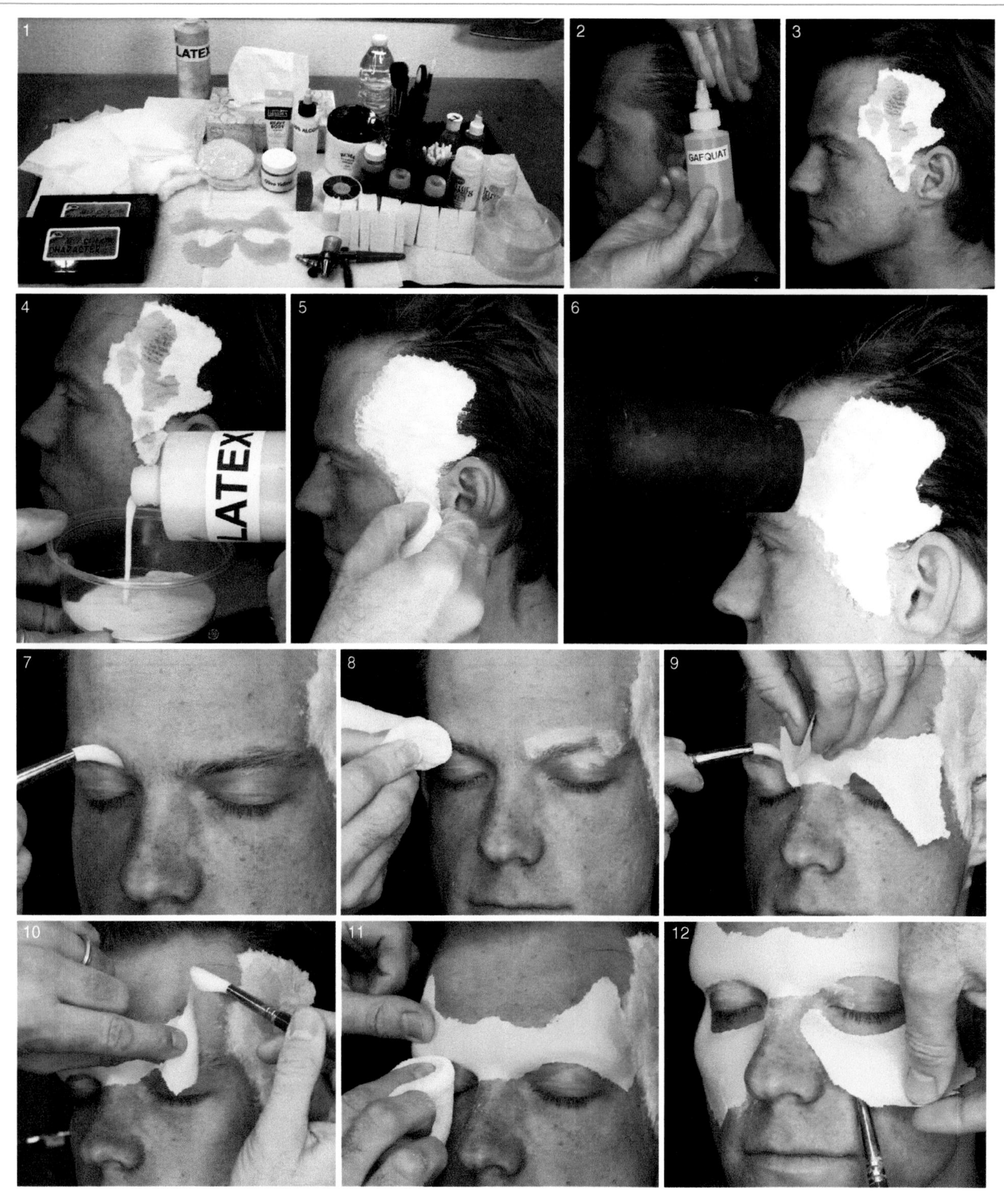

FIGURE 10.8 *Zombie makeup application.*

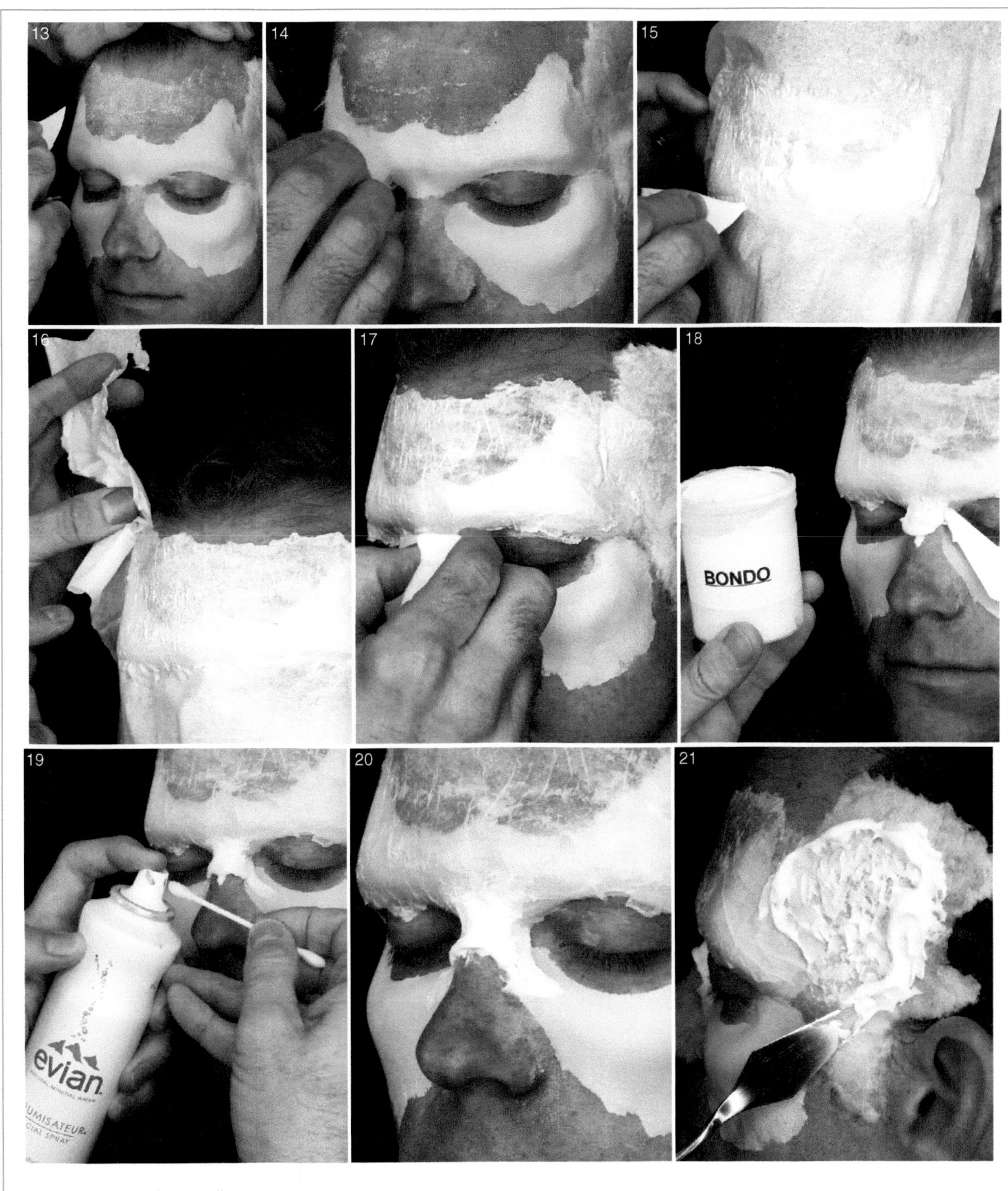

FIGURE 10.8 *(continued)*

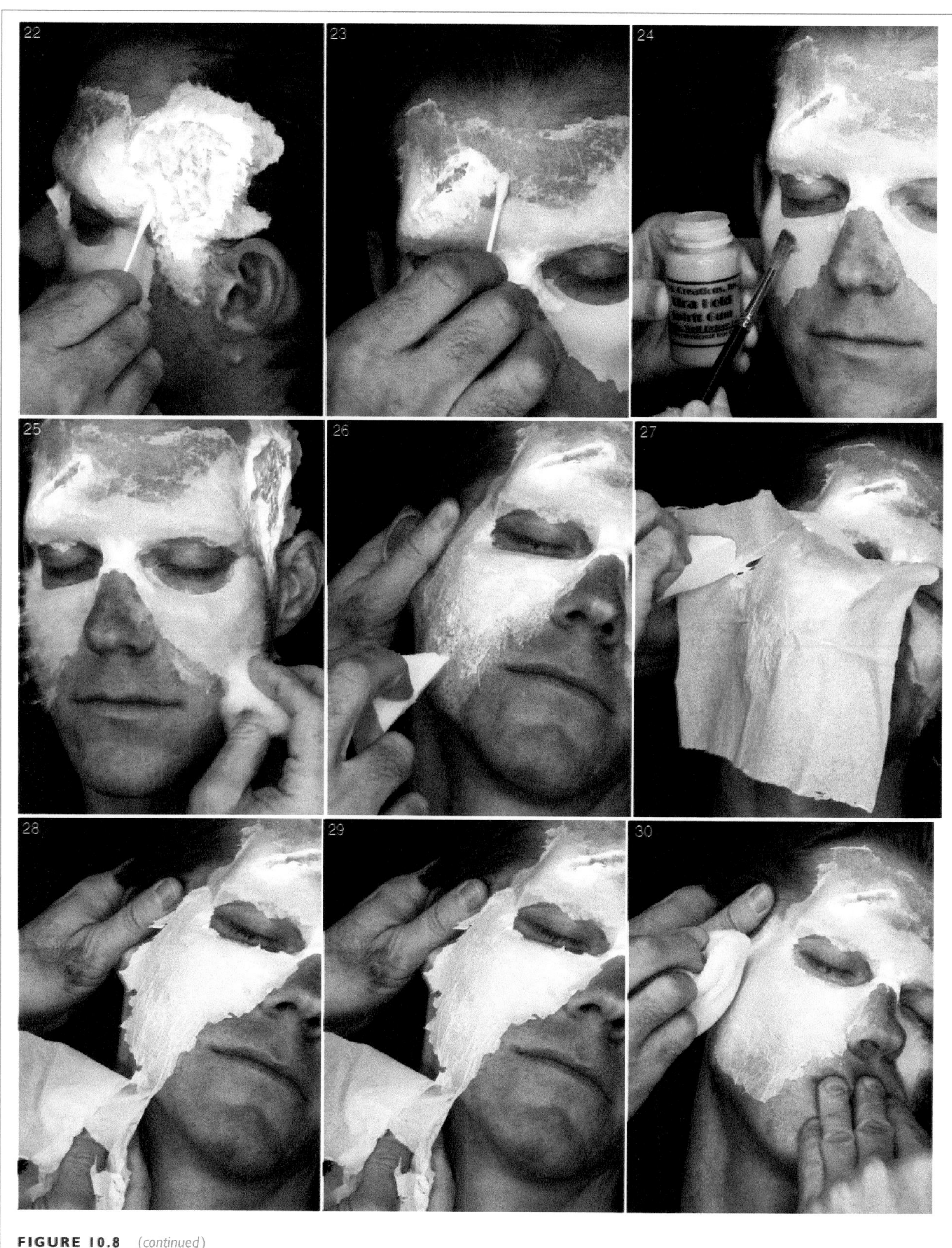

FIGURE 10.8 *(continued)*

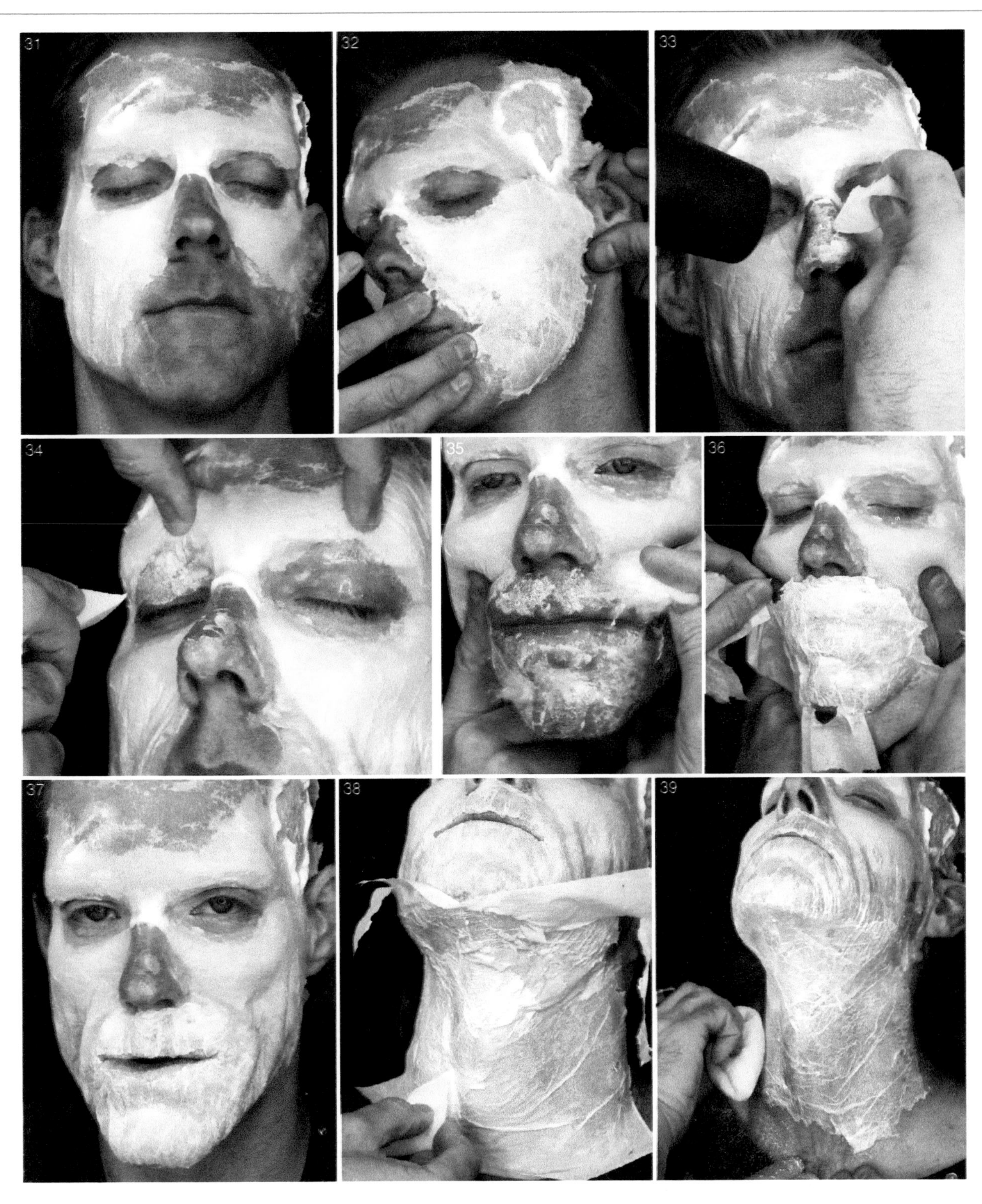

FIGURE 10.8 *(continued)*

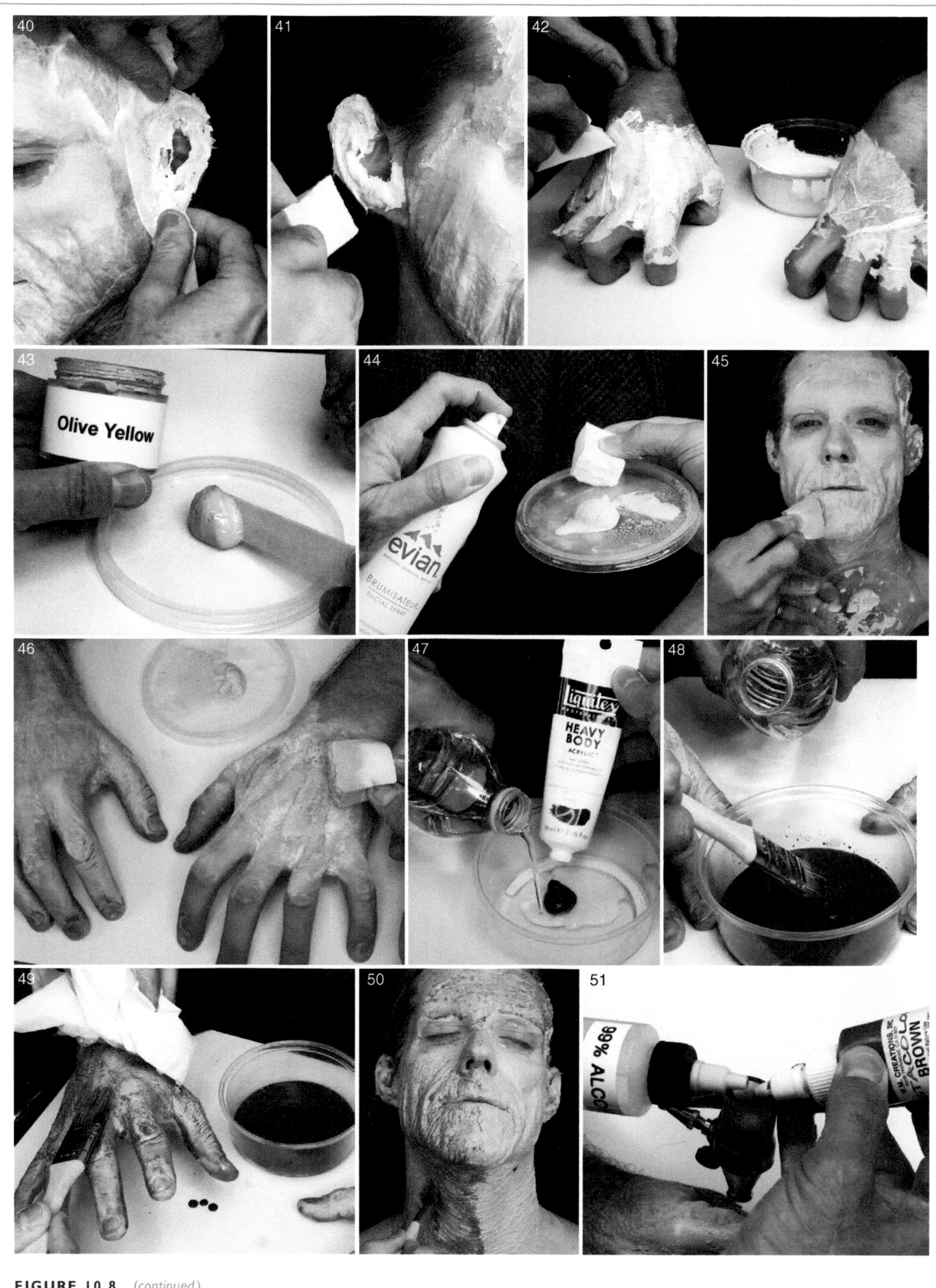

FIGURE 10.8 *(continued)*

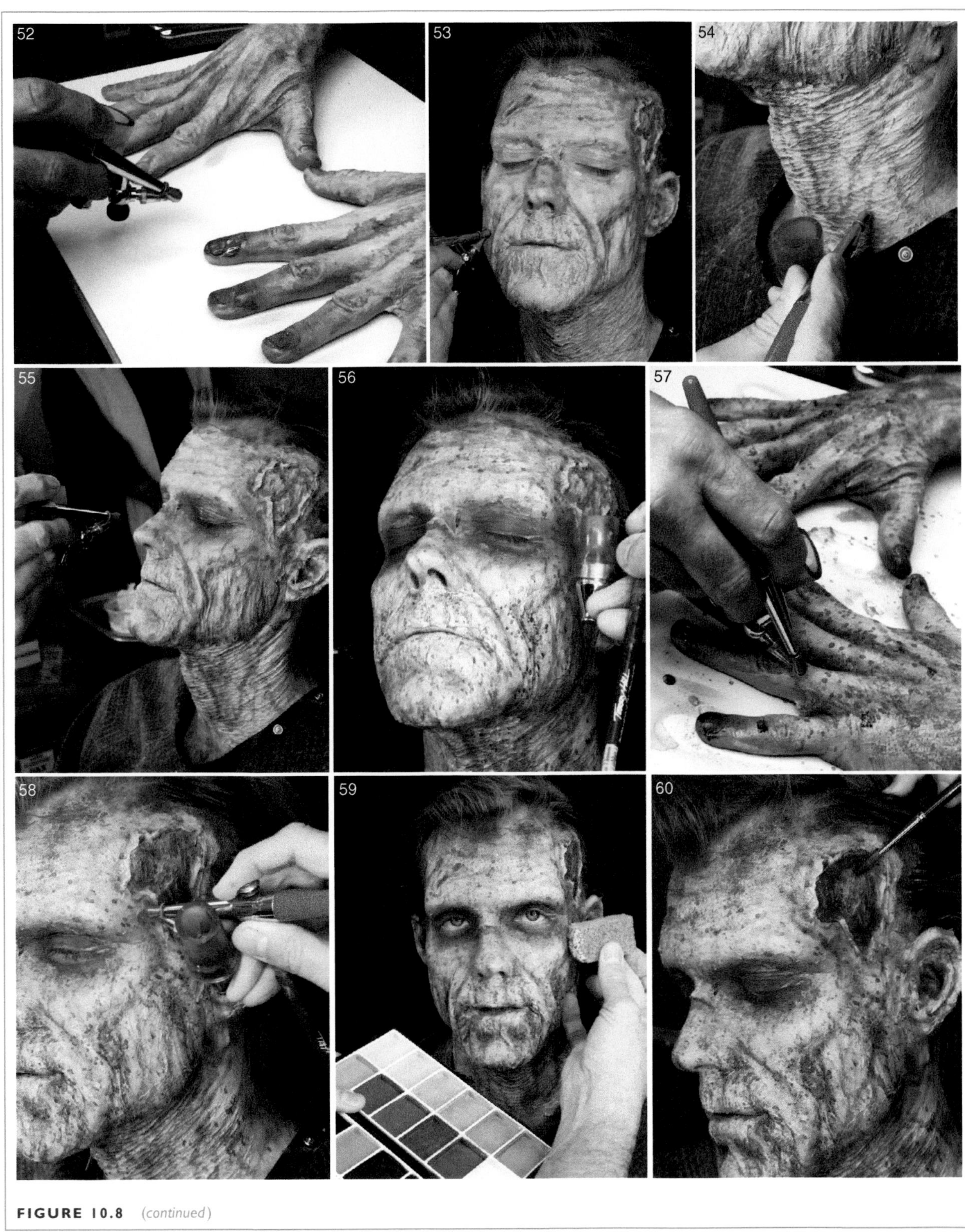

FIGURE 10.8 *(continued)*

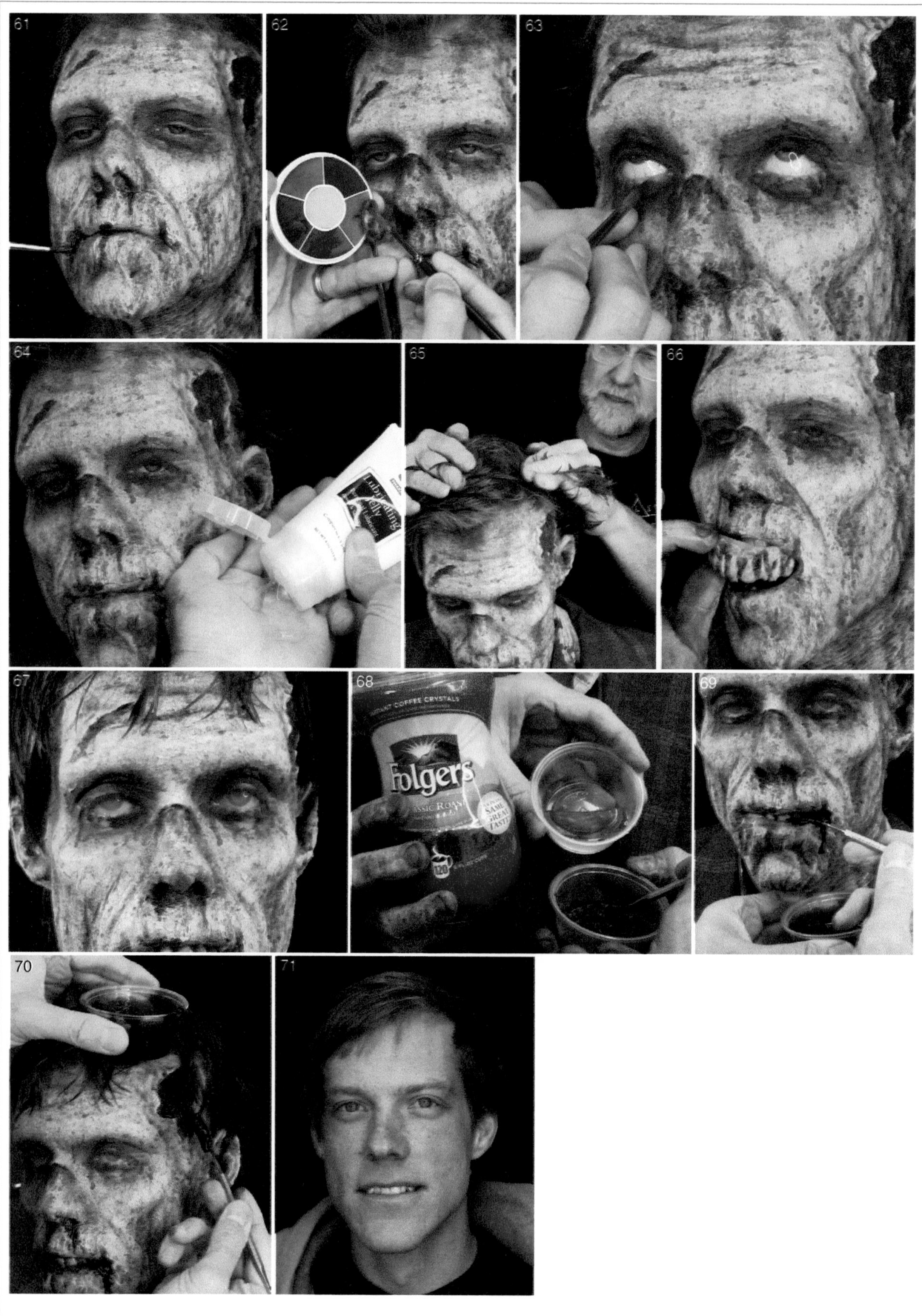

FIGURE 10.8 *(continued)*

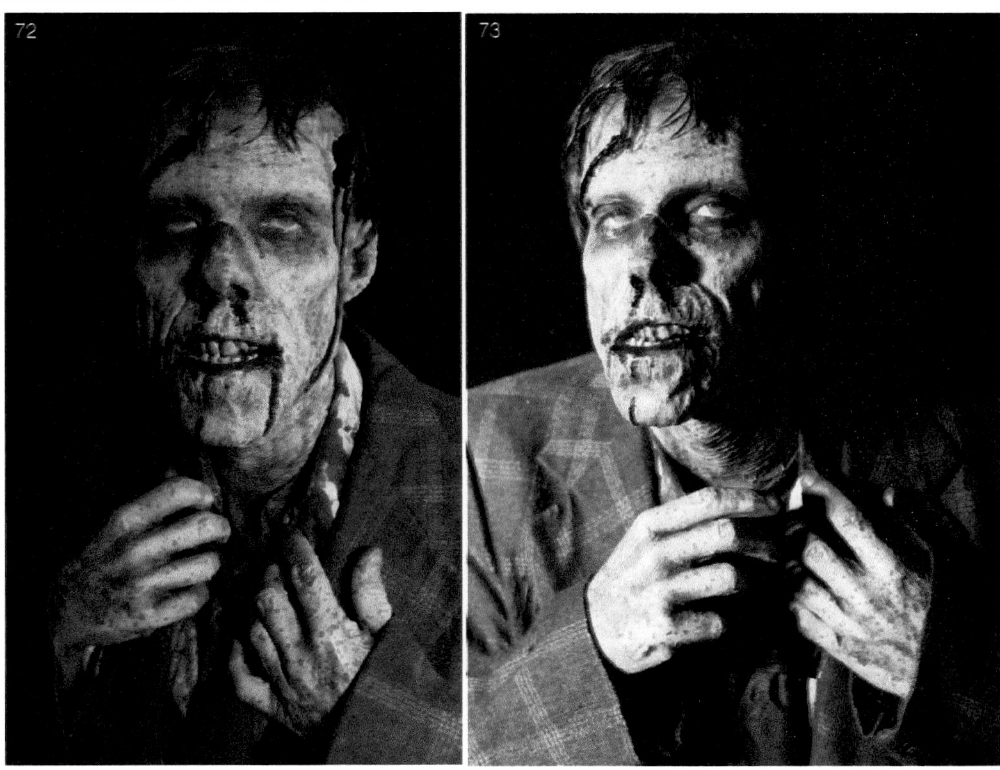

FIGURE 10.8 *(continued)*

3. Lay a torn piece of paper towel over the Gaf Quat area.
4. Decant latex into a deli cup.
5. Stipple the latex onto the skin and paper towel.
6. Dry the latex with a hairdryer.
7. Apply Telesis 8 adhesive to the eyebrows with a brush.
8. Powder the adhesive with No-Color Powder and a powder puff.
9. Glue down the forehead brow appliance with the Telesis adhesive, starting in the middle of the piece.
10. Glue both sides of the brow appliance down with Telesis adhesive.
11. Powder the edges of the appliance with RCMA No-Color Powder and a powder puff.
12. Glue both the cheek appliances down with Telesis adhesive.
13. While stretching the forehead back, stipple the skin and brow appliance with a generous coat of latex.
14. Press loose cotton into the wet latex.
15. After coating the cotton with latex, press 1-ply tissue into the wet cotton/latex and coat the tissue on the forehead area with latex using a white foam sponge wedge.
16. Tear the outer edge of the tissue from the forehead.
17. Stipple two additional coats onto and over the tissue on the forehead.
18. Apply Prosaide Bondo onto the nose bridge with a small metal spatula to create the nasal bone.
19. Wet a cotton-tipped applicator with water and smooth the Bondo on the nasal bone.
20. Sculpted Bondo nasal bone.
21. Apply Bondo with the spatula onto the paper towel attached to the temple area to create a large wound.
22. Blend the Bondo wound edges with a wet cotton-tipped applicator.
23. Apply another Bondo wound on the forehead and sculpt with a wet cotton-tipped applicator.
24. Apply spirit gum, with a brush, to both cheek areas, covering the appliance and the skin.
25. Stipple loose cotton onto the spirit gummed areas.
26. Stipple a coat of latex over the cotton area while stretching the skin back toward the ear.
27. Apply a 1-ply piece of tissue over the wet latex.

28. Tear the outer edge of the tissue from the cheek.
29. Stipple two more coats of latex onto the tissue area while continuing to stretch the cheek area. Dry with a hairdryer.
30. Powder with a powder puff and RCMA No-Color Powder. Release the stretch from the cheek area.
31. Before and after effect on cheek area.
32. Repeat process on the left cheek area.
33. Stipple latex onto the nose area while blowing air onto the area. This will create a broken skin texture on the nose.
34. Stipple three coats of latex onto the eyelid areas while stretching the eyebrows up. Powder and release.
35. Have the actor stretch the skin on his upper and lower lip/chin area horizontally while stippling cotton into a wet layer of latex.
36. Place 1-ply of tissue over a fresh coat of latex on the upper and lower lip/chin area. Coat with two additional layers of latex. Leave the center area of the lips uncoated with latex. This will help the actor open his mouth and make it simple to blend the tissue onto the lips with latex. Tear the excess tissue off.
37. Finished upper and lower lip/chin area.
38. Stipple a heavy coat of latex onto the neck and press a 1-ply layer of tissue into the wet latex while the actor tilts his head back.
39. Apply and dry two more layers of latex onto the neck area. Powder.
40. Apply a 1-ply layer of tissue on the ears after coating the area with latex.
41. Apply two more coats of latex onto the ears.
42. While having the actor curl his fingers under and stretch his hands, coat the area with a heavy layer of latex. Apply a 1-ply layer of tissue on both hands onto the wet latex. Coat with two more layers of latex. Dry and powder.
43. Decant a small amount of Olive-Yellow PAX onto a deli lid with a spatula or a tongue depressor.
44. Spray a generous amount of water onto a torn white sponge wedge and onto the PAX makeup.
45. Stipple a thin, translucent coat of PAX onto the face.
46. Stipple a thin, translucent coat of PAX onto both hands.
47. Place a quarter size dollop of Raw Umber Liquitex acrylic paint into an 8-oz. deli cup and pour 2 oz. of water into the container.
48. Mix the Raw Umber into the water with a 1-inch disposable chip brush.
49. Apply the thinned Raw Umber Liquitex Paint to the hands with the 1-inch brush, blotting any excess color with a tissue.
50. Apply the thinned Raw Umber Liquitex Paint to the face with the 1-inch brush, blotting any excess color off with a tissue.
51. Pour ⅛ oz. Brown liquid Stacolor and ¼ oz. 99% alcohol into the cup of the Paasche Airbrush.
52. Airbrush the end of the fingers, contour the hands (front and back) with the Brown Stacolor.
53. Airbrush the contours on the face with the Brown Stacolor.
54. Airbrush small and large veins on the skin with the Brown Stacolor.
55. Airbrush the eye sockets with the Brown Stacolor.
56. Continue the detailing with the Brown Stacolor. Deposit small dots/blotches onto the face by turning the air compressor down to 6–10 psi (pounds per square inch), slightly depressing the air trigger and tilting the airbrush at a 45-degree angle. Thin the Stacolor liquid down with 99% alcohol if necessary.
57. Load the airbrush with a thinned down Stacolor liquid (⅛ oz. GBB Beard Stipple and ¼ oz. 99% alcohol) and continue the contouring and detailing of the hands.
58. Continue the detailing of the face with the GBB color.
59. Add highlights to the face and hands with a #1 Stacolor (a high-value skin tone) from the Full Color kit and an orange stipple sponge.
60. Detail the makeup with browns, blacks, and dark red Stacolor activated with 99% alcohol and a round brush.
61. Add drool from the eyes, nose, and mouth with thin Stacolor GBB color from the Full Color palette.
62. Mix green and dark red crème lining colors from the Ben Nye FX Bruise color wheel together on the end of a metal spatula.
63. Blotch around the eyes with the lining colors and a round makeup brush.
64. Rub a generous amount of lubricating jelly between the palms of the hands.
65. Coat the hair with the lubricating jelly, rubbing it into the scalp and styling the hair.
66. Insert zombie dentures (see Making Dentures).
67. Dead eye contact lenses applied. *These must be prescribed and purchased through an authorized optometrist.*
68. Add a small amount of hot water to 4 oz. of instant coffee. Stir into a honey-like consistency.
69. Add to the mouth and nose areas of the makeup.
70. Add a little coffee mixture to the old open wound areas.
71. Actor Jon Haas.
72. Finished Zombie makeup.
73. Finished Zombie makeup.

BALD CAPS

One of the best methods of creating the effect of a bald head is to cover the hair with a latex or plastic cap. The cap is often worn plain, or hair can be added. Caps are also useful during the face and full-head casting process.

A bald cap can be made from a variety of different materials. Many of the new caps are made from synthetic products. These products offer the artist the ability to dissolve the edges with alcohol or acetone. The edges on these caps are nearly invisible, blending perfectly into the hairline area. The caps made from latex are the most economical, but require the topical addition of products like Prosaide or Bondo to fill in the cap edge and blend to the skin. The edges of caps made from Glatzan, and Baldeze, can be blended using acetone, and those made from Super Baldeze and Water-Melon (Michael Davy) with 99% alcohol.

Commercially made bald caps generally come in a one-size-fits-all. There are some excellent bald caps on the market for sale (Woochie, Kryolan, Michael Davy) that will eliminate the need to make a custom-fit cap. If, however, there is a need for repeating a bald cap makeup application for a commercial project (for theater, film, or television), it might be more economical to make your own.

Products used to make bald caps include:

- Balloon rubber
- Glatzan by Kryolan
- Baldeze by Mouldlife
- Super Baldeze by Mouldlife
- Water-Melon by Michael Davy
- Pliatex Mold Rubber by Sculpture House.

(There are two excellent DVD demonstrations on how to make a bald cap, one by Ed French, the other by Michael Mosher [themakeupguy.com].)

In making a latex or plastic cap, balloon latex or plastic cap material should be painted or stippled (a combination of the two is usually preferable) onto a positive plaster, ceramic, or plastic head suitably shaped to an average head size. Purchasing ready-made bald caps (either latex or plastic) will, of course, save a great deal of time (all bald cap products can be purchased from Kryolan, Alcone, and Monster Makers).

The following is a step-by-step process of making a bald cap on a Kryolan Red Plastic Head using balloon rubber:

Making a Latex Bald Cap (Figure 10.11)

1. Kryolan Red Bald Cap form.
2. Trim off numbers and any seams with an X-Acto blade.
3. Loctite 5-minute Epoxy Putty or another epoxy putty.
4. Mix and apply the Epoxy Putty to the seam of the bald cap plastic form to smooth out any imperfections.
5. Sand the entire plastic form with coarse 60–80 grade sand paper.
6. Mix 4 oz. of Heavy Body Ivory Black or Mars Black Liquitex acrylic paint and 2 oz. of Prosaide together in a container and stipple the mixture onto the entire plastic form with

FIGURE 10.9 *Kryolan Glatzan plastic bald cap material, ceramic cap head, plastic cap head.*

***Source:* Photograph provided by Kryolan Corporation.**

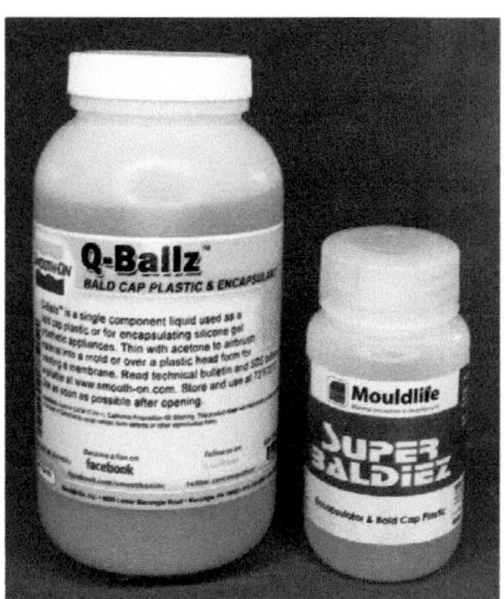

FIGURE 10.10 *Baldeze and Q-Ballz.*

an orange stipple sponge. This will give the head form a textured surface which will transfer onto the rubber bald cap when made. Let dry for 2 hours.

7. Drawing the hairlines. Locate the lines as shown in the photo with a white drafting pencil or white eyebrow pencil. For a more accurate hairline of the subject follow the steps below:

   a. Take a plastic wrap wig form tracing.
   b. Or place a cheap rubber novelty bald cap onto the subject's head.
   c. Trace out the hairline with a black permanent maker.
   d. Remove the cap and cut on the black line with scissors.
   e. Turn the cap inside out.
   f. Place the cap on the plastic head form and trace the hairline.

8. Spray the head form with three heavy coats of Krylon Crystal Clear Spray. Be careful not to let the spray run. Dry thoroughly between layers. Let dry for 2 hours.

9. Spray the head form with two light coats of Epoxy Parfilm and wipe the excess off with a tissue after spraying the last coat.

10. Balloon latex and 12 latex makeup sponge wedges. The 12 sponges will be used for each layer of latex stippled onto the head form.

11. Decant the balloon latex into an 8-oz. container.

12. & 13. Stipple the first layer of balloon latex onto the head form with the first makeup sponge wedge. Start at line 1 on the head form and fill in the whole head.

14. Dry each coat with a hairdryer before applying the next coat.

15. Stipple the balloon latex with the second sponge on top of the first (line 1) dry layer. Keep the sponge wet with latex when stippling, this will keep the first layer from lifting off the form. Dry.

16. Stipple the third coat ⅛ inch away from line 1 and dry.

17. Stipple each coat onto the entire head form.

18., 19., & 20. Continue stippling each coat onto the entire head, applying each layer ⅛ inch away from the previous coat.

21. Twelve coats of latex finished. Let the entire bald cap dry for at least 2 hours before removing it.

22. Materials: Finished latex bald cap, 1-inch brush, RCMA No-Color Powder, and powder puff.

23. Powder the entire latex bald cap liberally with powder and the powder puff.

24. Gently pull up the edge in the back of the cap using the 1-inch brush and powder.

25. & 26. Continue using the brush and powder to loosen and remove the edges of the bald cap.

27. & 28. Carefully pull the latex cap from the front of the head form and peel it back off the form.

29. Heavily powder the interior of the bald cap with powder and the powder puff.

30. Finished latex bald cap.

31. Strengthening and "vulcanizing" the latex. Heat an oven to 100 degrees and turn the oven off. Stuff the bald cap with paper towel. Put the bald cap onto a piece of paper towel and place it into the oven. Close the oven door and allow the oven to cool down for at least 30 minutes. Do not cure the bald cap at more than 100 degrees. This will cause the latex to de-laminate and bubble on the surface.

Applying the Bald Cap (Figure 10.12)

1. Makeup and set-up materials: PAX for bald cap coloration (Shibui, Lt. Bald Cap Undertone & MV002), lubricating jelly—if necessary, Beta Bond, spray water, tissues, cotton-tipped applicators, makeup brushes, comb, small scissors, 99% alcohol, Ben Nye Color Wheel FX Bruise, cover cloth, RCMA No-Color Powder, Stacolor Liquids (GBB Beard Stipple & Brown), Kryolan Large Bald Cap (save the tissue which the bald cap is wrapped in), Bondo, torn white sponges, torn orange stipple sponges, Stacolor Kits (Character & Full Color), CC measuring cups, Kryolan RMG Kit (not shown: airbrush and compressor, wax paper makeup paint palette).

Bald Cap PAX Makeup Formulas

Skin Tone MV002

(Skin color code developed by Matthew Mungle.)

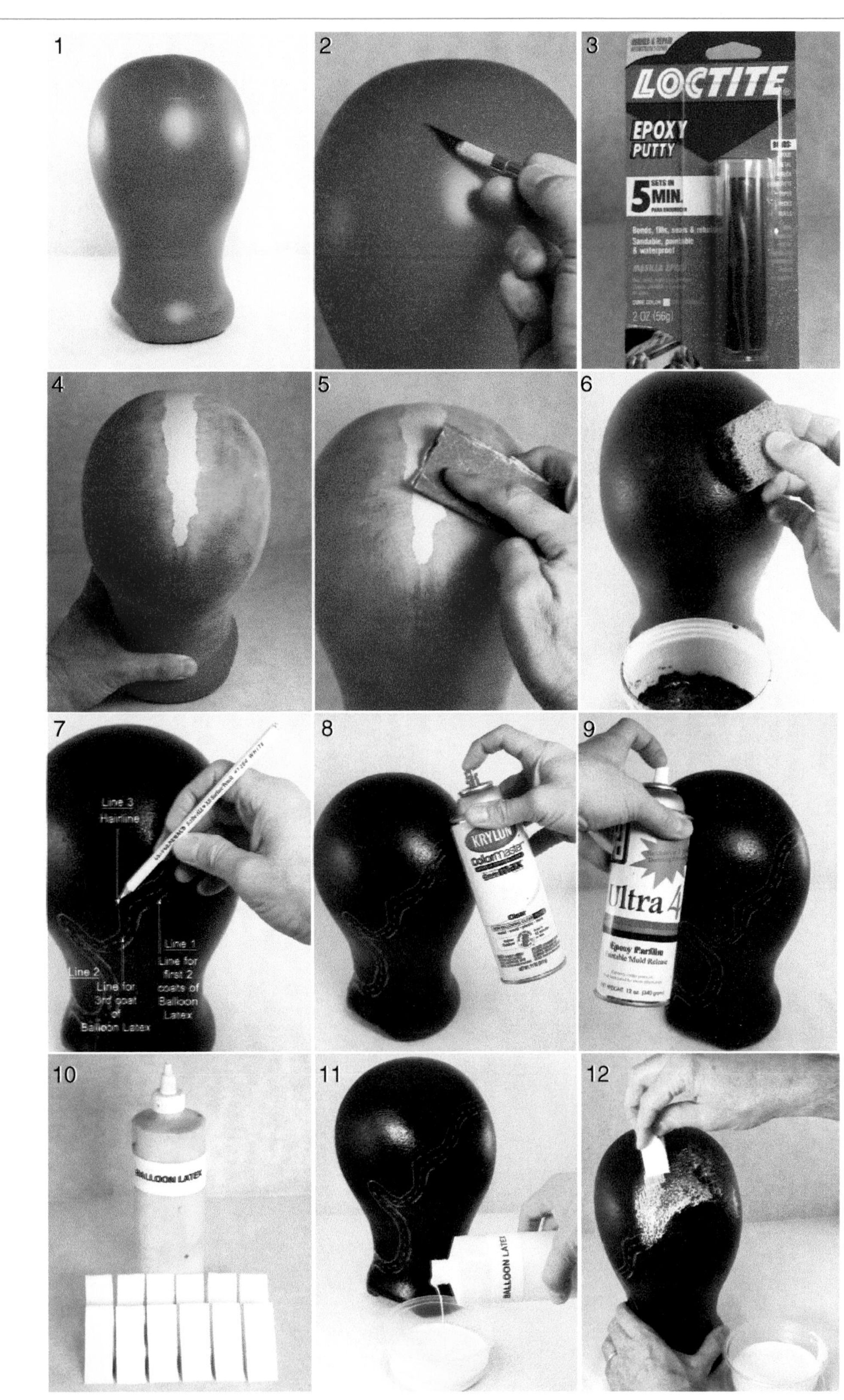

FIGURE 10.11 *Making a latex bald cap.*

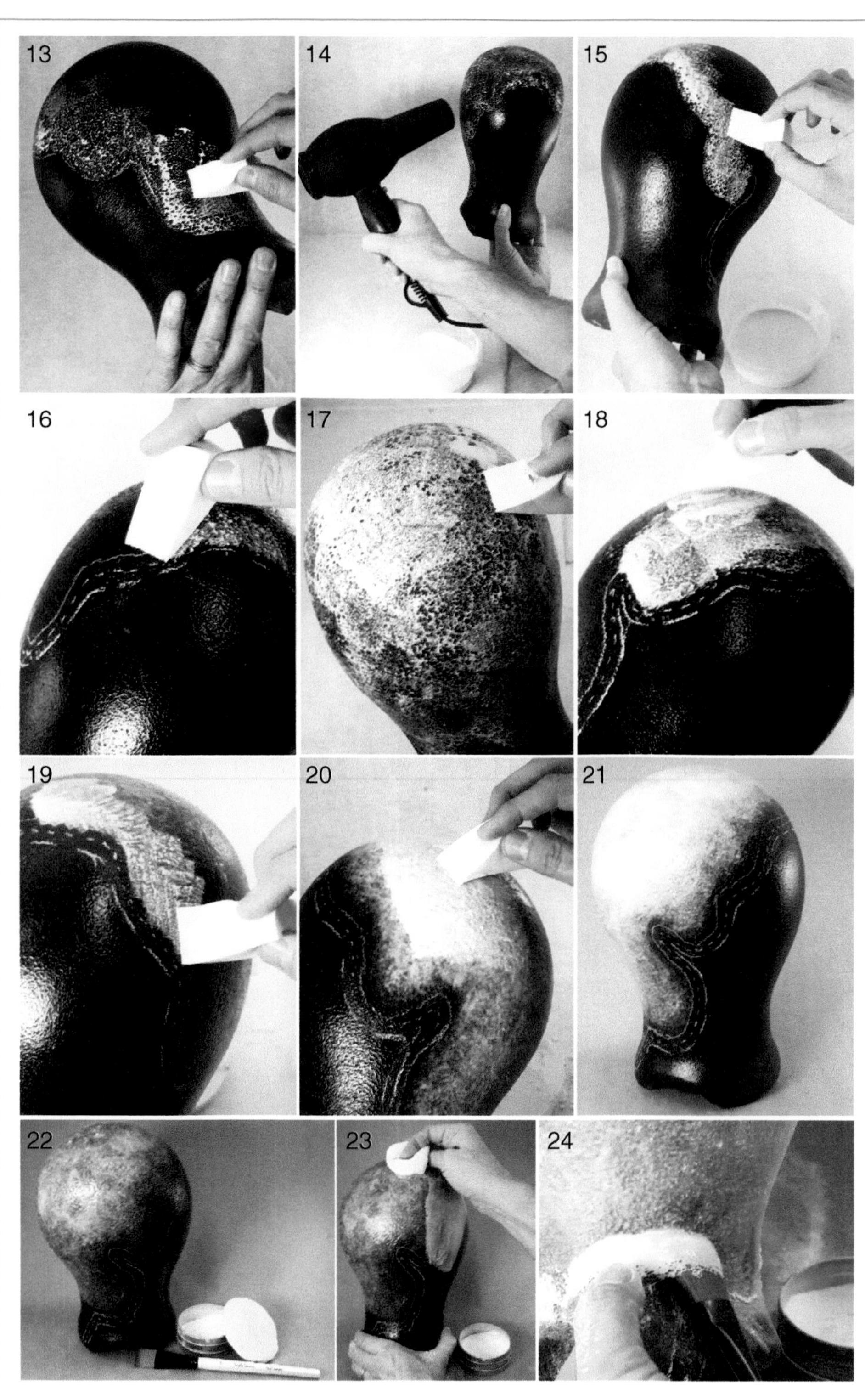

FIGURE 10.11 *(continued)*

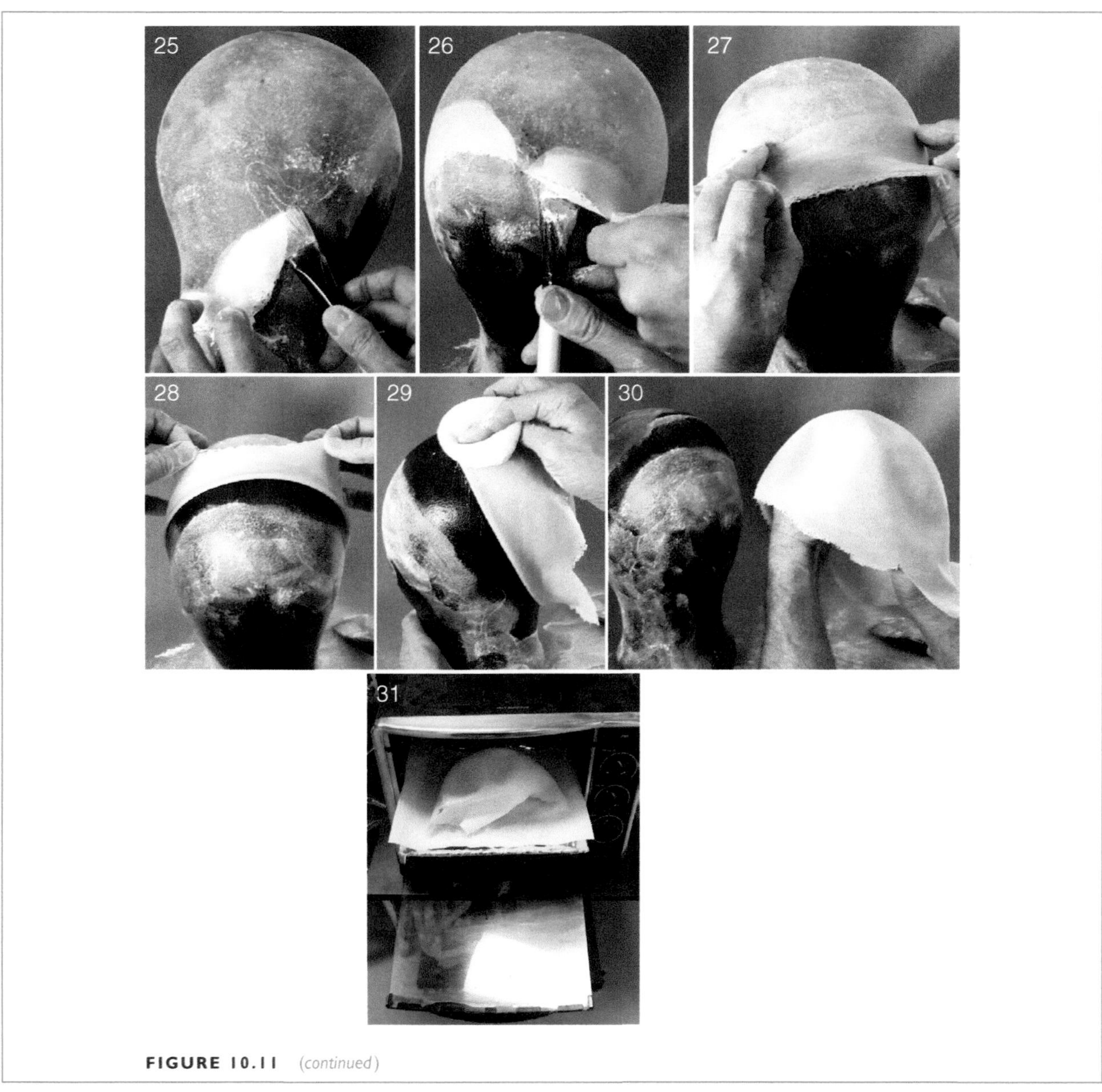

FIGURE 10.11 *(continued)*

Liquitex Tube Paints

40 grams—Titanium White

20 grams—Raw Sienna

8 grams—Burnt Umber

3 grams—Red Oxide

5 grams—Raw Umber

76 grams—Prosaide

Shibui

Liquitex Tube Paints

35 grams—Titanium White

11 grams—Raw Sienna

4.5 grams—Burnt Umber

1 gram—Red Oxide

52 grams—Prosaide

Lt. Bald Cap Undertone

Liquitex Tube Paints

42 grams—Titanium White

9 grams—Raw Sienna

4 grams—Burnt Umber

2 grams—Red Oxide

20 grams—Raw Umber

77 grams—Prosaide

2. Remove the bald cap from the package, save the tissue, and cut a slightly larger curved opening in the front of the cap.
3. Cap front cut with a larger opening.
4. Spray the hair with water and comb it back away from the forehead.
5. Decant Beta Bond into a small CC measuring cup.
6. Paint a small amount of Beta Bond onto the sideburns with a cotton-tipped applicator.
7. Flatten sideburns.
8. Pull bald cap onto the head. Soften any wrinkles or creases out of the bald cap with a hairdryer.
9. Apply a small amount of Beta Bond onto a cotton-tipped applicator.
10. Apply a small amount of Beta Bond onto the sideburn area and to the underside of the bald cap to tack the cap down. Repeat on the other side.
11. Tack down the sides of the bald cap.
12. Apply a light amount of Beta Bond to the back side of the bald cap and to the skin at the center back of the neck where the cap will be adhered. Dry with a hairdryer.
13. While the actor tilts his head back slightly, press the cap down to the skin.
14. Trim the back of the cap toward the ear.
15. Apply Beta Bond underneath the bald cap and onto the skin along the back hairline.
16. With the actor's head slightly tilted to the side and towards you, press the bald cap into the skin. Repeat this to the other side.
17. Mark the area around the ear with a Sharpie.
18. Cut out the ear area. Take care to cut the cap as close to the inside shape of the ear as possible. You can always cut it larger if needed.
19. Continue the cut to the back of the neck area.
20. Push the hair back under the bald cap with the handle of a makeup brush.
21. Glue down the neck area with Beta Bond. If needed, use a pair of tweezers to pull up to reposition or unfold an edge.
22. Glue down the sideburn area after cutting the bald cap away.
23. Continue trimming the bald cap ½ inch from the temple area.
24. Glue the temple area of the bald cap down with Beta Bond.
25. Repeat the same process on the opposite side of the cap.
26. Trim the bald cap to ½ inch from the top hairline in front. Glue and adhere the bald cap.
27. Place the tissue paper included in the bald cap package (or any tissue) onto the front of the bald cap and trace out the hairline with an eyebrow pencil.
28. Cut along the traced hairline. Discard the top part of the tissue.
29. Apply Prosaide Bondo to the edge of the bald cap with a small, white foam sponge wedge. Do not create too much texture on the skin and cap, just enough to conceal the bald cap edges.
30. Continue the Bondo application along the edge of the entire bald cap. Dry with a hairdryer.
31. Powder the Bondo edge with a powder puff and RCMA No-Color Powder.
32. Stipple Shibui PAX onto the entire bald cap, with a torn white foam sponge wedge, leaving ¼ inch of hairline showing through the bald cap.
33. Dry the PAX with a hairdryer.
34. Apply a coat of Lt. Bald Cap Undertone PAX over the previous coat of Shibui PAX with a torn white foam sponge wedge.
35. Before and after application of the Undertone color.
36. Wet a small white foam latex sponge wedge with water.
37. Apply Shibui PAX color to the edge of the hairline out onto the skin. The PAX must be blended and tapered onto the skin without leaving a hard edge.

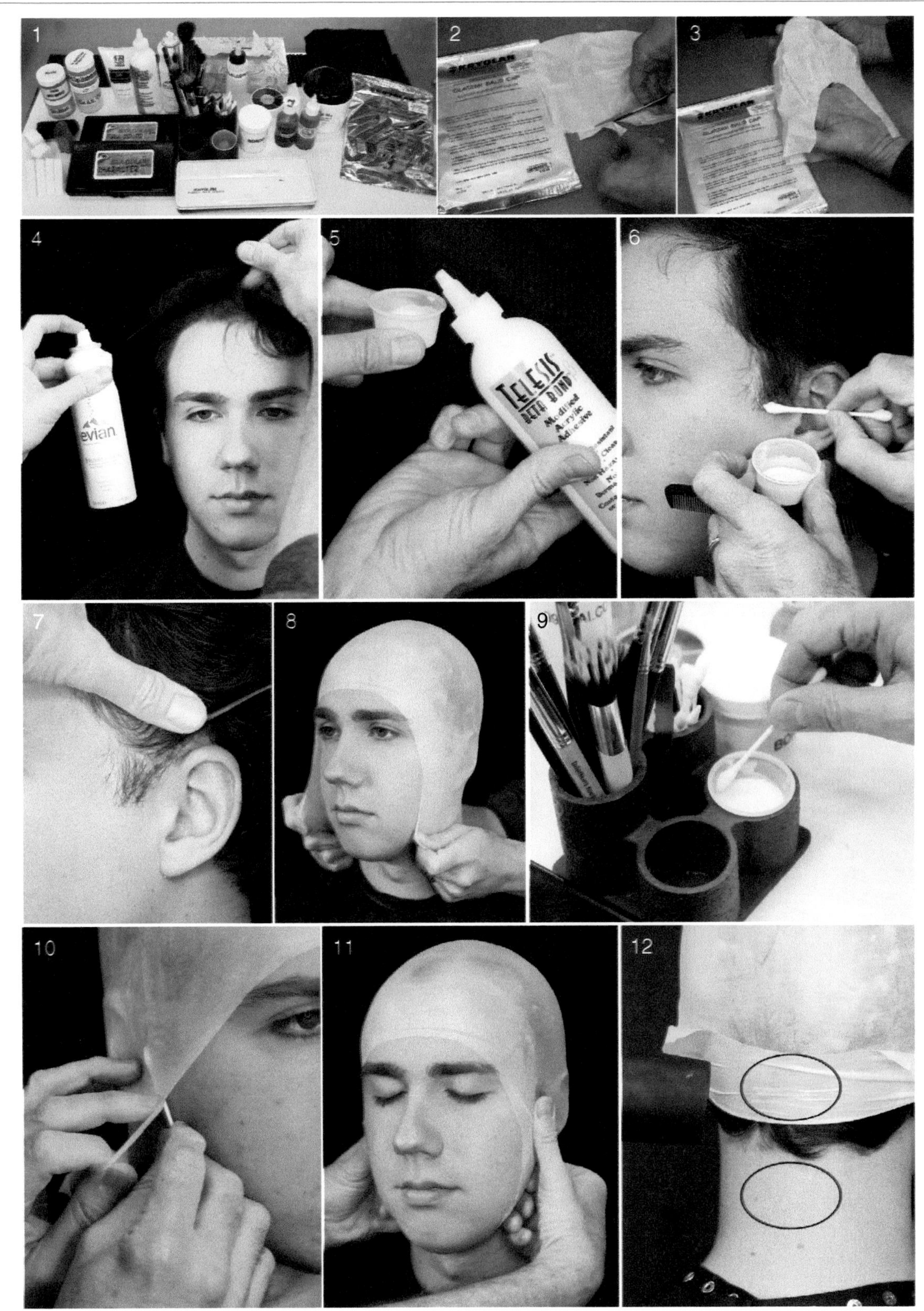

FIGURE 10.12 *Applying a bald cap. The latex cap is made of extra-thin latex, with an unusually long nape, which can be shortened if you wish. Complete instructions for applying the cap come with it. Application by Special Effects Makeup Artist, Matthew Mungle. Model, Connor Sullivan. (See also Plastic and Rubber Caps in Appendix A.)*

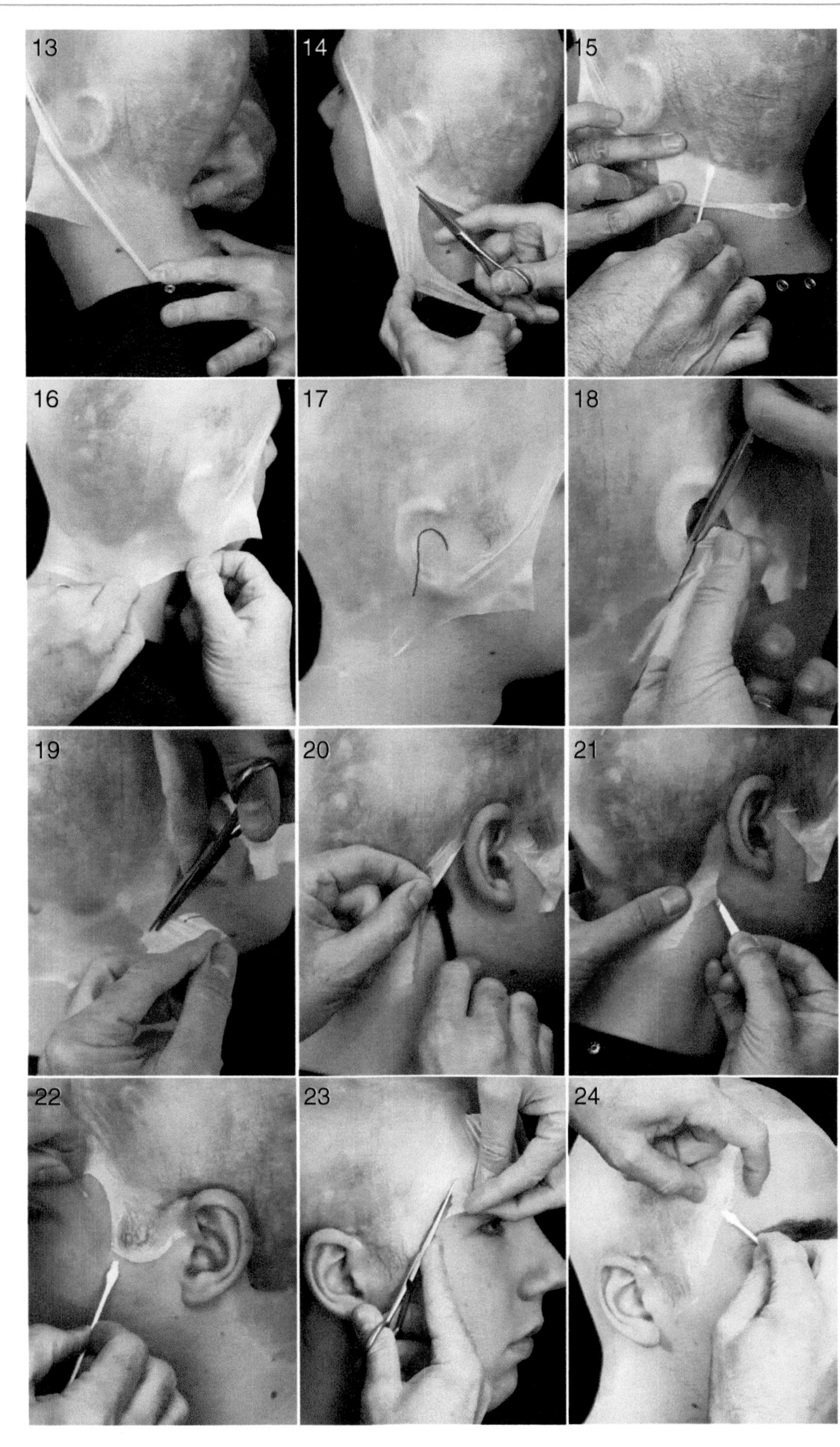

FIGURE 10.12 *(continued)*

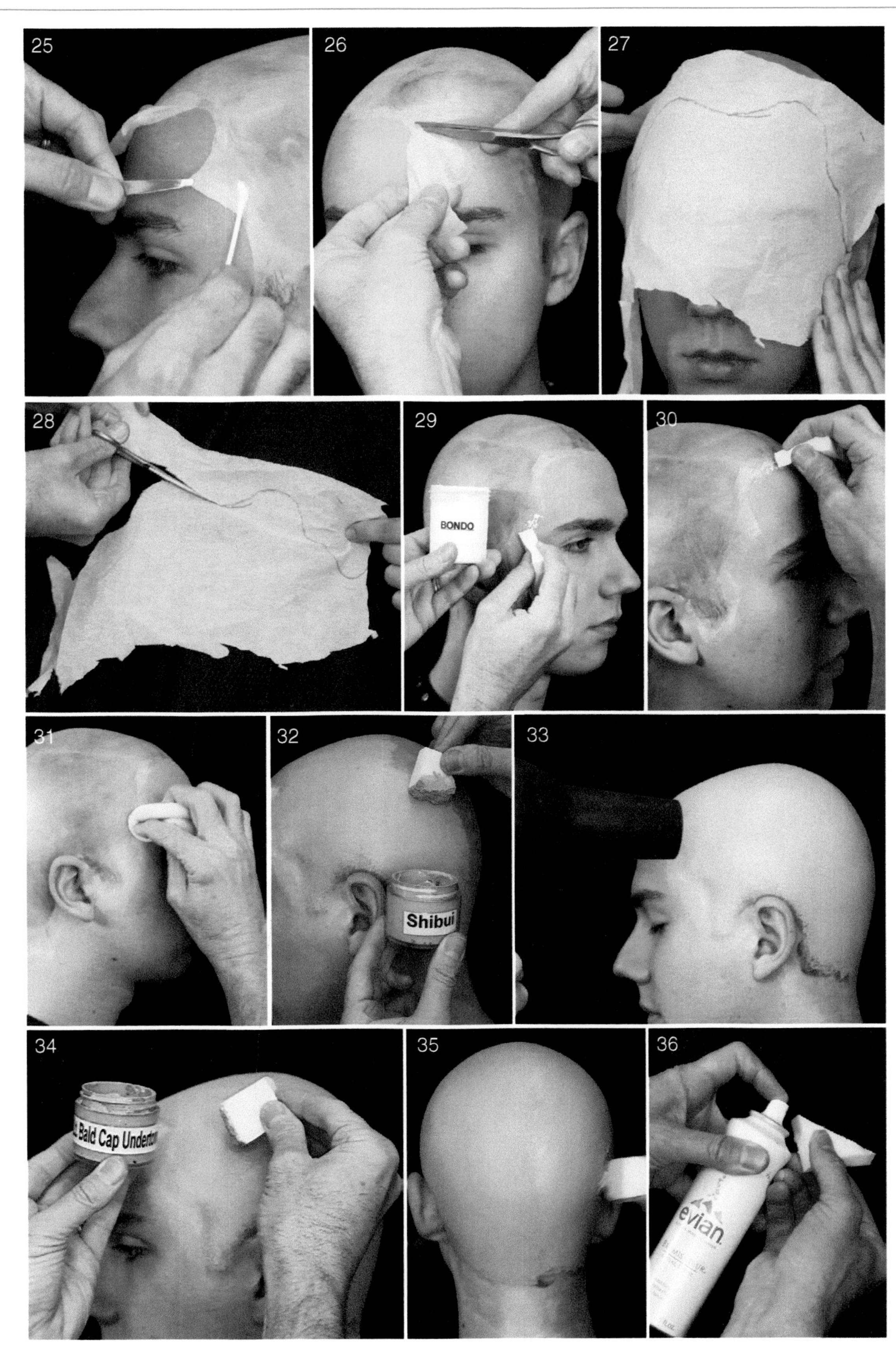

FIGURE 10.12 *(continued)*

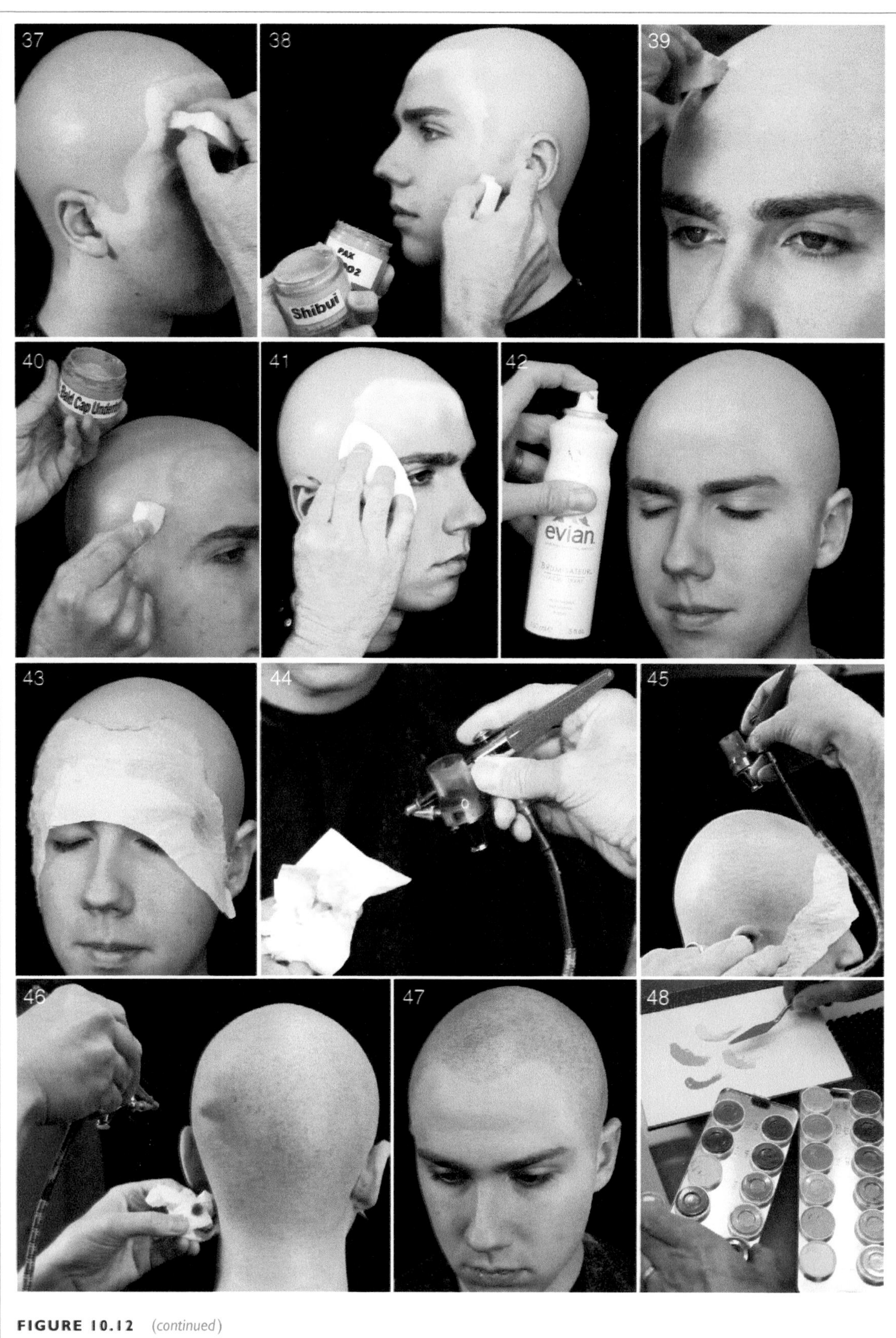

FIGURE 10.12 *(continued)*

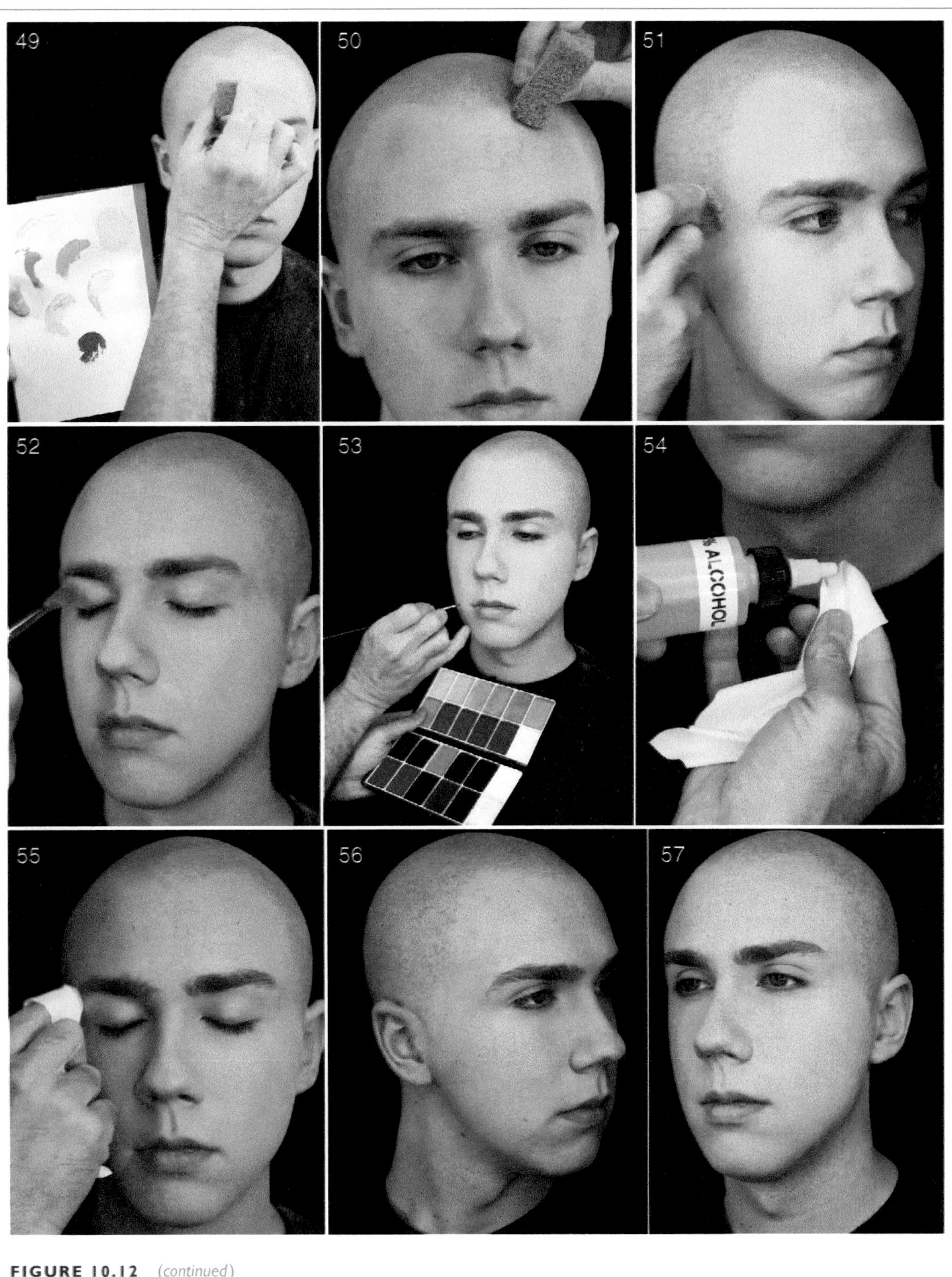

FIGURE 10.12 *(continued)*

38. Pick up a dab of Shibui and a dab of MV002 PAX with another small, wet, white foam sponge wedge and paint this combination onto the bald cap, starting at the Undertone color and outward onto the skin. Do not leave a harsh edge on the skin area.
39. Continue painting the bald cap and skin areas.
40. Reapply a light coat of Lt. Bald Cap Undertone to define the hairline. It is not necessary to cover the entire cap with this color again. Dry with a hairdryer.
41. Powder the whole bald cap with RCMA No-Color Powder and a powder puff.
42. Spray a light mist of water onto the front of the bald cap.
43. Place the tissue paper stencil cut (in step #28) over the forehead of the bald cap onto the hairline area.
44. Load the airbrush with Stacolor GBB Beard Stipple & Brown liquid colors and thin down with 99% alcohol (⅛ oz. color to ¼ oz. alcohol).
45. Turn the air compressor pressure down to 6–10 psi, tilt the airbrush at a 45-degree angle, and lightly press the valve to let out a small amount of air which will deposit small dots of color onto the bald cap. Test this on a tissue before airbrushing the bald cap.
46. Continue the spattering technique all over the bald cap.
47. Remove the tissue stencil from the bald cap. If the tissue sticks to the bald cap, lightly spray the area with water to remove.
48. Using the spatula, scoop out the desired Krylon RMG colors onto a wax paper palette.
49. Using a torn orange stipple sponge, pick up small amounts of skin tone colors to stipple and cover the PAX area up to the hairline and onto the skin. Stippling is a tapping motion. Blending is a rubbing motion.
50. Application of RMG colors onto the skin and bald cap. Stipple these colors onto the face as well.
51. Stipple a brick color on with an orange stipple sponge to add a natural coloration back into the duller skin tones.
52. Use a round brush to blend the RMG makeup under the eyes, onto the eyelids, and around the nose areas.
53. Stacolors (alcohol-based makeup) are used to add any blemishes and spots to the face where needed.
54. Apply a small amount of 99% alcohol onto a tissue.
55. Clean the eyebrows with the tissue, removing any excess makeup base.
56. Finished bald cap.
57. Finished bald cap.

FIGURE 10.13 *Christopher Walken. Wig attached over bald cap. Gelatin nasolabial fold and jowl appliances. Stretch and stipple aging (old age stipple) around eyes. Makeup by special makeup effects artist Matthew Mungle. Actor Christopher Walken in Blast from the Past.*

Source: Photograph courtesy of Matthew Mungle.

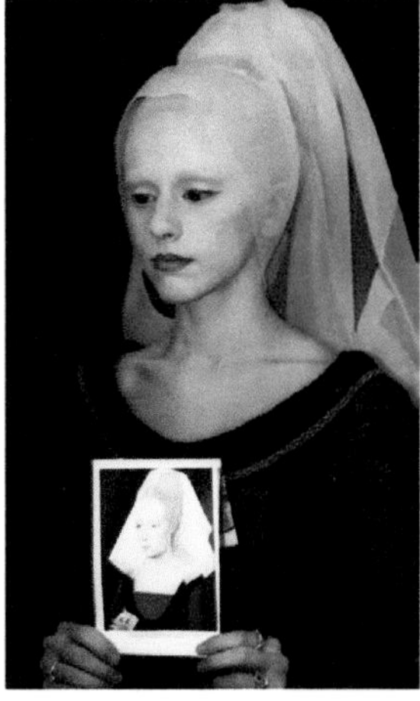

FIGURE 10.14 *Historic makeup recreation of a fifteenth-century portrait. Headpiece attached over bald cap.*

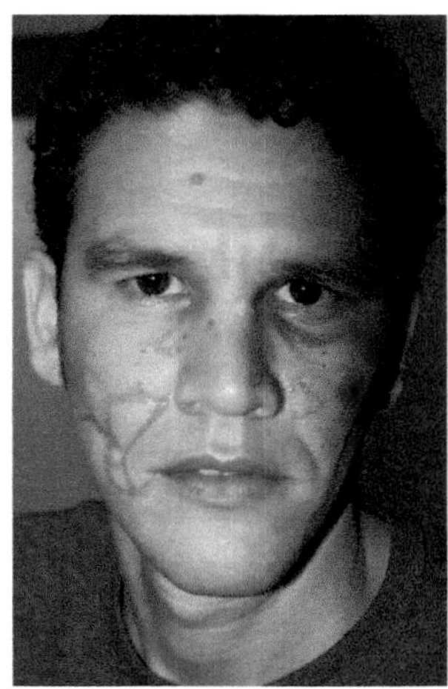

FIGURE 10.15 *Black eye, bruise, scar on model Pedro Reyes Cardona.*

BLACK EYE

A black eye involving only swelling and bruising can be simulated with paint (see Figures 10.16 and 10.17). It may involve only the orbital area or the cheekbone as well. In either case, it changes color as it ages. There is more red at first, but then the inflammation subsides, leaving a deep purple color (giving the "black" effect), medium or dark gray, and the greenish yellow color typical of bruises which are no longer inflamed.

The various stages of a black eye can be simulated by mixtures of red, purple, black, white, and greenish or lemon yellow (try Ben Nye bruise wheels and Kryolan 24-color Dermacolor palette, and alcohol activated color palettes by Primiere Products, Inc., Temptu, and W.M. Creations Stacolor). The purple can be deepened with black, and if the mixture is not red enough, red can be added. Or it can be stippled with black and red. Black and white can be mixed for the gray. For the yellowish tinge, lemon yellow can be mixed with just a little light gray (white with a touch of black) or stippled with light gray. All of the color can be applied with a brush or with a small black stipple sponge.

If the cheekbone is to be involved, you can highlight it just below the corner of the eye. The area immediately below the eye (including the lower lid) and the superciliary bone above the outer corner of the eye can also be highlighted. For light-skinned characters, white can be used for these highlights and stippled down later. For dark-skinned characters, it would be better to use a color a few shades lighter than the base. Gray shadow can then be stippled below all of the highlights and in the eye socket. Purple and black stipple can be added when appropriate. The shape of the darkened area will usually be a somewhat irregular oval. All edges of both highlights and shadows should be kept soft.

To begin, choose a bony area of the face above or below the eye as the impact point. This point can easily be highlighted creating the illusion of swollen skin (remember, light colors protrude while dark colors recede). Then, take your stipple sponge and cut it into several different shapes, some pointed, some rounded off. Take the pointed stipple sponge and apply a small amount of red to the bruised area. Do not make it a solid color! Using another sponge, stipple purple in a smaller area around the point of impact, overlapping the red in some areas (a fresh bruise is more red and pink in color so use the purple judiciously). Now, take a clean latex sponge and lightly blend the colors out in feather-like strokes creating streaks and swirls, giving the appearance of interesting patterns of broken blood vessels. Blend the two colors together in some areas, leaving them separate in others. You can, at this point, repeat the previous steps to intensify the colors. When you are finished, powder the bruise with translucent powder and brush away any excess. Then mist over the entire area with water (i.e. Evian aerosol spray) to reduce the powdery look and bring out the natural-looking colors.

Fresh bruises are mostly pink and reddish in color, turning purple and red, then purple and blue as they get older. The next stage is slightly greenish, then it turns yellow, and finally disappears as the blood pigments are absorbed gradually into the bloodstream. To make the older bruise, simply follow the same steps using more purple and blue, adding green and yellow around the edges.

BRUISES

Even when accompanied by swelling, a bruise can usually be simulated with paint. For light-skinned characters, red,

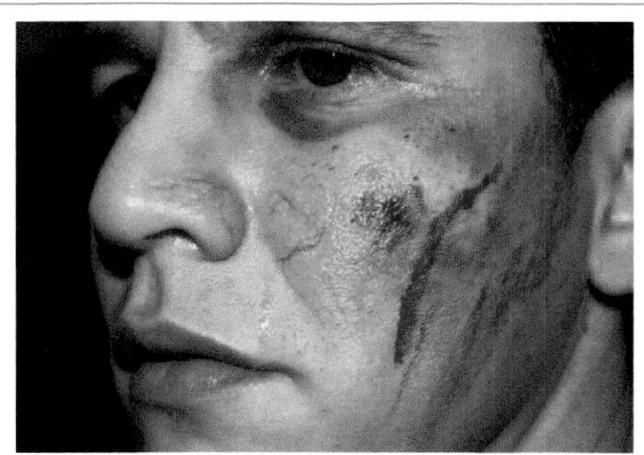

FIGURE 10.16 *Bruises and scrapes. Model Pedro Reyes Cardona. Broken capillaries around the nose are created with K-Y Jelly and yarn fibers.*

gray, purple, greenish yellow, and light cream or ivory can be used. The fresher the bruise, the more red; the older it is, the more yellow. For darker-skinned characters, the colors should be adjusted to the color of the skin. The color being used can be either dabbed on the bruised area and then blended together with a brush, or stippled on. In either case, make sure that all edges are soft. If the bruised area is to be very swollen, you may want to build it up first with derma wax, silicone putty, or gelatin (gelatin kits are available from Kryolan, Ben Nye, Paramount; for gelatin recipe, see Chapter 11, Figure 11.10).

BURNS

Minor burns can be simulated by stippling the skin with red makeup applied with an orange texture sponge or textured latex sponge. For blister burns, one or two layers of latex can be applied and dried with a hairdryer. Fingers can be used to then pull up from the skin small circular areas to create full or broken blisters. Color can then be added and a little petroleum jelly or K-Y gel painted on to create the wet sensitive skin under a broken blister.

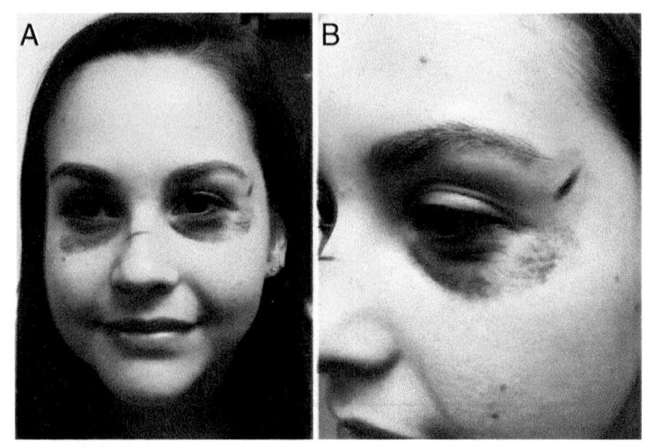

FIGURE 10.17 *Black eye and facial cuts created with alcohol-based effects palette. Model Sarah Scott. Makeup artist, Ben Rittenhouse (Head of the Special Effects Makeup Artist Program at the Academy of Makeup Arts in Nashville, TN).*

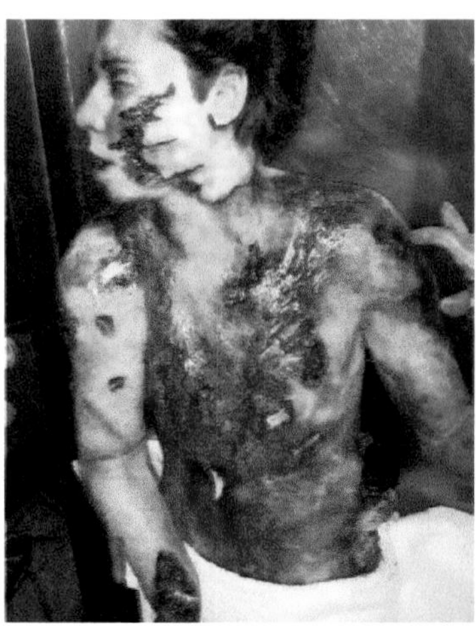

FIGURE 10.19 *Burn victim from the* CSI *television show. Makeup by Matthew Mungle.*

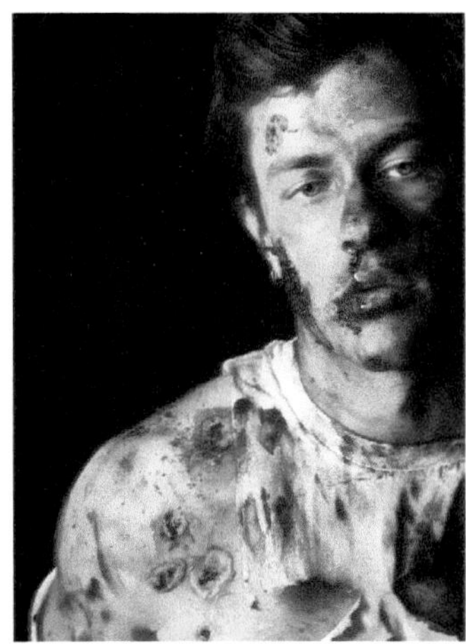

FIGURE 10.18 *Burn victim. Makeup using liquid latex, Ben Nye Bruise Wheel, stage blood, scab blood paste, black pressed eyeshadow.*

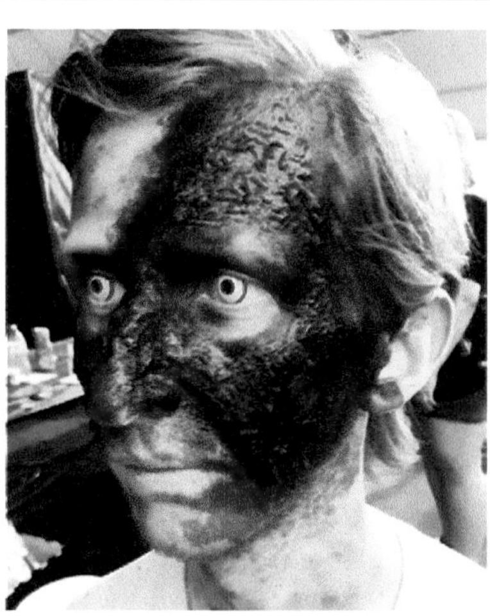

FIGURE 10.20 *Severe facial burn. Makeup artist, Rebecca Morgan.*

Cleansing tissue placed over the latex and then covered with another layer of latex will give more body to the hanging burnt skin. Cotton can be used with the latex for burnt flesh. For deeper, more dramatic burns, coat the skin with 2-part silicone gel (Skin-Tite by Smooth-On, 3rd Degree by Alcone, Artex by Kryolan, and Sculpt Gel by Mouldlife), which can be removed and used again. Makeup can then be applied over the latex.

Skin Burn (Figure 10.21):

1. Model: YuJung Shen.
2. 99% alcohol and cotton facial pad.
3. Decant 99% alcohol into a small spray bottle. Spray the cotton pad.
4. Clean the area of the face where the burn will be located with 99% alcohol.
5. Skin-Tite Silicone Ultimate Wound Kit: Parts A & B, 4 color pigments, Thi-Vex thickener, mixing sticks, 2-oz. mixing cups.

6. & 7. Decant equal amounts of Part A and Part B in separate containers.

8. Add a small amount of light flesh colorant to Part B. Mix well.
9. Add Part B into Part A. Mix well. Remember to scrape the sides and bottom of the bowl frequently.
10. Add one, two, or three drops of Thi-Vex thickener as needed. Mix well.
11. Apply Skin-Tite silicone directly to the skin. Use a wooden craft stick or other applicator.

12. & 13. Continue adding silicone until the desired thickness and shapes are created. Skin-Tite will cure within 5–6 minutes of application and will be ready to accept color.

14. Mix another batch of silicone. Repeat steps 6 and 7. Add a small amount of red colorant.
15. Blood red-colored silicone can be applied using a small metal spatula.
16. Skin Illustrator On-Set Palette alcohol-based makeup.

17. & 18. Apply the Aged Blood color with a brush.

19. & 20. Using the same Skin Illustrator color, apply makeup with a stipple sponge.

21. Mix another batch of Skin-Tite. Add a small amount of red and brown colorant to create a dark red mixture. Apply with a cotton-tipped applicator.

22. & 23. Using the Skin Illustrator On-Set Makeup Palette mix a dark purple color and apply to the wound using a small brush and stipple sponge.

24. Close-up of skin burn so far.
25. Mehron Bruise Wheel. Use the colors: Bloody Rose, Burnt Maroon, Midnight Sky.

26. & 28. Create a black eye using a small brush and the three colors listed in step 25.

29. Finished silicone skin wound.

Cuts, Wounds: Superficial cuts can be painted on with or without the use of artificial blood. Deeper cuts usually require building up the area with wax or putty, then cutting into it with a dull instrument, such as a palette knife. Plastic sealer can be painted over the construction at this point if you wish. Various materials, such as derma wax, putty wax, silicone gels, gelatins, scar plastics, tissue and latex, Prosaide (Prosthetic) transfers, and Bondo paste can also be used to create open wounds. And various non-makeup items can be combined with those materials to produce interesting effects.

The inside of the cut can be painted red with RMG, alcohol-based FX palette colors, and cream FX color wheels. For the most realistic and dramatic effect, the wound opening should be filled with stage blood (unless of course the character is a zombie which would require any variety of colored liquids other than red). For a cut that is still bleeding, a few drops or even a stream of artificial blood can be added to the cut with an eye dropper which can be allowed to flow out, then smeared over the wound and onto the skin surrounding it.

In some areas, such as the neck, where building up with putty or wax may not be practicable, latex can be painted directly onto the skin and allowed to dry thoroughly. The skin can then be pushed together into a crease in the middle of the strip of latex. The latex will stick to itself, forming a deep crease that can be made to look like a cut with the addition of red makeup. For a horizontal cut in the throat, be sure to use a natural crease in the skin if there is one. Pinching of the skin is not recommended but is sometimes done.

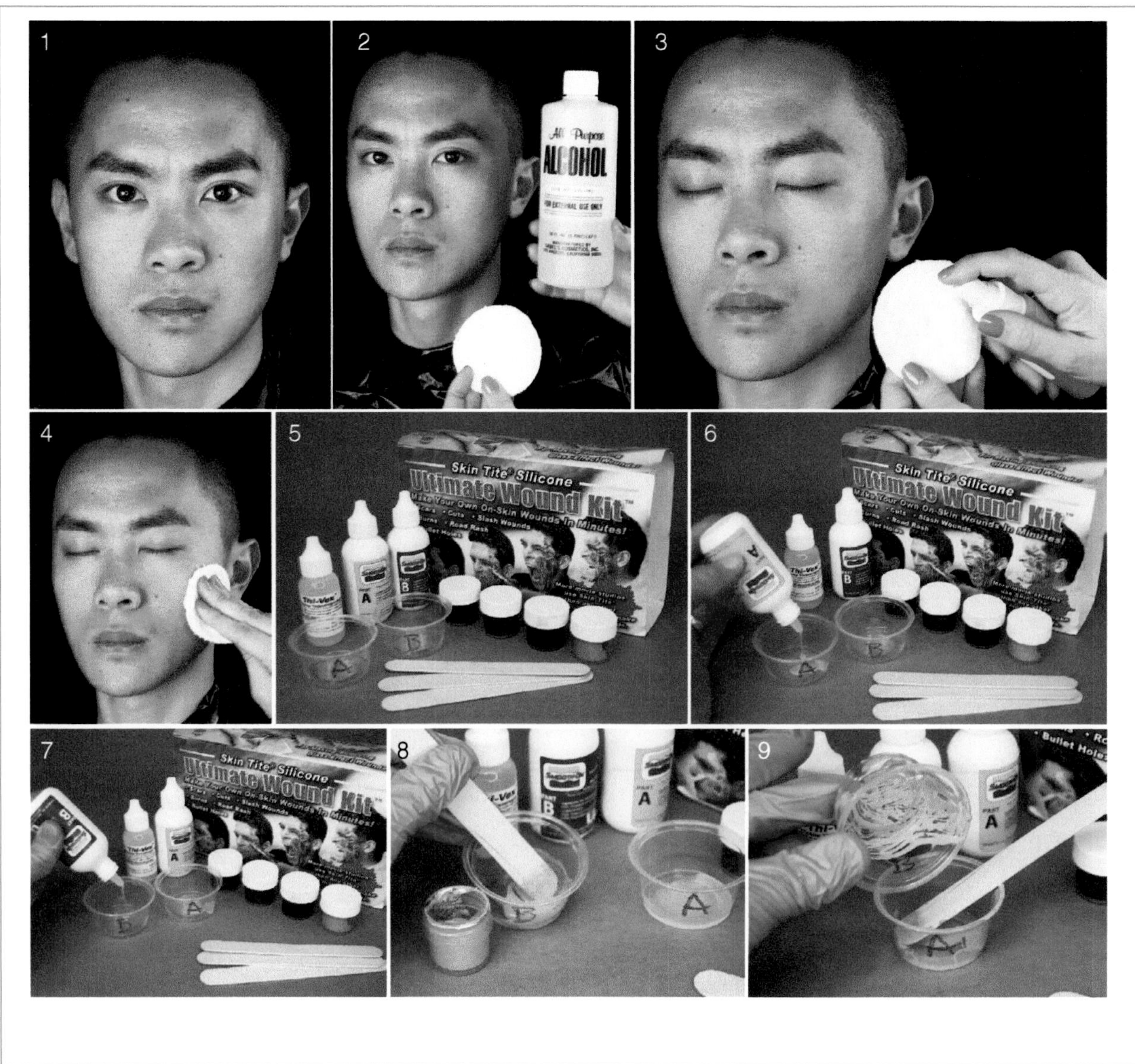

PROSTHETIC TRANSFERS

Deeper and more realistic cuts and scars can be created with a *prosthetic transfer*. The process, originally developed by Christien Tinsley for the film, *The Passion of Christ* (2004), allows the artist to create small prosthetic appliances without the need of a face, head, or body cast. Multiple pieces can be made ahead of time and stored for usage. The 3-dimensional pieces are sculpted from non-sulfur oil-based clay on a flat surface, molded in silicone, then made from thickened Prosaide adhesive.

How to Make a Prosthetic Transfer Cut/Wound

1. Figure 10.22 – Materials: Mold Star 30 Platinum Silicone Rubber Part A & B; non-sulfur oil-based clay sculpt of a wound/cut; mixing containers; mixing Sticks, Prosthetic Transfer Material, prosthetic transfer paper and release film; release agent (the small bottle); Ease Release 200 spray mold release.
2. Silicone Part A & B; the sculpt of a wound or cut; a small box of foam core to contain the silicone.
3. Place the box over the sculpt and use hot glue to seal the edges. Spray the sculpt generously with Ease Release 200 and allow to dry.
4. Measure 2 oz. of Part A and 2 oz. of Part B into separate cups.
5. Pour A into a larger mixing container. Pour Part B into Part A.

FIGURE 10.21 *Skin burn using 2-part silicone.*

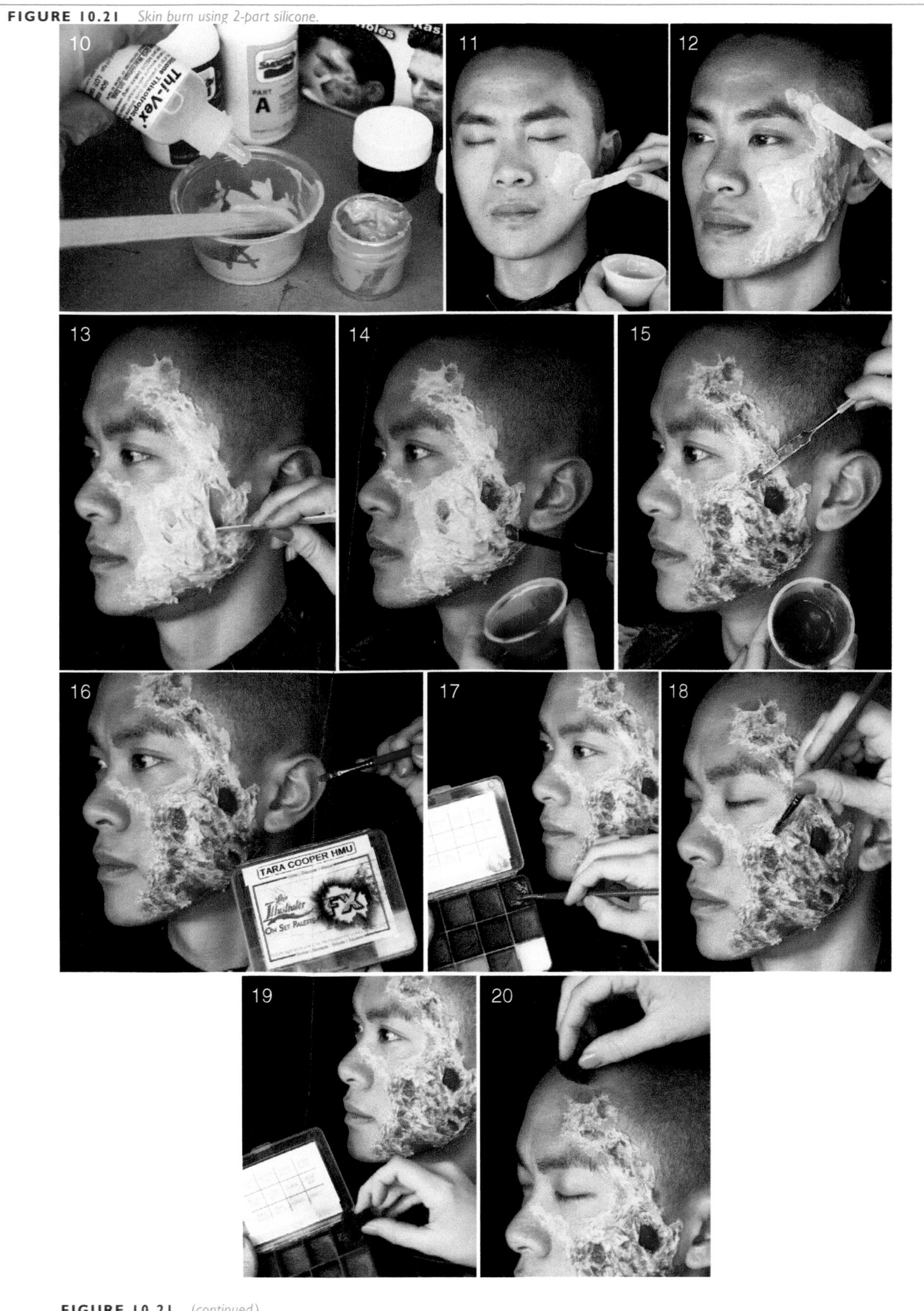

FIGURE 10.21 *(continued)*

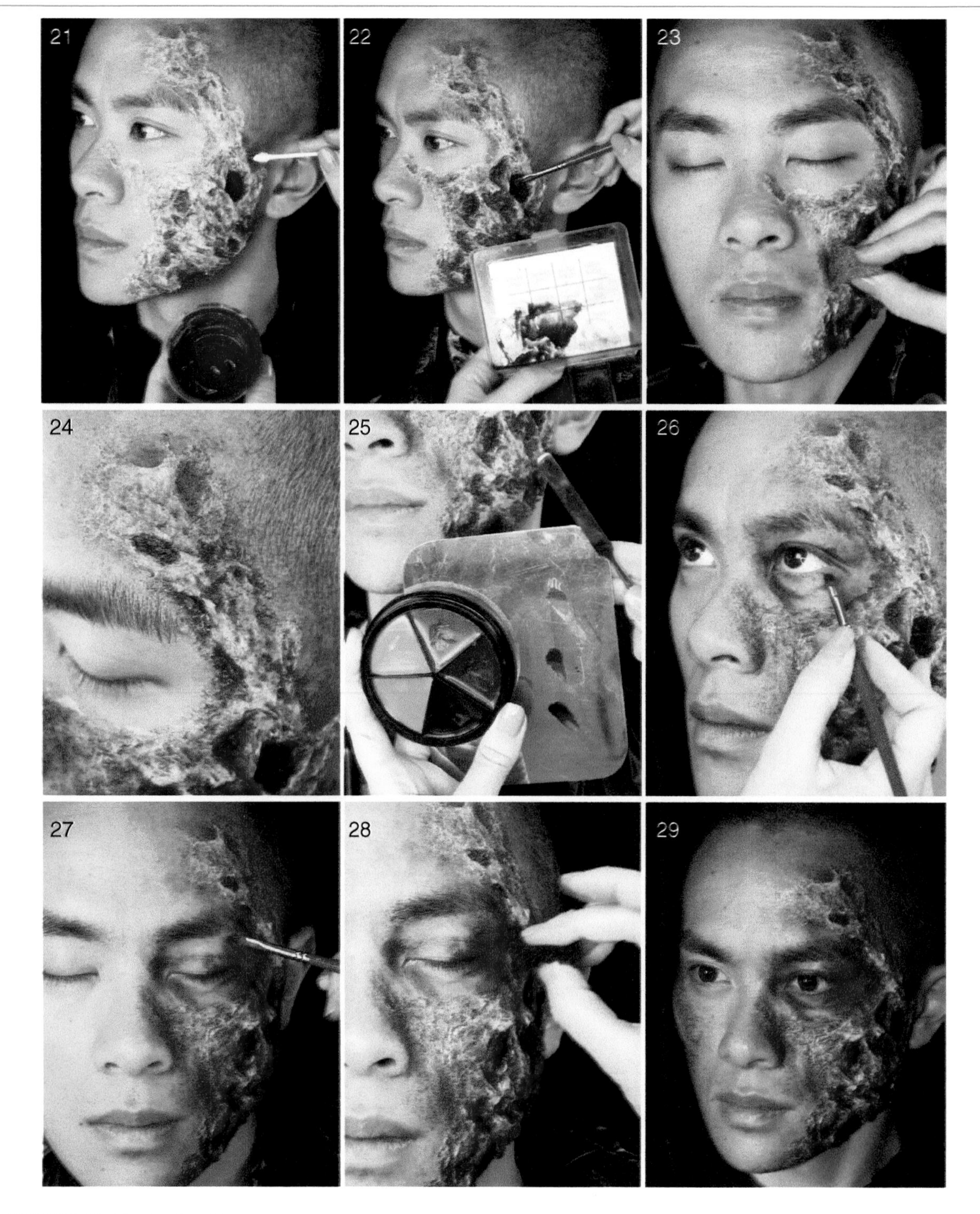

FIGURE 10.21 *(continued)*

FIGURE 10.22 *How to make a prosthetic transfer.*

6. Mix thoroughly for 5 minutes. Scrape the sides and bottom regularly to incorporate all of the silicone. This product has a working time (Pot Life) of 45 minutes.

7. Pour the silicone over the sculpt starting at the lowest point in the mold. Allow the silicone to cure for 6 hours. (Note: Different products have different curing times. Be sure to check the manufacturer's specifications.)

8. & 9. Carefully remove the box.

10. Separate the silicone negative mold from the positive sculpt.

11. Materials: Mold Release from Prosthetic Transfer Material, negative silicone mold, 1-inch chip brush.

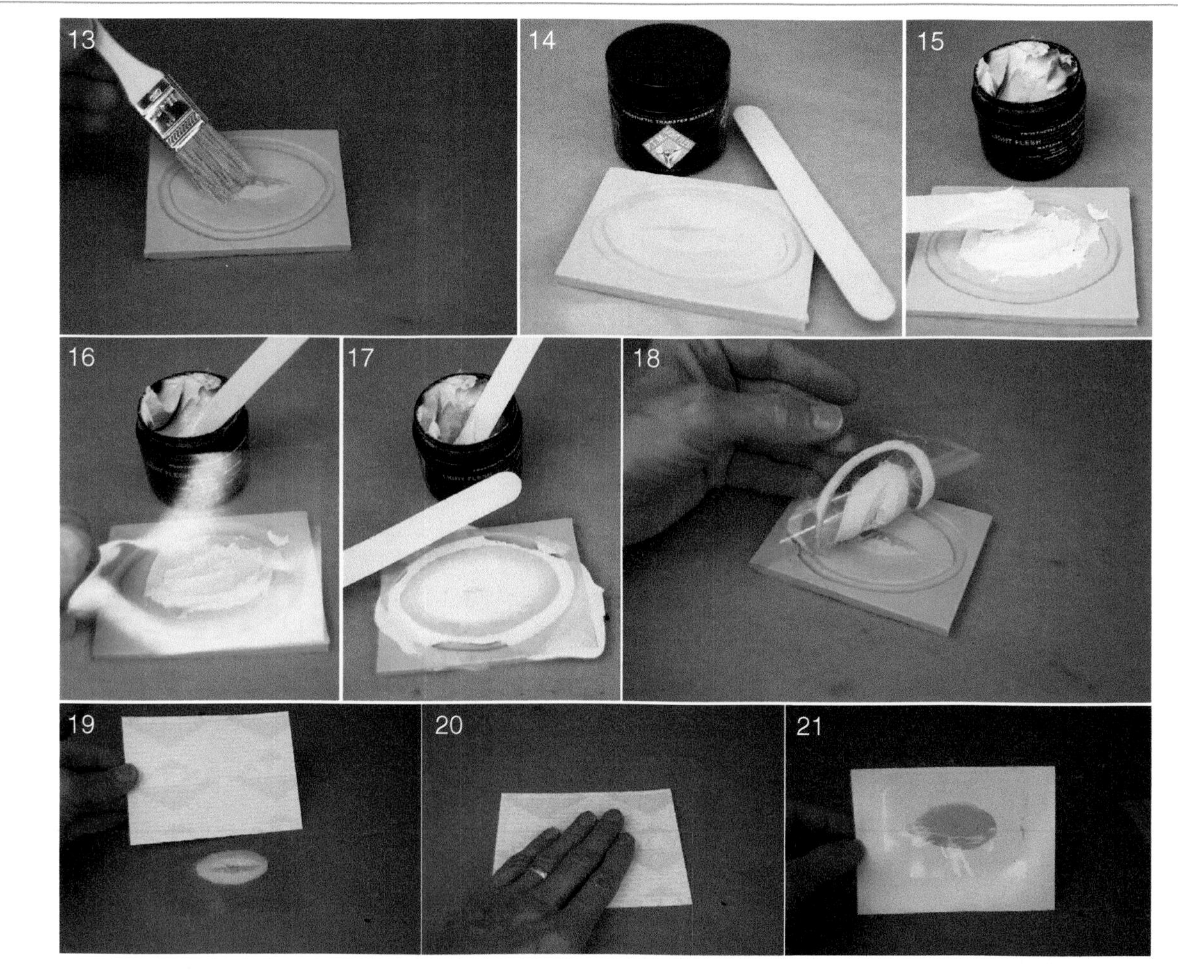

FIGURE 10.22 *(continued)*

12. Apply two drops of the Mold Release into the negative mold.

13. Brush the Mold Release into the mold, covering the entire surface. Let dry for 5 minutes.

14. Prosthetic Transfer Material (also known as P.T.M., Bondo, Pro-Bondo, Prosaide Transfer Material), negative mold, craft stick.

15. Spread a small amount of P.T.M. into the mold using a wooden craft stick. The material must be pressed into all areas to avoid air bubbles. The material should create a slight mound on the surface of the mold.

16. Place a sheet of clear release film onto the mold. Both sides of this film have a non-stick surface. Other manufacturers may produce this film with only one side having a non-stick surface. To test which side is non-stick, mark a short line on each side with a permanent marker. One side will be solid, the non-stick side will bead up.

17. Using the craft stick as a squeegee, drag the long edge of the stick across the surface of the film. (The stick must be longer than the mold is wide.) Squeegee in one direction, turn the mold 90 degrees and repeat in the other direction. The stick will displace the excess P.T.M. and distribute it in the trough equally all the way around. The P.T.M. will now have a flat surface.

    - Place the mold in the freezer for 15–60 minutes (depending on the size; smaller molds can remain in the freezer for the shorter amount of time; a larger mold, longer amount of time).

18. When the color of the product turns darker, remove the mold from the freezer and remove the Prosaide Transfer from the mold. It will still be attached to the plastic film. Allow the piece

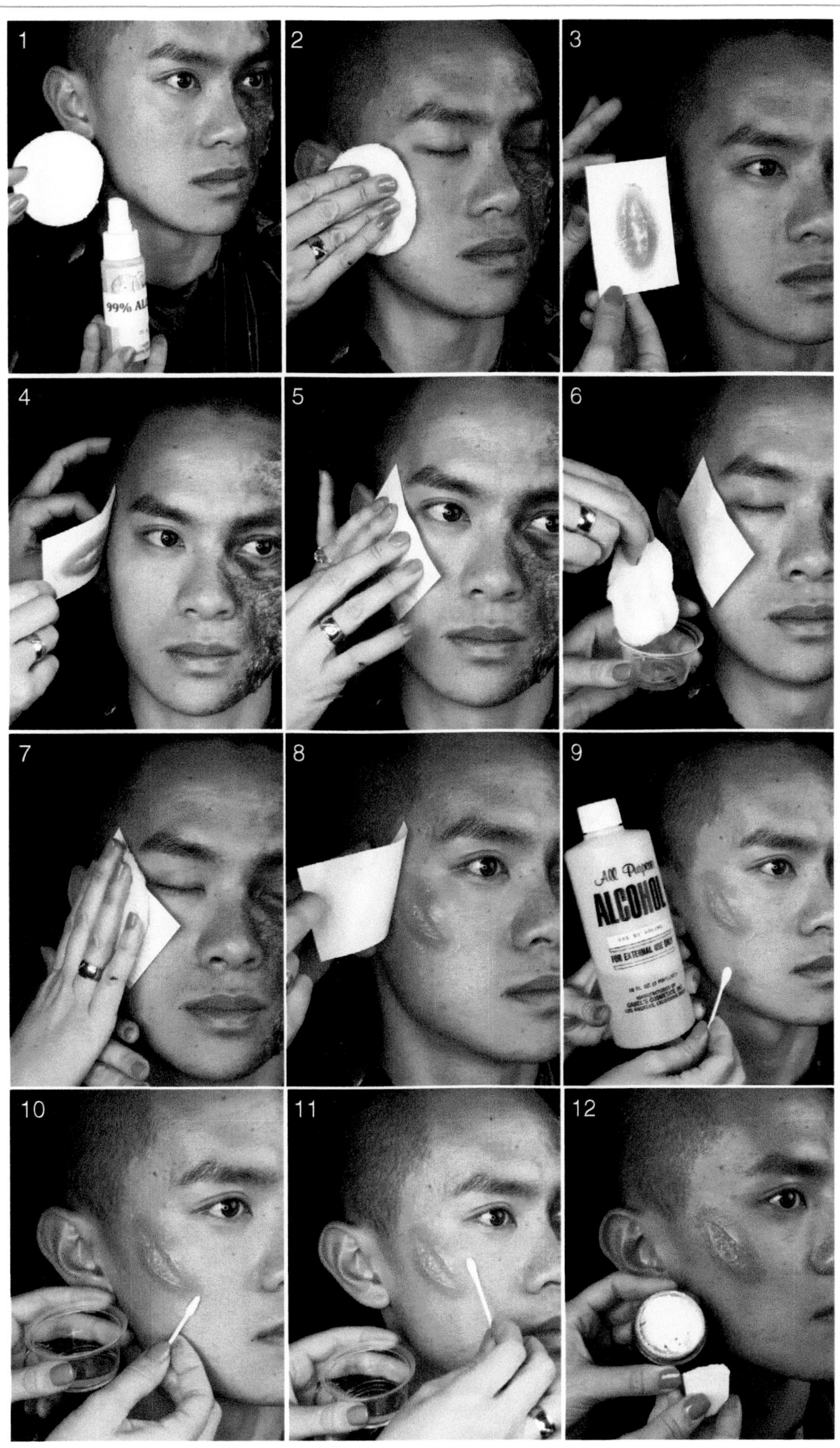

FIGURE 10.23 *How to apply the Prosaide Transfer cut/wound.*

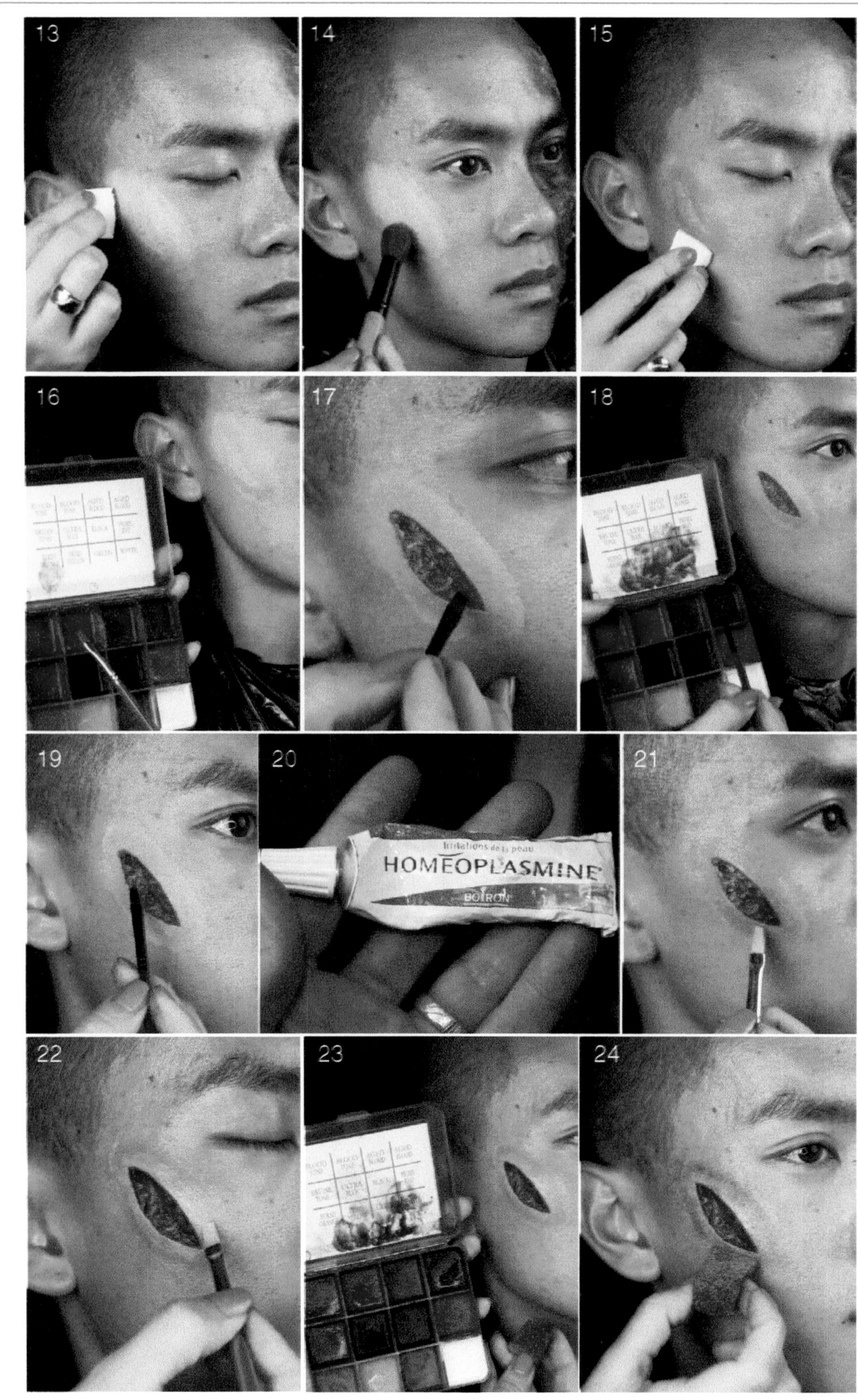

FIGURE 10.23 *(continued)*

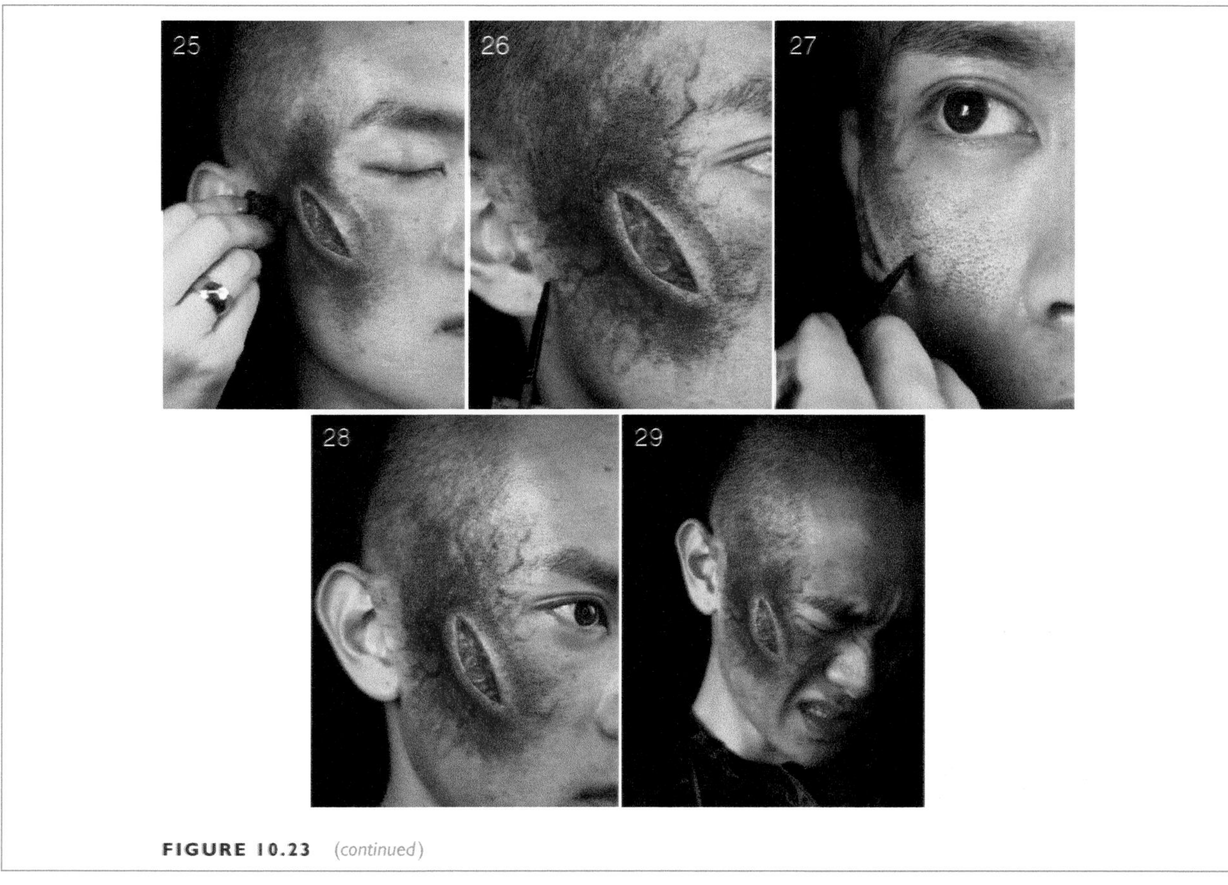

FIGURE 10.23 *(continued)*

to dry in the open air, under a light bulb, or in fruit/vegetable dehydrator. At this time the dimensional positive side will be facing up. The flat side will remain attached to the plastic film. The piece can be set aside or stored until the application.

19. Clean the dimensional side of the "transfer" with 99% alcohol on a cotton swab to remove any residue of the mold release, then paint the surface with a small amount of Prosaide adhesive and let dry. Place the shiny side (the plain white side) of the transfer paper onto the "transfer."
20. Firmly press the paper onto the "transfer."
21. Now the transfer is between the clear acetate film and the white transfer paper.

Applying the Prosthetic Transfer Severe Cut

1. & 2. Figure 10.23 – Clean the skin with 99% alcohol.

3. The prosthetic transfer or Prosaide Transfer Appliance attached to the transfer paper. The clear acetate film has been removed.

4. & 5. Apply the prosthetic transfer appliance by simply pressing it onto the skin. The Prosaide remains sticky and will adhere to the skin without extra adhesive. For a more secure appliance, first paint a thin layer of Prosaide adhesive on the flat side of the "transfer," allow it to dry (it will be clear and tacky when it dries), then apply it to the skin.

6. & 7. Press a wet towel, cotton pad, or sponge against the transfer paper. Allow the paper to become saturated. Warm water is suggested.

8. After a few minutes peel the paper away from the prosthetic.

9., 10., & 11. Blend the edges using a cotton swab and 99% alcohol.

12. & 13. Lightly powder the appliance with a no-color setting, finishing, or blotting powder.

14. Brush off extra powder.

15. Wipe the powder with a wet sponge.

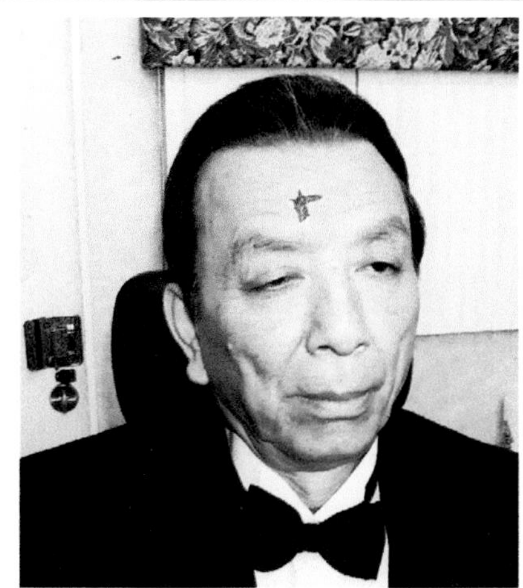

FIGURE 10.24 *Gelatin bullet hole for Actor James Hong in the film The Art of War. Applied with Prosaide, airbrushed with RCMA RMGP thinned with 99% alcohol. Colored with blood paste and liquid blood. Appliance was applied, then digitally removed until the actual shot was fired. Makeup by Adrien Morot and wig by Mark Boley for Steve Johnson's XFX, Inc.*

16. Skin Illustrator Bruise Effects Palette.
17., 18., & 19. Color the interior of the wound with various colors of Blood Tone, Aged Blood, and Black.
20. & 21. Apply homeoplasmine, makeup primer, or clear foundation liquid to the outer fleshy area of the wound to remove the powdery effect of the setting powder. This will return it to a moist skin texture that will blend with the surrounding skin.
22. Apply a highlight around the edge of the cut. This will resemble the pale color of the swollen area that surrounds a fresh cut.
23. Skin Illustrator Palette and a small orange sponge (activate with 99% alcohol).
24. Apply a light stippling of red around the appliance.
25. Continue adding color until the wound area represents your design.
26. Veins are painted onto the wound.
27. Veins are painted onto the wound.
28. Finished makeup.
29. Finished makeup.

EYE BAGS

These are invaluable aids to aging and are one of the simplest pieces you can make (Figure 10.25). Again, you should work from photographs of real people (see Figure 8.15). Some pouches will be fairly smooth and definitely pouch-like. Others will be somewhat flat and look like a mass of fine wrinkles. There are countless variations. If there is a definite line of demarcation or definitive crease line to the pouch you wish to make, then it will not be necessary to leave a thin edge on the bottom of the piece, though there should be one at the top. As usual, remember to give it skin texture. Because this area of the face is soft and pliable, it is of benefit to the performer to make eye pouches from a flexible product:

- Foam latex
- Gelatin
- Silicone
- Bondo and Prosthetic Transfer Material.

Each of these products has its advantages and disadvantages:

- *Foam latex* is very light and flexible, but requires a lengthy preparation of a formula with five ingredients, blended carefully in a mixer, poured into a 2-part gypsum mold and cured in an oven for up to 8 hours (4 hours of baking and 4 hours to cool). The edges must be masked by stippling with Prosaide, which can be difficult for beginners. Prosthetics from foam latex can be used only once.
- *Gelatin* is a very flexible, translucent product, blends nearly imperceptibly into the surrounding skin, also has a mixture of five ingredients (can be purchased as a ready-to-use product), and the edges blend easily with witch hazel. Somewhat heavier than foam latex. Can be made in a 1- or 2-part mold and cures/dries in a matter of minutes. Disadvantage: is affected by heat and perspiration. Can be used only once.
- *Silicone* is a very flexible, somewhat translucent product that blends nearly imperceptibly into the surrounding skin, has a 2-part mixture often mixed together in equal proportions, and can be used in a 1- or 2-part mold. Cures within 40 minutes. Can be used again if carefully removed.
- *Bondo* and *Prosthetic Transfer Material* are created from Prosaide adhesive and Cabosil. They are each quite flexible, and easy to make (can be purchased as a ready-to-use product) (working with foam latex will be discussed in Chapter 11).

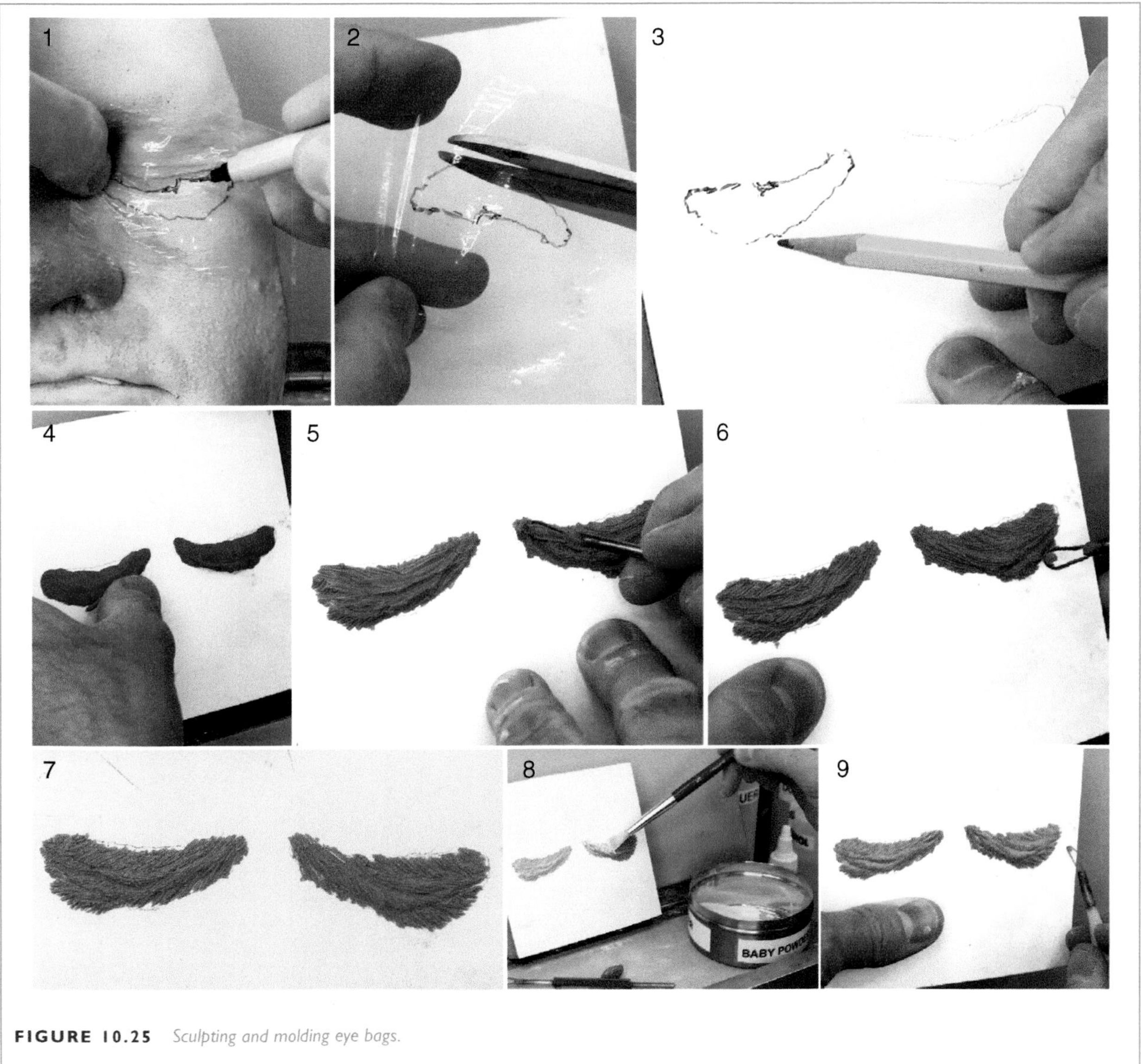

FIGURE 10.25 *Sculpting and molding eye bags.*

Sagging eye bags can be constructed in the same manner as the Prosaide Transfer deep cut. The following is a step-by-step process for creating eye bags using Bondo (Figure 10.25).

1. Trace a pattern on a piece of plastic wrap with a black Sharpie where the desired eye bag will be placed.
2. Cut the pattern out of the plastic wrap with a pair of scissors.
3. Trace the pattern on a plastic or Formica board with a pencil.
4. Block the eye bags out with Chavant NSP (sulfur-free) Brown clay.

5. & 6. Sculpt wrinkles and contours into the clay with a rake sculpting tool.

7. Sculpted eye bags before smoothing and texturing.
8. Lightly smooth out the sculpting with baby powder and a brush.
9. Continue any sculpting details with a small wire loop sculpting tool on the edges of the appliances.

10. & 11. Place a piece of plastic wrap over the sculpting and use a pin to sculpt small wrinkle lines into the clay.

12. Use a soft bristle brush and baby powder to blend and smooth the surface of the clay.
13. Spray the sculpture with a light coat of Krylon Crystal Clear in a well-ventilated area. Do not inhale the fumes.

FIGURE 10.25 *(continued)*

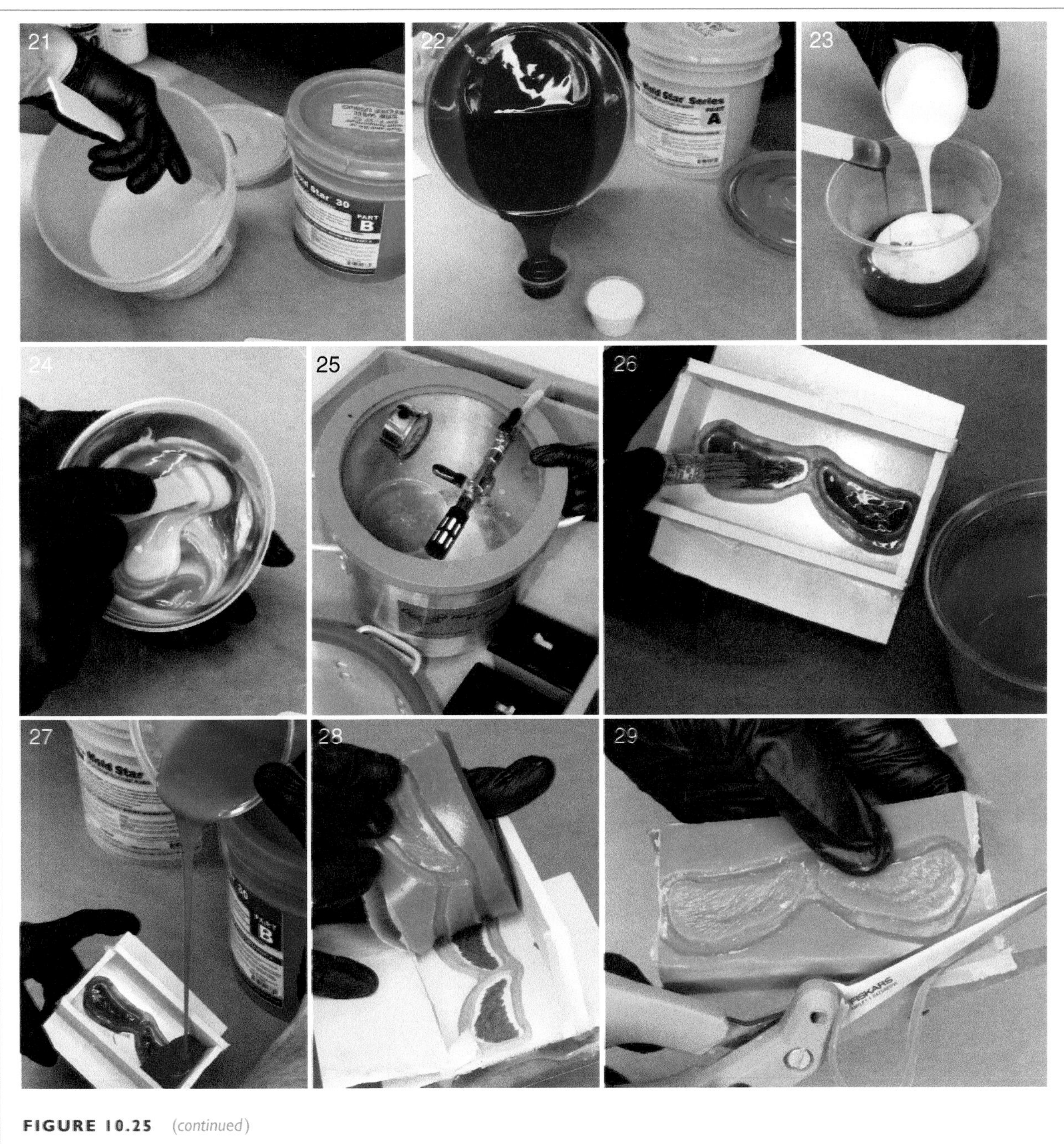

FIGURE 10.25 *(continued)*

14. Finished sculpting.
15. Build the flashing around the eye bags with Kleen clay snakes.
16. Trim the clay around the inside and outside of the flashing. Leave a $\frac{1}{8}$-inch space around the clay eye bags.
17. Re-spray with a light coat of Krylon Crystal Clear in a well-ventilated area. Do not inhale the fumes.

Making the Mold

18. Materials: Hot glue gun, four pieces of foam core cut in $1\frac{1}{2} \times 4$ and 2-inch sizes, eye bag sculptures.
19. Hot glue the foam core to the board to create a leak-proof box.
20. Materials: Mold Star 30, 200 Spray Release, sculpture, deli cups, vinyl gloves, paint stir sticks, tongue depressor and $\frac{1}{2}$-inch disposable brush.

21. Stir Mold Star 30 Part A and B with a paint paddle. *Do not* cross-contaminate product by using the same paint paddle for both Part A and B.
22. Pour out 2 oz. Part A and 2 oz. Part B into small deli cups.
23. Pour Part A and B together in a 32-oz. deli cup.
24. Mix the two components together for 2 minutes.
25. Vacuum the silicone in a vacuum chamber (if available) to remove any trapped bubbles.
26. Paint a light coat of the silicone onto the eye bag sculptures and flashing.
27. Pour the silicone into the box slowly and from a high point to break any trapped bubbles.
28. After the silicone has set (10 hours) pull from foam core box.
29. Trim silicone edges with scissors.

Making the Bondo Eye Bags

1. Spray the silicone eye bag mold with a light coat of Epoxy Parfilm.
2. Materials: Deli cups, Cab-O-Sil, Prosaide, W.M. Creations Soft Sealer, brush, tongue depressors, and metal spatula.
3. Measure out 2 oz. of Cab-O-Sil into a deli cup.
4. Pour in 2 oz. of Prosaide into same deli cup.
5. Stir the product until it becomes a smooth thick consistency. Set aside. There are various pre-mix, plasticized, pigmented Bondo formulas available from special makeup supply companies. (See *Bondo* or *Transfer materials* in Appendix B.)
6. Decant ¼ oz. of Soft Sealer into a small cup.
7. Paint the Soft Sealer up to but not over the edge of the eye bag sculpture with a brush.
8. Dry with a hairdryer for 1 minute.
9. Paint a second coat of Soft Sealer up to but not over the first edge. Dry with a hairdryer for 1 minute.
10. Spatulate the Bondo formula into the mold, being careful not to trap any air bubbles.
11. Spatulate from the middle of the mold out to one side of the mold to remove any excess Bondo.
12. Spatulate from the middle of the mold out to the other side of the mold to remove the remaining excess Bondo. Let dry for 2 hours or until Bondo turns clear.
13. Paint one additional coat of Soft Sealer over the appliance up to but not over the flashing.
14. Dry with a hairdryer for 1 minute.
15. Powder the appliances with RCMA No-Color Powder.
16. Remove the appliances with a pair of tweezers and powder the appliances.

Applying eye bags is presented in Figure 10.7, Character makeup with old age stipple.

PERSPIRATION AND TEARS

The effect of perspiration can be created by applying glycerin, Kryolan's Sweat, or Paramount's Glycerin (can also be purchased at the local pharmacy) over the finished makeup. These products can be applied with the fingers, with a stipple sponge, or with a manual spray bottle.

Tears, if unable to be produced by the actor, can be induced by either rubbing Kryolan's Menthol Tear Stick under the eyes or by using a Tear Blower filled with menthol crystals to blow vapors into the eyes (available at Frends Beauty, Namie's, and Alcone).

PIMPLES/ACNE

Although pimples can be created three-dimensionally with latex, derma wax, sesame seeds, etc., they can also be created more successfully as a Prosaide Transfer. When applying a Prosaide Transfer, clean the skin with 99% alcohol first. Apply the transfer, then color it using alcohol-based FX palettes. In order to determine the appropriate shade, observe the color of real pimples. The pimples, varying in size and irregularly placed, can then be modeled with highlights and shadows, using a very small brush.

If there are to be a lot of them, and the whole area that they cover is to be reddened, the reddening can be done first by stippling, to whatever degree is appropriate. For a few fairly large pimples, begin with a round, reddish spot a bit larger than the raised portion of the pimple in order to create the effect of an inflamed area around the pimple. To visually increase the raised portion of the pimple, place a small, round highlight in the center of the reddish spot. Then, with a tiny brush, shadow around the bottom of the highlight as if you were modeling a sphere. The edges of all three colors in the pimple must be soft.

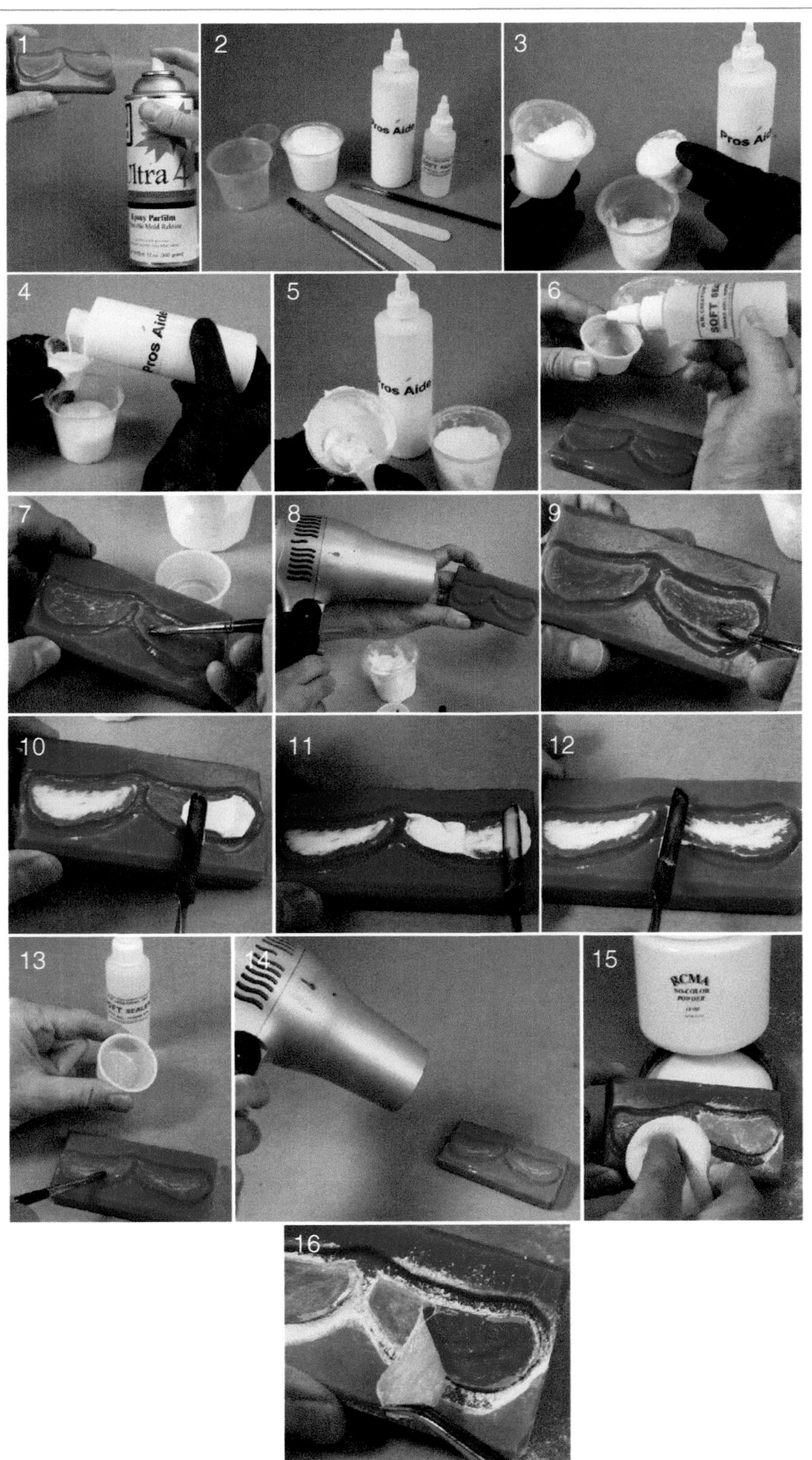

FIGURE 10.26 *Making the Bondo eye bags.*

FIGURE 10.27 *Kryolan Tear Stick.*

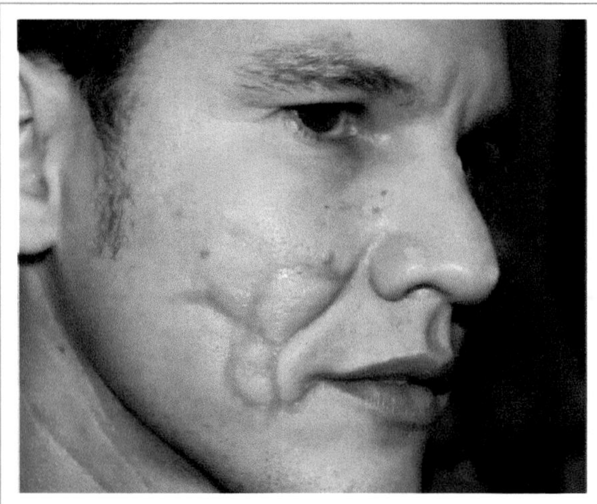

FIGURE 10.28 *Rigid Collodion scar. Model Pedro Reyes Cardona.*

SCABS

Scabs can best be made with Bondo (Prosaide adhesive thickened with Cab-O-Sil). Easily sculpted directly on the skin, this product once dried can be easily painted with cream makeups, and alcohol-based FX color palettes (Figure 10.8, Zombie makeup).

Fresh scabs will often begin as areas of coagulated dried blood. They are nearly black in color at the center and appear more red at the edges. Choose a dark red blood product that dries with a slight sheen (Ben Nye Fresh Scab, Mehron Coagulated Blood, Fresh Scratch by Kryolan, Fleet Street Bloodworks). Build up several layers at the center, blend the edges slightly to reveal the red coloration and let dry completely. Finish with a spray sealer or spray bandage.

SCARS/WELTS

One method for creating scars of the type illustrated in Figure 10.28, is to paint the area to be scarred with nonflexible Collodion (a Kryolan product) before any makeup is applied. As the Collodion dries, it will wrinkle and draw the skin. If the scar is not deep enough, successive coats can be applied. Each coat should be allowed to dry completely before another is added. The makeup is then applied as usual.

A better method is to apply alcohol-based color palette foundation (see Appendix A) to the skin first and apply the Collodion over it. Use only 99% alcohol to activate this type of makeup. Makeup may or may not be needed over the Collodion, depending on the effect you want. For additional protection to the skin, a barrier product like Top Guard by Premiere Products, Inc. should be used before applying the makeup or scar material. *Avoid using Collodion close to the eye.*

For recent scars that still retain a bit of red or pinkish color use pigmented Collodacolor by Michael Davy (see Appendix B).

Collodion scars can be peeled off or removed with acetone. Because dermatologists consider this prolonged creasing of the skin undesirable, this method of making scars cannot be recommended. In addition, Collodion may irritate the skin, though applying the Collodion over the makeup rather than directly to the skin should cause less irritation. However, if there is any irritation at all, this method should not be used. Another method is to pour or brush latex onto glass and, with a palette knife swirl it and shape it into the size and kind of scar you want. Then allow it to dry, or force-dry it with a hairdryer, powder generously as you peel it off the glass to keep the edge thin, and apply it to the skin with Prosaide adhesive. When you complete the makeup, color the scar with alcohol-based foundation and FX colors or with RMGP. It is a particularly good technique for arena staging. For greater dimension, combine the latex with cotton or tissue.

Three-dimensional latex scars can be colored intrinsically using cosmetic grade pigments. Form the raised scars by pouring pigmented latex into a plaster negative mold (#1 industrial molding plaster), allow to dry, powder, remove from the mold, and trim the edges. First, apply a skin barrier to the actor's body where the scars are intended to be attached, then coat the scars and the skin with a pressure-sensitive, silicone-based adhesive (Telesis V by Premiere Products, Inc.) and allow both to dry for 5 minutes. Firmly press the scar onto the actor's skin. Apply makeup to the scar and blend to match the actor's skin color, then powder. Use a strong, gentle solvent to remove the appliance (Super Solv by Premiere Products, Inc., see Appendix A).

Similar techniques can be used to make scars with plastic scar material (Tuplast by Kryolan), or plastic sealer. The plastic, as in the latex process, can be poured or painted into a negative plaster or silicone mold. The mold must first be sealed with two light coats of Kryolan Crystal Clear and Ease Release 200 Spray, and allowed to dry thoroughly between coats. Once it is cured, the plastic can be removed and attached to the skin with one of the pressure-sensitive adhesives. Another technique is to pour or smear the plastic onto glass, then swirl with an orangewood stick to make bumps or ridges similar to the latex process mentioned above. When the plastic scars are pulled off the glass, both sides should be powdered, as with latex pieces. When the scars are applied to the skin with Prosaide or Telesis adhesives, the edges of the plastic can be dissolved and blended into the skin by brushing them with acetone. The makeup can then be applied. The plastic scar can be left without makeup or can be partially or completely made up with appropriate colors. As with latex, materials such as cotton or string can be used in the plastic scar.

Gelatin and Bondo can also be used for making scars. A surgical scar, for example, could be easily and quickly duplicated directly on the skin with both materials. Or it could be made on glass or another smooth surface first, then attached with Prosaide.

Ready-made silicone and vacuform mold of scars and wounds can be found at Frends Beauty Supply, at www.fxwarehouse.com and at prosthetictransfermaterials.com.

Prosaide Transfer scars, which can be attached with medical adhesive and painted directly on the skin, can be used quite successfully (see "How to Make a Prosthetic Transfer Cut/Wound").

Scar Transfers (Figure 10.29)

1. Facial scars created with Prosaide Transfer Material.
2. Forearm scarring (cutting scars) made with Prosaide Transfer Material.
3. Scars are sculpted using sulfur-free, oil-based clay. Notice the research images behind the makeup artist.
4. Sulfur-free soft clay ¼-inch high trough is made around the scars. Then a 1-inch wall of the same clay is built around the sculpted scars and the trough.
5. Silicone is mixed and poured into the molds.
6. The clay is cleaned from the silicone molds. Notice the location of the ¼-inch trough surrounding the sculpts.
7. The silicone molds are sprayed with Epoxy Parfilm sprayable mold release.
8. Prosaide Transfer Material (see Appendix A) is spread into the mold. The product must be forced into the details to avoid air pockets.
9. Clear plastic transfer sheet is placed onto the Transfer Material.
10. Using a small squeegee (a flexible piece of plastic, a wooden craft stick, etc.), spread the Prosaide Transfer Material evenly across the surface of the mold. The squeegee should be longer than the molds and pulled across the surface in one direction, then in the opposite direction, forcing excess material into the trough around the sculpt.
11. Place the mold into the freezer.
12. Remove the scars from the silicone mold. The scars will stay attached to the plastic sheet.
13. Some FX artists dehydrate Prosaide Transfers in vegetable/fruit driers.
14. Prosaide Transfer ready to be applied to the skin.
15. The Prosaide Transfer is transferred from the clear plastic sheet to the paper-backed transfer sheet and pressed onto the skin. The paper is dampened to help the Prosaide Transfer release.
16. The transfer is now adhered to the arm.
17. The transfer scars are painted.
18. The advantage to making and using Prosaide Transfers is the ability to prepare many multiple prosthetics and store them for extended periods of time.
19. Prosthetic transfer scars are being applied to the skin of the performer.
20. A precisely labeled "Face and body" map of the exact locations for the placement of the various body scars. This is particularly useful when continuity during the filming process is necessary.
21. Prosthetic transfers being applied to the face of the performer.

STAGE BLOOD

There are many qualities and colors of stage blood manufactured for a variety of effects: arterial, veinal, wet, dried, pooling, scab, squirting, running, shiny, thick, thin, dark, red, blue, brown, transparent, opaque, gel-formula, nonstaining, eye, and edible. It must perform in a manner that is visually appropriate

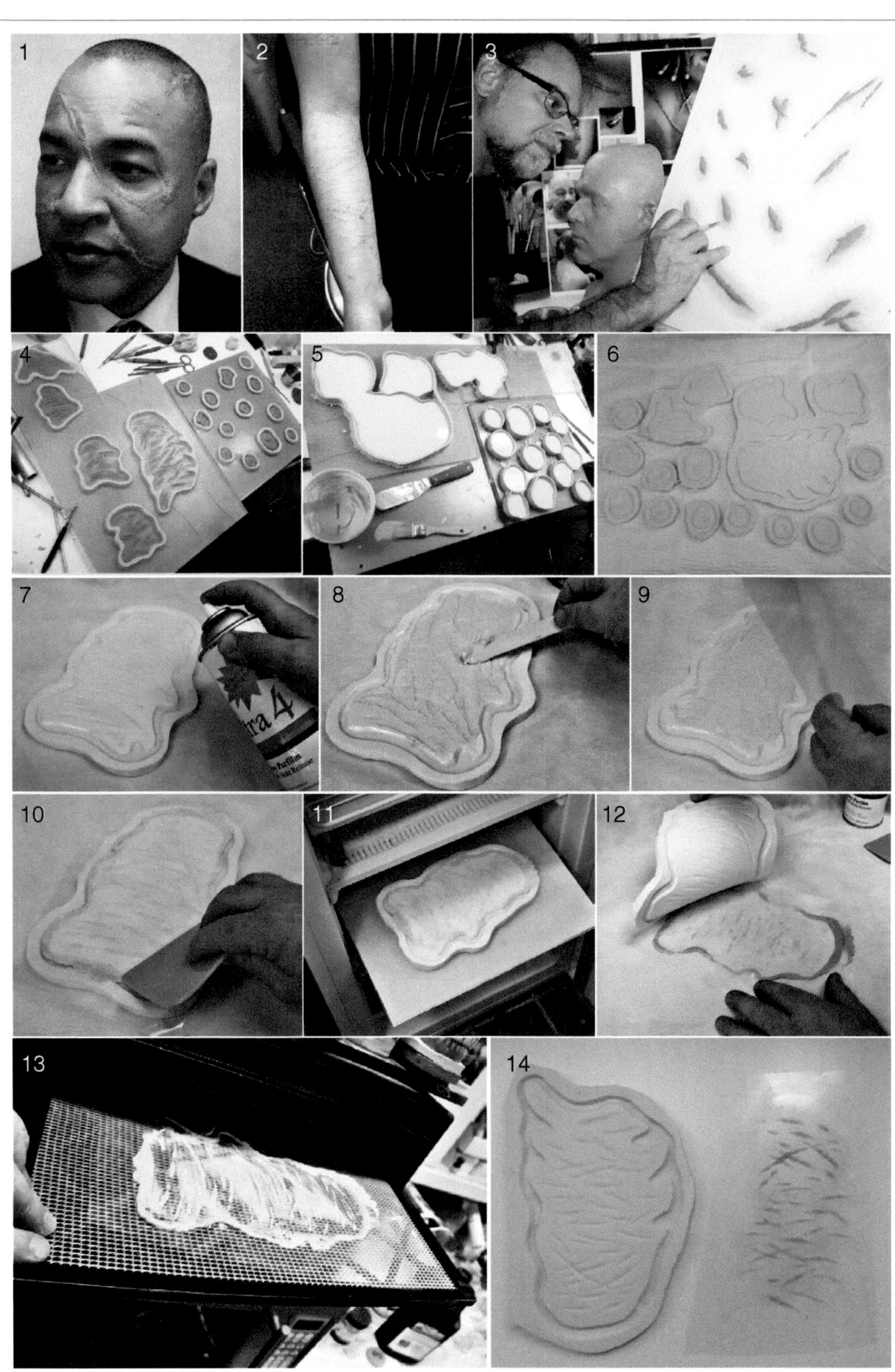

FIGURE 10.29 *Scar transfers by Stephan Tessier.*

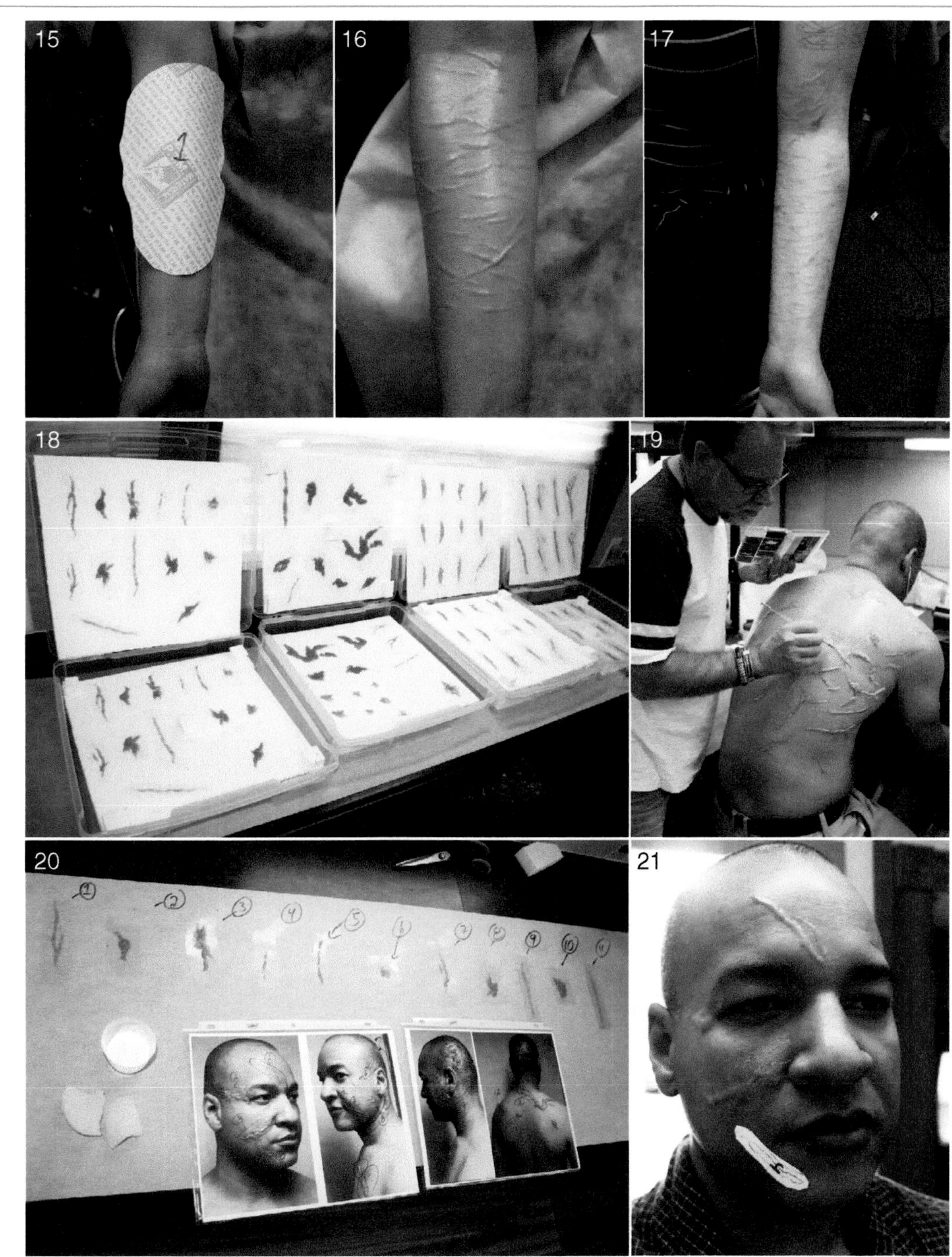

FIGURE 10.29 *(continued)*

FIGURE 10.30 *Types of blood products: Bloodworks Drying Pastes, Kryolan-Eyeblood, Mehron-Stage Blood, Ben Nye Fresh Scab, Kryolan-Show Blood, My Blood-Mouth Blood, Fleet St. Bloodworks—Drying Blood Fresh, Blasco Blood, Monster Makers-Red Blood Powder, K.D 151 Products—Dark Blood Jelly, Hawgfly-Original Formula, and Thick & Scabby (not included here).*

for the intended effect. Should you choose to develop your own recipe, here are a few suggestions:

1. Avoid liquid detergents and soaps with the hopes of creating a washable blood. Mixing colorants into soaps has the reverse effect. Acting as a surfactant, the soap breaks down the surface tension of the fibers allowing the colorant to penetrate deeper into the garment. It may also cause the blood product to foam.
2. Create a blood product that remains flexible and shiny and peels off the skin or other smooth surfaces by mixing your colorant into Phlex-glu, for example.
3. Karo Syrup and food coloring are a simple and effective product. The syrup will suspend the dye and keep it from staining fabrics (it is important to test blood products on fabric samples before using them on finished costumes). This is also safe as mouth blood.
4. Produce a no-drip blood by mixing 1 tablespoon peanut butter with ¼ teaspoon of vegetable oil, add two drops of water and red and blue food coloring as needed. Safe as mouth blood.
5. Use Hershey chocolate under blue gels or dark stage lighting. Safe as mouth blood.

FIGURE 10.31 *Karo Syrup, chocolate syrup, and food coloring.*

6. If blood comes into contact with the costume, be sure to choose fabrics that are washable. Dry cleaning will often lock in the stain. Always test the fabrics before using any blood product. To remove blood products from costumes, immerse them in warm soapy water as soon as they come off stage. It is always a good idea to have a costume double or back-up costume when they are repeatedly exposed to blood products.

Stage and movie blood can be delivered in a number of ways: gelatin capsules, sponges, blood bags, squeeze bottles, squirt guns, syringes, plastic tubing, specialty knives, and exploding squibs.

TEETH/DENTURES

False teeth or dentures for theatrical, television, and film design are often the most subtle, yet critical, detail for the ultimate transformation of an actor into the character he or she is performing. Other times the character might be played so broadly that teeth become a comic, or to the contrary, horrifying, aspect to the overall design. Whatever the desired effect, the teeth must be comfortable for the wearer, the materials the dentures are made from must be medically safe, and the performer must be able to speak without impediment (if the intention is to use their natural speaking voice). Historical and character research are critical to the design of any set of dentures for a play or movie. It is a given that the audience will expect to see Dracula wearing fangs. What kind of fangs, how long, and where they are placed on the denture (i.e. an extended canine over the third tooth, or in place of the lateral incisor next to an enlarged central incisor) are important questions to ask. A more subtle choice would be how to change the look of the teeth on an actor playing a Civil War officer of the 1860s. Some questions you might ask are: How old is the officer? What was his diet? Did he smoke? If so, was it cigarettes, a cigar, a pipe, or "chew"? How long was he away from home? How did he take care of his teeth? Did the army issue toothbrushes? When was the toothbrush manufactured for the general public? These questions and more would inform the design of the dentures for this character.

Once the performer is fitted with dentures he/she must be reminded that the teeth are just for acting; they're not for eating or any other personal daily activity. They are just for appearance.

The process for making false teeth/dentures begins with the taking of a cast of the performer's teeth (see below). Once the teeth cast has been cleaned up and the base has been filed or sanded smooth, the modeling of character dentures can begin.

There are two ways to create dentures for theater/film/television: one way is to build them directly on the teeth cast using store-bought or handmade acrylic teeth; the second is to sculpt the teeth in sulfur-free clay on the teeth cast then mold them in silicone and fill the mold with acrylic dental medium.

The following examples demonstrate two techniques for creating character dentures for actors in performance.

Teeth Casting Materials

- Bottled water (one for alginate and one for actor)
- Dental alginate in bag and decanted into a large deli cup
- Upper and lower dental teeth casting trays
- Water vial, alginate scoop, two dental bowls, metal spatula, and paper towels
- Vinyl gloves, disposable ½-inch chip brush
- Die Keen Green Dental Stone
- Petroleum jelly
- Dental vibrator.

Teeth Casting (Technique by Matthew Mungle) (Figure 10.32)

1. Materials: Bottled water (1 for alginate and 1 for actor), dental alginate in bag and decanted into a large deli cup, upper and lower dental teeth casting trays, water vial, alginate scoop, 2 dental bowls, metal spatula, and paper towels (not pictured: vinyl gloves, disposable ½-inch chip brush, and dental vibrator).
2. Vinyl gloves should be worn during this project. Pour out 1½ oz. water into small vial and into mixing bowl.
3. Pour two scoops (2 oz.) of dental alginate into bowl with water.
4. Mix water and alginate together in bowl. Alginate should be thick and not run off the spatula. Alginate sets in approximately 2 minutes so work quickly.
5. Load upper dental tray with thick alginate.
6. Pour water over alginate.
7. Form a small trough in the front with your finger.
8. Insert tray into actor's mouth pulling upper lip over tray and pressing tray into teeth.
9. Hold tray in place until alginate is set.
10. Have actor close their lips around the tray and blow. This will loosen the alginate from the teeth.
11. Remove tray from the mouth.
12. Place a wet paper towel into tray to keep the alginate moist.
13. Repeat steps 2 to 12 for lower teeth cast.
14. Green Die Keen pictured. This hard stone will be mixed with water to make the positive teeth cast. Blow the moisture out of the alginate teeth cast with canned air.
15. Mix the Green Die Keen (1 oz. water to 3 oz. Green or Blue Die Keen Stone).
16. Place lower teeth cast on a dental vibrator and add the Die Keen Stone with a disposable ½-inch chip brush starting at the back of the cast and letting the material flow into the teeth impression. If a dental vibrator is not available, slowly load the stone into the impression and tap the tray on a table repeatedly to work the material into the teeth. Be very careful not to trap any bubbles in the casting.
17. Repeat the process with the upper teeth cast.
18. Load the tray with additional stone.
19. Immediately turn the cast upside down on a flat surface coated with petroleum jelly for easy removal. This will create a flat back to the cast when it hardens.

FIGURE 10.32 *Teeth casting (casting by effects makeup artist Matthew Mungle).*

FIGURE 10.32 *(continued)*

20. Clean up any excess stone with a sculpting tool and let set for at least 3 hours.

21. Remove dental casts from alginate.

22. Grind the excess stone off the sides of both upper and lower cast. Pictured is a wet grinding wheel. A Dremel tool may also be used to achieve this step.

23. Finished teeth casts.

MAKING DENTURES

Example #1 (by Matthew Mungle) (Figure 10.33)

1. Plastic store-bought upper and lower acrylic teeth.

2. Hold each tooth securely with a pair of needle nose pliers and grind the back of the tooth off with a grinding bit attached to a Dremel tool.

3. Before and after grinding tooth.

4. Fitting tooth onto dental cast. Re-grind if necessary. Grind the additional teeth.

5. Materials: Buffalo tin foil 6 inches wide—.001 inch Dental Cast, Ground Down Plastic Teeth.

6. Tear a piece of Buffalo tin foil, 4 inches x 2 inches, and place on the upper dental cast.

7. & 8. Fold the foil over the teeth on the cast.

9. Tap the foil into the teeth cast on the front and back with a shortened ½-inch chip brush.

10. Before and after application of foil onto cast. Repeat the process on the lower teeth cast.

11. Generously apply petroleum jelly to the foil and the stone dental cast with a brush.

12. Materials: Vinyl gloves, CC measuring cups, Jet or equivalent dental polymer and monomer—tooth color and gum color, dental casts, tweezers, plastic teeth and, metal spatula.

13. Measure ½ oz. of polymer (dental acrylic powder) into CC measuring cup.

14. Add ½ oz. of monomer (dental acrylic liquid) into CC measuring cup.

15. Mix material together. This product sets in approximately 3 minutes depending on the room temperature so you must work *quickly*.

16. & 17. Dip the back side of each tooth into the acrylic mixture. Arrange teeth into the desired look on dental cast using tweezers.

18. Fill in the back space behind each acrylic tooth with the acrylic mixture. The mixture should not cover more than ⅛ inch of the original teeth in the back.

19. Repeat the same process on the lower teeth.

20. Finished teeth placement.

21. & 22. Mix Gum color acrylic as in steps #13–15 and fill in gum area on lower and upper teeth.

23. Finished gum and teeth placement. Let teeth cure for 2 hours.

24. Gently pry dentures from teeth cast with a metal sculpting tool and remove the foil from the back of the dentures.

25. Grind the sharp edges of the dentures down with a grinding bit and a Dremel tool.

26. Dentures ready to be polished.

27. Buff dentures with polishing wheel and wet pumice or a polishing wheel on a Dremel tool.

28. Polished dentures.

29. Materials: AcrylStains (Character Dental & Ocular FX Stains) or other denture stains, dentures, fine-pointed round brushes, and wax paper palette.

30. Use shade Brown stain diluted with thinner to add translucent color washes to the teeth.

31. Add diluted Clot color to stain gums and around teeth.

32. Add diluted Nicotine stain to teeth where desired.

33. Finished teeth.

34. Finished teeth on actor.

Example #2 Teeth (by Stephan Tessier) (Figure 10.34)

1. Plaster positive of upper and lower teeth.

2. Use Die Keen Dental Stone to make the dental positives. (Tip: It is rare that Dental Stone teeth molds are not broken when the acrylic dentures are removed. It is recommended that a silicone negative of the original cast be made, just in case.)

FIGURE 10.33 *Making dentures Example #1.*

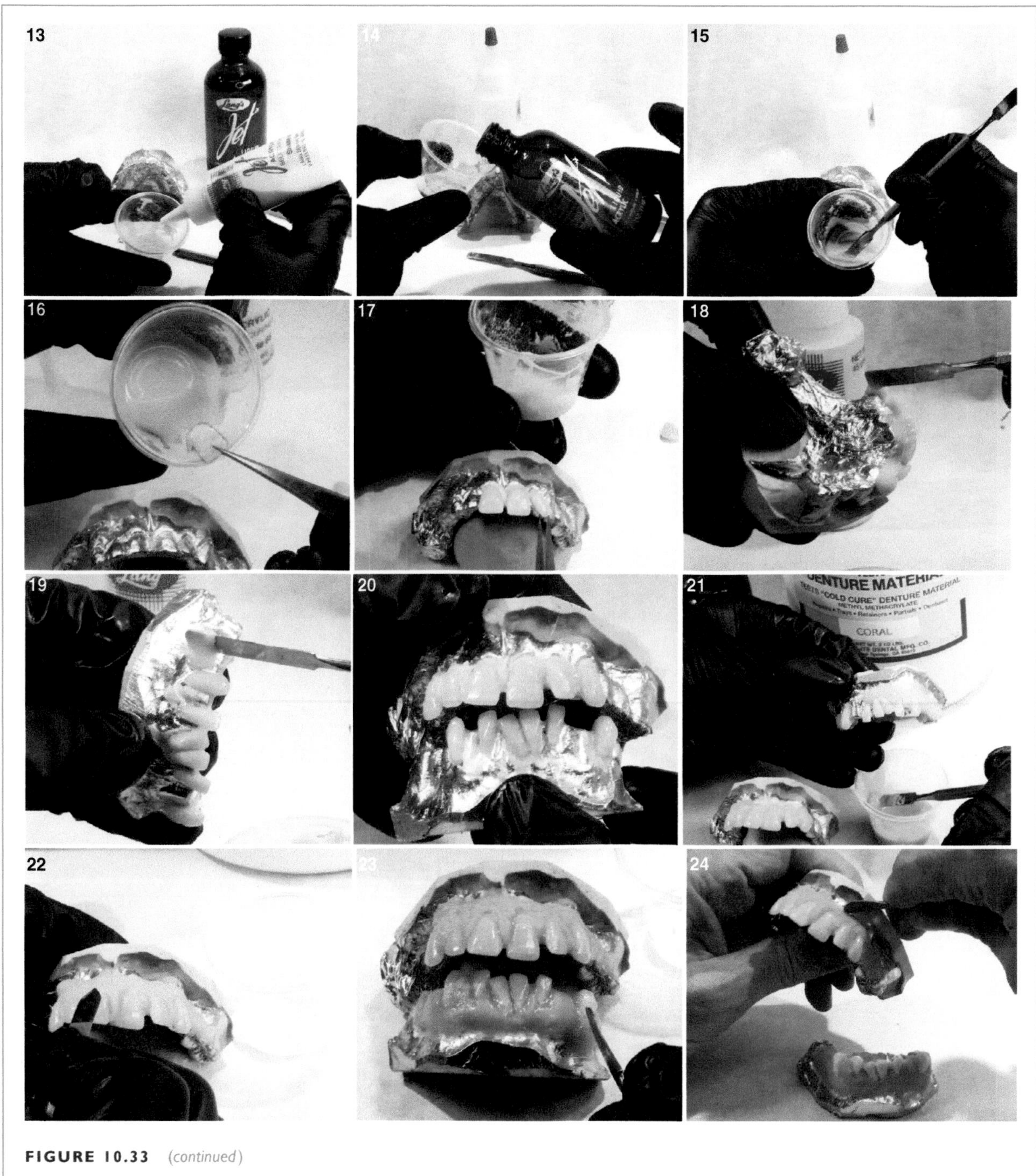

FIGURE 10.33 *(continued)*

3. Paint the surface of the Dental Stone teeth with two to three coats of Alcote Dental Separator.
4. Use sulfur-free clay to sculpt the teeth.
5. Sculpting the teeth.
6. Close-up of the sculpted teeth.
7. Interior view of the sculpted teeth.
8. Build a clay wall around the sculpt.
9. Pour silicone mold-making compound (Bluestar V-1065) into the mold.
10. Remove the clay walls and turn over, exposing the gray plaster teeth mold.

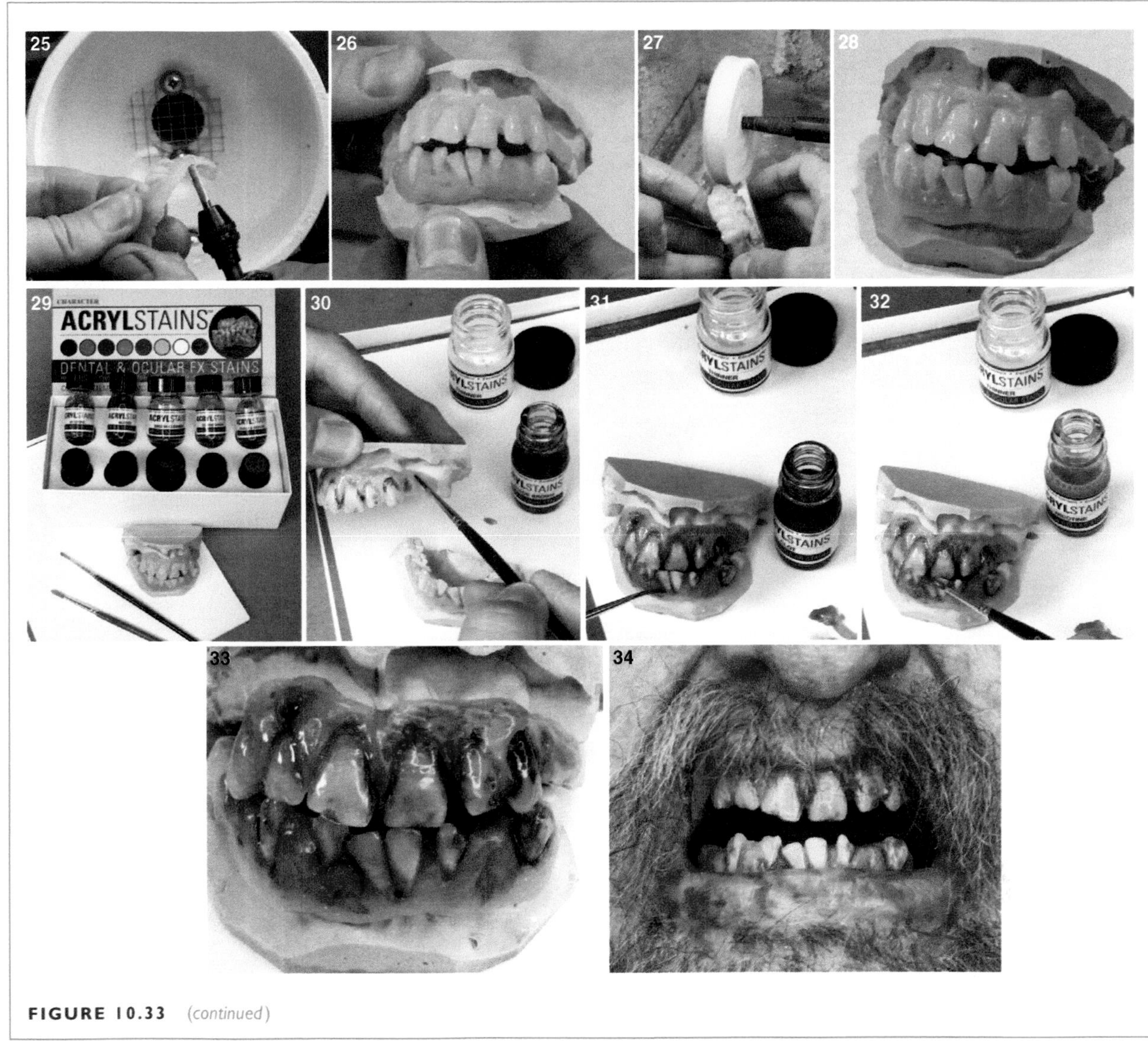

FIGURE 10.33 *(continued)*

11. Remove the plaster teeth and clean the residual clay out of the mold.
12. Mix the 2-part Flexacryl denture material to manufacturer's directions.
13. Pour the liquid denture mixture into the negative silicone mold.
14. Press the clean plaster positive teeth molds into the silicone molds. Allow the acrylic denture material to cure completely.
15. Remove the positive dentures from the silicone mold. The edges of the acrylic gums will need to be ground smooth, then polished.
16. Paint the teeth with acrylic denture stains (Minute Stains by Taub Dental, AcrylStains by Premiere Products, Inc.). (Tip: Alcohol-based colors by Skin Illustrator can be used to paint dentures, but it must be sealed with a clear dental varnish by Minute Stains, for example.)

17. & 18. Finished dentures.

19. Denture covers made of vacuform dental plastic. These were stained yellow to create yellowed teeth.
20. Vacuformed teeth covers with added metal braces.
21. Model wearing the dental braces.
22. Dental vacuform machine.

FIGURE 10.34 *Making dentures Example #2.*

FIGURE 10.34 *(continued)*

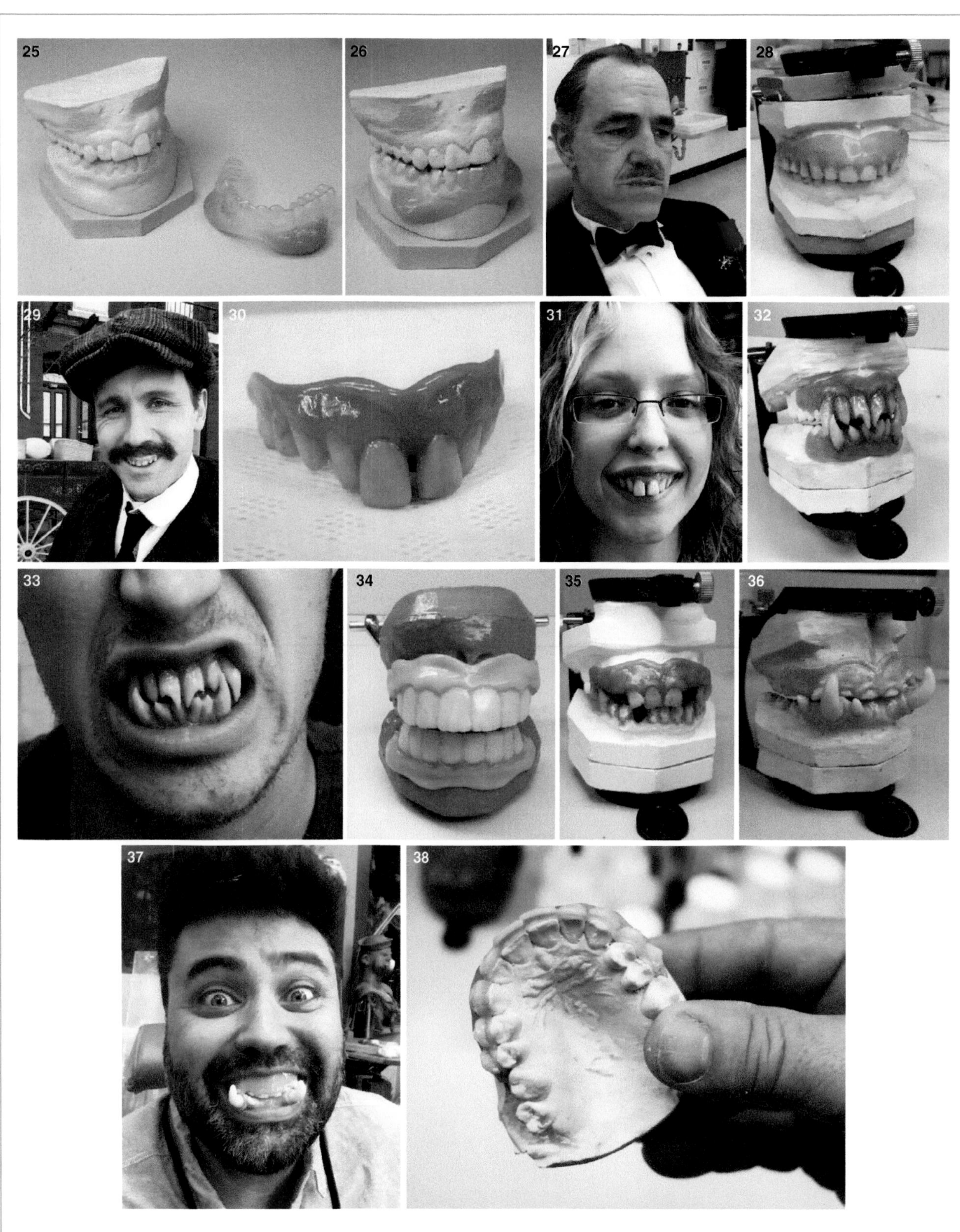

FIGURE 10.34 *(continued)*

23. Keystone vacuform plastic.

24. Vacuform plastic or Splint Material at .5mm thickness should be used.

25. & 26. Lip plumper made with acrylic dental compound on the vacumform dental plastic.

27. Lip plumper being worn by actor Deano Clavet as a Don Corleone look-alike from *The Godfather.*

28. Set of small teeth.

29. Small teeth worn by actor Émile Prouix-Cloutier in the movie, *La Bolduc.*

30. & 31. Extra-large front teeth with a space. Teeth worn by this actress.

32. & 33. Werewolf teeth.

34. Set of large teeth (i.e. Jim Carey in *The Mask*).

35. Set of rotten teeth.

36. & 37. Set of monster teeth with large lower fangs.

38. False teeth or dentures are generally made without wrapping around the edges of the performer's teeth.

WARTS/MOLES

Warts can be made with nose putty, derma wax, gelatin, molded latex, silicone, polyurethane, or latex foam. Nose putty, derma wax, and gelatin warts can be built up directly on the skin, whereas molded latex or foam warts must, of course, be molded first, then attached with spirit gum. Makeup can be applied to the wart with a small, flat shading brush. It can then be powdered along with the rest of the makeup.

Nonmolded latex warts, however, can be constructed directly on the skin by the following method:

1. Dip a small metal spatula into a container of Prosaide Bondo (by W.M. Creations) or Cabo-Patch (by ADM Tronics). This product is a thickened Prosaide made into a paste by mixing equal amounts of Prosaide adhesive with Cab-O-Sil. It can be tinted to the desired color with pigmented cosmetic powder or Revlon ColorStay foundations.
2. Pick up a small amount of thickened Prosaide paste and place it onto clean skin (clean with 99% alcohol).
3. Using the metal spatula, form the paste into the desired shape. Allow the paste to dry. When dry it will remain tacky (all products made with Prosaide remain tacky when dried). Powder.
4. Apply cream or alcohol-based foundation, or RMG Rubber Mask Grease Paint to the desired color.
5. Powder the wart carefully and brush off excess powder with a powder brush.

The advantage of making a wart by this method is that it is unlikely to fall off or to be knocked out of shape if accidentally touched.

This process can also be accomplished using Kryolan's Tuplast, 300 Bloom Gelatin (can be purchased in ready-to-use cubes), 2-part silicone gels, Sculptgel, Altex and 3rd Degree.

Since gelatin has a natural, flesh-like appearance, it is likely to require less makeup than other materials and may sometimes require none at all. When color is needed, add a small amount of flocking in red and natural skin tones to the gelatin. Flocking keeps the gelatin translucent. Other pigments like cosmetic powders can be used, but they tend to make the gelatin opaque and less skin-like. Gelatin moles and other small skin abnormalities can be attached with Prosaide and Telesis adhesives. Any blending can be accomplished using witch hazel and a small brush.

Moles can also be made by mixing liquid latex with alfalfa or chia seeds (and with scrapings from the top of an appropriate shade of brownish cake makeup if you want the mole to be colored), then pouring or spooning enough for one mole onto glass (or other smooth surface) and letting it dry. When it is dry, the top of the mole should be powdered, but the bottom must not be. If you want to attach the mole directly to the skin before applying any makeup, brush a spot of clear latex onto the skin and let it dry. Then carefully lift the mole off the glass with tweezers and press it onto the spot of dried latex on the skin.

BROKEN CAPILLARIES

To suggest broken blood vessels, lightly cover the area around the nose, nasolabial folds, and cheek with a small amount of K-Y Jelly. Imbed a mixture of short red, silk, rayon or wool fibers cut from a piece of fabric or yarn into the K-Y. Allow to dry (see Figure 10.16).

CHAPTER 11

PROSTHETIC MAKEUP

The most effective method of creating most three-dimensional additions to the head, face, and neck is to use molded prosthetic appliances. For the stage, this type of makeup is not always practical since actors normally do their own makeup, and the creation of molded prosthetics may require the services of a professional makeup artist.

However, the actors and young makeup artists who want to experiment with casting prosthetic appliances can certainly do so and will no doubt find it both interesting and useful. Whether the actors learn to make their own or have them made for them, the advantages of using this type of makeup are obvious—it can provide three-dimensional additions to the face impossible to achieve by painting, or with nose putty, derma wax, or other direct constructions. The pieces can be sculpted and resculpted on a plaster head until they are perfect and can then be reproduced indefinitely; and, unlike direct additions to the face, they can (for the stage, at least) be used several times.

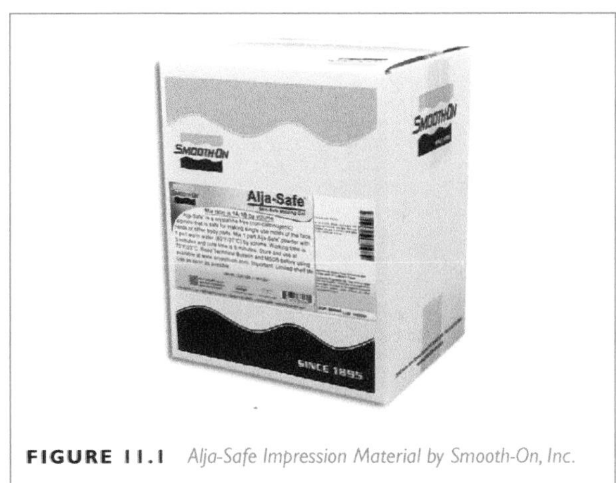

FIGURE 11.1 *Alja-Safe Impression Material by Smooth-On, Inc.*

FIGURE 11.2 *Smooth-Cast 385 Mineral-filled Casting Resin.*

CASTING FOR PROSTHETICS

The first step in creating a three-dimensional appliance is to reproduce the actor's face, or some part of it, in plaster, urethane plastics, or epoxy resins. To do this, a negative mold is made with a flexible impression material of either alginate or silicone (see Appendix A), as illustrated in Figures 11.4 and 11.5.

Preparing the Subject

When casting the face, head, or bust, it is best to have the subject sitting in an upright position, *not lying down*, to maintain an accurate facial structure. Straws, inserted in the nose, should *never* be used. A barber or dentist chair is ideal, but any chair with a high supportive back will suffice.

A plastic makeup cape or even an extra-large plastic trash bag can be used to protect the clothing. It may need to be taped to the skin at the neckline. The solidified alginate/silicone can be easily removed from the plastic later.

If a full face, the entire head, or a complete bust is to be cast, a plastic or a latex bald cap can be used to protect the hair. These can be purchased from any number of makeup supply companies or can be made specifically for the model (due to the fact that the edges of the bald cap used for this purpose do not need to smoothly transition into the skin and can be cleaned and reused, it might be advantageous to purchase one. (See Figure 10.12). In any case, after the cap has been positioned and secured on the head with spirit gum or Prosaide adhesive, it's a good idea to mark the model's hairline on the cap with an indelible ink pencil (available in art stores). After the impression material has been applied, cured and removed, the marked hairline will later be visible on the cast.

A. Face casting materials (Figure 11.4)

1. alginate (40 oz. for a full ¾ face cast)
2. pitcher of water (40 oz. for above mix + a little extra if the product remains too thick)
3. warm water for plaster bandages
4. flexible plastic bowls for mixing alginate, and plaster
5. pre-measured plaster (Hydrostone or Ultracal 30)
6. pre-cut plaster bandages (two to three 6-inch wide rolls)
7. large kitchen mixing spoon or metal spatula
8. disposable rubber gloves (latex, vinyl, or nitrile)
9. bald cap (rubber or plastic)
10. adhesive and adhesive remover (spirit gum or Prosaide) and applicator
11. sponge

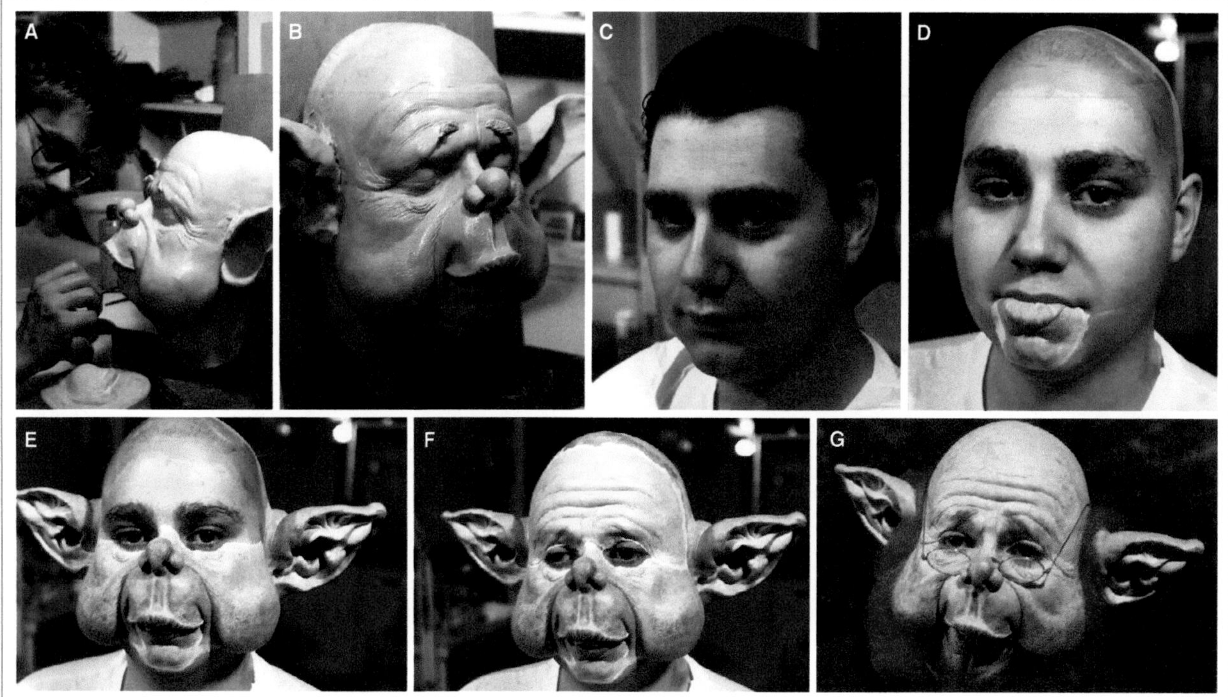

FIGURE 11.3 *Foam latex gnome. By TEXA FX Group using GM Foam System for a French children's television show. A. & B. Clay sculpt by Stephan Tessier. C. Subject, Olivier Xavier. D. Application of Glatzan bald cap, foam cheeks, and chin using Prosaide adhesive. For perfect edges, brush Prosaide on the skin and let dry; apply prosthetic; paint a little 70% isopropyl alcohol onto appliance edge (it will soak through and reactivate the glue); seal edges with Prosaide. E. & F. Forehead and ears are attached and painted with PAX, PAX Wash, and a touch of Rubber Mask Greasepaint. G. Wig and beard are pre-shaped on a form and set with Krylon Crystal Clear then applied with matte spirit gum.*

***Source:** Makeup and photographs by Stephan Tessier ofTEXA FX Group of Quebec, Canada.*

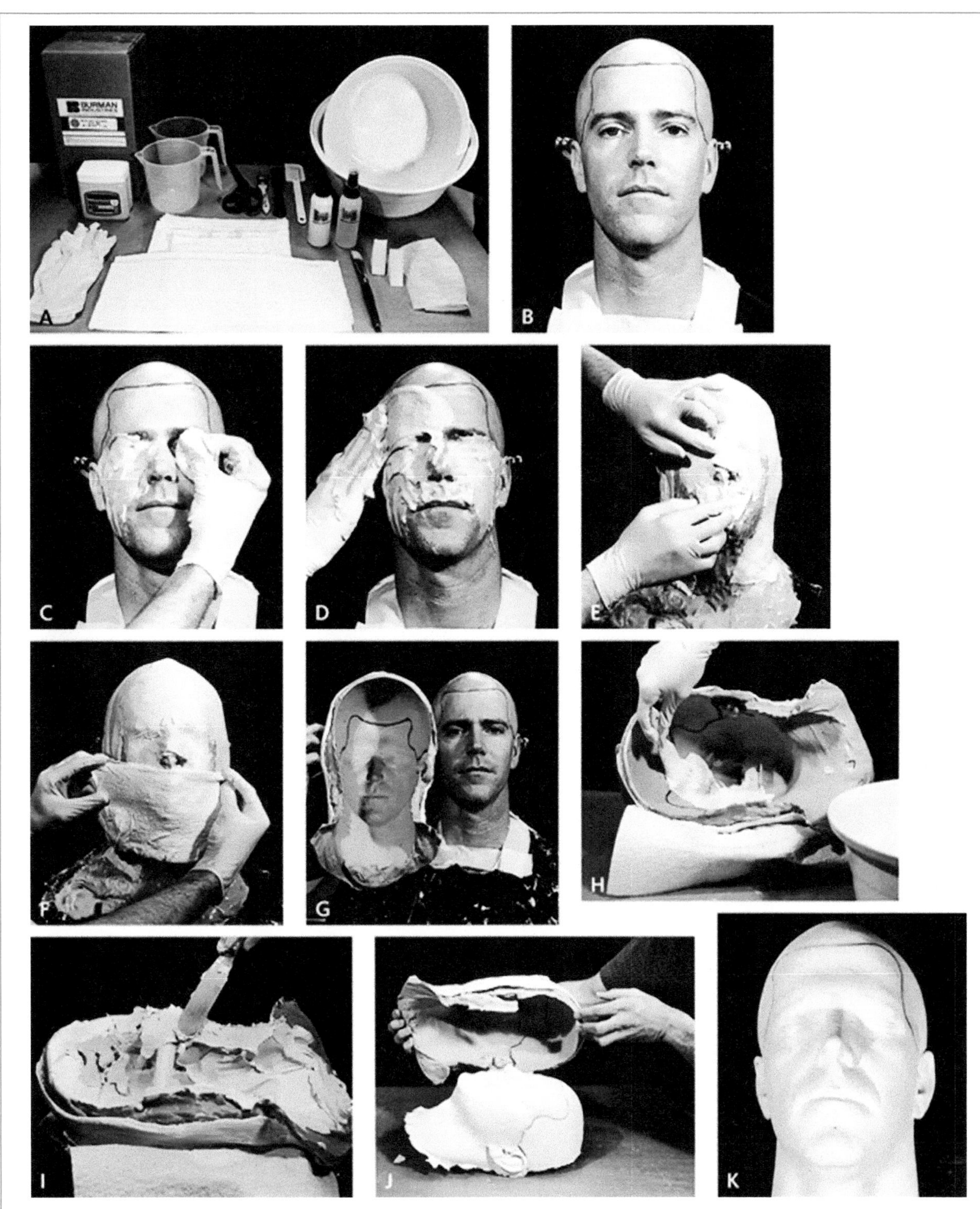

FIGURE 11.4 *Face casting with alginate.*

12. 1-inch disposable brush
13. scissors (small and large)
14. release agent (petroleum jelly or Body Double Release Cream)
15. measuring cup (at least 4-cup capacity)
16. indelible ink pencil
17. plastic cape (a cover-up to protect the model)
18. plastic container filled with crumbled newspaper or towel, used as a "nest" for the plaster/alginate face negative
19. scales (for weighing plaster and water)
20. pre-cut 4-inch x 4-inch pieces of burlap cloth.

B. Applying the bald cap in preparation for alginate/ silicone cast.

C. & D. Alginate/silicone application.

E. & F. Strips of plaster bandage being laid over solidified alginate/silicone.

G. Face cast removed.

H. Brushing first layer of plaster or Dental Stone into negative mold.

I. Adding the handle.

J. Removing alginate from plaster cast.

K. Finished and cleaned face cast. (Casting by Matthew Mungle. Model, Michael Cristillo.)

Preparing the Model for a Face Cast

While the face requires no special preparation, a light coat of petroleum jelly or Body Double Release Cream is recommended on the eyebrows, eyelashes, any exposed hair, and cap (do not forget the cap). At this time it is essential that it be made clear to the subjects that they are in no danger:

- It must be explained to them that if for any reason the alginate/silicone interferes with their breathing, they need only remove the alginate from their noses or mouths with their hands, or if feeling claustrophobic to expel their breath forcefully through their nose, open their mouths and break the mold. Most subjects, once they have confidence in the operator, find the process pleasant and relaxing.
- It is important that the facial muscles be relaxed during the mold-making process. A smile or the raise of an eyebrow can add an unwanted expression to the mold. The model should be sitting upright with the head slightly back, supported by a headrest.
- It is to everyone's advantage, especially with nervous subjects, to let them watch a mold being made on someone else first, clearly explaining the entire process as it unfolds. Having the actor view a commercially produced video of the entire casting process on a DVD or on YouTube may also help alleviate any fears.
- It is usually best to work in a private room that is relatively quiet. It is also desirable for the person or persons doing the casting to avoid casual conversation with others unrelated to the work being done. Knowing that he or she has the operator's undivided attention helps to give the subject confidence.
- Classical music, or any other music enjoyed by the model, playing in the background sometimes helps to break the silence and may calm your subject.
- Giving the subject a pencil and paper as a means of communication can add to a sense of security. The subject can also be given appropriate hand signals to enable the operator to ask questions and get "yes" or "no" responses without the subject's having to answer by writing.

Negative Alginate Mold

The primary type of facial casting material used is an alginate impression material, a seaweed derived powder, which when mixed with water becomes a flexible material easily removed from the skin. The setting time of different types of alginates may vary depending on the temperature of the room and water. A cool room and cold water will slow the setting time whereas a warmer room and water hasten the setting time. A silicone impression material such as Body Double SILK by Smooth-On can be used in the same manner as the alginate. The main advantage of using silicone is the fact that it will hold its shape indefinitely. Alginate, on the other hand, will begin to slowly dry and therefore begin shrinking as soon as it is removed from the face.

It is recommended that you mix a small batch of the impression material to test the setting time before casting your subject's face. Various impression materials require different mixing proportions and set-up times. For this casting process (Figure 11.4), Alja-Safe Alginate (see Appendix A, *Alginate*) was used. A face cast using Body Double SILK is presented later in this chapter (Figure 11.5).

As with any creative project, it is very important to have all the materials laid out before starting the face casting procedure. Your work area should be clean and organized. It is advisable to protect the work surface, the floor, and your own clothing by covering each with protective materials. This process is time-sensitive: the alginate will set up in approximately 5 minutes, the plaster bandages may take 15 minutes, the plaster may take 20 minutes, and all the while, you must keep your model comfortable. (Note: Once you start this process, there is no time to stop for an item you have forgotten.)

For a small face cast prepare the following:

- The alginate and water should be measured and placed in separate mixing bowls at approximately a 1:1 ratio:
    - for a face cast, place 3 cups (½ lb.) of alginate powder in a bowl;
    - measure 2.75–3 cups of cold water (depending on how thick or runny you like the alginate) into a separate container.
- The plaster bandages should be cut, organized into various lengths, and set aside:
    - You will need at least two or three 6-inch wide rolls that often come in 5-yard lengths. Using craft scissors, cut the rolls into 12-inch strips, leaving a few 6-inch pieces for covering the nose area (tearing the plaster bandage creates a lot of excess powder);
    - Prepare a bowl of warm water for dipping the plaster bandages. (Tip: Adding salt to the water accelerates the curing time of the bandages.)

Make the cast using Hydro-Stone (you may also choose another product from the plaster comparison chart, Figure 11.6).

(Note: Plaster of Paris lacks the strength and structural integrity for prosthetic makeup projects and should be avoided.)

- Measure by weight five 1 lb. bags of Hydro-Stone (in a class setting, try using small brown paper sandwich bags). Place a bag on the scales and pour the Hydro-Stone into the bag until the scale reads 1 lb. Repeat five times.
- Weigh an appropriate amount of water to mix with the Hydro-Stone based on the plaster comparison chart (Figure 11.6). In this case, if 5 lb. of plaster equals 100 parts (100 over 5), then 28–32 parts of water equals "x" pounds of water (28-32 over x).

$$\frac{100}{5} = \frac{28-32}{x}$$

To find x, multiply 5 x 30 (the average of 28–32), then divide by 100 to find x. In this proportional equation, x equals 1.5 pounds of water per 5 pounds of plaster. Remember to subtract the weight of the water container from the total.

(Note: Preparing the plaster to the specifications of the manufacturer will provide you with the confidence that the plaster will cure and harden to the manufacturer's standards. It will also assist you in managing your budget by allowing you to order exact amounts of the product. For example, if you are planning for a class of ten students, you will know to order at least 50 lbs. of plaster or stone.)

(Tip: Many professionals do not measure the plaster to the exact manufacturer's formula as mentioned above. Plaster or stone is often dusted onto the surface of the water until the absorption of the plaster into the water begins to subside, creating what amounts to a dry creek-bed on the surface. While this method is often more expedient, and allows the artist better control of the consistency of the plaster, it will, most likely, require a few extra bags of plaster.)

- Prepare a rectangular-shaped plastic dishpan by filling it with loosely crumpled balls of newspaper or something soft. This will make a soft supportive "nest" in which to lay your mother mold and alginate negative before filling it with plaster. (Tip: Make sure the nose area is supported with an extra cushion of paper.)
- The final step is to prepare the model as mentioned above.

FACE CASTING WITH ALGINATE IMPRESSION MATERIAL

(Note: When applying alginate to the face, two people should work together, one on the left side and one on the right. Many professionals who work solo have learned to apply the product with ease, but in a classroom format it is always helpful to have a partner. Alginate impression materials set quickly, some within minutes, so it is to your advantage to apply it as rapidly as possible. Should you decide to patch a hole or add to a thin area, remember that wet alginate will only stick to wet alginate. Once it cures it will not stick to itself. This is another reason to work quickly.)

To avoid surface bubbles on the plaster face cast, be sure to gently press the alginate into the eye cavities, around the edge of the nostrils, and into the corners of the mouth.

Step 1. Mixing the impression material (1 minute) (Figure 11.4)

Pour the alginate powder onto 2.75 cups of cold water and mix *quickly* until smooth. Add the remaining water if the product is too thick. The consistency should be of a viscosity that is easy to move around the face, but not so watery that it flows off onto the makeup cape. The mixing process should take no longer than 1 minute (some artists use their hands, some a large metal spatula, and others an electric hand mixer).

Step 2. Covering the face (4 minutes)

a. Starting with the eyes, gently but quickly spread the alginate impression material with your hands into the eye sockets, along the sides of the nose, over the nose bridge, tip, and around the nostrils and septum (placing it as close to the nostrils as possible, but not covering them, of course). Now cover the cheeks, the forehead, the mouth and chin, along the jawline, and onto the neck. It is advisable to wear vinyl or nitrile gloves when working with alginate and plaster bandages. This will make it easier to remove the gloves rather than spending time to clean your hands.

b. The alginate will slowly and constantly be moving down the face. It is necessary to keep moving it upward before the product sets up.

c. If you are a student, it is advised that you pay special attention to the detailed demonstration by your instructor to meet the requirements of the course. It is also advisable to watch as many online videos as possible before attempting this process for the first time. There are many variations for the face casting process. You must decide which techniques meet your personal and/or class goals.

d. It is recommended by some effects artists that you imbed small strips of a fibrous material such as baby flannel or cotton balls (unrolled) into the wet surface of the alginate. This will create a bond between the alginate and the plaster bandage that will hold the two together once they are removed from the face.

Step 3. Applying the plaster bandages (Making the mother mold)

a. Start by holding groups of three 12-inch lengths. Dip the plaster bandage into the warm (salty) water, lightly squeeze out the excess water, and opening it out to its full length, fold over 1 inch of the long edge and apply it to the top edge of the forehead (avoid over agitating the bandage in the water, you do not want to wash out all of the plaster). Continue with the rest of the pieces, first covering the outer edge, then filling in the interior of the face.

b. Place the plaster bandages *gently* on the face. Remember that the face and impression material are flexible and can be easily distorted. Smooth the bandage onto the surface of the alginate, working out any air pockets. Activate the plaster by lightly rubbing the surface until you no longer see the weave of the gauze base.

c. You may or may not want to include the ears in your mold. Covering only the front part of the ears with plaster bandages, however, will make removing the cast easier.

d. Support the bridge, the nose tip, and the septum with one or more of the smaller pieces of bandage. Working carefully around the nostrils, pinch and twist the bandages together, placing them over the bridge of the nose, over the tip, and onto the septum. This twisting will add greater strength. *Avoid covering the breathing holes.*

e. Plaster bandages undergo a geothermic reaction in order to cure. This means they will heat up as they set. This setting time will take approximately 15 minutes (according to the US Gypsum website). The heat reaction will peak in about 10 minutes and will cool rather quickly. You can monitor this reaction by simply touching the surface of the bandage. Your model will feel no discomfort as the impression material will act as a buffer to this reaction.

WARNING!: Never apply plaster bandages directly onto the skin. Even though you may have covered the face with the petroleum jelly separator, small facial hairs, eyelashes, mustaches, and beards may get trapped in the open weave of the plaster impregnated gauze, rendering it extremely difficult and painful to remove!

Step 4. Removing the mother mold and alginate

a. Remove the alginate and plaster bandage mother mold together by first asking the model to lean forward slightly, bring the hands to the face to support the mask and move all of the facial muscles (smile, frown, etc.) to aid in loosening the mold. Quickly expelling air from the mouth into the mold will assist in the alginate separating from the face.

b. The mold can then be removed easily. It is best to loosen it first near the ear to let in the air. Remove it carefully and slowly, running your fingers around the edges between the skin and the alginate. The alginate does not stick to skin but may stick to hair and the cap if they have not been coated with petroleum jelly.

c. When the negative mold is finished, the positive plaster cast should be made immediately to prevent the alginate from shrinking due to the loss of moisture.

FACE CASTING WITH SILICONE

An impression of the face can be made using a *silicone* product called Body Double (by Smooth-On). The process is exactly the same as using alginate. Body Double is a 2-part

FIGURE 11.5 *Face casting with Body Double SILK (silicone impression material).*

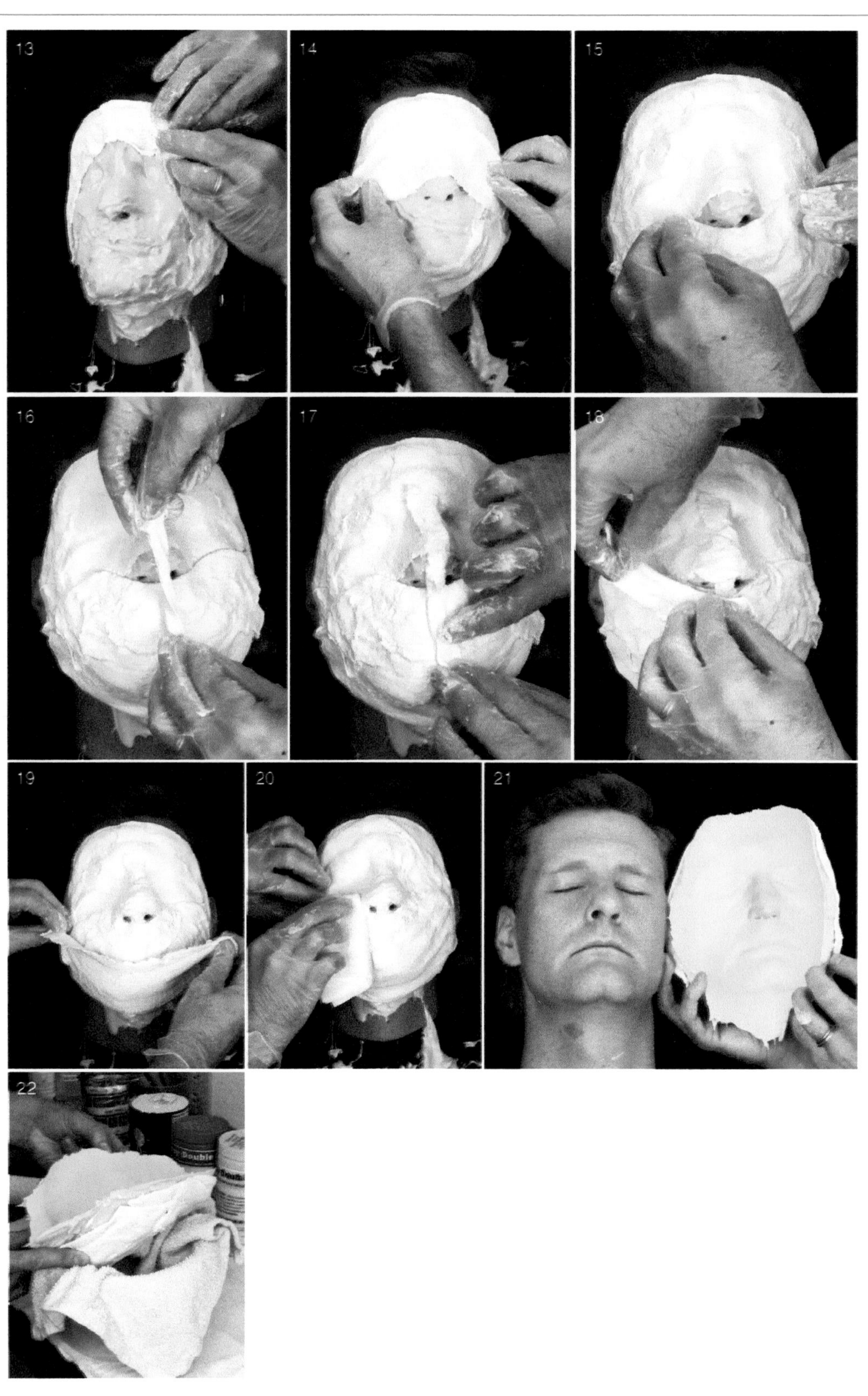

FIGURE 11.5 *(continued)*

mixture (Part A and Part B) combined in equal proportions by volume. The silicone cures in a similar time frame as the alginate, so once the parts are thoroughly mixed, there is a 5–6 minute working time before the product begins to thicken and set. The major advantage to working with silicone impression material is that it does not dry out, does not shrink, and does not need to be used immediately. Multiple plaster positives can be made easily, if needed (see Face casting with silicone, Figure 11.5).

1. Materials: vinyl gloves, plaster bandages (eight stacks of 4 x 10-inch bandages, three layers thick; one stack of 1 x 4-inch bandages, three layers thick; and two stacks of 1½ x 4-inch bandages, three layers thick), 2–5-oz. and 1/16-oz. deli cups, small metal spatula, large spatula, plastic or nylon cover cape, face cast container with cloth towel or newspaper to rest face cast in, 4-quart water container with warm water and ½ oz. of salt added, and paper towels.
2. Actor draped with cover cape and Body Double Release Cream applied to eyebrows and eyelashes. Wearing vinyl gloves is highly recommended.
3. Measure Body Double SILK (5 oz. Part A and 5 oz. Part B).
4. Part A and Part B of SILK poured into a 16-oz. deli cup.
5. Mix SILK parts completely with a large metal spatula.
6. Start application of SILK on nose area, working product into the creases around the nostrils and eye area. Be careful to avoid trapping air pockets in these areas.
7. Continue application onto the full face. (Note: Body Double SILK has a 7–8-minute working time.)
8. Use a small metal spatula to work SILK around nostril openings.

9. & 10. Use a tongue depressor to apply a thick application of SILK to outer edge of the face. Wait at least 4 minutes before application of plaster bandages.

11. Clean spatulas with a paper towel.
12. Pick up three pieces of plaster bandages (4 x 10 inch) for each application. Keeping them together, dip them into the warm salted water. Fold over the top ½ inch to create a thicker edge, then place on the outside perimeter of the face cast.

13., 14., & 15. Apply plaster bandage to the SILK face cast. Add additional layers, massaging bandage into the face cast to activate the plaster in the gauze. Continue until the full-face cast is covered. Leave the nose area exposed.

16. & 17. Dip the 1 x 4-inch piece of plaster bandage into salted water and twist the middle of the piece, applying it to the septum (middle area) of the nose.

18. Dip the 1½ x 4-inch piece of plaster bandage into the salted water and apply to the side of the nose. Repeat the process on the opposite side of the nose.
19. Use the remaining plaster bandage strips to reinforce the outside edges of the face cast.
20. Use a folded paper towel to blot off any moisture from the plaster bandage and to hasten the curing time.
21. After the last piece of plaster bandage has dried, have the actor slightly move his facial muscles then gently remove the face cast.
22. Place the Body Double SILK face cast into the face cast container.

*Mfr	Parts water per 100 parts plaster needed by weight	Manufacturer's name for product	Setting range, in minutes	Dry compressive strength, lb. per sq. in.
USG	64–66	Industrial Molding Plaster	25–30	2,000
USG	54–56	Pattern Shop Hydrocal	20–25	3,200
USG	40–43	Industrial White Hydrocal	20–30	5,500
USG	35–38	Ulracal 30	25–35	7,300
USG	28–32	Hydro-Stone	20–25	11,000
USG	21–23	Super X Hydro-Stone	17–20	14,000

*USG = USG Corporation, 125 S. Franklin, Chicago, IL 60606. (Call 1.800.621.9523 for the nearest distributor.)

FIGURE 11.6 *Plaster comparison chart.*

POSITIVE ULTRACAL-30 FACE CAST

1. Figure 11.7 - Materials: water, mixing bowl, 1-inch disposable chip brush, metal spatula, Ultracal 30, scissors, ten 2 x 3-inch and six 2 x 2-inch burlap pieces, Body Double SILK face cast, vinyl gloves (not pictured: Stanley planer) (Figure 11.7).
2. Measure out 3 oz. of water into mixing bowl.
3. Measure out 8 oz. of Ultracal-30 powder into water.
4. Mix the Ultracal and water with a metal spatula.

5. & 6. Paint a heavy coat of Ultracal 30 into SILK face cast. Be careful not to trap bubbles on the surface of the silicone face cast.

7. & 8. Pour a little water into mixing bowl and clean the sides of the bowl with the brush.

9. Pour the cleaning water into a trash bin, *not* down the drain. All plaster/stone products will clog drains.
10. Clean the 1-inch disposable chip brush to be used again.
11. After the first coat of Ultracal has set for approximately 10 to 20 minutes and the surface becomes matte, mix another batch of Ultracal as in steps #2 to #4 and paint a thin coat onto the first layer of Ultracal.
12. Wet a piece of 2 x 3-inch burlap with Ultracal.
13. *Gently* press the wet burlap into the mold and repeat the process with the remaining five pieces of 2 x 3-inch burlap until the inside of the face cast is covered. Be very careful not to press too hard when laying the burlap into place.
14. Dip additional 2 x 3-inch burlap pieces into the Ultracal and roll into a tube shape.
15. Lightly press the burlap/Ultracal tube shaped pieces around the edges of the mold. This creates a stronger mold edge.

16. & 17. Mix an additional thick batch of Ultracal with 2 oz. of water and 6 oz. of Ultracal and spatulate the material onto the edge and center of the mold.

18. Dip the 1-inch brush into water and smooth out the Ultracal mold.
19. Let set for 4 hours or overnight and remove from the negative face cast.
20. Shave the sharp edges of the mold off with a Stanley planer.
21. Finished Ultracal face cast.

POSITIVE SMOOTH-CAST 385 FACE CAST

1. Figure 11.8 - Materials: Body Double SILK—Measured out 2 oz. A and 2 oz. B, one 5-oz. deli cup, SILK face casting and metal spatula (not Pictured: Mann 200 Release Spray).
2. Mix A and B Body Double SILK product together and fill in the nostril holes from the outside of the face cast.
3. Turn face casting over and *carefully* fill in the nostril holes from the inside. Make sure no additional product gets onto the nose area.
4. SILK can be cured faster by blowing the area with hot air from a hairdryer.
5. After the SILK has cured inside the nose, spray the whole interior of face cast with the Mann 200 Release+ Spray.
6. Materials: Smooth-Cast 385 A & B, paint stirring paddle, gram scale and a 32-oz. deli cup (not pictured—½-inch disposable chip brush and paper towels).
7. Open Part B and stir with paint paddle. Shake Part A vigorously. (Note: Use this product in a well-ventilated area. Using a fan to blow away the fumes can be helpful.)
8. Weigh out 1,000 grams Part B.
9. Clean edge of Part B container with paper towel before closing lid.
10. Pour in 200 grams Part A.
11. Clean edge of Part A container with paper towel before closing lid.
12. Stir Part A and B together with paint paddle, making sure to scrape the edges and bottom of the container. Mix for 2 minutes.
13. Paint the 385 product into the SILK face cast with a ½-inch disposable chip brush. This ensures there will be minimal bubbles on final face cast model.
14. Pour remaining 385 into face cast.
15. Aluminum fold may be used to close top and bottom of face cast if necessary.
16. Let 385 dry overnight and remove from SILK casting.
17. Grind any sharp edges off 385 face model with a grinding bit and Dremel tool while holding a vacuum nozzle near to collect any grinding dust.

FIGURE 11.7 *Making the Ultracal-30 face cast in the negative alginate mold.*

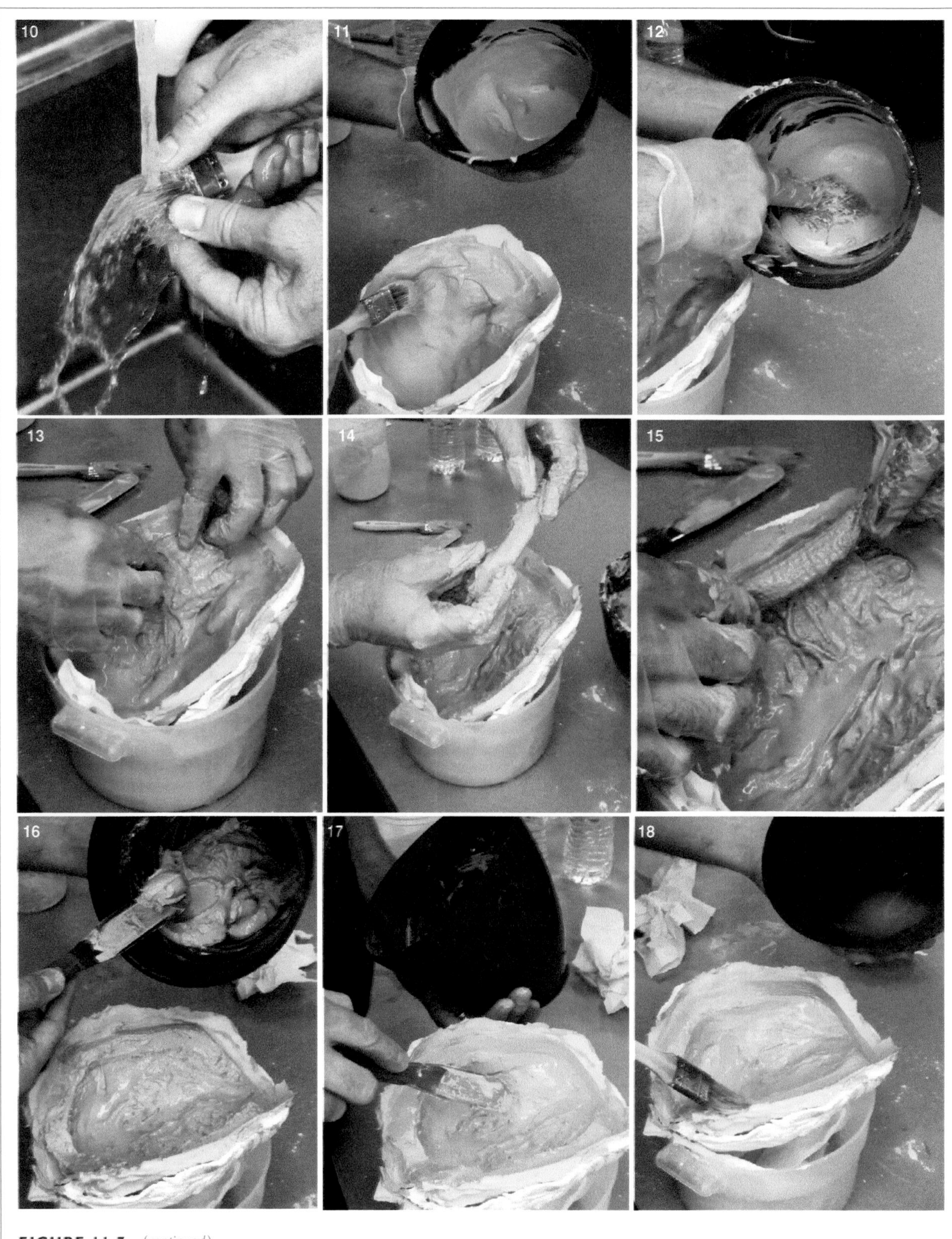

FIGURE 11.7 *(continued)*

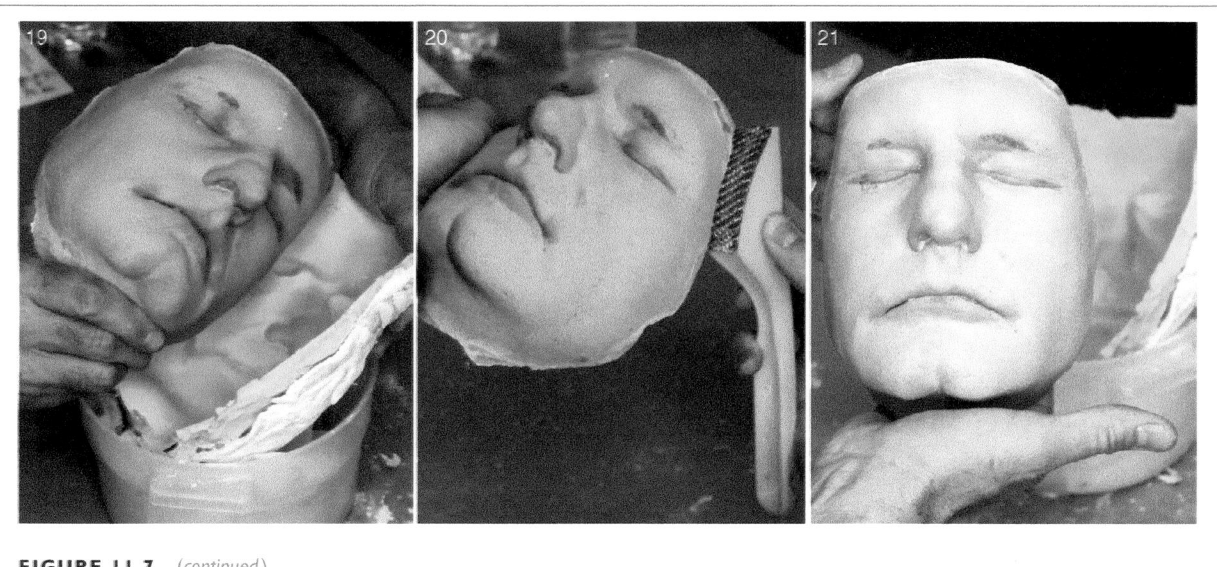

FIGURE 11.7 *(continued)*

(Smooth-Cast urethanes cure to a hard, non-porous smooth surface which allows silicones and gelatins to separate from the mold more easily than from plasters.)

CLAY MODELS: CREATING A NOSE IN SILICONE AND GELATIN

The sculpting of individual features like the nose for the character Cyrano de Bergerac (Figure 11.50) is done with a sulfur-free artists' modeling clay (Chavant NSP Medium, Monster Clay, see Appendix A), which requires no special technique. Sulfur-free clays will have no negative effects when working with silicones and other products when creating prosthetic makeups. You will do it largely with your fingers, and clay modeling tools for creating the details. Be sure the clay is perfectly smooth, completely blended at the edges, and modeled in exactly the form you want the nose to take. You can simulate skin pore texture by dotting the clay with a tiny round-tipped stylus and using texture stamps (see Appendix A). Wrinkles can be created by gently scoring the surface with a sculpting tool or straight pin.

All clay models should be textured. Remember that the slightest mark on the clay will be reproduced on the finished piece.

Modeling the Clay

The actual modeling of the clay nose should follow these four suggestions:

- Accurately follow the natural nose structure.
- Carefully blend the edges.
- Limit the clay addition to as small an area as possible.
- Add skin texture.

The prosthetic nose need not cover the entire nose. On the contrary, the smaller the area it covers, the easier it will probably be to work with. A tilted tip or a small hump, for example, does not require modeling a complete nose. If the piece you make involves the nostrils, they can be cut out of the piece after it has been cast in order to permit normal breathing.

The following demonstrations will include step-by-step instructions for making prosthetic noses:

- The first demonstration (see Figures 11.9 and 11.10) is a nose for an aging male character. This nose will be made from *gelatin*. The molds will be made from Ultracal 30, a standard, durable gypsum stone used in the process of making prosthetic makeup appliances (the entire makeup is demonstrated later in this chapter).
- The second demonstration (see Figure 11.11) is a nose made from *liquid latex* and the mold from #1 Molding Plaster.
- The third demonstration (see Figures 11.48 and 11.49) is a nose created for the character Cyrano de Bergerac (from the play by Edmond Rostand). This nose is made from *platinum silicone* called Dragon Skin FX-Pro (from Smooth-On, Inc.) and the mold from a plastic resin called Smooth-Cast 385 (also from Smooth-On, Inc.).

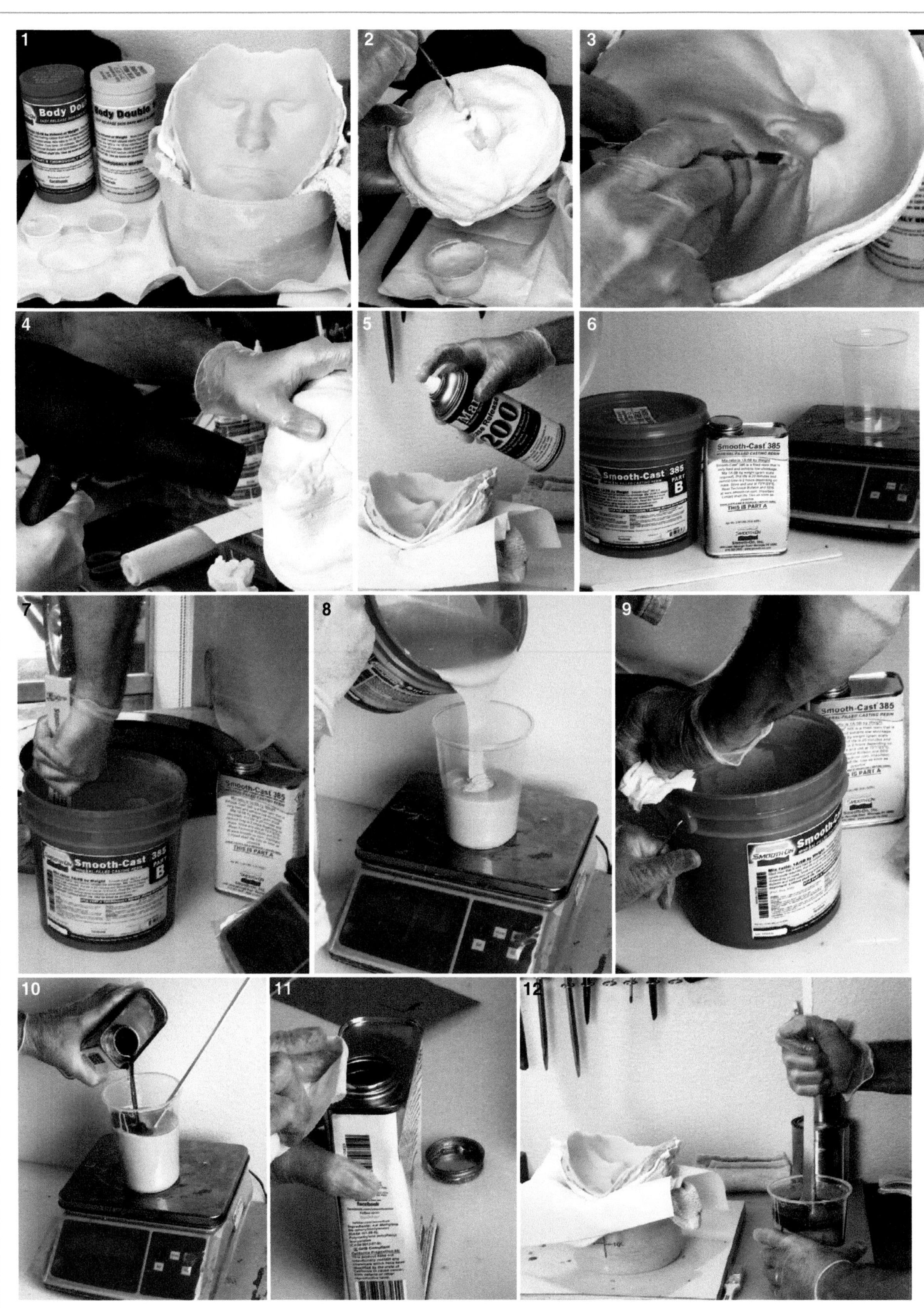

FIGURE 11.8 *Making the positive face cast using Smooth-Cast 385.*

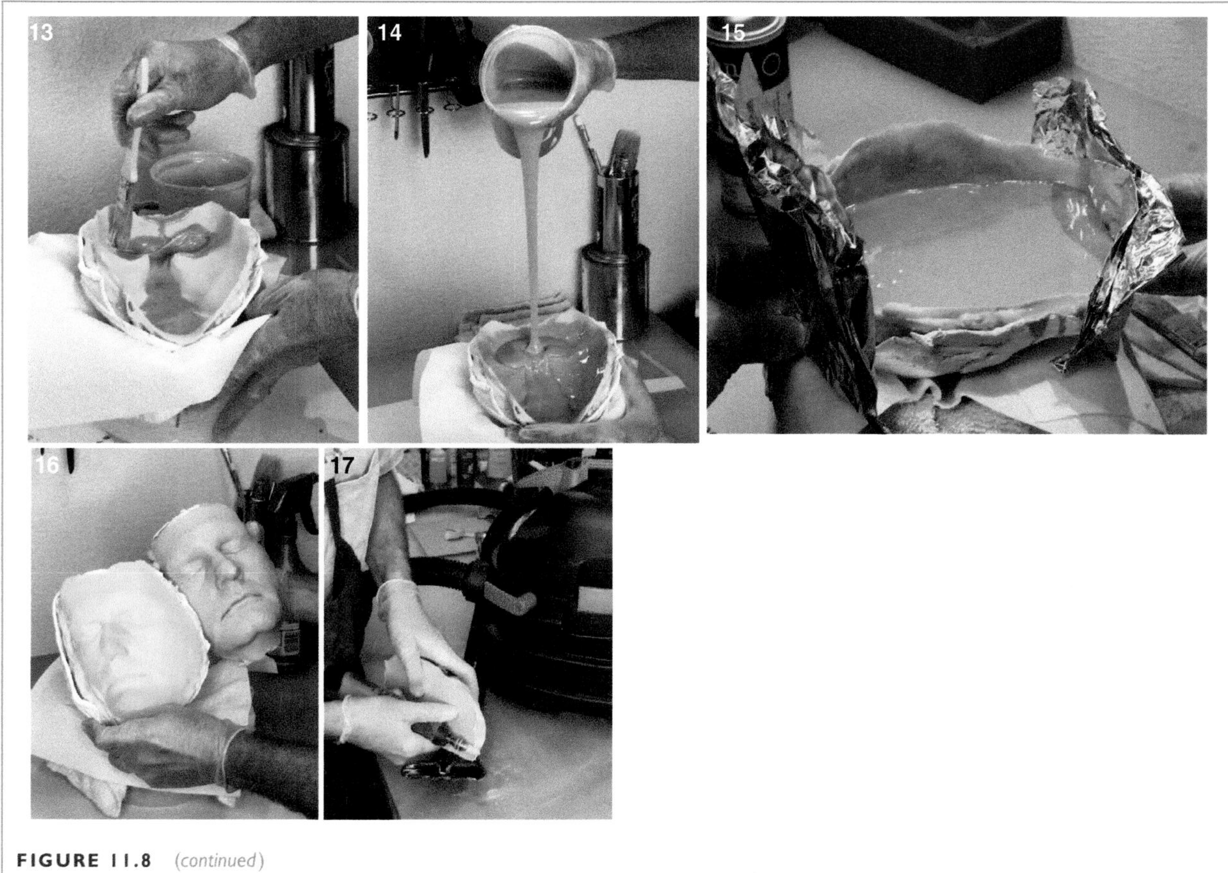

FIGURE 11.8 *(continued)*

The Gelatin Nose

Sculpting the Nose (Figure 11.9)

1. Spray the face cast with Krylon Crystal Clear in a well-ventilated area. Do not breathe the fumes.
2. Draw the outline of the desired nose with a pencil.
3., 4., & 5. Start sculpture by adding small amounts of clay to the surface of the Ultracal face cast.
6. Smooth out the clay with your finger, blending the clay edges onto the Ultracal face cast.
7. Use a wire loop sculpting tool to contour and blend the edges of the clay.
8. Create the nostril with the wire loop sculpting tool.
9. Use a soft bristle brush and 99% alcohol to smooth out nose sculpture.
10. Pore texture added with texture stamps.
11. After covering the clay with plastic wrap use a ball stylus tool to tap pores into the nose.
12. Create wrinkle lines at the top of the nose with a pin.
13. Add additional texture with the ball stylus if needed after removing the plastic wrap.
14. Gently smooth out the nose sculpture with a brush and baby powder.
15. & 16. Fill in the nostril area with soft sulfur-free clay to prevent any undercuts.
17. Clean the edges of the nose sculpture with lacquer thinner and a short-bristled brush.
18. Spray the sculpture with Krylon Crystal Clear in a well-ventilated area. Do not breathe the fumes.
19. After drilling the indented registration keys in the positive face cast (see Cyrano nose molding, Figure 11.48, images 28, 29, 30, 31, and 32), build up soft

sulfur-free clay snakes as flashing around sculpture. Keys are used to keep multi-part molds from shifting when placed together.

20. After smoothing out soft sulfur-free clay, clean indented keys out and cut clay ⅛ inch from the edge of the sculpted nose (see Figure 11.48 the Cyrano nose molding example for more details).
21. Spray the sculpture with Krylon Crystal Clear in a well-ventilated area. Do not breathe the fumes.
22. Pour lacquer thinner into a small bowl.
23. Clean keys and "cutting edge" of the sculpture with a small soft-bristled brush and lacquer thinner. The cutting edge is the exposed plaster between the nose clay and the flashing clay.

Ultracal Positive

24. Cut the bottom out of a 32-oz. deli cup with an X-Acto tool.
25. Cut the top rim off the deli cup with scissors.
26. Hold the trimmed cup onto the flashing and mark the contours needed with a Sharpie.
27. Trim the deli cup to the marked contour lines with scissors.
28. Press the trimmed deli cup into the flashing of the mold and seal the edge with soft sulfur-free clay.
29. Paint a very light coat of petroleum jelly into the indented keys and an even lighter coat on the "cutting edge" around the sculpted nose.
30. Mix a batch of 3 oz. water to 8 oz. of Ultracal-30 powder and paint onto the sculpture and flashing of the face cast. *Be very careful* not to trap bubbles on the surface of the clay, keys, and "cutting edge."
31. Use canned air to gently blow any small bubbles out of the wet Ultracal stone.
32. Paint more Ultracal onto the area to build up the thickness to ½ inch. Let this coat set for approximately 10–20 minutes or until the Ultracal loses its shine. Be careful not to dislodge the deli cup from the clay.
33. Mix another batch of Ultracal as in step #30 and paint a thin coat onto the set Ultracal.
34. Dip small burlap squares (2 x 2 inch) into the Ultracal mixture and gently tap them onto the previous layer of Ultracal.
35. After application of six burlap squares, pour the remaining Ultracal into the mold.
36. Let the mold set for 4 hours or overnight.
37. Cut the deli cup with a pair of scissors.
38. Remove the cup from the mold.
39. Gently pry the negative mold off the positive mold with a screwdriver.
40. Open mold.
41. Clean the flashing and sculpted nose clay out with a tongue depressor or wooden sculpting tool.
42. Remove as much clay as possible from the positive mold.

43. & 44. Shave all the sharp edges from the negative mold with a Stanley planer.

45. Clean all the clay from the negative mold with lacquer thinner.
46. Clean all the clay from the positive mold with lacquer thinner.
47. Finished molds.

1. Making the Gelatin Nose (Figure 11.10). Materials: Acryl 60, Prosaide, Sorbitol, Glycerin, microwave safe container, measuring cup, Zinc Oxide powder, Ben Nye Fair Facial Powder or Joe Blasco Ruddy Light Skin Facial Powder, metal spatula, CC cup, distilled water, red and tan flocking, 300 Bloom Gelatin, measuring spoons.
2. Measure 3 oz. of Sorbitol liquid and pour into a microwave safe container.
3. Measure 3 oz. of Glycerin and pour it into the container.
4. Measure ½ teaspoon distilled water and add to the Sorbitol & Glycerin. Stir together with a tongue depressor.
5. Measure 2 oz. of 300 Bloom Gelatin. A lower bloom of Gelatin may be used but the resulting gelatin will be weaker. Store-bought Knox Gelatin is 75 Bloom.
6. Add ¼ teaspoon Zinc Oxide powder.
7. Add ½ teaspoon of Joe Blasco's Ruddy Light Skin or Ben Nye Fair facial powder.
8. Add ¼ teaspoon red flocking.
9. Add ¼ teaspoon tan flocking.

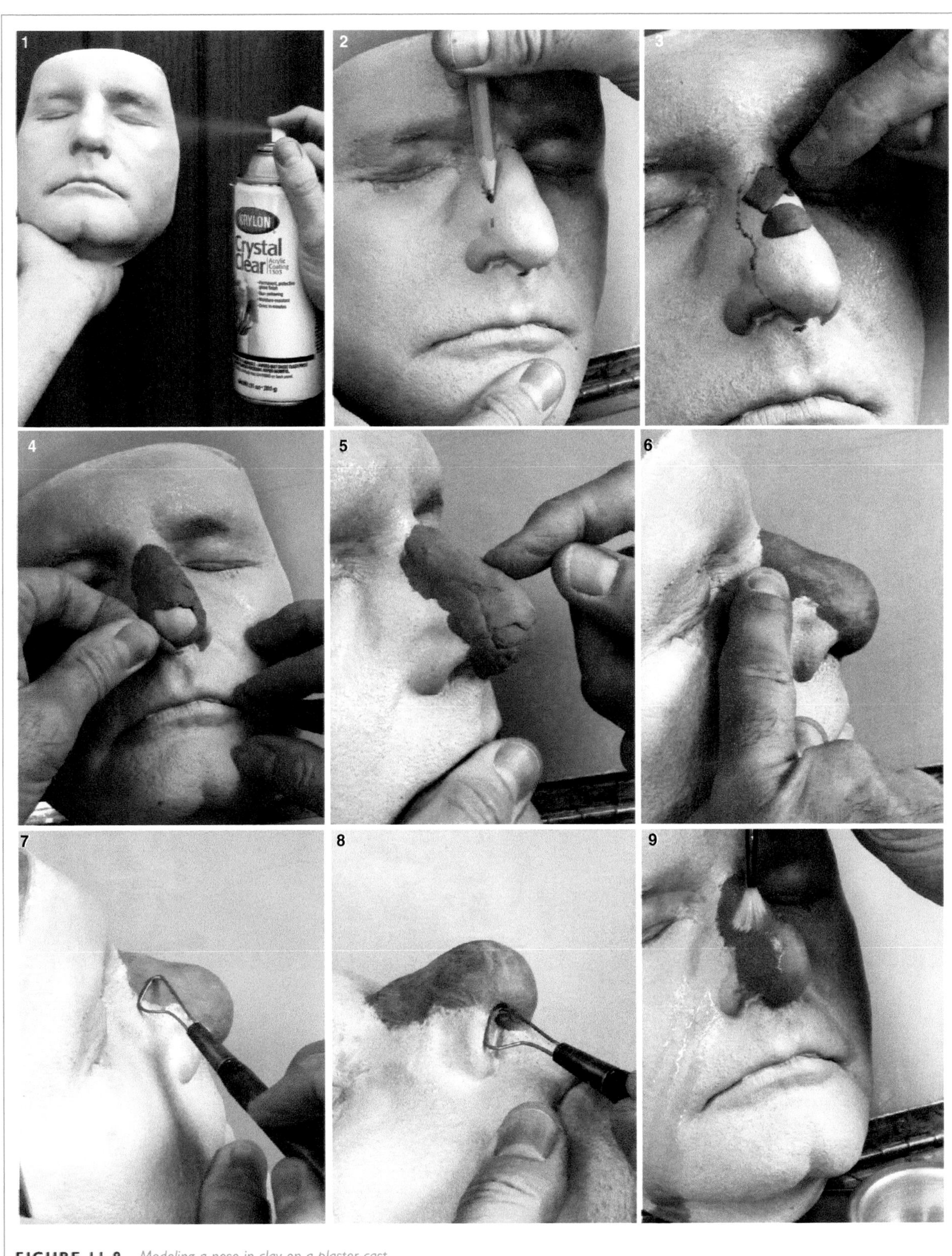

FIGURE 11.9 *Modeling a nose in clay on a plaster cast.*

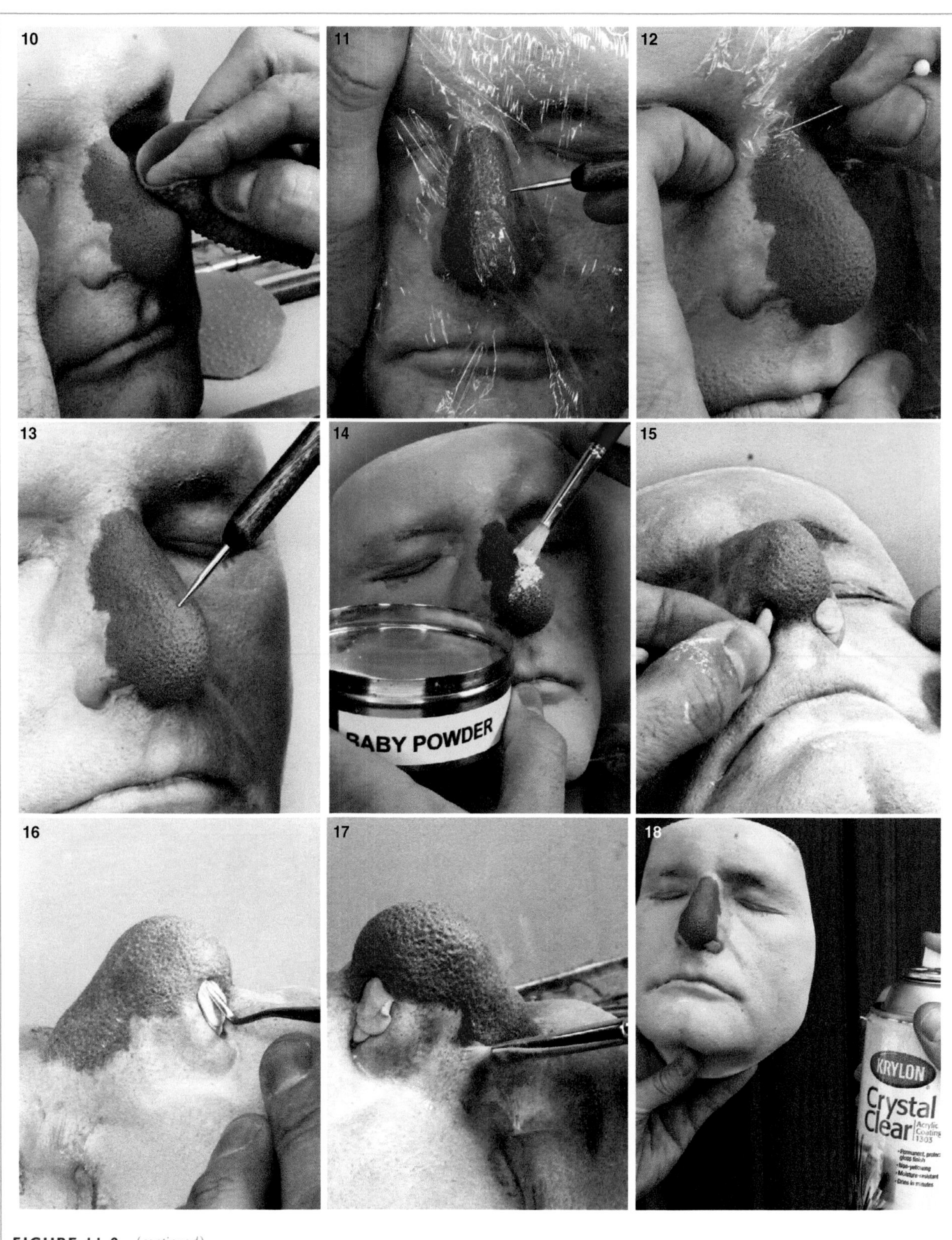

FIGURE 11.9 *(continued)*

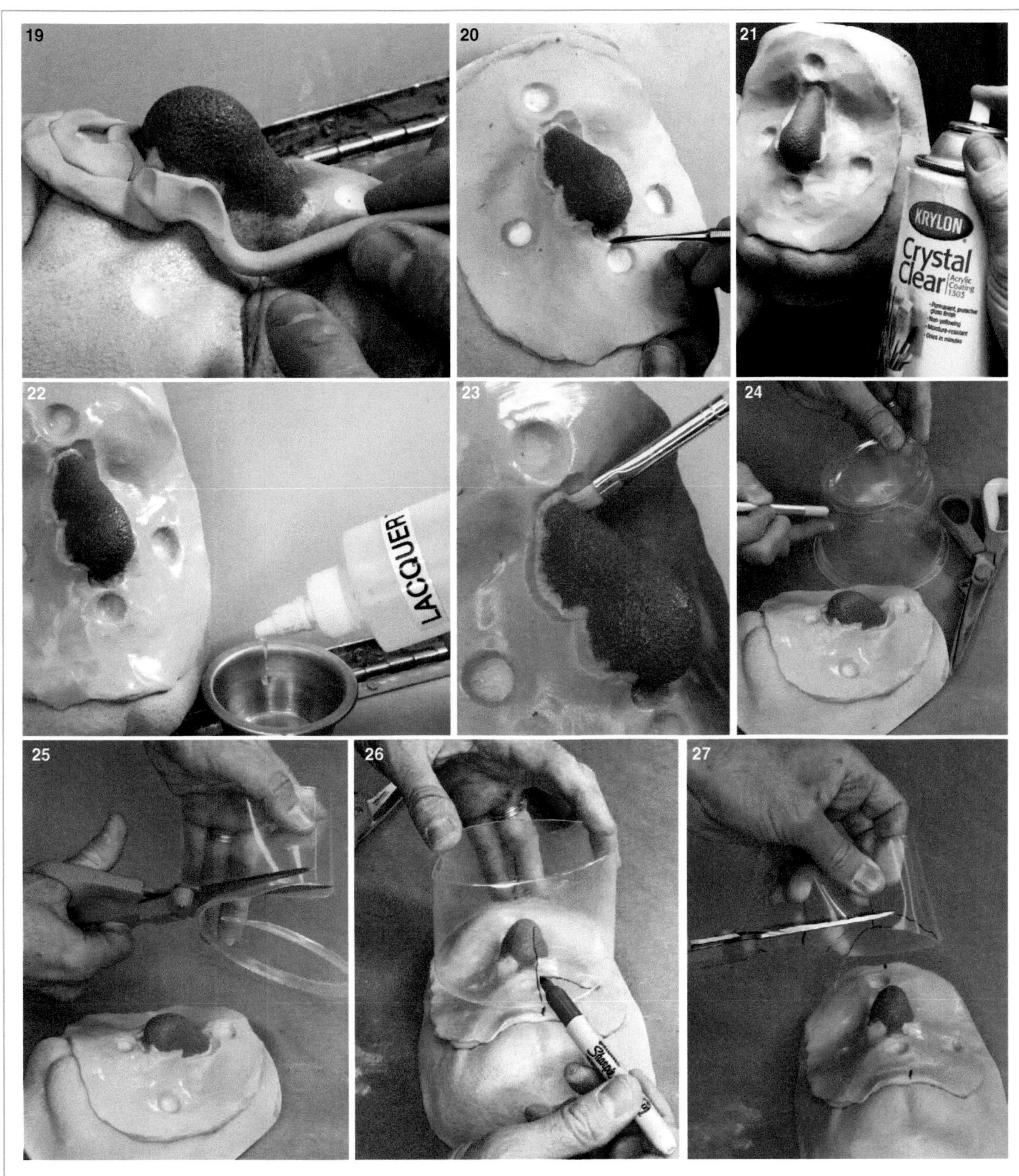

FIGURE 11.9 *(continued)*

FIGURE 11.9 *(continued)*

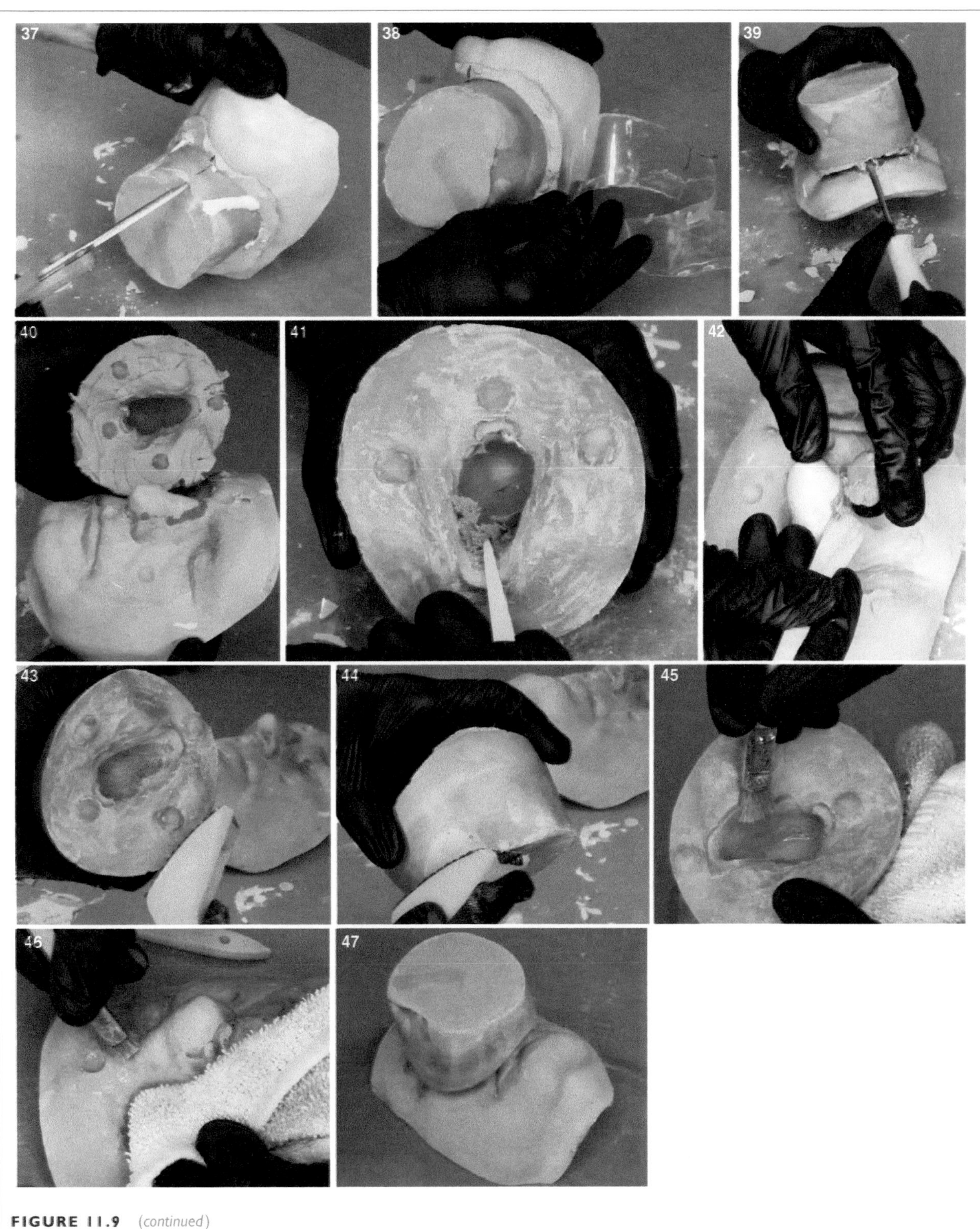

FIGURE 11.9 *(continued)*

FIGURE 11.10 *Gelatin making and running the gelatin nose.*

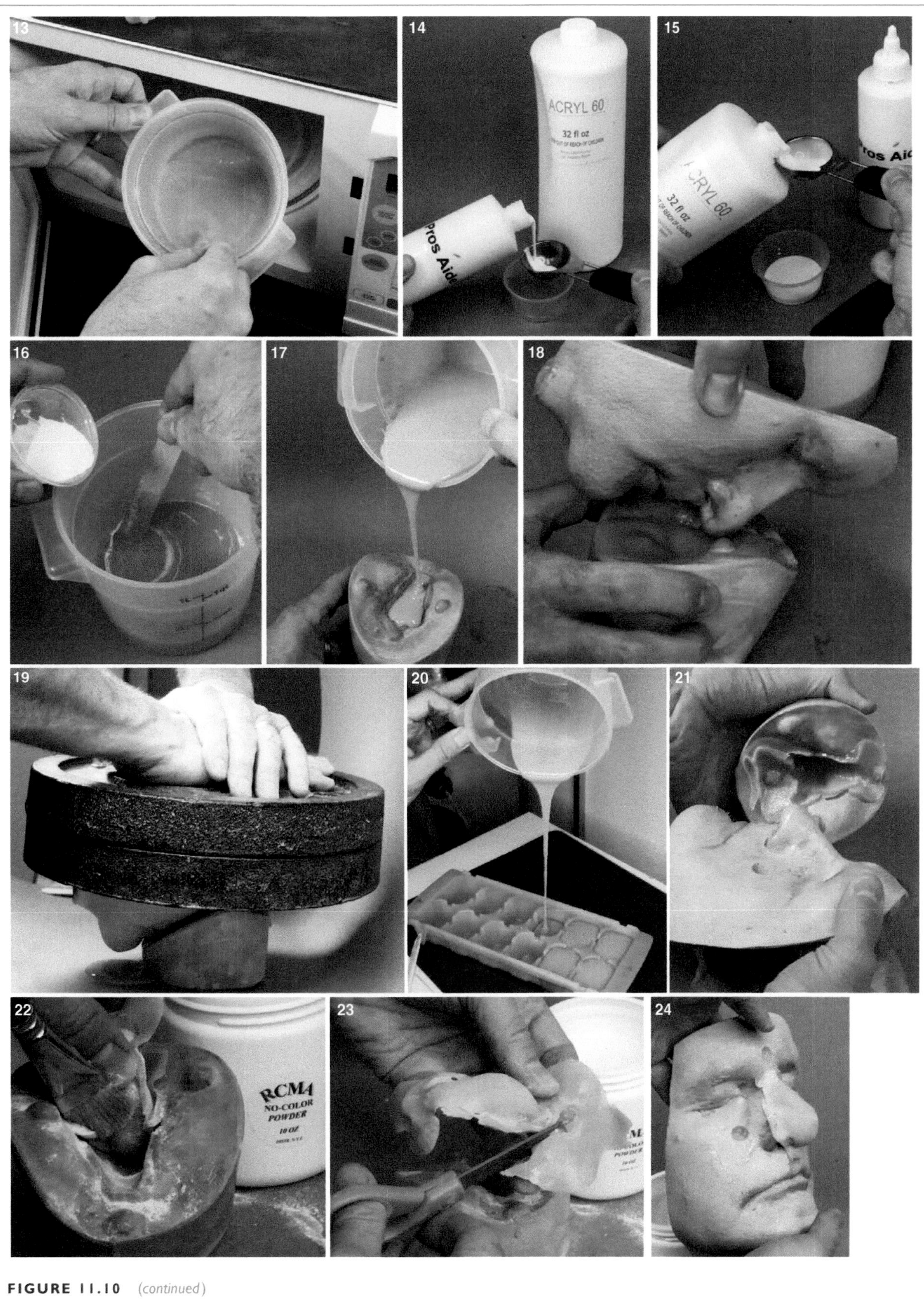

FIGURE 11.10 *(continued)*

10. Stir all the ingredients together with a tongue depressor and let set for 2 hours.
11. Spray the positive and negative molds heavily with Epoxy Parfilm release spray. Do not let the Parfilm spray puddle in the tip of the nose.

12. & 13. Heat the Gelatin mixture in a microwave for 30-second intervals, stirring the mixture at each interval. Heat the mixture for a total of 3 minutes. Do not let the mixture boil at any time.

14. Measure out 1 tablespoon of Prosaide into a small deli cup.
15. Add 1 tablespoon of Acryl 60 to the Prosaide and stir the mixture.
16. *Slowly* add the Prosaide / Acryl 60 mixture into the warm gelatin, stirring constantly when adding.
    - Running the nose
17. Pour the warm gelatin into the negative nose mold. *Be very careful, this mixture is extremely hot and can burn the skin.*

18. & 19. Close the mold and place a 50# of weight on top. This will keep the edges of mold completely sealed

20. Pour the remaining gelatin mixture into an ice cube tray and let cool. The cooled gelatin cubes can be stored in a plastic bag and used again (Figure 10.5).
21. Open the nose mold.
22. Brush generously with RCMA No-Color Powder as the gelatin nose is removed from mold.
23. Trim the excess flashing from the nose appliance. *Do* only the flashing *not* the edge of the appliance. (Note: Save all the trimmed gelatin materials which can be re-melted and reused again.)
24. Finished gelatin nose.

See Figure 10.7 for applying the gelatin nose.

The Latex Nose

There are four basic criteria for a useful, workable latex nose:

- It must be rigid enough to hold its shape without wrinkling or sagging.
- The blending edges should be tissue thin.
- The blend should, if possible, take place on a solid, rather than a flexible, part of the face (on the sides of the nose, that is, rather than on the cheeks or the nasolabial folds).
- It should be made in a very dry gypsum negative mold.

The first two of these criteria depend on the distribution of latex in the plaster cast and will be discussed below. The third requires careful placement of the clay used in building up the nose on the plaster cast. The fourth allows time for the liquid in the liquid latex to absorb into the surface of the gypsum plaster. This action will allow the rubber particles in the latex to collect on the surface, creating a thin yet stronger product.

MAKING A POSITIVE LATEX CAST

There are two techniques for making latex prosthetic pieces from the plaster molds:

- Painting method, known as a "slip cast." The liquid latex is painted into the mold, often with a cotton-tipped applicator.
- Filling the cavity with liquid latex and waiting for the buildup of rubber on the walls of the negative mold, before emptying the excess liquid. This is called a "slush" mold.

For either method, two types of liquid latex can be used: balloon latex or mask latex. These types of latex have high amounts of rubber solids and can usually be purchased in either flesh or natural white, which is almost transparent when it dries. It can also be tinted to your exact color specifications with:

- latex pigment concentrates
- Universal Paint tints (Cal-tints II)
- cosmetic grade pigments
- acrylic paint (Liquitex is best!!!)
- food coloring.

It is always useful to try to match the latex to the skin color of the performer. If it is too different it will be more difficult to cover. Remember, the solidified latex will always dry darker than the liquid latex.

The main requirements for a positive latex piece are:

- Make the central part of the piece thick enough to hold its shape.

FIGURE 11.11 *Making a slip rubber nose.*

- The edges must be thin enough to blend into the skin without an obvious line.

The Brush-in Technique, the "Slip Cast" (Figure 11.11)

Layers of latex are painted into the negative plaster mold, which requires no surface preparation. The type of applicator used is a matter of choice.

- Inexpensive brushes should be used.
- A soft-bristled brush lets the latex flow on more easily, but it is also very difficult to clean; and unless extreme care is taken, it will probably not last very long.
- A stiff bristle is easier to clean but doesn't give as smooth a coat of latex.
- A flat, medium-stiff bristle is perhaps the most generally practical.
- A cotton-tipped applicator is inexpensive, easy to use, spreads the latex smoothly onto the surface, and can be disposed of easily.

Taking care of your brushes:

- Brushes in use should be kept in soapy water and washed out thoroughly with soap the moment you have finished with them. Once the latex has solidified, it can seldom be removed from the brush.

(Note: Before painting in the first coat of latex, be sure the interior of the mold is clean and dry. If any separator or clay residue remains on the plaster surface, it will inhibit the absorption of the liquid in the latex into the plaster, therefore slowing drying time. You will also want to estimate about where you want the edge of the nose to be and to mark that with a pencil on the plaster. Then you can be sure to keep the latex thin along that line.)

Subsequent coats are painted in after the preceding coat is completely dry. Each coat can begin a little farther from the edge in order to provide a gradual thinning. The number of coats needed depends on the thickness of each coat. You will probably need a minimum of five, depending on the thickness of the latex and the requirements of the particular piece.

1. Making a Slip Rubber Nose (Figure 11.11). Materials: Negative Ultracal Nose Mold (from Cyrano Makeup Application section), container for balloon latex, seven cotton-tipped applicators, and balloon latex.
2. Dip a cotton-tipped applicator into balloon latex.
3. Apply one light coat of latex into the entire negative nose mold up to, but not over, the sculpted texture on nose.
4. Dry with a hairdryer.
5. Apply a second layer of latex on top of first dry layer of latex, 1/32 inch away from the edge and into the entire nose. Dry with hairdryer.
6. Continue applying five more coats of latex into entire nose mold keeping each layer 1/32 inch away from the edge of the previous dry layer. Dry each layer after application. More than seven coats of latex may be used if a thicker slip rubber nose is desired.
7. Repeat step #6.

Remove the Latex Nose from the Negative Mold

8. Materials: Finished balloon latex layers in negative nose mold, RCMA No-Color Powder, #6 (or similar) flat brush, and straight pin (not shown).
9. Before removing the latex piece, be sure it is completely dry. Powder the dry latex in the negative nose mold. In deep molds, such as noses, drying may sometimes take several days. Forcing hot air into the mold with a hairdryer can speed up the drying considerably. *Do not put the mold in the oven.*
10. Pull up the top edge of the latex carefully with the straight pin.
11. Insert the brush, with powder under the latex edge, and begin to pull up the latex nose. (Note: It is of utmost importance at this stage to keep the delicate edges of the piece from rolling.)
12. Continue removing the latex nose using more powder. Sometimes the piece comes away easily, sometimes it has to be pulled, but it will come. If you do have to pull hard, however, be sure not to pull it by the tissue-thin edge, which is likely to tear. Also, avoid pulling so hard that you stretch the piece permanently out of shape. As soon as you are able to loosen a little more of the piece, grasp it farther down to pull out the remainder. Tweezers can be helpful.
13. Finished slip rubber nose.

The Slush Mold

With the slush method:

1. Pour a small amount of the latex into the mold and gently slosh it around to build up layers of the latex. This is done by holding the plaster mold in the hand and moving or rocking it so that the latex runs first up to the edge as marked with a pencil. Subsequent movements should keep the latex nearer and nearer to the center and slightly farther and farther from the edge.
2. If you have a problem making the latex go exactly where you want it to, you can maneuver it with a clean modeling tool, a cotton-tipped applicator, or an orangewood stick (a slender, rounded stick, originally of orangewood, having tapered ends and used in manicuring, especially to push back the cuticles or clean the fingernails).
3. When you think you have built up enough thickness, drain off the excess latex or take it up with cleansing tissues or an absorbent cotton swab. Absorbing the excess out of the mold instead of pouring it out, avoids a buildup of latex along the edge at the point at which it is poured.

(Tip: You can avoid the whole problem of excess latex by pouring in a little at a time.)

Eyelids

Sagging eyelids are very helpful in aging youthful eyes. Unless the eyelids are part of an overall prosthetic makeup design, successful aging of the eyelids can best be accomplished using the "stretch and stipple" method of creating wrinkles (see Figure 10.6, Sissy Spacek from the film *Blast from the Past* and Figure 10.7.36, Character Makeup).

In modeling the lids, work from photographs of older people, using more than one, if you like, and combining the most useful and adaptable features of each. The foam latex or silicone eyelids can be attached to a forehead/brow or a nose/brow appliance (see Figures 11.12a and 11.12b). This design makes it possible to attach ventilated eyebrows or aged brows made from crepe hair onto the latex piece (see Figures 11.16d and 15.18). (See Figure 10.7.83 for crepe hair applied over the natural brow).

Ears

Rubber and silicone ears can be slipped over the actor's real ears very simply. Small ears or parts of small ears can be enlarged—as they must be at times. Ear tips can be used as seen on the character Legolas Greenleaf, a Sindarin Elf of the Woodland Realm in the film *Lord of the Rings* (see Figure 15.38). Full ears were made of silicone for Puck, also known as Robin Goodfellow, in Shakespeare's *A Midsummer Night's Dream* (Figure 11.13).

The technique in making ears, partial or complete, is to make an appliance that will fit over the natural ear. This requires a 2-piece or 3-piece plaster or resin mold: a mold of the performer's actual ear, and a 1- or 2-part mold of the sculpted ear.

Step 1: Make an impression of the natural ear of the performer first in alginate.

Step 2: Create a positive in plaster or resin.

Step 3: Model the clay ear on the plaster cast of the actor's natural ear with sulfur-free Chavant or Monster Clay. Blend the edges of the ear sculpt (where it will meet the performer's skin) into what will be the surrounding skin. Spray with a light coat of Crystal Clear by Krylon.

Step 4: Drill ½-inch round shallow registration keys into the base of the plaster ear cast.

Step 5: Lay the ear sculpt horizontally onto a bed of very smooth water-based clay called wed clay. Place the back of the ear as flat as possible against the wed clay. Build up from the clay bed to the center of the edge of the ear, creating a new clay bed. The surface of the clay bed should be very smooth and should connect to the ear edge at a 90 degree angle. The sculpted ear will appear imbedded or buried in the clay bed, but only up to the edge of the ear.

Step 6: Score a line around the ear onto the wed clay bed approximately 1 inch from the edge of the ear with a small metal sculpting spatula, creating a rectangular box-like shape around the ear. In the space between the score line and the ear create ½-inch round shallow indentations in the clay (you can use the end of a large makeup powder brush). At least two on either side of the ear. These will be the keys that keep the final multi-part mold pieces securely connected during the making of the ear prosthetic.

Step 7: Build a short wall of clay (at least 1 inch tall and ¾ inch wide) around the ear and along the score line. This wall should also butt up against the base and be half buried in the wed clay like the ear. There should be 1 inch of space all around the ear sculpt.

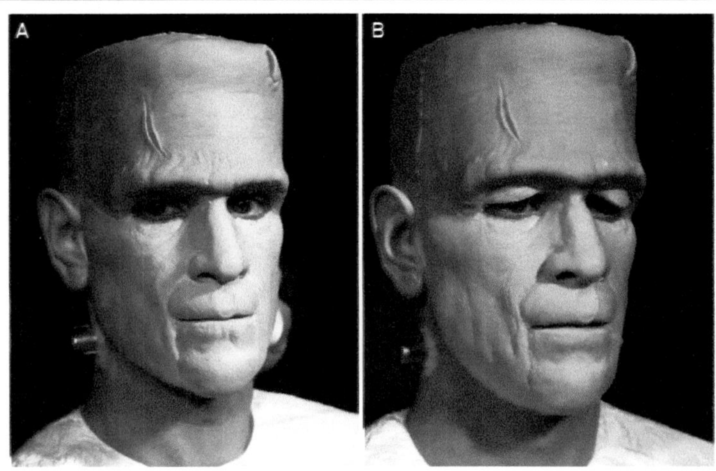

FIGURE 11.12 *Frankenstein makeup in foam latex.*

Step 8: Prepare and mix the plaster as in the face casting process demonstrated in Figure 11.7.

Step 9: Apply a layer of plaster with a chip brush on the visible side of the ear and base. Fill the trough created by the short wall and slowly build the plaster up to at least ½ inch thick. Apply at least three layers. Allow the plaster to set slightly between each layer. (Do not, however, allow the plaster to cure completely between layers.) After the third layer, dip a small piece of burlap into a small batch of fresh plaster and lay on the surface of the ear mold. The burlap should be completely contained within the edges of the mold. Add one more plaster layer to finish the first side of the mold. Smooth the surface of this last layer with a wet sponge or a kidney-shaped plastic or metal sculpting tool. Let cure completely.

Step 10: Remove the wed clay wall from the plaster mold. Remove the rest of the wed clay bed.

Step 11: Turn the mold over onto the plaster side and gently clean off any residue of wed clay from the other side of the ear sculpt and from the plaster mold with a soft brush.

Step 12: Spray the exposed clay with a light layer of Crystal Clear. Paint a thin smooth layer of petroleum jelly onto the plaster surface and into the round keys as a separator.

Step 13: After propping up the mold with wed clay to keep it horizontal and parallel to the work bench, build another short 1-inch clay wall around the outside of the plaster mold to contain the next layers of plaster. Add a small ⅛-inch rolled "tube" approximately 1 inch long made

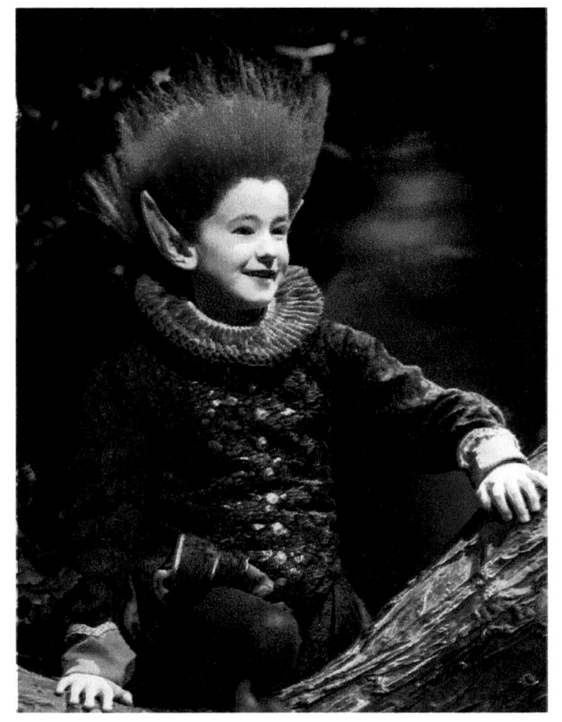

FIGURE 11.13 *Foam latex gnome. David Evans as Puck in the 2016 Glyndebourne Festival Opera production of Benjamin Britten's Midsummer Night's Dream, directed by Peter Hall. Photograph by Robert Workman. Prosthetic ears by Alison Rainey, Sarah Piper, Colette King, and Kerri Watters. © Courtesy of The Glyndebourne Festival.*

FIGURE 11.14 *Glenn Close as Albert Nobbs in the 2011 Rodrigo Garcia film, Albert Nobbs. Makeup by Matthew Mungle, Lynn Johnson; wig created by Martial Corneville. Image provided by Glenn Close. In this image a nose tip was applied and ear lobes were enlarged with silicone appliances.*

from wed clay and place it on the plaster connecting the tip of the ear to the clay wall. Lightly press this onto the plaster and connect it to the tip of the ear and to the wall. Seal these two connections to keep them from separating from the cast during the application of plaster layers. This tube will become a channel to expel air during the making of the silicone ears.

Make sure the wall is secure and the edges are sealed.

Step 14: Repeat the plaster layering process as before. Allow to cure completely.

Step 15: Carefully pry the mold apart with a large screwdriver. Be patient!

Step 16: Carefully remove the sculpted ear and original ear cast. Remove the sculpting clay off the original ear cast. Clean the interior clay from the mold using a wooden sculpting tool. Remove any excess clay with a tooth brush or short-bristled chip brush (you will need to use scissors to cut the bristles to about 1 inch in length).

In these ear molds you can make a set of prosthetic ears from liquid latex, foam latex, or silicone. For a hollow liquid latex ear you will need only the two parts that formed the prosthetic ear. For a foam latex and silicone ear, you will need two or three parts: the original ear cast on a base and the 2- or 3-part prosthetic ear mold.

The Latex Ear

The latex ear is made by pouring liquid latex into the cavity formed by the 2-part ear mold. This mold must be held tightly together with a mold strap or gaffer's tape to keep the latex from escaping through the seams. When using liquid latex, the escape channel at the tip of the ear must be filled with clay before pouring in the latex. There are two ways to approach the liquid latex ear:

1. Fill the cavity completely with mask latex. Allow it to stay in the ear for 30 minutes, then pour it out, allowing it to drain completely. Then allow the ear to dry completely. This might take several days. Using a hairdryer or placing the mold in a wig dryer will speed up the drying time.
2. Pour into the mold cavity just enough mask latex to cover the surface of the interior of the mold. Rotate the mold until the entire surface is covered. Carefully paint the edges of the mold where the ear will attach to the performer's body to keep that edge thin. Extra latex can be poured out. Dry completely and add another two layers. (Note: you will never know if the amount of latex you use will create a sufficiently thin, yet sturdy prosthetic ear. At some point you will have to open the mold and see for yourself. If you keep detailed records of the amount of latex used, by weight and/or volume, and the drying times, you will soon develop the correct formula for a successful prosthetic ear.)
3. The latex ear can be painted with PAX Paint or Rubber Mask Grease paint (RMGP).

The Silicone Ear

Making the ear from silicone requires the use of the 2- or 3-mold parts.

1. Spray the interior of the molds with 200 Mold Release Spray. Then secure the two mold parts of the prosthetic ear together with a mold strap or c-clamps. Stand the mold on end with the cavity opening up.
2. Prepare Part A and Part B of the Dragon Skin 20 or Platsil Gel-25 platinum silicone. Each of these silicones requires equal amounts of Part A and Part B by volume to cure properly, making them very easy to use. They can be colored to match the performer's skin tone with Revlon ColorStay liquid foundations (see Figure 11.49 for preparing and adding color to silicone). The Dragon Skin has a working time of 25 minutes and will cure in 4 hours. The Platsil Gel-25 has a working time of 5 minutes and will cure in 1 hour.

3. Once the silicone is colored and mixed, it can be poured into the mold. When you see the silicone coming through the exit hole at the tip of the ear, plug the hole with clay. This will ensure that there are no air pockets in the mold. Keep pouring until the ear cavity is full.
4. Once the cavity is full, place the third part of the mold in place. This is the plaster cast of the performer's ear. It will act as a cap on this mold. Once in place, put a small heavy object like a stage weight or barbell weight on the top to hold it in place if you can, otherwise the mold can be held together with straps, mold bands, or gaffer tape. This will put pressure on the mold and seal it while silicone cures. Some silicone will no doubt ooze out of the seams. This is why it is important to make sure the mold parts are securely held together.

The Foam Latex Ear

Foam latex is purchased in a kit with five components: a high solids foam latex base, a foaming agent, a curing agent, a gelling agent, and wax release agent (see Figure 11.19 and 11.20 for instructions on working with foam latex).

1. Paint the interior surfaces of all three molds with a light coating of the release agent.
2. Prepare the foam latex as per the kit instructions.
3. Using a rubber spatula, spoon the foam latex into each side of the mold. Quickly clamp the mold pieces together using c-clamps or mold straps.
4. Place the entire mold in an oven at 140 degrees for 3–5 hours. (This, of course, is an estimate.)

Things you should know about foam latex:

- Foam latex is extremely light and moves perfectly with the expressions of the face.
- Foam latex appliances can only be used once.
- You need a dedicated oven for this product. Foam latex gives off toxic fumes, so you cannot use the oven again for cooking food.
- Foam latex is a difficult product to use. It is sensitive to variations in room temperature, time, and humidity in the mixing process, and curing process.
- Once you use foam latex in a mold, you can never use that mold to make silicone appliances. The sulfur used to stabilize the latex keeps the silicone from curing.
- Foam latex is opaque. Human skin is translucent. Gelatin and silicone are also translucent and easier to create realistic skin. It takes a skilled hand to create the transparent layers of paint to create the look of real skin.

Chin

Receding chins can be built up or straight ones made to protrude; round chins can be made more square or square chins rounded. Goatees can be pasted on prosthetic chins as well as some real ones and will not need to be remade for each performance. Frequently a chin can be combined in the same piece with a scrawny or a fat neck.

If the chin addition is to be very large, a foamed latex, gelatin, or silicone prosthetic would be preferable (see Figures 11.15, and 11.34).

Wrinkled Forehead

A wrinkled forehead can be modeled in clay on a plaster cast of the actor's head and a negative plaster mold made from the clay positive. To replicate advanced aging effects the forehead is usually one part of a full-head prosthetic. Foam latex, gelatin, and/or silicone appliances can then be made from the negative plaster molds. Ready-made foam latex forehead pieces are available at a variety of online Special Effects Makeup companies.

Effective aging of the face can also be accomplished by the stretch and stipple method. This process utilizes a special latex formula called "Old Age Stipple," "Old Age Stretch & Stipple," and Green Marble Aging Concentrate (by Premiere Products, Inc.). This method produces the most subtle and natural aging effects on the skin (see Figure 10.7). Stronger skin wrinkling effects can be achieved using liquid latex with cotton or tissue (see Figure 10.8).

Neck

It is possible to age the neck effectively from the front with paint, but the profile is difficult to change. A prosthetic appliance will, however, produce an old neck from any angle. You can have prominent muscles and sagging flesh, transverse rolls of fat, or sagging jowls. For this type of construction, however, foamed latex, gelatin, or silicone should be used. (See Figure 11.47 and the *Little Big Man* images in Figure 11.37.) An aged neck can also be effectively created with the stretch and stipple technique (see Figure 10.8).

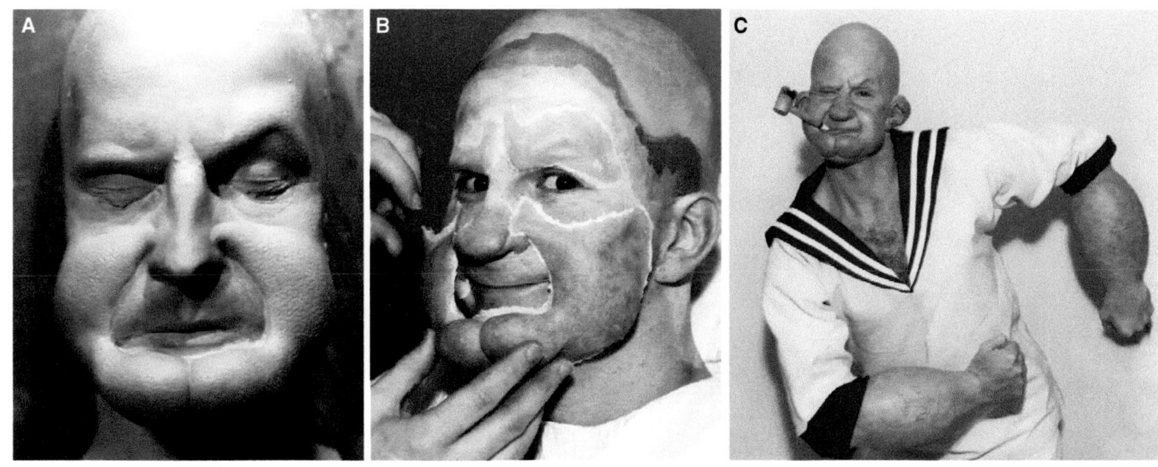

FIGURE 11.15 *A. Clay sculpt for a prosthetic makeup of Popeye by Stephan Tessier. B. Foam latex prosthetic chin being applied to the model. C. The character Popeye in full makeup and costume.*

Hands

Wrinkled and veined hands can be made up successfully with makeup. The use of color, and highlights and shadows, to enhance the bones, knuckles, veins, nails, and surface topography can be very effective with practice. This is an excellent painting exercise to do on your own hand. They are portable and always there when you need them!

Old Age Stretch & Stipple and Green Marble Aging Concentrate (by Premiere Products, Inc.) are both excellent products to produce a subtle and realistic aged wrinkle look on not only the hands, but also the face and neck.

[See latex Old Age Stretch & Stipple in Chapter 10 for a subtle effect or with a buildup of latex and tissue. The demonstration by Special Effects Makeup Artist Matthew Mungle utilizes the latex and tissue, and latex and cotton technique in the zombie makeup application (Figure 10.8).]

FOAM LATEX

Although the hollow, shell-like latex pieces work well on bony parts of the face, their hollowness may become apparent on softer areas where there is the possibility of considerable movement. This problem can be overcome through the use of foamed latex, with which it is possible to make three-dimensional, extremely soft, lightweight, spongy facial features that look and move like natural flesh.

Working with foam latex involves the combining of three to five compounds (based on the particular manufacturer's formulation) in various amounts in a specific order over a given amount of time. The procedure is considerably more complicated than the slush-mold process previously described. The following ingredients are needed to make a foam latex appliance:

- a relatively thick, creamed natural latex base with a high concentration of solids and ammonia;
- a curing agent containing sulfur to vulcanize and preserve the foam and other agents that keep the foam cell structure from breaking down;
- a surfactant or foaming agent to aid in lowering the surface tension of the latex, enabling it to froth more easily;
- a gelling agent that converts the foam from a liquid to a solid;
- and a waxy, mold release agent.

Foam latex is sold in a kit. The shelf life for the latex base is approximately one year, although with regular attention (weekly vigorous shaking) it will last nearly twice that long. The components, however, will last quite a long time with little attention.

Closed Molds

For foamed latex appliances it is necessary to use multiple molds: at least a positive and a negative instead of the one open mold used with liquid latex. The positive mold duplicates the actor's own features, the negative mold duplicates the clay sculpture and corresponds to the single

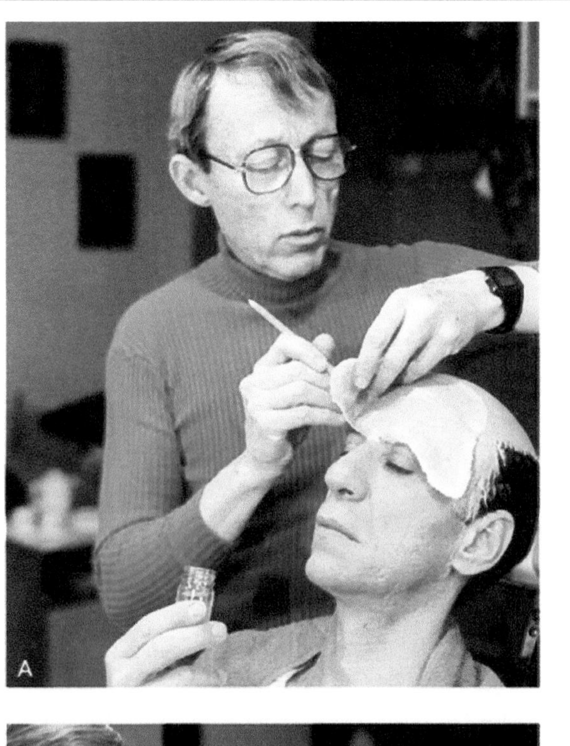

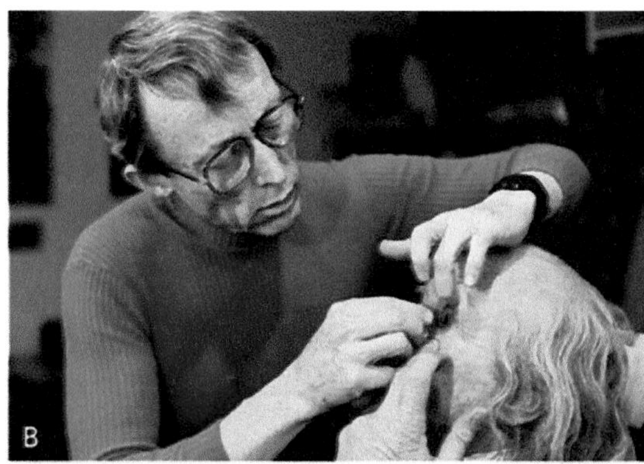

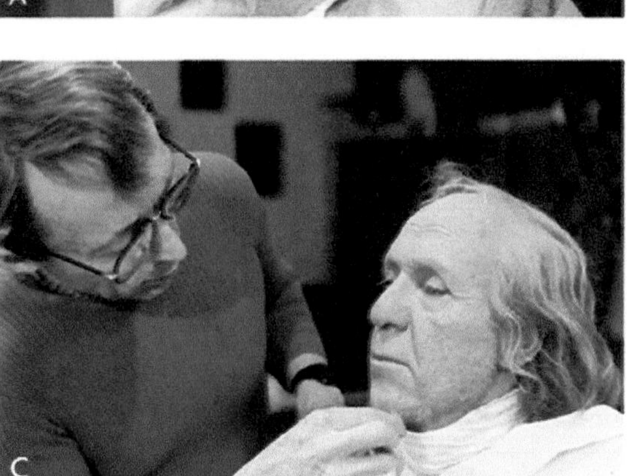

FIGURE 11.16 *a–d Foam latex prosthetic makeup. A. Dick Smith applying H-10 (Gafquat 734+ mustache wax + alcohol) to F. Murray Abraham to smooth and control the hair before applying the plastic bald pate (bald caps cover the entire head). The bald pate was made from a Union Carbide plasticizer called VYNS. The plastic bald pate and forehead appliance were then glued on with Dow 355 Adhesive (this product has been discontinued, substitute Prosaide, Telesis adhesives, or others, see Appendix A—Adhesives.) B. Contact lenses, with the arcus senilus hand-painted around the edge of the iris designed to add an aging effect to the eye, are inserted. C. Applying beard stubble. Stubble is made from short (½ inch or smaller) lengths of crimped (kinky) yak hair. Attach hairs by hand into a slightly tacky Secure Adhesive (Factor II) applied over the PAX Paint. Give the adhesive a matte finish by slowly mixing in the matting agent Cab-O-Sil. D. F. Murray Abraham as Solieri for the film, Amadeus. Makeup created by Dick Smith.*

mold used for painted-in latex pieces. When the two molds are fitted together or *closed*, the space or spaces between them will correspond precisely to the clay sculpture of the character or appliance that has been built up on the plaster cast. This space is then filled with foamed latex. The molds are usually made with Ultracal 30 or Dental Stone (see Appendix A), which is harder, less porous, and more durable than plaster. Instructions for making a closed mold can be seen in Figure 11.44.

Foaming the Latex

The companies that make latex for foaming have their own formulas for combining the various ingredients (either three, four,

FIGURE 11.17 *Molded latex forehead prosthetic.*

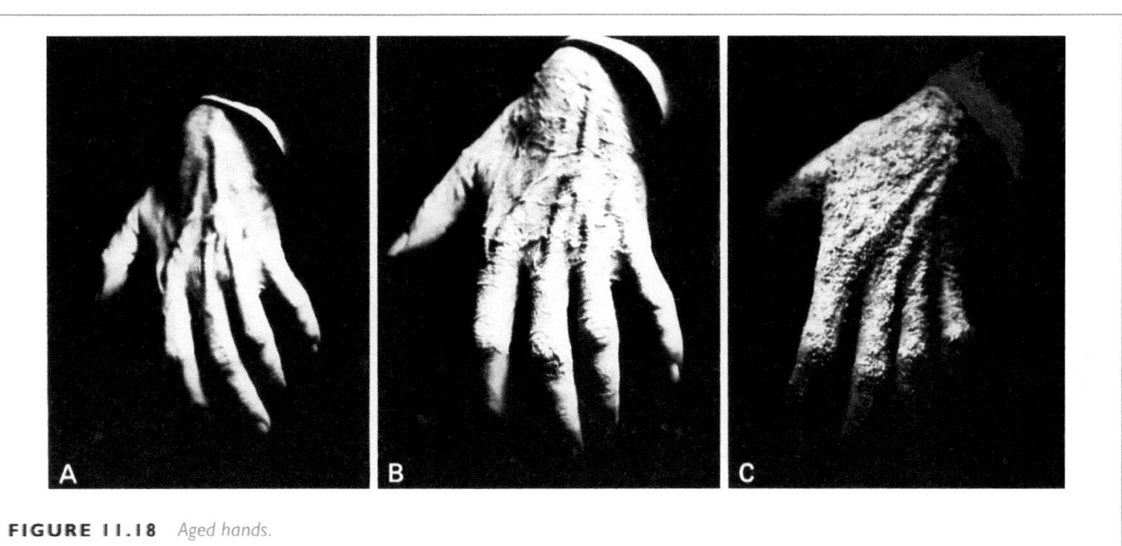

FIGURE 11.18 *Aged hands.*

or five depending on the brand) in order to produce the foam. Whenever you use any foam latex for the first time, carefully follow the directions that come with it. Any experimentation should wait until after you have observed the results produced by following the manufacturer's instructions. When you do begin experimenting with variations in the procedure, be sure to keep a precise record of all such variations, including all materials used and exact amounts of each, temperatures (both room and oven), humidity, beating times, and volume of foam. Date each entry and comment on the results. If the results are not entirely satisfactory, you might include any suggestions that occur to you for changes to be made in the next experiment.

With each new experiment, only one variation should be made.

When "running" a foam batch, it is the amount of ammonia in the foam that most affects the gelling process. Excessive amounts of ammonia will keep the foam from gelling, too little will cause it to "set up" in the bowl. When difficulties arise in the foamed latex process they are often caused by:

- the amount and speed with which the ammonia evaporates from the foam, which may be traced to such diverse sources as room temperature and humidity
- the speed of the mixer, the depth of the mixing bowl, the type of beater used (improper foaming), and even the rotation speed of the mixing bowl
- other sources, which can include too short a curing time

- too low or too high an oven temperature (foam too soft or too hard with an unpleasant odor)
- baking time
- and excess moisture in the mold. This might be caused by molds that have not thoroughly dried, or by release agents that have not thoroughly dried. The effects may cause latex skin becoming detached from the foam on or after removal from the mold.

Since formulas vary from brand to brand and since you will be following the instructions for your particular brand, the information given here is intended primarily for those who are not acquainted with the process but would like to have some idea of what is involved.

A detailed recipe for specific amounts of the various ingredients will be included in the manufacturer's instructions.

To transfer the foam to the mold:

There are two ways to transfer the foam latex into your negative mold:

- by pouring, the "open pour" process
- by injection

The *open pour* method works well on small appliances (noses, eye pouches) and for those no larger than the size of a face cast. You can also use a spoon to scoop foam into the mold, being careful to avoid adding large bubbles. Filling deep cavities and wrinkles by spooning or spreading the foam with a spatula or brush before pouring the remaining foam will help alleviate the possibility of trapped bubbles (see Figure 11.19).

Foam injection guns can be used to transfer foam into larger molds. The design of the mold must include at least one injection hole (large enough to accommodate the gun nozzle) and vent holes for displaced air and excess foam. When using the injection method, the positive and negative molds must first be assembled and clamped or strapped together before the foam is injected (see Figure 11.20).

(Note: the following description is a general process for mixing a batch of GM Foam Latex.)

FOAM LATEX PROSTHETIC MADE IN AN "OPEN POUR" MOLD

1. Figure 11.19 - The GM Foam Latex Kit is comprised of the high grade foam latexase, foaming agent, curing agent, gelling agent, and the mold release.
2. The variable-speed Sunbeam mixer, mixing bowl, and digital scale.
3. In an effort to establish consistency in room temperature and humidity the foam latex room should have a hygrometer, and a temperature gauge. A timer is also a necessary component.

To mix the compounds:

4. & 5. Before beginning the mixing process, paint the mold release onto the positive and negative molds. Allow the waxy mold release to dry completely. The surface will reveal a white powder when it has dried.

   (Note: Many professions prepare the molds with the product Alco-Wax, a mixture of 5-parts alcohol and 1-part Carnuba wax.)

6. When the release agent is completely dry, remove the residue by brushing it away using a chip brush.

   (Note: For this project the GM Foam manufacturer's recipe for one batch is being expanded approximately 2.5 times in an effort to accommodate the larger mold.)

7. Use a digital gram scale, weigh out 40 grams of curing agent into the mixing bowl.
8. Add 85 grams of foaming agent.
9. Weigh and add 375 grams of the foam latex base.
10. The three ingredients are now blended together in the following manner:
    - 1 minute at speed 1,
    - 7 minutes at speed 12 to create volume in the foam,
    - 2 minutes at speed 8 to stabilize the foam,
    - 3 minutes at speed 4 to de-ammoniate the foam,
    - 3 minutes at speed 2 to refine the cell structure.

    (Note: If you want to intrinsically color your latex to match the skin tone of the performer, add the appropriate amount of colorant during the foaming process and before the gelling agent is introduced. Colorant can be obtained from the manufacturer. Pigment dispersions, made specifically for coloring latex are recommended. Universal color tints are not recommended for foam latex appliances. Polypropylene glycol contained in the colorants causes the foam cell structure to break down.)

11. Measure 35 grams of gelling agent.
12. With the mixer running, reduce the speed to 2 and continue at this speed for 1 minute. Slowly add the gelling agent to the foam over the first 30 seconds of that minute.
13. "Back bowl" for the next 30 seconds. Back bowling is the process of slowly spinning the bowl with your hand against the natural spinning direction of the mixing bowl.
14 Reduce the speed to 1 for 30 seconds. Using a large rubber spatula gently scrape the sides of the bowl and mix the foam to completely incorporate the gelling agent.
15. Turn the mixer off and remove the bowl. Using a 2-inch chip brush, gently and quickly brush the foam into all of the details of the negative mold.
16. Pour the remaining foam into the negative mold cavity.
17. Slosh the foam around the interior of the mold.
18. Once the foam has been added, place the positive mold into the negative, allowing the weight of the positive to settle into the foam (this should take only a few moments). Then press the two parts together, closing the mold. This will automatically squeeze out the excess, leaving the space between the molds filled with the foam latex.
19. Secure the two mold parts together using a mold strap.
20. Wait until the foam latex has completely gelled. When gelled, the foam will produce a skin and collapse when touched, but the interior will no longer feel like liquid.
21. After giving the foam time to gel (usually 10–20 minutes) place the mold into the designated foam oven. This mold, because of its size, will be baked for 6 hours at 185 degrees Fahrenheit. In this exercise, the oven and the mold were allowed to heat up together.
22. When the baking is complete, allow the oven and the mold to cool completely; however, the mold should remain slightly warm to the touch. Removing the mold while it is still hot can cause cracking and damage to the plaster (stone).
23. Remove the mold strap.
24. Remove the excess foam from the exterior of the mold.
25. Carefully pry open the mold using extra-large screwdrivers. Be patient! Pulling the mold apart too quickly may cause damage to the foam. The foam piece will usually stick to one side or the other, but it could stick to both sides. Allow the mold to open slowly. Air needs to enter the mold to release the suction.
26. Gently separate the molds.
27. Remove the foam latex appliance. To preserve the delicate edges, powder the foam generously and start working the foam loose from the edges of the piece. Avoid excessive handling of the edges before they are powdered. Pull off any ragged edges of the piece but not too closely or too evenly (never cut edges). They should be very thin and somewhat irregular.
28. When the foam is completely separated from the mold and the flashing, it should be washed in Simple Green soap cleaner to remove any remaining sulfur (which may irritate certain types of skin), and to clean the surface of excess release agent. Gently squeeze out all of the water from the foam appliance, place it between a cloth towel and press the remaining water from the piece. Let the appliance dry overnight.
29. The finished foam latex prosthetic used to create an animatronic puppet. This character is based on the Vogon creatures from the film, *The Hitchhiker's Guide to the Galaxy*. The skin was painted with thin glazes of PAX Paint.

FOAM LATEX PROSTHETIC MADE IN AN "INJECTION" MOLD

This example uses a "single batch" of GM Foam Latex. The example, Figure 11.20, is a small part from a large animatronic character.

1. Preparation of the foam latex work area: Sunbeam variable-speed mixer and bowl, foam latex recipe work sheet, digital gram scale, GM Foam Latex Kit, small waxed cups.
2. The interior sides of the 3-part injection mold made from Ultracal 30 are painted with Alco-Wax release agent (5 parts 99% alcohol and 1 part Carnuba wax). Place the mold in front of a fan to dry. When the wax is dry, paint a second layer and allow that layer to also dry completely. Brush the excess powder from the mold and polish the surfaces with a soft cloth.
3. Close the mold using a mold strap. Notice the entry port built into the mold. This hole is where the nozzle of the injection gun will be placed and where the foam latex will enter the mold. Next to the entry port is a pry hole. The pry holes are most often placed at opposite sides of the mold. These holes are where the pry bars are placed when separating the mold pieces after it has been cured in the oven.
4. The foam latex worksheet. When running foam latex, time, temperature, and humidity must be monitored

FIGURE 11.19 *Foam latex open pour mold.*

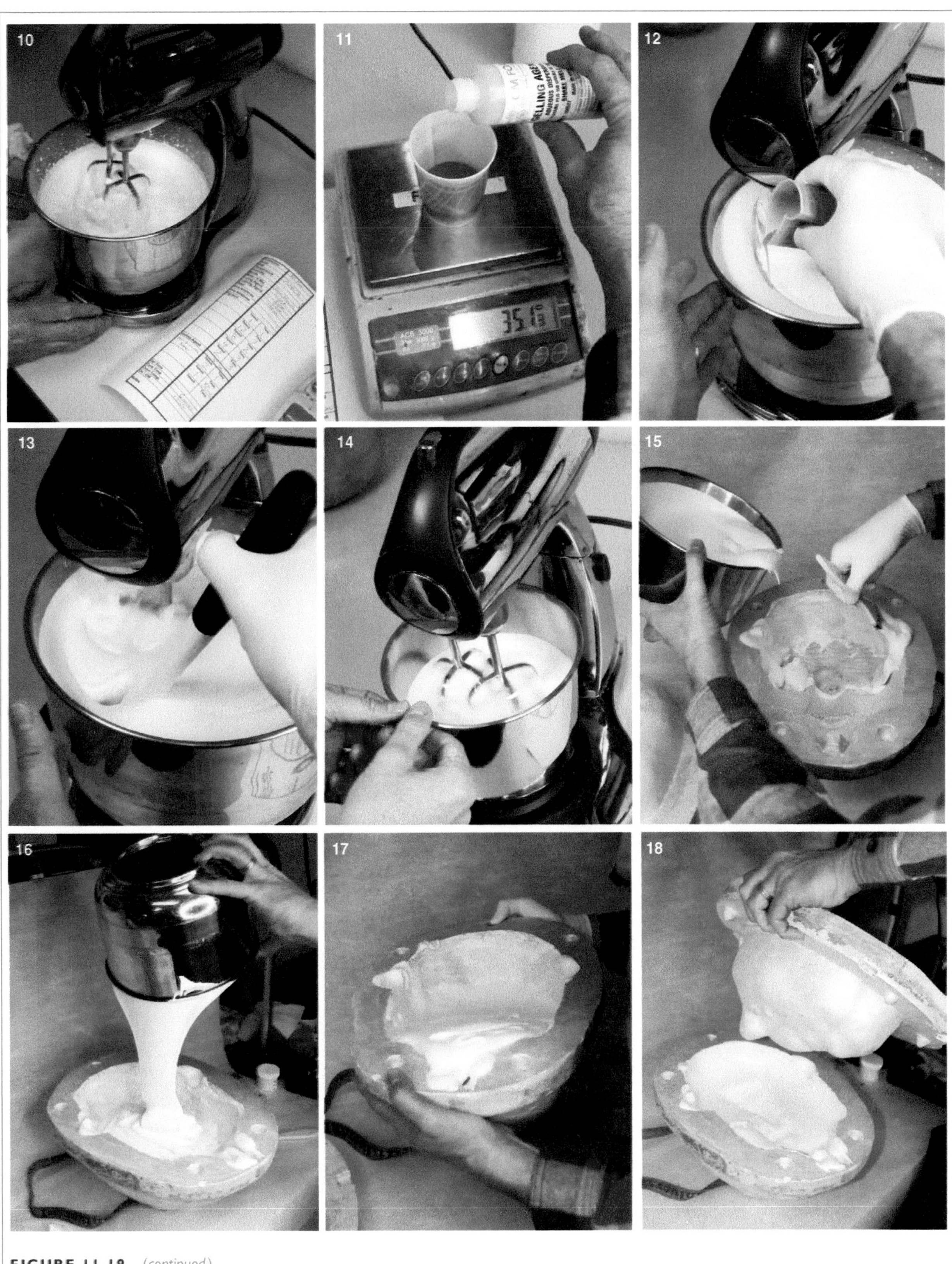

FIGURE 11.19 *(continued)*

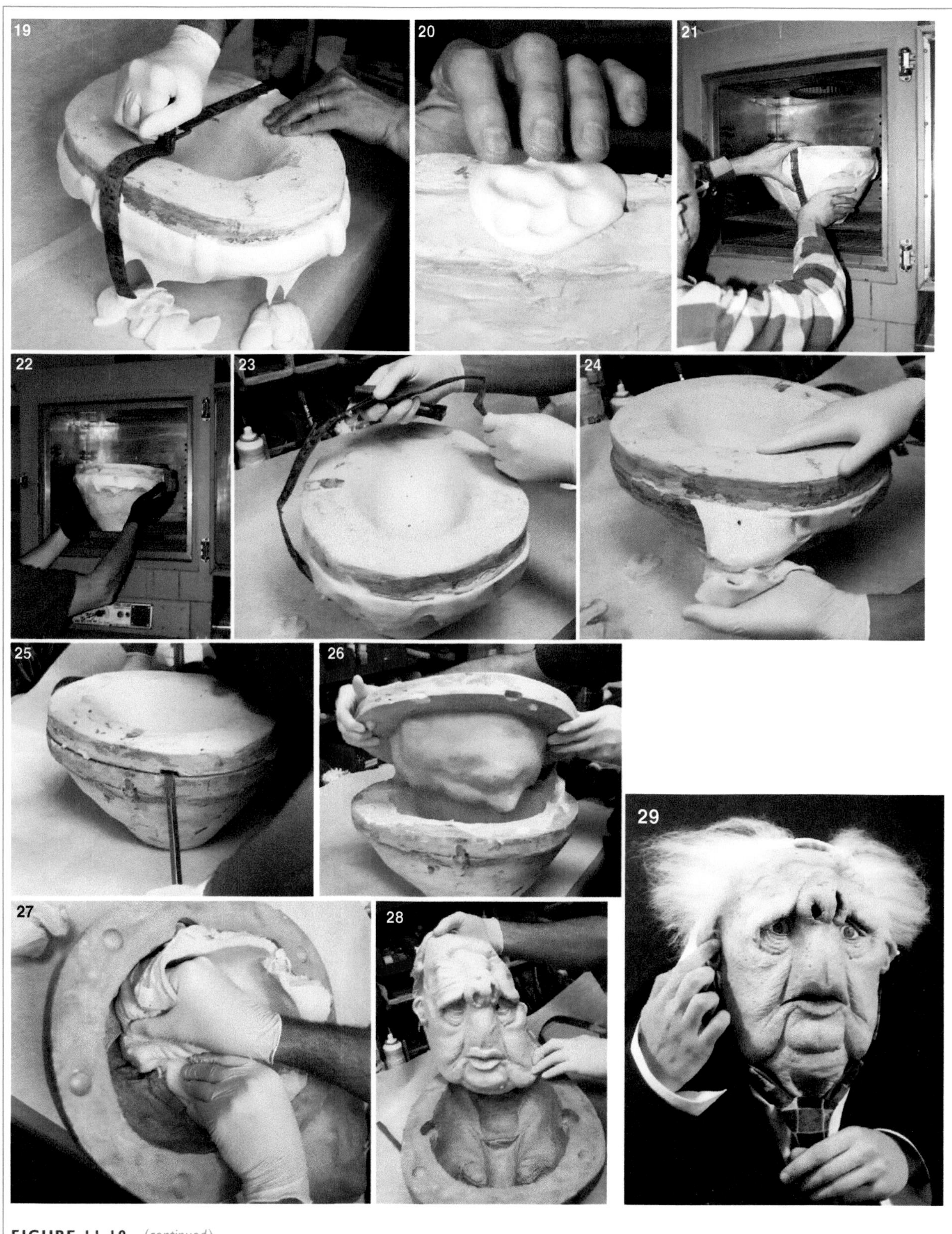

FIGURE 11.19 *(continued)*

throughout the work day. In an effort to run foam that is reliable on a regular basis, these variables must remain consistent. Keeping accurate records of each foam latex "run" is one of the most important and useful exercises to developing consistent foam latex prosthetics. Any variables in the recipe should be noted after each "run."

5. Add 15 grams of curing agent to the mixing bowl.
6. Weigh 30 grams of foaming agent into the mixing bowl.
7. Add 150 grams of the foam latex base.
8. Mix these three ingredients together with the Sunbeam mixer in the following manner:
   - 1 minute at speed 1 to blend the ingredients,
   - 6 minutes at speed 7 to create volume,
   - 4 minutes at speed 4 to de-ammoniate the foam,
   - 5 minutes at speed 1 to refine the foam.
9. Weigh 14 grams of gelling agent.
10. Slowly pour the gelling agent into the foam over 30 seconds at speed 1 for 1 minute. Scrape the sides with a rubber spatula and continue at speed 1 for 30 more seconds.
11. Back bowl for 1 minute of the last 5 minutes to help fully incorporate the gelling agent into the mixture. This will also aid the refining process.
12. Remove the bowl from the mixer and pour the foam into the injection gun. This must be done quickly before the foam begins to gel. If the foam gels too quickly, it will not flow into the mold. If this happens, note the number of minutes the foam took to gel. Adjustments can be made to the amount of gelling agent and/or the amount of time for the de-ammoniating process. Run another batch using slightly less gelling agent or slightly less time de-ammoniating the foam. Be sure to keep accurate records of your process.
13. Replace the tip of the injection gun and notice the air space between the foam and the tip.
14. Remove the extra air by pressing on the handle until the air is displaced with foam and a small amount of foam is released through the nozzle tip. This is called "burping" the gun.
15. Place the nozzle tip into the injection hole of the mold and slowly, yet firmly, push on the handle until the mold is full. Wait a few minutes until the foam has gelled.
16. Place the mold in the oven. Cure the mold at 150 degrees Fahrenheit for 4 hours. Turn the oven off and allow the oven and the mold to cool for several hours.
17. Remove the mold from the oven. The mold should be warm to the touch. If it is too hot to handle, the rapid cooling may cause damage to the mold. Carefully pry the mold apart and remove the prosthetic.
18. Remove the foam latex prosthetic. Abnormalities to look for may include air pockets where the skin separates from the foam interior. This is often caused by moisture in the mold: moisture from a fresh mold that has not been dried sufficiently, or moisture caused by a release agent that has not been dried completely. After removal, wash the appliance with Simple Green soap to remove excess sulfur and release agent residue.

(see *Foam latex*, Appendix A).

REPAIRING FOAM LATEX

The best material with which to make repairs is more foam latex. Mix a small batch and spatula it onto tears, seams, holes, or other imperfections, allowing it to gel, and set it back in the oven to cure. Check the piece every 30 minutes until the foam bounces back when touched. To protect your foam appliance, include an extra mound of foam to check for doneness. Another product that can be successfully used for patching small imperfections is Prosaide (see *Adhesives*, Appendix A).

Allowed to thicken naturally (simply leave the lid off a small bottle) or thickened with Cab-O-Sil or Cabosil (fumed silicone dioxide used as a thixotropic agent), Prosaide can be applied with a small metal spatula, dried with a hairdryer, and then powdered.

It is possible but not necessary to clean foam appliances by washing them in soap and water to remove the separating agent and any chemicals remaining in the foam. These chemicals may cause irritation on highly sensitive skin. The process may damage the delicate edges, so care must be taken. Add two to three drops of Ivory Liquid detergent or Simple Green per gallon of water and squeeze the foam with your fingers for a few minutes. Rinse well under fresh water until the water runs clear. To remove excess water, press the foam between paper or cloth towels and return it to the plaster positive until completely dry. Should the edges begin to curl and fold over onto themselves, generously add powder and carefully unfold the edges. (Note: If for any reason you should want to change the color of your foam latex appliance, simply dip it in fabric dye intended for natural fibers.)

FIGURES 11.20 *Foam latex prosthetic made in an "injection" mold.*

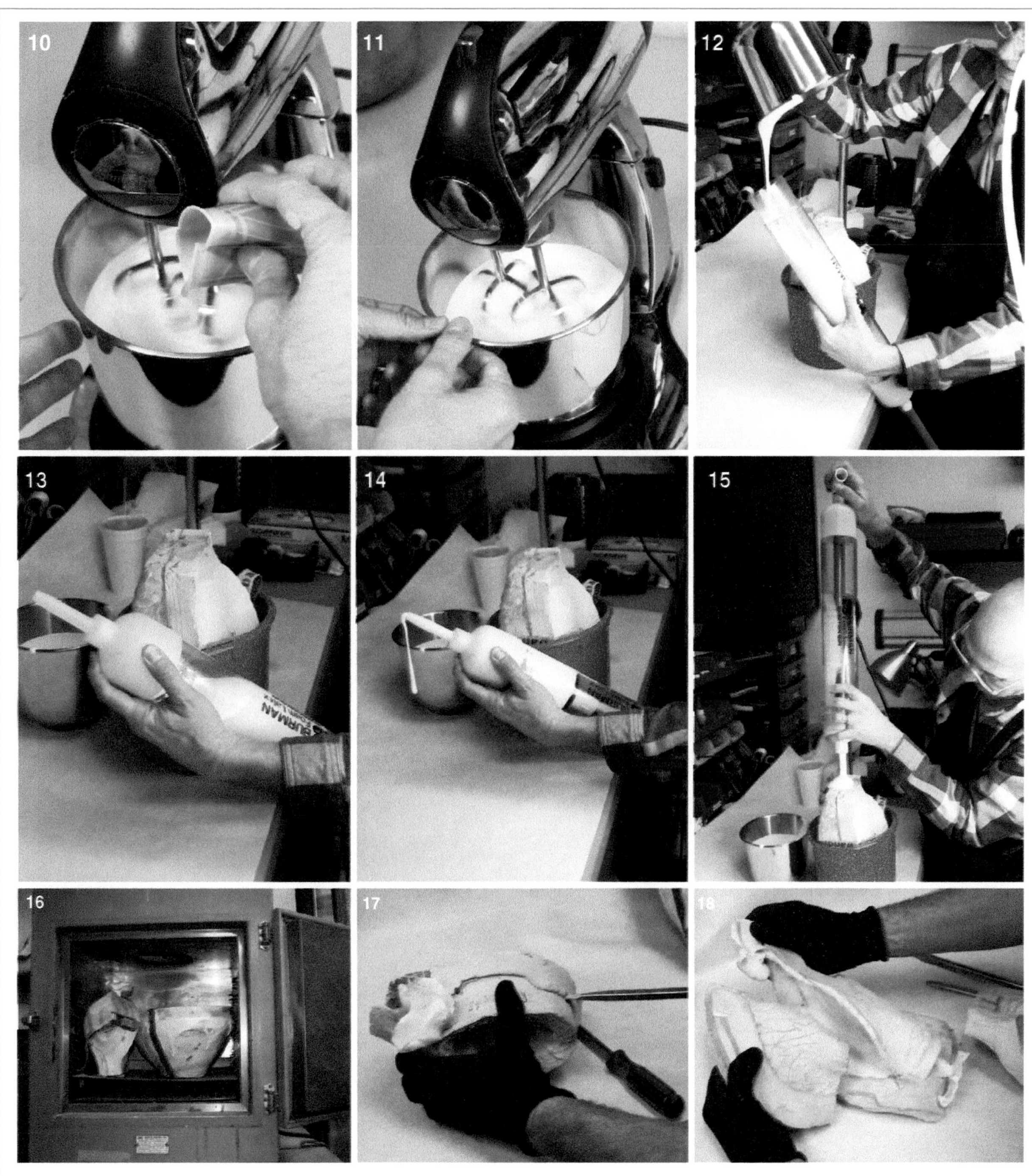

FIGURE 11.20 *(continued)*

BIOGRAPHY OF MAKEUP ARTIST DICK SMITH

By 2001, Dick Smith was a professional makeup artist for 56 years. In 1940 he entered Yale University to pursue a career in dentistry, but after seeing *Dr. Jekyll and Mr. Hyde* with Spencer Tracy, his interest began to change. He found a book on stage makeup and transformed himself into Mr. Hyde, scaring his classmates. From then on, when time permitted, he made himself up as the Frankenstein monster, the phantom, the werewolf, the mummy, Quasimodo, etc.—each time testing his work on hapless Yale men. Makeup became his passion.

After being discharged from the army in 1945, Smith moved to New York and tried to find work in film as a makeup artist. After 6 months of rejections, he was finally hired by NBC-TV in New York. He was the first staff makeup man in the television industry. During his 14 years at NBC, Smith taught himself about all types of makeup, invented quick-change techniques for "live" television and makeup colors for color television, ran a department with as many as 20 artists whom Smith trained, and created countless beauty, character, and appliance makeups. In 1956 Smith moved from New York City to Larchmont, New York, with his wife and two sons, where he spent the next 37 years preparing his creations in the basement of his home. In 1959, after leaving NBC, Smith became director of makeup for David Susskind's television productions for two years. Two dramas, *Moon and Sixpence* and *The Power and the Glory* starring Sir Laurence Olivier, were the most memorable. After Susskind lost his drama series to the new television game shows, he produced his first film, which became Smith's first work with film as well. The film was *Requiem for a Heavyweight* starring Anthony Quinn, who played a battered old prizefighter.

In the 1960s Smith created the makeup for a number of films including *Mark Twain Tonight* for television (which won the Emmy for makeup), *Midnight Cowboy* and *Little Big Man* starring Dustin Hoffman (who was aged to 121 years), and others. With the 1970s came the era of "special makeup effects," which refers to a physical change in the performer's face while the camera is rolling, caused by a special makeup device or technique. Smith started it all using bleeding bullets in *The Godfather* and many macabre effects in *The Exorcist.*

In this new era, Smith and other artists like him no longer worked on a film from beginning to end. After *Godfather II* and *The Sunshine Boys* in 1975, he would only create special makeup or effects and was on the set for their filming. Additional makeup artists would handle all other makeup. The following films required such special work from Smith: *Taxi Driver, Marathon Man, The Sentinel, The Deer Hunter, Altered States, Night Hawks, Ghost Story, The Hunger, Amadeus* (won US and British Academy Awards for makeup), *Starman, Poltergeist III, Everybody's All American*, and *Dad*. Smith was makeup consultant for *Death Becomes Her* in 1991 and *Forever Young* in 1992.

Dick's life work, *The Advanced Professional Makeup Course*, is a 700-page illustrated home study course sold to students and professional makeup artists around the world. Since 1992, he has lectured twice yearly at a school in Tokyo, which has developed a course in special effects based on his written work. For Making and Applying a Foamed Latex Appliance on Dustin Hoffman as the 120-year-old man in the film *Little Big Man* (Makeup created by Dick Smith, S.M.A.), see Figures 11.21–11.41.

(Photographs of Figures 11.21, 11.22, 11.23, 11.24, 11.25, 11.27, 11.28, and 11.29 by Mel Traxel, Cinema Center Films. All others by Dick Smith.)

Application of Foam Latex Pieces

Foamed latex pieces can be attached with Prosaide, Prosaide II, silicone adhesives, prosthetic adhesive, or Premiere Products Telesis adhesives. (*Spirit gum is not recommended because of its tendency to react to salt in perspiration, compromising the adhesive bond.*) Unlike a "shell" latex appliance, foam latex pieces *and the appropriate adhesive* must be attached to the entire surface area of skin covered by the piece. Because most of the pressure-sensitive adhesives have similar working properties, Prosaide will be used for this application method:

Step 1: Clean the face of all makeup, dirt, and skin oils with 99% alcohol on a cotton swab.

Step 2. Hold the foam latex appliance against the face to check for proper placement. Starting at the center of the face and working toward the edges, brush on Prosaide to just outside the edges of the appliance. Let the Prosaide dry slightly, then press the piece into the adhesive (having two people working will expedite the process). The various drying times of the different adhesives will determine how large an area can be covered at one time. For an even stronger bond, paint adhesive to both the face and the inside of the appliance and allow it to dry before application (Prosaide stays quite tacky when it is dry). It is important to attach the appliance symmetrically.

FIGURE 11.21 *Dustin Hoffman as the 120-year-old Little Big Man.*

FIGURE 11.22 *Making a plaster cast of Dustin Hoffman's head and shoulders.*

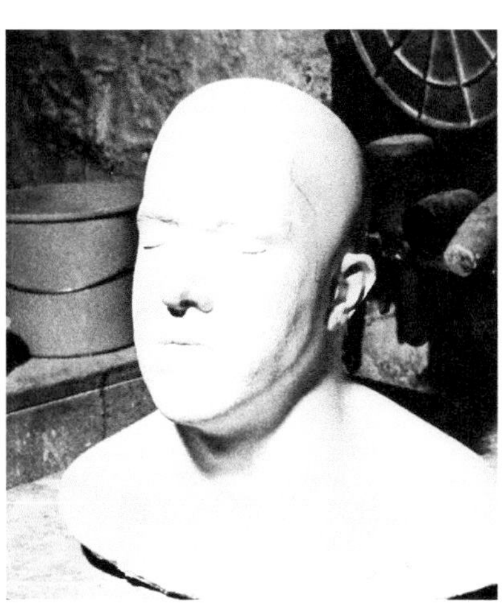

FIGURE 11.23 *Plaster model of Dustin Hoffman's head.*

FIGURE 11.24 *Makeup artist Dick Smith making the clay model for the face and neck.*

FIGURE 11.25 *Rough model of Dustin Hoffman's head will later be broken down into eight parts—brow, nose, upper lip, eyelids, bags, lower lip, chin, and sides of face and neck.*

FIGURE 11.26 *Finishing the outer surface of the mold of the face and neck section. This exterior part of the mold is made of hard plaster.*

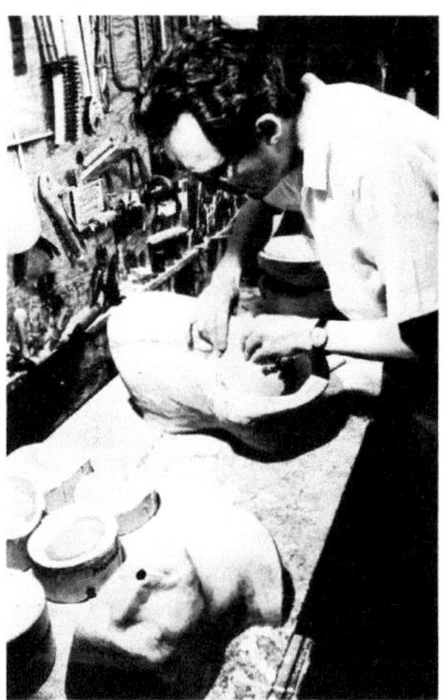

FIGURE 11.27 *Removing foam latex. After the mold has been baked to cure the foam latex and the positive cast of Dustin's face has been lifted out, the foam latex mask section is then carefully removed. (Pouring foam latex into the mold is illustrated in Figure 11.19.)*

FIGURE 11.28 *Making molds of clay models of bags, chin, and nose.*

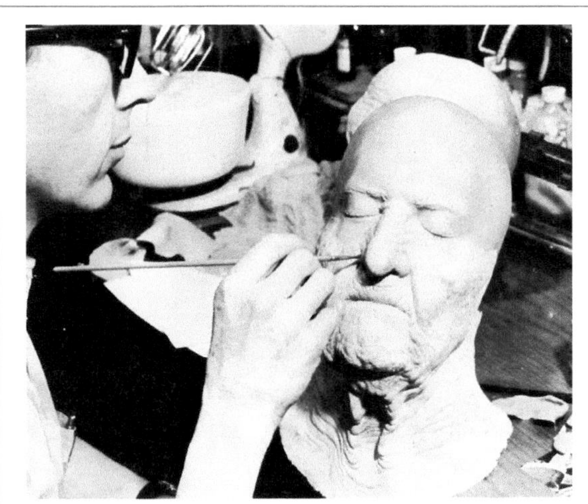

FIGURE 11.29 *Painting "liver spots" on the foam latex mask.*

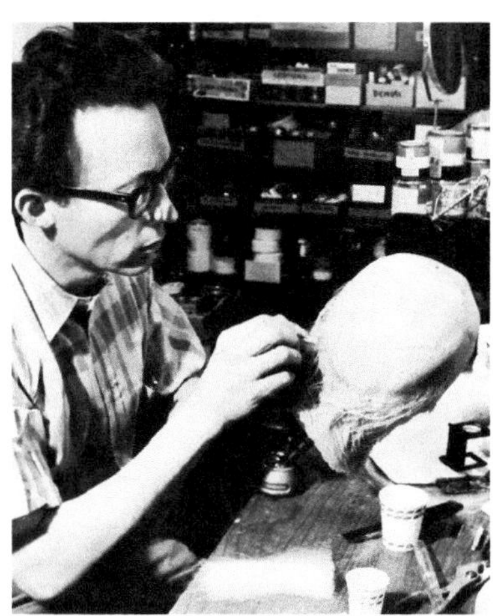

FIGURE 11.30 *White hair being "punched" hair by hair into the back section of the mask.*

FIGURE 11.31 *Finished mask sections.*

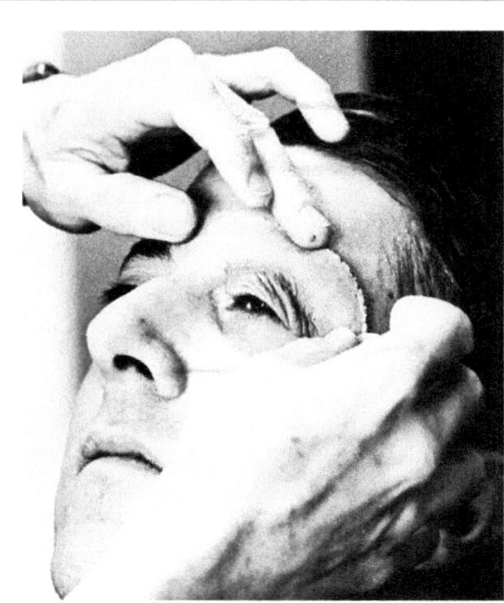

FIGURE 11.32 *Attaching foam latex eyelids and brow to Dustin Hoffman. Piece is made thin enough and with folds sculpted into it so that it blinks naturally.*

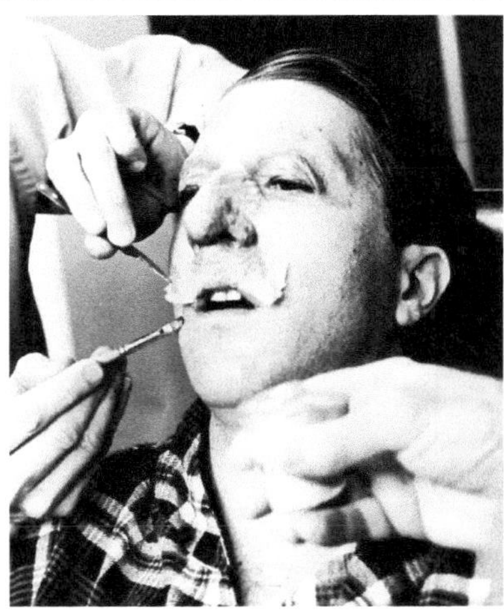

FIGURE 11.33 *Nose and lip piece. Dick Smith used Slomon's Medico Adhesive to attach the prosthetic pieces. Artists now use Prosaide and Telesis adhesives.*

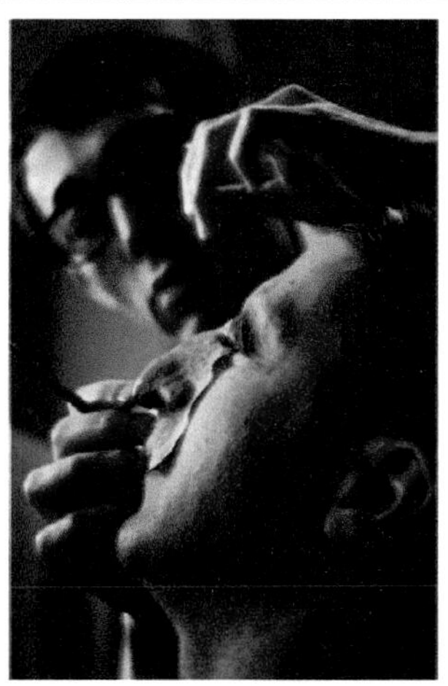

FIGURE 11.36 *Attaching the nose and lip piece.*

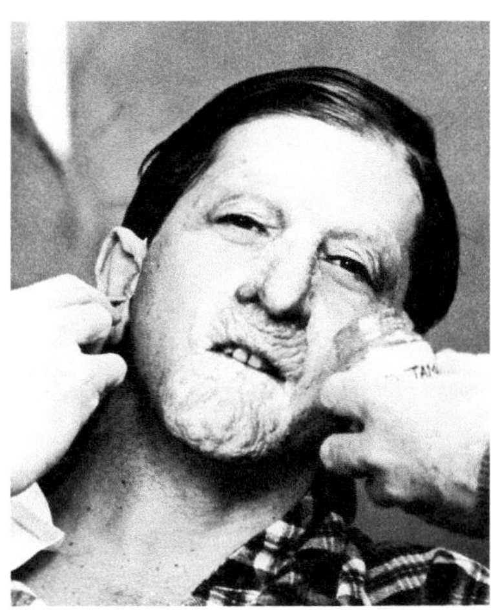

FIGURE 11.34 *Attaching the ears. Made of slush-mold latex. All others made of foam latex.*

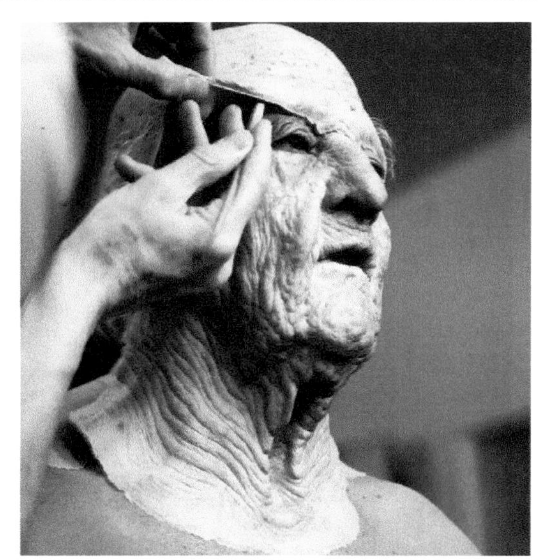

FIGURE 11.37 *Applying adhesive to the interior of the forehead section.*

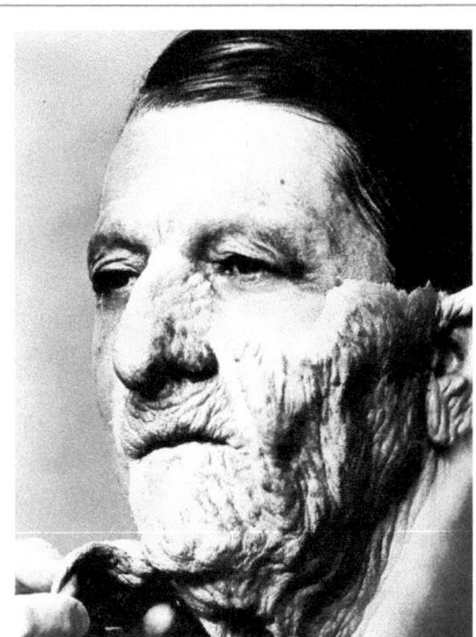

FIGURE 11.35 *Attaching large foam latex pieces for cheeks and neck.*

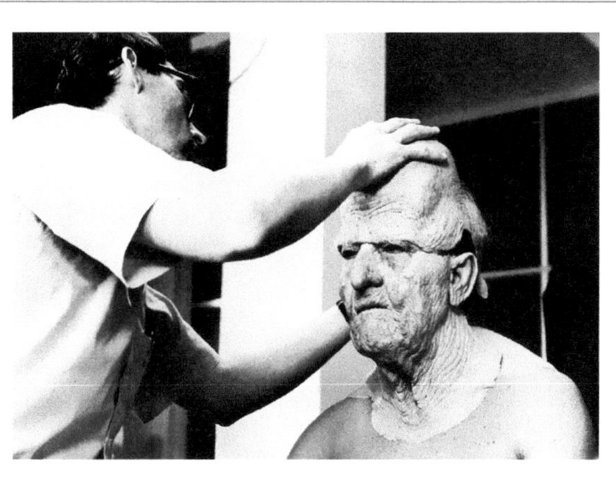

FIGURE 11.38 *Head piece being put on. This piece was constructed of two overlapping sections of foam latex.*

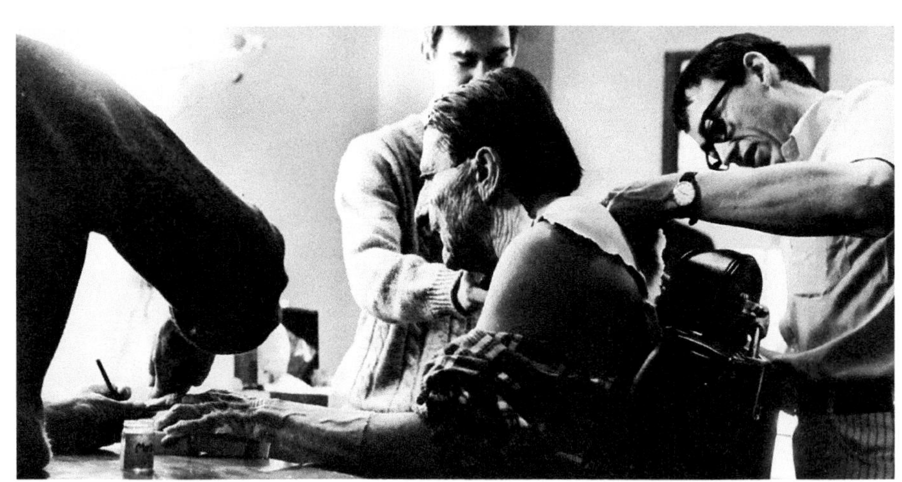

FIGURE 11.39 *Applying shoulder hump and hands.*

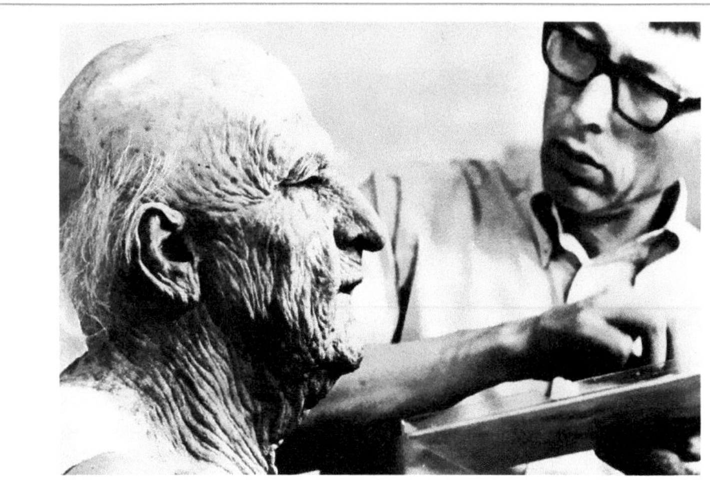

FIGURE 11.40 *Final tough-up of foam latex makeup.*

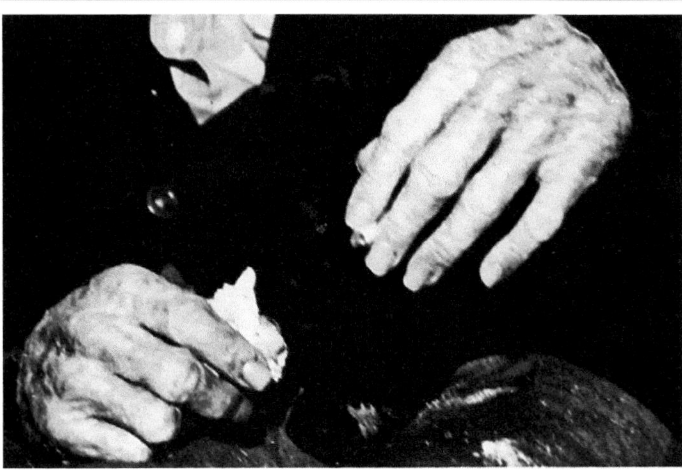

FIGURE 11.41 *Hands with latex gloves and fingernails.*

Step 3. To more easily apply adhesive behind your appliance, bend the ferrule of your brush at about ¾ inch above the bristles to an angle of approximately 45 degrees (see Figure 6.5.7). Use a powder puff to complete the adhesion by pressing it against the appliance, otherwise your fingers will stick to the glue.

Step 4. Once the appliances are glued, seal the edges by stippling them with Prosaide using a piece torn from a red stipple sponge or latex blending sponge. Allow it to dry, then powder with a translucent setting powder.

Painting Foam Latex

Two products commonly used for coloration on foam latex are RMGP (a castor oil-based appliance makeup) and PAX Paint (a mixture of Prosaide and Liquitex artist acrylic paint). These two products can be used separately or in combination (see Figure 10.12 Applying a Bald Cap). Because they have glycerin and/or other lighter oils that absorb easily into the foam, regular cream foundations are not recommended. They have a tendency to be absorbed by the foam latex, turning them dark with an unnatural gray, lifeless cast. Some silicone-based cosmetics can be used but test these first.

Rubber Mask Greasepaint

Rubber mask grease can be applied to the pieces with a sponge or with brushes. The degree of coverage that can be achieved ranges from highly opaque to extremely transparent. It can be used straight from the container or thinned with castor oil or the cosmetic fluid GP-20 (diluted with water) for transparent glazes. This glazing technique provides the makeup artist with the ability to create layers of natural-looking skin coloration for intimate theater settings and for television and film (see Figure 10.3).

After the foundation colors are applied you may then want to adjust the color generally or locally (as with rouge, for example) by stippling on additional color with a coarse stipple sponge (make a custom-shaped stipple sponge from a 1-inch by 2-inch block of polyurethane foam). Along one long side draw eight to ten irregular shapes in a variety of sizes and cut or tear away the background or negative space, leaving the shapes on the surface (see Figure 10.7.8).

This helps to add texture and skin discoloration while relieving the flatness of the rubber mask grease foundation. To finish, press powder into the makeup to set it and remove the shine. If variations in surface sheen are required this can be accomplished by adding more or less powder in certain areas. Glazes can now be added to the powdered makeup for further texturing.

PAX Paint

PAX, developed by the Academy Award-winning makeup artist, Dick Smith, is made by mixing 1-part Prosaide to 1-part Liquitex acrylic artist paint. This creates an opaque flexible paint that moves equally well on the skin as it does on appliances, better in many ways than RMGP. Mixed with non-toxic Liquitex paint in earth-tone colors (burnt sienna, raw umber, burnt umber, raw sienna, red oxide, yellow ochre, titanium white, and black), PAX Paint is relatively safe to use on healthy skin.

It is extremely durable, an excellent cover for appliance edges, it photographs well, and does not rub off on costumes! As with RMGP, apply and blend PAX with a patting motion using a firm polyurethane foam applicator. Any makeup or adhesive can be used on top of PAX.

What makes this product appealing is also its biggest disadvantage. The strength of its adhesive properties causes some difficulty in removing it from the skin. It is, therefore, not recommended for application near the eye area. Gentle, yet strong, prosthetic adhesive removers specifically formulated to remove PAX are available and work quite well (see *Adhesives* and *Solvents*, Appendix A).

(Note: It is the responsibility of the artist to collect all scientific data relating to any product with which the artist or the subject might come into contact with and to use good judgment in determining how or whether to use the product.)

PAX can be modified in a variety of ways. The following are some suggestions for using PAX:

- Mix Prosaide with Liquitex Matte Medium to form PAX Medium, a colorless material that when added to PAX can produce a paint with varying levels of transparency. Adding various levels of transparent coloration to the appliance will help you create a more realistic-looking skin. It will also assist you in blending the paint off into the skin around the eyes, the edges of the face, and off the edges of the appliance should you choose to use makeup on the skin.
- Add water (or PAX Extender, see *PAX*, Appendix A) to PAX Paint to produce a thinner, even, more transparent product. It can be thinned as much as 24 parts of water

to 1-part PAX and used as a wash to tint areas of the face (i.e. sunburns). Thinned PAX Medium can be used as a sealer over makeup on pre-painted bald caps to protect them during the application process.

- Add more Prosaide to your original recipe to create a stronger adhesive bond. Adding less will make a paint that is easier to remove.
- Any product, except acetone, can be applied over PAX.
- Since PAX products dry with a slight shine and the surface remains a bit sticky, it is important to powder with a slightly translucent setting powder (choose a slightly warm tone).
- Avoid applying layers of thick PAX over soft foam. This will cause unnatural folds and wrinkles and the surface will appear thick-skinned and heavily made up.

ADVANCED MOLD MAKING

Occasionally it will be necessary to make molds for aging or changing the features of an actor's face. In this case a mold must be made without any undercuts to make what is called a *wraparound prosthetic appliance*. The following materials are needed for mold making and sculpting:

Alginate (40 oz.)	Water (60 oz.)	Water for plaster bandages
Plaster bandages	Ultracal 30	Krylon Crystal Clear Acrylic Spray
Metal or kitchen spatulas	Wood rasp	Disposable rubber gloves
Chavant NSP Medium clay	Brushes	Clay sculpting tools
99% alcohol	Drill	Router key bit
¼-inch and Q-inch drill bits	Burlap (pre-cut into 4-inch squares)	
Water (Wed) clay		

1. Starting with a full-face cast mounted on a formica board or on the top of a counter (Figure 11.42a), sculpt out all the undercuts around the jawline and neck area with water clay (see Appendix A). An undercut (Figure 11.42b) is an area of hard plaster that curves under the cast and therefore would make a negative mold impossible to remove from a positive mold without breaking a delicate edge. With water-based clay, sculpt all of the undercuts out of the face cast (Figure 11.42e, far left image). Undercuts may appear in the back of the jawline, around the neck area, between the cheekbones and the ear area, and around the nostrils.
2. The next step is to take an impression of this form with alginate and reproduce it in a harder plaster, Ultracal 30 (UC). In order to mold the flared-out face cast you will need to spray the whole form with two or three light coats of an acrylic spray such as Krylon Crystal Clear Acrylic Spray (see Appendix A) and paint the plaster with a light coat of petroleum jelly to keep the alginate from sticking to it.
3. Mix 40 oz. of alginate into 60 oz. of water and coat the cast with an even coat (¼- to ⅓-inch thickness) (Figure 11.42c).
4. After the alginate has set, gently remove it from the face cast and place it back. This will ensure that the alginate and plaster bandage mother mold will come off in one piece.
5. Cover the set alginate in plaster bandage as you would with a face cast (refer back to face casting in Figure 11.5) to create a mother mold, supporting the shape of the alginate (Figure 11.42d).
6. Once the plaster bandage has set, carefully remove the alginate/plaster bandage mold together (Figure 11.42e).
7. Measure 1 cup tepid water into a plastic mixing bowl and sift in 2 cups UC. Let set for 1 minute. Mix thoroughly by hand, using rubber gloves. Tap the bottom of the bowl with your hand to release any excess bubbles that may have accumulated in the UC. Paint the UC mix into the alginate negative with a 1-inch disposable brush and follow by building up the thickness as the material starts to thicken (Figure 11.42f). This layer should be at least ¼ inch thick. Let set, usually about 5–10 minutes.
8. Mix 2 cups tepid water with 4 cups UC and let set for 1 minute. Mix and paint one light coat onto the set UC. Dip two layers of burlap squares into the UC mix and gently press into the negative alginate mold. Continue this procedure, overlapping burlap squares, until the whole mold is covered. Roll two layers of burlap saturated with UC and reinforce the edges of the mold (Figure 11.42g). Place a metal pipe into the back of the mold and reinforce with burlap. An additional small batch of UC may be mixed and painted onto the surface as a finishing coat.
9. After the mold has set for at least 3 hours it can be pulled and cleaned (Figure 11.42h). Let this mold set overnight. The mold is now ready to sculpt on.

SCULPTING

To sculpt an old age or character face, begin by building up high and low areas, cheekbones, nasolabial folds, jowls, and neck waddles (Figure 11.43a) in Chavant NSP medium-density clay (see Appendix A). The thickest area of your sculpture could be up to 1 inch, the thinnest area should be no thinner than 1/32 inch. It is important to look at the sculpture in different lighting situations (i.e. full frontal, side lighting, etc.) to estimate the curves of folds and wrinkles. It is very important that the edges of the sculpture be blended out, creating a smooth transition between clay and plaster. Edges can be cleaned with a brush or cotton-tipped applicator and acetone. A brush and 99% alcohol may be used to smooth out any rough areas of clay.

Various sculpting tools may be utilized to achieve different wrinkles and folds (Figure 11.43b). Textures may be added with rubber stipple sponges, sculpting tools, or from rubber latex skin-texture pads (Figure 11.43c) described in the Clay Models section of this chapter. Slight over-texturing of pores into the clay will assist the plaster or stone in duplicating details in the negative.

MAKING THE NEGATIVE MOLD

After you are satisfied with your sculpture you will need to make a negative mold of it to capture all the details of the clay (Figure 11.44):

1. Drill indented keys into the mold with a rounded router bit and drill. These indented keys will stabilize the negative mold, make the positive a tighter fit, and keep it from shifting around when placed in the negative mold (Figure 11.44a). Surface keys, where stone meets stone, can also be utilized to stabilize the positive into the negative mold. It may be necessary to shave off any undercut areas around the nose and eyes in order for the negative to be removed without chipping.

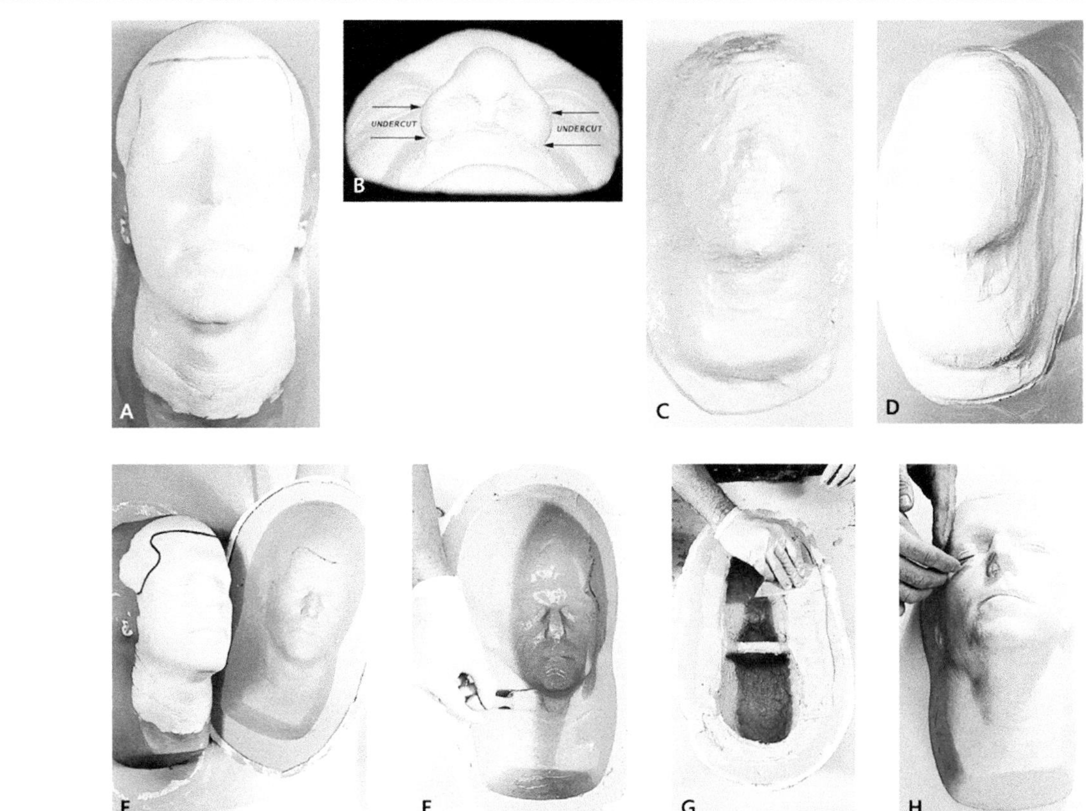

FIGURE 11.42 *Making a new cast without undercuts (called a flared positive). A. Water clay used to eliminate undercuts from original cast. B. Close-up illustrating undercuts on nose area. C. Alginate applied to cast. D. Plaster bandage applied over alginate. E. Alginate negative removed from plaster positive. F. Brushing in first coat of Ultracal 30 into alginate negative. G. Attached handle and reinforcing with burlap to the edge. H. Cleaning flared positive.*

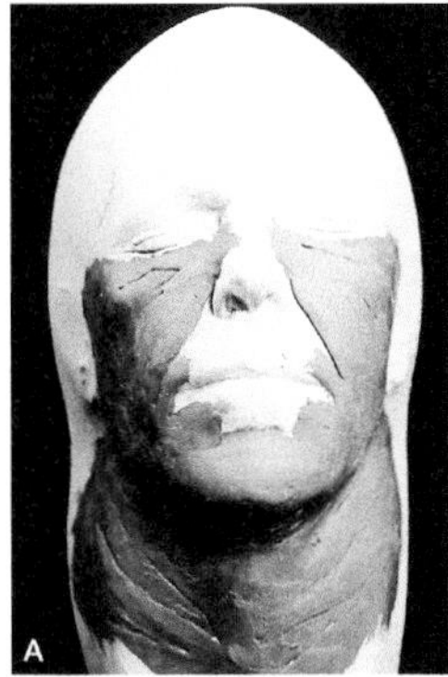

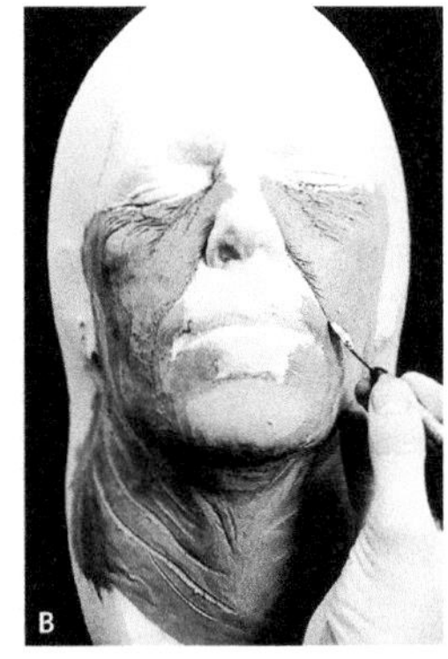

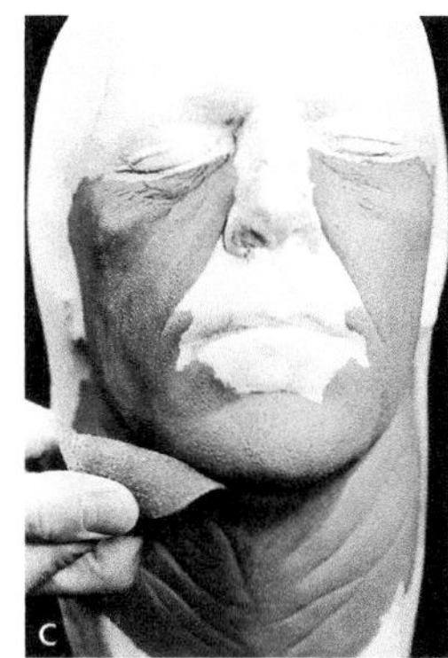

FIGURE 11.43 *Sculpting the wraparound appliance. A. " Blocking out" the appliance in clay. B. Sculpting wrinkles and folds. C. Texturing with texture pads.*

2. Using Chavant NSP medium clay, roll 12-inch-long, ¼-inch-wide snakes. These will be used to make the casing around the sculpture (Figure 11.44b). Clay should also encircle the indented or surface keys. Water clay can be used for larger areas. Stay at least ⅛ inch away from the edge of the sculpture with the clay casing.

3. Once the casing is completed, clean the stone area between the clay sculpture and the clay casing area with acetone on a cotton-tipped applicator. This will ensure that your edges of the final prosthetic appliance will be as thin as tissue. Then spray the sculpture with three light coats of Krylon Crystal Clear Spray. A light coat of petroleum jelly should be painted into all indented and surface keys only after they have been cleaned off with acetone. (Note: Acetone can be used to clean Ultracal 30 (UC) or plaster molds. Lacquer thinner can be used to clean epoxy, resin and urethane molds.)

4. Mix 1½ cups water to 3 cups UC. Tap the bottom of the bowl to release any bubbles from the mixture. Gently paint the surface of the sculpture with the UC and a disposable brush (Figure 11.44c), being careful not to trap any air pockets between the clay and the UC mix. You may want to blow a little air on the surface to relieve any bubbles. Continue patting the UC mixture on until it starts to thicken. This coat should be approximately ¼ to ⅓ inch thick.

5. After this first splash coat has set, mix 2 cups water with 4 cups UC and paint a thin layer onto the previous coat. Dip two layers of 4-inch burlap squares into the UC mix and gently apply this to the mold. Continue this process until the whole mold has been covered. Make small rolls of burlap dipped into UC and apply these to the outer edges of the mold for reinforcement (Figure 11.44d). With two rolls of burlap dipped into UC, make a bird's nest on top of the mold. Fill it with UC to create a flat surface. This will act as a pedestal when the mold is turned over.

6. Let this mold set overnight, then clean off the sharp edges with a wood rasp.

7. Open the mold by pulling or using a furniture clamp or C clamp and three blocks of wood (Figure 11.44e).

8. Remove all clay from both molds. Clean the clay residue off with 99% alcohol or acetone. *Be sure to use a respirator when using chemical solvents.*

(Tip: Use only wooden tools on the surface of the sculpted area to avoid damaging the stone.)

9. Use a ¼-inch drill bit, drill vent holes through the positive mold into areas where the casings were placed next to the sculpture. This will allow for the excess gelatin to run out of the mold, creating a thinner edge on the prosthetic appliance (Figure 11.44f).

10. This same process is used to make a nose appliance mold (Figure 11.44g).

MAKING A GELATIN WRAPAROUND APPLIANCE

Mixing Gelatin (see Figure 11.10 for mixing gelatin)

Supplies needed:

Sorbitol

Glycerin

Distilled water

Gelatin (300 Bloom)

Zinc oxide

Joe Blasco Ruddy Light Skin Powder or any colored powder

Red flocking

Large tongue depressor or stirring utensil

Small strainer

Large microwavable bowl

Cups

Measuring spoons

Measuring cup.

(Remember, this mixture will be extremely hot. Do not let it touch the skin.)

Making the Gelatin Appliances (Figure 11.45)

Once the positive and negative molds are made, either a foam latex appliance or a gelatin appliance may be produced.

The advantage of a gelatin appliance:

- it requires a lighter makeup application, provided the gelatin color is a close match to the actor's skin color
- it moves more like real skin
- the materials are less expensive and
- the appliance is less time-consuming to produce.

The only disadvantage:

- gelatin can melt on the face if the actor tends to perspire freely. There are steps, however, that can be taken to prevent this from happening (see step 3 under Applying the Gelatin Appliance):

1. To pour and remove a gelatin appliance from a stone mold, you will have to coat the mold with a releasing agent. Spray vegetable oil, which is available in grocery stores, is the most economical choice. However, a more effective releasing agent is Epoxy Parfilm (see Appendix A) or the combination of the two. Spray the positive and negative molds with a heavy coating of the release agent and let it set for at least 30 minutes. The release agent will soak into the plaster and pickle the mold (Figure 11.45a). After 30 minutes, spray a lighter coat onto both molds making them ready to accept the hot gelatin mixture.
2. Heat the pre-mixed gelatin formula and carefully pour it into the negative mold (Figure 11.45b). Pick up the mold and roll the gelatin around onto all the sculpted areas.
3. Quickly press the positive into the negative (Figure 11.45c) and place barbell weights or any heavy object onto the positive mold only (Figure 11.45d). Let set for at least 45 minutes. Time will vary depending on the thickness of your mold.
4. Remove the weights and open the mold. Carefully pull the gelatin away from the molds and powder both sides with baby powder (Figure 11.45e). To keep the gelatin appliances from wrinkling or the edges from being folded under, place the appliances on a vacuform face cast or on a face cast covered with plastic. The appliances must be kept in a sealed plastic bag away from heat and humidity until ready for use (Figure 11.45f).

Applying the Gelatin Appliance

1. Clean the skin with a tissue dampened with 99% alcohol. Be careful not to get alcohol near the eyes (Figure 11.47a—model before makeup application). Clean the front and back of the gelatin appliances with a tissue dampened with acetone.
2. Apply a pre-made rubber bald cap or bald pate with Beta Bond adhesive (see Applying a Bald Cap in Chapter 10). Then add "stretch and stipple" old age (old age stipple) on the forehead and around the eyes.
3. Start the application of the wrap around the gelatin appliance:
    - Applying adhesive to the skin and back of the appliance. Prosaide and Beta Bond are two types of adhesives that work well with gelatin appliances (see Appendix A). The adhesives are contact glues (pressure sensitive) and work best when both sides are allowed to dry, then are pressed together. If re-gluing or re-setting the piece is necessary, 99% alcohol may be used as a solvent to lift the appliance off the face. No extra glue will be necessary to tack that area back down.

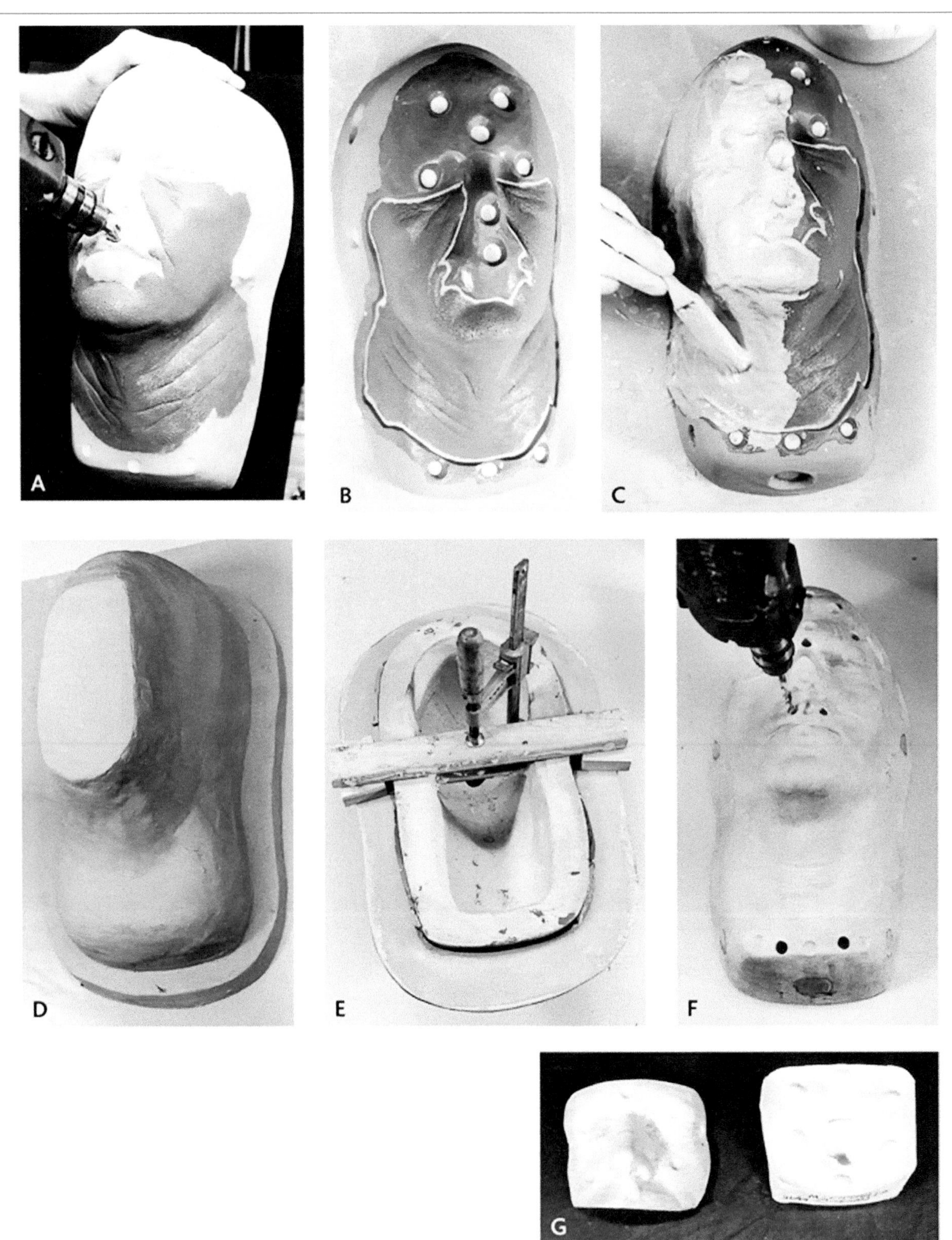

FIGURE 11.44 *Developing a negative mold for the prosthetic appliance. A. Drill keys into the positive. B. Add a clay casing around the entire sculpt and cast (both light and dark gray indicate the casing). C. Brushing on the first coat of Ultracal 30 over the entire sculpt. D. Burlap reinforcement is applied over entire sculpt. Use burlap to build the bird's nest on top and to reinforce edges. E. Opening mold with furniture clamp and wood. F. Vent holes being drilled. G. Positive cast of original nose with negative cast of new nose.*

Source: Photos courtesy of Matthew Mungle.

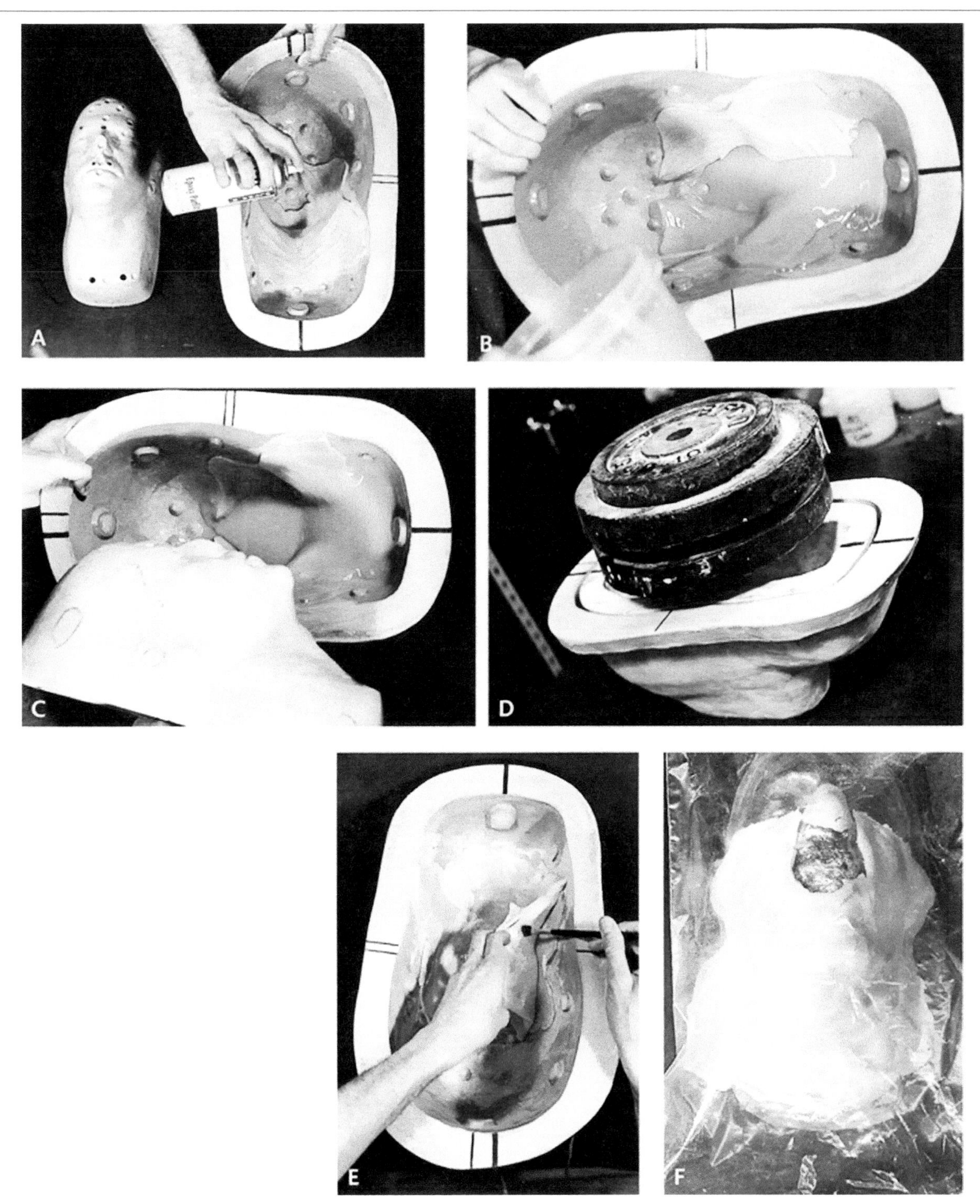

FIGURE 11.45 *Making the gelatin appliance. A. Negative mold being sprayed with mold release. B. Gelatin mixture being poured into mold. C. Positive mold being pressed into negative mold. D. Weights applied to positive. E. Powering the gelatin appliance as it is being removed. F. Store the gelatin appliance in a plastic bag on the form.*

FIGURE 11.46 *Materials used for applying the gelatin appliance. Brushes; sponges (white foam and stipple sponges); tissues; brush and adhesive holders; adhesives (Beta Bond, Prosaide and Spirit Gum, see Appendix A under Adhesives); adhesive removers; 99% alcohol; acetone; Old Age Stipple (see Appendix A); witch hazel astringent (available at drug stores); cotton-tipped applicators; plastic sealer (W. M. Creations Sealer A); Stacolor (see Appendix A); Rubber Mask Greasepaint kit; scissors.*

- Begin at the chin and work up to the cheeks and eyes of both sides of the face (Figure 11.47b). Finish the application by gluing the neck down. Gluing is best achieved in small sections to ensure the whole appliance has been glued down. Press any bubbles out between the appliance and the skin.
- *If the actor perspires freely*, it is advisable to coat his or her skin with five coats of plastic sealer such as Sealer A from W.M. Creations, Inc. (see Appendix A) to prevent the perspiration from attacking the gelatin and melting it. The back of the appliance may also be coated with plastic sealer.

4. Make sure all the appliance edges are glued with adhesive.
5. With a cotton-tipped applicator and witch hazel, blend or "melt" the edges of the appliance into the surrounding skin (Figure 11.47c).
6. Apply any additional pieces. For this makeup example, a nose tip and ear lobes were also applied (Figure 11.47d).
7. After application and blending of all appliances are complete, apply a light coat of Prosaide or Beta Bond adhesive to all the edges with a cotton-tipped applicator. Let the adhesive dry.
8. To protect the gelatin appliance:

   Stipple a light application of Sealer A with a small torn white foam sponge or red stipple sponge over the edges only. The whole appliance may be coated with sealer.
9. Add life to the gelatin:

   Apply a light, translucent application of Stacolor Pink-6205 (see Appendix A–*Alcohol-based makeup*), thinned with a very small amount of 99% alcohol with a torn red or orange stipple sponge (Figure 11.47e). Because the skin

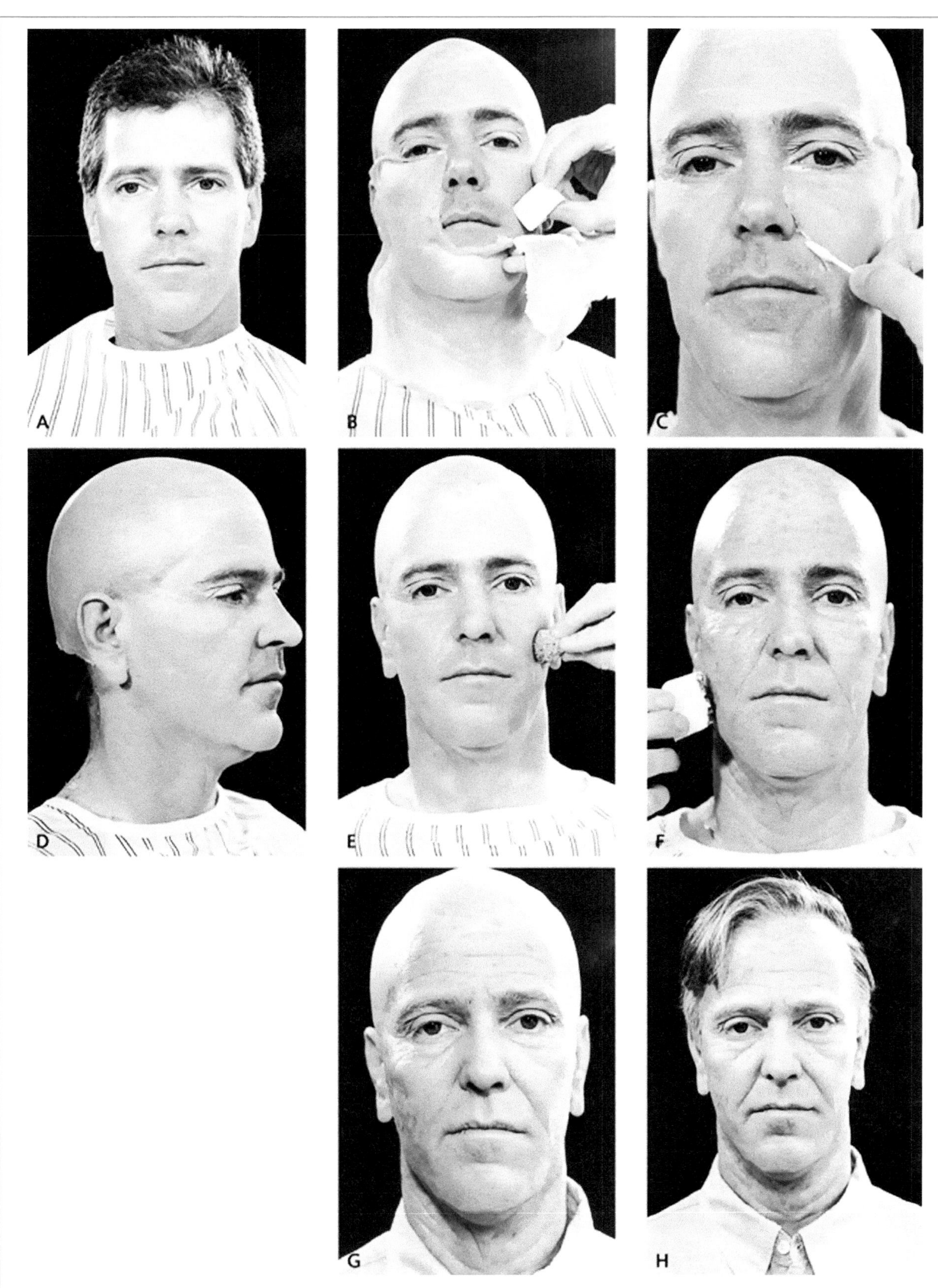

FIGURE 11.47 *Applying gelatin appliances. Makeup by Matthew Mungle. Wig made, styled, and applied by Stuart Artingstall. Model, Michael Cristillo.*

contains enough red pigmentation, Stacolor is applied only to the gelatin. Stacolor is used for this step because it does not rub off when you begin to apply the skin tone foundations. When skin-toned Stacolors are used instead of makeup, the appliance becomes smudge-proof, waterproof, and grease (oil) free. (REEL Creations Palettes, Skin Illustrator Palettes, and TEMPTU tattoo colors may be substituted in this step).

10. To create skin depth and aging effects:

    - Apply RMGPs with a torn white foam sponge. It will be necessary to apply at least three to four different shades of makeup bases to accomplish the look of skin discoloration and old age spots.

    - Thin the makeup bases with either castor oil, GP-20% or 70% alcohol to create a translucent color application, thus achieving a more realistic skin tone effect. *Heavier application of makeup on gelatin appliances is not necessary* (Figures 11.47f).

11. Finish the makeup with additional shading and wrinkle lines. Extra reds may be added to give more life to the prosthetic appliances (Figure 11.47f).

12. Aging eyebrows and eyelashes with hair white or a light makeup base (Figure 11.47g).

13. Apply a properly cut and styled lace-front wig and glue it down with spirit gum to finish the prosthetic makeup (Figure 11.47h).

14. Remove the gelatin appliance:

    - First using the proper remover suggested for Beta Bond (Beta Solv) or Prosaide (Prosaide Remover). Prosaide may also be removed with 70% alcohol and a flat brush. Carefully apply the solvent with a medium-soft brush to the edges of the appliance and slowly work the solvent under the appliance until it is freed from the skin.

    - Once the appliance is removed, the remaining residue can be removed by soaking a small powder puff in Isopropyl Myristate and gently rubbing the area until it disappears. The Isopropyl Myristate leaves an oily film and is milder for the skin than products such as Detachol, which tends to leave the skin red and dry.

    - Latex "stretch and stipples" are best removed by first coating the area with liquid hand soap.

    - Allow the soap to set for a few minutes, then apply a warm wet towel to the area. This process can be repeated until all of the makeup is removed.

    - Adhesive residue may be removed in the same manner with adhesive removers.

15. Taking care of the skin:

    The skin can then be cleaned with a mild medicated cleanser (Noxema, for example), and treated with a 100% pure aloe vera gel and Vitamin E cream.

Matthew Mungle

Academy Award-winner Matthew Mungle was born in Durant, Oklahoma, in 1956. Matthew was one of four children born to Atoka dairy farmers Jene and Becky Mungle. As a boy, Matthew recalls seeing *Frankenstein*, *Dracula*, and *Creature from the Black Lagoon*. In 1964, with the release of *The Seven Faces of Dr. Lao*, Matthew credits the film as being his greatest influence and the deciding factor in becoming a makeup effects artist. After reading the Fourth edition of Corson's *Stage Makeup* book, he began experimenting with face casts and prosthetics on willing family members.

After attending Oklahoma State University as a theater arts major for 2½ years, Matthew followed his dream to Hollywood to begin learning his craft. He arrived in the fall of 1977 and applied and was accepted into Joe Blasco's Makeup Center. Matthew credits Joe Blasco with his professional start in the industry and today is a voice to a new generation of up-and-coming makeup artists hoping to find a working niche in the industry.

"If you want to be a working makeup artist, it's important to learn and perfect all areas of the craft." (Matthew Mungle)

Matthew's professional career began on low-budget projects, which would teach him to think fast on his feet. It would not be long until he achieved his first major success with *Edward Scissorhands* in 1990. With over 100 film and television projects to his credit, Matthew has worked on a number of box office successes—Bram Stoker's *Dracula*, earning him his first Oscar in 1992; *Schindler's List*, earning him another Oscar nomination in 1993; Oliver Stone's *Natural Born Killers*; *Outbreak*, *Primal Fear*, and aging James Woods to 72 in *Ghosts of Mississippi*, earning him his third nomination in 1996.

"Aging" and character makeup have been one of Matthew's strongest calling cards and one which has proven to be exceptionally challenging. His fascination with making someone young look old prompted him to research more viable methods such as gelatin (which was originally used in the 1930s but later abandoned when the hot lights would cause it to melt). With today's less intensive lighting and faster film speed, Matthew has given new life to this nearly translucent substance, which when applied correctly looks and moves like real skin. Today's silicones used for prosthetic appliances have replaced gelatin as a more user-friendly material.

Matthew's additional film credits include work with Mike Meyers in, *Austin Powers* (1996), working with Meryl Streep on *One True Thing* (1998) and *August: Osage County* (2012), Aging Sissy Spacek and Christopher Walken in *Blast from the Past* (1999), and with Jack Nicholson in *The Bucket List* (2007). Matthew had the great fortune to work with Glenn Close and Janet McTeer on *Albert Nobbs* in 2011, making both look like men with subtle prosthetic changes and dental apparatuses. *Albert Nobbs* earned Matthew his fourth Oscar nomination in 2012. Matthew also extended his talents into the realm of television, which would garnish him with 26 Emmy nominations and six wins for *Citizen Cohn*, *X-Files*, *Six Feet Under*, and *John Adams*, to name a few.

Although his work schedule dictated much of his time, Matthew and his business partner and husband, John E. Jackson, decided, in 2017, to move their studio from North Hollywood, California to Austin, Texas where they now live and work. Matthew continues to work on smaller and more challenging projects while also lecturing and teaching. He still creates all the prosthetics and masks for the Broadway musical *Wicked*, which he started in 2003.

SILICONE

The translucent appearance of the human skin has been a challenge for makeup artists for many years. With the introduction of silicones, it is now possible to create the color of skin in a more lifelike appearance without the use of lights and makeup. Designing a prosthetic piece in silicone can be a very simple procedure. A basic understanding of the material, however, is foremost in completing any silicone project.

There are four different grades of silicone elastomers defined by their usage:

- industrial grade
- food grade
- medical grade
- implant grade.

Industrial grade includes the varieties of 1-part RTV (room-temperature vulcanizing) silicones found at local building supply or hardware stores. Squeezed from a tube or sprayed from a can, these silicones are used as caulking compounds and aerosol lubricants and coatings.

Tested for their ability to remain in contact with the skin surface or pierced through the skin's surface, products made from *medical-grade* silicones range from prosthetic reconstructions to catheter implants and blood-carrying systems to silicone-coated syringe needles. Silicone products tested for their ability to safely remain inside the body are considered *implant-grade* silicones. Other products, such as baby bottle nipples, candy molds, watch bands, and three-dimensional prosthetic devices used to enhance age and character makeups, are made with *food-grade* silicone. It is this latter group that is of interest for this discussion.

Two basic types of RTV silicone elastomer systems fall under the heading of food-grade silicone: tin condensation cure and platinum addition cure silicones. They are differentiated from one another by the type of chemical reactions used for their curing process. Tin cure systems employ a silanol polymer and use tin as a catalyst, while the platinum system utilizes vinyl polymers and platinum catalysts. Both polymers react with their curing reagent and are accelerated by the catalyst producing a silicone elastomer. The chemical reaction inherent within the tin system produces ethyl alcohol as a by-product that quickly evaporates. Inevitably, this small loss of material results in some slight shrinkage as curing occurs and the alcohol evaporates. This is why tin silicones exhibit more shrinkage than platinum cure systems. This chemical reaction in which the molecules combine with the evolution of a by-product is usually called a condensation process, hence the name for the product line. All of the platinum silicones rely on the additional reaction between the vinyl polymers and hydride curing reagent to create a silicone elastomer. This entire process is aided and accelerated by the platinum catalyst. Heat may also be utilized to greatly accelerate the platinum curing process without compromising the physical properties of the material. One advantage to this reaction is that there is no by-product formed in this chemical reaction, making it virtually odorless. The final result is a translucent, flexible, skin-like product that, when filled with the appropriate pigments and then applied to the body, becomes indistinguishable from the actor's own skin.

Tin condensation cure silicones generally cure at lower temperatures than platinum; therefore, they cannot be accelerated by the addition of heat! The benefit to a tin system is it will cure practically anywhere, against virtually any mold surface, using any mold release. It is by far the simplest silicone elastomer to use. Tin silicones will actually cure in a mold that has been contaminated by latex, if a little care is taken to clean the mold. One negative side to tin silicones is they are generally not recommended for extended contact with skin tissue. This problem is easily solved, though, by the addition of a layer of medical-grade brushable silicone to the inside of the prosthetic (between the appliance and the skin).

Platinum silicones in general exhibit superior physical properties such as tear strength and elasticity. This is the reason they are generally the material of choice for any prosthetic appliance that is to come into contact with skin. The negative side to platinum silicones is that they are very susceptible to contamination. They will not cure with any exposure to various sulfur-based products, such as foam latex, latex gloves, and Roma Plastilina. If you choose a platinum silicone, you must create a new sculpt using the proper sculpting medium (sulfur-free Chavant or Monster Clay), fabricate a new mold using all of the proper casting compounds (choose a resin or epoxy product over stone), pigments, mold releases (Mann's Ease Release 200), and mixing equipment (stainless steel, clear polypropylene—avoid glass and polystyrene containers). Many professional FX artists use polypropylene deli cups purchased from restaurant supply companies.

Making a Silicone Nose (Figure 11.48)

1. Sculpting the nose—Materials: Smooth-Cast 385 Face Cast, 99% alcohol, Chavant NSP Brown Medium Clay (always use Non-Sulfur Clay when working with Platinum Silicone products), Sculptex Non-Sulfur Clay, baby powder, texture stamps, sculpting tools and brushes (Figure 11.48).
2. Clay can be heated by placing a 75-watt bulb above the clay.
3. Start the nose sculpting by adding small amounts of softened clay onto the face cast nose.
4. Begin to build the false nose by adding more clay.
5. Blocked out nose.
6. It is very important to look at the nose from all angles and in different lighting conditions.
7. Continue to add contour and character to the nose.
8. Once the clay nose is blocked out use a small wire loop sculpting tool to smooth out the surface of the nose. The sides of the clay nose should taper to a thin blending edge and the nostrils should cover any undercuts in the area.
9. Use a smaller wire loop sculpting tool to carve out the nostril areas.
10. Probe the sides of the nose with a pin to make sure there will be *no* undercuts on the sides of the nose. An undercut will lock the negative onto the positive mold.
11. Smooth the surface of the clay nose with your fingers.
12. Decant a small amount of 99% alcohol into a container.
13. Use a brush and 99% alcohol to continue smoothing the surface of the clay.
14. Texture pads, available in a variety of styles, are used to add skin textures to the clay.
15. Use a texture pad to press pores into the surface of the clay.
16. Cover the clay with plastic wrap and use a ball stylus sculpting tool to tap deeper pores into the sculpture.
17. Continue creating pores in the sculpture.
18. Use the small wire loop sculpting tool to create longer dash marks in the clay.
19. Create wrinkle lines by using a straight pin.
20. Carefully remove the plastic from the sculpture.
21. Use a brush and baby powder to lightly smooth out the texture.
22. Finished sculpted clay nose.
23. Use a softer sulfur-free clay (from Reynolds Advanced Materials) to fill in the nostril areas.
24. Continue filling in the nostril area with a soft clay.
25. Clean the edges of the clay nose sculpture with 99% alcohol or lacquer thinner.
26. Add additional texture or wrinkle lines if necessary.
27. Spray the finished sculpture with one light coat of Krylon Crystal Clear. Use this spray in a well-ventilated area and do not inhale it.
28. Mark mold key positions on positive with a Sharpie. These keys should be spaced so the negative mold will not

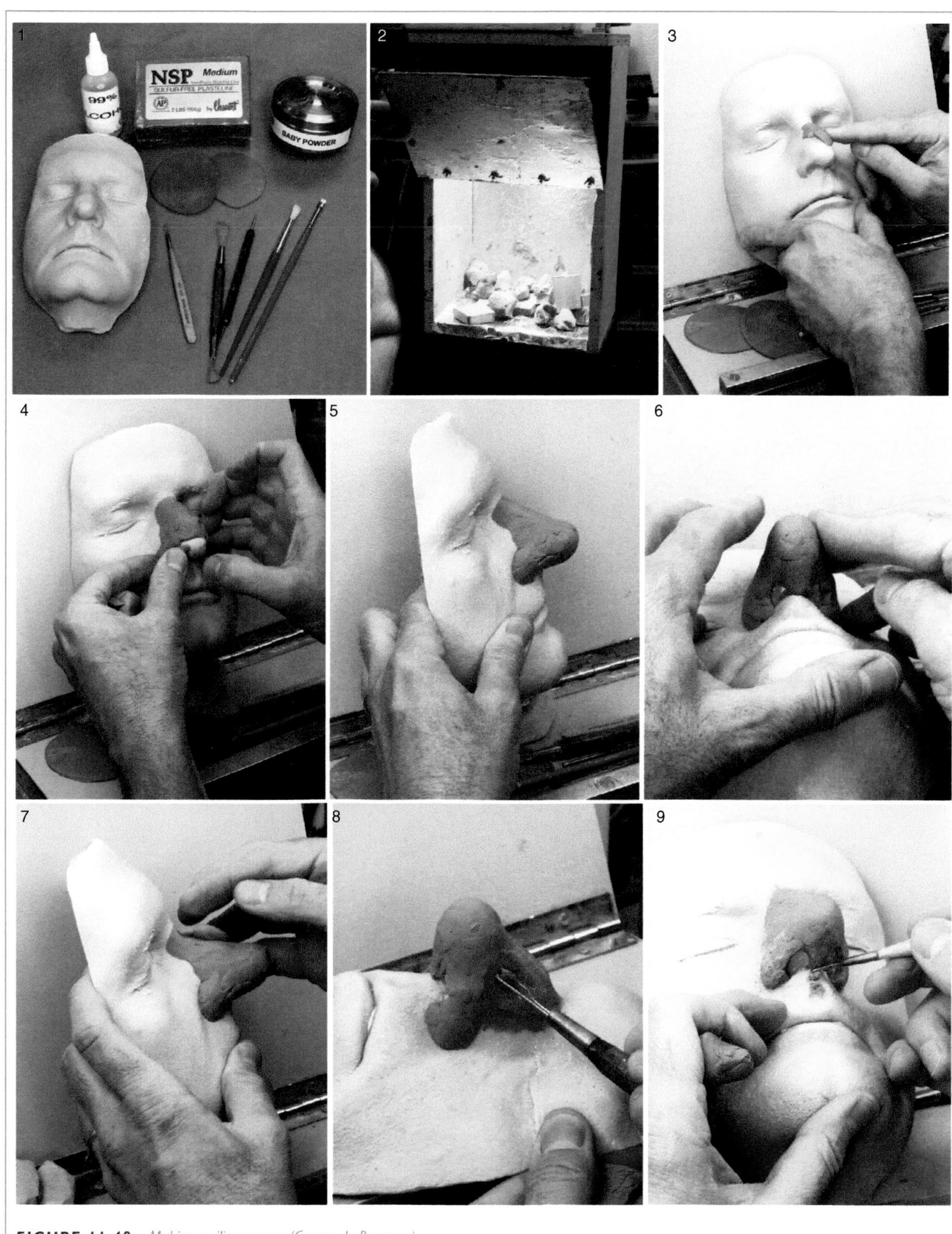

FIGURE 11.48 *Making a silicone nose (Cyrano de Bergerac).*

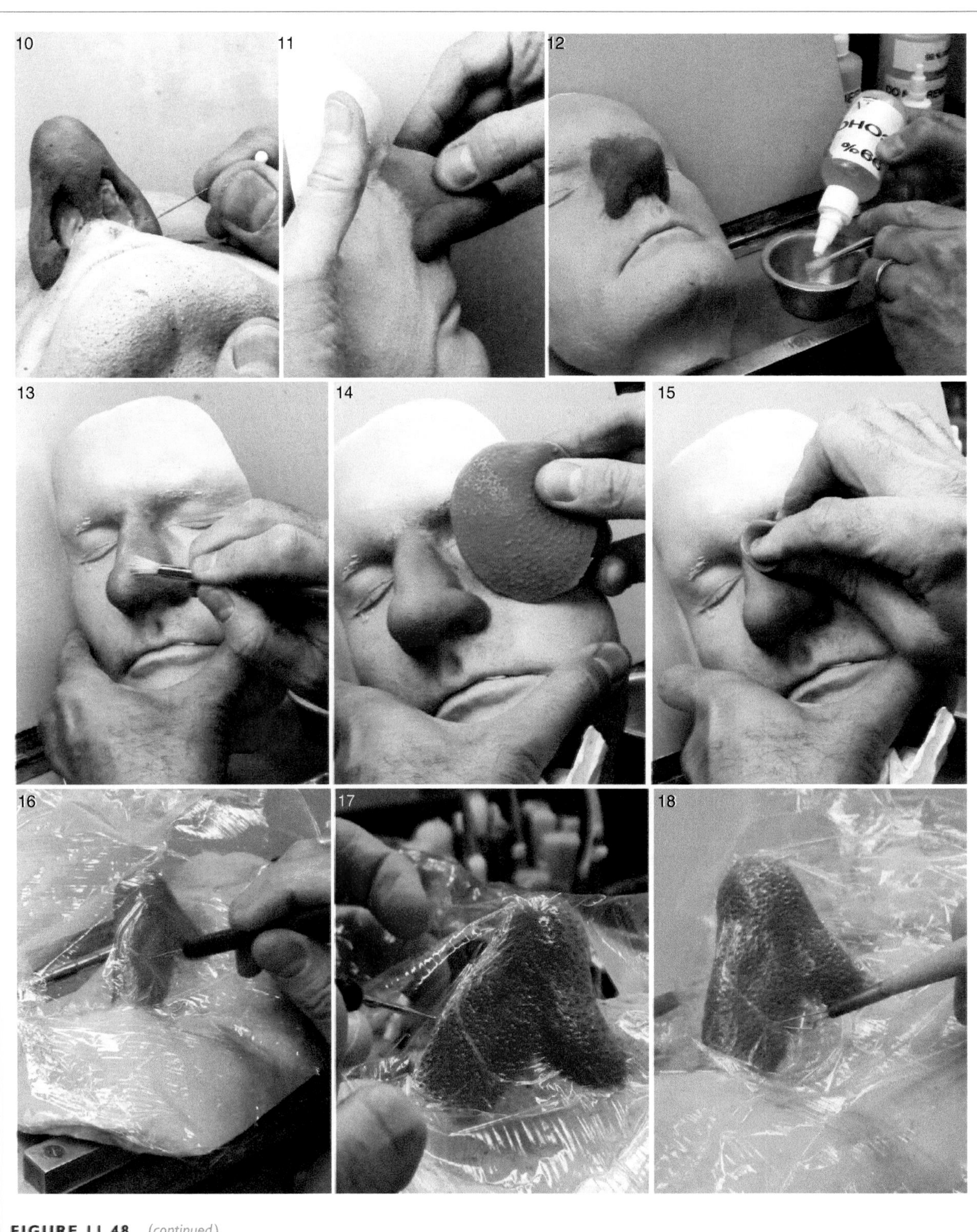

FIGURE 11.48 *(continued)*

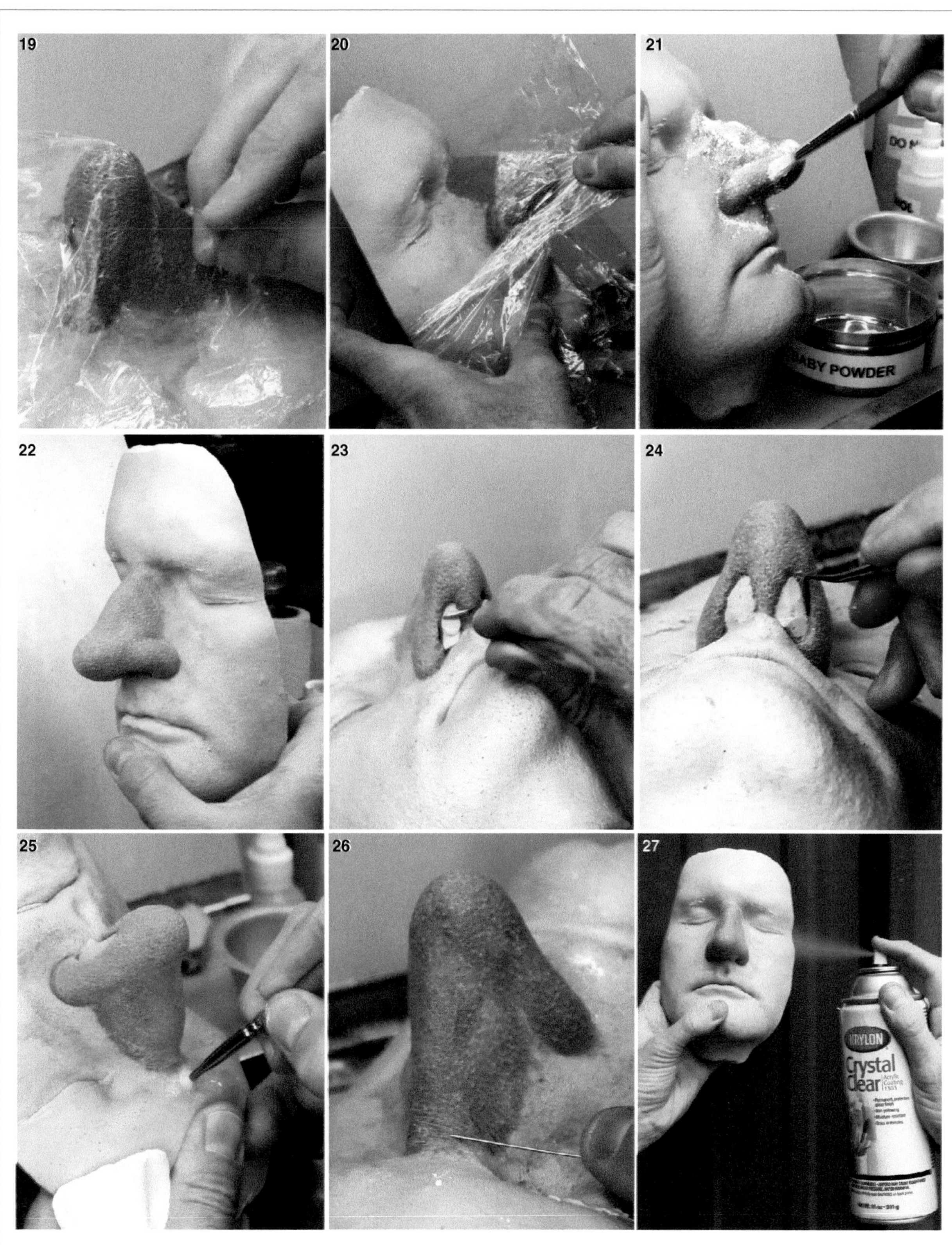

FIGURE 11.48 *(continued)*

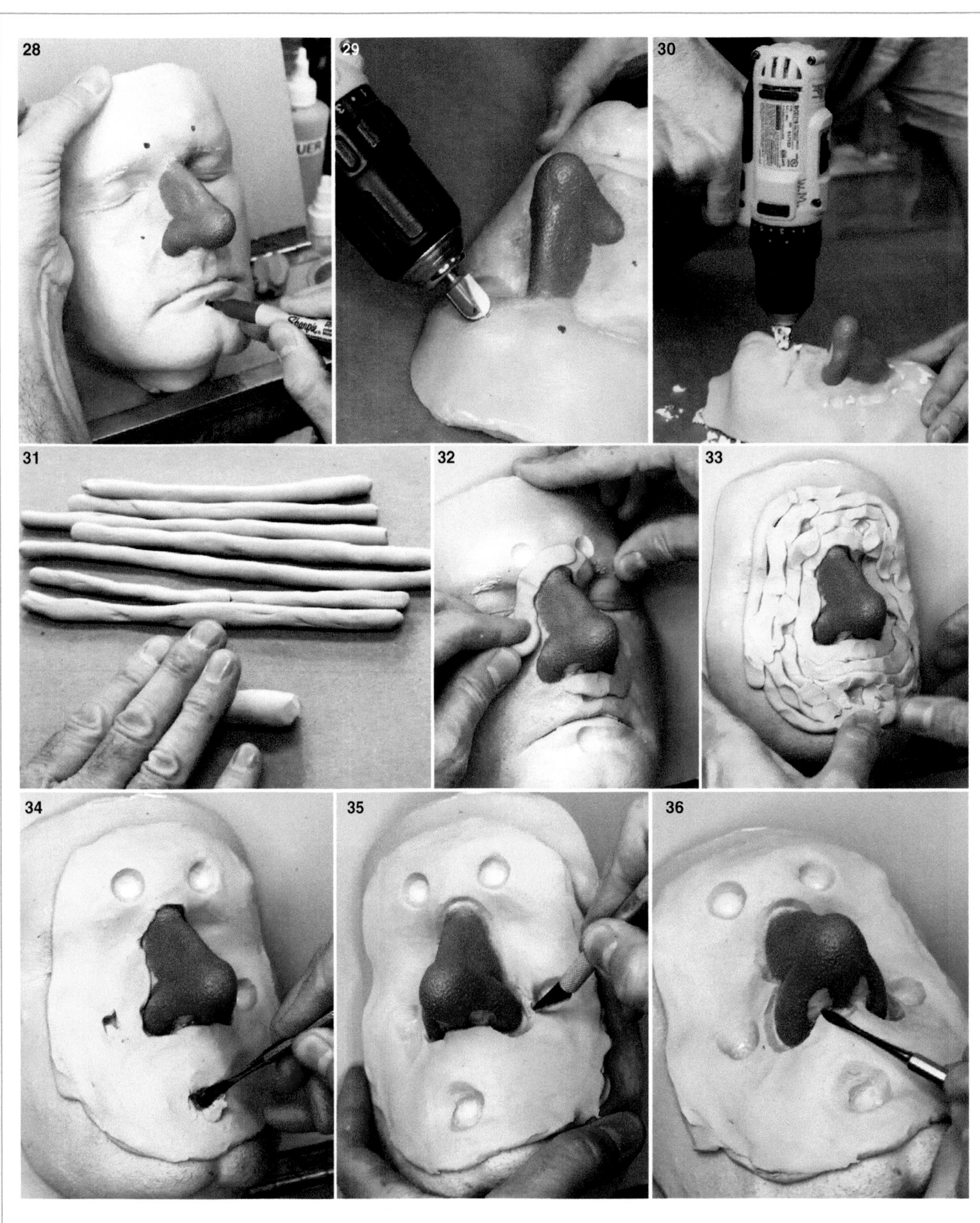

FIGURE 11.48 *(continued)*

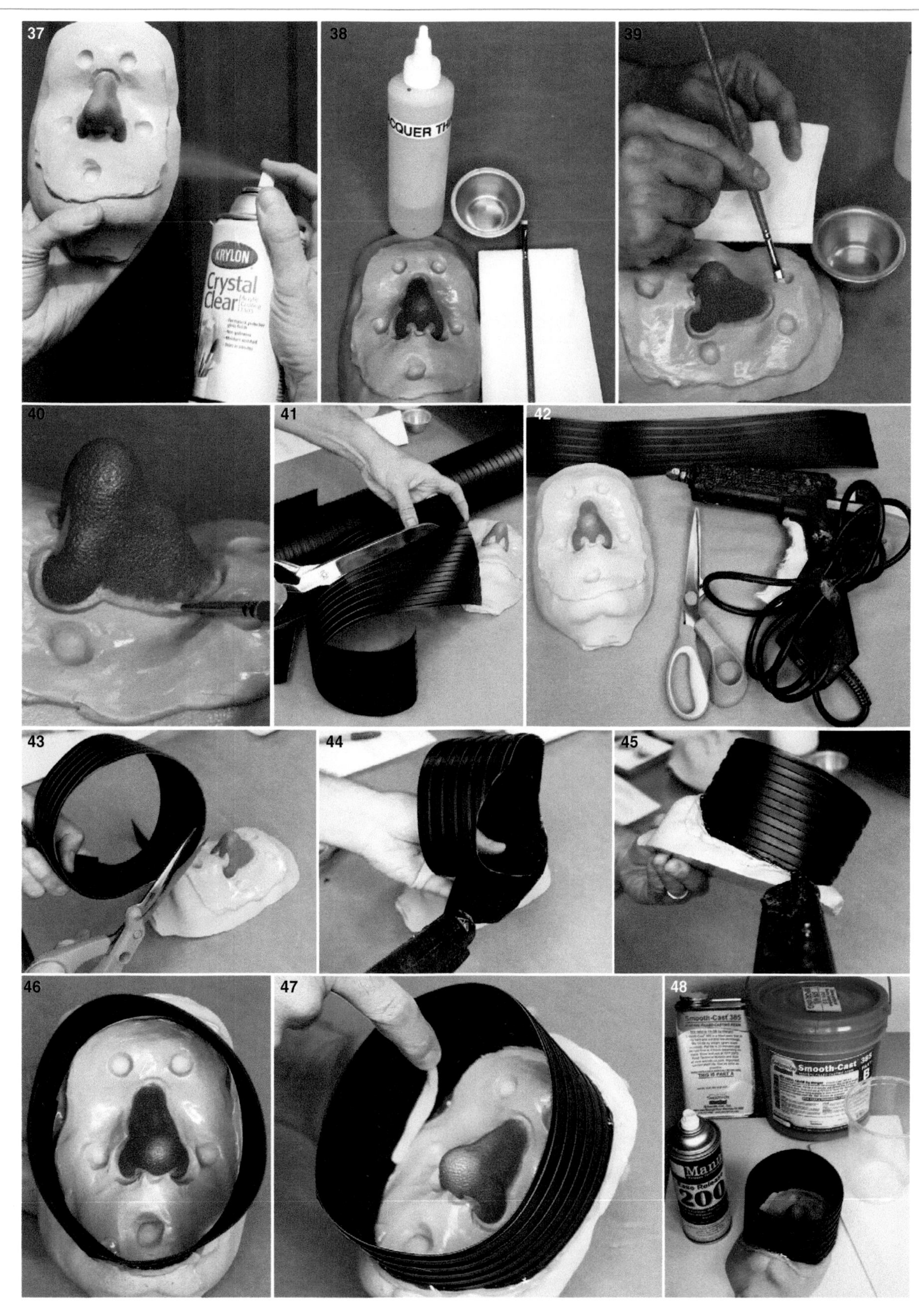

FIGURE 11.48 *(continued)*

FIGURE 11.48 *(continued)*

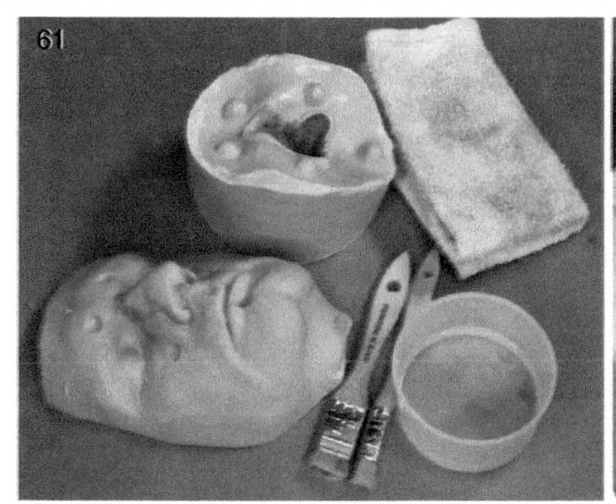

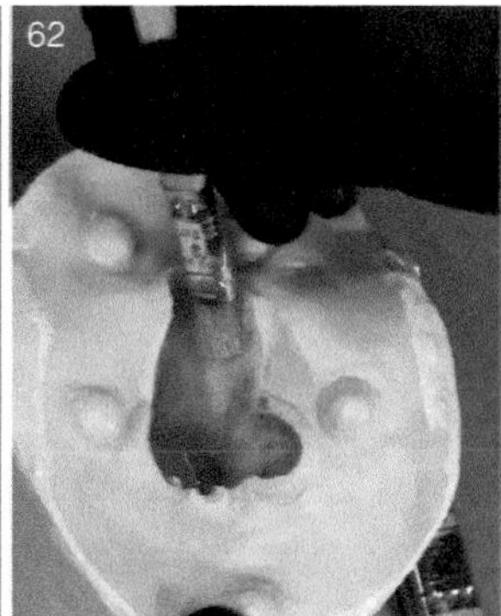

FIGURE 11.48 *(continued)*

"rock" or cause an uneven closure when the negative is created.

29. Drill indented keys with a router bit (Core Box or Round Nose router bit) attached to a hand drill. A Dremel tool may be used for this step using a 911 Aluminum Oxide Grinding Stone. This key should be an indented half sphere.
30. Continue drilling round indentations.
31. Roll out "snake" shaped clay for use as flashing on the positive mold.
32. Start application of clay up to but not touching the edges of the sculpture.
33. Finish the mold out with the sculptex clay "snakes."
34. After smoothing the clay out, use a sculpting or dental tool to cut out and remove the clay from the indented keys.
35. Use an X-Acto blade to cut the clay ⅛ inch from the edge of the nose clay at a 90-degree angle around the sculpted clay nose. This will create the "cutting edge" which will result in a thin blending edge on the final silicone appliance.
36. Blend the flashing clay into the clay-filled nostril.
37. Spray the whole model with a light coat of Krylon Crystal Clear again.
38. Materials: lacquer thinner, small bowl, edge cleaning brush, paper towel and sculpture.
39. Clean the indented keys with the brush and lacquer thinner. Wipe the brush off after cleaning each hole.
40. Very carefully clean the "cutting edge" area between the nose sculpture edge and the clay flashing with the brush and lacquer thinner.

Making the Mold (Negative Cast) from Smooth-Cast 385 Plastic Resin:

41. Cut an 18-inch x 4-inch piece of vinyl runner mat. This will be used as the retaining wall around the sculpture.
42. Materials: face cast with sculpted nose, scissors, hot glue gun, pre-cut vinyl runner mat.
43. Cut the mat to fit the contour of the clay flashing area.
44. Glue the mat together at the end with the hot glue gun. *Be very careful, this product gets very hot.*
45. Place the contoured mat onto the clay flashing and seal the edge with hot glue gun.
46. Finished glued mat.
47. Seal any area with clay that might leak.
48. Materials: Smooth-Cast 385, 200 Spray Release, 32-oz. deli cup, Paint Stir Stick & Face Cast with 49. Sculpture with Mat Wall, ½-inch disposable brush.
49. Spray the sculpture, flashing, and wall with Ease Release 200 spray.
50. Mix 1,000 grams Part B and 200 grams Part A Smooth-Cast 385 product as described in the previous casting steps (see Figure 11.8) and *carefully* paint the product onto the sculpture and surrounding area. Make sure not to trap any air bubbles on the sculpted nose as this will show on the final prosthetic appliance.

51. Slowly pour the 385 product from a high point into the top of the sculpture. This will break any small bubbles from being trapped in the mold.
52. Finished positive and negative molds. Let set for 5 hours or overnight.
53. Remove the vinyl runner mat from the negative mold.
54. Carefully pry the positive and negative molds apart with two screwdrivers at the same time, lifting the negative mold off the positive mold.
55. Pull the molds apart.
56. Start cleaning the soft sulfur-free sculptex clay from the mold with a tongue depressor or a wooden sculpting tool. *Do not* use metal tools, they will scratch the surface of the negative mold resulting in a compromised silicone prosthetic appliance. Get as much clay off as possible.
57. With a smaller piece of tongue depressor, scrape the NSP clay out of the nose area.
58. Remove as much clay off both positive and negative molds as possible.
59. Grind the sharp edges off the negative mold with a grinding bit and a Dremel tool.
60. Grind the sharp edge off the back of the negative mold also. Use a Shop Vac to vacuum the dusk and particles as you work.
61. Materials: positive and negative molds, cloth towel, ½-inch and 1-inch disposable brushes cut down to ½ inch, container with lacquer thinner.
62. Clean all clay from the negative nose sculpt and flashing area with lacquer thinner using the ½-inch and 1-inch cut disposable brushes.
63. Finished positive and negative molds.

Running the Silicone Nose - (Figure 11.49)

1. Materials: Dragon Skin FX-Pro, Slacker, 200 Mold Release Spray, tongue depressors, Revlon Color Stay Foundation 320-True Beige, 50 lb. weights, deli cups, and red flocking (not pictured: Vacuum Chamber and 50# Lifting Weights or Stage Weights).
2. Silicone color skin match sample made ahead of time using Revlon Color Stay Foundations and Dragon Skin FX-Pro.
3. Matching actor's skin tone with silicone color samples.
4. Spray the Smooth-Cast 385 negative and positive Cyrano nose molds with 200 Mold Release Spray.

Measuring the Silicone:

5. Measure out 2 oz. of Part A Dragon Skin FX-Pro.
6. Measure out 2 oz. of Part B Dragon Skin FX-Pro.
7. Pour Part A into larger deli cup.

Adding Color to Match the Performer's Skin Tone:

8. Add a dollop of Revlon 320-True Beige makeup foundation into Part A.
9. Add a pinch of red flocking.
10. Mix the colorants into Part A.

Mixing the Silicone:

11. Add Part B to the mix and stir for 1 minute to thoroughly mix both parts. Scrape the edges and the bottom of the cup while mixing with a tongue depressor.

Degassing the Silicone:

12. Vacuum the mix in a vacuum chamber for approximately 1½ minutes. If a vacuum chamber is not available, roll the product around in the cup to break any bubble from the mix.
13. Pour the mix slowly from a high point onto the top of the nose area and let it flow into the mold.
14. Press the positive into the negative.
15. Place 50# of weights onto the mold. Let cure for 1 hour.
17. Remove the weights and pry the molds apart with a screwdriver.
18. Molds pulled apart.
19. Cut the excess silicone from under the nose.
20. Finished nose with the silicone flashing removed. Do not cut the edge of the silicone nose. If the silicone needs to be removed, carefully tear the flashing from the nose using your fingers.

21. & 22. Powder and remove the silicone nose.

FIGURE 11.49 *Running the silicone.*

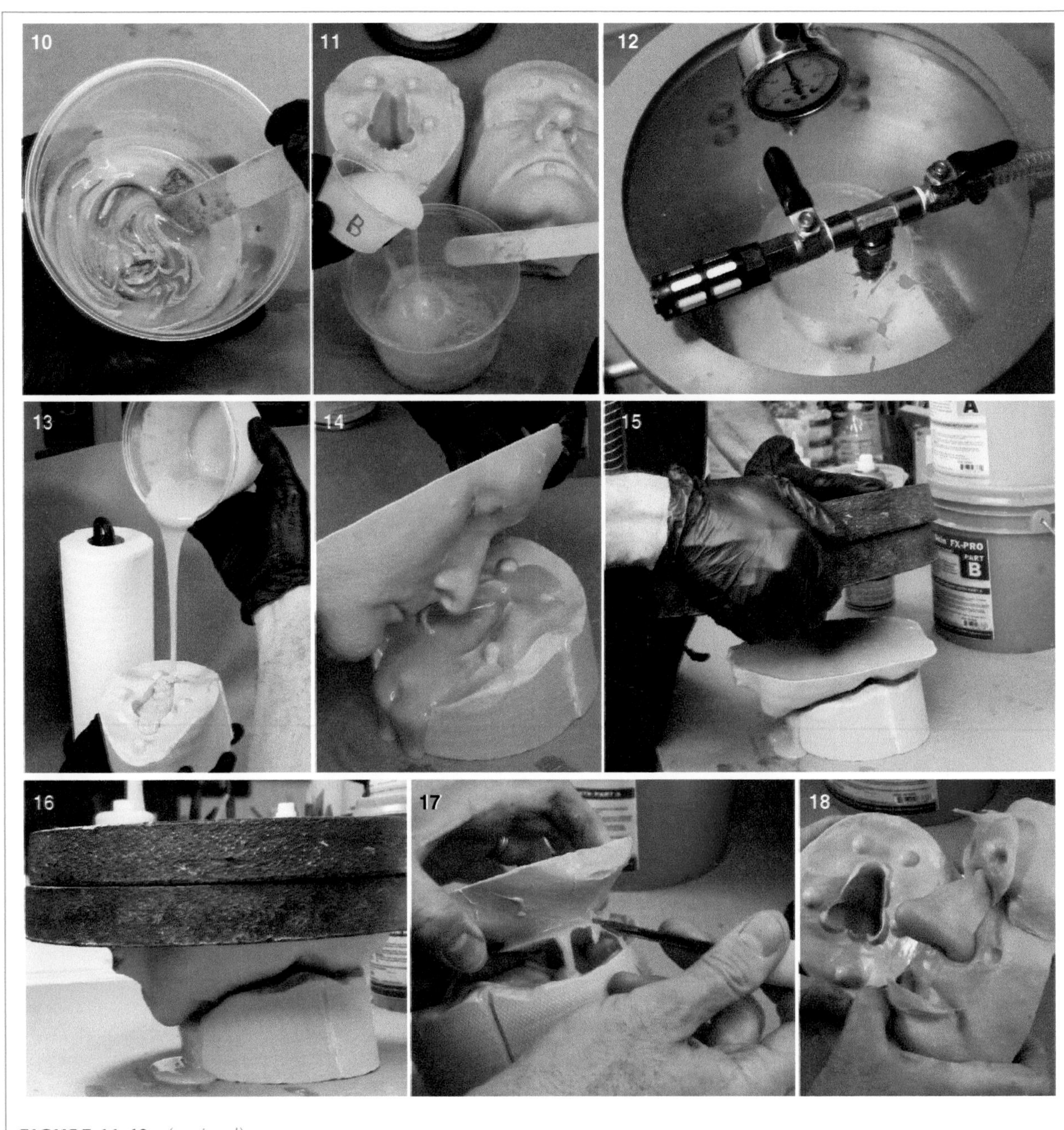

FIGURE 11.49 *(continued)*

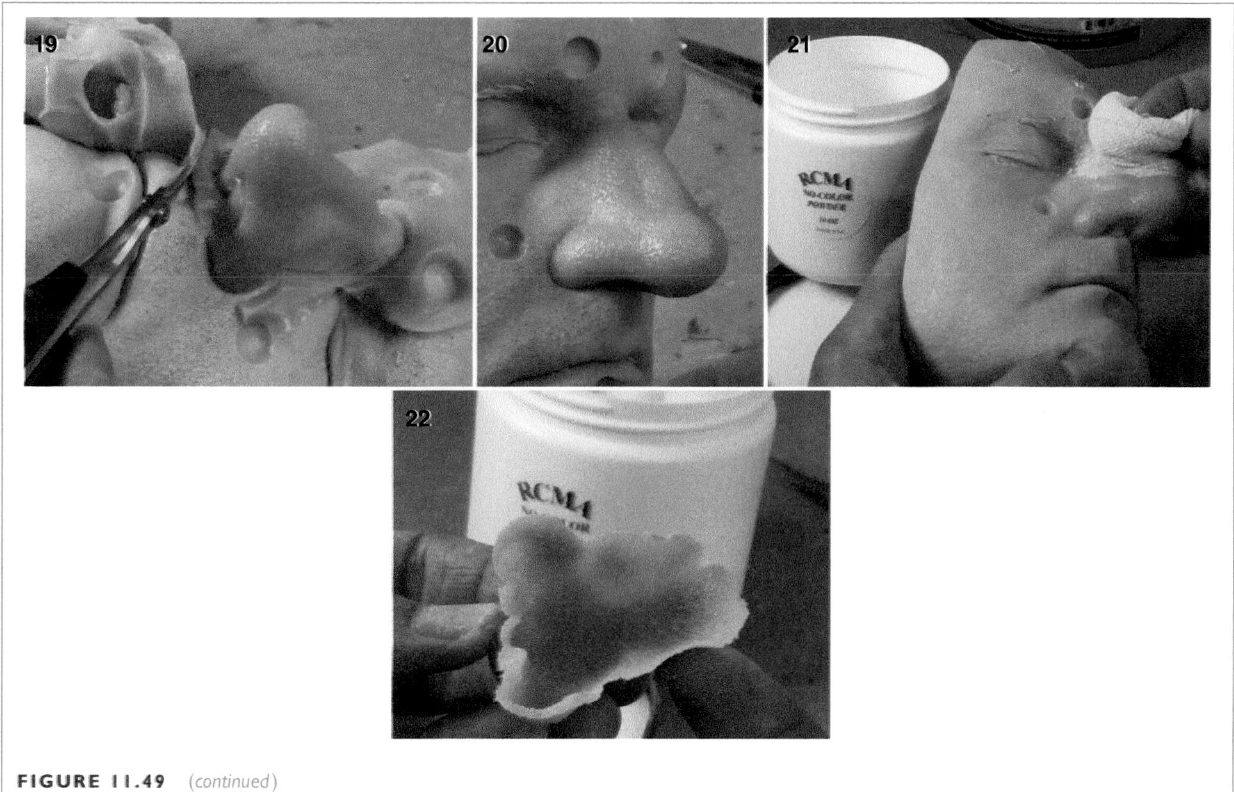

FIGURE 11.49 *(continued)*

CYRANO MAKEUP APPLICATION

1. (Figure 11.50). Makeup set-up materials: dressed wig and facial hair, tissues, 99% alcohol, powder puffs, RCMA No-Color Powder, Skin-Tite Platinum Silicone Kit, brushes, hair-cutting scissors, tweezers, comb, cotton-tipped applicators, CC measuring cups, Krylon RMG Kit, silicone nose, torn and cut white foam sponges, torn orange stipple sponge, Stacolor Kits (Character and Full Color), spirit gum, and small cup holder.
2. Cut out the nostril holes from the silicone nose (see Figure 11.50[2]).
3. Clean the silicone nose (inside and outside) with 99% alcohol and a tissue.
4. Clean the actor's nose with 99% alcohol and a tissue.
5. Decant a small amount of Part A Skin-Tite into a small CC measuring cup.
6. Decant the same amount of Part B Skin-Tite into the same small CC measuring cup.
7. Mix Part A and B Skin-Tite together with a clean metal spatula. This product has a 5-minute cure time.
8. While Skin-Tite is setting, place the silicone appliance onto the actor's nose and powder with No-Color Powder and a powder puff. This will leave an outline where the Skin-Tite Silicone will be applied.
9. Apply the mixed Skin-Tite to the actor's nose with a cotton-tipped applicator slightly past the area of the powdered outline of the nose.
10. Place the silicone nose onto the Skin-Tite and lightly press with your finger, starting at the center of the nose outward to make sure the entire nose is adhered securely.
11. Dab a little more Skin-Tite onto the edges of the nose with the cotton-tipped applicator. Press a powder puff with a small amount of No-Color Powder onto the edge to texture and blend the Skin-Tite onto the actor's skin. Let cure for 2 more minutes before continuing.
12. Blotch the silicone nose with LIP color Stacolor activated with 99% alcohol with a brush to add redness to the nose.

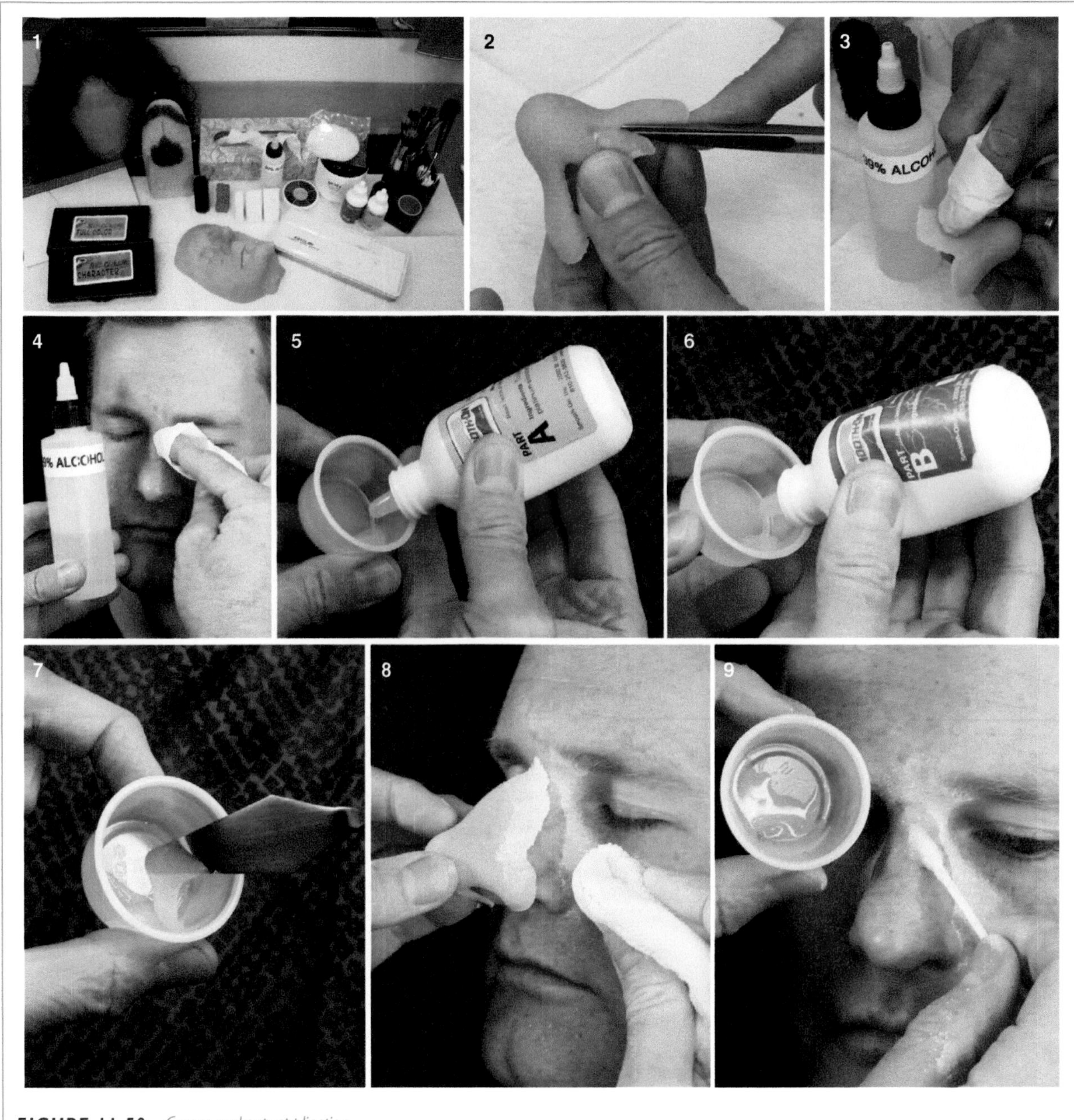

FIGURE 11.50 *Cyrano makeup application.*

13. Spatulate the appropriate skin tone colors plus a brick color Krylon RMG onto a wax paper makeup palette. Appropriate skin tones will vary according to the character design.
14. Stipple the RMG onto the skin and nose with an orange stipple sponge. This places tiny dots of makeup base onto the skin and does not cover the real skin tone completely.
15. Stipple the dots of RMG on the skin with a white foam sponge. This evens out and blends the makeup, removing any excess makeup base. Do not rub the base color.
16. Stipple the nose with the RMG base color with a medium-size round stipple brush.
17. Stipple a brick color RMG onto the cheeks, nose, and forehead with a large-size round stipple brush.

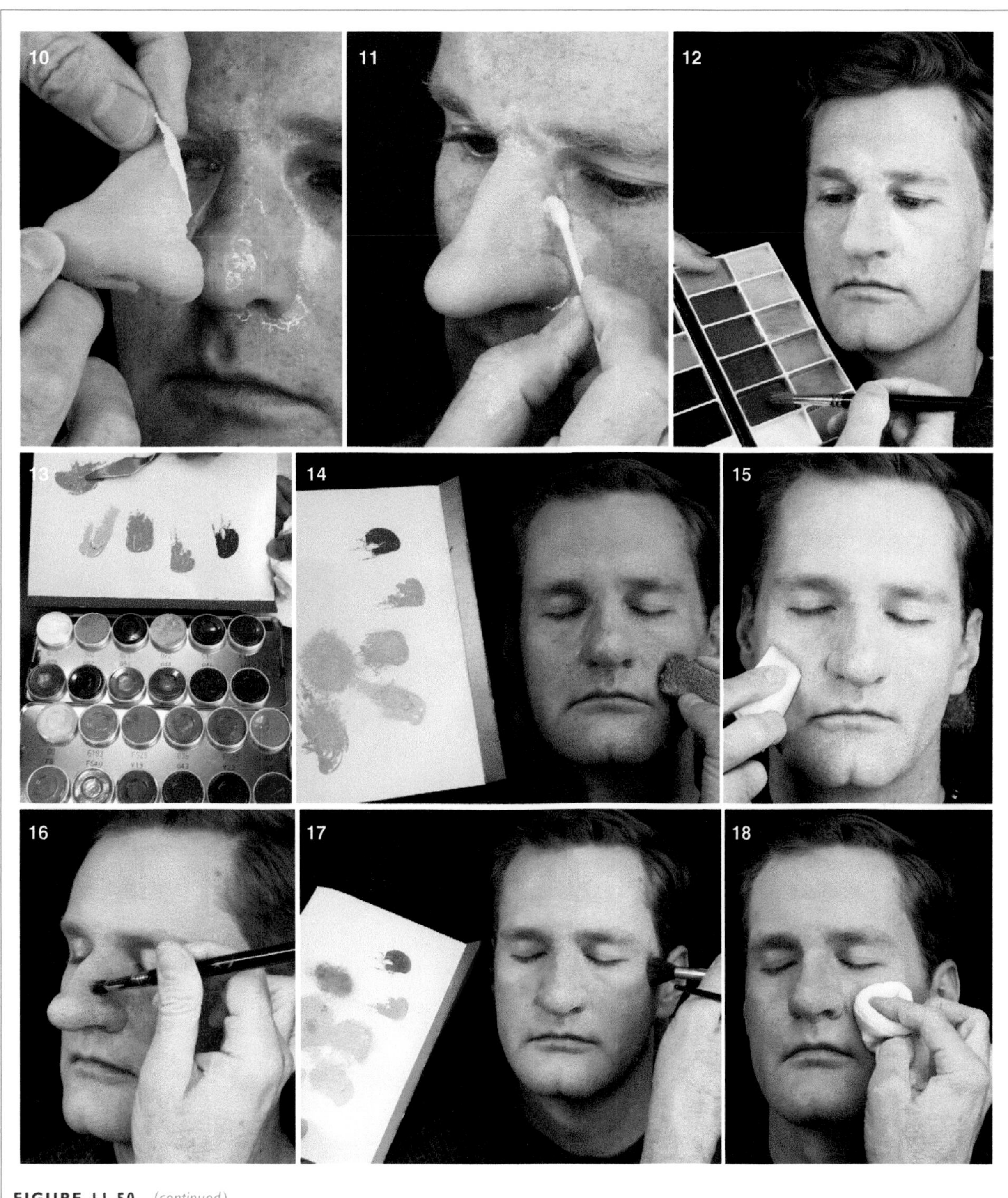

FIGURE 11.50 *(continued)*

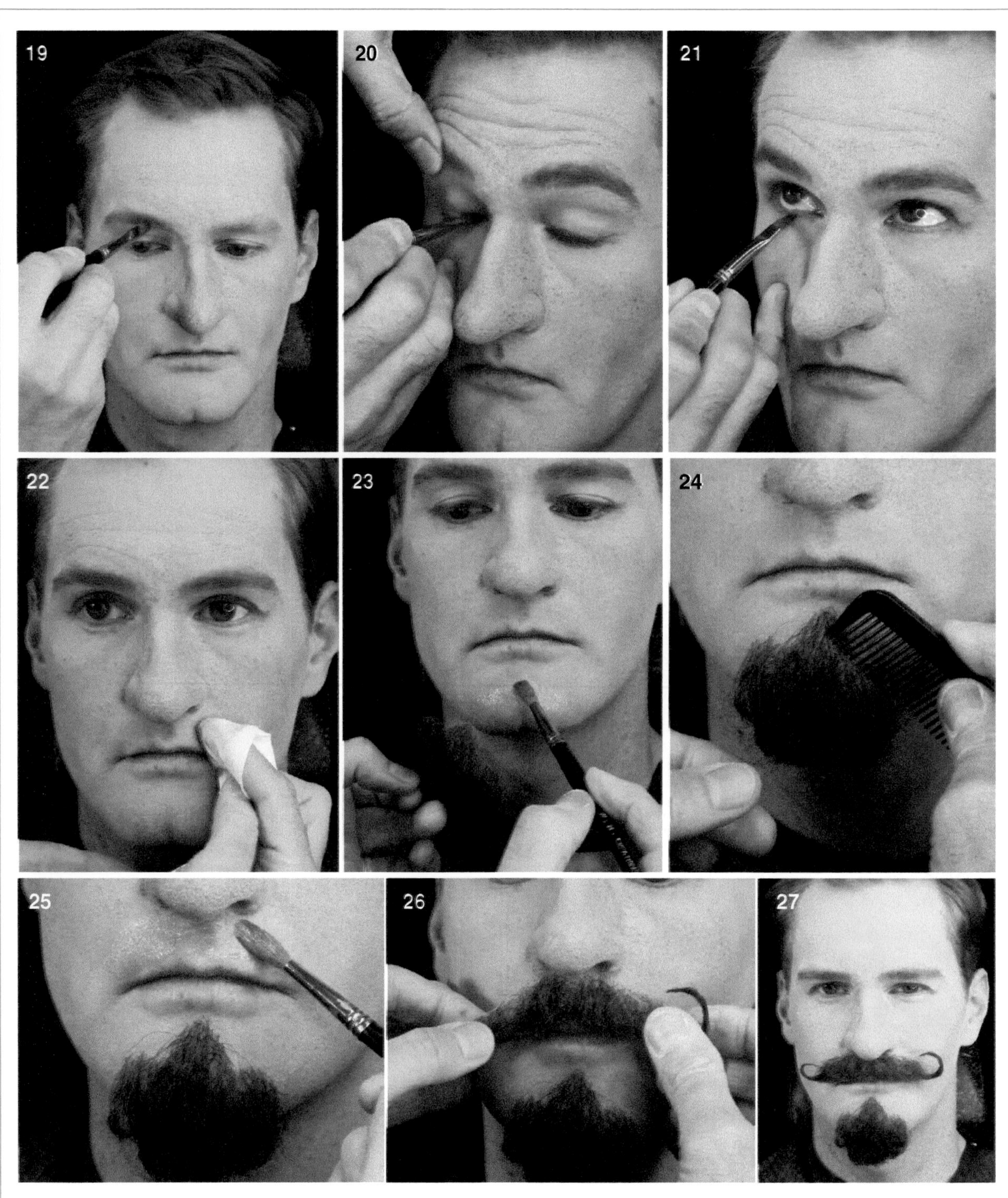

FIGURE 11.50 *(continued)*

FIGURE 11.50 *(continued)*

18. Powder the whole face and appliance with RCMA No-Color Powder and a powder puff.

19. Carefully paint the eyebrow hairs with a blackish-brown Stacolor color and a brush.

20. Line the upper eyelids with a water-based liner.

21. Line the lower lids with a water-based liner.

22. Clean the upper lip and chin, where the mustache and goatee will be glued, with 99% alcohol and a tissue.

23. Apply a generous amount of W.M. Creations Extra Hold Spirit Gum to the area where the goatee will be placed. Tap the adhesive area with the brush to matte the spirit gum.

24. Press the goatee into place, lift it up once and then replace it to the skin. This transfers the glue onto the back of the goatee lace. Press the lace, not the hair, into the skin with a comb.

25. Apply a generous amount of W.M. Creations Extra Hold Spirit Gum to the area where the mustache will be placed. Tap the adhesive area with the brush to matte the spirit gum.

26. Press the mustache into place, lift it up once and then replace it to the skin, having the actor slightly smile.

This transfers the glue onto the back of the mustache lace. Press the lace, not the hair, into the skin with a comb.

27. Finished makeup before wig application.
28. Wig application: Have the actor place two fingers under the front of the wig and place it onto his forehead as you pull the wig down and back. Secure the wig with hairpins where necessary.
29. Glue the front and sides of the wig down with spirit gum.
30. Finished look before costume.
31. Finished Cyrano de Bergerac look.
32. Remove the silicone nose by carefully peeling the nose off from the edges. The nose can be saved and reused multiple times for a stage production.
33. Remove the mustache and goatee with 99% alcohol. Use gel-formula RJS Adhesive Remover (see Appendix A) to clean the spirit gum from the skin. Use 99% alcohol to clean the adhesive from the wig and facial hair lace.

CHAPTER 12

BEARDS AND MUSTACHES

The first step in constructing a beard or a mustache is to make a rough sketch of what you have in mind. Presumably you will have done this based on your research when designing the makeup. Illustrations in this book and in your morgue should be helpful. The style you choose will, of course, depend on the period of the play and on the personality of the character.

You can make or buy beards or mustaches of real, synthetic, or yak hair ventilated on a lace foundation. This type of beard is the quickest to apply, the most comfortable to wear, and the most convincing. It is also the most expensive, but it will last for many performances, if not for many years. If you will be using a beard or a mustache for only a few performances and if your budget is limited, you will probably want to use crepe hair. In any case, you should become proficient in the technique of applying it.

HAND LAYING THE BEARD

Human Hair, Animal Hair, and Wool Crepe

Crepe hair is hair that is tightly crimped by means of weaving it on strings, then boiled or steamed to set the curl. It can mimic and/or resemble beard textures of all kinds. There are generally three types of crepe hair: human, yak, and wool. Both human and yak crepe can be set and styled just like any other human hair, and are perfect for hand laying a beard. Wool crepe cannot be styled like human hair, but has a suitable beard-like appearance and texture and is the most economical choice for smaller budgets. In the following demonstration, human crepe hair will be used to create a full beard. If you are using crepe wool, you will notice that the fiber lengths are shorter and do not respond as well to curling irons as human hair. However, colors can be just as easily mixed and, by placing them in a drawing card or hackle, can be used exactly the same way as human hair. No further preparation is needed.

1. Products needed for laying on a beard (left to right): Drawing card, hackle, hair-cutting scissors, lengths of crepe hair braids in various colors, 5-pronged lift/teasing comb, hair brush, electric curling iron, flat iron, and thermal stove (Figure 12.1).
2. Human hair crepe comes tightly woven on two strings in a figure eight pattern.

   To use it, find the beginning of one hair section and carefully pull it off the strings without disturbing the hair too much. It might be necessary to cut the strings, in which case be very careful not to cut the hair itself.
3. Once the hair section is off the strings you can see the characteristic coil shape. Cut off a 4 inch length for an approximate 6 inch finished length.
4. The texture can now be adjusted to your liking, for design and ethnicity. This is achieved by holding the crepe on one end and pulling the hair crepe through a hot curling iron.

   (In this image an electric curling iron is being used.)
5. A marcel iron can also be used to adjust the texture of the crepe hair.
6. Observe the crepe carefully as it changes texture. This might require two or three passes with the iron to achieve the desired results (keep in mind to treat the ends of the crepe as well).

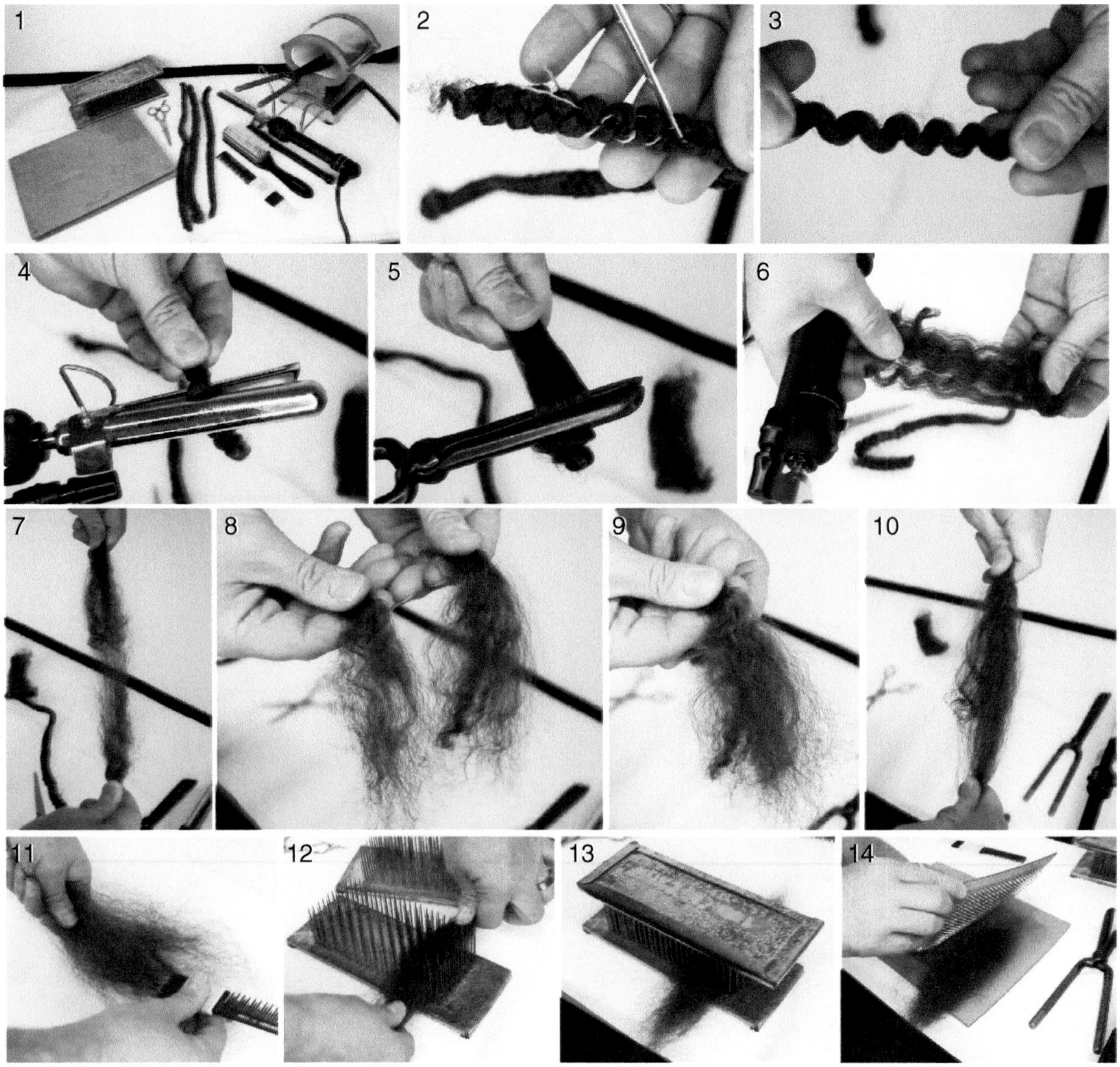

FIGURE 12.1 *Preparing crepe human hair.*

FIGURE 12.2 *Preparing crepe wool using a steam iron to adjust the amount of texture.*

7. Once the desired texture has been reached, fluff the hair up by holding both ends and pulling it apart. You may have to shake your hands slightly while pulling the hair apart.
8. Crepe hair pulled apart into two lengths.
9. Re-laying the hair on top of itself, lengthwise. There is no need to concern yourself with the directions of the tips and roots.
10. Repeat this process with all colors until the hair has a uniform texture. There should be no clumps remaining in the hair.
11. Comb through the hair with the 5-pronged lift comb to organize the hair before placing it in the hackle.
12. Place the hair into a drawing card, or into a hackle.

FIGURE 12.3 *Constructing a beard with crepe hair and spirit gum. Straightened hair is built up gradually in layers, using two or more shades of hair. All loose hairs are pulled out before the final trimming. Notice how the thinner hair on the cheek blends into the skin. Makeup artist, Richard Corson.*

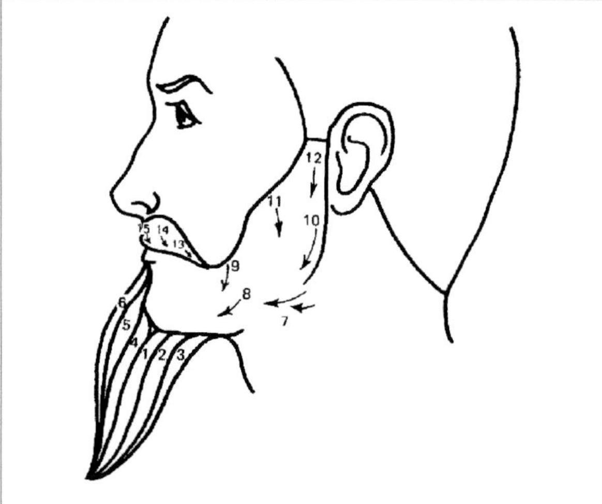

FIGURE 12.4 *Diagram for applying crepe hair beard. Layers of hair are applied in the order indicated by the numbers.*

13. Place the two parts of the hackle together. This will hold the hair in place.

14. Hair can also be placed in a drawing card.

Figure 12.5 demonstrates the process of hand laying a beard with crepe hair. Assemble all of your materials and lay them out so that you have an easy workflow and can reach all of them easily. Keep your station hygienically sound and clean at all times as this can be a relatively messy process.

(Note: The beard should be laid over the finished makeup. Keep in mind that the makeup must be fully set and as thin as possible under the area where the beard is applied.)

Skin-safe adhesives such as Mastix, a matte spirit gum by Kryolan, and the Telesis 5 Silicone Matte Lace adhesive are both ideal for laying hair goods.

1. Materials: Hackle with four hair colors (dark brown, reddish-brown, gray, and a gray/brown mix); spirit gum (Mastix); three brushes for applying adhesive (1 round, 1 x ¼ inch flat, 1 x ¾ inch flat); hair-cutting scissors; 4-pronged pick comb; 99% alcohol; small cups for glues and thinners; protective cape; paper towels; ¾-inch flat foundation brush for removing the beard (not pictured).

   (Note: Position yourself in front of the performer to more easily reach the chin and mandible areas.)

2. Pull a small amount of hair (about 15 to 20 hairs) from the hackle or drawing card.

3. Cut the end square (straight across). Some artists cut the hair at a slight angle for easier handling when applying it to the contours of the face.

The Gluing Process

4. Apply a small amount of spirit gum (matte adhesive is preferred) to the skin under the chin. This should cover approximately ½ x 1 inch space. (Tip: It is best if the actor is *not* freshly shaven. The alcohol in the spirit gum might irritate the face for a few seconds.)

5. Hold or pinch the hair between your thumb and index finger. Fan the hair slightly by pushing your thumb against your index finger. Press the ends of the freshly cut hair into the adhesive and lightly press with the tip of the scissors or brush handle. Be careful to avoid gluing the instrument to the performer's skin.

6., 7., & 8. Apply hair starting at the chin, then work up along the jawline to the sideburns. Repeat the procedure: pull a small amount of hair from the hackle, cut the hair ends with the scissors, apply adhesive to a small area, and lightly press the hair into the spirit gum. The hair should look as though it is growing out from the skin. It should not look flattened against the face.

9. Press the hair gently onto the adhesive with the tip of the scissors.

10. Feel free to mix the hair colors according to the particular design. The last layers of hair should be slightly lighter than the base color. This helps provide a more natural look. Gray hair can also be added as a top layer.

    Note: Follow diagram (Figure 12.4) for a suggested glue pattern. Mix hair colors as you see your design requires. Most beards will look much more natural if the colors are mixed, but not totally blended.

    The amount of hair you apply into the actor's beard should be about one-third more than the final desired beard density, because depending on how well you have applied the hair, you could lose about one-third in the combing and styling process.)

Styling the Hand Laid Beard

11. Gently comb through the beard using the 4-pronged pick comb to remove any stray hair and to begin the styling process. This will remove the hairs that did not get glued down sufficiently.

12. & 13. Trim and shape the beard periodically through the process using hair-cutting scissors. Cut the hair approximately 20% longer than the desired length. For example: if you want a 3-inch finished beard length, trim it to approximately 3⅝ inches.

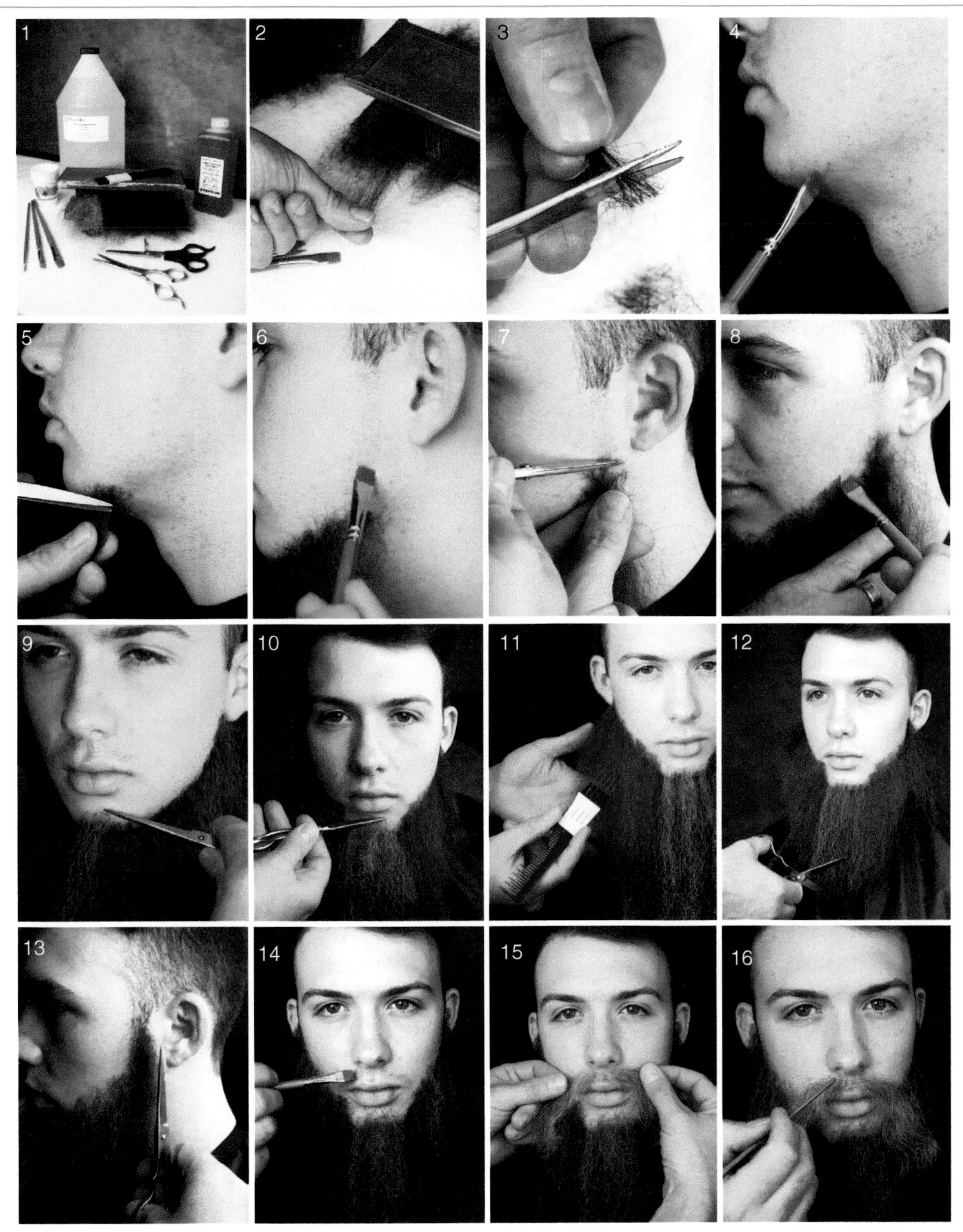

FIGURE 12.5 *The hand laid beard using crepe hair.*

FIGURE 12.5 *(continued)*

FIGURE 12.6 *Crepe hair beard and mustache. Beard constructed on latex, using four colors of crepe hair—light gray, medium gray, light gray-brown, and blond. Makeup by Bill Smith.*

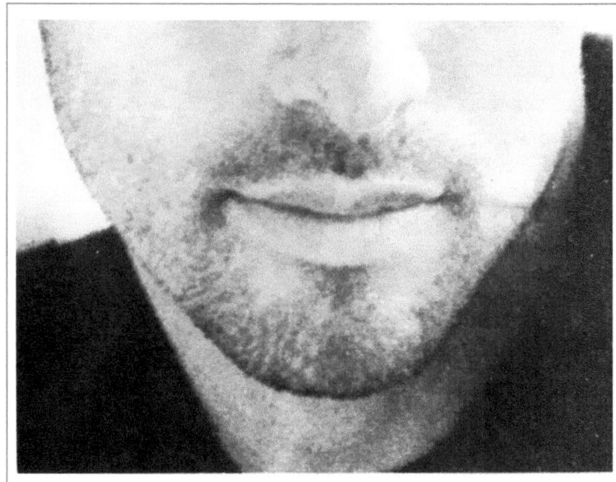

FIGURE 12.7 *Beard stubble.*

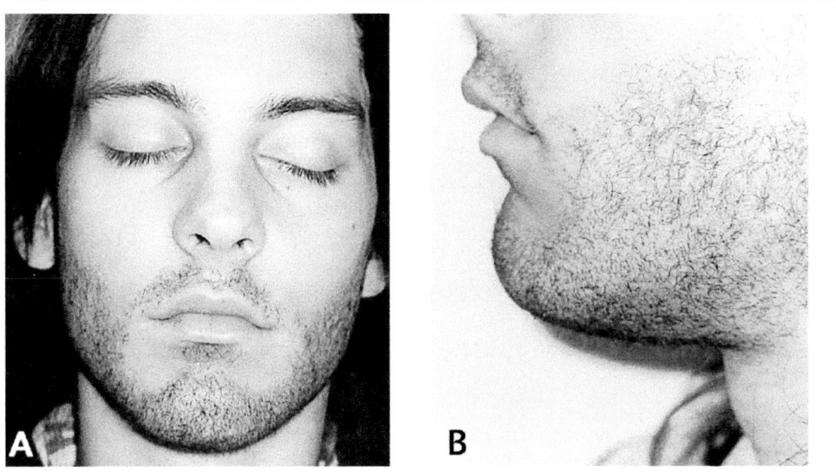

FIGURE 12.8 *Beard stubble applied with Naturo Plasto Mortician's Wax on actor Toby Maguire in the film, Ride With the Devil. Makeup by Jeff Goodwin at Transformations Makeup FX.*

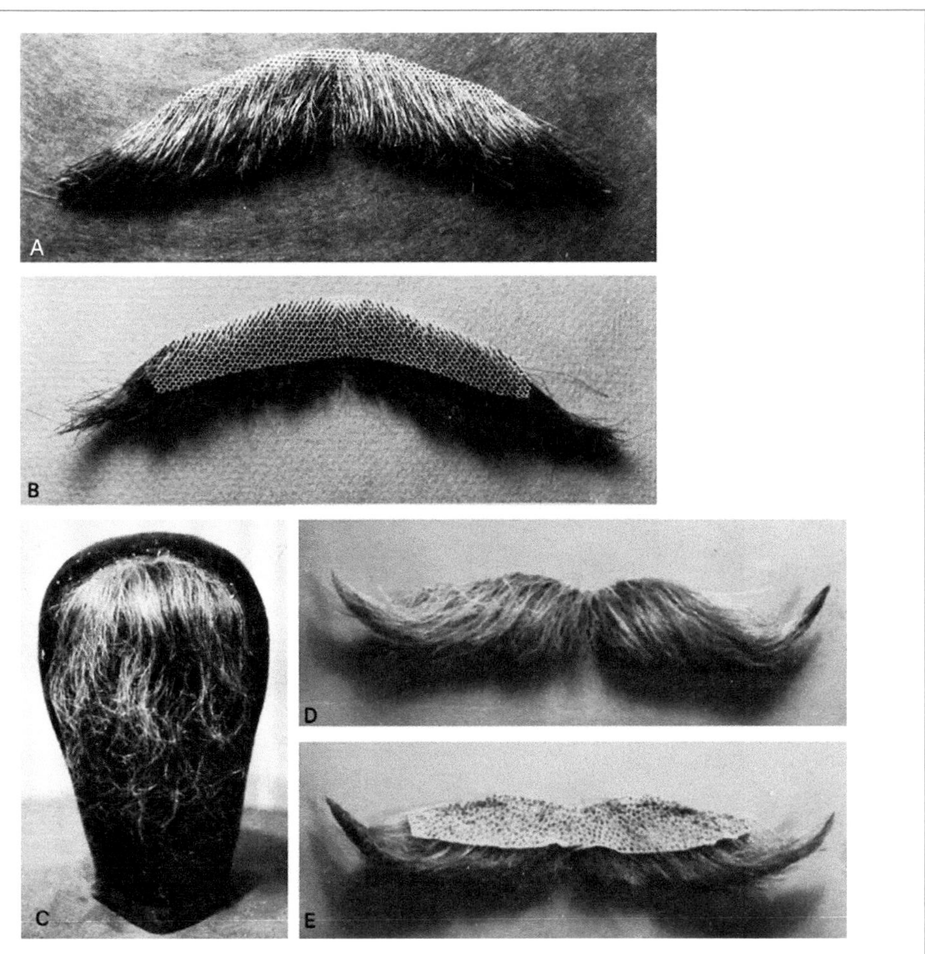

FIGURE 12.9 *Ventilated mustaches. A, B. Front and back of mustache ventilated on lace. C. Mustache (on wig block) ventilated on lace, shown before trimming. D, E. Front and back of mustache ventilated on gauze.*

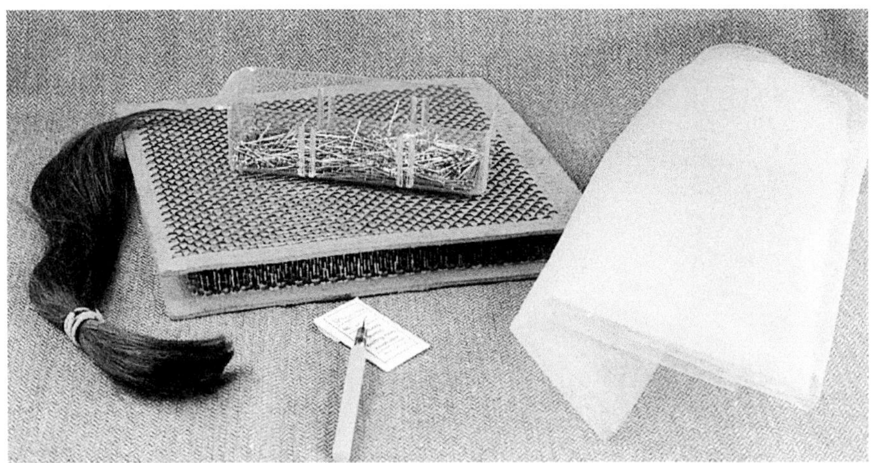

FIGURE 12.10 *Ventilating tools. (clockwise from left) Human hair hank, a set of drawing cards, silk or dressmaker pins, fine netting, ventilating needle holder, ventilating needle packet. (Drawing cards, ventilating needle and holder from Kryolan; netting from De Meo Brothers.)*

14. Apply the pre-made ventilated mustache (this mustache was made using a blend of the three colors used in making the beard) (see Figure 12.17, Ventilating a Mustache). First apply the spirit gum (Mastix) to the area above the upper lip. Keep the adhesive within the shape of the wig lace. Allow it to become slightly tacky.
15. Gently place the mustache onto the adhesive. Make sure it is centered on the performer's face.
16. Use the rounded tip of a makeup/adhesive brush to press the lace, not the hair, onto the adhesive. The lift comb is also a useful tool for this process. The key is to avoid pressing the mustache hair into the spirit gum.
17. Trim the mustache using hair-cutting scissors.
18. The finished beard.

REMOVING THE HAND LAID HAIR

Use only skin-approved removers that correspond to your gluing system.
For spirit gum use appropriate spirit gum remover, or isopropyl alcohol.
For Telesis glue, use Premier Products Inc.'s Super Solv.

19. Dip the ¾-inch flat brush into the 99% alcohol.
20. Starting at the sideburns, use the alcohol to dissolve and soften the spirit gum.
21. Gently pull off the hair until the entire face is clean. The residue can be removed using the alcohol and cotton balls or cotton rounds.

BEARD STUBBLE

A makeup effect mimicking a 1 to 3 day beard growth can be achieved by cutting textured human hair, or crepe hair, into very small pieces.

1. Cut the hair in the palm of your hand.
2. Spread the cut hair out on a paper towel or clean surface. Mix colors as desired or cut different colored hair and keep them separate, it all depends on your design. Protect your actor's costume or clothing by using a barber's cape, or shampoo cape.
3. Start by applying small amounts of adhesive to the skin. Use a similar gluing pattern to the one used with the hand laid beard, but you can apply adhesive in a wider area depending on the size of your brush, or area of application.

   (Depending on the adhesive you choose, wait for the adhesive to get tacky; again, experimenting before applications can be useful.)
4. Use a dedicated blush or powder brush for this task and dip it into the mix of cut hair, the hair will be picked up by the brush.

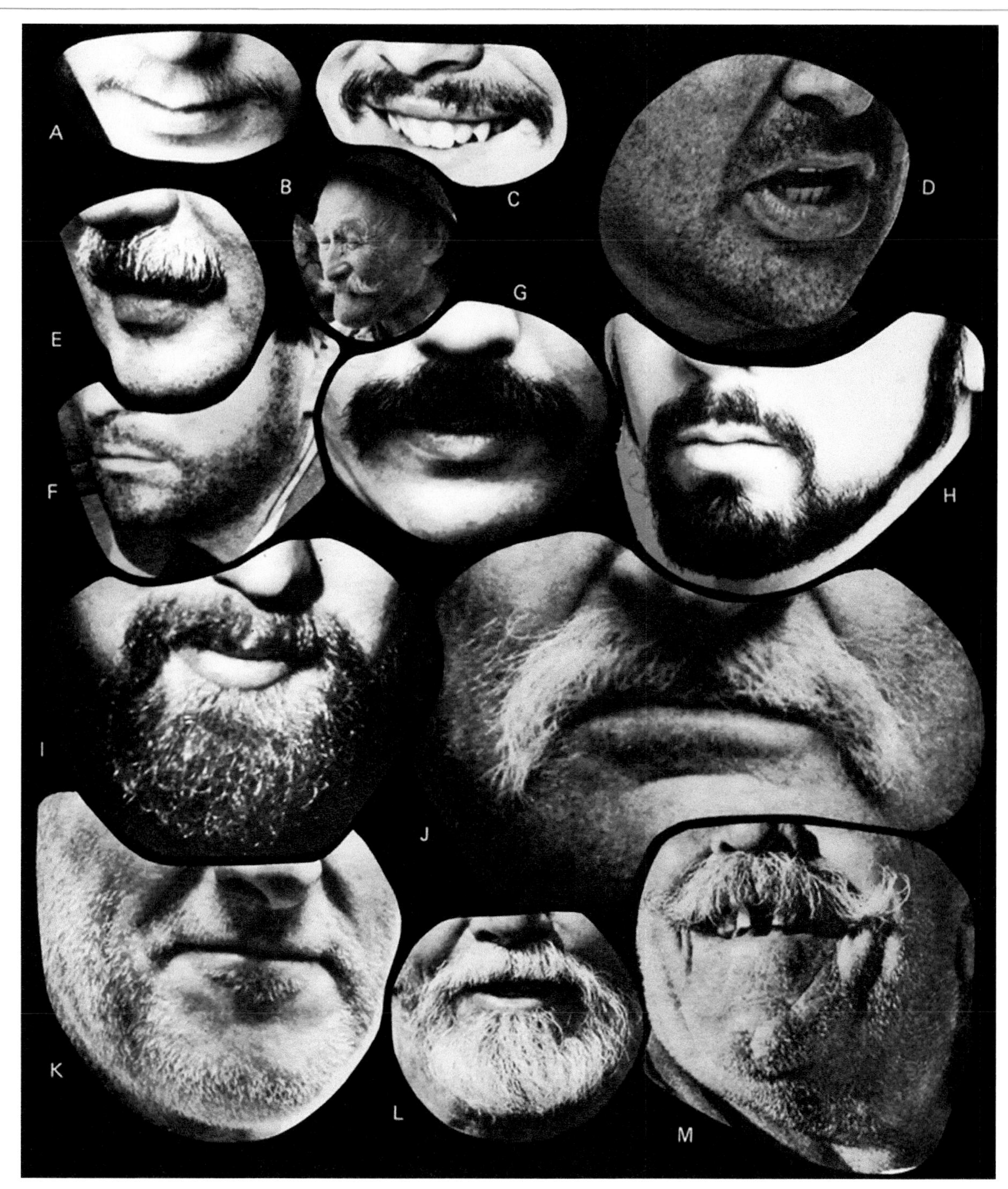

FIGURE 12.11 *Mustaches and beards.*

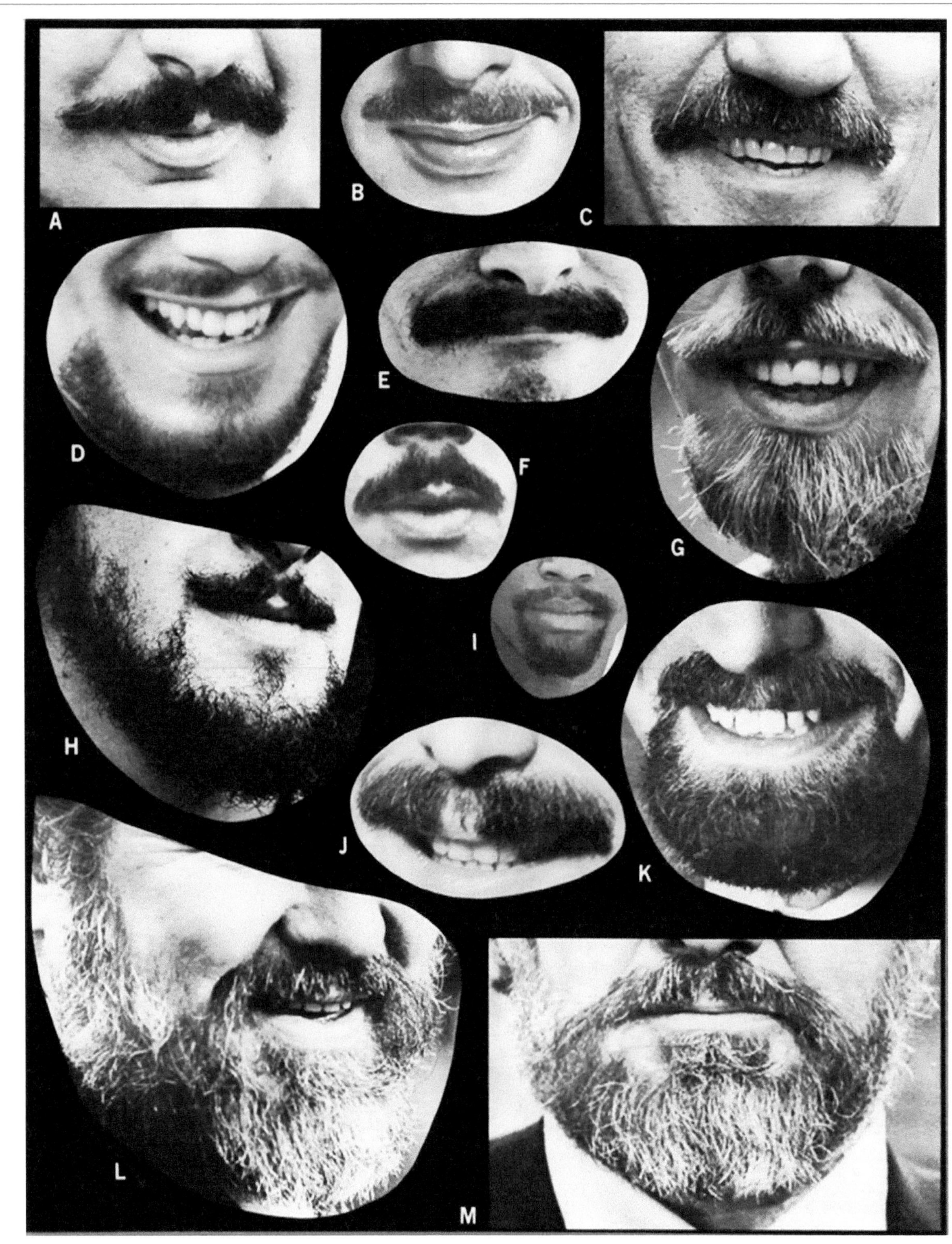

FIGURE 12.12 *Mustaches and beards.*

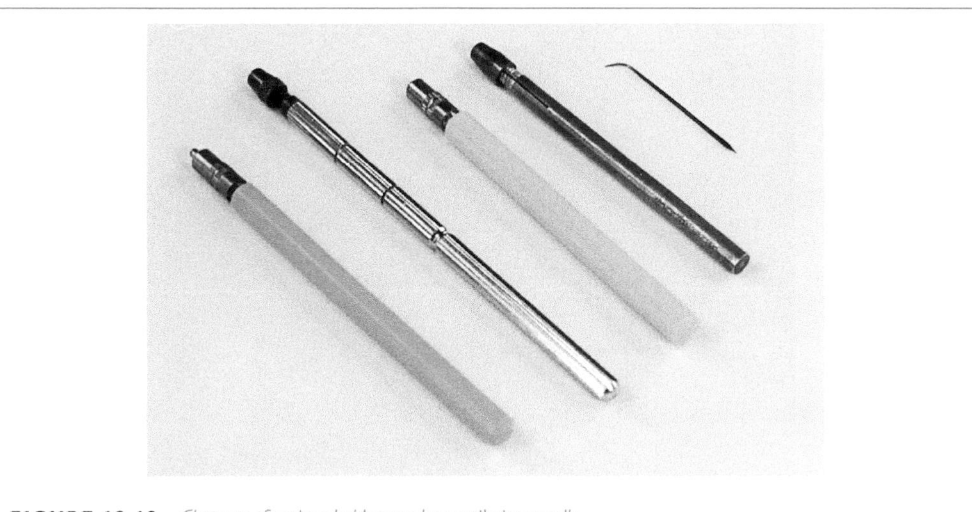

FIGURE 12.13 *Close-up of various holders and a ventilating needle.*

FIGURE 12.14 *Using the drawing card for ventilating. A. Hair is placed on the drawing card with root end toward you. Notice that the angle of the metal teeth on the card is curling away from you. B. The two halves of the drawing card are firmly pressed together. C. Pinch a small amount of hair at the root end and draw it from the card.*

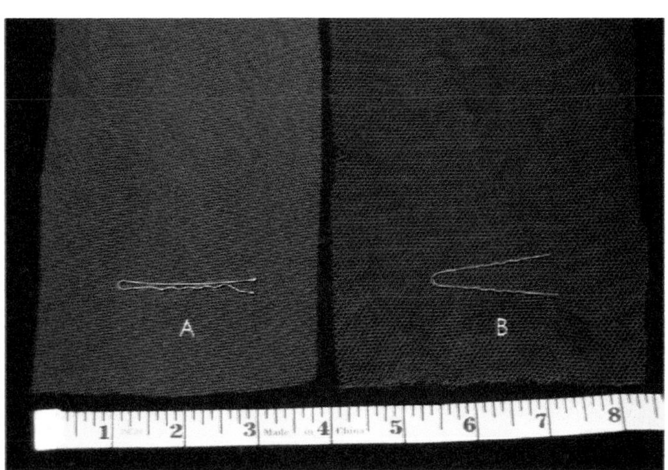

FIGURE 12.15 *Fronting laces. A. Super Lace "Theatrical Quality" from De Meo Brothers. B. 20 Denier Swiss Lace from The Wig Department (formerly Hugo Royer), United Kingdom.*

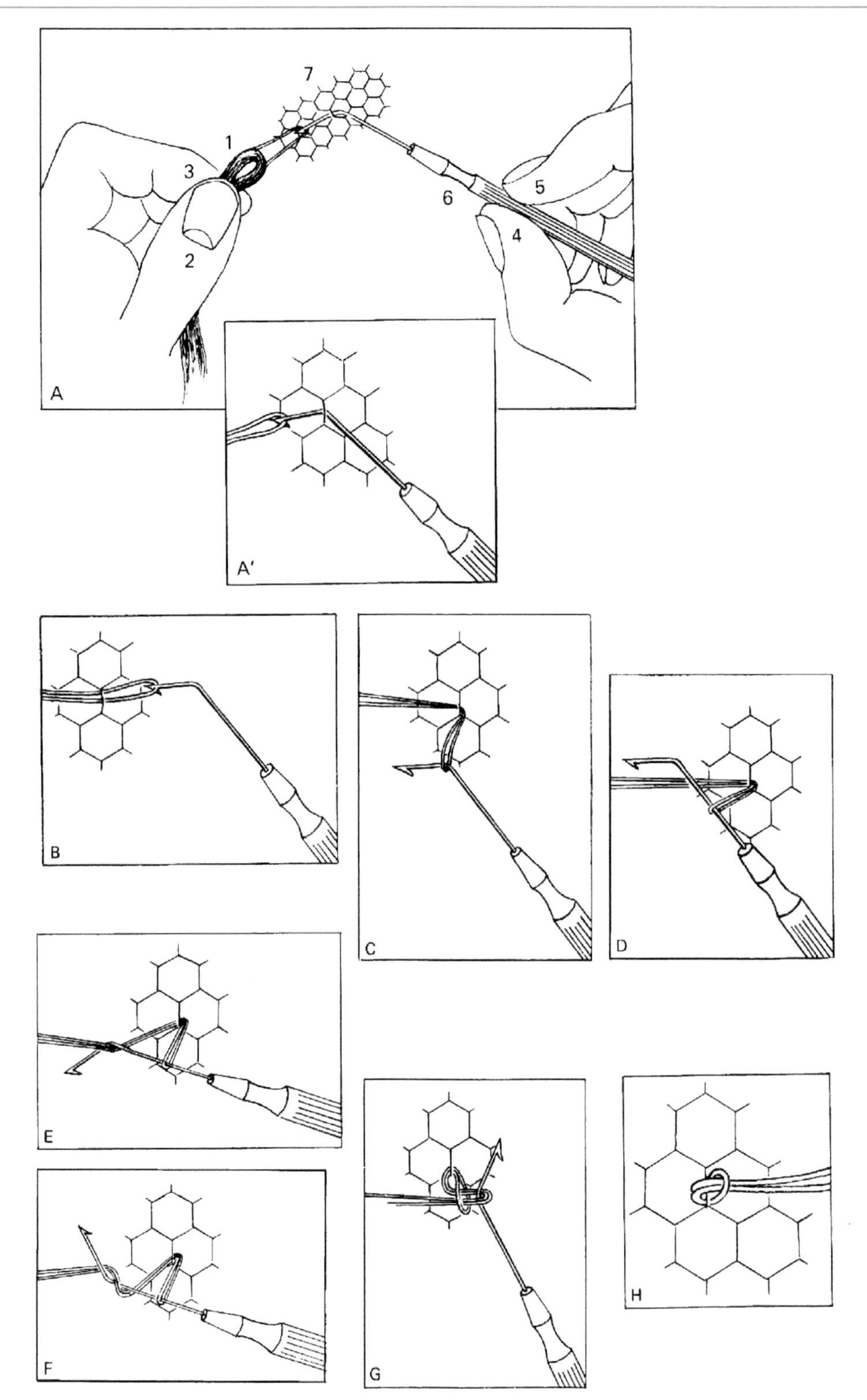

FIGURE 12.16 *Correct handling of hair when ventilating. This diagram shows the progressive positions of the ventilating needle in relation to the hair and the lace when creating the knot used by wigmakers to ventilate hair into wig lace. Notice in Diagram A that the cells are 6-sided and stack one on top of the other creating a row. When arranging lace onto the beard block and/or mustache pattern, this row of cells is placed vertically on the center line of the block. Size of the lace is greatly magnified.*

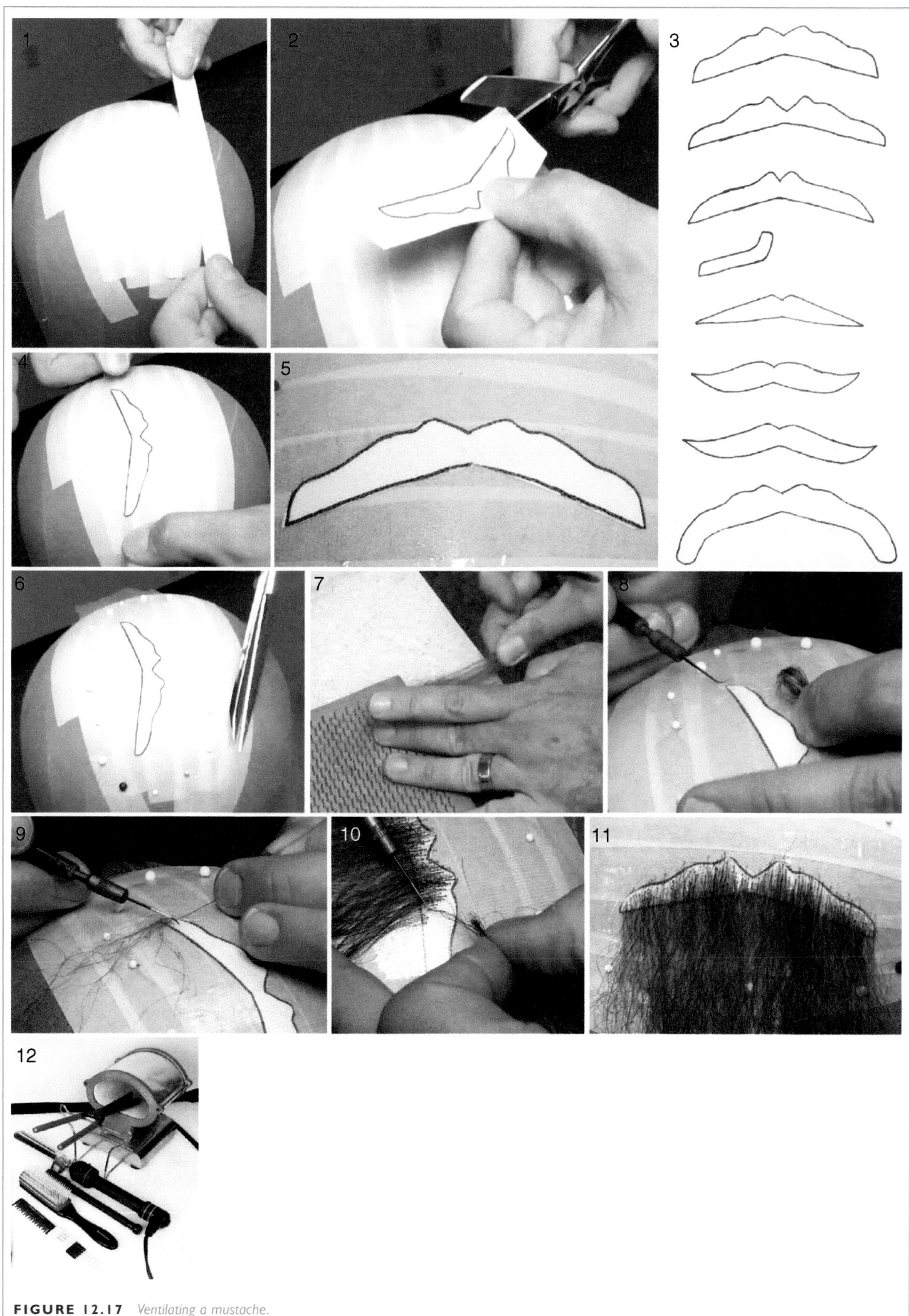

FIGURE 12.17 *Ventilating a mustache.*

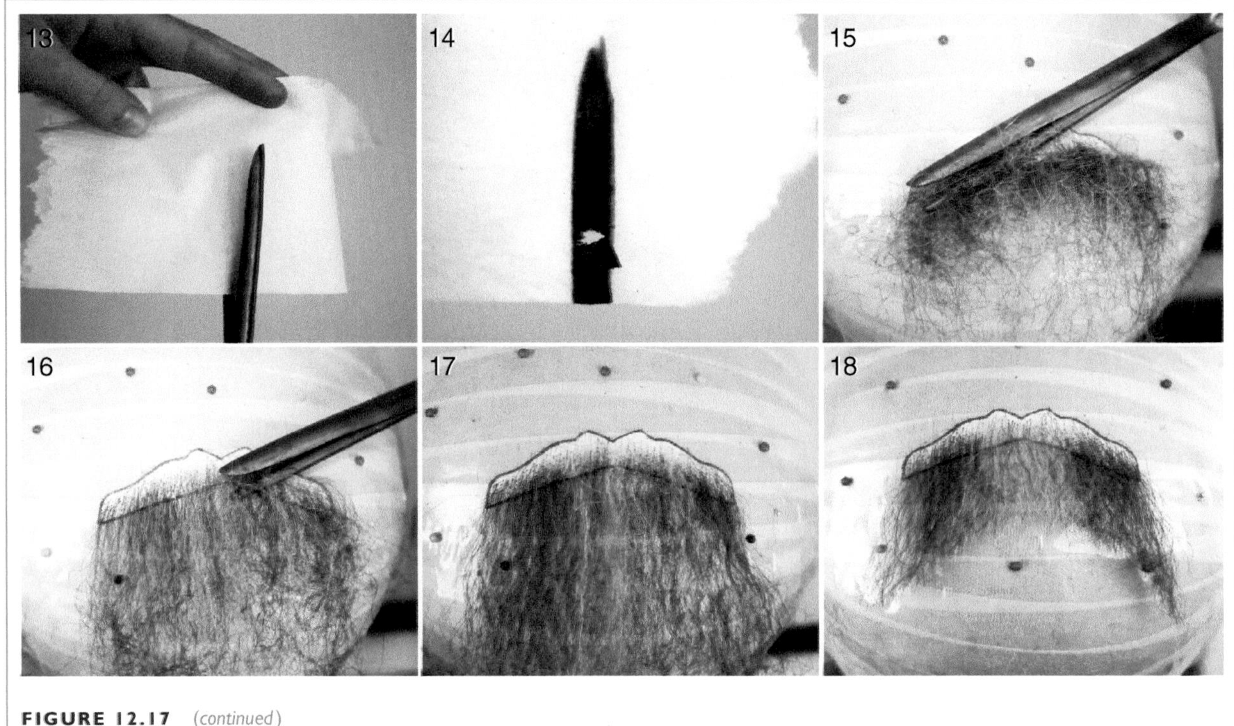

FIGURE 12.17 *(continued)*

5. Quickly apply the hair to the skin with a light pressing or gentle tapping motion. Press the brush with hair directly onto the tacky-glued area. You should be able to observe the hair being adhered to the skin. You can adjust the density by applying more hair to the area while the adhesive is still tacky.
6. Allow the adhesive to dry, then use a clean powder brush to brush off any excess hair. Adhesives suitable for applying beard stubble to the skin include matte lace adhesives such as the Telesis systems (by Premier Products Inc.) and or matte spirit gums. In a pinch the eyelash glue Duo can be used but it tends to leave a slightly shinier surface on the skin.
7. For removal follow the manufacturer's recommendation. Popular choices are Super Solv for the Telesis system, spirit gum remover from Kryolan, and any oil-based makeup remover if you use Duo as your adhesive.

A *beard shadow* effect can be achieved by cutting the hair to an almost powdery consistency. Start by applying a very translucent underpaint of gray, or light brown, to the beard area according to the design. A cream-based makeup, such as Kryolan Supracolor, will work well. Vary the translucency and density slightly in areas to achieve a natural look. You can add dimension by stippling the colors lightly onto the skin using a prepared stipple sponge. Lightly powder the makeup to set it, then apply the finely cut hair over the adhesive in the same manner as the beard stubble process described in the previous section.

The techniques in this chapter can be easily adapted for eyebrows and body hair. For creatures and monsters you can experiment with different fibers to achieve the desired hair effects.

VENTILATING FACIAL HAIRPIECES

Ventilating, also known as "knotting", is the process of tying hair in a knot onto a fine lace. The art of creating ventilated facial hairpieces is necessary if the facial hairpieces are to be used repeatedly to retain a consistent look, or for a reccurring production.

The first step in creating any ventilated piece is to create a pattern, or tracing, of the area to be ventilated. This is called a *hairline tracing*. A hairline tracing can be created for eyebrows, a mustache, sideburns, a full beard, or an entire hairline for a wig (see Figure 12.19).

FIGURE 12.18 *Full beard in sections. Sideburns, mustache, and beard made of real hair ventilated on nylon net. These pieces can be recombed, straightened, or curled and used in various combinations, as illustrated in Figure 12.21.*

WIG LACE

Foundations for beards, mustaches, and goatees are commonly made from wig lace. Wig lace can be manufactured from nylon and/or silk and is generally sold in "theatrical" and "film" qualities. Wig lace is measured in deniers (from 15–40), the linear mass density of a fiber. The smaller the number, the finer the fiber. Film-quality lace is generally listed as 20–30 denier, and the newer high-definition lace can be even finer at 15 denier (see Chapter 13 for more information). This ultrafine lace can be difficult to work with and takes a very delicate and experienced hand to avoid tearing the fibers during the ventilating process. Facial hair for the theater is made from a somewhat stronger, more durable lace with a higher denier. The higher quality nets are thin, fairly stiff, and somewhat transparent, so that when they are glued to the skin they become invisible from a short distance (Figures 8.38, 12.15, 12.20).

1. Ventilating a mustache. Figure 12.17 – Prepare for making a mustache by applying overlapping strips of masking tape to the top of a canvas wig block.
2. Design a mustache shape and draw it on a piece of white paper. Cut this shape out with a pair of scissors. This shape should fit perfectly on the model. Similar to creating a head and a beard hairline tracing, tape a small piece of plastic wrap to the upper lip and draw the mustache shape with a permanent marker. Transfer that shape to white paper.
3. Diagram of a variety of mustache shapes. These can be reshaped and resized for any model.
4. Using clear shiny tape (cellophane or scotch brand), attach the mustache shape to the wig block. Cover the shape completely with overlapping pieces of tape. The shiny tape is preferred by many artists.
5. Place small-celled wig lace over the mustache shape and secure with round glass/plastic headed pins. Imbed the pins completely into the surface of the canvas block. The lace should be placed in a manner where the cells of the lace align (north to south) with the center line of the mustache.
6. Trim the excess wig lace from around the mustache pattern. Leave at least 2 inches of lace all around the pattern.
7. Draw a small amount of hair from the *drawing card.*
8. Fold the top 2 inches of the hair into a loop and hold this between the thumb and forefinger. Pick up one side of the lace cell (see diagram in Figure 12.16) with the hooked point of the ventilating needle.
9. Begin ventilating hair into the lace. It is a good rule of thumb to begin ventilating at the lower edge of the mustache.
10. Ventilating nearly complete. The ventilating needle is seen here picking up one hair at a time.

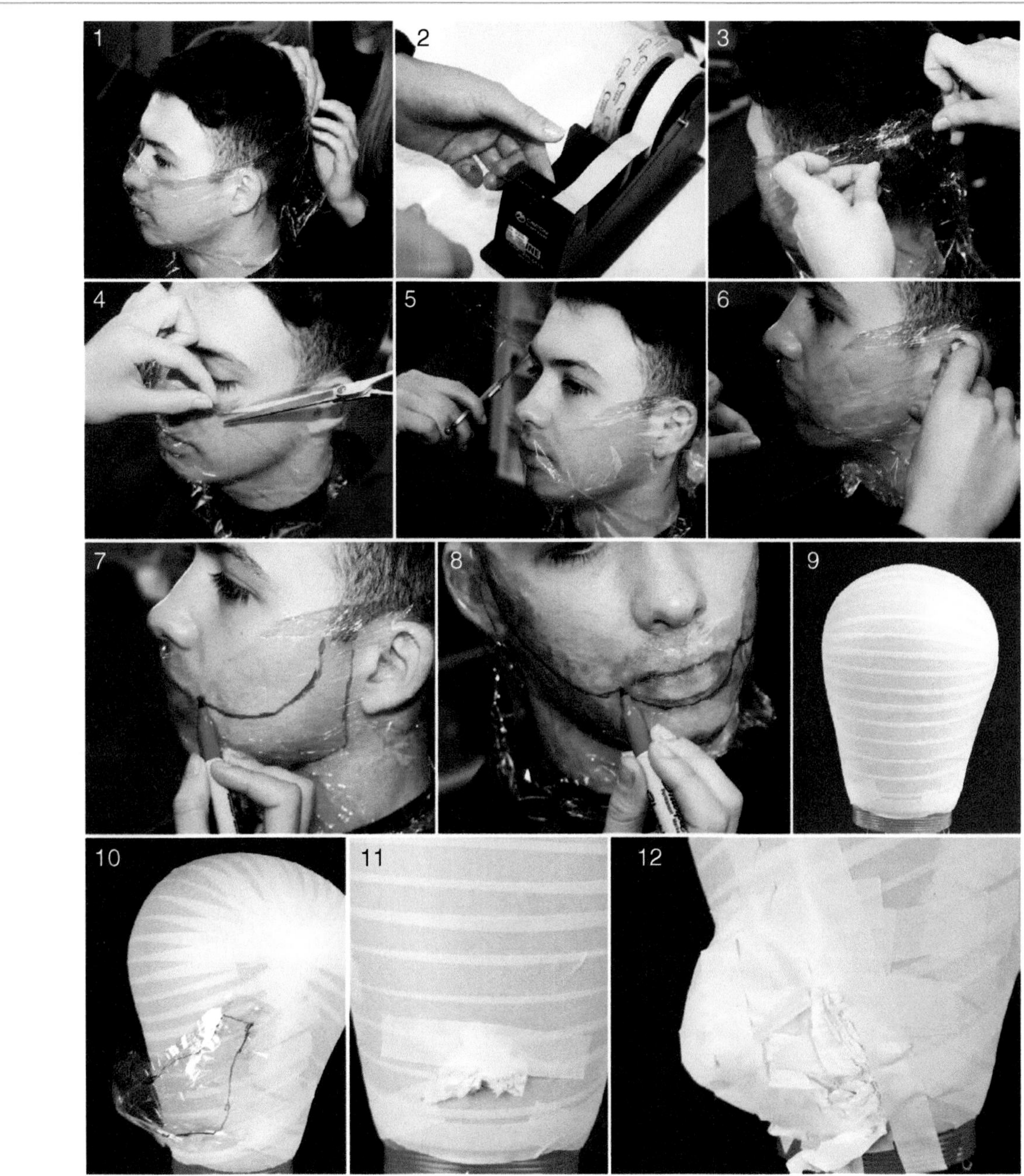

FIGURE 12.19 *Making a beard.*

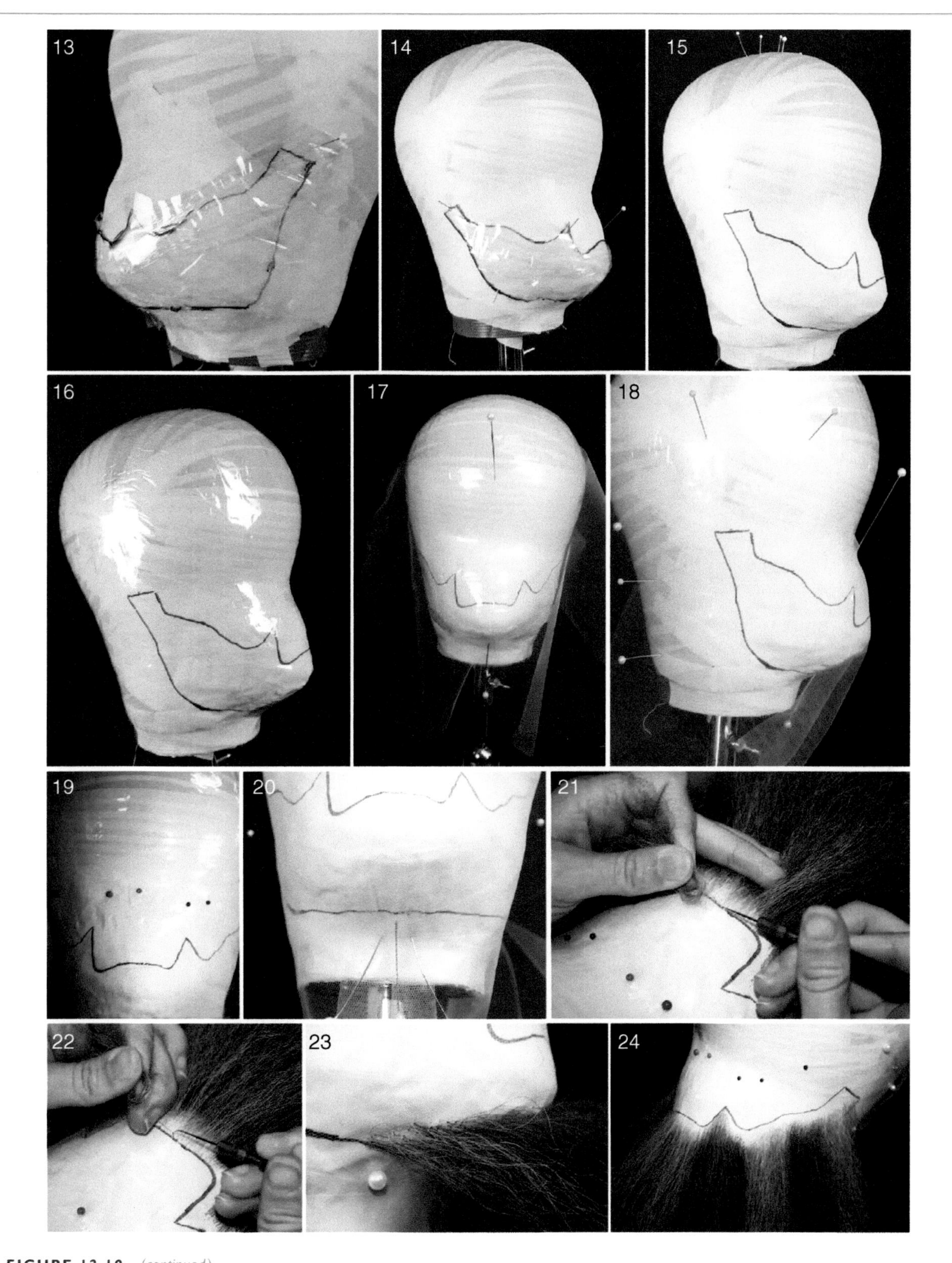

FIGURE 12.19 *(continued)*

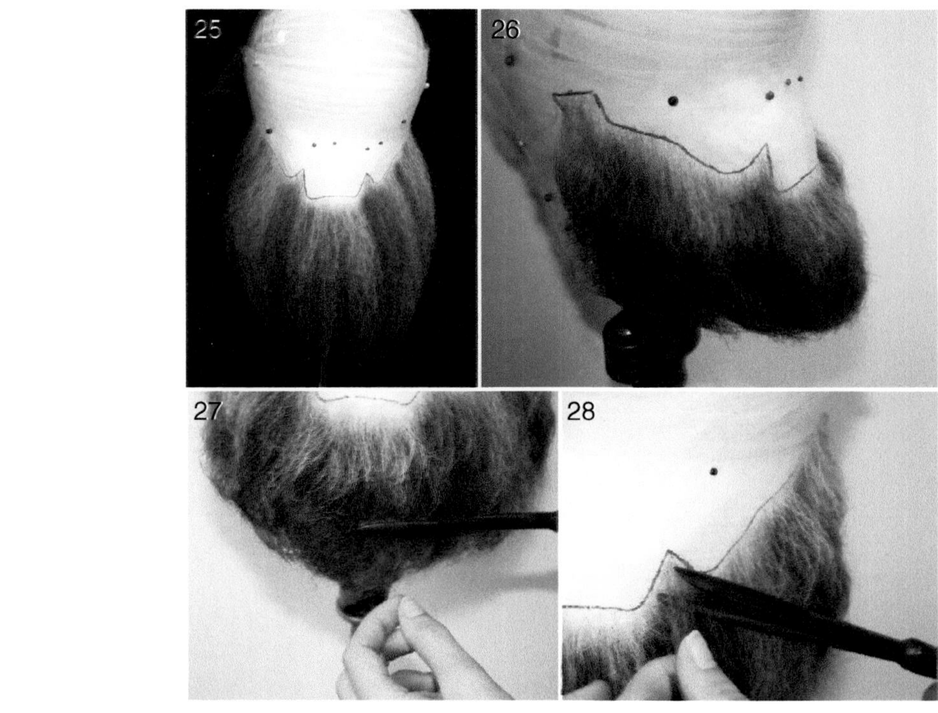

FIGURE 12.19 *(continued)*

11. Ventilation of the mustache is complete. Notice how the hairs at the top edge of the mustache are staggered above and below the line. When creating a natural-looking mustache or other facial hair, a staggered or feathered edge is preferred. At this stage, the mustache should be backcombed aggressively. The hair will look quite matted.
12. Curling and styling tools: Thermal stove and flat iron; electric curling iron; hair brush; 5-pronged lift comb.
13. Test the curling iron on a white tissue.
14. Here the curling iron has burnt the tissue and is too hot to use on hair.
15. Using the curling iron on a mustache that has just been hand ventilated. Notice how unorganized and matted the hair is at this stage in the process. Remember to backcomb the mustache before using the curling iron.
16. Start near the knots, pick up a small amount of hair in the curling iron, and gently draw the iron down the length of the hair. The iron should be opened and closed quickly as it moves through the hair. This action gently organizes the hair, leaving it with a natural curl.
17. The mustache after the hair has been organized with the curling iron.
18. Trimmed mustache. This is a general trimming. The final trimming and shaping should happen after it is applied to the performer (the mustache will be applied in Figure 12.20).

MAKING A HAIRLINE TRACING FOR A BEARD

Tools that are used to take a hairline tracing in Figure 12.19 are:

- Felt markers
- Scotch tape (clear/shiny)
- Food-grade cling wrap.

In this example, a full beard tracing will be taken. The mustache is not included (see Figure 12.19).

Begin by positioning your model in a comfortable chair with room for you to stand and work in front and to the sides of your model.

1. Unroll a length of cling wrap or plastic wrap about 30 inches long, and try not to let the plastic fold up on itself. Place the halfway point of the plastic film onto the center of the chin and gently stretch the film towards the crown of the head. Make sure to not cover the nose. Basically, wrap the chin, mouth, and sideburn area in cling wrap.

2. Tape dispenser with both masking tape and clear shiny tape.
3. Overlap the cling wrap edges at the crown of the head so that it holds onto itself. This will allow you to have your hands free to work. If you are working alone, you can place a piece of Scotch tape at the overlap of the crown just to reinforce it a bit. Again, make sure that your model can breathe freely.

4. & 5. Trim the plastic wrap along the top edge to just below the nose with scissors.

6. Take individual lengths of Scotch tape, about 4 to 6 inches each, and start applying the tape to the cling wrap in the design area, allowing the long edges of each piece to slightly overlap. The pieces will vary in direction according to where you are working, but you want to make sure that the edges are slightly overlapping at all junctures so that cling wrap is completely covered. The end product has no exposed cling wrap. The tape is providing form to the cling wrap against your model's features, essentially creating a form-fitted mold of your model's chin.
7. Using a fine-point permanent marker, trace the hairline of the beard onto the taped surface. You can follow the natural beard line of the model which, even if freshly shaven, can be seen through the Scotch tape and cling wrap, or create a beard outline based on your own design. The beard line should continue below the jawline.
8. The markings on the left and right sides of the face should be symmetrical. Get into the habit of marking the tracing with your model's name and the date you took it, and any other information needed such as show information or other details before it is removed.

(Note: Using your markers, you can include helpful markings such as indicators showing growth direction with small arrows, and potential color changes can be noted, swirls, etc. by using different colored markers.)

This same technique can be used to take a mustache, eyebrow, or sideburn tracing.

CREATING A CUSTOM PADDED BEARD BLOCK

Purchasable blocks can be made from wood or canvas. These blocks can also be full heads on which you can build a custom padded chin (see details below). There are also specialized chin blocks specifically designed for building facial hair in both wood and canvas. Custom foamed blocks can be made from face casts when needed, and in rare cases a plaster cast can be used.

To make the custom padded beard block you will need the following:

- A canvas head
- Masking tape
- Scotch tape (clear/shiny)
- Tissue paper (the gift wrap type)
- T pins
- Permanent marker (Sharpie).

9. In preparation for making the padded beard block, a canvas wig block is completely covered with strips of masking tape. The strips of tape should overlap in a pattern as demonstrated in Figure 12.19.9.
10. Remove the beard tracing from the model, then cut away the excess plastic around the marked edge of the beard tracing with scissors. Leave approximately 1 inch of space between the marked line and the cut edge. Gently place the beard tracing you created onto a prepared canvas block, at the chin area. Notice the void between the plastic shape and the block. This is the area that you will need to "pad out." This term is used to describe the building up of the chin to match that of your actor.
11. Start padding the chin by adding a layer of crumpled tissue paper to the chin area, holding it in place firmly with masking tape covering all the tissue paper. Work in small and thin layers, adding more and more tissue paper to the chin. Check your progress often by placing your molded tracing over your layers until it fits smoothly over the padded block.
12. Once you reach a point where the tracing fits very well and only small air pockets are visible through the tracing, you can take a T pin and poke through the tracing in a gentle stabbing motion, leaving small marks on the masking tape to indicate where you need to add more padding. The more precise and smooth the fit of your tracing and padding is, the better the facial hair will fit.
13. Wig block is padded to perfectly receive the plastic wrap tracing. The beard tracing should fit smoothly on the built-up wig block. There should be no air pockets or uneven surfaces. Once you are satisfied with the fit and the shape of the padded block, remove the tracing and add a final layer of masking tape. Use the same overlapping pattern as discussed earlier to create a smooth surface.
14. After the chin and jawline have been built up properly and the chin area has been covered with a new layer of masking

tape, start trimming the molded tracing to the exact outline of the hairline. Using scissors, cut along the line indicating the exact shape of the beard. If for any reason you want to make some alterations to the shape of your beard, it is easy to do that at this point. Now, pin the molded tracing to the beard block. Make sure it is perfectly centered on the block.

15. Transfer the finished edge of the plastic beard tracing to the taped surface of the block with a permanent marker. Then remove the plastic beard tracing.
16. Cover the entire surface of the block with overlapping strips of clear shiny tape, making sure that this layer has a smooth and even surface. This will prevent the masking tape from rolling, peeling, and getting dirty during the beard making process.

    (Note: The same procedures can be used for other facial hair, such as a mustache or sideburns. It is unlikely that these areas will need to be padded as they have fewer contours.)

BLOCKING THE LACE

Materials Needed:

- Wig fronting lace
- Pins, either sewing pins, or wig points for wooden blocks
- Sewing needle and thread in the color of the beard, or invisible thread for the full beard.

For a Full Beard or Goatee:

17. Drape wig lace onto the block and over the beard shape. This is called "blocking the lace." Position the lace with the grain of the cell pattern running north to south. Place a pin about 1 inch above the center beard line. Stretch the lace slightly downward and under the chin. Hold it down with another pin about 2 inches away from the bottom of the hairline. Make sure the lace conforms to the curves of the chin and lays flat and taut without deforming the lace pattern in any direction.
18. Pinlace in place as indicated on the left and right sides of the face. Place pins outside the style lines at approximately 1 inch from the line. Work symmetrically, left to right.
19. Secure the lace to the beard block by placing pins at intervals of about 1 inch around the entire outline of the beard shape. The lace should lay flat against the form without any wrinkles.
20. Begin forming two to four symmetrical darts under the chin to shape the lace to the block. The point of the darts, known as the "apex," should not extend beyond the tip of the chin. Pin and hand sew the two darts (use a whip-stitch) with the invisible thread by Gütermann.

If the lace now conforms perfectly to the beard block, you are ready to start ventilating.

VENTILATING THE BEARD

21. Ventilating the beard. After drawing a small amount of hair from the drawing card or hackle, fold over the top 2 inches of hair into a small, tight loop. Place the hook of the needle under the lower side of the cell and "hook" one hair, pull it through, and follow the diagram in Figure 12.16 for creating the knot.
22. After drawing the hair through the loop, complete the knot by pulling the hair through the loop, tightening the knot.
23. Close-up of the beard ventilation and color mixing.
24. All facial hair and wigs should be made using a mixture of at least three or more hair colors. This beard is made with a mixture of three colors plus the carefully placed mixed gray tones.
25. Front view of the completed beard before it has been styled.
26. Completed beard after being cut, shaped, and styled.

27. & 28. A curling iron is being used to shape and style the beard.

Preparing the Hair

It is important to know which part of the hair is the root and which is the end. This is more important, however, for wigs than for facial hair. Place one side of the drawing card on the table in front of you so that the teeth are bent away from you. Place a small amount of the hair in the drawing card so that there are 2 to 2½ inches of the *root* end of the hair (facing toward you) hanging over the edge. Place the other half of the drawing card on top of the first side with the hair in it, again making sure that the teeth are pointing away from you. Press down on the drawing cards over the hair so that the teeth mesh together. This will allow you to "draw" the desired amount of hair from the card to ventilate into your project (Figure 12.14a, b, and c).

Place the ventilating needle in the holder. Practice holding your needle as you would a pencil. Roll the needle between your fingers so that the hook on the needle goes toward you and then away from you. Put the needle down in a safe place to prevent it from rolling off the table.

Figure 12.16 illustrates the ventilating technique. Always keep in mind, in ventilating, that your hands must be pulling against each other from the moment the needle catches the hairs until the hairs are knotted. Releasing the tension of the hairs before the knot is tied will probably result in their slipping off the needle. Releasing it before the ends of the hair are completely free of the knot may result in a loose knot, which will then have to be tightened by pulling it with the fingers.

The canvas block with the prepared netting can be held in your lap on a soft pillow or by a wig clamp attached to a counter. (Note: If you find the hair difficult to grip, spray a bit of water on it with a mister.) This is the procedure for ventilating:

1. Pull a small amount of hair out of the drawing cards (Figure 12.14c). Go down the bundle of hair approximately 2 inches and bend it over. This is known as the *turn over.* Pinch the hair (A1) between the thumb (A2) and index finger (A3) of your left hand approximately ¼ inch to ½ inch down the turn over (Figure 12.16a). Allow the ends of the hair to be loosely supported in the rest of your fingers. At first the tension of your pinch will be very tiring, but once you get used to the process, you can tighten and ease up as needed. Now you are ready to ventilate.

2. Take your ventilating needle (A6) in your right hand and hold it as you practiced (Figure 12.16a). Slide the needle through a hole on the netting, passing under or *catching* a bar and come out through the next hole (A7) (Figure 12.16a). Bring the bundle of hair to the needle and catch a few hairs on the ventilating hook (the number depends upon the size of the needle). Pull the hair out of the bundle a short distance (A). With both hands in tandem, slide the hair back through the holes, under the bar, taking care to keep the hook from catching the lace or netting. That can be done by rolling the needle slightly with the thumb and the forefinger in a counterclockwise direction and, at the same time, pushing the needle gently upward against the strand of the lace under which the hook must pass, enabling the smooth side of the needle to pass freely under the strand of the lace without the hook becoming caught in the net. This may take a little practice, but will soon become automatic.
   Then withdraw the hook far enough to clear the lace comfortably (B), but be careful not to draw it too far, or you may pull out the short end of the hair from between the thumb and index finger.

3. Now that you have a loop of hair attached to the needle, move the needle forward and catch the hair in the neck of the needle as illustrated in Figure 12.16C. Roll the hook of the needle away from you so that the hair is wrapped around the neck. With both hands in tandem, pull the hair and needle toward you and swing the needle to the right. You should see or feel the hair on the neck slide up the neck and be caught by the hook of the needle (Figure 12.16D and E). Drop the hook behind the hair and twist the needle one half turn clockwise (Figure 12.16F). Leave your left hand stationary and pull the hair that is held by the hook through the loop of hair still on the needle (Figure 12.16G). Pull the hair all the way through to the right and out of your left hand. If you tighten the tension of the hair in your left hand as you pull the hair out with your needle, the knot will tighten to the bar of the net. You should have a nice, clean knot (Figure 12.16H). The hairs will then lie in one direction, moving away from the left hand. Always move the right hand in the direction you want the hairs to lay.

As you become more comfortable and familiar with the process of ventilating, you will loosen your grip by relaxing your hands, resulting in the elimination of much of the motion in your left hand, letting the right hand and needle do the lion's share of the work. If you are left handed, reverse the hands as described above and pull the hair out toward the left.

The most important part of ventilating is to stay calm and focused and to take regular breaks. Novice as well as experienced ventilators should develop stretching exercises to reduce muscular tension and to avoid more serious physical conditions such as tendinitis and carpal tunnel syndrome.

In making a mustache, always begin at the outer corners and work along the bottom and upward. The top hair should always be the last to be knotted in. When the hair is in, trim the net about ¼ inch beyond the hair. The lace immediately under the nose may have to be trimmed closer than that, but avoid trimming it too close since the edges will eventually ravel and will have to be cut down still further.

You may want to do some preliminary trimming of the mustache before trying it on, for when you finish the ventilating the hair will probably be as long as that in Figure 12.9c. When you are learning to trim and style beards and mustaches, carefully study photographs before you do any trimming at all. If you can find a photograph of exactly the style you want, so much the better. Cut the hair carefully with a good pair of barber's shears, a little at a time. Be sure to try on the mustache before doing the final trimming.

CUTTING AND STYLING OF VENTILATED FACIAL HAIR

Tools Needed for this Task:

Regular hair-cutting shears
Thinning shears
Rat-tail comb
Regular hair-cutting comb
Marcel curling irons in various sizes
Marcel iron oven
Hair spray
Tissue paper or TP.

It is easiest, and recommended, to create facial hairpieces using a pre-textured hair such as crepe hair. If you do so, you can move ahead into styling. If, however, you have chosen hair that doesn't have a texture to it, then you will need to create a texture. This texture will vary according to ethnicity.

1. To create a texture you will need to heat your marcel irons in the marcel oven.
2. Using your rat-tail comb, begin by vigorously backcombing each facial hairpiece until they look almost matted (Figure 12.17.15).
3. Once your iron is heated, you will want to test it on some tissue paper by placing the tissue paper into the iron as if it were hair. If the iron burns, or leaves scorch marks on the tissue paper, the iron is too hot for the hair (Figures 12.17.13 and 12.17.14). It is extremely important to double check the iron temperature *every* time it comes out of the oven, because if the iron is too hot, you can easily burn the hair off. Inversely, if the temperature is too low, the hair will not hold a curl, or transformation. It is recommended that you keep a small sample of the hair you are working with to check the iron's temperature before laying it into the facial hairpiece.
4. Once you are comfortable with the temperature of the curling iron, insert the curling iron into the backcombed hair at the root of the facial hair (Figures 12.17.15 and 12.17.16), and with a clapping motion rapidly open and close the curling iron around the hair. The heat of the curling iron will set the hair in an irregular fashion. It will likely take a few passes over each section to get to a desired texture.
5. Once you have treated all of the backcombed hair in this way, use a wide-toothed comb and gently start combing out the backcombing. You will see that the hair has taken on an irregular wiry texture (Figure 12.17.17).
6. If the texture needs to be more intense, repeat the above steps from backcombing onward as often as necessary to achieve your desired texture.

Trimming the Facial Hair:

1. Using your regular hair-cutting shears, begin cutting the excess hair to give it the basic shape of your design. It is recommended to leave about 25% more length than the desired final result.
2. Use your thinning shears to do the final 25% trimming as they won't leave cut marks, and will result in the hair looking more natural.
3. At this point you might want to use your heated curling iron to gently bend the tips of the hair under, and give the facial hair their final direction. It is a fine dance that you have to do between your curling iron work and hair cutting to get the desired result.
4. Once you are satisfied with the results apply a *light* mist of hair spray, but don't overdo it.
5. Remove the facial hair from the block, and trim the excess lace off. Leave approximately ¼ inch of lace beyond the knots. It is easier to trim more off than it is to begin again, so start cautiously.

APPLICATION OF VENTILATED PIECES

A full beard can be applied in one piece or, if desired, cut into sections—usually three for actors or five for singers—each section being applied separately. In dividing the beard into sections, cut the lace very carefully, avoiding, if possible, cutting any of the hair. (Figure 12.18 shows a beard cut into three sections, plus a mustache.)

1. Items needed (Figure 12.20):

Appropriate adhesive such as matte spirit gum or Telesis glue systems:

Glue brushes

Rat-tail comb

Barber cape or shampoo cape

Damp piece of chamois leather about 3 x 3 inch in size (not shown).

(Note: It is advised that anytime you work with adhesives you protect the actor's costume or clothing; it is very difficult and sometimes impossible to remove glues out of fabrics, so take precautions.)

2. & 3. Dry fit the beard by holding it up to the model's face. This will allow you to practice placing it where it fits best. Visually note the area where you will need to apply the adhesive.

4. Starting at the center of the chin, apply spirit gum, covering an area from one side of the mouth to the other. Let the adhesive get tacky. The time it takes for the spirit gum to get tacky depends on the type and the consistency of the adhesive, so it is beneficial to do a small test area for timing. (Note: Aim to use the thinnest layer of adhesive possible.)

5. Attach the beard to the chin area first. When the glue is at the right consistency, lightly press the facial hair into the glue. Using the tip of the rat-tail comb under the hair, press only the lace into the adhesive. You will also notice that the lace as it comes into contact with the glue will get translucent and seems to disappear into the skin. Film lace tends to disappear better than heavier lace.

6. Now, apply more adhesive to the cheek.

7. Placing the tip of the comb under the hair, press the lace into the adhesive.

8. Apply adhesive to the sideburn area.

9. Press the lace into the adhesive with the tip of the comb.

10. Apply a small amount of adhesive to the top edges of the lace wherever it has not been adhered well. Gently press the lace into the adhesive.

11. & 12. Dry fit the mustache.

13. Apply adhesive to the upper lip area, keeping it within the lace edge of the mustache.

14. Place mustache onto the adhesive.

15. Using the tip of the rat-tail comb, press the lace into the spirit gum.

16. Model wearing the completed mustache and beard.

DRESSING VENTILATED PIECES

When the beard or the mustache is securely attached, it can be combed with a wide-toothed comb. But remember, in combing any hairpiece, always to hold the comb at an angle so that there is no possibility that the teeth will dig into the net foundation and tear it. This means holding it at the reverse angle from the one usually used in combing your own hair. Also, when the hair is fairly long, always begin combing at the ends and work toward the roots. Human hair in hairpieces of any kind becomes matted and tangled much more easily than the same hair would while growing on the head. This is because half of the hair is going against the natural direction of growth. In other words, the hair is knotted somewhere between the roots and the end, both of which are extended outward. A human hair is not quite the simple, smooth filament it appears to be—there are little scale-like projections, all going in the same direction. You can usually feel the difference by running a hair quickly between your thumb and forefinger in the direction of growth and then against the direction of growth. When hairs are not all going in the same direction, these tiny scales catch onto each other and cause matting. Therefore, special care is needed in combing any kind of hairpiece made from human hair.

If the hair does not naturally fall just as you would like it to, comb it with water, set it (pushing it into waves or making pin curls—on the ends of beards or mustaches—for example), and let it dry before recombing it. When the hair is dry, spray it with hair oil or hair spray, or apply a gel or cream dressing, then comb the hair and do whatever trimming and shaping may be needed. If you want the hair to look dry or unhealthy or dirty, you can use colored powder or cake makeup to dull it.

Human hair can also be curled with a curling iron if you prefer. Heat should never be used on synthetic hair. Steaming is preferred. In order to maintain the wave in synthetic hair, it may be necessary to spray it with hair spray. The ends of a mustache can be shaped with mustache wax, derma wax, or hair spray.

REMOVING FACIAL HAIR

Items Needed:

Remover brush, soft bristled and appropriate in size

Appropriate glue solvent (remover)

Cotton balls or soft tissue

Shampoo cape to protect the actor's costume.

To remove the beard or the mustache, dip your remover brush into the solvent, and press the bristles into the lace edge. Be careful not to drip the solvent over other things. Start by applying the remover on one edge of the facial hairpiece, and work the brush under the lace with a gentle circular motion to dissolve the glue, and the facial hair will come off quite easily.

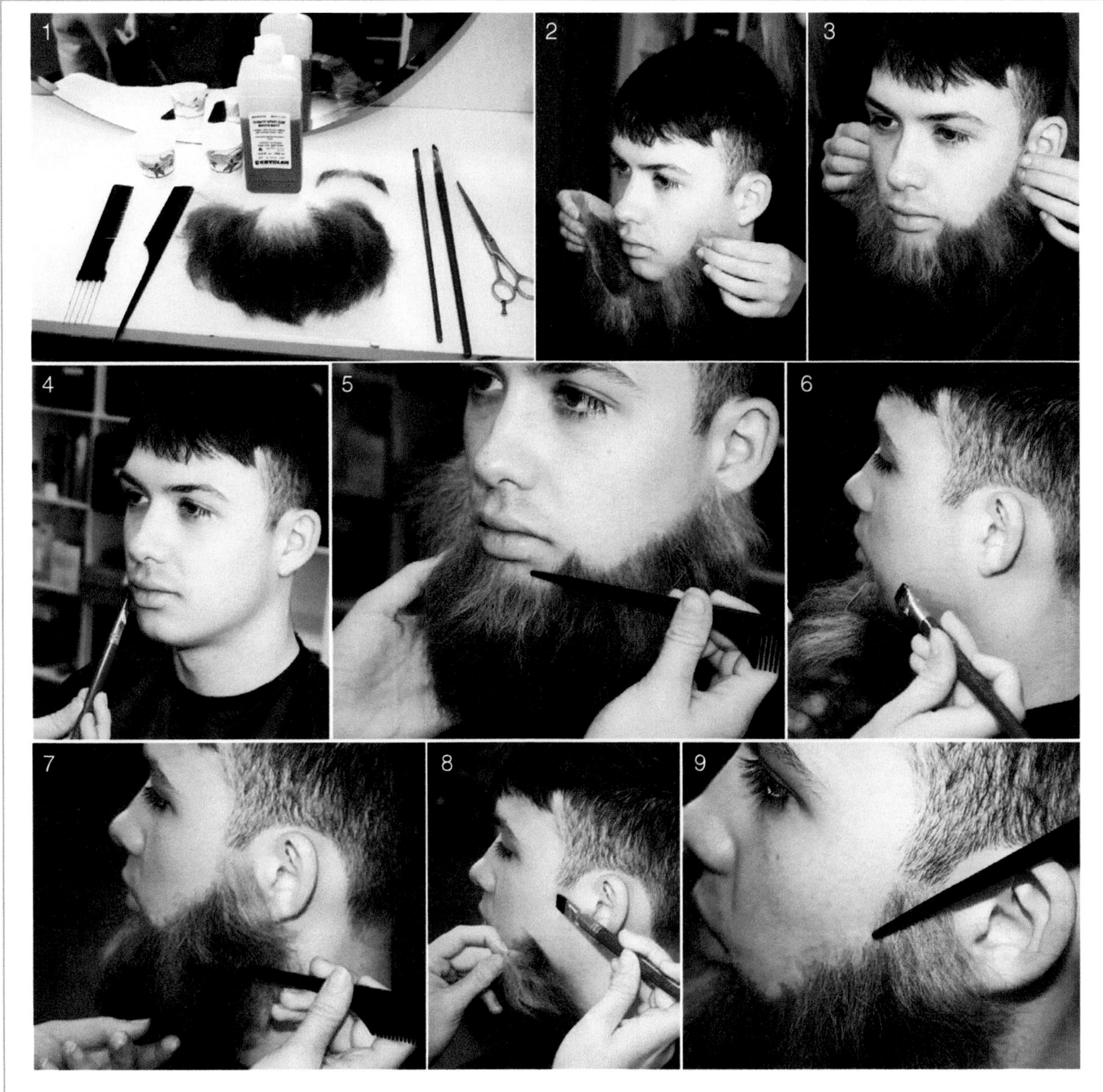

FIGURE 12.20 *Applying ventilated facial hair.*

Don't force it, let the remover do the work. Any good lace or net is very delicate and requires considerable care in handling to avoid stretching or tearing it. Keep flooding it with the remover until the gum is softened and the lace comes up by itself.

Once the facial hair has been removed, set it aside in a safe location. Use cotton balls dipped in small amounts of solvent to remove any remaining glue residue from the actor's skin. Be extremely careful when removing facial hair around the eye area, so as not to get solvent in the eyes. Never remove facial hair by pulling it off your actor without using a glue solvent, as you risk damaging the skin as well as the facial hairpiece.

(Note: Use the solvent appropriate for the gluing system you have chosen. Protect your actor's costume or clothing with your shampoo cape.)

CLEANING AND SANITIZING FACIAL HAIR

1. Items needed:

   Appropriate solvent for your chosen glue system

   91% isopropyl alcohol

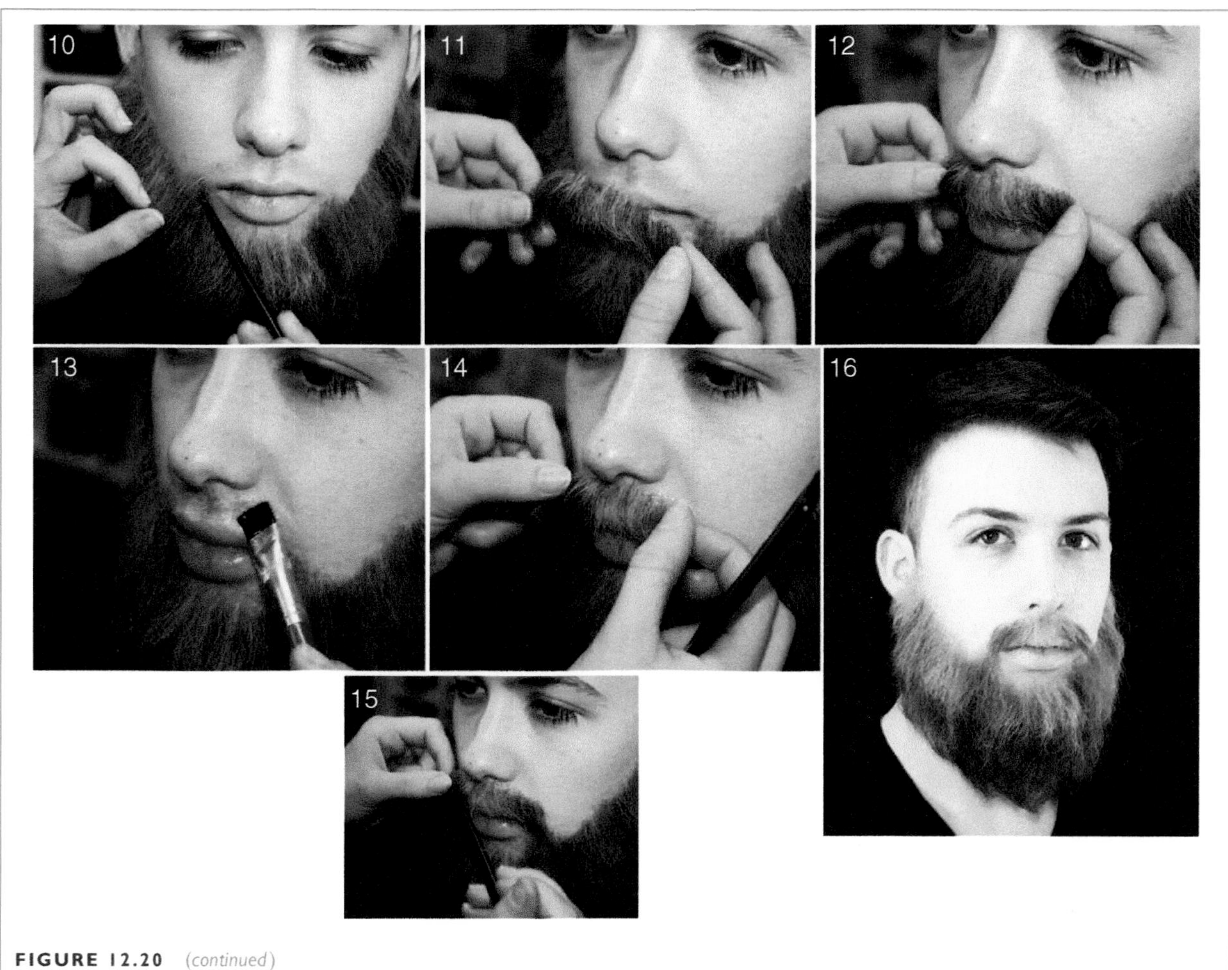

FIGURE 12.20 *(continued)*

Soft-bristled toothbrush

Saucer, or plate

Paper towels.

The used facial hair should be cleaned as soon as possible after the application to remove any remaining glue on the lace and to sanitize it for next use.

2. Add just enough of the appropriate glue solvent to lightly cover the saucer, or plate.
3. Place the facial hair with the lace side down into the remover and let it sit for a few minutes.
4. Take the facial hairpiece out and place it onto a double layer of paper towels.
5. Using the soft-bristled toothbrush, dipped into remover to moisten it, press the brush into the hairpiece, and use a very soft circular motion, massaging the facial hairpiece into the paper towel. The paper towel will absorb the softened glue residue, and lift it off the lace and hair. Repeat two or three times with a fresh paper towel (or part thereof). Be careful not to overly disturb the style of the facial hair. Once the facial hair appears to be clean you will want to sanitize it.
6. Using a separate saucer (or clean the one you've used), pour a light layer of isopropyl alcohol into the saucer.
7. Lay the facial hair, lace side down, onto the alcohol. You can lightly tap the hairpiece with the toothbrush to remove any last glue or solvent residue. The isopropyl alcohol will not remove your styling.
8. Lift the hairpiece out and pat it dry between a few paper towels, being careful not to rub or disturb your styling.

Let the facial hair air dry, and store appropriately.

FIGURE 12.21 *Versatile beard. Late nineteenth-century beard styles made by combining the four ventilated hairpieces shown in Figure 12.18. The same hairlace wig was recombed and used throughout.*

9. Your ventilated facial hair is now ready for the next use. Restyle only if necessary.

Storage of Facial Hair:

1. Facial hair should be stored in a well-ventilated area. *Never* store hairpieces in ziplock plastic bags as they do not allow airflow and mold can grow in humid climates.
2. You can pin facial hairpieces onto cork boards, or pin them on regular printer paper and store them in binders.

Additional Thoughts:

- Consider building full beards in four sections: the goatee, two large sideburns and the mustache. This technique allows the four sections to be used a full beard, or as individual pieces (see Figure 12.18).
- Play with color choices, and don't match the beard color too closely to the actor's main hair color, as this can look artificial.
- Don't ventilate the facial hair too thickly. Vary the texture slightly in areas.
- Don't overblend colors, as this could result in the beard color looking muddy.
- Historical hairstyles vary greatly, even within a historical period, so take the time to carefully research your design.
- Remember—longer facial hairpieces can be cut shorter, and can be adapted to fit different periods.

CHAPTER 13

WIGS

The hair is always an important element in any makeup and is invaluable as a means of suggesting period, personality, and age. There is so much effort required for collecting research, developing a character analysis, and creating makeup designs that failure to make the hair suit the character can compromise an otherwise effective makeup. If you are creating a likeness of a famous individual, then the appropriate research should guide you in the right direction. If you are creating a new character, then your research should include several style possibilities for that character. Thorough research and planning are vital to the design process and will serve you well in your collaborations with the costume designer, director, makeup designers, lighting designer, and the actor, as you develop a style that is appropriate for the character. You have many options with which to achieve the hairstyles. You can use the actor's natural hair, you can use wigs, or you can use a combination of the two.

If your actor's hair is not suited in length, texture, or color for styling in the ways the role they play demands, a wig is a good option. If you are doing historical period productions or are working with large groups of people, wigs can be an expedient choice and help maintain continuity.

NATURAL HAIR

Cutting

There are times when cutting the hair is the simplest method of achieving the correct hairstyle for a character. If actors are being sent to have their hair cut, present the hair stylist with visual references of the desired style. It would be advisable to meet with the hair stylist beforehand, or attend the styling appointment, to answer any questions that may arise.

Occasionally the style required might be so unflattering to modern eyes (though appropriate for the period) that actors may well object to having their hair cut. This can also occur if actors are involved in a play and doing commercial or film work at the same time where they are expected to maintain a certain style for continuity purposes. In most professional settings, the actor's manager and production representatives will work out any physical appearance issues as part of the actor's contract. The solution to an appearance issue may be using a wig, or hairpiece.

Coloring and Texturing

Another design option for creating the hair for a character is the addition of color. There are three methods for accomplishing this: permanent, semi-permanent, and temporary color.

Permanent color is as the name implies. To minimize the chances of irreparable damage to the actor's hair, it is *strongly* recommended that a professional cosmetologist who has experience coloring hair make such a change. Please note, hair that has never been exposed to harsh chemicals, as those involved in coloring, permanent waves, or relaxers, will take the color much better than hair that has been processed. Be aware that over-processing can cause damage to the hair.

Semi-permanent color is often used to temporarily color graying hair to help it blend in with the natural hair color. Semi-permanent color can be used to change an actor's hair color if the run of the performances is limited to one or two weekends,

FIGURE 13.1 *Johnny Depp as Sweeney Todd from the film, Sweeney Todd: The Demon Barber of Fleet Street. The actor is wearing lace hairpieces and extensions in combination with his own hair. The lace pieces were applied to the front hairline and curly extensions were clipped onto his own hair, then pinned in place. The worksheet explains that his natural hair was curled with Redkin Fresh Curl Boost before the extensions were added. Makeup design by Ve Neill.*

Source: Courtesy of Paramount Pictures.

SWEENEY TODD MAKE-UP STEPS

1. CLEAN FOREHEAD WITH KIEHLS BLUE ASTRINGENT.

2. APPLY LACE FRONT HAIRPIECE AND EXTENSIONS

3. BOOST FROM ROOTS TO END WITH REDKEN FRESH CURL BOOST AND TWIST AND SCRUNCH AND HOLD DRYER TO DRY THEN CLIP PIN IN PIN CURLS.

4. COVER RED SPOTS WITH PALE YELLOW

5. APPLY BEN NYE CS-3 SHADING CRÈME TO EYES,CHEEKS & FOREHEAD.
USE 20-30-40 TO SHADE UNDER CHIN.
CONTINUE WITH DARK COLORS AROUND EYES.
PURPLE, CHARCOAL AND RED.

6. APPLY MEDIUM FOUNDATION
KETT HYDRO AIRBRUSH MAKE-UP FOUNDATION
7 DROPS OF HO3
7 DROPS OF HO1
7 DROPS OF MIXER AIR COLOR
AVOID SIDE BURN AREA.
CLEAN AIRBRUSH WHEN DONE

7. AFTER AIRBRUSH APPLY SIDE BURNS ON RIGHT SIDE THEN GO TO THE LEFT SIDE

FIGURE 13.2 *Makeup application worksheet for Johnny Depp in the film, Sweeney Todd: The Demon Barber of Fleet Street.*

Source: Courtesy of Ve Neill.

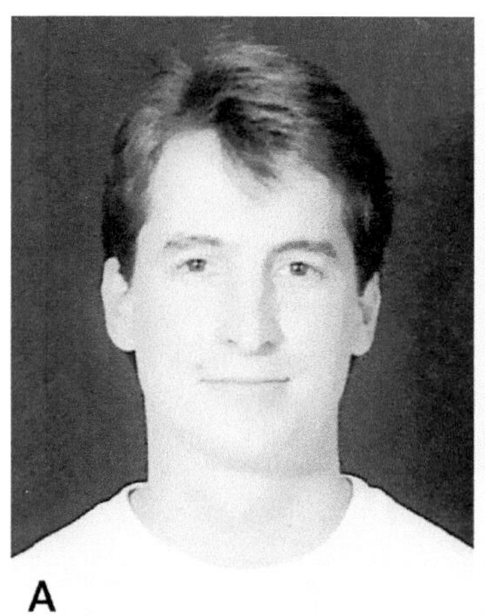

A B

FIGURE 13.3 *Opera student makeup. Matthew Smith as Mangus in the opera The Knott Garden at the Cincinnati Conservatory of Music. Before and after. Makeup: wax nose, wig, facial hair by Lenna Kaleva.*

or if using permanent color is not an option. If you intend to use a semi-permanent color for an extended run, expect to refresh or re-color the hair every week and a half to two weeks. This will largely depend on how often the actor washes his or her hair.

Temporary hair color comes in a variety of forms including liquid, mousse, spray, gel, and alcohol-activated palettes. It is available at most beauty supply stores and websites, and is the easiest coloring option. It simply washes out with regular shampoo. You can successfully change the hair color from light to dark with this product but lightening dark-colored hair would best be achieved with a spray-on color. Temporary color should not be used if actors have a tendency to perspire profusely. The color will lift from the hair as they sweat and it will stain the skin and the clothing.

You should always follow all directions. Preparation and careful application is a must with hair-coloring products. Some of them will stain the skin and all will stain fabrics. In the case of most permanent colors, it is important that you also use proper ventilation as the chemicals involved often have a very harsh scent. As always, if you do not feel comfortable doing the coloring yourself, contact a professional.

For characters whose hair would be expected to look dull and lifeless, face powder the color of the hair can be dusted on, or a little cake makeup, liquid body makeup, or a palette of hair paint of the desired shade can be applied with a sponge. If the hair is to look stiff and matted, it can be heavily sprayed with a liquid setting lotion or hair gel, shaped with the fingers, and dried with a hairdryer and diffuser. When a stringy, dirty appearance is called for, using hair conditioner not only creates that look, but the actor can condition their hair at the same time.

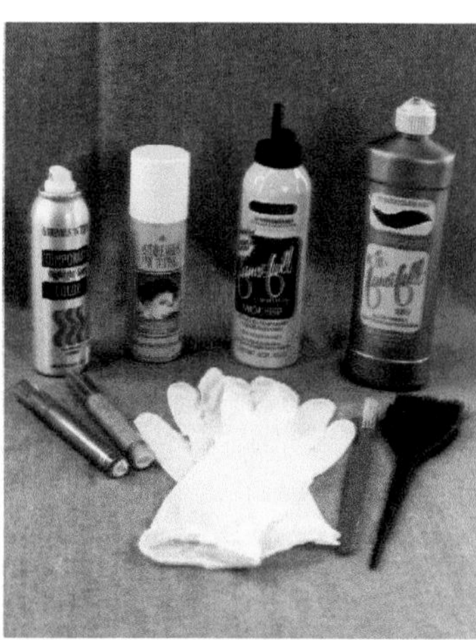

FIGURE 13.4 *Coloring products and tools. Steaks 'N Tips Temporary Highlight Spray Color, Fanciful Temporary Haircolor Mousse and color rinse.*

Graying

There are many products on the market for adding gray color to natural hair. There are sprays, sticks, creams, liquids, and alcohol-activated palettes. They come in many shades, including silver and white, but do not always look natural on everyone. One of the major concerns with hair whiteners is that flat white and gray can often appear to have a bluish cast or can turn chalky on dark hair colors. Hair whitener applied over dark hair may require a warmer yellow or orange tone mixed into a base. It is to your advantage to test your colors under performance lighting when possible.

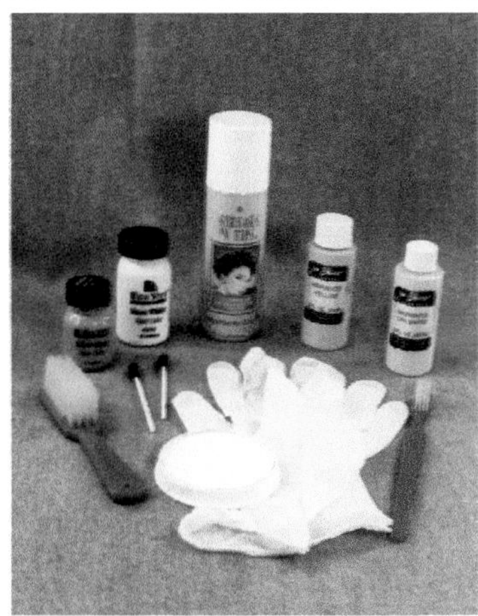

FIGURE 13.5 *Graying products and tools. Ben Nye Hair Color in Snow White and Silver Gray, Streaks 'N Tips Temporary Highlighting Colors, Joe Blasco Hairwhite Yellow and Off-White, Kryolan Aqua color White.*

When choosing a graying product, consider the hair styling process prior to and after it is grayed. Most problems occur when petroleum- or oil-based hair styling products are used. With the exception of aerosol colorants, most graying formulas will simply not adhere to these styling products. Even when using spray-ons it is difficult to retain the intensity of the color after the hair has been combed or brushed through. If gray hair color needs to be applied over styling products, a water-soluble brand will provide a more suitable surface on which to paint.

Aerosol colorants are not recommended for actors if head coverings and touching of the hair are part of the action within the performance. These spray-ons, when dry, can produce a rather comical powder-puff effect, sending dust-like particles floating through the air. Color sticks can be substituted for adding streaks or coloring specific areas. Liquids can also be used for overall graying effects, but will, on occasion, come off on hats.

No matter what kind of graying product you use, it is important that you avoid blending color into the skin around the hairline. A medium- or soft-bristled toothbrush is an excellent tool to assist you in accurately applying fine streaks of color in the hair. Toothbrushes are particularly useful for applying small amounts of color to the hairline at the temples and sideburns and to eyebrows and facial hair. A disposable mascara wand is another handy tool that will allow you the same control. For covering larger areas, a very soft-bristled brush, such as a baby brush, can be used. Be sure to protect the costume by covering it with a smock or cape. Many of the graying products have an oil base and will not easily wash out of the clothes.

Here are some tips for applying color to the hair:

1. Spray-on products can be used as directed or sprayed into a small container and applied with a toothbrush. If the spray-on color is to look natural, it is important that you carefully comb through the style after the color has dried.
2. Liquid colors should also be applied with a brush or toothbrush by pouring the color into a bowl or dipping the brush into the color, blotting the excess on a towel or tile, and brushing the color into the hair. Liquid color can be combed after it has dried. (Note: Liquid graying products must be mixed well or shaken vigorously before application.)

   The alcohol-activated hair paint palettes are moistened by adding 99% alcohol and they can be applied with the same tools as the liquid colors. Alcohol-based makeup resists rubbing off and moisture once it is dry.
3. Stick colors should be applied by carefully drawing the color through the hair. Comb or brush as necessary.
4. Cream or pancake makeup of the appropriate color can also be used and applied with a makeup brush or with a toothbrush. The pancake makeup will require water to make it work. Dip the brush into the water, tap off the excess liquid, and scrub the brush over the pancake. Apply as with liquid color.

Shoe polish is not recommended as it can damage the actors' hair (some actors, however, find shoe polish a useful tool). Using white powder or cornstarch is also discouraged, as it will have the same dusty effect as spray-on hair color.

HAIRPIECES

A hairpiece is by definition small (see Figure 13.6). It would be added to existing real hair, or a wig, and integrated into a hairstyle. Hairpieces can come in all sorts of different shapes and styles, from small round pieces to rectangular pieces, and even dome-shaped pieces can be found. Hair extensions fall in this category as well. The pieces should be matched in color and texture, as closely as possible, to the main hair. When building a hairpiece notice the base shape, or area to be covered. Estimate the length you want, and the color that you need to match, before you purchase the hair. You can measure, or trace the needed shape and transfer the measurements, or tracing, onto the canvas block.

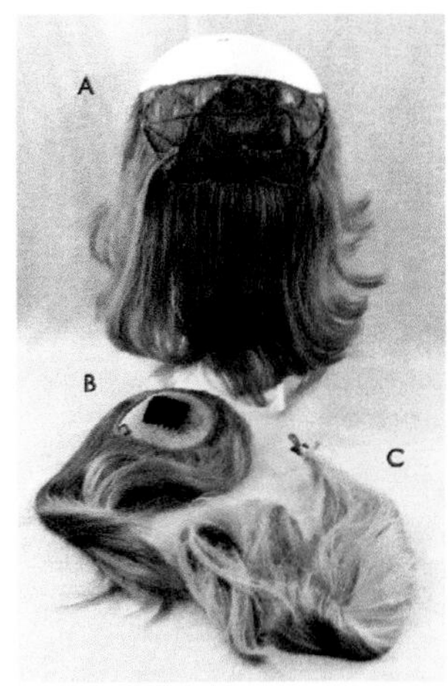

FIGURE 13.6 *Hairpieces. (top to bottom) Handmade hairpiece from weft, chignon, hair extension.*

FALLS AND CHIGNONS

Falls are hairpieces used to lengthen the back of the hair. A full wig can be used as a fall if it is set back on the head and the natural hair in the front is blended into the style.

A chignon is a hairpiece that is used as an addition to the natural hair. It can add height, volume, and depth to a style. It can be used as extra curls, braids, or buns.

A switch is a type of chignon that is also used as an addition to the natural hair. It comes in the shape of a ponytail and is made of wefting. It can be shaped into a bun, but it is most often used as a braid or a length of curls. It is also quite useful when you need to lengthen an existing ponytail. Attaching falls and chignons to existing wigs can improve the versatility of any company's wig stock.

MAKING AND USING HAIRPIECES

Take measurements of the anticipated shape of the hairpiece.

This exercise will demonstrate how to build a rectangular hairpiece 3 inches wide by 5 inches long (see Figure 13.7). Materials Needed:

- Masking tape
- Clear tape
- Canvas block and table clamp
- Sewing pins
- Sewing needle and thread in appropriate color
- Hair weft in appropriate color
- Tape measure
- Pencil and eraser
- Finger shield.

1. The canvas wig block has been covered with overlapping strips of masking tape. Mark the 3- x 5-inch shape of the hairpiece onto the top of the wig covered wig block. The taped area will need to be somewhat larger than the hairpiece. This is necessary to protect the canvas block from getting permanent marks on it.
2. The final hairpiece pattern shape has been drawn onto the masking tape..
3. Two lengths of 4 oz. commercially made human hair wefting is being used. One length is measured to fit around the outer shape of the rectangle, the other length is cut to the length of the inner zig-zag section. Wefting is often sold in a double strand with a zig-zag machine stitching holding the two strands together. If the hairpiece appears too dense the double strands can be separated by releasing the stitching.
4. Begin by laying the weft along the outer edge of the rectangular shape drawn on the wig block.
5. Pin the weft to the four corners of the outer rectangle first. Slightly overlap the ends, then cut the weft.
6. Sew the ends of the weft together using a needle, a finger shield, and matching thread.
7. Fill in half of the inside of the rectangle in a triangular pattern, starting at the perimeter to the center intersections, then reverse the direction of the weft. Pin securely.
8. Now pin the other half in the same manner, making sure that the weft touches at each central intersection and is securely pinned down.
9. Once the pinning is completed, begin sewing each intersection.
10. When all intersections have been securely sewn to each other, your hairpiece is finished.
11. Finished hairpiece.
12. If you are going to place your hairpiece directly onto a person (not into a wig), you will need to lift the piece

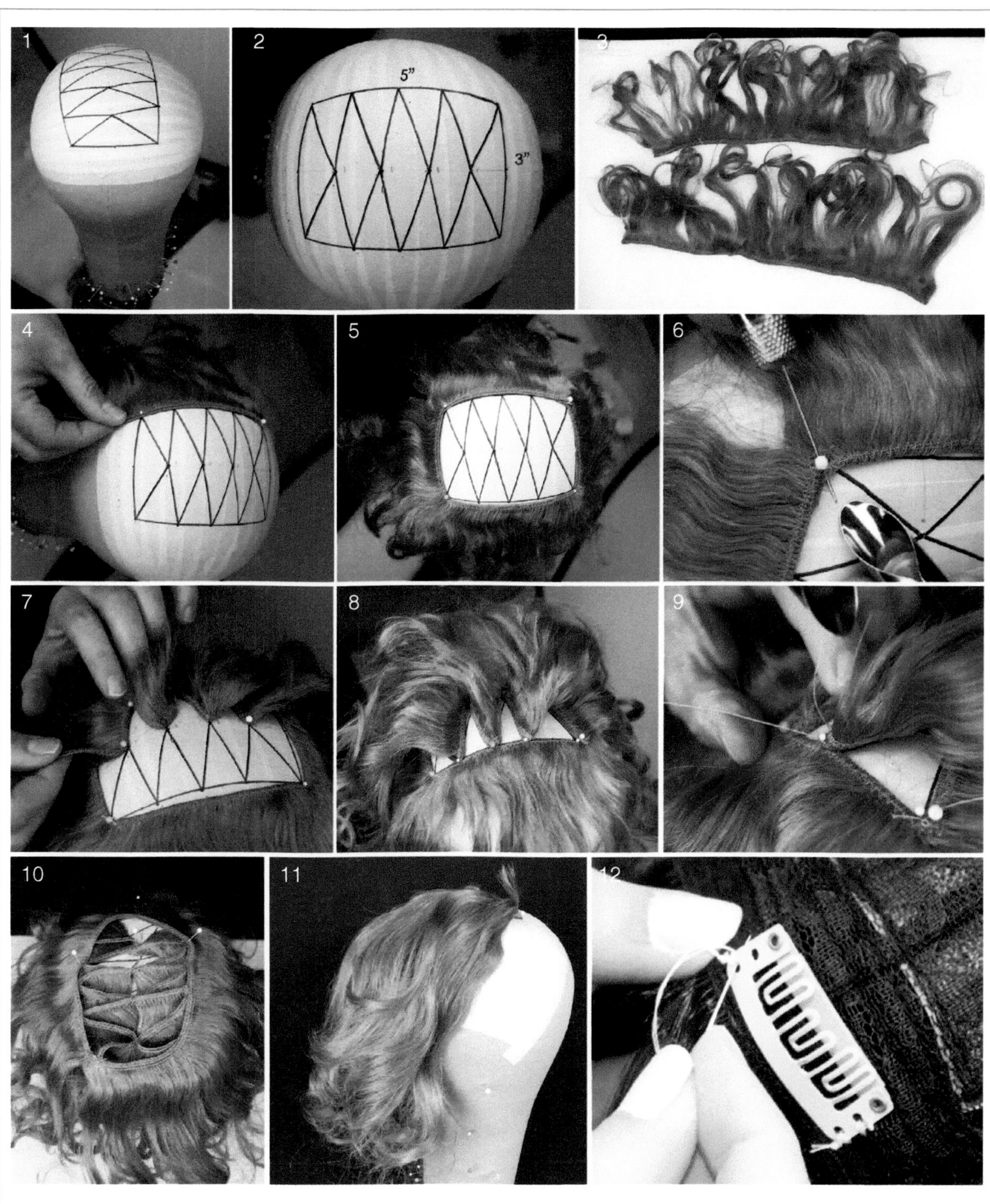

FIGURE 13.7 *Making and using hairpieces.*

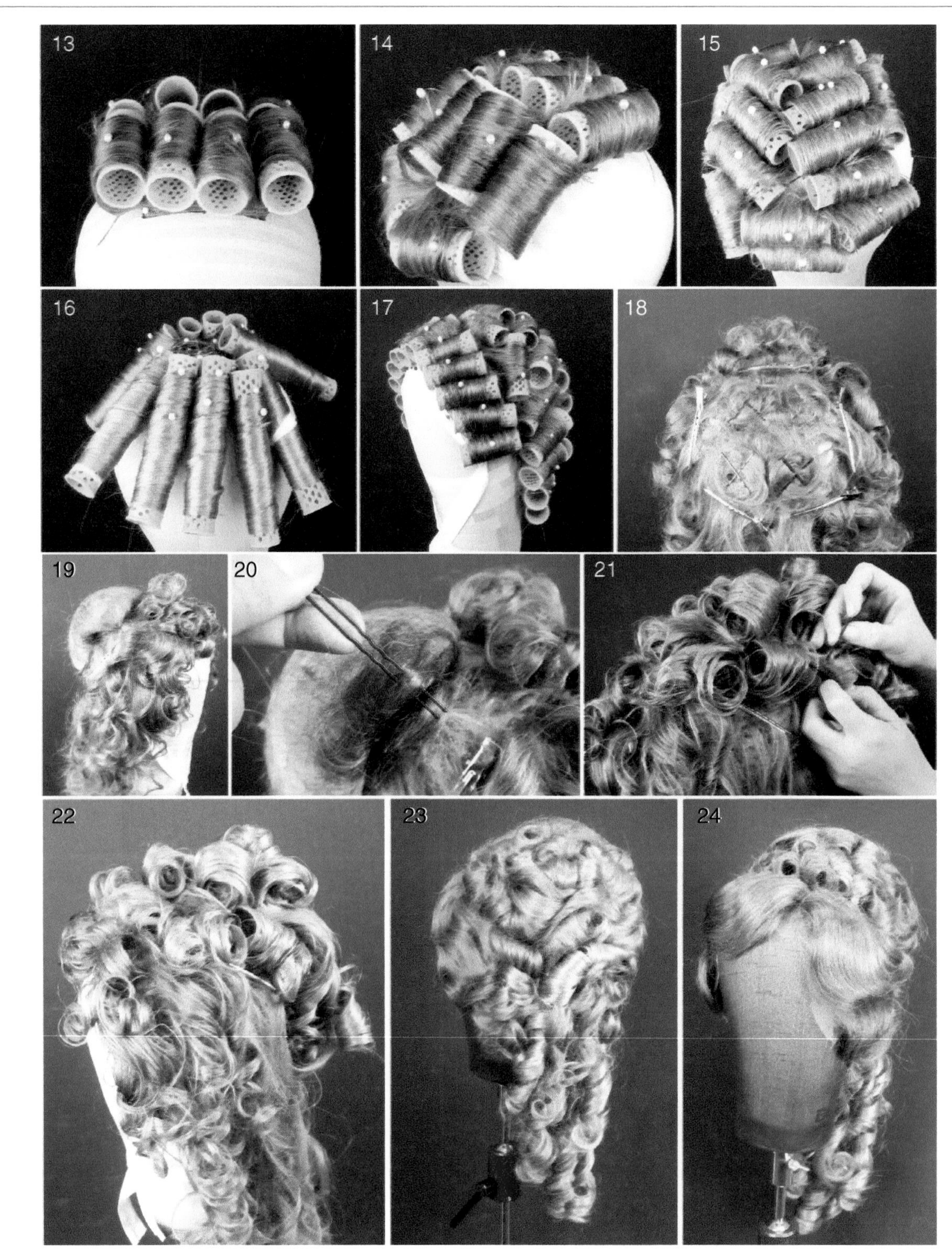

FIGURE 13.7 *(continued)*

from the block and sew toupe clips along the edge of the backside of your hairpiece, before you style it (image by Epic Cosplay).

If you are adding the hairpieces to a wig, you can style them at this juncture.

The following hairpieces are being prepared to be integrated into a base wig that will become a hairstyle from the Edwardian period.

After they have been set in rollers, lift each one from their block, and use hairpins to integrate it into the wig.

13. Small hairpiece, set in yellow rollers.
14. Second small hairpiece set in rollers.
15. Third and largest hairpiece set in rollers.
16. This hairpiece is a chignon and longer than the other three. It is being curled with spiral rollers and will become the long curls that hang onto the shoulder.
17. The base wig in curlers.
18. In an effort to create extra height on a wig, a stuffed pad of loose hair called a *rat* is first attached to the wig. The wig is prepared to accept the rat by creating a flat area with a circle of pin curls.
19. The rat is placed over the pin curls.
20. The rat is secured to the wig with hairpins.
21. After removing the hair rollers, the hairpieces are attached to the wig with hairpins, bobby pins, and/or hair clips.
22. The base wig with hairpieces.
23. The completed Edwardian-style wig (back view).
24. The completed Edwardian-style wig (front view).

ANATOMY OF A WIG

The ultimate compliment to a wigmaker and wig stylist is when no one can tell the actor, or person, is wearing a wig. Your work should never be distracting from the performance of an actor either on stage, or on the big screen, and should not be too difficult for the actor to work in. Our work should be supporting the actor in their character.

In general there are two main styles of wigs in the entertainment industry—custom-made wigs which are mostly handmade, and commercial wigs which are usually made using machines.

Both types have a few subcategories that we will be exploring in this chapter.

Commercial wigs, or those that you can buy in a local wig store, are generally mass fabricated in the eastern regions of the world (you can check the labels). The hair will either be a synthetic fiber, like Modacrylic or Kanekalon, or it will be human hair.

It is important to know that most synthetic wigs are not heat resistant, and cannot be curled using a curling iron. In recent years there have been synthetic fibers coming onto the market that can tolerate a moderate amount of heat, but follow the manufacturer's recommendation and test each fiber, regardless of the claims on the packaging.

FIGURE 13.8 *Faith Prince as Ursula from the Disney Theatrical Productions Broadway production of The Little Mermaid. This wig used a variety of hairpieces to create this gravity defying wig. Hair and wig design by David Brian Brown. Makeup by Angelina Avellone.*

Source:* *Photograph by Joan Marcus.

Human hair wigs can be treated and styled just like any human hair. This type of wig, with proper care, will last a long time.

Another aspect of wigs to familiarize yourself with are the various fronts. This means whether the wig has lace at the front hairline (called a lace-front wig), or has a hard sewn edge (known as hard-front wigs) (Figure 13.11).

Lace-front wigs are designed to have a natural transition into the human skin by the addition of a very fine lace at the front of the wig where the hairline is located (Figure 13.12). The ultimate goal is that the lace and the ventilated hairline blend into the skin, giving a natural appearance.

You can purchase or build both lace-front wigs and hard-front wigs. In general, commercially made lace- and hard-front wigs will have a much thicker appearance than fully custom-made wigs. There is simply more hair built into a commercial wig. While this might sound advantageous (more hair for the money), that amount of fullness often appears unnatural. The quality of the work also makes a significant difference. The lace on machine-made lace-front wigs is designed to last a long time. It is thicker, and will show more than a truly custom-made lace-front wig. High-quality wigs will need to be re-fronted more often, because the lace is finer, but it will not be as visible.

Let's take a look at how a traditional commercial hard-front wig is constructed. You will usually see two main sections.

1. The top of the wig consists of a harder plastic (Figure 13.9a). The hair is inserted by a machine and is intended to give the illusion that the hair is growing out of the scalp.
2. The second section, or back of the wig, is where wefts (Figure 13.10) are sewn to vertically aligned elastic ribbons.

You may also find elastic adjustment ribbons to make the wig slightly bigger or smaller.

Take a look at the hairline of a hard-front wig (as in Figure 13.19) and observe how the weft is sewn to the underside of the wig foundation. This is done to disguise the hard-front of the wig. Study how thick the materials are, and how they contribute to the overall thickness, and weight, of the wig.

A commercial lace-front wig will have a lace material (often a plastic or hard synthetic lace) attached in front of the wig, and a ventilated hairline, trying to duplicate a natural hairline. The back of the wig can still have a wefted section (see Figure 13.10).

The anatomy of a custom-made wig can vary greatly. Whether creating period wigs, medical wigs, partial wigs, wigs to resemble male balding patterns, or wigs to cover hair loss, each one will have its own characteristics. Every wigmaker will develop their unique patterns and techniques, and will take into consideration the ultimate use of each wig they create.

Let's start by analyzing how a wig sits on a human head, and how the set of measurements are related to the fit of the wig, and wig prep.

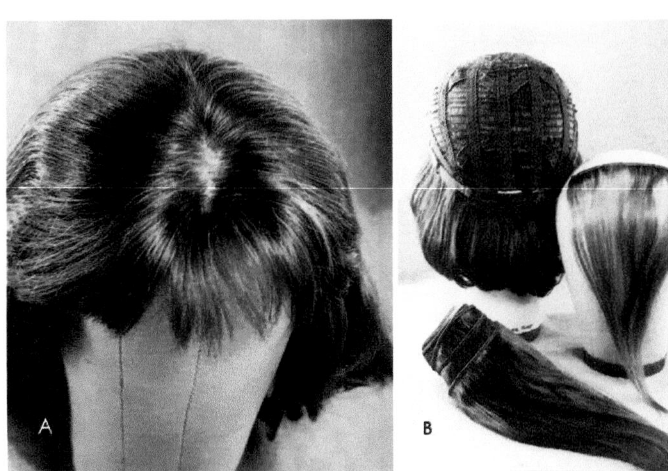

FIGURE 13.9 *Commercially made wigs. A. Rubber crown of a commercially made wig. The hair has been punched into the rubber. B. Wefting (clockwise from the left) A commercially made wig, a short piece of weft, wefting as it can be purchased in a bundle. The elastic at the center back of the wig is used to tighten the wig to fit the actor.*

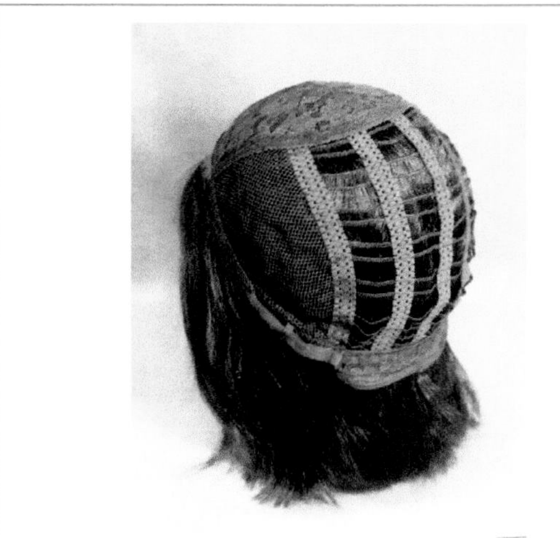

FIGURE 13.10 *Interior construction of a commercially made wig showing the rows of machine applied wefting.*

FIGURE 13.11 *Hard-front wig worn by actor Andrew Carlson as Cyrano de Bergerac.*

FIGURE 13.12 *Lace-front wig worn by actor Brendan van Rhyn as Frank N. Furter.*

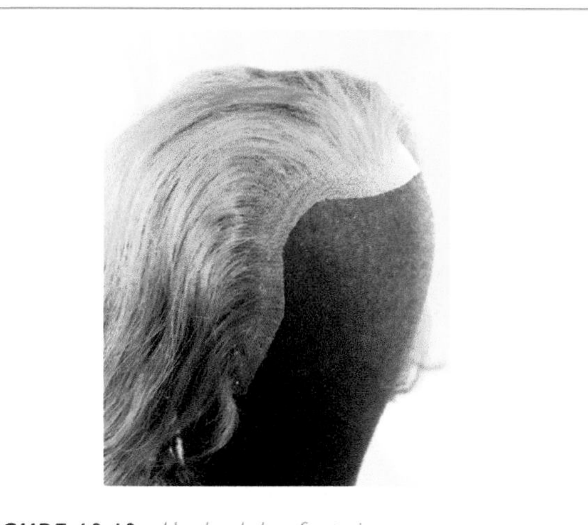

FIGURE 13.13 *Handmade lace-front wig.*

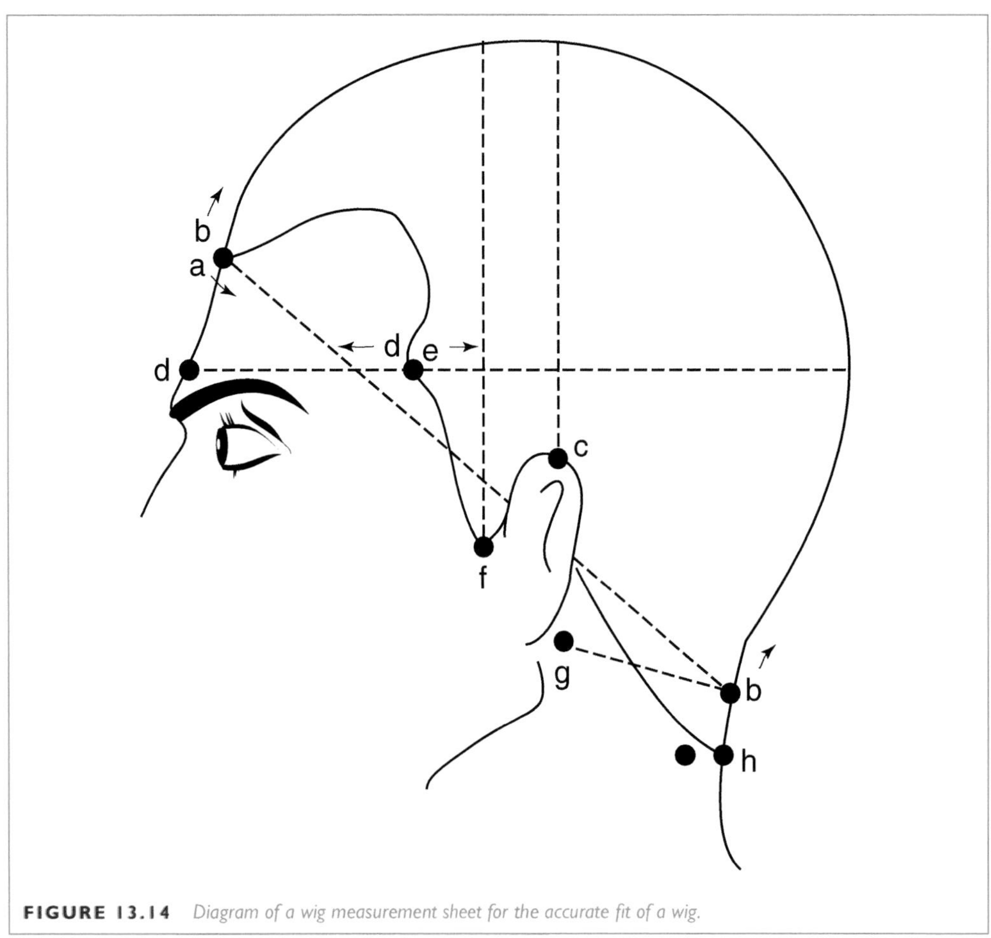

FIGURE 13.14 *Diagram of a wig measurement sheet for the accurate fit of a wig.*

WIG MEASUREMENTS AND INFORMATION

(Note: Remember to add an extra ½ to 1 inch to your measurements if the performer has hair that reaches center back or longer *or* is at least shoulder length and thick!)

a. Around the head (hairline) _________
b. Over the top (hairline to nape) _________
c. Ear to ear (over the top) _________
d. Temple to temple (front) _________
e. Temple to temple (back) _________
f. Sideburn to sideburn (over the top) _________
g. Bottom of ear to bottom of ear (back, over nape) _________
h. Nape (back, bottom hairline on neck) _________

Hair information:

Color number: human _________ synthetic _________
Highlights human _________ synthetic _________

Texture: ______________________________
(thick, fine, naturally curly …)

Length: ______________________________
(top of shoulders, center back, short man's cut …)

Other notes:

Wig Measurement Information Sheet (Figure 13.14)

The first step in this process of adding a natural hairline to a wig is to take a set of measurements, and a tracing.

On an average head, the widest point a wig will need to fit is around the circumference from the point approximately 1–2 finger widths below the hairline in the center of the forehead, over the ear and to the back center of the head above the occipital bone. This will be noted as the head circumference—measurement "a" on the measurement sheet.

Follow the instructions on the measurement sheet (Figure 13.14) for a full set of measurements. Over time, and with practice, you might find additional measurements to include.

Wig-making Kit

- ventilating needles
- sewing needles
- tape measure
- retractable tape measure
- sewing cotton
- thimble
- mounting tongs
- stitch catcher
- mounting hammer
- block pin
- comb.

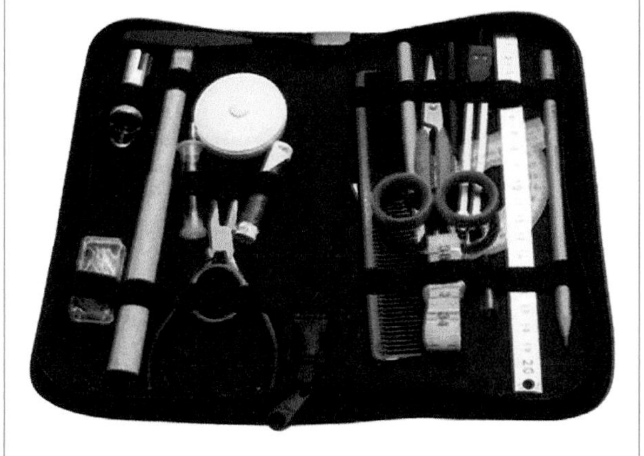

FIGURE 13.15 *Fischbach & Miller Wigmaker Tool Kit.*

ADDING A NATURAL HAIRLINE

Transforming a commercial hard-front wig into a lace-front wig suitable for theater or film applications.

Materials Needed:

- Commercial wig—best without a plastic skin top
- Wig fronting lace
- Seam ripper
- Small scissors
- Sewing needle and thread in the base color of the wig
- Thimble and needle catcher
- Ventilating needle
- Various combs
- Tape measure
- Pencils and felt markers
- Masking tape and clear tape
- Hair to ventilate the front in the colors of the wig
- Canvas block in the size determined by your circumference measurement
- Sewing pins
- Table clamp to hold the canvas block.

Adding a Natural Hairline to a Store-bought or Commercial Wig

There are almost as many variations of adding a natural hairline to a commercial wig as there are wigmakers. Here is a simple version.

In order to take a hairline tracing, follow the steps in Figure 13.19 (and see Figure 13.18). The measurements and hairline tracing should be taken over a "wig prep."

"Wig prep" is a term used to describe the process of preparing the performer's hair for the application of the wig. It includes covering pin curls with a nylon wig cap (see Figure 13.20).

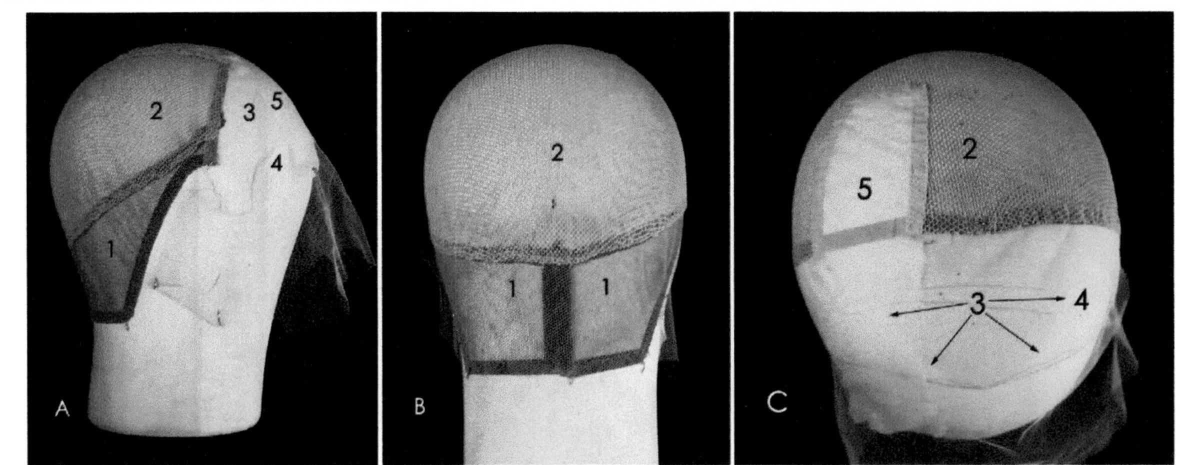

FIGURE 13.16 *Anatomy of a custom-made wig foundation. A. 1—The Nape is made from cotton lace by Atelier Bassi Art.525.38.70242.210; 2—The crown area is made from cotton lace by Atelier Bassi Art. 525.38.70025.210. B. 1—The Nape Lace; 2—The Crown Lace. C. 2—Crown Lace; 3—The front of this wig base is made from two layers of fronting lace. The front lace bottom layer is made from Atalier Bassi 100% PA 6.6 Monofil Art. 525.38.84046.697 and cut back to about ⅛ inch behind the hairline. The arrows point to the edge of this bottom layer of lace; 4—The top layer fronting lace is Atelier Bassi 100% PA 6.6 Monofil Art.525.30.82041.C2.697. This layer will transition to the fine hairline; 5—The silk used to create a "part" in the hair is DeMeo Brothers Domestic SILK Gauze 8XX, 29 inches wide.*

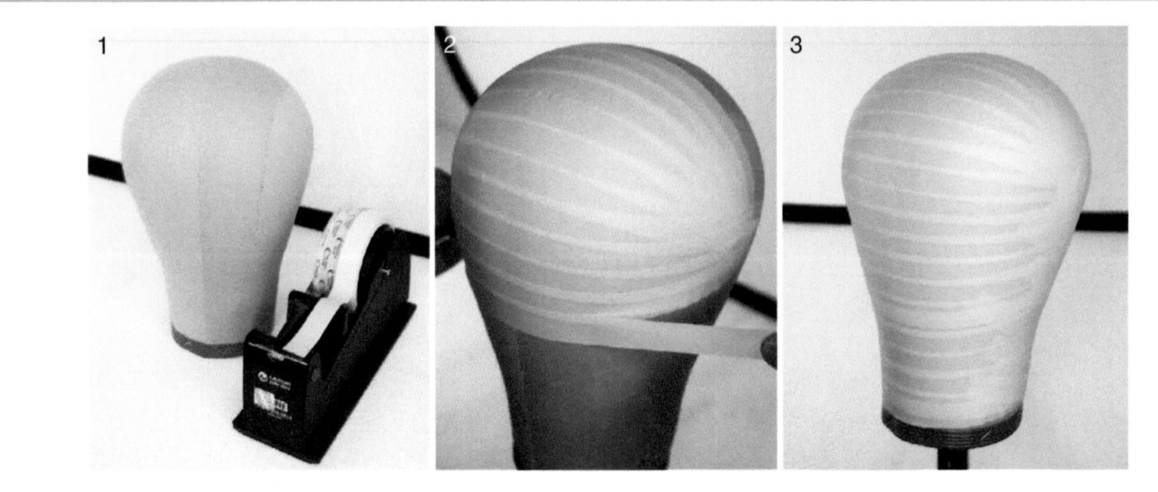

FIGURE 13.17 *Covering the canvas block.*

First, start by covering a canvas block with masking tape (Figure 13.17).

1. Products needed to cover a canvas wig block: canvas wig block, masking tape.
2. Cover the canvas block with slightly overlapping strips of masking tape (this will be accomplished in the same fashion as in Chapter 12).
3. Canvas wig block completely covered with masking tape.

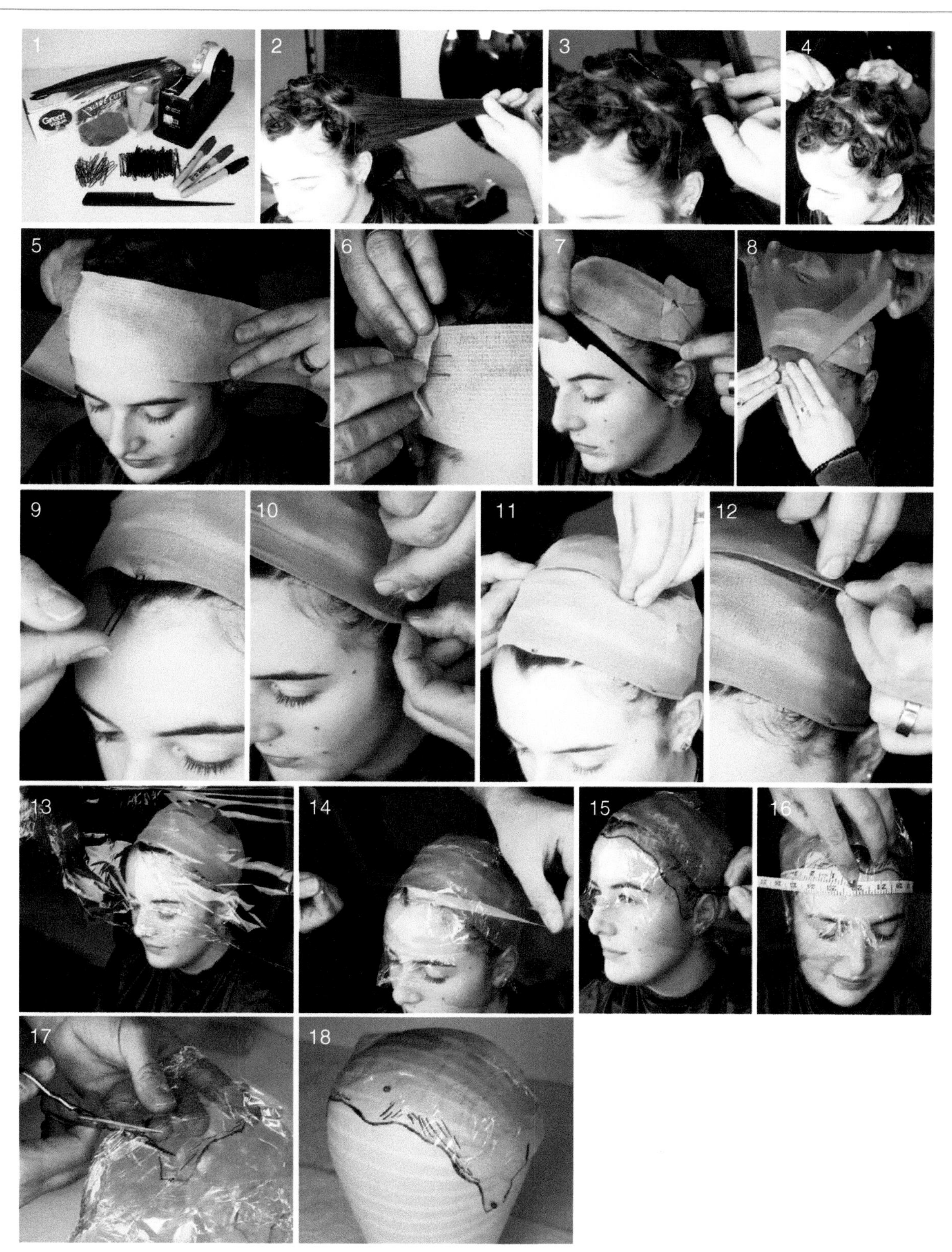

FIGURE 13.18 *Making a hairline tracing used for fronting a wig.*

1. Products needed for making a hairline tracing: clear cling (plastic) wrap, clear shiny Scotch tape, wig cap, elastic bandage, hairpins, bobby pins, rat-tail comb, permanent markers (see Figure 13.18).
2. Prepare the hair for making pin curls. Section off a length of hair.
3. Wrap the hair around your fingers creating a tight coil.
4. Use two bobby pins to control the curl.
5. Starting at the center of the forehead wrap the entire hairline with the elastic bandage.
6. Use the hairpins to control the ends of the bandage. Move the bandage up to the hairline.
7. Use the handle of the comb to control any loose hairs, pushing them under the bandage.
8. Apply the wig cap, covering the bandage and all of the pin curls.

9. & 10. Secure the wig cap with hairpins at the center front, at the sideburns, and behind the ears.

11. & 12. Fold up the excess wig cap at the crown of the head and secure with two hairpins, one on either side of center front.

13. Unroll a 30-inch length of cling wrap and wrap the hairline. Overlap the ends at the center back and secure with a piece of tape.
14. Apply 6-inch (or longer) lengths of the clear Scotch tape to the entire forehead and top of head. Continue from sideburn to sideburn. The entire head can be covered at this time from the forehead to the nape of the neck to create a full-head hairline tracing.
15. Transfer the natural hairline onto the plastic using the permanent markers. You might add other markings that indicate hair growth direction, cowlicks, and swirls.
16. Before removing the hairline tracing, take a series of head measurements and write them on wig measurement sheet (see Wig Measurement Sheet, Figure 13.14).
17. Remove the hairline tracing from the model and cut along the exact hairline marked on the plastic tracing.
18. Place the hairline tracing on a prepared canvas wig block. Make sure that the hairline sits in a natural position. You can use the measurement sheet and measuring tape to double check the placement. (Refer to how the hairline tracing and beard block were made in Chapter 12.) Once you are satisfied with the position of the tracing, trace and transfer the hairline with a permanent marker to the prepared canvas block.

(Note: To ensure the marker doesn't dull or rub off and to keep the masking tape clean, cover the entire block in Scotch tape (clear/shiny) in the same fashion as the section on making a beard block in Chapter 12.)

Look closely at the hard-front hairline of the store-bought wig. You will either see that there is hair thickly ventilated around the hairline onto a fabric tape, or you may see weft wrapped around the tape onto the inside of the wig. The process for preparing a commercial wig to receive the wig lace for fronting a wig is seen in Figure 13.19.

1. A commercial store-bought wig placed on a canvas wig block.
2. View of the inside of the commercial hard-front wig. The front edge of this wig shows that the ends of the wefting have been folded around the tape edge of the wig foundation.
3. Using hair-cutting scissors remove all of the hair, revealing at least ¼ inch on the front seam, exposing the fabric wig tape that is underneath the hair. *Don't cut the wig tape off in this process*, only the hair, as it could make the wig fall apart and force unnecessary repairs.
4. Turn the wig right-side-out and remove the hair (cutting it with a pair of hair scissors) from the front edge of the wig to approximately ½ inch away from the taped edge, as shown in Figure 13.19.

   (Note: If the commercial wig has a ventilated front, you may have to open the knotted hair and remove them from the tape one stitch at time. WARNING—This can be a tedious process. Try using a small sewing needle or a ventilating hook to untie the knots.)

5. Once the wig tape is cleared of hair, place the prepared wig on the canvas block approximately 1–1½ inches behind the transferred hairline. Make sure that the wig is straight and centered on the block. Use a tape measure to verify by measuring the distance from the edge of the wig down to the edge of the block. Adjust the wig until it looks like it is sitting on the head naturally. Once you are satisfied with the fit of the wig in relation to the hairline, secure the wig firmly to the block just behind the exposed tape using three to five sewing pins.

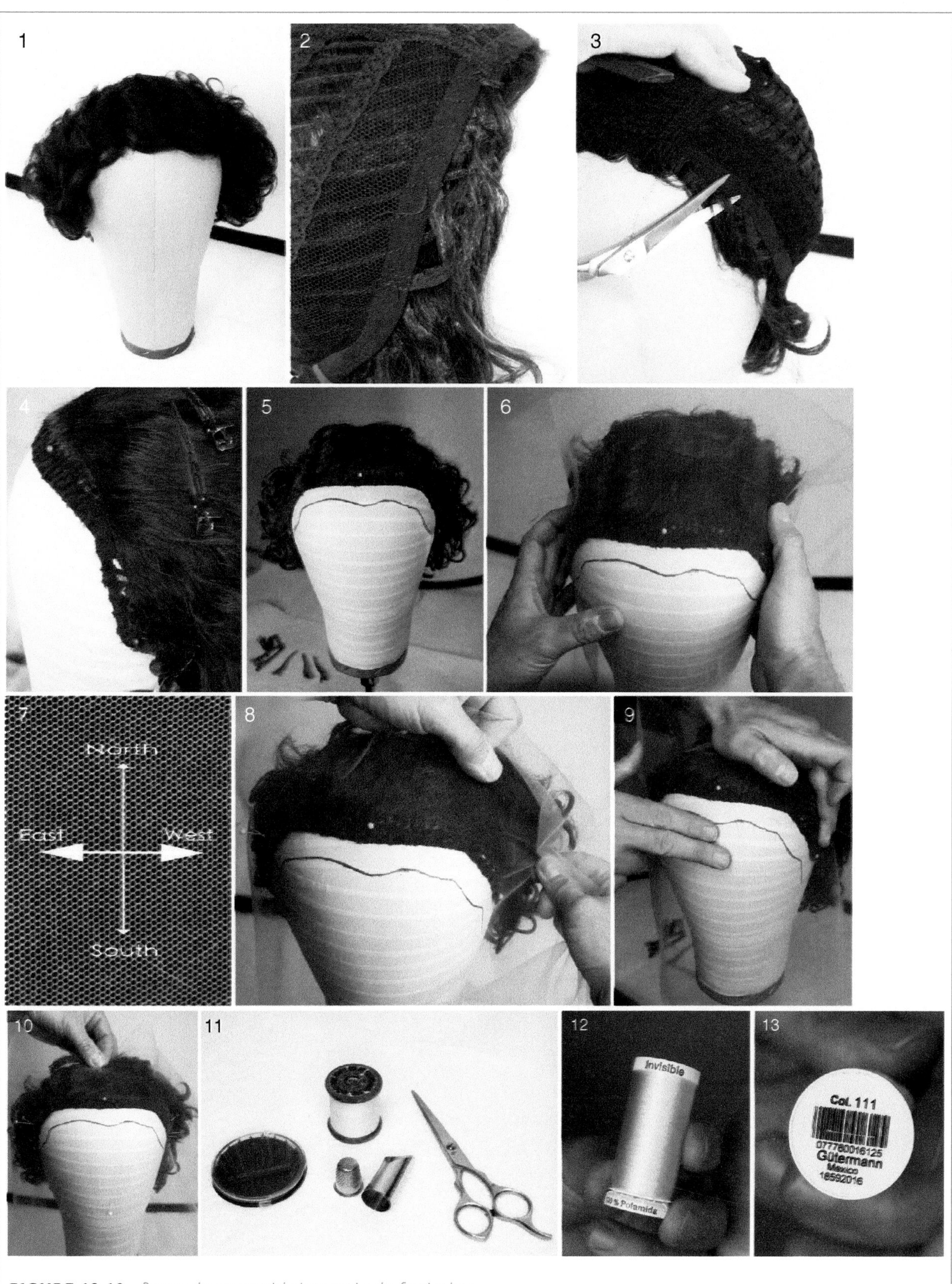

FIGURE 13.19 *Prepare the commercial wig to receive the fronting lace.*

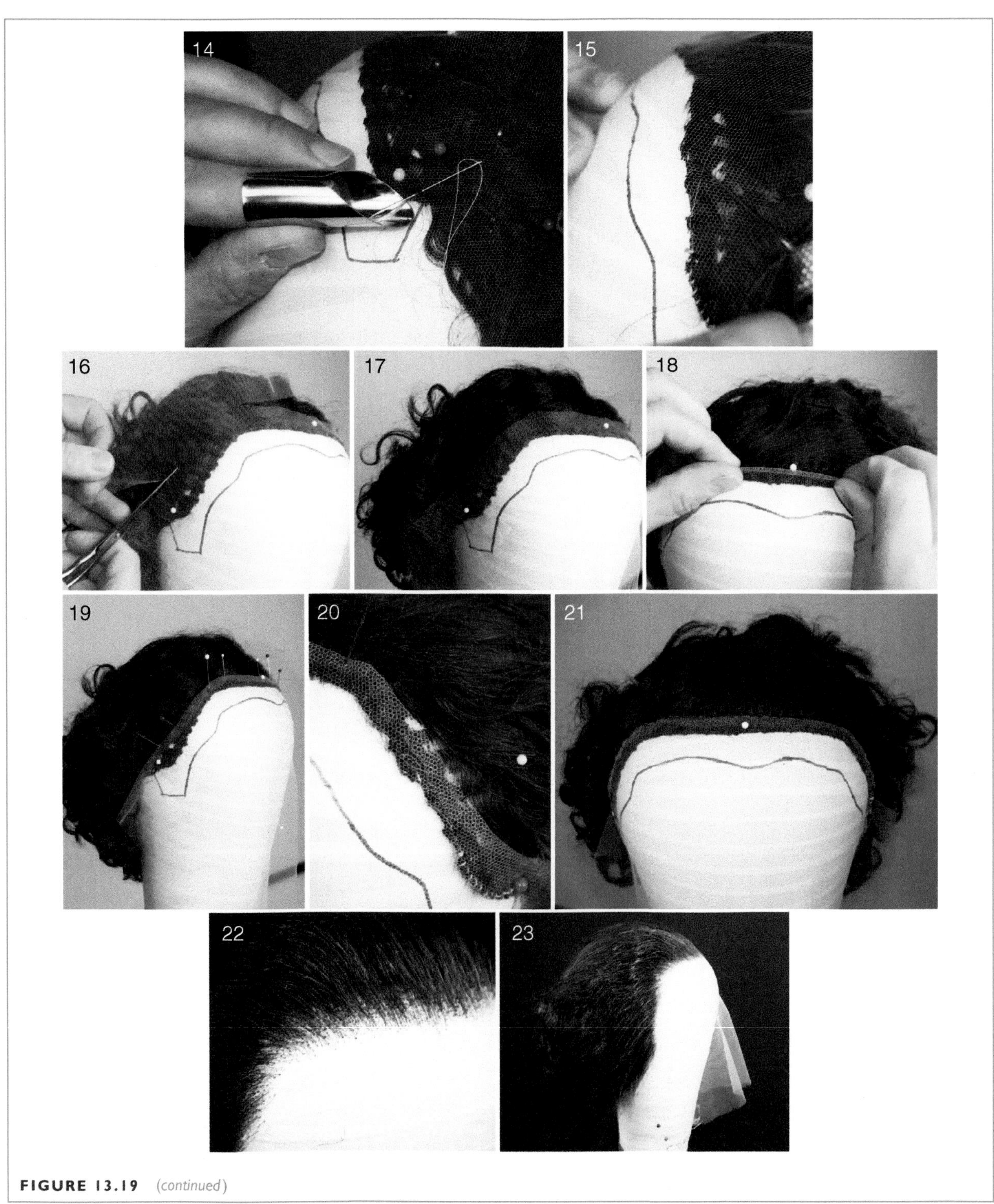

FIGURE 13.19 *(continued)*

Laying on the Lace

6. Position the lace on the block and check that the piece is big enough, and covers the entire hairline, going past the hairline by a few inches.

   Position yourself in front of the wig block so you are looking toward the forehead.

7. Look closely at the lace, and observe the direction of the hexagons to determine how they are running. If they stack up on top of each other and form a straight line it is termed "north to south," when they line up next to each other left to right, it would be termed "east to west." Begin by cutting a piece of lace about 8 inches deep (lace grain north/south) x 15 inches wide (lace grain east/west).

8. Lay the lace, centered on the forehead of the block, and pin the lace on one side with three to four pins just past the clear tape above the ear. Stretch the lace across the forehead area over to the other side of the wig, being careful to have adequate tension, but not misshape the lace pattern. Pin the lace on the other side with three to four pins as on the first side.

9. The most important tension points are about two fingers' width below the hairline on the forehead, and the same distance behind the hairline on top.

   WARNING—If these points are not properly tensed, the result could be a front that lifts at the edges, or puckers on top.

10. Now add a pin directly center front at the bottom of the lace approximately where the nose of the face would reside. Gently stretch the center of the lace toward the back of the head so that the lace lays flat over the exposed wig tape. Add a pin center back to hold the lace down. Stretch the lace diagonally left from the center backward and secure with a pin. Repeat the same action on the right side, working all sides until the entire lace piece lays flat against the wig tape.

    Now remove the pin at the nose area and observe how the lace reacts. If the lace pulls up, or doesn't maintain its flatness two fingers' width over the entire wig tape, you will need to unpin and restart the process. Be patient with this process, it takes practice to get the correct tension.

    Once the tension is correct, and the lace remains flat across the wig tape, place several pins to hold down the front lace at the outer edge, but don't pin too close to the hairline.

    Now you are ready to stitch the lace to the wig using a clear (invisible) nylon thread.

11. Sewing supplies to connect the lace to the wig front: assorted needles, thimble and finger guard, hair-cutting scissors, and invisible thread.

12. & 13. Invisible thread by Gütermann.

14. Begin stitching the wig lace to the wig front on one side of the block at the sideburn edge (in front of the ear) where the wig meets the lace. Sew the edge of the tape closest to the hairline. With a fine whip-stitch, secure the lace to the wig, tying a knot every few inches to prevent the lace from coming undone should the thread break at any point.

15. Work your way across the length of the wig tape, keeping your stitching even. Because the invisible thread is difficult to see, a short example of the type of stitch used for this exercise was done in an opaque sewing thread. This can be seen at the lower edge of this image.

16. & 17. Once you have the front edge stitched, remove the back pins and trim the back edge of the lace, closest to the wig. Leave sufficient lace, about ¾ inch, to allow for a small extension the width of the wig tape.

18. Fold the lace back over itself onto the wig tape so the cut edge is to the inside.

19. & 20. Secure the folded lace in place with a few pins. Stitch the newly folded lace in the same manner as the front edge.

21. After the folded edge is completely sewn, you are ready to begin ventilating the front.

    See ventilating techniques in Chapter 12.

22. Close-up of the completed wig front.

23. The completed wig.

PUTTING ON AND SECURING A WIG

1. In preparation for putting on and securing a wig, the first step is to control the performer's hair by making as many pin curls as possible. Each pin curl is controlled with one or more bobby pins (see Figure 13.20).

2. Apply a wig cap over the pin curls. Control stray hairs by moving them under the cap with the handle of the rat-tail comb.

3. & 4. Secure the wig cap with hairpins placed first at the center front, then two at the sideburns, and two more at

the nape of the neck. Notice the technique for inserting hairpins. Start with the hairpin in a position perpendicular to the head, pushing it through the wig cap, then wrap the pin under a pin curl and push in place.

(Note: Some wig designers wrap the pin curls with an Ace bandage before applying the wig cap (see Figure 13.16, step 5). This is done so that you have lots of areas to secure the wig to the actor's head. Steps 1–4 in this process are called "wig prep.")

5. There will usually be extra fabric at the crown of the wig cap. Fold the fabric in on itself, creating a smooth tuck, and control the fold with one or two hairpins.

6. Carefully place the dressed wig onto the performer's head. Adjust the wig until it settles in place as it was designed to fit.

7. & 8. Secure the wig with hairpins placed at the front edge slightly above the sideburn area. The next pin will be placed on the opposite side at exactly the same place. Notice again the technique. The pin is gently pressed through the wig lace perpendicular to the wig, then wraps around one of the pin curls and is pushed in place.

9. & 10. Repeat the placement of the hairpins at the back of the wig behind the ears. If the wig is a good fit, this should be enough pinning to secure it. If the wig remains slightly

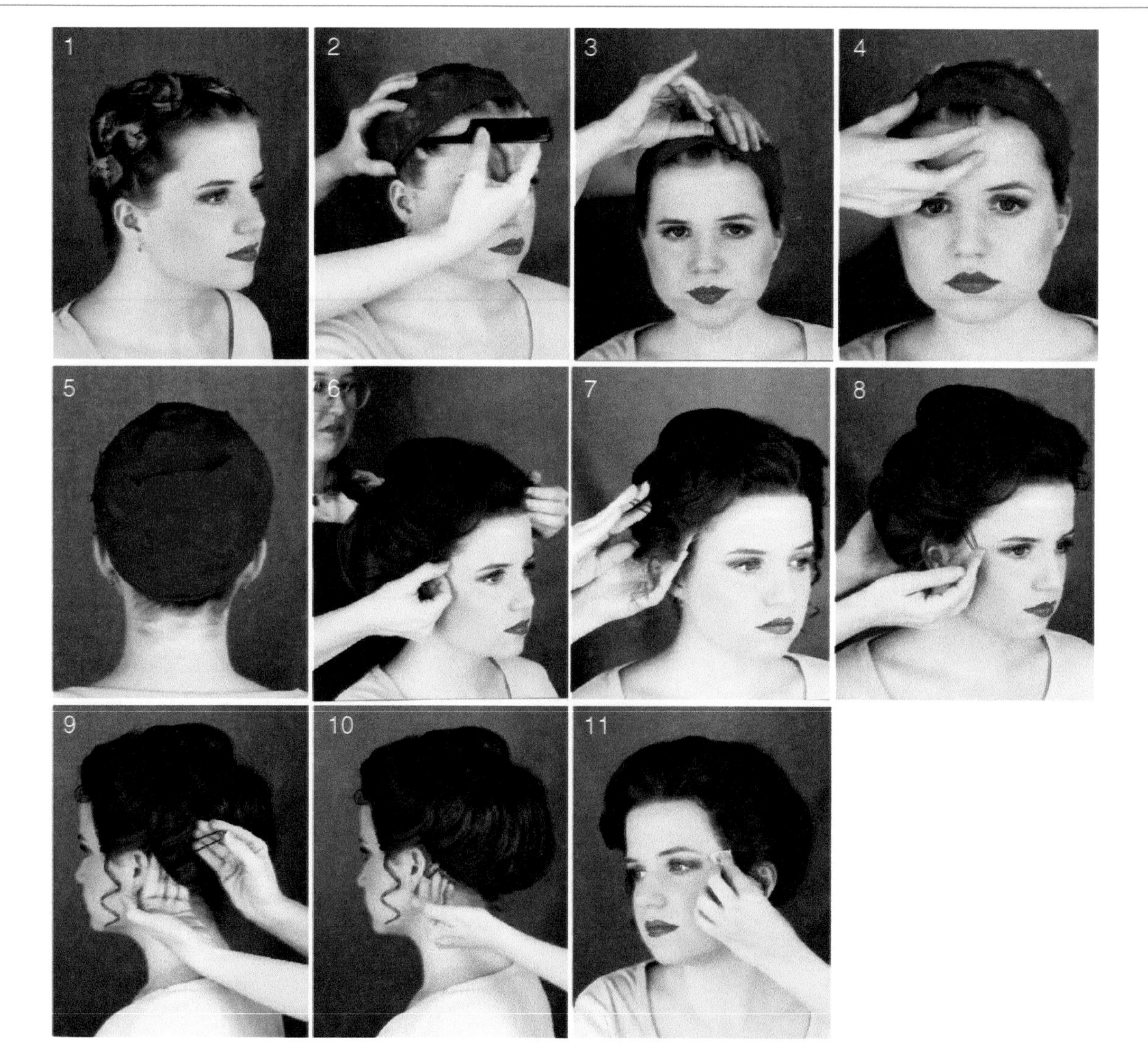

FIGURE 13.20 *Putting on and securing a wig.*

loose or the performer has particularly strenuous activity on stage, then more pins can be inserted.

11. Apply a small amount of matte spirit gum to the skin at the sideburn area. Allow the adhesive to become tacky. Gently lay the wig lace against the adhesive and press with a piece of damp leather chamois.

REMOVING THE WIG

To remove the wig, work in the exact reverse process of putting on the wig. You will need the following tools:

- Spirit gum remover or 99% isopropyl alcohol
- Tissues
- Cotton balls
- Cotton-tipped applicators
- A medium-size hairpin
- A brush.

If you have a lace-front wig that has been glued to the face, you must start by loosening or removing the spirit gum. First, dampen a cotton ball with spirit gum remover or alcohol. Make sure it is wet, but not dripping. It is recommended that you keep tissues close by, as you do not want any remover to fall into the eyes of the actor. Gently press the cotton ball with the remover onto the lace at the glue line.

Once the spirit gum begins to dissolve, take a medium-size hairpin or cotton-tipped applicator soaked in the remover and carefully slide it under the lace. When sliding a hairpin under the lace, move it in the direction that the hair naturally grows, then gently separate the lace from the skin.

Now remove the anchor pins from the wig to release it from the head. Lift the wig up and away from the head and carefully place it on the wig block. Remove the pins from the wig cap. Put the wig cap where it will be washed or keep it with the wig to be used again. Take out the pin curls and brush out the hair. The actor should never remove the wig on their own.

CLEANING WIGS

The process for cleaning and conditioning human hair wigs can be identical to caring for your own hair. After taking down the style and carefully brushing through the wig, wash it in warm water using a mild shampoo and a light conditioner, then rinse well. Towel dry and carefully comb through the wig using a wide-toothed comb. Allow the wig to dry thoroughly or place it in a wig dryer before putting it away. The process of washing a human hair wig will remove all of the curl, so be sure to leave plenty of time if you need to restyle it for the next performance.

Synthetic wigs can also be cleaned and conditioned. After taking down the style and carefully brushing through the wig, wash it in cold water using a mild shampoo. Use a light conditioner on the wig and rinse well in cold water. Towel dry and carefully comb through the wig with a wide-toothed comb. Allow it to dry thoroughly. Washing a synthetic wig in cold water will retain its curl. Washing a synthetic wig in warm or hot water will make the curl fall or come out completely. Using a conditioner on a synthetic wig will help to control frizz and static electricity.

The following are two suggestions that may dispel any myths about caring for a synthetic wig:

1. Do not wash a synthetic wig in the washing machine. You will do severe damage to the wig, and it will take you days to comb out all of the tangles.
2. Do not use a fabric detergent or fabric softener on a synthetic wig. They are too harsh, they do not completely rinse out, and your actor may be sensitive to the chemicals.

FIGURE 13.21 *Synthetic wig for Beau Bridges as P. T. Barnum for A&E. This ¾ wig is attached to a hard bald cap with side pieces and frontal border added on the actor. Made of white, gray, platinum, golden blond, and light brown hair ventilated on classic cotton cinema lace. Wig by Richard G. Hansen of Les Ateliers in Montreal.*

ATTACHING MICROPHONE BATTERY PACKS TO THE WIG

There are times when battery packs for head-worn microphones must be concealed in the wig. Wigmakers are often asked to develop creative solutions to locate these wireless technologies where they will be perfectly concealed, yet easily accessed. There are no doubt as many solutions to this problem as there are wig designers, but the following is one successful example of how a wireless microphone and transmitter were designed to attach to a performer's wig cap and then be concealed by the wig. In this example (Figure 13.23) the choice was made to include a double microphone and double transmitter as a hedge against a technical failure of one part of the system.

1. The battery pack/transmitter holder was designed as a lightly padded circular pouch with a pocket designed to hold the transmitters. Each transmitter is secured by an elastic strap with the antennae located at opposite sides to avoid any interference.
2. Wig designer, Serret Jensen, attaches the battery pack/transmitter to the wig cap of singer, Chanel, in preparation for her performance in the Zach Theatre production of *Lady Day*.
3. The battery pack holder is designed with a circular flange of black horsehair stitched to the perimeter of the pouch. Hairpins are inserted through the horsehair braid into the pin curls to secure it to the top of the head.
4. The microphone wires are carefully wrapped around the pouch and secured with hairpins. The two microphones are secured to the forehead with a medical tape called Tegaderm Film.
5. Tegaderm Film is a medical-grade sterile, waterproof adhesive film. Cut into a small square and used to "tape" the microphones to the forehead, it will successfully hold the wires in place through an entire performance without worrying about them coming loose.
6. A mesh wig cap is placed over the microphone/transmitter holder and secured with hairpins.
7. The singer is ready to be wigged. Notice how the wig caps are applied to slightly reveal the hairline.
8. The wig has been applied, completely concealing the battery/transmitter pouch. The microphone can be seen peeking through the wig.

FIGURE 13.22 *Puck and Oberon from the 2016 Glyndebourne Festival production of the Benjamin Britten opera, A Midsummer Night's Dream. Head of Wigs, Sheila Slaymaker. © Glyndebourne Production Ltd.*

Source: Photo: Robert Workman.

Learning how to design hairstyles, and dress and care for wigs is an important part of the makeup process. If you also know how to construct wigs, you are in an advantageous position. In the professional theater, actors are not usually expected to style, care for, or remove their own wigs. In the nonprofessional theater, however, both actors and makeup artists may sometimes be expected to do all three. A thorough knowledge of the techniques involved with hair design and construction for both natural and synthetic wigs will not only contribute greatly to the effectiveness of the makeup, it will positively affect the quality of the entire production.

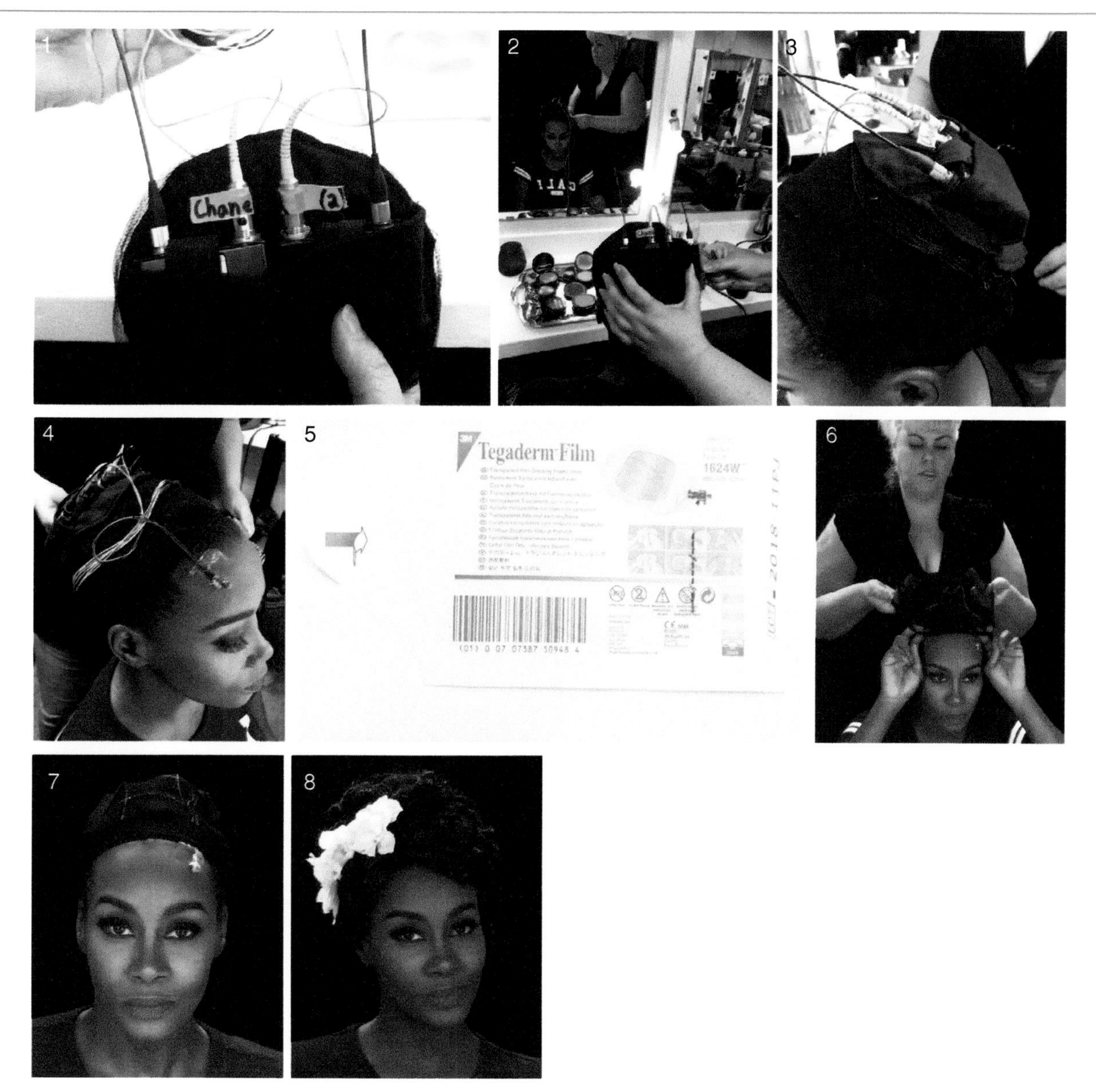

FIGURE 13.23 *Attaching microphone battery packs to the wig. Wig and makeup by Serret Jensen. Singer/actor - Chanel.*

CHAPTER 14

CROSS-GENDER MAKEUP

Men and women may apply cross-gender makeup in theatrical productions for a number of reasons:

- Because the script requires it (Rosalind, Portia in Shakespeare's *As You Like It*)
- Because it has become an established convention (Kabuki Theater)
- Because the particular production requires it (Hedwig in *Hedwig and the Angry Inch*)
- Because the performer chooses to do it (Drag Queens and Kings)
- Because the director has arbitrarily decided to have a particular character played by the performer of the opposite sex (Richard III played by a woman).

MEN AS WOMEN

A successful male-to-female makeup change requires, first of all, careful casting. The actor must be able to convincingly portray the female character he was selected to perform. Harvey Fierstein as Edna Turnblatt in *Hairspray*, Wilson Jermaine Heredia as Angel in RENT, and Brian Bedford as Lady Bracknell in *The Importance of Being Ernest* are examples of successful male-to-female cross-gender makeup design. The basic approach is to follow the general principles of female corrective or character makeup and techniques drawn from classic drag makeup, noting a few special problems. An actor with a strong chin and a rugged jawline may find it difficult to be transformed into a convincingly attractive ingénue (without prosthetic makeup). Beard shadows can be concealed, eyebrows can be thinned or blocked out, and lips can be painted on, but little can be done about a bone structure that is strongly masculine—except, of course, to create a strong woman. Given an actor with a softer bone structure, however, a convincingly female face is not difficult to achieve. Good acting is surely an effective ingredient in these transformations.

Eyebrows

If the eyebrows are too thick, they can be narrowed and reshaped by removal, by blocking out part of them, or by completely blocking them out and painting on new ones, as was done for the makeup in Figure 14.11 (Lola, from the musical, *Kinky Boots*).

Beard Shadow

An actor playing a female part should shave immediately before applying his makeup. Then, if any trace of beard shadow remains, it can be counteracted with an application of beard neutralizer (usually orange in color). This beard cover should be lightly powdered, with the excess powder dusted off before the foundation is applied. A cream, cake, or liquid foundation can be used over the beard cover, but it should be sponged or patted on, not stroked on, in order to avoid smearing the beard cover.

Lips

Techniques for changing the shape of the lips begin with lining the lips with a lip pencil. Simply create the new shape, blend the pencil onto the lip and fill in the new lip shape with one or more lipstick

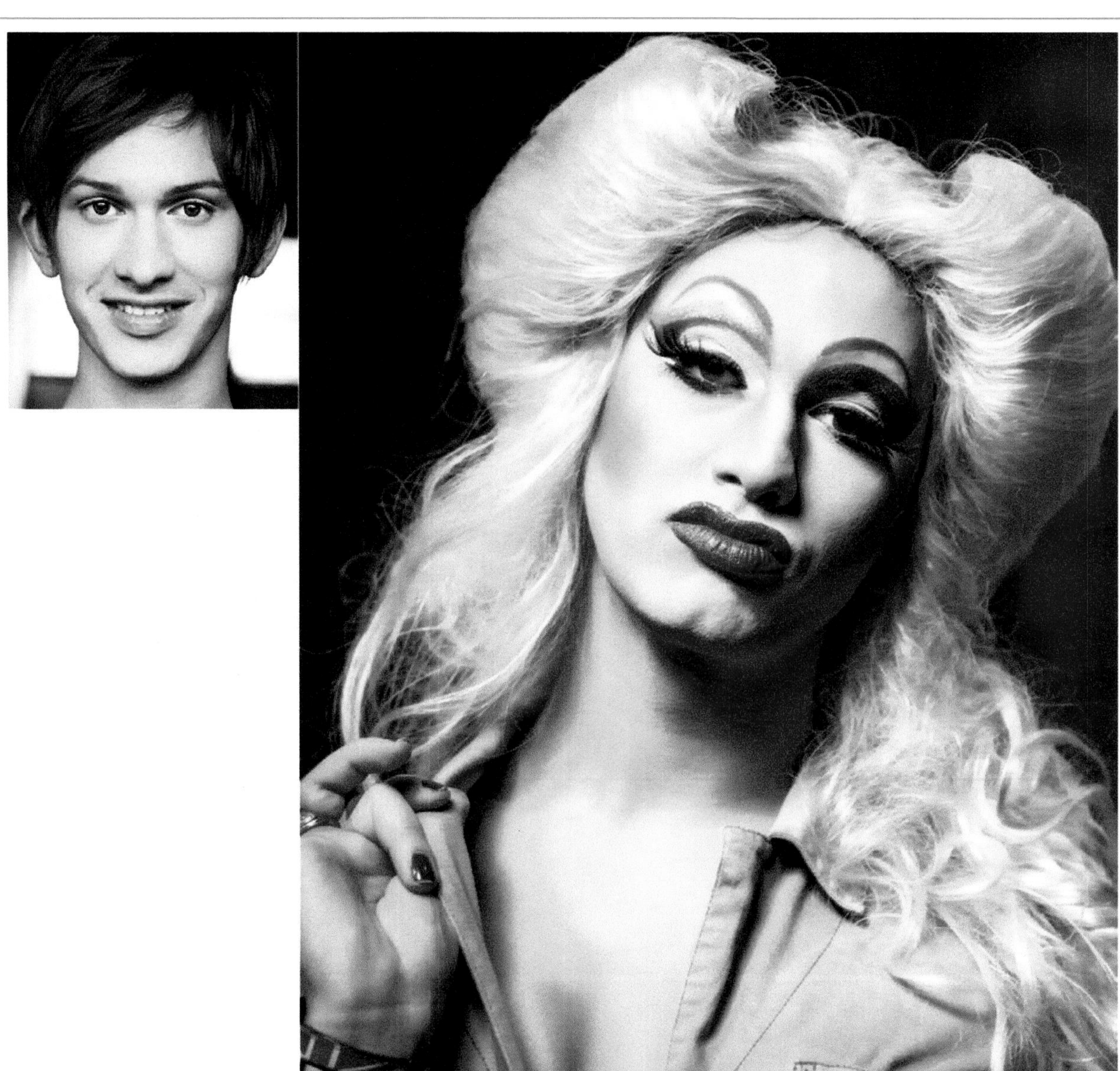

FIGURE 14.1 *A. Jerick Hoffer (aka. Jinkx Monsoon). B. Jerick Hoffer as Hedwig in the Seattle Theatre Group production of Hedwig and The Angry Inch.*

Source: *Photograph by Christopher Nelson (with special permission from Jerick Hoffer/Jinkx Monsoon).*

colors (see Figures 8.28 and 8.29). Matte, soft sheen, or glossy finishes can be applied, depending on the character. If the desired lip shape is smaller, less wide, or thinner, covering the unwanted areas with foundation (full-coverage) and/or concealer will camouflage those areas.

For a more natural design, it may be that the lip shape needs no change at all and appropriate lip color will suffice. In this case, lining the lip with a neutral color lip pencil before the lip color is applied is always suggested. This will create a longer-lasting lip color and keep the lip color from migrating past the lip line.

Hair

If the actor's hair is not long enough, or if for some other reason (a receding hairline, for example) it cannot be suitably dressed for the female character, a wig can be worn.

If a complete physical transformation is requested, a full prosthetic makeup can be created (see Figure 14.9). Examples of this are two endearing characters in modern film history, Robin Williams as *Mrs. Doubtfire* and John Travolta as Edna Turnblatt in *Hairspray*.

FIGURE 14.2 *Brian Bedford as Lady Bracknell in The Importance of Being Earnest, at the Stratford Festival 2009.*

Source: Photograph by David Hou (Courtesy of the Stratford Festival).

FIGURE 14.3 *Diego Montez as Angel in Rent.*

Source: With permission from Marcio Del Nero/Editora Globo Brazil.

FIGURE 14.4 *Model and makeup artist Cody Sadler in casual drag makeup. Natural eyebrows shaped by plucking.*

FIGURE 14.5 *Cristofer Jean as Lady Capulet in Shakespeare in Love. Oregon Shakespeare Festival 2017. Costume design by Susan Tsu.*

WOMEN AS MEN

When women are made up as men, the changes required may involve facial structure, coloring, hair, and the possible addition of beards and mustaches.

Facial Structure

Since soft curves tend to make a face look more feminine, and angles more masculine, exaggerating whatever angular features the woman already has will help to give a more masculine look.

The angle of the jaw can be modeled with highlights and shadows to give it a less rounded and more square, muscular look; and the chin, if it is softly rounded, can be similarly "corrected" to appear more angular. The nose, if it is small and feminine, can be modified with highlights and shadows, or a new one created with gelatin, silicone, or latex to make it look more masculine. However, using corrective makeup for lengthening or broadening or both may give the nose a sufficiently masculine look—at least from the front. Enlarging the nostril openings with a dark pencil, and placing a shadow in the crease of the nostril (where it connects to the face) will also create a stronger, more

FIGURE 14.6 *The Club (Front l–r) Julie J. Hafner and Joanne Beretta; (middle l–r) Carole Monferdini and Gloria Hodes; (top l–r) Terri White, Marlene Dell, and Memrie Innerarity. Circle in the Square production of the musical, The Club. 1976.*

Source: Photograph by Martha Swope. Copyright Billy Rose Theatre Division, The New York Public Library for the Performing Arts, 1976.

FIGURE 14.7 *Glenn Close as Albert Nobbs. A silicone nose tip, ear lobes, and wig complete the transformation. She wore no makeup in this film.*

Source: With permission of David Polick of Roadside Attractions. Photos by Patrick Redmond.

angular nose. All of this, of course, will have no effect on the profile.

A softly rounded forehead can be made to look more masculine by highlighting the frontal bone to give it greater prominence and by shadowing the inner corners of the eye socket just below the frontal bone. Lightly shadowing the temporal fossa area may also be helpful in squaring off a rounded forehead. Emphasizing the top of cheekbones and flattening the side planes of the face with a contour color from the high cheekbone to the jawline, by modeling them with highlights and shadows, can also be useful in creating a more angular face. Studying the faces of the cast of the Off-Broadway production of *The Club* will reveal various techniques for creating successful transitions from female to male: deeper color foundations, bronzers, fuller brows, angular features, and facial hair all assist in the transformations (see Figure 14.6).

For her role as Richard III at the Stratford Festival, Seana McKenna accepts and takes on the role of Richard III with all of his obvious physical anomalies: the hump of a hunchback, the withered arm, the limp, and thinning, stringy hair. Ms. McKenna talks about acting as a transformative experience, both physically and spiritually. Her emotional interpretation is to play him "as he is examined in the script: an outsider, using animal imagery, someone who pretends to be human, but remains inhumane." She plays him "not as a woman or a man, but a villain, a handicapped, somewhat deformed villain." "If people thought I was male, female, transgendered or undefinable, that was alright." She questions, "What is Richard III?" "He is an actor … an imposter who imitates life, but feels nothing."

FIGURE 14.8 *Seana McKenna as King Richard in Richard III.*

Source: Photograph by David Hou. (Courtesy of the Stratford Festival Archives. Permission from Seana McKenna.)

To begin the transformation her makeup required a bald cap to completely cover her own hair. A wig, long and stringy, with thinning hair and receding hairline was worn over the cap. The makeup required a certain amount of discoloration throughout to resemble a somewhat diseased skin texture, and scars at the temples that would indicate a difficult birth … as with forceps. Eyebrows are slightly thicker with less of an arch and lips were of a natural skin color.

Coloring: The foundation color should be slightly warmer than is usually used for women. If a beard is not going to be worn, a slight beard shadow will give a more masculine look (see Chapter 12). If you use color in the cheeks, apply a bronzer on the areas of the face that tend to be warmed by the sun, as you would for men. It is usually better not to use color on the lips (a light coat of Chapstick may be all that is necessary). Some artists will slightly darken the upper lip.

Eyeshadow and eyelash makeup should also be avoided. The eyebrows should not be darkened excessively, but they nearly always need to be made fuller. A slight angle in the brow will give a more masculine look than a soft curve. Experiment with various eyebrow shapes before deciding which one is most effective. Eyebrows can sometimes be reshaped convincingly by filling them out with an eyebrow pencil applied very carefully with a sketching technique, using short, light strokes to give the effect of natural hair. If this doesn't prove satisfactory, crepe hair eyebrows or, preferably, real-hair eyebrows ventilated on lace can be created and applied.

Beards and mustaches: When appropriate, beards and mustaches can, of course, be very helpful in achieving a masculine look. They can be constructed of crepe hair, but real or synthetic hair, ventilated on lace, is preferable. (For instructions in making beards and mustaches, see Chapter 12.)

Hair: The hairstyle should, of course, be one that is appropriate for men—or for the particular man being portrayed. A wig may or may not be required. For short hair with sideburns, a handmade lace-front wig may be necessary. If the hair can be longer and need not have close-cropped sideburns, a good ready-made men's stretch wig with synthetic hair may be satisfactory. This, however, requires careful, professional styling to maintain a convincing look.

Celine Dion look-a-like makeup in Figure 14.9 uses foam latex prosthetics for the transformation from male to female. The foam latex pieces are glued to the face with silicone adhesive Telesis 5 + thinner. The edges are stippled with two

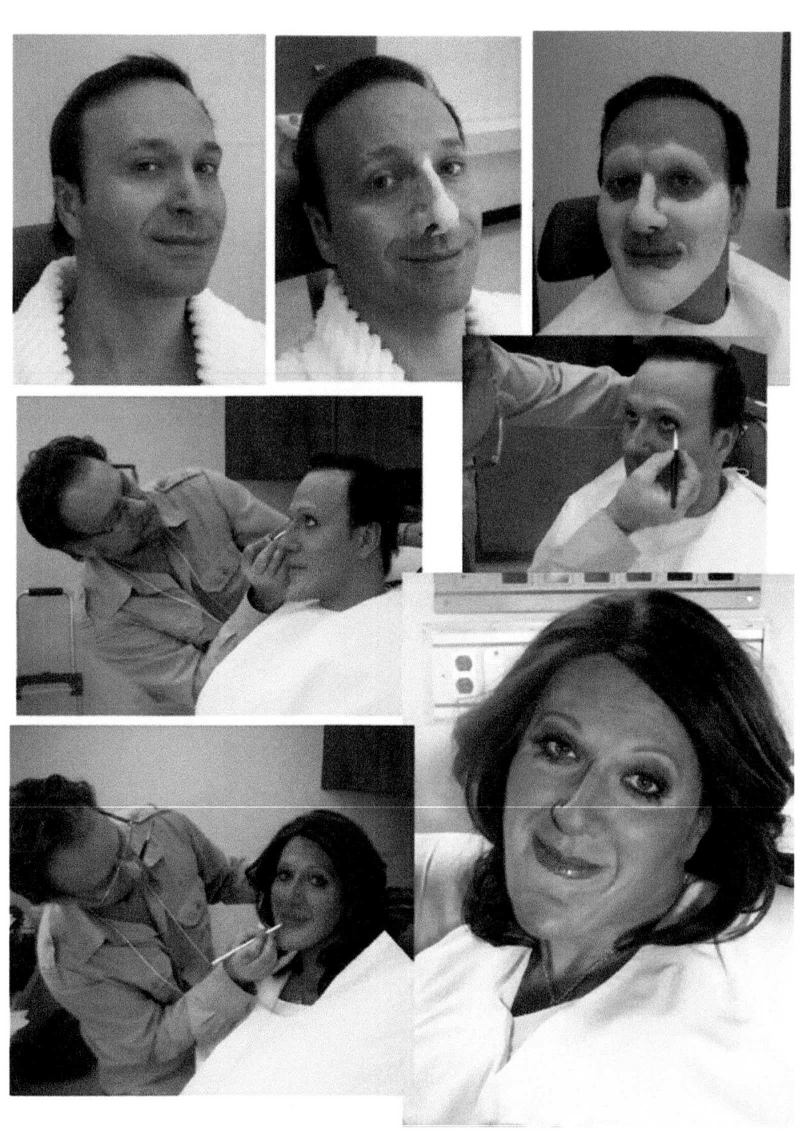

FIGURE 14.9 *Foam latex prosthetic cross-gender Celine Dion look-a-like makeup. Model Joël Legendre. Makeup artist, Stephan Tessier.*

light coats of Prosaide adhesive all over the edges, dried, then powdered. PAX Paint was used as the base, then finished with the airbrush and Skin Illustrator color to create a flawless beauty skin tone. The makeup is adjusted with Rubber Mask Greasepaint (RMGP), followed by regular beauty makeup, false lashes, eyeliner, and lip color.

PLANNING THE MAKEUP

In planning a gender-reversal makeup, it's a good idea to make pencil drawings of the character on tracing paper, over a photograph of the actor or actress in order to make sure, first of all, that an effective makeup can be done, and second, what actually needs to be done. This will save a great deal of time in experimenting on the face with various makeup possibilities.

1. Female to Male makeup application (Figure 14.10). Marika Klein—Model/Performer.
2. Apply The Body Shop All-in-One Mattifying Skin Perfector/Primer used under the foundation to smooth out pores, cover blemishes, and eliminate shine.
3. MAC Studio Sculpt Gel Foundation (SPF 15). NW25.
4. Mix the foundation and the primer together on a makeup palette to create a more sheer, light coverage.
5. Apply foundation mixture with a foundation brush.
6. Make Up Forever Full Cover Concealer: Ivory 6.

7–11. Apply concealer to the chin, lip edges, under the nose, and eyelids.

12. Apply MAC Blot Pressed powder with a sponge wedge.
13. Apply blot powder to the chin, lip area, and eyelids.
14. Apply concealer under the eyes using a small foundation brush.
15. Set the concealer with blot powder.

16., 17., & 18. Apply highlight to the high cheekbone, the brow bone and forehead, and the jawline. Use a small foundation brush. MAC Studio Sculpt Foundation: NC15.

19. MAC Studio Sculpt Gel Foundation: NW43 & NW45.
20. Mix the two foundations on a metal palette.
21. Apply this contour to the cheek plane from the cheekbone to the jawbone. The contour should be stronger at the cheekbone and gradually lighten to the jawbone. This plane should appear as flat and rectangular as possible. For a female face, sculpting the cheekbones with a contour, blush, and highlight accents and shapes the cheekbone and brings color to the face. In creating the male face, less color and less shaping are applied to create a more angular facial structure.
22. Contour placed at the temple.
23. Contour placed along the planes of the nose. This will create a strong, more angular nose.
24. Create a soft jowl shadow.
25. Contour the sides of the nose.
26. Contour around the crease of the nostrils.
27. Create a soft nasolabial fold.
28. Choose a dark brown character cream. Ben Nye Cream Color: Copper Brown.
29. Darken around the nostrils.
30. Contour the edges of the mouth.
31. Contour under the lower lip and place a dimple on the chin. These are naturally occurring on this model.
32. Create frown lines between the eyebrows and deepen the eye sockets at the inner eye.
33. The makeup application so far.
34. Choose a medium brown shadow. Ben Nye Pressed Eyeshadow: Cork and Ash Brown.
35. Create a subtle under-eye aging effect.
36. Contour the outer edge of the eyelid.
37. Lightly apply the dark brown press shadow as liner to the lower lash line using a very small, domed shadow or lip brush. Ben Nye: Ash Brown. This liner is thicker at the outer edge, tapering to nothing as it follows the lower lash line toward the inner eye.

38. & 39. Softly powder the eyelids and forehead using MAC Blot powder: Medium on a triangular sponge.

40. Brush and organize the brow hairs with a clean mascara wand.
41. Shape and fill in the eyebrows using a sharp-edged angle brow brush and a medium brown shadow. Ben Nye pressed eyeshadows: Ash Brown. The brows should be relatively straight, and fuller than the model's natural brows.
42. Choose a pressed contour powder. MAC Powder Blush: Blunt.
43. Apply the pressed contour powder to the cheek plane using a large flat brush.
44. Apply a natural color to the upper lip with a lip pencil. MAC Lip Pencil: Spice. Apply tinted Burt's Bees Balm: Zinnia, to the lower lip.
45. Draw on sideburns using the small angled brow brush and a dark brown/black pressed shadow.

46.–49. Final makeup and costume: model with cigar; model without facial hair; model with mustache; model with mustache and goatee.

FIGURE 14.10 *Female to male makeup. Makeup artist, Tara Cooper (this makeup is inspired by the character makeup used in the Circle in the Square production of The Club).*

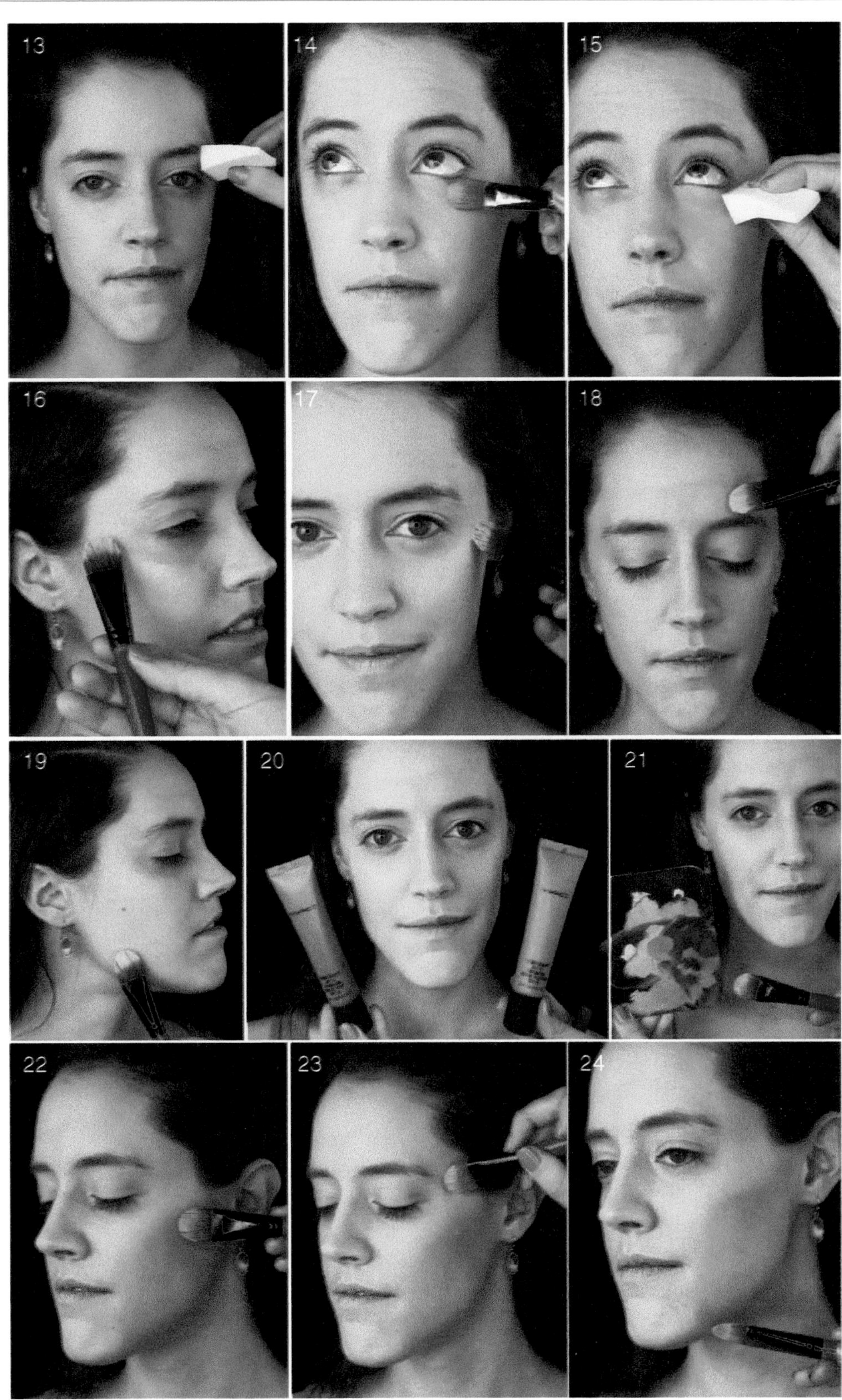

FIGURE 14.10 *(continued)*

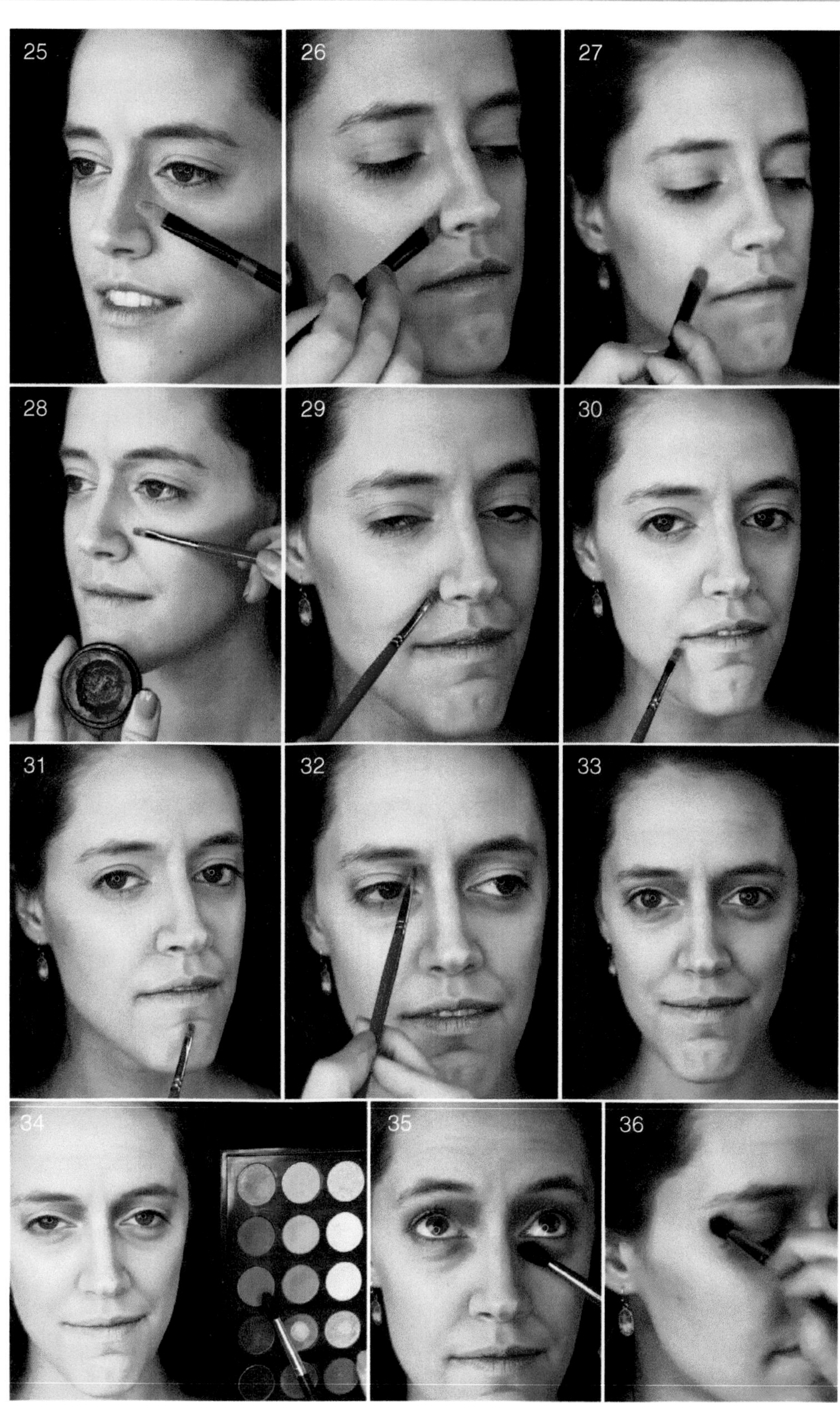

FIGURE 14.10 *(continued)*

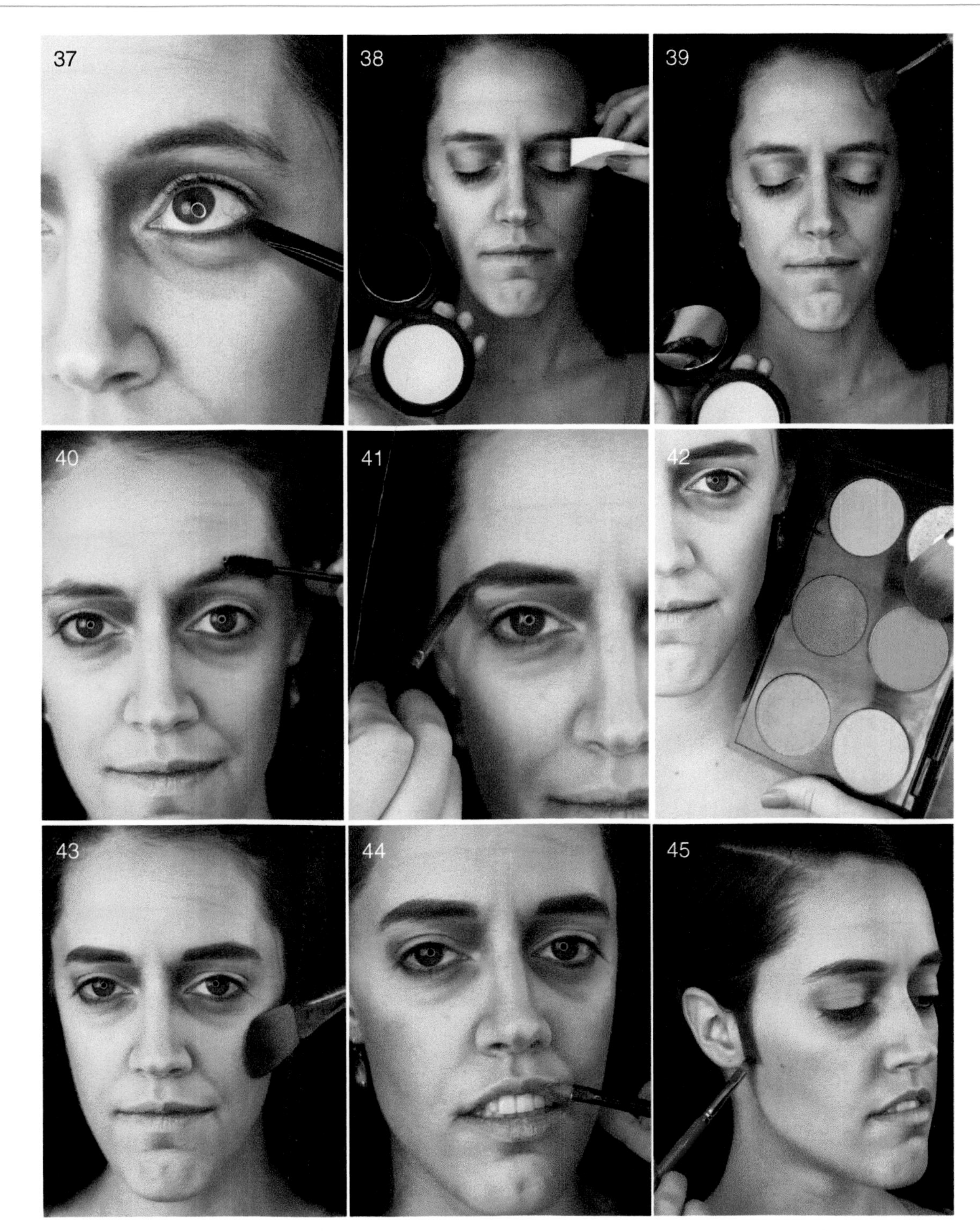

FIGURE 14.10 *(continued)*

FIGURE 14.10 *(continued)*

FIGURE 14.11 *Male to female makeup. Lola, from the musical Kinky Boots. Makeup artist, Caleena Hunt. Model/Performer, Joseph Harrington III.*

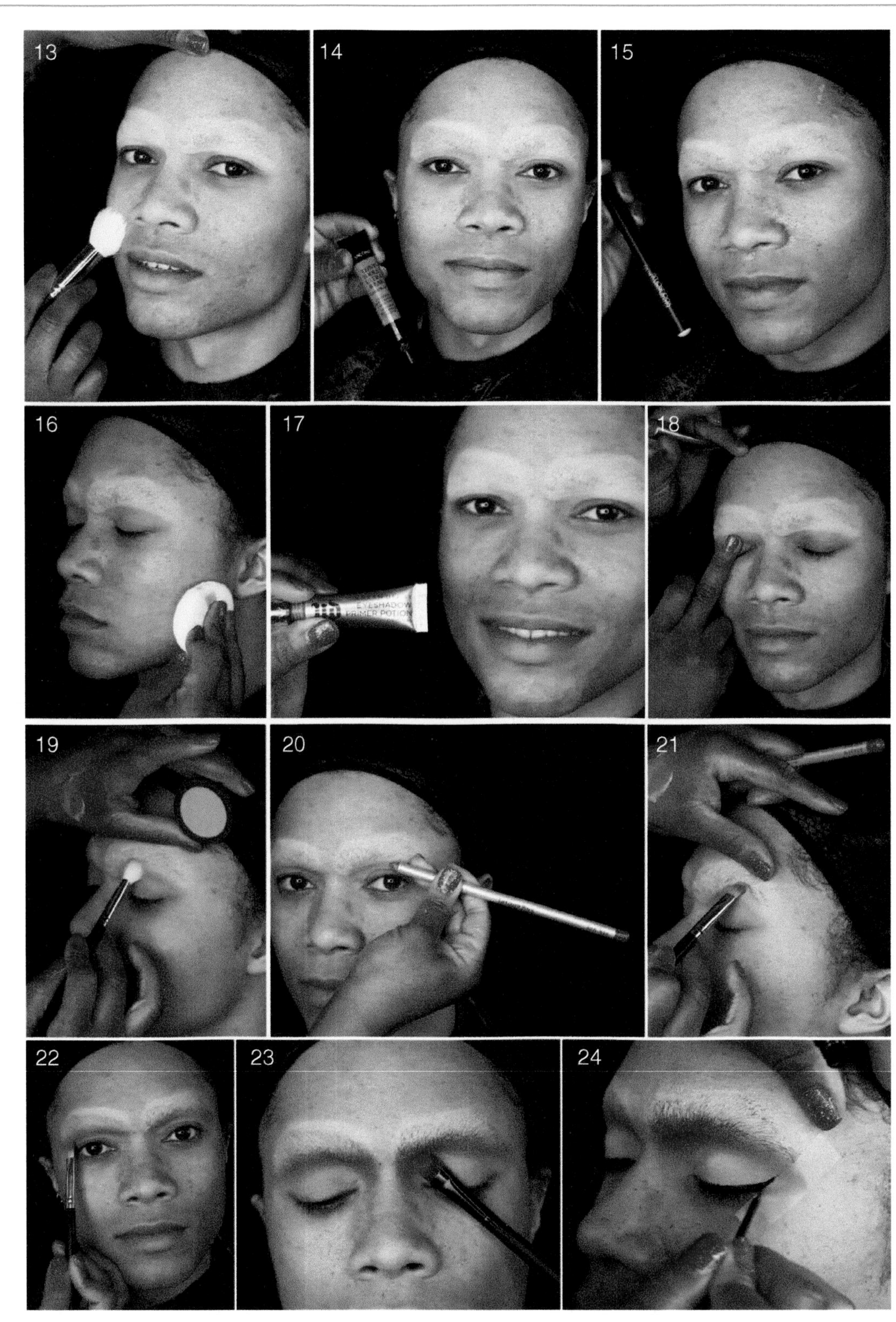

FIGURE 14.11 *(continued)*

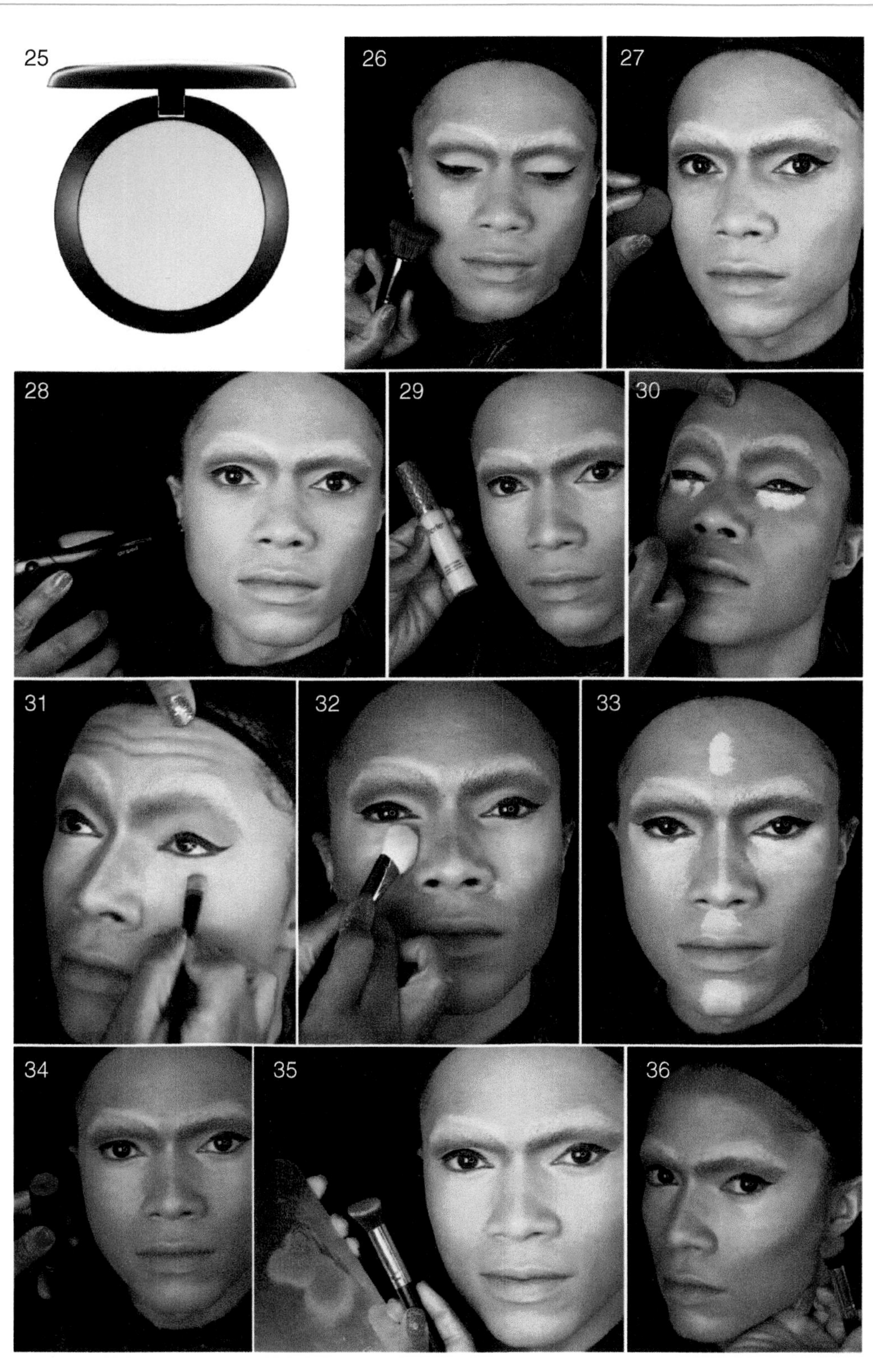

FIGURE 14.11 *(continued)*

FIGURE 14.11 *(continued)*

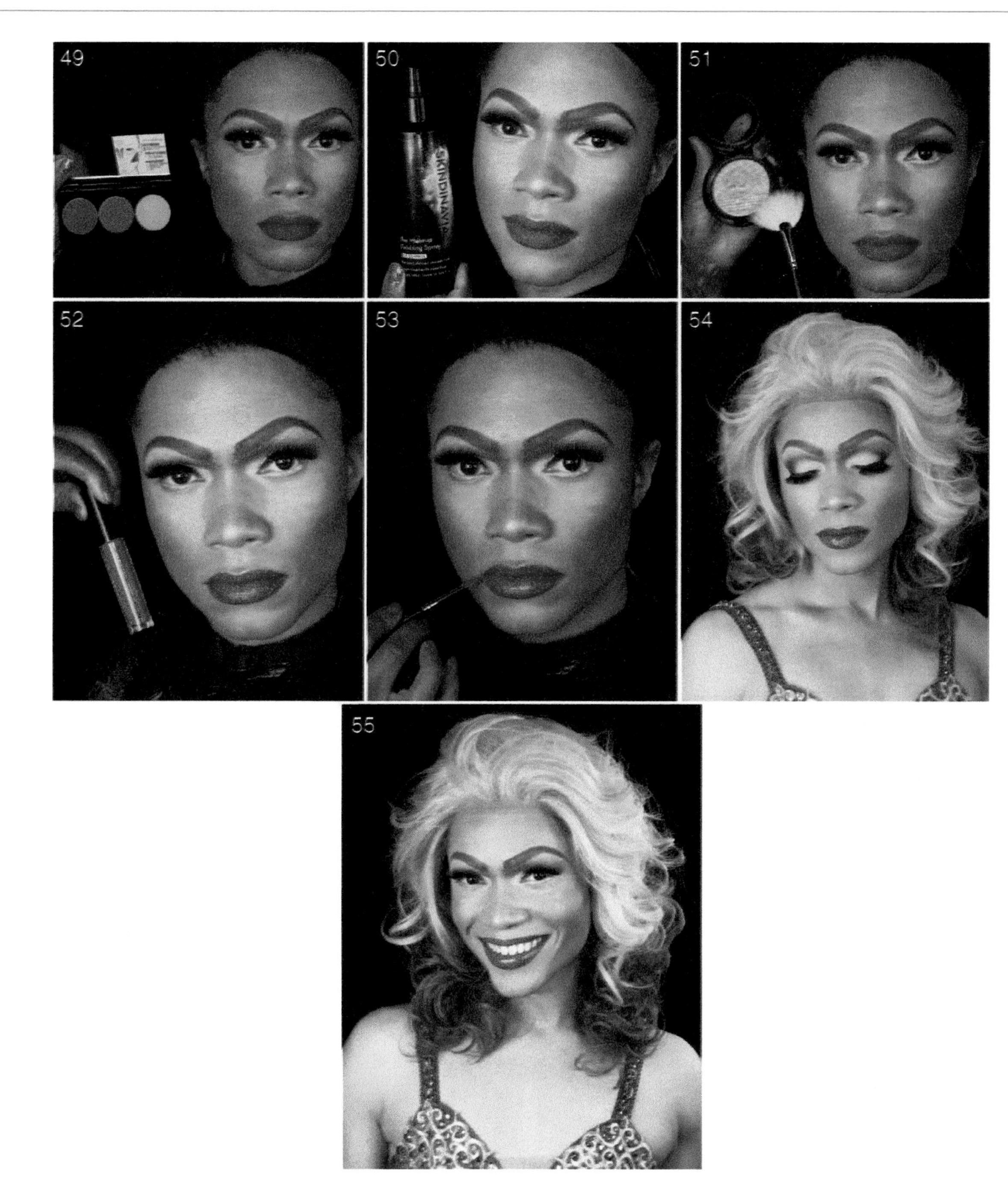

FIGURE 14.11 *(continued)*

1. Male to Female makeup application (Figure 14.11). Model/ Performer: Joseph Harrington II.
2. Hair is braided in preparation for the wig cap. (Assisted by Vanessa J. Lopez.)
3. Arrangement of the braids.
4. Application of the wig cap.
5. Cleaning the brow area with 99% alcohol.

6. & 7. Cover the eyebrows with Elmer's Glue Stick. First, the glue is applied against the natural hair growth to cover all sides of the hair. Then, the brow hairs are flattened smooth.

8. Dry the glue between applications with a hairdryer set to "cool."
9. Clean the excess glue from the edges of the eyebrows using a cotton-tipped applicator and water.
10. Powder the eyebrows between applications of glue until they are smooth (Ben Nye Neutral Set Powder).
11. Apply MAC Concealer C-15.
12. Apply Embriolisse Lait Crème moisturizer over the entire face. Allow the moisturizer to absorb into the skin for at least 15 minutes.
13. Apply a light layer of Becca Backlight (Illuminating) Primer.
14. Lancôme Camouflage/High Coverage Corrector in Orange-Red used here as a beard cover or blue/black color neutralizer (also used as tattoo cover). Apply this product only to the areas where the beard or mustache grow.
15. Apply red color corrector by Smashbox to red areas and blemishes. Blend.
16. Lightly powder the beard cover and color corrector using a small powder puff and a no-color powder.

17. & 18. Eyeshadow primer by Urban Decay applied to the upper lid area.

19. Apply Ben Nye "Natural Blush" pressed color over the entire lid up to the brow.
20. Create an eyelid crease just under the natural brow with Ben Nye Lip Colour Pencil: Spice.
21. Blend out the crease down onto the lid with a small, domed shadow brush.
22. Lightly apply MAC Full Coverage Foundation NW-20 onto the lid.
23. Accentuate the crease with Ben Nye Lumiere Grande Color: Cherry Rose.
24. Create the perfect eyeliner extension by first applying a piece of magic tape at an angle from the outer edge of the lash line toward the end of the brow. Liquid eyeliner is being used in this image.
25. MAC Full Coverage Foundation (NW 35).
26. Apply foundation to the entire face using a flat-topped foundation brush.
27. Blend the foundation with a Beauty Blender-type foam sponge. Lightly dampen the sponge before use. Blend the foundation using a tapping motion.
28. To create an even smoother surface, use an airbrush. (Cordless Airbush by TEMPTU Air SilkSphere: Desert Sand.)
29. Shape Face Concealer by Tarte: Light Sand.
30. Brush on concealer under the eyes.
31. Carefully blend concealer with a small, domed blender brush.
32. Apply setting powder to the under-eye area. Use a medium-angled or domed blush brush.
33. Now apply concealer at the center of the forehead, nose, upper lip, and chin. Blend.
34. Contour foundation by Interface: Cognac.

35. & 36. Place a small amount of contour foundation on a palette. Use a flat-topped angled stipple (blender) brush to apply contour under the cheekbone and across the forehead at the hairline.

37. Place contour along the jawline to minimize a strong, angled jawbone. Blend the contour under the jaw to create a shadow.
38. Place contour on either side of the nose and in a V-shape under the tip of the nose. Use a very small angled brow brush or domed shadow brush.

39. & 40. Carefully blend the contour color on the forehead and cheek into the foundation. Use a blending sponge.

41. Using a small angled brow brush and a dark brown pressed shadow, shape the eyebrows.
42. Using a white eyeliner pencil, draw a line under the lower lash line.
43. Apply MAC eyeshadow: Brun to the outer corner of the eyelid and up onto the crease. The crease should be created above the natural crease of the performer to help open up the eye.
44. Shape the lips by first lining them with a dark lip color (Ben Nye: Vino) and blend onto the lip with a lip brush.

45. & 46. Apply Cailyn Extreme Matte Tint lip color: Pure Lust to the entire lip. Then add MAC Retro Matte lip color: Quite The Standout as a highlight (this is painted within the boundaries of the lip at the sides and to the top and bottom edges of the lips). Allow to dry thoroughly.

47. Add a narrow cream highlight along the center of the nose.
48. Reinforce the contour on either side of the highlight. Softly blend (tap the nose softly with the sponge blender once or twice, just to soften but not completely blend out the lines).
49. Using the Smashbox "Deep" contour palette, strengthen the highlight under the eyes with the Warm Highlight, the cheeks and forehead with Bronze, and under the cheekbone with the Deep contour.
50. Set the makeup with a light mist of Skindinavia Finishing Spray.
51. Place a warm peachy-cream shimmer highlight to the top of the cheekbone.
52. & 53. Add a glossy highlight to the lips with Cailyn Tinted Gloss: Art Touch.
54. Finished makeup.
55. Finished makeup for the character Lola, from the Broadway musical *Kinky Boots* (this is a recreation and is not from the Broadway production).

CHAPTER 15

NONREALISTIC MAKEUP

Nonrealistic makeup comprises makeups not only of fantasy characters such as monsters, demons, and gnomes, but also various human-looking creatures designed in stylized forms like clowns, zombies, and vampires. Nonhuman characters like the mandril, Rafiki from *The Lion King* (Figure 15.1), the lizards from *Seascape*, and the felines like those from *Cats* (Figures 15.2 and 15.3) are all part of makeup designs defined by the term "Nonrealistic."

FIGURE 15.1 *Mukelisiwe Goba as Rafiki from The Lion King from Disney Theatrical Productions Broadway production. Photograph by Matthew Murphy.*

NONREALISTIC STYLES

The nonrealistic styles can range from theatrical realism or *theatricalism* (Figures 15.4 and 15.5a) to nonrealism. When this nonrealism results from imposing a particular style on the design of the makeup, it is referred to as *stylization* (Figure 15.5b).

Stylization. In designing a stylized makeup, you might begin by thinking in terms of using line, color, and form to heighten, exaggerate, simplify, clarify, satirize, symbolize, or perhaps amuse. Instead of consulting photographs for inspiration, you might consult paintings (Figure 15.6), drawings (Figure 15.7), prints, caricatures, masks (Figure 15.8), mosaics, toys, sculpture, or stained glass. Then, from your various ideas, you could select for your designs those that seem best suited to the character, the play, and the style of production.

For a stylized production of a French farce (i.e. George Feydeau's *Flea in Her Ear*) using black and white sets and costumes, for example, black and white makeups are an obvious, but potentially amusing, choice. For a Medieval morality play like *Everyman*, you might design makeups to look like mosaics (Figure 15.9) or stained glass. For the production of a play by Brecht (*The Caucasian Chalk Circle*, *The Good Person of Szechwan*), you could relate the makeups to the work of German artists of the period, like Gabriele Münter and George Tappert.

FIGURE 15.2 *Fantasy character: Female feline. Makeup by Rick Geyer. Makeup and wig design by Paul Hadobas. Model, Amanda Elliot.*

Source: Courtesy of Ben Nye Cosmetics.

FIGURE 15.3 *Fantasy character: Male feline. Makeup by Rick Geyer. Makeup and wig design by Paul Hadobas. Model, Robert Luke.*

Source: Courtesy of Ben Nye Cosmetics.

FIGURE 15.4 *Frank N. Furter in The Rocky Horror Show.*

Source: Photograph by Jesse Kate Kramer (test shoot). Frank N. Furter—Brendan van Rhyn. South Africa. An example of theatricalism.

FIGURE 15.5 *Mephistopheles. Makeup in two different styles. A. Theatricalism. B. Stylization. Makeup by Richard Corson.*

FIGURE 15.6 *Contemporary portrait. Reproduction by Chin Hua Yeh.*

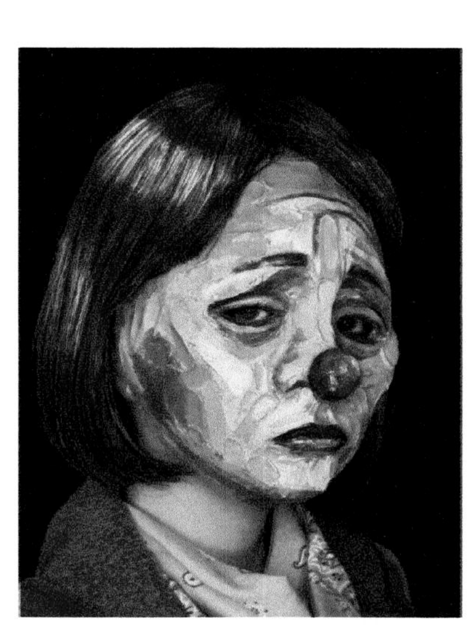

FIGURE 15.8 *Stylized latex mask by Jesse Rose Lowerre.*

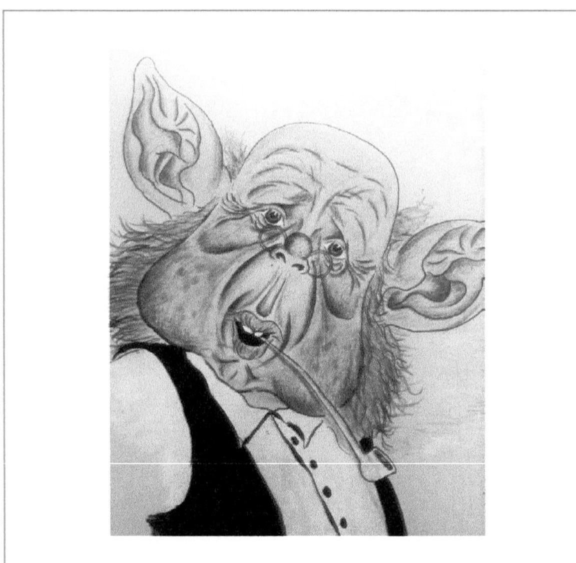

FIGURE 15.7 *Gnome drawing. Courtesy of Stephan Tessier.*

FIGURE 15.9 *Thirteenth-century mosaic head. San Marco, Venice.*

RELATING THE MAKEUP TO THE AUDIENCE

In addition to relating to the style of the production, to the play, and to the character, a nonrealistic makeup should also relate to the audience. Stock characters in the Beijing Opera, for example, are well known to audiences (see Beijing Opera, Figures 15.13 to 15.17). As soon as they appear on stage their often exaggerated makeup and costume define them immediately as specific character types in the story.

Although audiences are usually quite willing to go along with innovations in style, there are certain areas of resistance the actor or the makeup artist should be aware of. Our ideas about some nonrealistic characters may be rather nonspecific and are thus open to fresh interpretation. But our ideas about other nonrealistic characters, such as those in *Alice's Adventures in Wonderland* and *Through the Looking Glass*, for example, are not so flexible. Sir John Tenniel created visual images of the characters in *Alice* (Figure 15.10) that have become the definitive representations of those characters, and most audiences will tend to relate to them more readily on stage if they look rather like the ones with which they're familiar. Likewise, the iconic image of the Frankenstein monster (Figure 15.11) (high, extended forehead, heavy, overhanging brow, gray-green skin color, and neck bolts) created on Boris Karloff by legendary makeup artist Jack Pierce will remain forever part of our collective cultural memory.

In Figure 15.12, makeup artist Joe Dulude II painted the entire body of the actor with Kryolan Supracolor 074 in his version of the Frankenstein monster. The following is an outline of his process:

1. Accent areas on the arms, legs, chest, face, and back with Kryolan UV Dayglow Aquacolor UV-Blue. Over the heart use Kryolan Supracolor 079 and in the center of that highlight with Kryolan UV Dayglow Aquacolor—UV—Red. Accent center with white.
2. Powder entire body with Kryolan Neutral Set loose powder—the more, the better.
3. Apply Obsessive Compulsive Cosmetics Loose Colour in Cavu Blue all over the blue around the heart and up onto the face and head. Apply OCC Loose Colour in Cherry Bomb over the red of the heart. Powder all down again with the Neutral Set.

FIGURE 15.10 *The duchess from Alice's Adventures in Wonderland. With Alice, Cook, Baby, and Cheshire Cat.*

Source: Illustration by Sir John Tenniel.

FIGURE 15.11 *Frankenstein makeup by Stephan Tessier (foam latex prosthetic makeup).*

4. On the blue side of the face Brun and Carbon from MAC was used to do the contours and Gesso to do the highlights. On the flesh side of the face, crème colors from a MAC Fall 14 Trend Forecast Eye palette was used. The colors were Grey Matter, Toasted Chestnut, Tortoise, and Organic. This was a limited item that no longer exists. The colors were all gray/muted greens, gray, and one burgundy.
5. For the scars—they were drawn in with OCC Colour Pencils. Black Dahlia, a dark burgundy, was used for the wound itself. The stitches were drawn in with tarred pencil, black, with feathered, white, to highlight. Make Up For Ever Flash Color palette in red was used to accent the scarring and make it look more fresh.
6. The makeup was powdered with Neutral Set and then the entire body was sprayed with Kryolan Fix Spray.

BEIJING OPERA

There are four main character types in the Beijing Opera: Sheng, Dan, Jing, and Chou. Each character has various physical, vocal, and personality traits. For example, Sheng is a male character with a variety of types: The types of male roles are called Laosheng, Hongsheng, Xiaosheng, Wusheng, and Wawasheng.

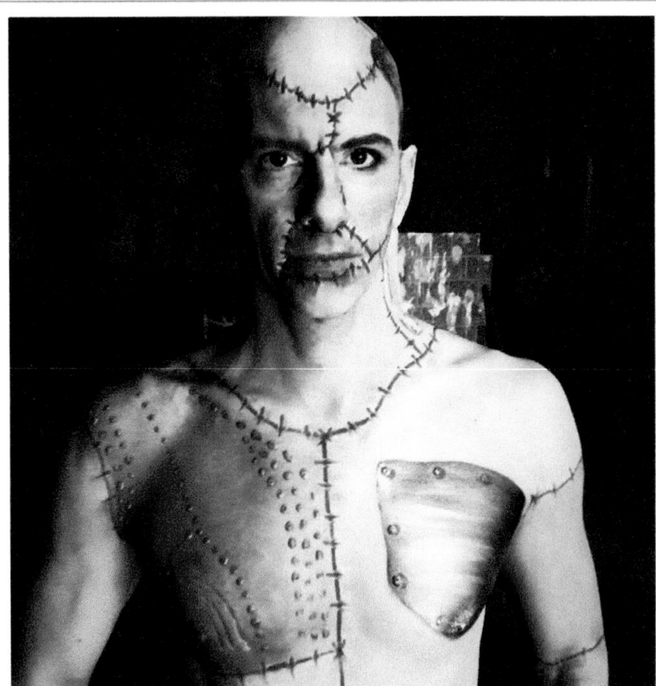

FIGURE 15.12 *Mary Shelley's Frankenstein by Eggtooth Productions.*

Source: Courtesy of makeup artist, Joe Dulude II.

FIGURE 15.13A *Beijing Opera makeup. The foundation for the character Wu Xiaosheng is a white cream-based makeup (CreamBlend by Mehron in White), applied with the hands. It is patted with the fingers into an even, smooth surface. A red cream makeup (CreamBlend by Mehron in Red can be seen in the mirror) is applied starting at the eyebrows and blended to a very pale pink at the jawline.*

FIGURE 15.13B *Beijing Opera makeup. The Wu Xiaosheng performer is fitted into the many layers of his costume.*

The performer in Figure 15.13 is playing a Wu Xiaosheng, a handsome young male, with no beard, wearing an elaborate costume with extremely long pheasant feathers. These feathers distinguish him as a warrior. He sings in a rather high-pitched shrill voice and is quite athletic on stage.

The performer in Figures 15.14, 15.15, and 15.16 is seen here playing the Jing role, a dignified, middle-aged official or scholar, and is being trained in the art of makeup application by the Master Makeup Artist.

The white and gray makeup foundation is completed by the Master Makeup Artist on one half of the face. The student performer will complete the makeup, then apply the black details.

Dan is a term for the female roles in Beijing Opera with six subcategories: Zhengdan, Gui mendan, Wudan, Laodan (old woman), Huadan, and Daomadan.

The performer in Figures 15.15, 15.16, and 15.17 is playing a Zhengdan (also known as Quingyi), a main female role. It is the most important role in Beijing Opera. She is serious, dignified, and decent, mostly seen as mothers and wives. The role is always dressed in yellow clothes and sings with a pure, high-pitched voice.

FIGURE 15.13C *Beijing Opera makeup. The Wu Xiaosheng character is being fitted into his headpiece.*

[These photographs were taken at a dress rehearsal of student performers at the Hong Kong Academy of Performing Arts.]

FIGURE 15.13D *Beijing Opera makeup. The Wu Xiaosheng character on stage (center in blue).*

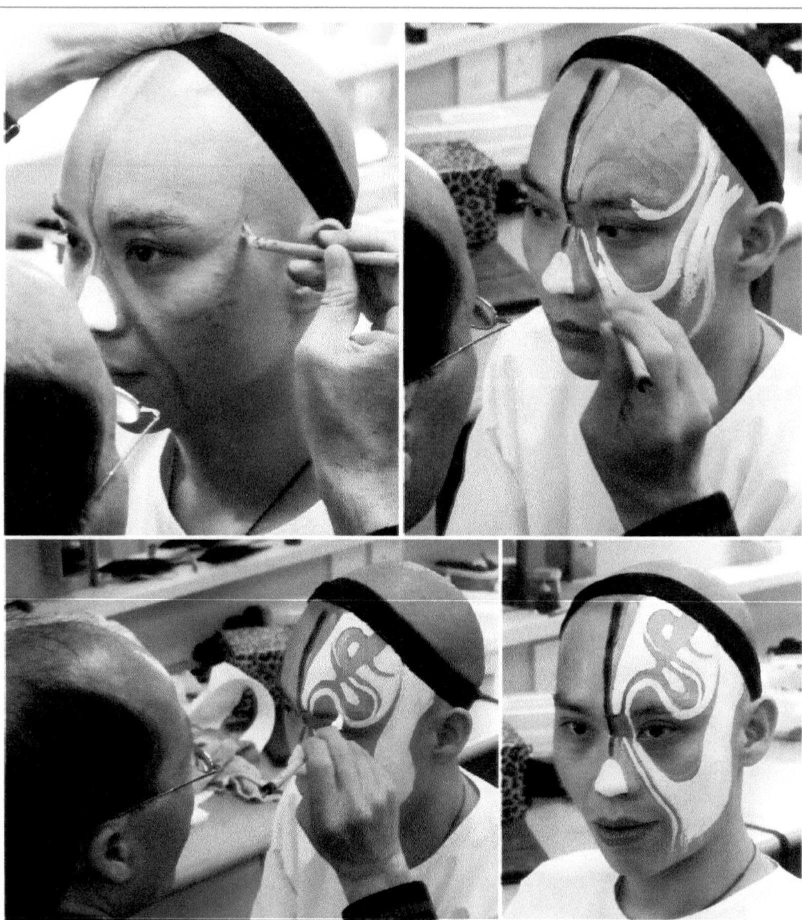

FIGURE 15.14 *Beijing Opera makeup. This performer is playing a Jing role: a dignified, middle-aged official or scholar with a deep, gruff voice and grotesquely painted face. The character has a forceful personality on stage. He wears a black beard and the black and white makeup characterize him as brave (black), yet deceitful (white). There are three types of Jing: Tongchui, a good singer and loyal general; Jiazi, a good acting role; and Wujing, a more physical role that displays a skill in martial arts and acrobatics.*

FIGURE 15.15 *Members of the Beijing Opera, with the Jing character (center).*

FIGURE 15.16 *Beijing Opera character Jing posing after the performance with the performer playing Quingyi.*

FIGURE 15.17 *The performer playing Quingyi.*

NONREALISTIC AND NONHUMAN CHARACTERS

Makeups for nonrealistic and nonhuman characters may or may not be nonrealistic in style. Sometimes—as when an actor is playing a cat, for example—there is no choice since an actor simply cannot be made up realistically as a cat. But the actor can be made up quite realistically as a gnome (see Figure 15.18) or a werewolf (Figure 15.19).

The following suggestions may provide some ideas for dealing with a variety of nonrealistic characters. When referring to these suggestions, bear in mind that the descriptions are based largely on literature, art, folklore, and cultural history; and though they may sometimes be stated dogmatically, they represent only a convenient point of departure. You may wish to vary them to suit your purpose.

Angels: First determine the style of the production and the sort of angel required. If an ethereal angel is called for, you may wish to work with pale lavenders, blues, or whatever color seems appropriate. The features will probably be idealized human ones. A Guardian Angel would certainly be personified as warm, nurturing, and protective, where the Angel of Death might appear as a skull with horns, wearing flowing black robes.

FIGURE 15.19 *Werewolf by Matthew Mungle. Makeup for the "CSI" television show.*

FIGURE 15.18 *Fom latex gnome (foam latex prosthetics by makeup artist, Stephan Tessier).*

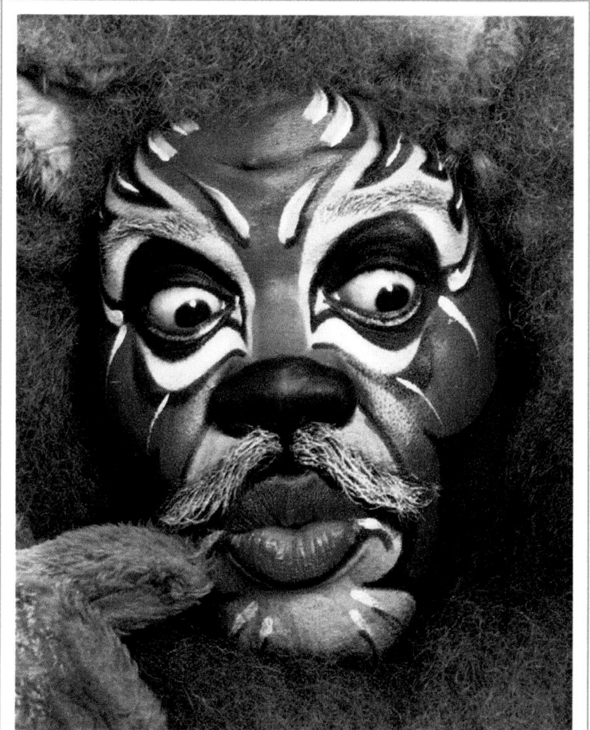

FIGURE 15.20 *The Lion, from the National Tour of The Wiz. Actor, Tedd Ross.*

Source: Photograph by Martha Swope. Copyright Billy Rose Theatre Division, The New York Public Library for the Performing Arts, 1976.

FIGURE 15.21 *Sea creature mask by Marika Klein (latex).*

FIGURE 15.22 *Rabbit makeup by Rebecca Morgan.*

But if you were doing *Angels in America*, the angel could achieve the most serious effect required only with a realistic makeup, a white costume, and enormous wings.

Animals: When animals are played by humans (Figures 15.20 and 16.26), the style of the makeup may be either realistic or nonrealistic. Papier maché, latex, thermoplastics, or heads and masks can be used and sometimes should be, if the style of the production permits. You may prefer merely to suggest animal features on a human face. That can be done in a completely nonrealistic or a modified realistic style with paint (Figures 15.22 & 15.23), or the paint can be combined with three-dimensional makeup. Natural wigs and/or synthetic fur can also be used. Split lips can be drawn (Figure 15.22), foreheads can be lowered, real or painted whiskers can be added, and paws can be made from gloves.

1. Rabbit Makeup (Figure 15.23). Model—Kelly Bland.
2. Eyebrows are covered with glue stick.

3. Flatten the glued eyebrows using a metal makeup spatula.
4. Continue to flatten the eyebrows using the stick end of an eyebrow brush wand.
5. Clean the glue from the surrounding skin using a wet cotton-tipped applicator.
6. Powder the brows with a no-color setting powder.
7. Clown white.
8. Apply clown white to the face using a foundation brush.
9. Fill in the eye area with a pink cream makeup.
10. Shade the forehead area with the pink cream in the shape of the eyebrows.
11. Add pink to the tip of the nose.
12. Lightly apply pink to create the cheek shadow. This creates a triangle from the corner of the mouth, angling slightly upward to the middle of the cheek, then to the edge of the nostril.
13. Create an eyebrow-like outline around the eye with short hair-like strokes. Outline the lower shape of the eye in a similar manner, painting on hair-like strokes using black cream liner.
14. Create the eyebrows by first painting a solid brow shape. Begin shaping and shading the cheek and mouth areas with grayish-black hair-like strokes.
15. Breaking up the solid eyebrow line with hair-like strokes in an upward direction. Notice the pink shading around the upper lip and cheek area. There is a subtle pink shadow in the space between the upper lip and nose.
16. Create the two large front teeth by painting around them with the black cream makeup.
17. Draw in a sharp line at the center of the upper lip.
18. Draw in the black hair-like shadow above the pink nose. At the same time shadow the sides of the nose, again with hair-like strokes.
19. Draw on three long whiskers on either side of the upper lip.
20. Draw on five dots on either side of the upper lip near the whiskers. Begin adding black eyeliner to the upper lash line.
21. Close-up of eyeliner.
22. Add black mascara to the upper eyelashes.
23. Completed rabbit makeup.
24. Completed rabbit makeup with character lashes.

Faded Feline Makeup Application (Figure 15.24)

1. The design by Paul Hadobas combines elements both feline and human, with dramatic touches of age and faded glamour.
2. Block out brows with wax. A mottled texture overall is achieved by stippling three shades of cream makeup, neutralizing the pink in the skin underneath while keeping it somewhat sheer. The muzzle is based with a red neutralizer mixed with white.
3. Additional cream highlights are added to flatten the nose, and bring out the cheekbones and brow. Cream contours are brush-applied to sides of nose, and softly blended.
4. After setting the blended cream with a neutral powder, the eyes begin to get shaped with an iridescent purple shadow.
5. The feline tip of the nose and muzzle are defined with liquid liner, as is the eye crease, bringing the inner corners in and down. Lite Auguste and Azalea under the lower lash will lend a teary-eyed quality.
6. Pressed shadows in shades of taupe and gray feather the lower lash line, and are also used to bring texture to the jawline. Silver shimmer powder (wet) on the eyelid, and dry blended softly just above the crease.
7. Mouth shape sketched in with pencil. Brows shaped with downward slant, first in pressed shadow in black, then given more crisp graphic "hair" in small, short strokes with pancake, in black, gray, and white.
8. Texture to the neck is done with cool brown pancake applied with the narrow end of a pre-cut foam sponge, then softened with pressed shadows in grayer tones. A pair of dramatic false eyelashes, selected for their density and ragged tips, are a big part of taking the "glamorous" quality over the top. The wig is added, and blends well into the painted texture at the hairline. Mole and whiskers have been sketched with a small liner brush in black pancake. The deep red on the lips has a smudge outside the liner to add to the effect of wear and tear. The additional fur-like texture

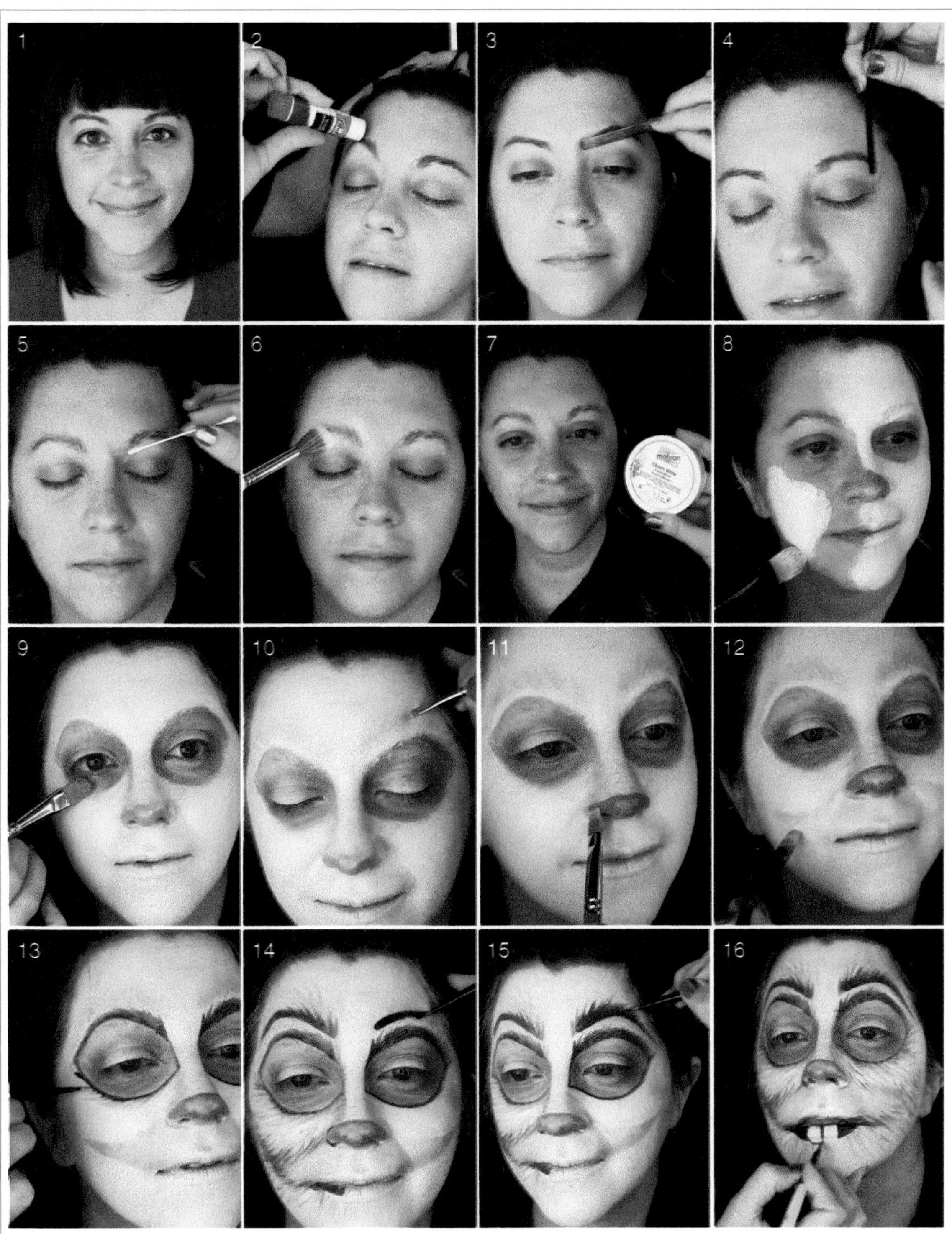

FIGURE 15.23 Rabbit makeup design by Rebecca Morgan (recreated by makeup artist Tara Cooper, model Kelly Bland).

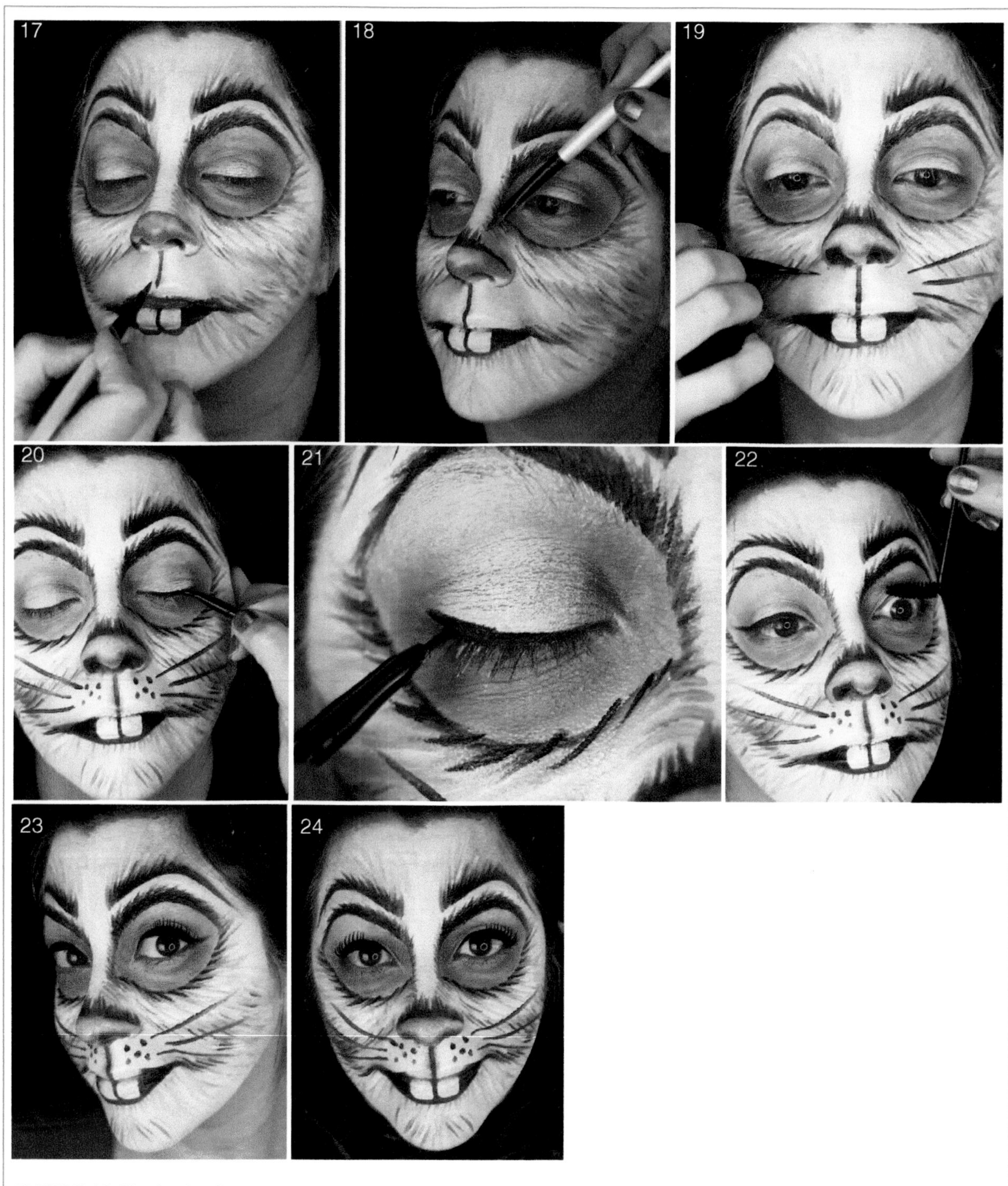

FIGURE 15.23 *(continued)*

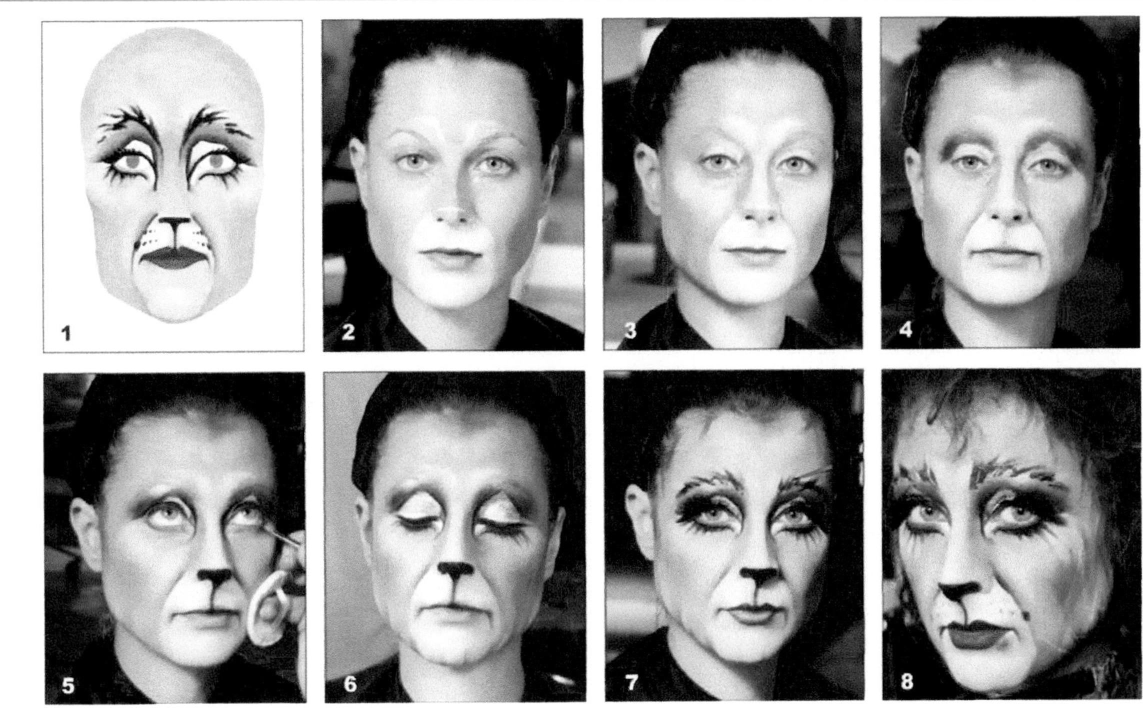

FIGURE 15.24 *Fantasy character design, Faded Feline, by makeup artist, Paul Hadobas. Model, Amanda Elliot.*

Source: Courtesy of Ben Nye Cosmetics.

is dry pressed shadow applied with a thick liner brush to taper it, and is complementary to the painted graphics on the body stocking. Judiciously applied glitter around the eyes makes the character come to life under the lights.

Product List for Faded Feline Makeup by Ben Nye Cosmetics

Foundations:
- P-14 Sallow Green
- P-15 Cadaver Grey
- SA-2 Golden Latté

Highlight:
- CL-1 White Cream Color

Shadow:
- SA-2 Golden Latté

Muzzle:
- White, plus NR-1 Red Neutralizer 1

Face Powder:
- TP-5 Neutral Set Powder (Colorless)

Powder Rouge:
- DR-12 Pink Blush

Lip Colors:
- EP-85 Espresso
- LS-33 Marilyn Red
- LS-53 Sangria
- LS-31 Hot Coral

Stripes (Pressed Colors):
- ES-30 White
- ES-302 Vanilla
- ES-39 Rich Sable
- ES-97 Greystone
- ES-62 Mossberry
- ES-99 Black

Eye and Brow Colors:
- LU-13 Royal Purple
- LU-14 Amethyst
- LU-16 Azalea
- P-101 Lite Auguste
- LXS-4 Silver Sparkle Pwdr
- LXS-20 Starry Night Pwdr
- EL-0 White Cake Eye Liner

EL-1 Black Cake Eye Liner
CF-23 Grey MagiCake
LE-1 Black Liquid Liner
MD-4 Silver Glitter
MD-10 Silver Prism Glitter
MD-1 Opal Ice Glitter

Uncle Jinxy Fantasy Animal Makeup (Figure 15.25)

1. Block out brows. Draw general guidelines with white pencil.
2. Apply Light Peach to center area of design and Dark Peach to outer area of design. Highlight forehead, nose, and chin with Ivory. Apply white to the muzzle. The muzzle is the brightest area of the design and appears to protrude from the face. Powder thoroughly with colorless powder, removing excess with powder brush.
3. Paint fake brow and line eyes with Dark Brown cake. Paint Rust cake under brow. Create "new" eyelids and highlight beneath brow with Yellow cake. Apply Light Orange pressed on lids above Yellow and contour sides of nose.
4. Create "new" eye crease with Dark Orange pressed; deepen with Mocha pressed. Define crease with Light Brown cake.
5. Line beneath lower lashes with White cake to open and brighten eyes. Line above Dark Brown eyeliner with White cake. Mix cake with LiquiSet in place of water for durability.

   Contour cheeks with Light Orange, Dark Orange, and Rusty Red pressed (light to dark from top to bottom).
6. Highlight forehead and "apples" of cheeks with Vanilla pressed to enhance roundness. "Wash" cheeks and forehead with Melon pressed.
7. "Wrinkles" extended beyond outer corners of eyes imply friendliness. Paint top wrinkle with Black cake, bottom with Light Brown cake.

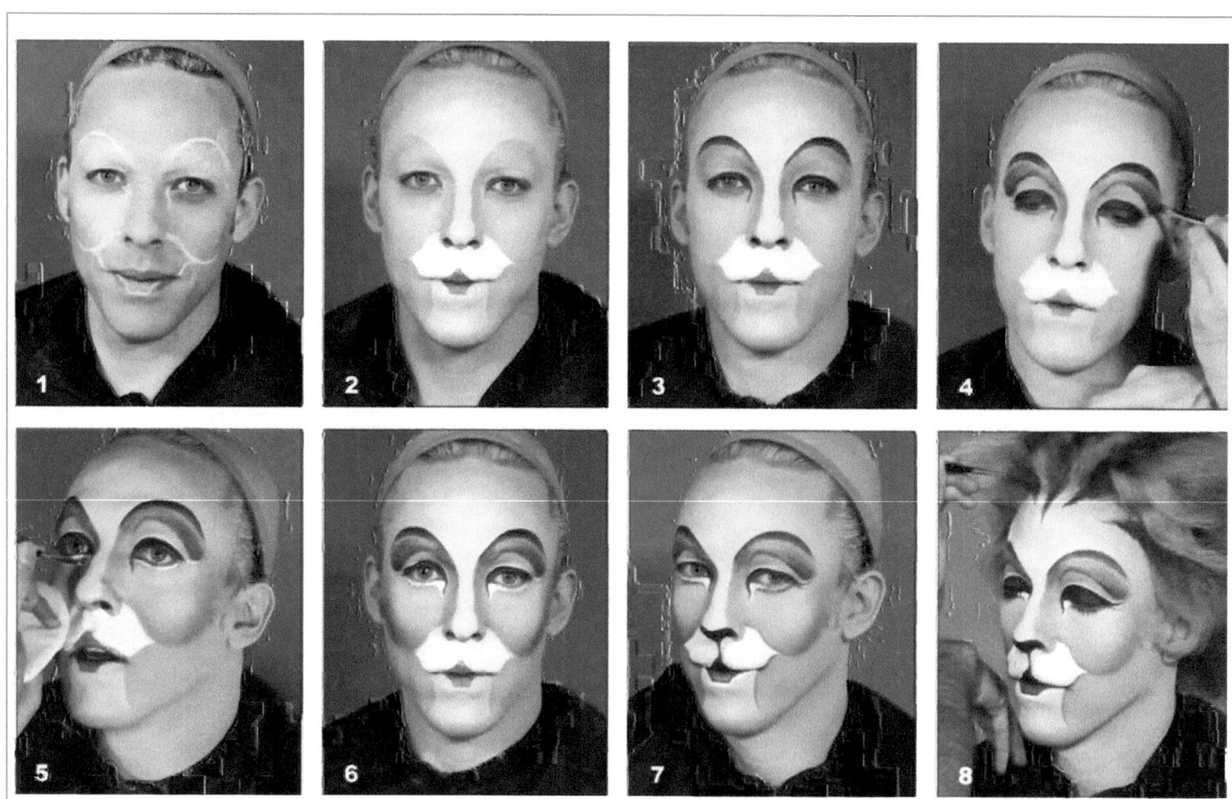

FIGURE 15.25 *Fantasy character: Uncle Jinxy. Makeup by Rick Geyer. Makeup and wig design by Paul Hadobas. Model, Robert Luke.*

Source: Courtesy of Ben Nye Cosmetics.

Line lower muzzle, lower lip and eyes with Black cake. Define top of muzzle, white "beard," and beneath cheek contour with Light Brown cake. Paint nose with Dark Brown cake. Add muzzle contour with Maize cake.

8. Add stripes at forehead with Rust and Red-Brown cakes, blending up and into wig stripes of same shade. Fade stripes onto forehead with Mocha pressed shadow.

   Paint stripes at chin with Yellow, Maize, and Light Brown cakes.

Product List for Uncle Jinxy Makeup by Ben Nye Cosmetics

Creams:

- MO-11 Mellow Orange Lite (Light Peach)
- P-2 Lite Pink + NT-4 Tattoo Cover 4 (Dark Peach)
- P-1 White Cream Foundation
- CH-0 Ultralite (Ivory)
- CR-7 Coral Cream Rouge

Pressed Powders:

- ES-39 Melon Shadow (Melon)
- DR-99 Orange Pop! (Light Orange)
- DR-98 Autumn Sunset (Dark Orange)
- ES-52 Mocha Shadow (Mocha)
- DR-2 Coral Red + DR-99 (Rusty Red)
- ES-302 Vanilla Shadow (Vanilla)

Cake Colors:

- EL-4 Dark Brown Liner (Dark Brown)
- EL-1 Black Cake Liner (Black)
- CF-89 Maize MagiCake (Maize)
- CF-9 Sunshine Yellow (Yellow)
- CF-19 Rust MagiCake (Rust)
- CF-26 Brown-Black + CF-52 Cranberry MagiCakes (Red-Brown)
- PC-135 Calcutta Cake (Light Brown)
- PC-1 White MagiCake (White)
- MC-1 MagiColor White Pencil
- TP-5 Neutral Set Powder (Colorless)
- LQ-2 Liquiset Mixing Liquid

(Note: Use water-based Cake colors for hard lines, or bold, solid coloring. Use Pressed Powders for more gradual shading and transparent coloring.)

Step-by-step Tiger makeup by Jasmin Walsh (Figure 15.27)

1. Tiger Makeup—Cameleon Face and Body Paint
   - BL3015 Pure White
   - BL3013 Strong Black
   - BL3012 Coffee
   - BL3024 Machiatto
   - BL3022 Almond
   - BL304 Banana Yellow
   - BL306 Orange Juice
   - Round (cut in half) soft, high-density sponge
   - Brushes—Rake brush
   - Round, fine-point brush—size 6
   - Cat's tongue brush (to be used as a dry brush)

2 Model—Elisangela Jnocéncio Gomes Borges. Using a damp sponge, load on the sponge a mixture of the yellow, orange, and almond, not picking up too much of any of the three colors, and blend them onto the nose, forehead, cheeks, and jaws, leaving the eyes, chin, and space for the muzzle without any paint.
   Continue applying in small amounts the different tones of brown and spread unevenly on the nose, forehead, cheeks, and jaws, and try to give a bit of texture to the base.

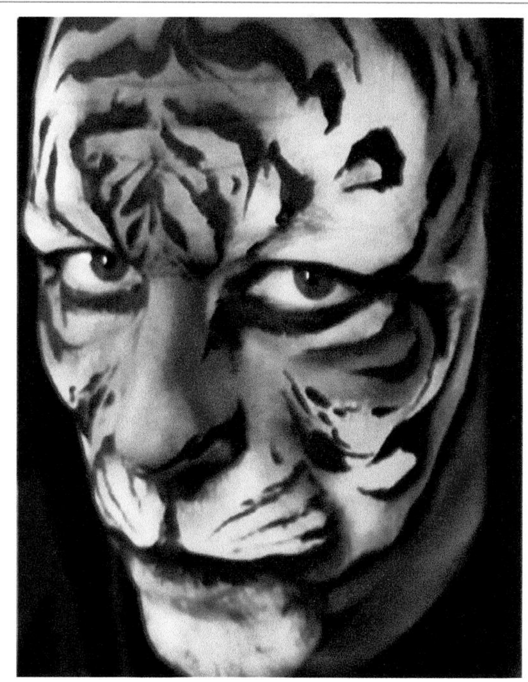

FIGURE 15.26 *Tiger makeup design and application by makeup artist, Jasmin Walsh. Model, Craig Walsh.*

3. With the clean side of the sponge, apply white to the eyes (going up to the forehead), muzzle, cheek, and chin area.
4. Once the white paint has dried, load a "rake" brush with white paint and create hair-like strokes from the white into the colored base.
5. Close-up of the "rake" brush, hair-like texture.
6. Load a round brush with pink and paint the nose.
7. Load black paint onto a fine, round brush and paint around the nose and paint a muzzle, and using a dry cat's tongue brush, blend a bit of the black to create some shading on the muzzle.
8. Still using the fine round brush and the black paint, paint around the eyes and start creating the tiger markings.

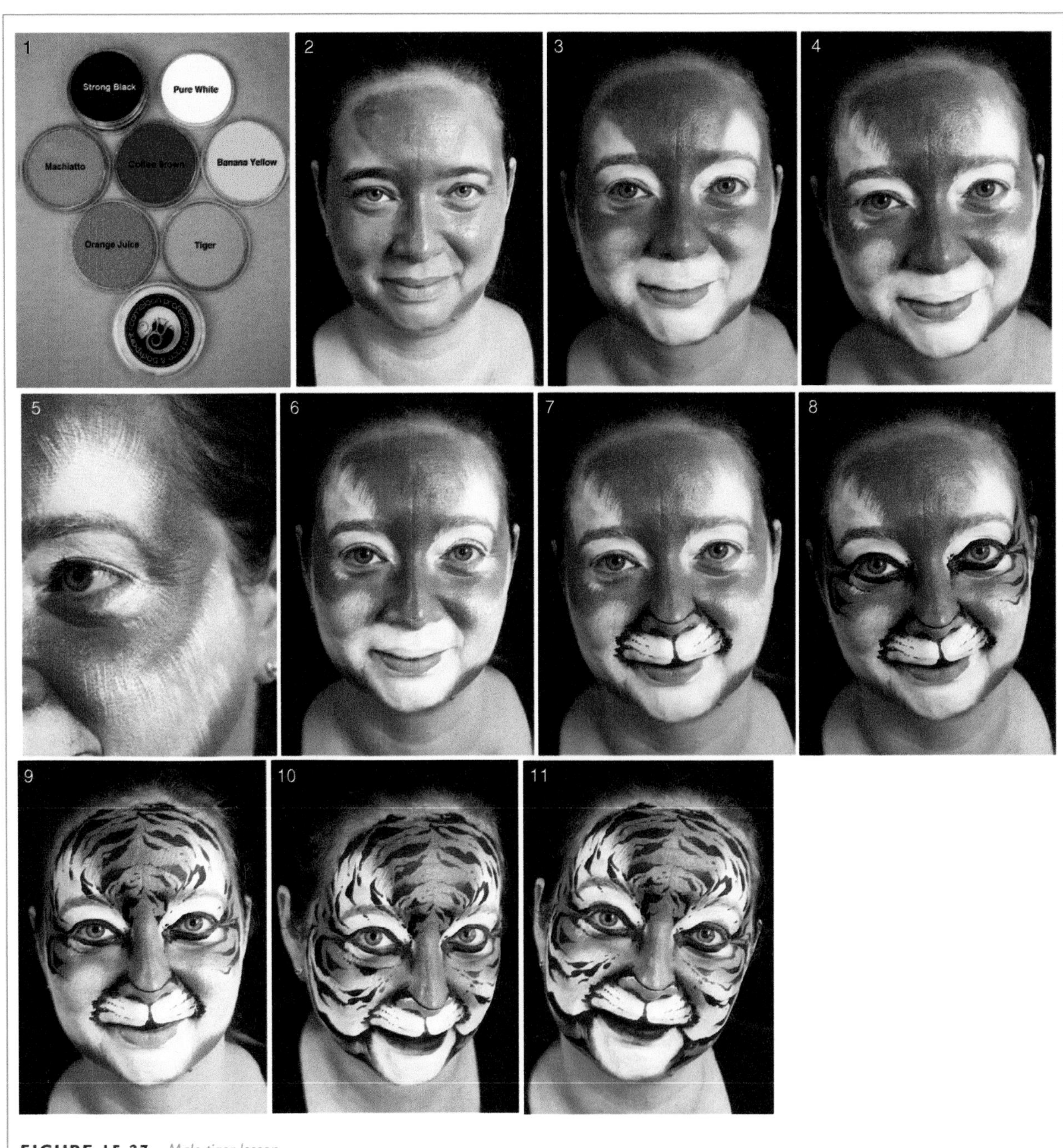

FIGURE 15.27 *Male tiger lesson.*

9. Paint on the forehead the tiger markings going from small to larger stokes and using thicker and thinner stokes as you go up from the eyes to the top of the forehead.
10. Paint the black markings around the jaw area and the bottom lip. On the bottom lip use the dry brush to drag and smudge the paint toward the chin, so that there isn't a straight line on the bottom lip. Finalize by adding some fine lines and dots on the tiger's nose in white paint.
11. Finished tiger makeup.

Birds: Bird faces can be built up with three-dimensional additions or completely stylized with painted details. Sometimes the two may be combined. Birds with small beaks and large eyes (owls, for example) are, of course, easier to do with paint than large-beaked birds. Brightly colored feathers can be attached with spirit gum. A complete mask would be more practical if the makeup had to be repeated. For smaller-beaked birds being done with makeup rather than masks, putty might be used instead of latex. Color can be as realistic or as fanciful as the birds themselves.

Clowns: Traditional circus clowns defined by organizations such as Ringling Bros. and Barnum & Bailey Circus are visually and emotionally represented by three traditional clown types: Auguste, Tramp (or sad) clown, and White Face. Professional clowns Lou Jacobs, Emmett Kelly, and Frosty Little are examples of these styles, respectively, and pride themselves on designing and applying their own makeups, never copying the makeup of another clown.

FIGURE 15.28 *Snow leopard by Mehron Cosmetics.*

Modern performing artists in the clowning or circus industry have developed a contemporary aesthetic, taking the classical tradition and modifying it for a modern sensibility. Defined by individual artistic expression, and thematic concepts rather than following strict traditions, the clowns of companies like Cirque du Soleil work with professional designers to create their characters.

a. Former Ringling Clown, Ben Schave (Figure 15.31).
b. Ben warms Mehron's Clown White between his hands before applying it to his face, neck, and ears.
c. Patting the makeup produces a smooth, even finish.
d. Moistening a cotton-tipped applicator.
e. The moistened cotton-tipped applicator is used to "cut out" the design details in the clown white foundation. He cuts out the brows, below the eye, bottom lip, and cleft in chin.

f., g., and h. Fill in the "cut-out" areas with Mehron's black foundation greasepaint.

i. Powder with a white sock filled with baby powder. Avoid inhaling the powder.
j. Remove powder with a large powder brush.
k. Ben uses a string to hold on his nose.
l. Ben Schave dressed in his "Agent Suit," knit bald cap, and wig.

Shakespearean clowns are represented by *fools* or *jesters*, and *buffoons* (or *bouffon*, a modern day French theater term coined by Jacque Lecoq to describe a specific style of performance work that has a main focus in the art of mockery), and require a makeup—either *realistic* or *theatrical*—appropriate for the individual character. Other clown types represented in theatrical stage performances, such as in the play *Coulrotropia* (the title is a slight deviation from the word coulrophobia, a fear of clowns) produced in Bristol England by Pickled Image Limited, are based on iconic designs interpreted by the actors to better suit their theatrical design aesthetic and characterizations.

Clowns by their nature, no matter how happy or sad, can for many people produce a sense of fear, creepiness, or even of horror. The film industry has certainly exploited humanity's fear of clowns. Films such as *Killer Klowns from Outer Space* (1988) take a humorous approach to the clown genre film, while *All Hallows Eve* (2013), *American Horror Story: Freakshow*, and Stephen King's *It* (1990; 2017) cross into the dark side of clowning.

FIGURE 15.29 *Emmett Kelly—Hobo Clown with permission of © Glenn Embree/mptvimages.com.*

FIGURE 15.30 *Contemporary clown makeup.*

The first step in designing a makeup for a circus clown is to decide what sort of clown you want—sad, happy, elegant, shy, brash, suspicious, ineffectual. Then design an exaggerated, stylized makeup to fit the conception. For a sad, Tramp clown, made famous by Emmett Kelly, for example, the curious expression of the eyebrows and the corners of the mouth slant downward (see Figure 15.29). His stylized beard stubble and tattered clothes are intended to draw empathy from the audience. A happy clown will, of course, have the corners of the mouth turned up. If your clown is to be an "Auguste" (see Figure 15.35), he will presumably have white paint accenting the eyes and mouth, pinkish cheeks, and a red nose. The "white face" clown or Pierrot, is a strikingly elegant, yet powerful, character and is usually the clown in charge. Bright and colorful expression painted on a background of pure white was performed by the iconic Ringling Bros. and Barnum & Baily Circus' "Boss clown," Frosty Little (see Figure 15.34). Sketching your design on paper first is likely to save time and result in a better makeup.

The incredibly dense cream makeup, clown white (see Appendix A) is most often used as foundation. All exposed areas of flesh should be evenly colored. The Ben Nye cosmetic company has named a cream character color "Auguste" in honor of the iconic clown type. Then with pencils, brushes, and shading colors, you can duplicate your design. Bulbous clown noses can be molded with latex or purchased ready-made. Red-rubber balls are sometimes used. The hair should be treated in a style harmonious with the rest of the makeup. A skull cap or a wig is usually worn.

Death: is usually pictured as having a skull for a head. The facial bones can be highlighted with white or ivory and shadowed with gray, charcoal-brown, or both. If the head is not going to be covered, a white skull cap or a plastic or a latex cap should be worn. The cap, which should cover the ears, can be painted the same color as the face and the edges blended carefully into the foundation. The eyebrows should always be blocked out (see Chapter 14).

If the makeup is to be luminous, the white paint can be dusted with fluorescent or phosphorescent powder (see Appendix A) before any shading is done. With fluorescent makeup, an ultraviolet ray must be used on a dark stage to cause luminosity.

If Death is to appear part of the time disguised as a human, a normal though pale makeup can be used instead of

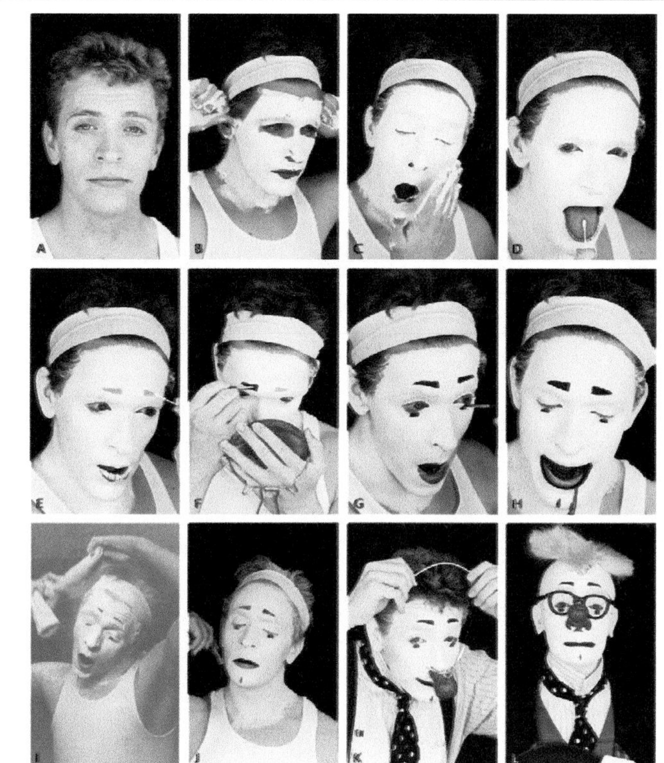

FIGURE 15.31 *Clown makeup lesson.*

FIGURE 15.32 *Coulrophobia clown makeup with permission from Pickled Image Limited production, Coulrotropia. Actors, Dik Downey and Adam Blake. Costume design, Linda Annaveld. Makeup, Dik Downey & Adam Blake.*

Source: Photograph by Adam D.J. Laity Bristol, England.

FIGURE 15.33 *Clown horror mask by Chibbi Orduña.*

white and the fluorescent paint or pigment applied only to the bones of the skull. Under normal stage lights the makeup will look normal, but under the ultraviolet ray the skull will appear. If the hands are to be visible, they should, of course, be made up in harmony with the makeup on the face. It is also possible to present Death in other ways—as a coldly beautiful or handsome person, perhaps, as a black-hooded figure with no face at all, or as a clown.

Devils and Demons: The conventional devil usually has a long face with sharp, pointed features, prominent cheekbones, long, hooked nose, well-defined lips, dark, upward-slanting eyebrows close together, and deep-set eyes. He may also have a mustache and a small, pointed beard. Conceptions of demons are usually less conventional and more imaginative.

Elves: Elves are usually pictured as very small with pointed or butterfly-shaped ears, large mouths, small, turned-up noses or long, pointed ones, and round or slanted eyes. The hair may be short or long. Older elves usually have beards. Red cheeks are appropriate for good-natured elves of any age. The film *Lord of the Rings* features the Sindarin elf, Legolas, from Mirkwood Forest, with sharp, pointed ears and long pale hair. He is neither tall nor short, has a delicate mouth, and a strong, aquiline nose.

Fairies: Fairies tend to be diminutive and graceful, unless they have turned bad, in which case they will appear more evil and witch-like. Wicked fairies (Carabosse in *The Sleeping*

FIGURE 15.34 *Frosty Little with permission from Sabrina Lowe, Director, Global Public Relations. Feld Entertainment, Inc.*

FIGURE 15.35 *Auguste clown makeup (by "Ambrose").*

Beauty, for example) are more like wicked witches and are sometimes played by men, giving them stronger, less feminine features. Emphasis in the makeup should, of course, be on wickedness—dark, slanting eyebrows, close together; evil, piercing eyes, etc. (see *Witches*). Good witches may tend to look more like fairies.

The skin color for good fairies is usually light and delicate—shell pink, lavender, orchid, pale blue, or green, gold, or silver are possibilities. Red shades, being more human, should be avoided. Metallic flakes or sequins are sometimes used. The flakes usually adhere to greasepaint. If they don't, you might try rubber mask grease, or you might use stubble paste (see Appendix A) as an adhesive. Sequins can be attached with a latex adhesive or spirit gum.

The features should be delicate and well formed. The ears may be pointed. A delicate lip coloring should be used but no cheek rouge. The eyebrows and sometimes the eyes may be slanted. The hair of female fairies is usually long and golden.

Ghosts: Ghosts are usually thought of as being pale and rather indistinct. Highlighting is, of course, essential in achieving an appropriate ghostly effect. As for the makeup, pale, bloodless colors—such as white or lighter, grayed tints of blue, lavender, greenish yellow, or yellowish green—might be used. The bone structure can be highlighted with white or pale tints of the base color and shadowed with gray, especially in the eye sockets, which should be the most deeply shadowed areas of the face. Hair on the head and on the face can be white or gray.

Gnomes: Gnomes are commonly thought of as living underground. They are always mischievous and nearly always unfriendly. They may be very ugly, even deformed. A long nose, prominent cheekbones, jutting brow and receding forehead, pointed chin, receding chin, fat cheeks, sunken cheeks, large ears, very bushy eyebrows, no eyebrows, pop eyes, small and beady eyes, and bulging forehead are possible characteristics. Older gnomes may have long and flowing beards. The skin may be very wrinkled and either very pale or very sallow (see Figure 11.3).

Goblins: Goblins are believed to be evil and mischievous. Rough and swarthy skin, slanted slits for eyes, enormous mouths, flat or long and carrot-shaped noses, extremely large ears, and pointed teeth are possibilities to be considered in the makeup.

Grotesques: Grotesques are ugly or comical creatures (human or nonhuman) that are in some way distorted or bizarre. The Weird Sisters in *Macbeth* are sometimes made up as grotesques.

Monsters/Beasts: This category covers a variety of creatures, from mechanical men to werewolves. If the monster or beast is to be animalistic, the hair should grow low on the forehead and perhaps cover a good deal of the face (see Figure 15.40). The nose usually needs to be widened and flattened. False teeth made to look like fangs will make the monster more terrifying. But if the creature is to appear in a children's play, it should be conceived with some discretion. Gory details, such as blood streaming from an open wound and eyes torn out of their sockets, might well be saved, if they are to be used at all, for adult horror plays. Foreheads can be raised and heads squared off, eyes rearranged, teeth made large and protruding, and so on. Skin-texture techniques—tissue with latex, tissue and spirit gum, latex and bran or cornmeal—can be used to good effect.

Ogres: An ogre is usually conceived to be a hideous monster who feeds on human beings. Prosthetic applications will undoubtedly be needed. You might consult the suggestions for making up a gnome and then exaggerate them.

Pan: Pan is the mythological Greek god of forests, flocks, and pastures. His head and body are those of an elderly man, and his lower parts are those of a goat. He is usually depicted with horns.

Pierrot: Pierrot and Pierrette are often made up with a white foundation covering all exposed flesh. Ivory or very pale pink can be used if preferred. The lips should be small and quite red with a pronounced cupid's bow. The natural brows should be blocked out, and high, arched ones painted on with black eyebrow pencil. The eyes should be well defined, and the rouge should be two round spots. For a more completely stylized makeup, rouge, lips, and eyebrows might all be in the shape of diamonds or other simple geometric figures. The design of the costume should harmonize.

Statuary: All exposed flesh should be made up; the color depends on the color of the material of which the statue is supposedly made. Grays, grayed blues, grayed greens, and grayed violets are useful for shadowing. Avoid warm tones unless the statue is of a color that would require warm shadows. Whether or not the makeup should be powdered will depend on the material of which the statue is supposedly made. If the finish would naturally be shiny, a cream or a grease foundation without powder can be used. A dull finish requires a water-soluble or a powdered cream or grease foundation.

Gold, silver, or bronze statues can be made with metallic body makeup. The effect is excellent, but the technique should be used with care (see discussion in Appendix A under *Metallic Makeup*).

Toys: Makeup for toys other than dolls—as, for example, tin or wooden soldiers or marionettes—can best be copied

FIGURE 15.36 *Demon carnival mask and makeup design by Luis Demetrio llanos Meola, owner of Selva Africana Taller in Baranquilla, Colombia.*

FIGURE 15.37 *Devil/demon latex mask by Sue McCorkle (latex, hair).*

from the actual toys. Their unreality should be stressed in order to counteract the obvious lifelike qualities of the actor.

Trolls: Trolls live underground or in caves and are usually thought of as being stupid, ugly, and hateful. They have been described as having large, flabby noses, enormous ears, rotten teeth, and disgusting skin. For the skin, the face might be covered with latex over mounds of derma wax. For a rougher texture, miller's bran could be added. (For wonderful illustrations of trolls, goblins, brownies, elves, and other fairy creatures, see *Faeries*, a book by Brian Froud and Alan Lee.)

Vampires: A vampire is a preternatural being that spends its days in a coffin and comes out only at night to drink fresh warm blood. The "vampire" fantasy popularized by Bram Stoker's *Dracula*, F.W. Murnau's 1922 film, *Nosferatu*, the *Underworld* films and the *Twilight* series present characters synonymous with the undead. Since they never see the light of day, they invariably have pale, bloodless complexions—with the exception of the lips, which are sometimes abnormally red. Dark hair is conventional, as are razor-sharp fangs. The face should usually be thin and rather emaciated.

Werewolves: Werewolves, or sometimes "lycanthropes," are legendary creatures known to shape-shift from human form into a supernatural wolf-like beast (see Figure 15.19). Popularized in movies such as *An American Werewolf in London* (1981), *Van Helsing* (2004), and *Underworld: Rise of the Lycans*

FIGURE 15.38 *Orlando Bloom as the Sindarin elf, Legolas Greenleaf. Lord of the Rings: Fellowship of the Ring (2001). Marjory Hamlin—prosthetics supervisor. Permission of Warner Bros. Entertainment, Inc.*

(2009), the transformation of the werewolves is as fascinating to an audience to watch as it is for the FX artist to create.

Witches: Traditional witches usually have sharp, hooked noses, prominent cheekbones, sunken cheeks, thin lips, small, sunken eyes, prominent, pointed chins, numerous wrinkles, straggly hair, clawlike hands, warts and hair on the face, and seldom more than one or two good teeth. The complexion may be light or dark, sallow or swarthy, gray or puce. It might even be yellow, red, blue, green, or violet.

Witches can, however, be good or bad, young or old, ugly or beautiful. And the makeup can be realistic or stylized. Whereas a wicked old witch (as described in the song "Ding Dong the Witch is Dead" from the film *The Wizard of Oz*) might have a face with green skin, a hooked nose, and an extended, pointy chin, Glinda, the good witch from the same movie, had a face of alabaster, rosy cheeks, and golden hair. A bad (but sophisticated) young witch, on the other hand, could have a face with a glint of steel, slashed with jet-black eyebrows over heavily lashed, slanted eyes. And then there are the three witches in Shakespeare's *Macbeth*, who symbolize the darkness of the human soul, who can be visually portrayed in any number of styles, limited only by one's imagination. Witches can also be comic masters of magic as seen in the film *Hocus Pocus* (1993), starring Bette Midler, Sarah Jessica Parker, and Kathy Najimy.

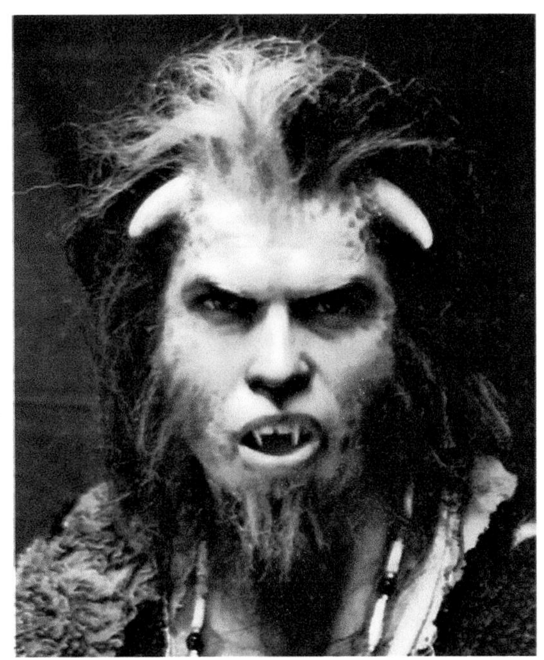

FIGURE 15.39 *Satyr. A brown cream makeup was set with a brown pressed powder. Makeup designed and applied by Paul Hadobas.*

FIGURE 15.40 *The Beast from Beauty and the Beast, The Victoria Theatre production. Victoria, Texas. Makeup artist, Nathan Jones.*

Zombies: Popularized in Michael Jackson's *Thriller* video, *Fear the Walking Dead* TV series, and the *Santa Clarita Diet* (Netflix), zombies are usually portrayed as flesh-eating relics of once-living humans. Zombie character designs are as individual as the artist creating the character. There are endless possibilities to inspire the makeup artists: the zombie's former professions, age, period in history, ethnicity, levels of decomposition, and by the circumstances of the demise of their former human selves. Their human lives may have ended by some dramatic or horrific event and possibly at the hands of someone they knew. Shooting, stabbings, mutilation, or being buried alive are all reasons for a zombie to return from the dead to avenge his/her premature death … or should we say *murder*. A well-designed zombie will surely be presented with some level of decay, both in their clothing and in their skin and hair. Skin texture may well be expressed in three dimensions using liquid latex, foam latex, gelatin, silicone, putty, or prosthetic transfers. The prosthetics can easily be created freeform directly on the face using softened gelatin, silicone, bondo (Prosaide adhesive thickened with Cab-O-Sil), and/or latex and tissue (see Figure 10.8 Zombie Makeup).

FIGURE 15.41 *Pan mask (latex) by Samantha Gashette.*

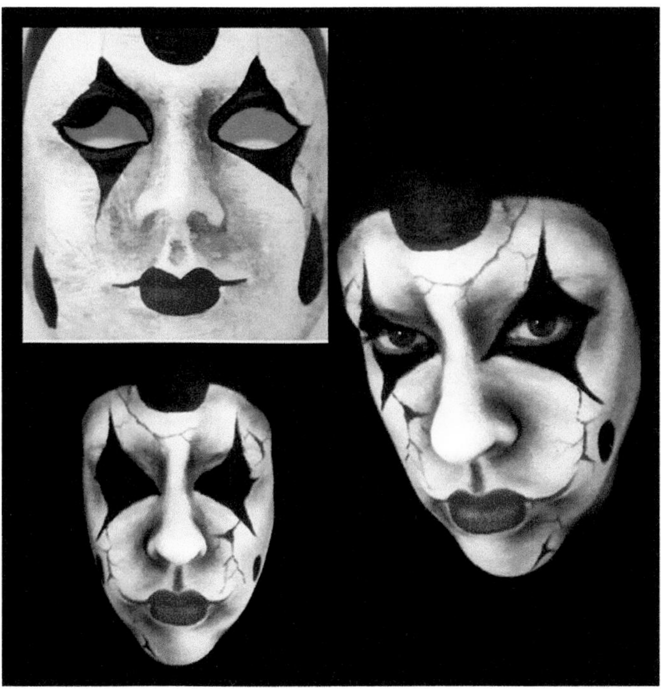

FIGURE 15.42 *Pierrot makeup by Rebecca Morgan with historic mask research.*

FIGURE 15.43 *Drácula di Dario Argento 2012 (licensed by Oscar Berrendo and Victoria Bernal at egeda Madrid, Spain). Actor Thomas Kretschmann as Dracula.*

FIGURE 15.44 *Zombie scientist full-face prosthetic, with sage-colored skin with yellow highlights and blue shadows. Makeup designed and applied by Paul Hadobas.*

FIGURE 15.45 *PopArt Zombie by makeup artist Marie-Laurence Tessier.*

FIGURE 15.46 *Makeup artist Marie-Laurence Tessier in her studio using the Snazaroo Face Paint Palette.*

FIGURE 15.47 *Snazaroo face and body paint.*

FIGURE 15.48A *Biker zombie. Silicone face prosthetic with sutures across the brow line and a full set of zombie dentures. Painted with alcohol-based makeup. Model, Louis Nergal. Makeup design and application by Raul Cuadra (Chile).*

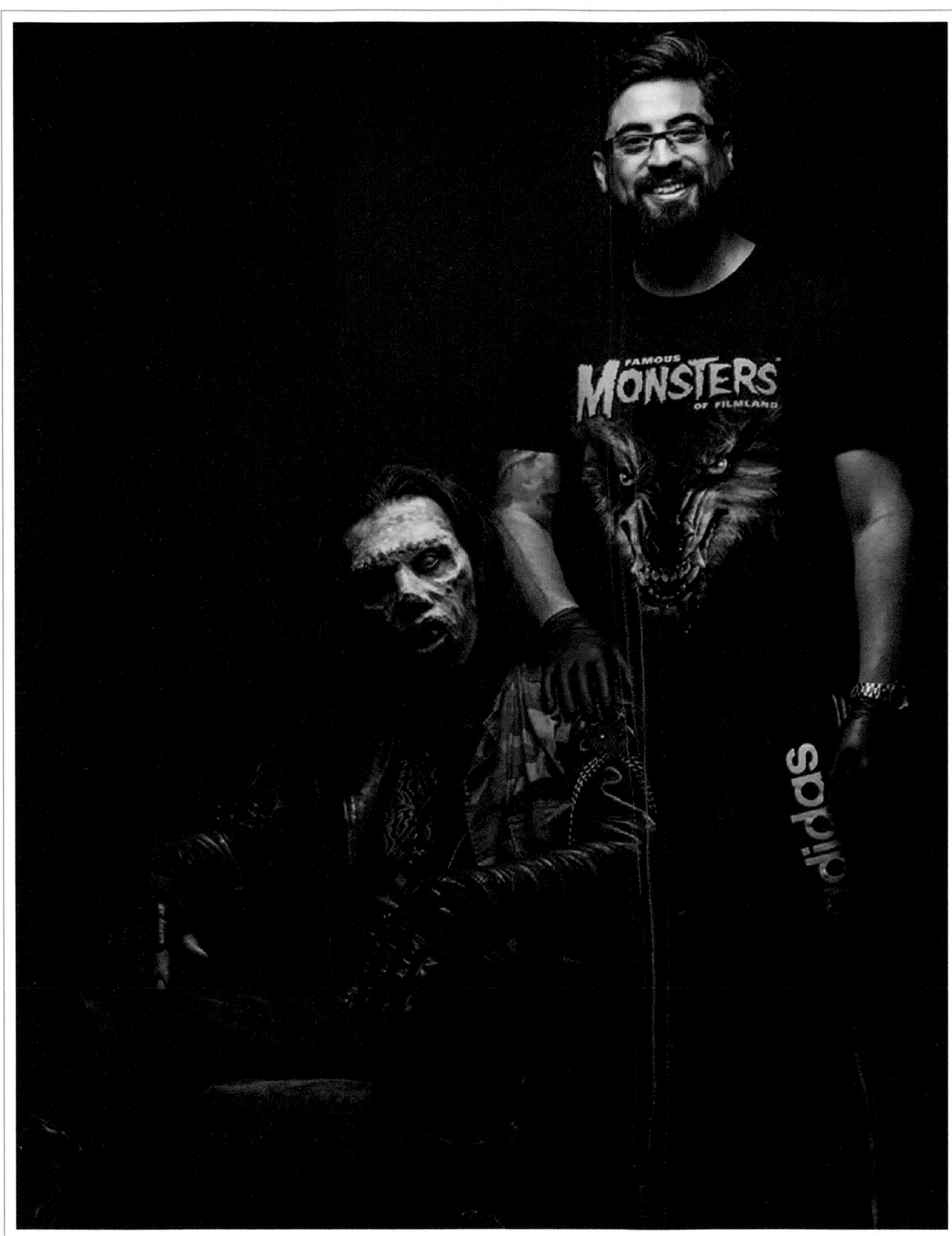

FIGURE 15.48B *Biker zombie. Makeup designed and applied on model Louis Nergal by Raul Quadra (Chile).*

APPENDIX A

MAKEUP MATERIALS AND GLOSSARY

This is a partial list of materials, terms, and vocabulary used in the makeup classroom and studio. It can serve as a starting point for creating a customized reference guide for the makeup student. The specific products in this appendix can be cross-referenced in the source appendix (Appendix B), along with additional vendors and their websites.

Acetone—A flammable liquid ketone (C3H6O) used mostly as a solvent. In the makeup profession acetone has been used to dissolve and blend edges of prosthetics. It has also been used to clean brushes and adhesive off the wig lace.

Acrylic—Acrylic polymers (plastic) are used in many products: fake acrylic nails, acrylic paints, and colorants to tint latex and PAX Paint (used to paint foam latex appliances).

Adhesive removers—liquid: Most adhesives will recommend a remover that works best with its properties. Some example removers are: Bond Off, Detachol, Isopropyl Myristate, Orange Solvent, RCMA Adhesive remover, and Super Solv.

Adhesive removers—RCMA, Telesis, and RJS products sell gel-formula removers that stay where you place them.

Adhesive tape (toupee tape)—A clear, two-sided tape that can be sold in strips or rolls. Remove the paper from one side, attach to a surface, then remove the paper from the other side to attach to a clean, oil-free face, or body.

Adhesives—The following products are some examples of adhesives (there are many choices on vendor websites where you can decide what properties will work best for your project).

Spirit Gum: An all-purpose amber-colored adhesive used most notably to attach hair products (mustaches, beards, and wigs), and simple prosthetics (nose, ear tips, chins). (Tip: after applying to the skin it should be tapped with a finger until tacky. It naturally dries a little shiny and is not particularly flexible and is not advised for application to soft, flexible skin surfaces. Many artists use a small piece of leather chamois to press the hair lace into the adhesive for greater contact and to cut down on the shine. Matte spirit gum is also available. Not a flexible product. The basic formula is isopropyl alcohol, resin, copal, and silica. SD Alcohol 35-A is the solvent and resin is the adhesive. Spirit gum was first produced in the 1890s.

Prosaide®: (see the website for all of the product options) This adhesive is used for attaching medical prosthetics and three-dimensional Special Effects Makeup appliances. Formulated for sensitive skin, non-irritating, water-based products. Once dry, the bond is waterproof.

Telesis Beta Bond and Beta Bond Plus (Premiere Products, Inc.): Acrylic bonding products, Beta Bond is used for vertical hold, Beta Bone Plus is used for horizontal bond. Beta Bond Plus absorbs powder, makes edges nearly invisible, and is tackier and more pliable than Beta Bond. Both are non-flammable. Remove with Beta Solv or Telesis Super Solv.

Telesis 5, 7, & 8 Silicone Adhesives (Premiere Products, Inc.): Telesis adhesives are medical-grade, pressure-sensitive adhesives especially useful on sensitive areas around the eyes and mouth. They are also produced in matte formulas for laying lace hairpieces. Non-flammable and non-toxic.

Sigma Bond (Premiere Products, Inc.): Acrylic-based and useful for attaching 2-part platinum silicone wound and scar appliances (like Alcone's 3rd Degree). It is a strong, safe, flexible, and easy-to-use product to adhere lace products to the skin. Easily removed with Super Solv adhesive remover.

FIGURE A.1 *Duo Striplash adhesive.*

FIGURE A.2 *Adhesive removers.*

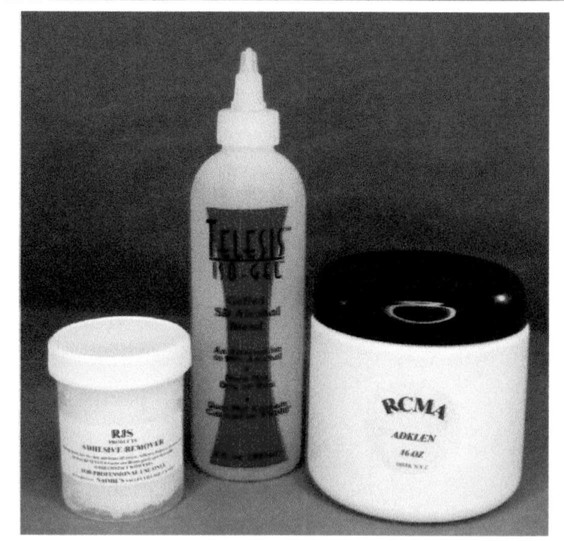

FIGURE A.3 *Gel adhesive removers.*

FIGURE A.4 *TEMPTU airbrush makeup pod system.*

Duo: An adhesive that is primarily used for attaching false eyelashes. It is a latex-free formula that is safe for sensitive skin and people wearing contact lenses.

Airbrush—The "brush" is a pen-like apparatus that is attached to an air compressor, and the force of the air distributes liquid cosmetics or paint. Some of the uses include high-definition (HD) camera work, temporary tattoos, stencil work, body painting, and painting prosthetics. There are companies that specialize in airbrushes and airbrush products. Some of the vendors are listed in Appendix B, Sources.

Airbrush cosmetics—Liquid cosmetics with a consistency that is compatible with the airbrush system. The pigment can be emulsified in different mediums—water, alcohol, or silicone.

Alcohol—99% Isopropyl is the usual strength for many makeup purposes, like cleaning adhesive residue or blending edges of some prosthetic appliances. The 70% strength can be substituted, but may not clean as effectively. They can be used to thin temporary tattoo inks, to revive dried inks, and to thin prosthetic colors (Although Rubber Mask Greasepaint [RMGP] may lose some of its workability). There are also types of cake cosmetics that are activated with 99% alcohol—these were alcohol-based liquids that were poured into containers and dried. You can also use 99% alcohol to remove prosthetics and clean wig lace. Alcohol can cause dryness and skin irritation. Available at drug stores.

FIGURE A.5 *Table-top airbrush holder.*

FIGURE A.6 *TouchUp Antishine by Mehron.*

Alcohol-based makeup—Used with 99% alcohol as a solvent. This product is applied with a brush or sponge and will not rub or sweat off.

Alginate—A non-reusable impression powder for taking face casts and duplicating molds. It comes in regular and

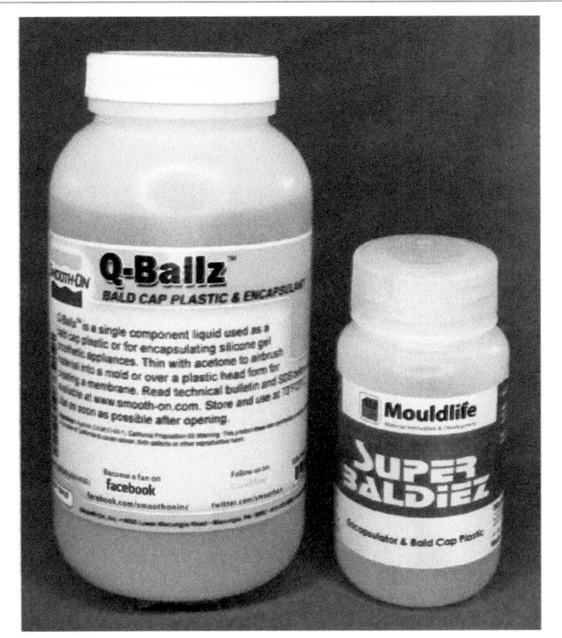

FIGURE A.7 *Encapsulator and bald cap plastic.*

prosthetic grade and in a variety of formulas based on working time. Available from dental supply stores, and various Special Effects Makeup vendors. See index listings for specific references and information.

Alja-Safe Alginate™—This product is manufactured by Smooth-On and contains no free crystalline silica, which is a carcinogen. Used to mold and cast. Cures quickly, makes accurate reproductions of faces and body parts.

Appliance—A generally accepted substitute name for a prosthetic.

Astringent—An alcohol-based skin care product used to help improve the skin's appearance by removing excess oils, cleansers and dirt, and minimizing pores. It is recommended to be used between cleansing and the application of moisturizer. Experts recommend a "toner," a milder, alcohol-free product, for drier skin types. Witch hazel is a natural plant-based astringent with known cleansing and healing properties.

Bald cap—See *Plastic and rubber caps.*

Barrier products—These are available in cream, spray, and paint-on versions. Barrier products are water- and perspiration-resistant formulas applied to the skin to reduce irritation from cosmetics and adhesives and to increase the adhesion of prosthetic devices. See Appendix B, Sources, for vendors.

Beard block—A shaped wooden block used for ventilating beards. Available from wigmakers' supply houses. A plaster

FIGURE A.8 *Barrier Spray by Mehron.*

FIGURE A.9 *Ben Nye products.*

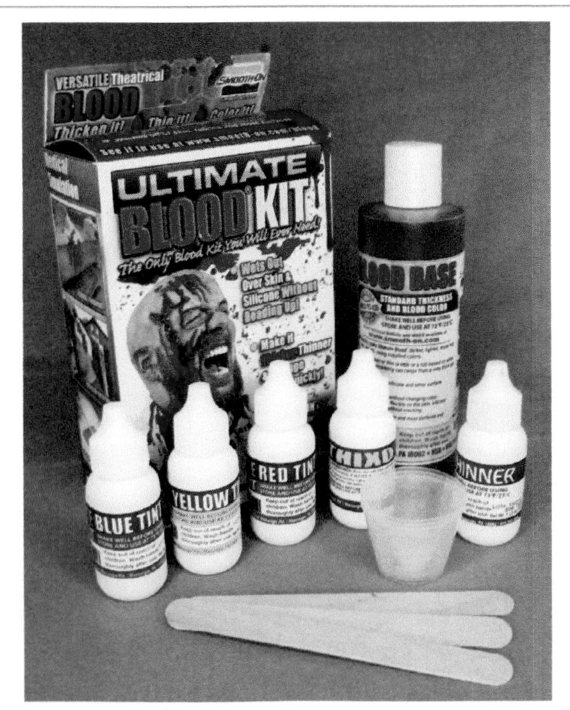

FIGURE A.10 *Ultimate Blood Kit by Smooth-On, Inc.*

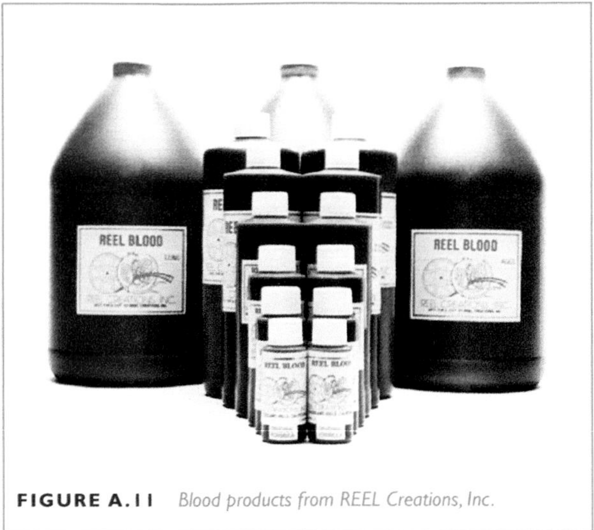

FIGURE A.11 *Blood products from REEL Creations, Inc.*

cast of the actor's head can be substituted if no beard block is available or if a more precise fit is required. The lace can be attached to the plaster with masking tape. If you want to use a wig clamp to work on the plaster head, embed a 1-inch pipe into the plaster while it is still wet—the pipe will fit over a standard clamp.

Black wax—This type of wax is used for blocking out teeth to make them appear lost, broken, or uneven. It is softened in the hand, then applied to a well-dried tooth or teeth. It can be removed with a dry tissue. Black tooth enamel (in a liquid form) serves the same purpose and is available from various vendors. Sometimes a black eyebrow pencil can be used for a temporary effect.

Blend (blending edge)—During the prosthetic application process, it involves making the edges of the prosthetic disappear into the surrounding area.

Blender—A type of transition piece for a prosthetic that is usually made from the same material as the prosthetic.

Body Double™—This is a platinum silicone-based product produced by the Smooth-On company. It is used for the

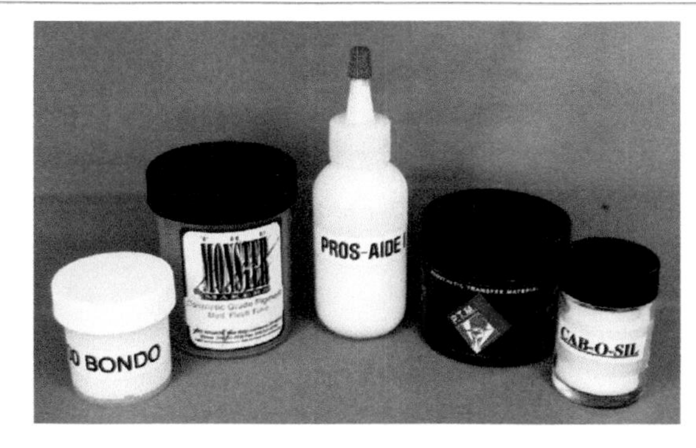

FIGURE A.12 *Bondo transfer products.*

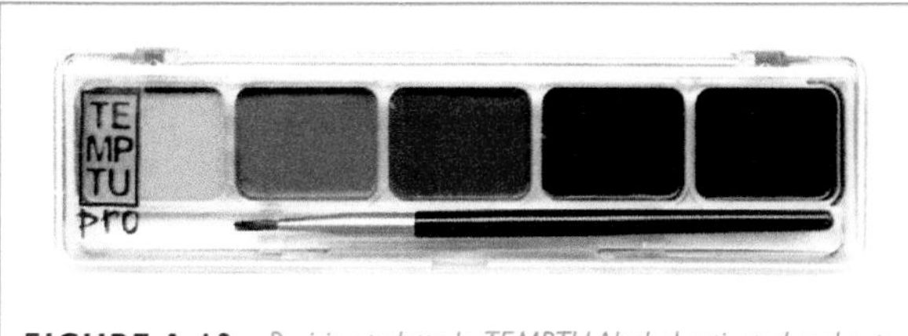

FIGURE A.13 *Bruising palette by TEMPTU Alcohol-activated makeup.*

molding and casting of the torso and head. It copies the form in perfect detail and the mold will last through many castings.

Body Makeup (see Chapter 6)—Available as an opaque liquid, a transparent liquid, or a powder. Opaque liquid body makeup is a greaseless foundation comparable to cake makeup. It can be applied with a sponge, brush, or airbrush and is removable with soap and water or makeup remover. See Appendix B, Sources, for vendors.

Bondo (PAX putty, PAX butter)—Thickened Prosaide used in the production of "transfer" prosthetics made popular my makeup artist Christien Tinsley. It is also used to fill in holes, build up shapes, or to smooth out and blend edges of prosthetic appliances and bald caps. It is made by mixing just enough Cab-O-Sil with Prosaide to prevent the mixture from running. Apply the mixture with a flat dental spatula or a small wedge of red stipple sponge. The name, PAX butter, refers to the same material when made with PAX Paint (colored). Can be removed with Prosaide removers.

Brushes, Chinese or Japanese—Watercolor brushes with a fine, sharp point. They are useful in accenting wrinkles and fine details in the makeup. Find them at art supply stores and websites.

Brushes, Dye—They are also referred to as hair-coloring brushes and can be found in various forms. Some are shaped like toothbrushes and can be used for applying spirit gum remover to ventilating lace when removing wigs, toupees, beards,

FIGURE A.14 *Brush cleaner by Crown Brushes.*

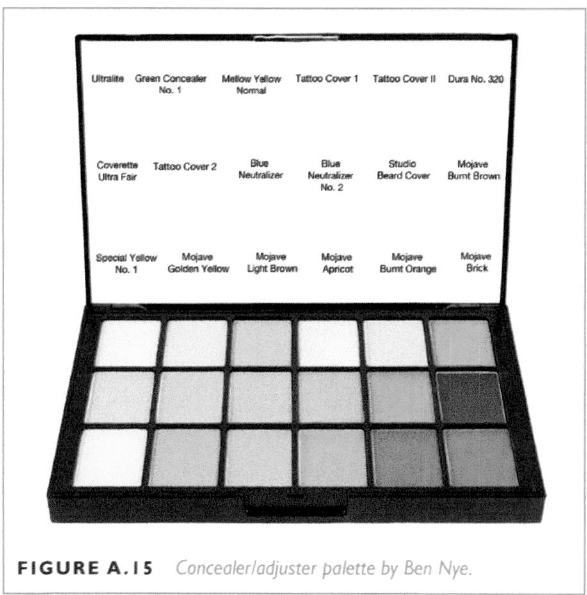

FIGURE A.15 *Concealer/adjuster palette by Ben Nye.*

and mustaches. See hair supply vendors, and makeup companies that carry hair supplies.

Burlap—An open-weave material, an un-dyed natural fiber, that is dipped into plaster and used to reinforce molds.

Cabo-Patch (see Bondo)—This is mostly used to help blend the edges and/or repair foam latex prosthetics.

Cab-O-Sil (fumed silica)—A fumed silica powder used as a thixotropic agent or thickener. Add it to Prosaide to make Bondo or to PAX to make PAX butter. It will thicken just about any liquid. It can also be used as a matting agent for most adhesives.

Cake makeup—A compressed powder in cake form that is water-soluble. It can be applied dry, or with a dampened sponge or brush. The cakes can be the dry or moist version. The moist cake is somewhat easier to blend and stipple with. See Appendix B, Sources, for vendors.

Camouflage crème—see *Concealer*, *Dermacolor*, and *Tattoo covers*.

Carcinogenic—A substance that is known to cause cancer.

Casting fiber—Made of long fibered hemp, this material is used for reinforcing plaster molds.

Castor oil—A highly emollient carrier oil that serves to bind together ingredients of cosmetic formulations such as Rubber Mask Greasepaint (RMGP). On its own it is ideal for coating latex appliances before applying crème makeups. It is also sold under the name Castor Sealer by the Ben Nye company and Castor Seal by Graftobian. Castor oil can be found in drug stores and pharmacy departments.

Castorsil—A mixture of Cab-O-Sil and castor oil. It makes a gel that is then mixed with an oil-based liner color to create a thicker, subtly tinted glaze used to color Old Age Stipple, prosthetic appliances, and three-dimensional latex and gelatin makeups. Glazes are more natural-looking than opaque colors and can be built up gradually.

Character powders—A variety of pigmented powders used on the face, body, and costume to resemble dirt, dust ash, charcoal, and grease. It is also available in white for specialty makeups. Powders also come suspended in solutions for spraying, painting, or sponging on skin and costumes. Check source websites for the range of types available.

Cholesterol cream—Find this product in the aisle with hair conditioning products. It is used to strengthen and condition dry and chemically damaged hair. It can also be used to flatten and keep the hair in place when necessary under a bald cap for a life casting.

Clown white—This is an opaque, highly pigmented, white makeup used primarily for clown makeup and other white makeups where full-coverage is needed. See Appendix B, Sources.

Collodion—A clear, viscous solution of cellulose nitrates in alcohol and ether. There are two types of Collodion—flexible and nonflexible. The flexible is used for building up three-dimensional shapes with cotton and other fillers. The nonflexible or rigid type shrinks as it dries and it is used directly on the skin for making scars or pock marks (see Chapter 10). It dries quickly and can be diluted with acetone, or rejuvenated with Hexane. Collodion can be peeled off the skin or removed with acetone. See the Kryolan and Mehron vendor websites for more details. Collodacolor, a pigmented Collodion, is available from Michael Davy Film & TV Makeup. A skin barrier cream or liquid is recommended for this product.

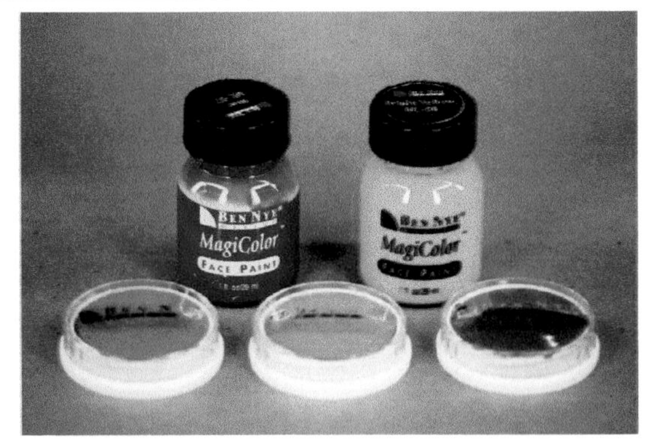

FIGURE A.16 *MagiColor face and body paints by Ben Nye.*

Concealer—An opaque, highly pigmented cream foundation used to camouflage or conceal skin discolorations, birthmarks, and tattoos. Available from professional makeup sources as well as street-wear makeup vendors.

Condensation-sure silicone—tin cure silicone, room-temperature vulcanization, RTV, silicone—for description and instructions see Chapter 11 on Prosthetic Makeup.

Cream makeup—A soft consistency, non-greasy makeup that can be applied with fingers, sponge, blender, or a brush. Some varieties contain silicone in their formulas for a longer-lasting natural effect. These products can be removed with facial cleanser, or makeup remover.

Crepe hair—There are two types, crepe wool and human crepe hair. Both can be used for making beards, mustaches, or eyebrows. Crepe wool and crepe hair comes in tightly woven braids and it is usually purchased by the yard. It is available from various companies and comes in the usual hair colors and some fantasy colors.

Cure (curing agent)—A chemical reaction where two or more chemicals after being mixed together change their physical characteristics from a relative liquid form to a relative hardened form. For example, the process or method of changing a substance like foamed latex by adding a curing agent to create a product with elasticity and strength. The entire process changes the liquid form of latex into a molded, solid form. Some latex is heat cured in an oven.

Dental acrylic powder—Mix this powder in a 1:1 ratio with dental liquid monomer to make teeth.

Dental impression plaster (Dental Stone)—This is used to make molds for teeth and it is harder than most plasters.

Dental tray—The plastic trays that are filled with alginate and placed in the mouth to make dental impressions. These trays should not be shared.

Depilatory—A chemical cream/lotion for the removal of unwanted hair and to avoid the negative effects of shaving. These products are carried by beauty supply stores and their websites.

Derma wax—A soft wax for building up areas of the face. It is easier to apply and to remove than nose putty but it has less adhesive properties. It can also be mixed with nose putty (see Chapter 10). It is available from various makeup companies and their distributors. Ben Nye's Nose and Scar Wax and Mehron's Putty/Wax are mixtures of derma wax and putty (see *Putty wax*). Kryolan has a special wax for street wear (called Dermacolor Skin Plastic) for concealing scars. The wax is then covered with Dermacolor makeup. Mehron has a sturdy wax compound mixed with fibers called Extra Flesh for creating warts, cuts, and scars.

Dermacolor—A very effective highly pigmented camouflage cream by Kryolan. It is designed primarily for street wear for both men and women to cover skin discolorations, such as birthmarks or uneven pigmentation. It can also be used for the stage to cover temporary or permanent skin discolorations that may be difficult to cover with most stage makeup. It can be used as a foundation color over the entire face or applied only to the discolored areas, then covered with stage makeup for the overall foundation. It has been used successfully by actors who are allergic to other kinds of makeup, and it has the additional advantage of being waterproof. This makeup is available in palettes and the colors can be mixed for a perfect match. They can also be thinned with alcohol, or cosmetic fluid GP-20, to create translucent skin colorations for truly natural effects (see Figure 10.3).

Detail layer—When working with the negative mold, this is the first layer applied inside (usually brushed on). This layer is applied in a thin coat and pushed into the details of the mold.

Drawing cards—Used in wig making for holding the hair in place as it is drawn out and then blended into its desired color.

Dremel—A brand name for a rotary tool that is used to drill, sand or grind.

Epicanthic fold—An elongated fold of the upper eyelid skin that extends over the inner corner, or both corners, of the eye.

Epoxy parfilm—A spray release for easy removal of gelatin from stone molds.

Extrinsic coloration—A coloration system, or product, that is added on or applied to a given surface.

Eyebrow plastic—This is a plastic in a stick form made by Kryolan. It is used for blocking out eyebrows.

Flashing—A gap that is left around the entire edge of a sculpted appliance. The gap is meant to be filled with the molding material and create a thin edge on the appliance.

Flocking—Fine nylon, or rayon, fibers in a variety of colors used to intrinsically color gelatin appliances. It can be mixed with K-Y Jelly and applied on the surface of the appliance to give a "capillary" look. Mixed with K-Y Jelly, it can also be applied directly to the skin to produce a similar natural effect. Available from various companies.

Foam latex—A multi-ingredient product used to make soft and flexible three-dimensional prosthetic makeups. It includes a natural latex foam base, microcellular foaming agent, curing agent, and gelling agent. Companies that sell foam latex kits and supplies will have their own instructions for using their products. Read the information in Chapter 11 and use Appendix B, Sources, for distributors.

Foundation—Makeup intended for application to the face and/or body that comes in a full range of colors providing an appropriate skin tone, and/or texture (natural, matte) for the performer and to serve as a base for contour and accent colors. Foundations are available in sheer to full-coverage in cream,

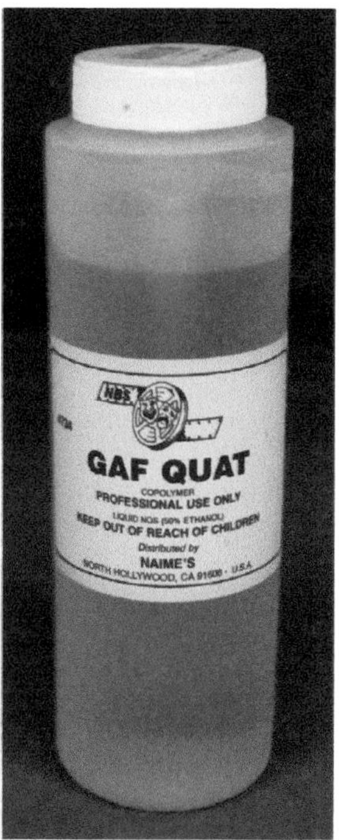

FIGURE A.17 *Gafquat.*

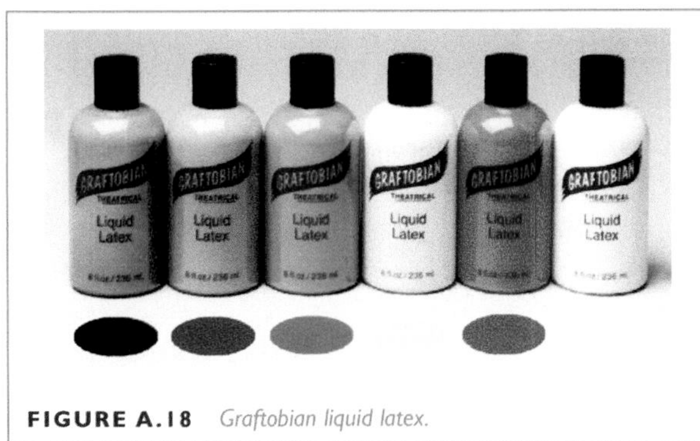

FIGURE A.18 *Graftobian liquid latex.*

cake, liquid, airbrush, and greasepaint makeup. Foundations (or bases) can be mixed together if the exact skin tone is not available in the ready-made selection.

Fuller's earth—A "clean" dirt that is used for dust clouds in special effects explosions and to simulate a dirty appearance on costumes and skin.

Gafquat 734—A resin that is found in commercial hair spray used to control hair. It is often used to flatten the hair under bald caps. It is mixed with mustache wax and 70% alcohol to make H-10.

Galloon—A narrow fabric tape used in wig-making and blocking wig lace while styling and cleaning the wig.

Gelatin (Gelatine)—A highly refined colorless, tasteless water-soluble protein made from collagen, often produced in sheets, granules, and powder form that is used in food products such as gummy bears, marshmallows, Jell-O, medicine capsules, and desserts. Can be used for certain types of quick three-dimensional skin additions. It is also used for manufacturing gelatin appliances for makeup effects (see Figure 11.10). It is produced in "Bloom values" (or Jelly strength) ranging from 30, the most soft, to 300, the most firm (and resilient). An industrial quality product called 300 Bloom gelatin is recommended. This gelatin is often mixed with glycerin, sorbitol, and zinc oxide to form a substance to create flexible, resilient, and translucent skin-like appliances. Also sold in ready-to-use cubes. Available from Burman Industries, Alcone, Monster Makers, and FX Warehouse. Other gelatin-based special effects materials include Mehron's 3-D Gel, Ben Nye's Effects Gel, Kryolan's Gelatin cubes, and Gelafix Skin, and Titanic Gelatin, available at Burman Industries, Namie's, Frends Beauty, and Alcone. Ready-made gelatin appliances can be found on various company websites.

Glatzan L.—A Kryolan product used for making bald caps. See *Plastic, film, liquid.*

Glycerin—A clear, slightly sweet, thick liquid recovered from the soap-making process. It is a gentle emollient for the skin and has natural antiseptic properties. It can be brushed, or sponged, onto the body to resemble sweat or tears and to make the skin shine. It can be used as a base for metallic powders. The powders can either be patted on over the glycerin, or mixed with it before it is applied. Mehron has a Mixing Medium that can be used with metallic powders as well as other dry pigments. Glycerin is also used as a "plasticizer" for making gelatin appliances (see Figure 11.10). Glycerin is available at drug stores and from most makeup distributors.

Greasepaint—A term derived from the use of petrolatum in the makeup. The original type of stage makeup that was used by performers to apply opaque coloring on the face. It can also be used to color prosthetic appliances and bald caps. Greasepaint (including Rubber Mask Greasepaint, RMGP, which uses a castor oil base) deteriorates with age. If any makeup smells rancid, throw it out. Mehron carries a soft, lanolin-enriched foundation paint. Kryolan's greasepaint comes in palettes and as individual sticks.

Green Marble SeLr™—Premiere Products, Inc. makes this product that seals makeups. It can be applied to the makeup and then have additional layers added to the makeup. For tanning effects it can be mixed with powders and pigments. Mix with Attagel to create an effective skin aging product (see Premiere Products Inc. website for instructions).

Gypsum—A mineral consisting of calcium sulfate that is used in making plaster.

H-10—This is a material used to flatten the hair at the hairline to eliminate the volume under a bald cap and to control the hair around the ears and the nape of the neck. It is made by mixing 1-part Gafquat 734 into 1-part mustache wax in a double boiler. After these products are mixed completely, remove them from the heat and slowly add 1-part 70% alcohol (all measurements are by volume). (Note: If you are using an open flame to heat, the flame must be extinguished before adding the flammable alcohol. H-10 is applied with a toothbrush or dental spatula. This substance will hold hair in almost any position. Do not use on hair when also using bald cap material that can be affected by alcohol.

Hackle—A base with a bed of long metal spikes that combines the functions of a comb and a brush. It can be used to blend hair colors together, or untangle skeins of hair. Available from wig-making suppliers.

Hair (human, synthetic, yak)—Human hair is available in lengths from 10 to 24 inches, it is sold by the pound, ounce, or gram, and it comes in a variety of colors. Prices can vary with the length and color. Styles can be set into human hair wigs using a special wig oven.

Synthetic hair is becoming more and more realistic in appearance and more expensive. It is sold by the ounce and can be styled using steam. Some wigs are a blend of human and synthetic hair.

Yak hair is sometimes used for wigs, but it is more frequently used for facial hair. It comes in natural, or white, and takes dye very easily. Because it has a coarse texture it can hold an extreme style.

Hair punching—This process pushes hair into a foam latex or silicone surface to resemble natural hair growth. The punching tool can be a large sewing/crafts needle with the top of the eye cut off to form a U-shape. There are specialized punching needles available from various companies.

Highlight colors—Highlighting colors can be used for contouring in corrective and character makeups. Many suppliers carry palettes of both highlight and shadow colors for a wide range of skin tones.

Hydrocal—Used for plaster projects, it is a neutral gypsum cement. The set time is normally about 25 minutes and it is stronger than plaster of Paris.

Ice powder—Simulates frost and ice when sprayed with water. It is best when used with Ice Gel.

Intrinsic coloration—Dry or liquid colorant added to a product in the mixing process, therefore becoming an essential part of that product.

Isopropyl alcohol—Also known as isopropanol, it is colorless and flammable. A common ingredient in antiseptics, disinfectants, and detergents. Used as a dispersal liquid/activator for makeup pigments.

Isopropyl myristate—Isopropyl alcohol and myristic acid. An emollient that aids skin absorption. It can also be used to remove prosthetics. Refer to the MSDS (material safety and date sheet) for more information.

Key—A key is attached to, or built into, plaster, stone, or silicone multi-part closed molds to ensure proper alignment and stability between parts. A key can be a small circular indentation, a wedge-shaped block, or a narrow slanted rail along the outer edge of the mold (see Chapter 11).

Kick—A term that refers to the point at which a substance begins to solidify.

Kryolan Crystal Clear™—A brand name clear acrylic spray used to coat clay sculptures to protect the clay surface during the mold-making process. Available at art supply and hardware stores and websites. (Krylon paint products are a different company than Kryolan Cosmetics.)

K-Y™ Jelly—This product is found in drug stores and pharmacy sections of big retail stores. It can be used for blending nose putty and derma wax. It can create a sheen on injury makeups. Mix it with red flocking and apply over foundation to create the effect of broken blood vessels.

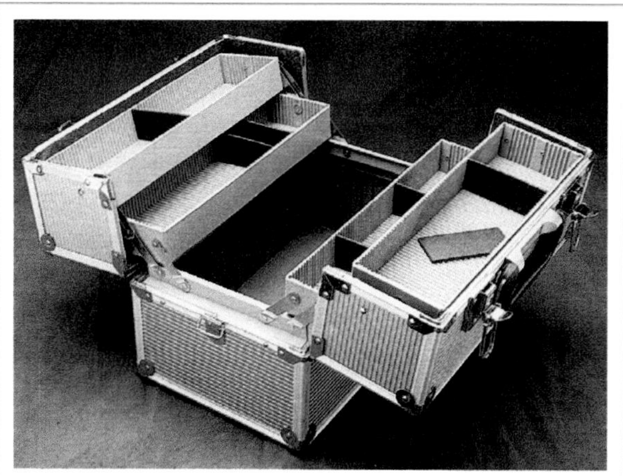

FIGURE A.19 *Makeup case from Kryolan.*

Latex (liquid)—Liquid latex can be used for building up flexible prosthetic pieces, making full-face masks, attaching crepe hair, or creating wrinkles and texture for age makeups. Latex comes in off-white or light tan and it can be colored by adding small amounts of concentrated vegetable dye, food coloring, cosmetic grade pigments, or pigment dispersions (highly recommended) to create whatever flesh tone is needed. White latex dries clear and colored latex normally dries darker. If your bottle of latex has a brush in the cap, always return the cap to the bottle as quickly as possible to avoid prolonged exposure to air. Once latex dries on a brush, the brush is ruined. Protect your own brush by using a coating of liquid soap, or citrus cleanser, to protect the bristles. Rinse the brush with distilled water to avoid curdling the latex.

Latex is sensitive to temperatures, it will freeze and become permanently solid. It has a shelf life so check your supply before you begin a project. Because latex can cause a burning sensation when applied to the skin, always test the product on the inner wrist before applying it to the face. Latex sensitivity is a common allergy, so test for reactions well before starting a makeup.

Latex caps—Used for creating a bald head effect. Also refer to *Plastic and rubber caps*. Ready-made caps are available from many companies and they come in different thicknesses. They can also be custom-made on appropriate plastic heads. Some caps can be removed with care and reused. The cap can be glued into place with appliance adhesives or medical adhesives.

Laying hair—Refers to when hair is being applied a small amount at a time and is held in place with adhesive. Example: hand laying a beard.

Lifecast—This usually refers to a 3-part process using alginate, plaster bandages, and a plaster positive to create a dimensional duplicate of a face, whole head, and/or body parts.

Lumiere™—A soft, shimmery, luminescent makeup from the Ben Nye Makeup Company. It comes in cream, cake, and powder and there is a variety of wheels and palettes available.

Matte adhesive—A non-shiny spirit gum, available from various makeup companies. Matte spirit gum can be created by mixing a small amount of TS-100 Matting Agent into regular spirit gum.

Menthol blower, crystals—Menthol crystals are placed into a small container that can produce fumes when blown toward a performer's eyes and produce natural tears. Available from Frends Beauty, Namie's, Kryolan, and various other sources.

Metallic Makeup—Metallic makeup in both cream and water-based formulas comes in gold, silver, silver-blue, silver-green, silver-lilac, bronze, and copper. Kryolan's metal-free metallic makeups include Metallic Aquacolor and Metallic foundations. Kryolan also has a nonmetallic liquid makeup, called *Liquid Brightness*, in gold, silver, and copper. It can be applied with a brush, a sponge, or the fingers, directly on the skin or over other makeup. It can also be mixed with other liquid makeup before it is applied. Either technique will give variations on the basic colors (red-gold, green-gold, silver-blue, etc.). Any unevenness can be smoothed out after the makeup is dry by stroking lightly with tissues or cotton. Although gold and silver powders (in solution) can be used on the hair for graying or adding brilliance, they are difficult to remove. Silver and gold hair sprays are preferable. Nonmetallic products that provide a lustrous sheen include Ben Nye's cream formula *Fireworks* in Gold Dust, Silver Satin, Diamond Ice, Ruby Lustre, Copper, and Bronze, and dry pressed colors called *Lumiere Grande Colors* in eight vivid shades. Kryolan also has an iridescent cream makeup called *Interferenz*. Under no circumstances should metallic spray paint by companies such as Krylon be used on the skin. WARNING! Do not confuse the commercial paint company, Krylon with the cosmetic company—Kryolan.

Methylcellulose—Mixing this product with warm water produces "slime." The thickness and stringiness can be adjusted to suit the desired effect. It can be tinted with water-based colorants.

Mineral oil—A clear, odorless oil derived from petroleum that is not known to cause allergic reactions. It is used as an emollient cleanser and emulsifier of dirt trapped in pores. It can also be sprayed on the face to simulate perspiration.

Mortician's Wax—This is also known as Naturo Plasto, and is similar to derma wax, cine-wax, and nose putty. It can be used for the same purposes as any of the variety of waxes meant for use in makeups. Check Appendix B, Sources, for vendors and websites.

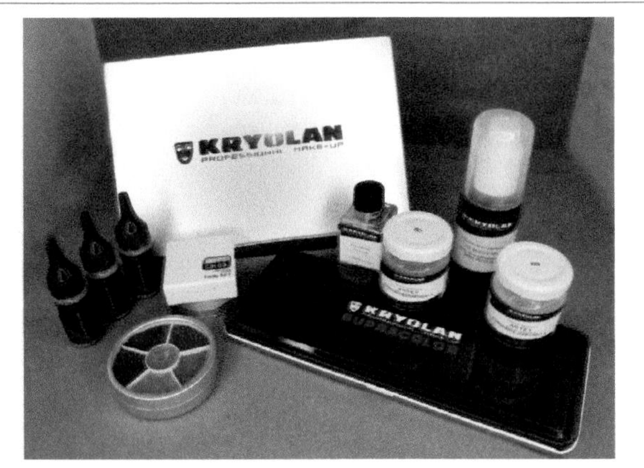

FIGURE A.20 *Makeup products by Kryolan.*

FIGURE A.21 *FX makeup palettes by Kryolan, Mehron, and Ben Nye.*

Mother mold—A rigid shell (like plaster bandages, Hydrostone, Ultracal 30) that helps the flexible material (usually alginate or silicone) keep its shape during the mold making process.

Moulage—An inexpensive impression material that will cast objects including props, masks, and faces. It can be reused many times and is useful for beginners who are still practicing. Moulage must be heated in a double boiler. This turns the otherwise rubbery product into a smooth, thick, pourable substance. In this state the moulage can be very hot! Take care to avoid burning

FIGURE A.22 *Alcohol-based makeup palettes.*

the skin when making a facial impression. Available from various companies.

Movie mud—A product that was created by Joe Blasco for simulating mud or dirt. There is also a product called Ultra Mud made by Ultra Material Products and it is mixed with water. Check websites for available products.

MSDSs—Material Safety Data Sheets are provided by companies to inform the public of the chemical ingredients used in the production of industrial products. Information on proper use of the product, personal protection, and possible physical hazards (including toxicity levels and carcinogenic properties) are also included.

Negative mold—The concave portion of a mold. A negative mold is made on a face, body part, positive sculpt or product. It can be made from aliginate, plaster or stone, and/or silicone. It has received the impression, rather than making the impression.

Neutralizer—A translucent cream-based product used to diminish the appearance of facial discoloration by employing color theory; specifically the use of complementary colors. Complementary colors, when mixed together, produce a neutral tone, a shade of brown. By applying the complementary color over a skin discoloration, that discoloration should be neutralized. It can be applied over or under the foundation. A foundation can also be adjusted by mixing it with a complementary color from an adjustor palette or correcting stick.

Nose putty—Used for building up the nose and other bony parts of the face. Available from various companies and websites. See Naturo Plasto Mortician's Wax and derma wax.

Old Age Stipple—A liquid latex mixture stippled onto stretched skin with a latex, synthetic, or red-rubber sponge that has been torn to create texture. When dried and powdered, Old Age Stipple forms a stiff, yet flexible, layer over the skin which buckles when the stretched skin is released. With gelatin as one of its ingredients, it is necessary to immerse Old Age Stipple in hot water for a few minutes to bring it back to a liquid state before application. Old Age Stipple can made in three grades: light for around the eyes; medium for the face; and heavy for the back of the hands. Can also be referred to as wrinkle stipple.
Basic Recipe:

90 grams (90 ml.) foam latex base

10 grams (5 teaspoons) talc U.S.P.

6 grams (2 teaspoons) loose pigmented powder or pulverized cake makeup

2 grams (1½ teaspoons) Knox unflavored gelatin

32.5 ml. (3 tablespoons) boiling distilled water.

Light Recipe:

1. Combine and stir together talc, powder or cake, and gelatin in an 8-oz. plastic, glass, or Styrofoam cup.
2. Add the boiling distilled water (tap water will change the pH of the latex and cause it to curdle) 1 tablespoon at a time (mixing after each) until the mixture is smooth.
3. Strain the latex mixture through tulle or wig lace to remove any lumps.
4. Slowly add dissolved powders to the latex. Stir rapidly to avoid lumps.
5. Pour the mixture into 2-oz. or 3-oz. glass or plastic jars and label them "stipple light" with the date.

Medium Recipe:

1. Combine the light recipe (the light recipe yields 140 grams) with either 60 grams of Winsor & Newton Acrylic Gel Medium or 50 grams of Acrylic Gel Medium thickened with 3 tablespoons of Cab-O-Sil.
2. Stir small amounts of the light stipple into the gel until they are combined thoroughly.
3. Pour into jars and label.

Heavy Recipe:

1. Combine 1 part (by volume) Medium Grade Stipple with 1 part (by volume) Sculpture House Pliatex Casting Filler clay.
2. Pour into jars and label.

(Note: When stronger adhesion is needed, combine 45 grams of Prosaide with 45 grams of foam latex base. See Chapter 10

FIGURE A.23 *Makeup removers.*

FIGURE A.24 *Monster Makers sulfur-free sculpting clay.*

for removal suggestions. This product must be stored in the refrigerator.)

Old Age Stipple is available from Ben Nye, W.M. Creations, Kryolan, RCMA and various other companies.

Old Age Stipple moistener—A mix of castor oil and 99% isopropyl alcohol applied with a foam latex sponge or the finger tips to the dried and powdered Old Age Stipple. This will turn the stipple translucent, which allows the skin's natural coloration to show through. It also prepares the surface to accept any type of foundation or liner color (PAX Paint is the exception—it does not need surface preparation on latex; Rubber Mask Greasepaint, RMGP, already has castor oil and doesn't need surface preparation either). Excess moistener can be taken off with a tissue before applying makeup. Also sold as Castor Sealer by Ben Nye.

OSHA—Occupational Safety and Health Administration, a division of the US Department of Labor that oversees safety in the workplace. Their goal is to prevent workplace injuries, illnesses, and deaths.

PAX Medium—A mixture of approximately equal parts of Prosaide and acrylic matte medium. PAX Medium will dry crystal clear and can be mixed with water-based or water-soluble coloring agents (food coloring, cake makeup, acrylic paint, etc.) to make translucent glazes for character coloration on the skin and prosthetics. (Note: Adding Titanium White to a PAX Medium glaze will minimize the translucency and lessen the effect.)

PAX Paint—This is a type of paint that is used to pre-paint prosthetic pieces and for prosthetic applications. It is made by mixing Liquitex acrylic paint with Prosaide adhesive in equal proportions (see Figure 10.12). Available ready-made from various sources. This product is not for direct application on the skin. When removing PAX colored appliances, soak the adhesive with the appropriate remover, or 70% isopropyl alcohol on a flat brush first. Then, carefully peel the appliance away from the skin. Remove the residue with a puff soaked in isopropyl myristate, which is gentler on the skin than Detachol. Clean the skin with a gentle cleanser and finish with 100% aloe vera gel.

Perspiration—Glycerin can be used to achieve the effect of perspiration by patting (not rubbing) it on the skin with the fingertips or mix with water in a spray bottle. Glycerin can be purchased at a drug store, in pharmacy sections, and from some makeup suppliers. See *Glycerin.*

Pigment—The term can refer to the coloration in skin tissue, or a dry substance used as coloring when it is mixed with a compatible fluid.

Plaster bandage—Rolls of gauze treated with plaster that are used in making molds with alginate and silicone. Different brands can be obtained from art, medical, and makeup suppliers.

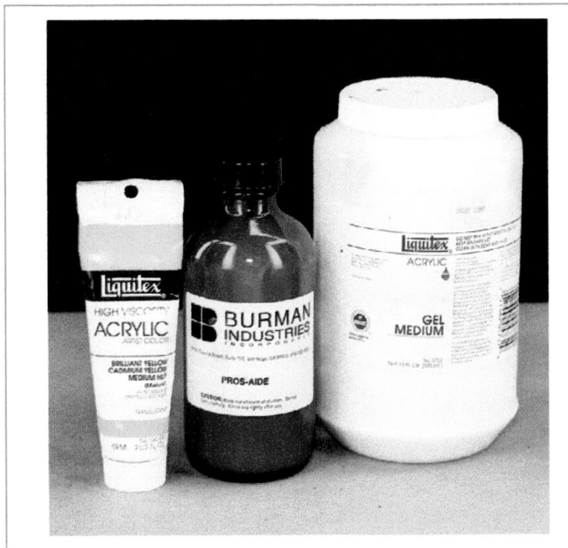

FIGURE A.25 *PAX Paint and PAX Medium components.*

Plastic and rubber caps—Used for a bald head effect. If the makeup you are using does not adhere to the cap, use Kryolan's Fixer Spray, or Glatzan L (matte finish) to coat the cap before applying the makeup. If a cap has lost its flexibility, warm it with a hairdryer. Use medical or prosthetic adhesives for securing rubber caps, and Prosaide adhesive for plastic caps.

Plastic, film, liquid—Kryolan carries a liquid plastic called Glatzan L that is used to make bald caps. It can also be painted on glass to make a plastic film in any shape or size. The film can be used for making eyebrow covers, scars, and sagging eyelids. It should be used in a well-ventilated room. Glatzan L matte can be used over Glatzan L for a matte finish. A Glatzan hardener is available for making stiffer plastic film. *The Glatzan liquid must not be used on the skin.* Glatzan that has become too thick can be thinned with acetone. For other cap materials check the websites in Appendix B, Sources.

Plastic (porcelain) head forms—Used for making plastic bald caps. Available from Alcone, Kryolan, and other makeup suppliers.

Positive—A negative mold is filled with material to create a positive replica of the negative impression.

Prosaide™—An adhesive used for appliances and other makeup purposes, safe to use on sensitive skin and resists moisture. (See *PAX Medium* and *PAX Paint.*)

Prosthetic adhesive or medical adhesive—A special adhesive for use with prosthetic appliances. Available from various makeup supply websites.

Putty wax—A soft putty made by melting nose putty and derma wax together (see Chapter 10). Mehron's Modeling Putty Wax and Ben Nye's Nose and Scar Wax are ready-made mixtures of derma wax and nose putty.

Registration key—Mold registration keys are carved, or imbedded, in both parts of a mold to keep them together and to help line up the halves accurately.

Release agent—A substance (like petroleum jelly) that is applied to the surface of the mold before casting begins to aid in the separation process.

Rubber Mask Greasepaint (RMGP)—A special castor oil-based greasepaint used for slip latex, foam latex, and gelatin appliances. Mineral oil-based products tend to absorb into the latex and turn slightly gray in color. A sealer must be applied to latex and gelatin appliances when crème makeups are used instead of RMGP.

Running foam—This term refers to the process of making appliances with foam latex.

Scar plastic—Available from RCMA as Scar Material and Blister or Scar Making Material. See *Tuplast* and *Gelatin*.

Sealer—A liquid plastic skin adhesive containing polyvinyl butyral, castor oil, and isopropyl alcohol. It is used to provide a protective coating for various makeup applications. It is an important item in any makeup kit. There are many different sealers in various types of containers and it is helpful to read the company's product information to see which one will match the needs of the specific project. See *Barrier products* also.

Separating agents (mold release)—Used between the positive and negative molds when casting to make it possible to separate them easily: petroleum jelly, Carnuba Wax, Polyvinyl Alcohol (PVA), Polysoft Mold Release, Epoxy Parfilm, Molder's Edge ME-301, NS Spray Petroleum, Pure Lube Mold Soap, and cooking spray are a few examples.

Shading colors—This term is used in two ways—to refer to contour colors used for shadowing, and to refer to all contour and accent colors. Shading colors, for both usages, are available from all makeup sources.

Silica—There are two types of silica or silicone dioxide: crystalline silica and amorphous silica. Silica is a basic component of soil, sand, granite, and many other minerals. Amorphous silica (hydrated silica) is used in a wide range of cosmetics and personal care products, including bath products, eye makeup, hair care products, makeup, setting powders, nail care products, oral hygiene products, and skin care products. Crystalline silica is found in rock, stones, sand, and clay and used in the manufacturing of concrete, bricks, and other building products. Crystalline silica is known to cause silicosis. Check the contents of the casting and mold-making materials such as Hydrostone and Ultracal 30, and use the appropriate protection to avoid the inhalation of crystalline silica particles

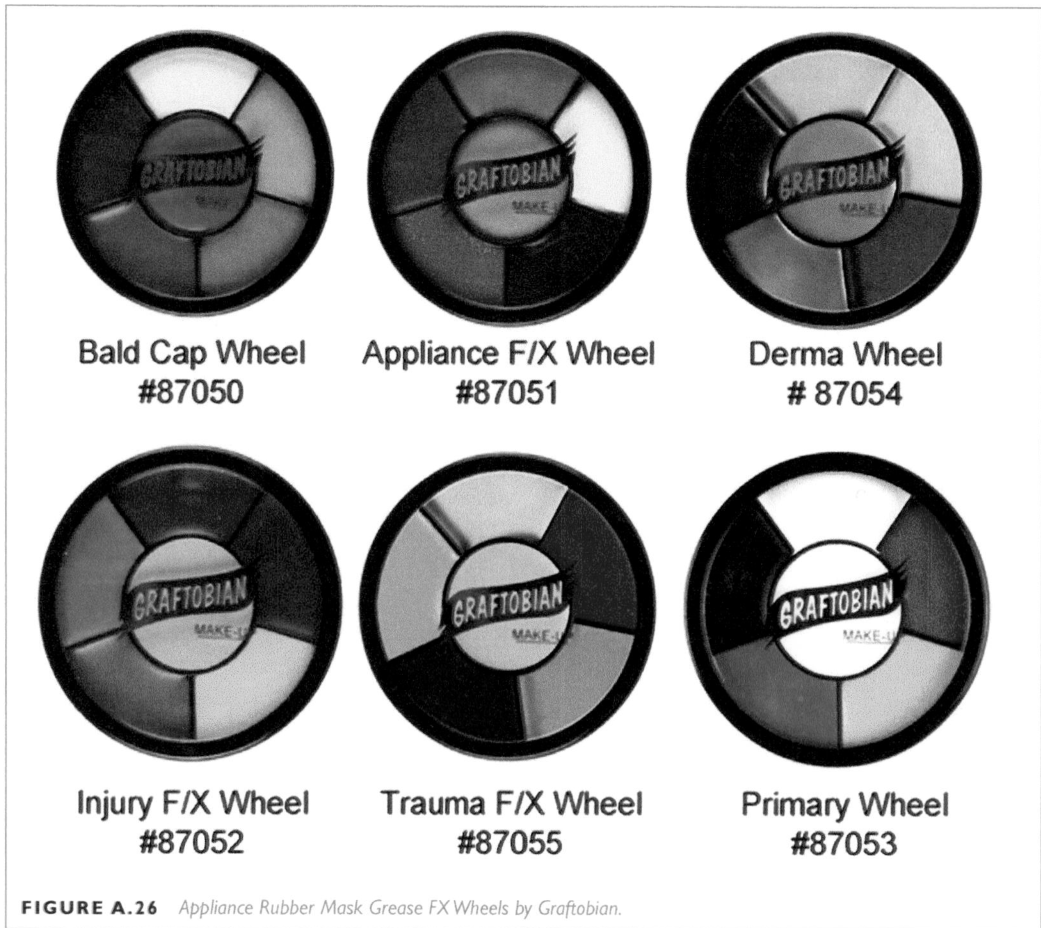

FIGURE A.26 *Appliance Rubber Mask Grease FX Wheels by Graftobian.*

(particle masks and respirators). The US FDA (Food and Drug Administration) report on amorphous silica states,

> Silica, amorphous, fumed (crystalline free) has a demonstrated lack of toxicity. The acute toxicity studies are toxicity category IV. The mutagenicity studies are negative. Silica, amorphous, fumed (crystalline free) is not classifiable, as to its carcinogenicity however, given its amorphous nature, it is not expected to pose a carcinogenic risk. Silicas are considered to be inert when ingested, and due to the high molecular weight it is unlikely to be absorbed through the skin. There should be no concerns for human health, whether the exposure is acute, subchronic, or chronic by any route.

Silicone—A room-temperature vulcanizing (RTV) rubber with a long shelf life. Its translucency gives it a lifelike quality. There are tin cure and platinum cure silicone products. Platinum cure is known for less shrinkage. Silicone can also be a component in some liquid makeup.

Silicone oil (DC 200 Fluid)—A mold release agent that is also useful when applied over a finished makeup application when a shine effect is needed. The product will not disturb the makeup.

Skin-Tite™—A silicone sculpting medium that is produced by Smooth-On and Reynolds Advanced Materials that can be sculpted on the skin for wounds and scars. It can be pigmented and used in a mold. Also used as an adhesive that is flexible and won't come off until it is taken off.

Slip latex—Latex, slush latex.

Sorbitol—A corn syrup derivative used in formula gelatin mixtures for gelatin appliances. Available from suppliers specializing in the special effects products.

Special effects—In reference to makeup, this term generally applies to the design, creation, and application of prosthetics and three-dimensional makeup effects.

Spirit gum—See *Adhesives*.

FIGURE A.27 *Setting sprays.*

FIGURE A.28 *Silicone rubber molds.*

Splash coat—In mold making when adding plaster into the negative, the first thin layer is brushed into the details and the rest of the plaster is then added as the splash coat.

Stipple—A process for adding texture, with paint or a latex mixture (see *Stretch and stipple*), to the skin. Applying color stipple can be accomplished with a black porous sponge, a red-rubber sponge, an orange sponge, a ripped-up foam latex sponge, toothbrush, chip brush, or a brush with irregular bristles. Running your finger across the bristles of a brush to spatter the color can also be called "flecking."

Stretch and stipple—A technique for aging the face, neck, and hands. A mixture of, primarily, liquid latex is applied to small areas of skin while the skin is stretched in the opposite direction of the desired wrinkles. The latex is forced dry with a hairdryer, powdered, released, and then applied to the adjacent section of skin. There are specific products available for this process, or mix from scratch (see *Old Age Stipple*).

Styptic—Stops bleeding from minor cuts, usually from shaving hair. Available as a pencil, powder, and liquid. Try the Frends Beauty, or Alcone, websites and local drug stores.

Tattoo covers—There are specific products made for covering tattoos by companies like Dermablend, Ben Nye, TEMPTU, and Mehron. Foundations and concealers can be used, and alcohol-based palettes for extended wear. The coverage process and types of products will depend on the intensity and color of the tattoo, and the skin tone of the model.

Tears—To induce natural tears, vapors from menthol crystals in a specially designed blower can be used. For applying artificial tears, drops of glycerin can be placed near the eye. Glycerin can be purchased at pharmacies and on some professional makeup websites.

Texas dirt—A body makeup that comes in powder form and is applied with a damp sponge. It can be removed with soap and water.

Texture stamp—Impression of various textures (i.e. the surface of an orange) taken by applying layers of liquid latex, or silicone, powdered, and removed, that can be used to impress textures into the surface of a clay sculpt.

3rd Degree™—This is a platinum-based silicone prosthetic material. It comes in a 2-part formula that is available in transparent, or pigmented, options. It can be sculpted directly onto the skin, cures in less than 5 minutes, and will not break down from heat or perspiration. Use medical adhesive to apply. Check the Alcone website for the full range of colors and associated products.

Thixotropy—A thixotropic agent, such as Cab-O-Sil, thickens other materials (see *Bondo*).

Tooth enamel—An enamel is applied to dry teeth to add color. It comes in a variety of colors like black, nicotine stain, rotten teeth, decay, gold, and natural white. The color can be removed from teeth by wiping with a cleansing tissue and then

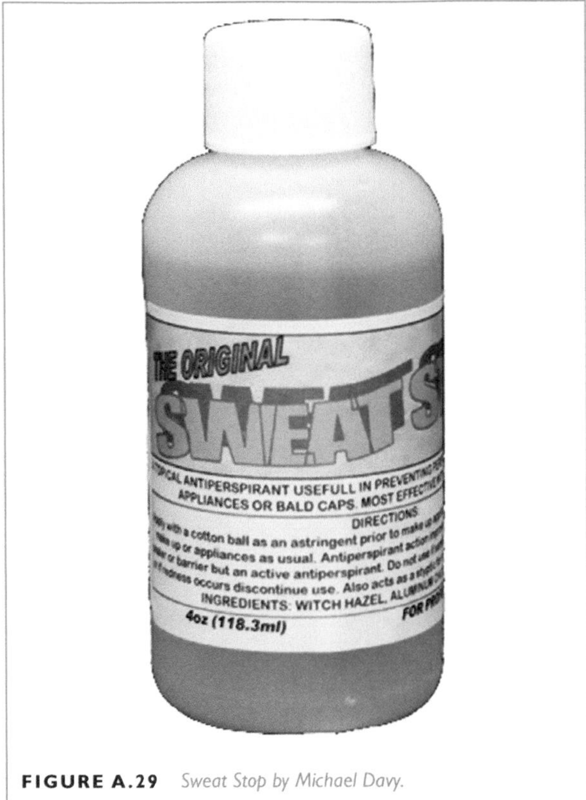

FIGURE A.29 *Sweat Stop by Michael Davy.*

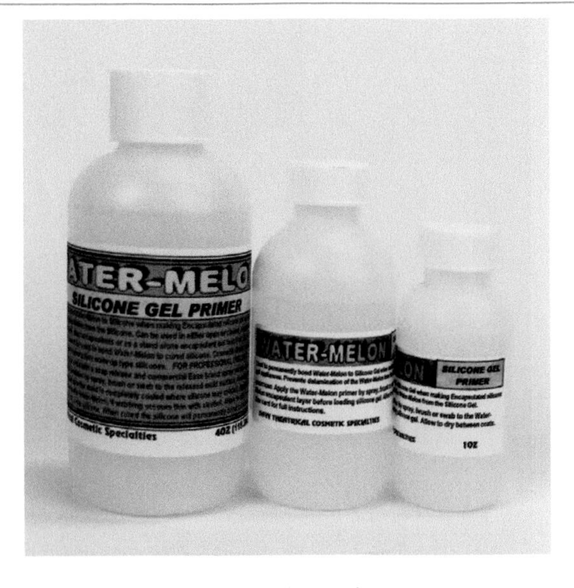

FIGURE A.30 *Water-Melon silicone gel primer.*

brushing the teeth. See vendors for products: PPI/Fleet Street, Ben Nye, and Mehron.

Toupee tape—A very thin, double-sided adhesive film for attaching bald caps, wig lace, facial hairpieces, and toupees. It can also be used for simulating scars. Available from hair/wig suppliers and some makeup websites.

TS-100—A clay-based matting agent usually added to spirit gum and other adhesives to remove the characteristic shine.

Tuffy head—A life-size rubber head (face and neck) that can be used for making beards with a latex base rather than making them directly on the face. If the beard is to be sprayed, it should be done while it is on the Tuffy head rather than on the face. See hair supply websites and some makeup websites.

Tuplast™—A thick, liquid plastic that can be used on the skin to build up three-dimensional scars. It can also be used in open molds to make three-dimensional molded pieces. (Eye pouches can be made in much the same way as in using gelatin. Edges can be dissolved with acetone for blending.) Available from Kryolan distributors.

244 fluid—A silicone brush cleaner designed to dissolve oils and grease. Also used for cleaning plastilina clay out of molds. It is safe on the skin and has no fumes. Can act as a release agent for molds.

Ultra ice—This is a clear gel that can build up ice effects on the skin. It is a flexible, sculptable gel that visually becomes part of the actor's skin. Facial movement and subtle expression is possible with the product on the face. See makeup websites like Alcone, Namie's, Frends Beauty, etc.

Ultracal 30—Gypsum cement-based powder that is mixed with water and used for making molds when casting foam latex and gelatin appliances. Available from Burman Industries and pottery or ceramics suppliers. Add Acryl 60 to increase its structural strength and hardness.

Ventilating—The process of hand-knotting hair onto wig-making lace to create natural-looking facial hair, wigs, or hairpieces (see Chapters 12 and 13).

Ventilating needles—These are used for knotting hair into lace for wigs and hairpieces. They are ordered by numbers, the smallest is usually 000 with the largest being an 8 (also called a chunking needle). There are specific holders that are bought with the needles. See websites for hair and wig-making suppliers.

Water-Melon—A bald cap plastic created by Michael Davy. This is a water-based cap vinyl that thins with water, and the edges can be dissolved with alcohol. It can be applied directly onto the skin, or slushed into plaster molds like latex. When applying without adhesive, use 99% alcohol to adhere it to the skin. There are Water-Melon tints for pigmenting before application. Available on Michael Davy's website, as well as pre-made Water-Melon caps.

Weaving frames—These are wooden frames that are used for hand-weaving hair into wefts.

FIGURE A.31 *Yak hair, wig, and beard by Joe Rossi..*

Weft—When hair is hand-tied, or machine sewn, into a binding material like silk, string, or elastic. The wefts are used for creating wigs, hair extensions, and hairpieces.

Wig block—Most commonly canvas, or wood, head forms used for wig making, facial hair, and styling purposes. They can also be made from castable, rigid polyurethane foam.

Wig lace—The net foundation used to make wigs, beards, and mustaches (see Chapters 12 and 13).

Witch hazel—An alcohol-based solution that is distilled from the bark of a witch hazel tree. It is used in lotion form as a soothing, mild astringent.

Yak hair—A yak is a large, long-haired ox. The hair is used for making wigs and facial hairpieces. It has a coarse texture and comes in white or off-white.

APPENDIX B

SOURCES OF MAKEUP MATERIALS

Note: The following lists are composed of a cross-section of makeup suppliers, wig and hair resources, schools, and publications and conferences. It is not comprehensive, and is intended as a place to begin research into these areas.

*Indicates vegan, cruelty-free, sustainable, and/or eco-friendly products.

Makeup Suppliers

1. ACCU-CAST ALGINATE

   www.accu-cast.us

   (855) 773-0460

   Life-casting supplies and kits with (optional) instructional DVDs. Buy directly from website, or find a local distributor.

2. ALCONE COMPANY

   www.alconeco.com

   info@alconeco.com

   (800) 466–7446, Store (212) 757–3734, Warehouse (718) 361–8373

   Store: 322 W. 49th St. (between 8th and 9th Avenues)

   N.Y., N.Y. 10019

   Headquarters and Warehouse:

   5–45 49th Ave.

   Long Island City, N.Y. 11101

   Makeup, skin care, tools, and brushes, FX supplies, wigs, facial hair, crepe hair, wig-making supplies, and 3rd Degree. Contact for a catalog.

3. ANASTASIA OF BEVERLY HILLS

   www.anastasiabeverlyhills.com

   (800) 310–3773

   Fashion makeup products. Shop on the website, or find local distributors.

4. APPEAL COSMETICS

   www.AppealCosmetics.com

   Creators of 100% fine mink eyelashes, and a line of lipsticks. Shop on the website, or find local distributors.

5. ARADANI STUDIOS, INC.

   www.aradanicostumes.com

   sales@aradani.com

   P.O. Box 160518

   Nashville, TN. 37216

   Prosthetic appliances include elf ears, horns, and costumes.

6. BAD ASS STENCILS

www.istencils.com

(877) 863–5227

70 Industrial Park Dr.

Franklin, N.H. 03235

Bad Ass Stencils are tattoo stencils designed by body painter Andrea O'Donnell. The website lists distributors.

7. BDELLIUM TOOLS

www.bdelliumtools.com

FAX (562) 404–3781

Nexagen Corporation

13246 Alondra Blvd.

Cerritos, CA. 90703

*Eco-friendly makeup brushes, anti-bacterial makeup brushes, cruelty-free lipsticks. They carry a wide range of types of brushes for various purposes, also offered in complete sets, and they have brush rolls. Shop the website. Pro classification available.

8. BEAUTYSOCLEAN

www.beautysoclean.com

(416) 848–1251, FAX (416) 848–1254

40–1110 Finch Ave. West, Suite 1230

Toronto, ON. M3J 3M2

Cosmetic sanitizer that comes in a mist, or wipes. Conditioning brush cleaner. Order online, or find a store.

9. BEN NYE CO.

www.bennyemakeup.com

(310) 839–1984, FAX (310) 839–2640

3655 Lenawee Ave.

Los Angeles, CA. 90016

Full line of theatrical and high-definition (HD) makeup and supplies. Order catalog; find local distributor.

10. BIODERMA

www.beautylish.com

French skin care products that are safe to use on the most sensitive skin types. The products protect and help with resistance to environmental elements.

11. BLOODY MARY

www.dearbloodymary.com

(305) 893–5650, FAX (305) 893–5674

Bobbie Weiner Enterprises LLC

P.O. Box 530128

Miami Shores, FL. 33153

*Products not tested on animals, and they do not contain animal products. FX makeup, face paint, camouflage, sports fan, kits, accessories, books, and videos. Order on website.

12. BLUEBIRD FX

www.bluebirdfx.com

Website only, lists distributors for purchasing products. Alcohol-based palettes and fluid inks come in 100 colors. They also carry adhesives, removers, and blood for HD work.

13. BRICK IN THE YARD

www.brickintheyard.com

1-888-676-2489

521 Sterling Dr.

Richardson, TX. 75081

Suppliers of mold-making products: casting resins, epoxy coatings, PlatSil gel silicone, adhesives, casting rubbers, DVDs and books, classes, and online demonstrations.

14. BTS

www.Behind-the-Seen.net

(818) 822–6250

1051 Glendon Ave. #124

Westwood Village, CA. 90024

*Organic skin care and foundations. Membership offers discounts. Makeup application tutorials on the website. Store offers skin care services.

15. BURMAN INDUSTRIES

www.burmanfoam.com

(818) 782–9833, FAX (818) 782–2863

13536 Saticoy St.

Van Nuys, CA. 91402

Special FX supplies, mold making, casting, cases and containers, sculpting, tools, brushes, books, and DVDs.

16. CAILYN

www.cailyncosmetics.com

Shop on the website, or with local distributors. Beauty makeup products with some HD quality foundations.

17. CHAVANT

www.chavant.com

(800) 242–8268

5043 Industrial Road

Wall Township, N.J. 07727

Check website for local distributors; direct ordering is possible with a full case minimum. Clay and clay modeling products.

18. CHELLA.COM

www.chella.com

(877) 424–3552

Online sales featuring brow, eyes, lipstick, and skin care products with tutorial videos on the website.

19. CINEMA SECRETS, INC.

www.cinemasecrets.com

(818) 846-0579

4400 W. Riverside Dr.

Suite 110

Burbank, CA. 91505

The products are offered on selected vendor websites; some stores carry their products.

20. COZZETTE INFINITE MAKEUP

www.roquecozzette.com

Online sales, Pro discount offered, check website for additional distributors. Products include brushes, eyeshadows, and foundations.

21. CROWN BRUSHES

www.crownbrush.com

(219) 791–9930

10769 Broadway St.

Suite B354

Crownpoint, IN. 46307

Online sales offer Pro memberships, and the products offered include: brushes, sets of brushes, professional makeup, and accessories.

22. DERMALOGICA

www.dermalogica.com

(888) 292–5277

1535 Beachey Place

Carson, CA. 90746

Online shopping for their skin care products, locate local distributors, information about their education center, classes and workshops offered.

23. DINAIR

www.dinair.com

(800) 785–4770

6215 Laurel Canyon Blvd.

North Hollywood, CA. 91606

The website offers Pro Card membership, airbrushes, kits, tanning, hair coloring, airbrush beauty makeup, video library of tutorials and demonstrations.

24. DONJER PRODUCTS, INC.

www.flockit.com

(800) 336–6537

13142 Murphy Road

Winnebago, IL. 61088

Complete line of flocking fibers for intrinsic coloring of prosthetic appliances. Shop online, or find local distributors.

25. DOUGLAS & STURGESS, INC.

www.artstuf.com

(510) 235–8411

Website offers a wide variety of art and mold-making supplies including: clay, body casting, adhesives, paints, thermoplastics, tools, waxes, books, and DVDs.

26. DOSE OF COLORS

www.doseofcolors.com

* Vegan and cruelty-free cosmetics. Featuring lips, eyes, face, and brushes for beauty makeup. Find stores and make online orders on website.

27. ECOBROW (by Marco Ochoa)

www.ecobrow.com

(310) 912–5977

489 S. Robertson Blvd., Suite 100

Beverly Hills, CA. 90211

Eyebrow color and control products. Shop online, or find a local vendor.

28. EUROPEAN BODY ART

www.europeanbodyart.com

Airbrushes, airbrush supplies, face and body makeup, waterproof blood, hair supplies, removers, cleaners, thinners, top coats, adhesives stencils, and tutorial DVDs. Shop online, or find local stores.

29. EVE PEARL BEAUTY BRANDS

www.evepearl.com

Skin care products, foundations, eyes, lips, brushes, kits, sets, and makeover guides for beauty makeup. Shop on the website, or find local distributors.

30. EYE INK FX

www.eyeinkfx.com

rbfxstudio.com

Professional hand-painted contact lenses.

31. FREEFORM CREATIONS, Inc. (Steve LaPorte)

www.freeformcreations.com

Find retailers that carry the signature utility bag and FaceMaker makeup products.

32. FRENDS BEAUTY SUPPLY

www.frendsbeautysupply.com

(818) 769–3834

5244 Laurel Canyon Blvd.

N. Hollywood, CA. 91607

There is an extensive inventory online and in the store. Makeup, nails, special FX, skin, hair care, accessories, and tools.

33. FUSE FX

www.fusefx.ca

Specializes in paints and pigments for silicone surfaces. Use the online store, or distributors with Canadian pricing.

34. FX WAREHOUSE, INC.

www.fxwarehouse.info (store information)

www.order@fxwarehouse.info (orders)

231 E. Girard Ave.

Fishtown, Philadelphia, PA. 19125

Special FX supplies, character makeup products, and tutorials.

35. GERDA SPILLMANN SWISS SKIN CARE

www.GerdaSpillmann.com

(800) 282–3223

Website carries skin care products and cosmetics. There is a list of local distributors.

36. GLOSSIGIRL (Stephen Dimmick, Creator)

www.glossigirl.com

* Vegan lipsticks carried by various distributors, including the Alcone Company.

37. GM FOAM

www.gmfoam.com

(818) 908–1087

13536 Saticoy St.

Van Nuys, CA. 91402

See website for distributors of their 4-part professional hot foam latex system.

38. GOTHIKA

www.gothikalenses.com

100 Cummings Center Dr. #245G

Beverly, MA. 01915

Shop online for theatrical contact lenses.

39. GRAFTOBIAN

www.graftobian.com

(800) 255–0584, or (844) 899–8797

510 Tasman St.

Madison, WI. 53714

HD and beauty products, face painting, FX airbrush, fantasy, theatrical, special FX, Halloween, tools and brushes on their website, or use a local distributor.

40. HATAMOO

www.HataMoo.com

The website is in Japanese and English, with an email contact option for their temporary tattoos.

41. HAUNTS FX

www.hauntsfx.com

email: hauntsfx@yahoo.com

(985) 513–4365

Foam latex appliances, FX supplies, body-painting supplies, moulage simulation wounds, Haunts FX, props, costumes, escape room props, and Special FX Makeup service.

42. HOOKUP TATTOOS

www.hookuptattoos.com

(661) 964–7937

The website offers a diverse selection of one-of-a-kind temporary tattoos; custom design services available.

43. HOT MAKEUP

www.hotmakeup.com

Beauty makeup supplies for the face, eyes, lips, and special collections.

44. HURT BOX by Brian Kinney

www.fullslap.com

(818) 395–7505

Online shopping and a list of vendors. Platinum silicone molds that can be used to cast bondo, latex, vinyl, gelatin, and platinum silicone appliances.

45. IMAGE EXCLUSIVE

www.imageexclusive.com

(702) 733-0400

856 East Sahara Ave.

Las Vegas, NV. 89104

This website offers a wide range of cosmetics, hair products, theatrical supplies, cases, chairs, and equipment. Shop online, or in the store.

46. INGLOT COSMETICS

www.inglotcosmetics.com

Place orders online or find local dealers. Eco-friendly reusable palettes, beauty makeup for the face, body, eyes, lips, nails, accessories, brushes, and cases.

47. IWATA

(503) 253–7308

Iwata Medea, Inc.

1336 N. Mason

Portland, OR. 97217

Locate a local dealer for airbrushes and spray guns. The website has a newsletter available and educational resources.

48. JAPONESQUE PROFESSIONAL MAKEUP SUPPLIES, INC.

www.japonesque.com

(800) 955–6662

Find a retailer on the website for their products: brushes, brush cleaner, lashes, brows, palettes, organizers, accessories, cases, and bags.

49. JOE BLASCO

www.megamakeupstore.com

This website carries the full line of Joe Blasco makeup products, as well as books, skin care supplies, and brushes.

50. KETT COSMETICS

www.kettcosmetics.com

(718) 352–1400

Shop online, or find a local retailer. HD makeup is a specialty along with airbrush kits and makeup palettes. They also offer videos and workshops.

51. KRYOLAN CORPORATION (US)

The website offers an extensive inventory of makeup, and locations for dealers. The products include: body and face, special FX, airbrush supplies, skin care, hair supplies, beards/mustaches/sideburns, Dermacolor, Aquacolor, Supracolor, HD, along with equipment and education.

52. LASHES IN A BOX

www.lashesinabox.com

Cruelty-free selection of false eyelashes made from human hair and synthetic blends. Online shopping and local store locations available.

53. LE METIER DE BEAUTE

www.lemetierdebeaute.com

The online site has online shopping and local retail options. There are beauty makeup products and skin care supplies.

54. MAC COSMETICS

www.maccosmetics.com

(800) 588-0070

Online shopping and store options are listed. Shop for makeup, primer and skin care, brushes and tools, nails, and fragrance. There is also a directory of makeup services offered for education.

55. MAKE UP FOR EVER STUDIO

www.makeupforever.com

(855) 575–3820

Look for local retail options, or shop online for: face, eyes, lips, brushes, accessories, special FX, and cleansers. The artistic line includes: powder pigments, liquid pigments, black light pigments, metal powder, glitter, and limited edition products. There are also academy locations for education.

56. THE MAKEUP SHOP

www.themakeupshop.com

Tobi Britton's makeup business features permanent makeup, makeup services, and classes. Online shopping not offered.

57. MEHRON, INC.

www.mehron.com

Shop online and find local distributors. Beauty products include skin prep and accessories. Performance products: face and body (Paradise AQ), Halloween (kits and special effects), Theatrical, Clowning and instructional guides.

58. MEL PRODUCTS

www.melproductsusa.com

(818) 982–1483

Shop online. MelPAX airbrush products, ESP (encapsulated silicone prosthetics), molds (SOS, Silicone On Set), bald caps, Mel skin, Perma Blood FX cream, gel Bondo/ prosthetic transfer cream, CC cup holders, tutorials, and podcasts.

59. MICHAEL DAVY

www.michaeldavy.com

(888) 225–7026

Separate website locations for products and orders. Order by email (download the form), order by phone, and find local vendors. There is a $50.00 minimum for retail orders. Products include: adhesives, Water-Melon (water-based cap vinyl), and plastic products.

60. MINK LASH PACK

www.minklashpack.com

Shop online. *These fur false eyelashes are 100% cruelty-free.

61. MODELROCK LASHES

www.modelrock.com

*Vegan and cruelty-free, shop online. Lashes, lip products, tools, and accessories.

62. THE MONSTER MAKERS

www.themonstermakers.com

(216) 671–8700

13957 West Parkway Road

Cleveland, OH. 44135

Online shopping for FX supplies, sculpting and molding, foam, latex mask making kits, videos, and books.

63. MORPHE

www.morphebrushes.com

Shop online for beauty makeup products and palettes, lashes, brush cases and belts, set bags, and tools.

64. MORPHSTORE

www.morphstore.com

Online shopping includes: foam latex pieces, adhesives and removers, animals, bald caps, contact lenses, prosthetics and masks, props, teeth, zombies/undead, and videos.

65. MUSE BEAUTY PRO

www.musebeauty.pro.com

(888) 393–3963

Kett airbrush supplies, kits, Viseart makeup products, brushes, tools, and workshops offered.

66. NAMIE'S BEAUTY CENTER

www.namies.com

(818) 655–9923

Website offers a wide range of makeup, airbrush supplies, skin care, bath and body, hair care, wigs and hairpieces, nails, tools, bags/cases/containers, and workshops.

67. NATIONAL FIBER TECHNOLOGY (NFT)

www.nftech.com

Manufactures custom-made hair, wigs, and fur fabrics. Sample packs available.

68. NIGEL'S BEAUTY EMPORIUM

www.nigelbeauty.com

(818) 760–3902

Online shopping from an extensive selection of makeup, FX supplies, skin products, tools, accessories, and tutorials.

69. NIMBA CREATIONS

www.nimbacreations.com

Online shopping for prosthetics in silicone and gelatin for people who do not want to make their own appliances. The website includes clear how-to videos on applying and painting all of their prosthetics.

70. OBSESSIVE COMPULSIVE COSMETICS (OCC)

www.occmakeup.com

(888) 622-0504

174 Ludlow St.

N.Y., N.Y. 10002

*100% vegan and cruelty-free, gluten-free, paraben-free, and silicone-free products. Shop online for lip tar (their signature product), pencils, skin care, eyes, glitter, nails, crème color, brushes, and sets. Call the store for makeup application appointments.

71. PARIAN SPIRIT BRUSH CLEANER

www.parianspirit.com

(818) 353–5298

*Environmentally friendly brush cleaning products. Online site has various sizes and container types. Find local vendors.

72. PREMIERE PRODUCTS, INC.

www.ppipremiereproducts.com

(800) 346–4774

*FDA (Food and Drug Administration) licensed, cruelty-free, vegan certified products. Email, phone, and online orders available. Products include: Telesis, Fleet Street, glazing gels and sprays, skin and hair illustrator, Green Marble SeLr, age stipple, and hair care.

73. PROFESSIONAL VISIONCARE ASSOCIATES

www.provisioncare.com

(818) 789–3311

Special effect contact lenses.

74. PROSAIDE

www.Prosaide.com

(201) 767–6040

Visit website to locate authorized distributors for their medical-grade adhesives.

75. PROSTHETIC TRANSFER MATERIAL

www.prosthetictransfermaterial.com

(818) 232–8363

Online shopping for transfer paper, two-sided release film, release agents, Hi-Ro slip molds, Red Drum blood products.

76. QOSMEDIX

www.qosmedix.com

(631) 242–3270

Website offers applicators, brushes, packaging, measuring, manicure, and pedicure supplies.

77. REEL CREATIONS, INC.

www.reelcreations.com

(818) 346–7335

Shop for powders, sparkle sprays, blood, body art kits, dirt, temporary hair color, palettes, transfer sheets, and stencils.

78. RESEARCH COUNCIL OF MAKEUP ARTISTS (RCMA)

www.rcmamakeup.net

(805) 526–7262

Locate a store, or shop online for foundation, palettes, highlight and contour, powders, cheek colors, creams, eyeshadow, thinners, and tutorials.

79. REYNOLDS ADVANCED MATERIALS

www.reynoldsam.com

Find retail locations on the website, or shop for life-casting, mold-making, and sculpting supplies. There are online tutorials offered, and locations for seminars.

80. ROYAL & LANGNICKEL BRUSH, MFG.

www.royalbrushstore.com

Online shopping for brushes, paints and mediums, tools and accessories.

81. RUBBERWEAR

www.getrubberwear.com

This website offers a DVD and the names of their distributors.

82. SIGMA BEAUTY

www.sigmabeauty.com

Retail locations are available on the website. Online shopping includes brushes and beauty makeup products.

83. SMOOTH-ON

www.smooth-on.com

(800) 762-0744

Web store and distributor locations. Products include: life casting, silicone, adhesives, foams, epoxy, casting, molding, colorants, tools, and equipment. Educational support from online videos and seminars.

84. STATIC NAILS

www.staticnails.com

Reusable pop-on manicure kits.

85. TATTOO PRO

www.airbrushtattoopro.com

Online tutorials, and shopping for stencils, airbrushes, and equipment.

86. TATTOOED NOW

www.tattooednow.com

Realistic temporary tattoos on the website. They also provide a custom design service using your design, or one their artists create.

87. TEMPTU

www.temptu.com

(888) 983–6788

Online shopping and store locations on the website. They offer a comprehensive line of airbrush supplies, airbrushes, air pods, hair and eyebrow colors, and makeup.

88. 9MM Sfx

www.9mmsfx.com

Kevin Carter's website for his custom, hand-painted contact lenses.

Wig and Hair Resources

1. ATELIER BASSI

www.atelierbassi.com

High-quality wigs, supplies, and makeup products, with a price list on the site. Order by email, or phone; the catalog can be downloaded.

2. BANBURY POSTICHE LIMITED

www.banburypostiche.co.uk

Apollo Park, Ironstone Lane, Woxton, Banbury

Oxfordshire, England OX15 6FE

(UK) 00 44 (0)1295 757400

sales@banburypostiche.co.uk

Professional hairdressing and wig-making materials.

3. CALIFORNIA MERCHANDISE COMPANY (CMC)

www.cmcwigs.com

(800) 262–9447

They carry wigs, hairpieces, extensions, costume wigs, facial hair, and accessories.

4. CHARLES H. FOX, Ltd.

www.charlesfox.co.uk (also https://uk.Kryolan.com)

22 Tavistock Street

Covent Garden, London, England WC2E 7PY

(UK) 00 44 (0) 20 7240–3111

5. DEMEO BROTHERS, INC.

www.demeobrothers.com

(973) 778–8100

Human hair suppliers.

6. FISCHBACH + MILLER

www.fischbach-miller.de/en/kontakt

Complete line of wig making tools and supplies, including human and synthetic hair, wigs, and makeup products. .

7. GIOVANNI & SON

www.giovanniandson.com

(818) 908–0183

Shop online for human hair.

8. GOLDEN SUPREME, INC.

www.goldensupreme.com

(800) 332–9246

Shop for thermal irons, stoves, stands, shears, and accessories.

9. HAIRESS CORPORATION

www.hairess.com

(219) 662–1060

The website offers a wide selection of wig accessories and supplies.

10. HIS & HER HAIR

www.hisandher.com

(800) 421–4417

Shop online for wigs, extensions, hairpieces, toupees, tools, and accessories.

11. JOHN BLAKE'S WIGS AND FACIAL HAIR

www.johnblakeswigs.com

(855) 452–9447

Find wigs, facial hair, and supplies on the website.

12. MANE-STA'

    www.mane-stalace.com

    (818) 763–6692

    This company offers a wig lace that is coated with an exclusive process that gives it endurance. The lace comes in three weights.

13. NATIONAL FIBER TECHNOLOGY (NFT)

    www.nftech.com

    Manufactures custom-made hair, wigs, and fur fabrics. Sample packs available.

14. ROCKSTAR WIGS

    www.rockstarwigs.com

    (281) 888–1232

    Extensive online shopping for Cosplay, lace-front wigs, hair extensions, and eyelashes.

15. WIG AMERICA CO.

    www.wigamerica.com

    (800) 338–7600

    Shop online for men and women's wigs, costume wigs, lace-front wigs, eyelashes, and accessories.

16. THE WIG DEPARTMENT

    www.thewigdepartment.com

    (UK) 00 44 (0) 7989 306556

    Swiss nets and laces, wig-making tools and equipment; order on their website.

17. WILSHIRE WIGS

    www.wilshirewigs.com

    (800) 927-0874

    Online store offers a wide variety of wigs, hairpieces, extensions, costume wigs, and accessories.

Professional Schools

Note: Academic institutions that offer Bachelor degrees are not included in this list. Check individual makeup vendor websites for educational workshops they may offer.

1. ACADEMY OF MAKEUP ARTS (AMUA)

   www.theamua.com

   (615) 925–9963

   830 Fesslers Parkway, Suite 114

   Nashville, TN. 37210

2. APRIL LOVE PRO MAKEUP ACADEMY

   www.aprillovepromakeupacademy.com

   (626) 285–3500, or (562) 924–2100

   903 East Las Tunas Dr.

   San Gabriel, CA. 91776

3. CHICSTUDIOS

   www.chicstudiosnyc.com

   (917) 974–8755

   139 Fulton St., Suite 600

   N.Y., N.Y. 10038

   (310) 916–6403

   1639 11th St., Suite 180

   Santa Monica, CA. 90404

4. CINEMA MAKEUP SCHOOL

   www.cinemamakeup.com

   (213) 368–1234

   3780 Wilshire Blvd., Suite 202

   Los Angeles, CA. 90010

5. COMPLECTIONS INTERNATIONAL ACADEMY OF MAKE-UP ARTISTRY (COLLEGE OF MAKEUP ART & DESIGN)

   www.cmucollege.com

   (416) 968–6739

   85 Saint Nicholas St.

   Toronto, Ontario, Canada M4Y 1W8

6. COSMIX

   www.cosmixinc.com

   (954) 564–4181

   3440 North Andrews Ave.

   Orlando Park, FL. 33309

7. DOUGLAS EDUCATION CENTER (TOM SAVINI)

   www.dec.edu

   (800) 413–6013

   130 Seventh St.

   Monessen, PA. 15062

8. EI SCHOOL OF PROFESSIONAL MAKEUP

   www.ei.edu

   (323) 871–8318

   6767 Sunset Blvd.

   Los Angeles, CA. 90028

9. FACE BODY ART

   https://facebodyart.com

   International Face Painting School (online program)

   Owner—Olga Masurev

10. JCI—John Casablancas Institute

    www.jcinstitute.com

    Suite #150—220 Cambie St.

    Vancouver, B.C., Canada V6B 2M9

    (between Cordova and Water Streets)

    1 (866) 688–0261 Toll Free

11. JOE BLASCO

    www.joeblasco.com

    (678) 519–4894 Atlanta Training Seminars

    makeupdept@joeblasco.com

    (407) 363–1234 Orlando Makeup School

12. THE MAKEUP DESIGNORY (MUD)

    www.mud.edu

    See website for additional locations.

    (818) 729–9420

    129 S. San Fernando Blvd.

    Burbank, CA. 91502

    (212) 925–9250

    65 Broadway, 15th floor

    N.Y., N.Y. 10006

13. THE MAKEUP INSTITUTE

    www.themakeupinstitute.com

    02 9698 9919

    53 Balfour St.

    Chippendale, Sydney, Australia NSW 2006

14. VANCOUVER FILM SCHOOL

    www.vfs.edu

    (800) 661–4101

    198 West Hastings St.

    Vancouver, B.C., Canada V6B 1H2

Conferences

1. COMIC CON

   www.comic-con.org

   San Diego, California

2. IMATS (INTERNATIONAL MAKEUP ARTISTS TRADE SHOW)

   www.imats.net

   Sponsored by *Makeup Artist Magazine* at various locations.

3. MAKEUP ARTIST DESIGN SHOW

   www.make-up-artist-show.com

   Dusseldorf, Germany

4. MONSTERPALOOZA

www.monsterpalooza.com

Pasadena, California

5. USITT (UNITED STATES INSTITUTE FOR THEATRE TECHNOLOGY)

www.usitt.org

The annual conference location changes each year.

APPENDIX C

HEALTH AND SAFETY

Monona Rossol, Health and Safety Officer
United Scenic Artists, Local USA829 (IATSE)
181 Thompson St., # 23 New York, NY 10012-2586 212/777-0062 Email: ACTSNYC@cs.com

Throughout history men and women have sacrificed health for cosmetic effects. Women in the court of Queen Elizabeth I persisted in wearing white lead paint (containing cerussite, a natural white lead carbonate) on their faces even though they knew it ruined their skin and made their hair fall out. In the eighteenth century, one well-known actress died from using lead-laden makeup.

Lead and Mercury

Today, acutely toxic chemicals like lead and mercury still are found in foreign cosmetics—even some sold in the US. For example, kohl, a mascara made of lead sulfide and antimony sulfide, has been used for centuries to make up children's eyes in the Middle East, India, Pakistan, and some parts of Africa. One US health department found that use of kohl caused high blood lead levels in eight children. Two of the children's mothers purchased the kohl in the US.[1]

For another example, several Mexican-made mercury-containing beauty creams are also used in this country. One is known to have caused elevated mercury levels in 104 people. Because mercury can penetrate the skin so easily, elevated mercury levels also were found in some persons who never used the cream but were close household contacts of cream users![2]

Mercury is still allowed in cosmetics by the FDA in eye-area products in very low concentrations (0.0065 percent) in order to prevent serious eye infections in users. Mercury preservatives in these very small amounts may cause allergies in a few people, but they are not enough to cause toxicity.

The fact that makeup containing high levels of lead and mercury are still on the market is reported here to emphasize the importance of using only US FDA ingredient-labeled makeup.

Hazards to Wearers

Despite FDA's regulations, some individuals will have reactions or allergies to makeup. Both ordinary consumers and performers are at risk. There are numerous documented incidents of makeup affecting individual actors adversely. One well-known example is Buddy Ebson's serious reaction to a shiny aluminum makeup which cost him the role of the Tin Man in the *Wizard of Oz* movie.

Hazards to Makeup Artists

If you are a professional earning a living as a makeup artist, you should have had training about the hazards of your materials if your employer is complying with the Occupational Safety & Health Administration's Hazard Communication Standard (29 CFR

1 *Am. Journal of Public Health*, Vol. 86, No. 4., April 1996, pp. 587–588.
2 Physicians' Bulletin, San Diego Dept. of Health Services, May 1996, Press Release # 31–96, CA Dept. of Health Services, Sacramento, The Mortality & Morbidity Weekly Report (CDC) 45(19), May 17, 1996, pp. 400–403, and ibid., 45(29), July 26, 1996, pp. 633–635.

1910.1200). Your employer is required to provide material safety data sheets (MSDSs) on each makeup product and to provide you with formal training about the potential hazards of your work.

A number of studies show that beauticians and cosmetologists suffer a higher incidence than average of lung problems like asthma and chronic bronchitis, more skin rashes, and more frequent kidney and liver damage. Some studies also show that they have a higher incidence of cancer and reproductive problems like toxemia of pregnancy and miscarriages.

No similar studies have been made of diseases of theatrical makeup artists, but it is clear that they are exposed to some of the same chemicals used by beauticians and cosmetologists. It is important, then, to understand the nature of these cosmetic chemicals.

How We Are Exposed

In order to harm you, makeup and beauty products must enter your body. They must do this by one of three routes of entry: skin contact, inhalation, or ingestion.

Skin contact: some makeup chemicals can cause skin diseases such as irritation, infection, and allergic reactions. Some makeup chemicals, hair dyes, and solvents also can penetrate the skin and enter the blood stream.

Inhalation of powders, aerosol sprays, and airbrush mists is another way makeup and cosmetic chemicals can enter your body. Studies have shown that inhalation of aerosol hair sprays can damage or destroy the tiny hair-like cilia which sweep foreign particles from the lungs. When the lung's defenses are weakened in this way, inhaled substances can cause even more damage.

The smaller the particles of dust or mist, the deeper they can penetrate the lung. In the deepest part of the lung, the air sacs (alveoli), are the most vulnerable. Face powder particles and airbrush mists are examples of small particles that can be deposited deep in the lungs. Studies show that tiny particles of inert minerals, such as those used in cosmetics (e.g. talc and kaolin), can remain in the alveoli indefinitely. (See also *Nanoparticles* below.)

Ingestion of lipsticks, wetting brushes with the mouth, and eating, smoking, or drinking while applying makeup can put cosmetic ingredients directly into your digestive tract. Cosmetics are also ingested when the cilia in the upper portion of the lungs raise mucous and dust particles up to the back of the throat where they are swallowed.

Skin Diseases

Acne: The most common reaction to cosmetics is an infectious reaction of the skin. Especially common is a condition known as "acne cosmetica," or cosmetic acne. (Cosmetic acne should not be confused with "acne vulgaris," which is associated with the onset of puberty.) Cosmetic acne usually is a mild condition. Small pimples appear and disappear intermittently and affect women from their twenties through their fifties. Other types of acne and skin infections can result if cosmetics support bacterial growth or irritate the skin.

Allergies: Many people develop allergies to chemicals in cosmetics. It is estimated that one person in ten is allergic to fragrances in cosmetics. Some of the preservatives and humectants (e.g. propylene glycol) also cause allergic responses in a few people.

Chrome and nickel compounds have been known to cause severe allergies and skin ulcers in industrial workers exposed to them. Chrome compounds can be found in some eye cosmetics, especially in blue and green hues. And while nickel should not be used in cosmetics, nickel allergy has been documented in hairdressers.

In fact, the percentage of the general population in the US that are allergic to nickel has risen in the last few years from 10 to over 14 percent. Experts think that intimate contact with nickel in metal alloys used in earrings and body piercing jewelry is the reason.[3]

The greatest potential for serious allergic reactions to theatrical cosmetics is in our use of natural rubber latex and foam products such as eye lash adhesives, Special Effects Makeups, and face-molding compounds.

Allergies to natural rubber are well known through the experience of doctors and other medical workers who wear latex gloves daily. Somewhere between 10 and 17 percent of medical professionals have developed the allergy. Symptoms may include: skin rash and inflammation, hives, respiratory irritation, asthma, and systemic anaphylactic shock. Between 1988 and 1992, the FDA received reports of 1,000 systemic shock reactions to latex. As of June 1996, 28 latex-related deaths had been reported to the FDA. As recently as 2000, a woman in England died from a reaction to latex hair extension glue.

While there are no systematic studies of special effects latex makeup allergies, this author can testify that her eyes have swelled completely shut on application of rubber latex eye lash adhesive. Many other people have reported similar experiences. Fortunately, there are synthetic substitutes for almost all natural rubber makeup products and latex gloves.

3 *NY Times*, "When Body Piercing Causes Body Rash," Denise Grady, Tuesday, October 20, 1998, p. F8.

Irritation: Chemicals which are caustic, acidic, or strong oxidizers can harm the skin by attacking its surface. Examples include sodium and potassium hydroxides which can be found in cuticle softeners and hair relaxers and removers. One example of a strong oxidizer is hydrogen peroxide which is used to lighten facial hair. Organic solvents such as alcohol and acetone also can irritate the skin or dry it out by removing natural oils.

Cancer: Sunlight is the major cause of skin cancer, and both natural and tanning-salon light can cause cancer. Some chemicals have been shown to cause it, too. One example is old fashioned carbon black, which was common in mascara until it was banned for use in cosmetics by the US Food and Drug Administration (FDA). Newer methods of manufacturing carbon black do not create the cancer-causing by products.

Many cancer-causing and highly toxic pigments are approved for use in artists' paints and materials. Some may even be labeled "non-toxic" because, used as directed, there should be no significant exposure. Using art products directly on the skin, however, is not a directed use and is not advised!

Eye Diseases

The skin around the eyes is more sensitive and more easily penetrated than facial skin. All types of skin diseases (infection, irritation, allergies, and cancer) which affect facial skin also can affect the skin around the eyes. The membrane covering the eye and lining the underside of the eyelids (the conjunctiva) can be affected by cosmetic chemicals, producing inflammation (conjunctivitis).

Scratching the eyeball during application of eye makeup is the most common eye injury related to cosmetics. Once an eye abrasion has occurred, the possibility of infection increases. The most important thing to remember about these infections is that they proceed with extreme rapidity and immediate treatment for all painful scratches is recommended. Although most scratches from mascara brushes do not result in infections, those that do can cause ulcers on the cornea, clouding of the cornea and, in rare cases, blindness.

Infections Transmitted

Makeups can provide a hospitable environment for many microorganisms. The preservatives in makeup are added to increase shelf life and they cannot prevent an infectious organism from one person to be transmitted to another.

Examples of a few of the microorganisms that can survive on makeup include: cold viruses; bacteria such as staphylococcus, streptococcus, and impetigo; fungal infections; and highly infectious viruses such as hepatitis A and herpes simplex. Hepatitis A in particular can remain active for months even on dry surfaces. And in 2004, a nasty case of scabies was transmitted from an infected Italian tenor to a New York City opera makeup artist causing pain, embarrassment, and financial loss because all her makeup and utensils had to be discarded.

The AIDS virus probably cannot be transmitted by makeup. But many other blood-borne diseases can be. Makeup and all personal items such as razors, nail care tools, and similar personal grooming items which might draw blood or contact acne or open sores should not be shared.

Label Reading Tips

Consumer makeup labels are required to carry a complete list of ingredients. An exception is occasionally granted by the FDA to certain manufacturers who claim that certain of their ingredients are trade secrets. These products can be identified when the phrase "and other ingredients" is included on the label. Trade secret ingredients should not be used by people with skin allergies since it may not be possible to find out what is in the makeup.

Professional makeup manufacturers are exempt from complete ingredient labeling requirements. Many, however, list their ingredients as a professional courtesy. These fully labeled products should be used exclusively. They make it possible to identify ingredients which may be causing symptoms and to choose products best suited for the intended theatrical effect.

"Not Tested on Animals." The FDA requires testing of all cosmetic ingredients. Products that claim not to be tested are only claiming that the product as a whole has not to been tested. But to sell a cosmetic product legally in the US, each ingredient must have been purchased from sources that provide tested and certified cosmetic grade chemicals. At some time in the past, each of these types of ingredients have been tested on animals for their ability to cause acute toxicity.

Natural ingredients. There is absolutely no reason to trust a "natural" ingredient more than a synthetic one. Somehow we have forgotten the millions of years and the millions of deaths it took mankind to distinguish between the mushrooms and the toadstools; the henna and the hemlock. We need to be reminded that the deadly allergies to rubber are caused only by natural rubber because proteins from the sap of the rubber tree are present. And if we trust natural minerals mined from the earth, we need to be reminded that asbestos and silica are natural minerals.

Both synthetic and natural ingredients can be hazardous. Be suspicious of any product label that induces you to prejudge the product's safety by its natural origins. Instead, you want the ingredients to be certified, tested cosmetic grade ingredients that are disclosed by name on the label.

Use as directed. Different FDA safety standards apply to makeup ingredients intended for use around the eyes, for lipsticks, and for face makeup. For example, lipstick ingredients must be tested for ingestion hazards. Eye makeup must protect against infection and be suitable for the especially thin and sensitive skin around the eyes. Makeups, therefore, are considered safe only when used as directed.

Cosmetic Ingredients

Most makeup ingredients fall into a few basic categories: minerals such as talc and kaolin, vegetable powders such as corn starch, oils and waxes, pigments and dyes, and preservatives.

Minerals. Face powders, makeups, and rouges are likely to contain minerals such as talc, kaolin (and other clays), chalk, zinc oxide, titanium dioxide, mica, and bismuth oxychloride. These minerals are harmless to the skin or by ingestion. They also do not cause allergies. They are only hazardous if they are inhaled from dusty products or from airbrushed makeups.

Industrial experience confirms that mineral dusts can irritate the eyes and respiratory system. Fine particles of titanium dioxide can cause lung cancer when inhaled. Talc, kaolin, and mica also can cause long-term lung damage. In addition, talcs in the past often contained significant amounts of asbestos. Anyone who collects antique containers of baby and face powders should never use them.

No law prevents manufacturers from using asbestos-contaminated talcs. Instead, a voluntary industry standard is honored. Nevertheless, a study of commercial cosmetic talcs found traces of asbestos in six of 15 samples.[4] Clouds of dust should not be created during application of talc or any cosmetic powders. Airbrushing makeup also causes inhalation of these ingredients.

Bismuth oxychloride added for a metallic or pearl lustre has produced photosensitivity (skin reactions provoked by sunlight) in some people. Mica can also be used for lustre.

Vegetable powders. To avoid the hazards of mineral powders, some manufacturers have switched to organic substances such as corn starch or rice flour. Like all powders, these are also capable of irritating the respiratory system. They are also more likely to cause allergies, especially in people who have food allergies.

Oils, fats, and waxes. Cream makeups, rouges, mascaras, and lipsticks are suspended in a base made of either oils and fats alone or oils and fats emulsified with water. There are dozens of cosmetic oils, fats, and waxes. In general, natural oils such as lanolin and cocoa butter are more likely to provoke allergies. Almost no one is allergic to oils derived from highly purified petroleum such as baby oil and Vaseline.

Some of the oily cream products also contain detergents which enable the makeup to penetrate the skin for a longer "hold" but which may also result in irritation.

Dyes and pigments are assigned names by the FDA. These names indicate whether they are approved for food, drugs, and cosmetics (for example, FD&C Yellow #5) or only for drugs and cosmetics (for example, D&C Red #7). Most cosmetic pigments and dyes have had some long-term testing and they are approved only for uses that will not expose consumers to amounts above a threshold for causing harm.

The colorants for cosmetics may not have long-term hazard testing, but they must be tested for purity. Colorants must be purchased from FDA-approved manufacturers with a batch certification. Once the package is opened and repacked this batch number is no longer valid and the color may not be used for manufactured products marketed in the US. When sellers say the ingredients have been "tested," it is important to ask what they have been tested for.

Lipsticks contain the most dyes and some dyes are associated with a form of dermatitis called "cheilitis." It is a drying or cracking of the lips, and usually is caused by eosin dyes which stain the lips. Commonly used eosin dyes are D&C Red #21 and #27, and D&C Orange #5. Experts recommend avoiding these staining lipsticks. Lanolin and perfumes also may cause cheilitis.

Additives & preservatives such as thimerosal (a mercury preservative), methylparaben, and other biocides are in small amounts, but are needed to extend shelf life and keep microorganisms from growing in the cosmetics. Most of these are quite toxic, but are in amounts small enough that most experts think that people will not be harmed.

Nanoparticles: A Brand-New Hazard[5]

Scientists have known for decades that small particles can be more toxic than larger ones when inhaled deep into the lungs. In recognition of this fact, the Environmental Protection Agency (EPA) sets more restrictive outdoor air quality standards for

4 Blount, A.M., "Amphibole Content of Cosmetic and Pharmaceutical Talcs," *Environmental Health Perspectives*, Vol. 94, 1991, pp. 225–230.

5 Information in this section derived from many sources including: The Bureau of National Affairs, 34(17), 4/22/04, pp. 440–446; ibid., 34(33), 8/12/04, pp. 846–847; BNA-Daily Environment Report, # 59, 3/29/04, pp. A7–A10: www.washingtonpost.com/2004Jul29.

soot and other particulate matter (PM). The standard sets a more restrictive limit for PM that is only 2.5 microns in diameter ($PM_{2.5}$) than is set for the larger 10 micron particles (PM_{10}). Research shows that the smaller the particle, the greater its association with respiratory and heart problems and stroke. Recent studies indicate that some inhaled nanoparticles can pass through air sac membranes directly into the blood where the particles can initiate clot formation.

Skin absorption. Studies on beryllium were among the first to show that small particles also can penetrate the skin. Researchers found that one micron-sized beryllium particle can enter workers' bodies through the skin, sensitize them to beryllium, and cause the deadly and untreatable disease called "beryllosis." This phenomena explains why workers who wore respirators fell ill while workers who wore both gloves and respirators stayed well.

Nanoparticles. Today, particles much smaller than one micron are being created in a hot new field called "nanotechnology." In this area of research, scientists manipulate atoms and molecules or grind substances so fine that the tiny particles have amazing and useful new properties. The particles can be made in a great variety of shapes: tiny fibers, balls, hollow tubes, and more.

The nanoparticles are measured in nanometers, a scale 1,000 times smaller than the micron scale. For example, $PM_{2.5}$ micron particles are 2,500 nanometers in diameter. However, the term "nanoparticle" is generally only applied to particles that are 100 micrometers (0.1 microns) or less. Products containing particles as small as 5 nanometers are already on the market. Tens of thousands of these nanoparticles will fit on the point of a pin.

Nano-Products. As expected, manufacturers put products containing nanoparticles in our hands before the hazards are studied. Products already available include wrinkle and stain-resistant fabrics, paints, pigments, cosmetics, special abrasives, carbon black in tires, clay particles in tennis ball polymers, digital camera displays, high resolution printer inks, and more.

Nano-Hazards. Preliminary animal experiments have shown that some nanoparticles are highly toxic. They were shown to enter the body and move through cellular membranes and damage the animals' lungs, brains, and other organs. Tests on titanium dioxide nanoparticles used in cosmetics, however, did not show these effects by skin contact. But the titanium dioxide was not tested by inhalation, and it should have been. Titanium dioxide is listed as a lung carcinogen by the National Institute for Occupational Safety & Health (NIOSH) and the International Agency for Research on Cancer.[6] Although nanoparticles are common in products today, they should not have been allowed in makeup and other consumer products until each has been tested for toxicity by all routes of entry.

Now the National Institute for Occupational Safety and Health has set a recommended exposure limit for titanium dioxide nanoparticles of 0.3 mgk/m_3 and have noted that the cancer-causing effect is not inherent to the substance, but instead, is a factor directly related to the small particle size and large surface area of the nano particles. And OSHA has a recommended (not enforceable) limit of 0.001 mg/m_3 (i.e. 1 $microgram/m_3$) for carbon nano tubes and all other untested nanoparticles. Since many makeup ingredients and pigments are now in nanoparticle size, these are the kinds of limits unions and workers should want applied to makeup work.

Protection from nano. Workers and consumers exposed to nanoparticle dusts can reduce but not prevent inhalation with ordinary air-purifying respirators or air filters. HEPA filters capture 99.97% of particles 0.3 microns (300 nanometers) in diameter and are much less efficient with smaller particles. Nanoparticles of 5 to 50 nanometers can be in consumer products—well below the size of particle use to test HEPA filters. Ventilation is the preferred method for protection.

In addition, nanoparticles probably absorb through the skin. And no one knows if they can permeate gloves effectively, but it is likely. More research should be done and soon.

Cosmetics. Of great concern is the use of nano-versions of pigments such as iron oxide and zinc oxide in cosmetics and sun screen products. In 2004, a joint report to the British Government by Britain's Royal Society and Royal Academy of Engineering strongly recommended that these nanoparticle-laden cosmetics be kept off the market until proven safe for use on skin.

In 2004, Linda M. Katz, Director of the US Food and Drug Administration's Office of Cosmetics and Colors, said the FDA was examining the nanoparticle issue and expected results within two years. But Katz admitted that the FDA didn't have a list of the cosmetics that contain nanoparticles and that product labels do not identify cosmetics containing nano-sized ingredients. Until this day, no report is available. In other words, consumers have no way to avoid products that contain them.

We are especially concerned that nanoparticles may be in the popular airbrush makeups which may be inhaled as well as skin-absorbed. For example, the FDA has spoken out against tanning booth spray color additives.

6 IARC: Titanium dioxide (IARC Group 2B) Summary of reported data, Feb. 2006, updated, March 10, 2006. It has been considered a carcinogen by NIOSH since 1988.

Airbrushed Cosmetics and Tanning Additives

The FDA's rules restrict various cosmetic ingredients and additives to specific body areas or external use. For example, ingredients approved for use on the cheek may not be approved for use around the eye or on the lips and mucous membranes. And most importantly, cosmetic ingredients and additives are not approved for inhalation.

The FDA's Office of Cosmetics and Colors referred to the restrictive nature of the approvals for cosmetic ingredients in 2003 when the new DHA-Spray Sunless "Tanning" Booths became popular. In these booths, consumers receive an airbrush mist or spray application of dihydroxyacetone (DHA), a cosmetic chemical which gives the skin the appearance of a tan.

DHA is regulated by the FDA as a color additive. On their website, the FDA explains the color additive rules:

The Food, Drug, and Cosmetic Act (FD&C Act), Section 721 authorizes the regulation of color additives, including their uses and restrictions. These regulations are found in Title 21, Code of Federal Regulations (21 CFR), beginning at Part 70. If a color additive is not permitted by regulation or is used in a way that does not comply with the specific regulation(s) authorizing its use, it is considered unsafe under the law. Such misuse of color additives causes a cosmetic to be adulterated.

DHA is listed in the regulations as a color additive for use in imparting color to the human body. However, its use in cosmetics—including sunless "tanning" products—is restricted to external application (21 CFR 73.2150). According to the CFR, "externally applied" cosmetics are those "applied only to external parts of the body and not to the lips or any body surface covered by mucous membrane" (21 CFR 70.3v).

In addition, no color additive may be used in cosmetics intended for use in the area of the eye unless the color additive is permitted specifically for such use (21 CFR 70.5a).[7]

FDA's advice. When exposed to an airbrush mist in the tanning booth, it is difficult to avoid exposure to DHA in ways for which it is not approved such as in the area of the eyes, lips, mucous membranes, or even internally by inhalation. Consequently, FDA advises you to ask the following questions when considering commercial facilities where DHA is applied by spraying or misting:

Are consumers protected from exposure in the entire area of the eyes, in addition to the eyes themselves?

Are consumers protected from exposure on the lips and all parts of the body covered by mucous membrane?

Are consumers protected from internal exposure caused by inhaling or ingesting the product?

If the answer to any of these questions is "no," the FDA says "Consumers should request measures to protect their eyes and mucous membranes and prevent inhalation." This, of course, is impossible. Wearing a respirator and patches over your eyes and mouth would defeat the purpose of a uniform tan. And clearly, FDA's advice applies to all the new theatrical and consumer airbrush makeup that includes color additive ingredients as well. Currently, we are not aware of any airbrush makeups for which all the ingredients are FDA-approved for use both on the skin (e.g. the cheek), around the eyes, and the lips and none that are approved by inhalation. Until such ingredients are developed, we cannot endorse the use of spray or airbrush tanning products or airbrush makeups for either theatrical or consumer applications.

Cancer-Causing Ingredient in some Airbrush Makeups

The cancer status of titanium dioxide (TiO_2) should be the final nail in the coffin for airbrush makeups. No matter how close the applicator is held to the skin, particles get into the air. Titanium dioxide never was approved by FDA for inhalation and now has been shown to cause lung cancer in animal studies. And none of the other airbrush makeup ingredients have been approved or tested by inhalation either. There may be other ingredients that can cause cancer when inhaled.

Titanium dioxide was listed by NIOSH in 1988 as a carcinogen by inhalation. In 2006, the International Agency for Research on Cancer (IARC) listed titanium dioxide as a 2B carcinogen, that is, possibly carcinogenic to humans. And the cancer effects are related to particle size with smaller particles being most toxic.

The good news is that IARC found no evidence that even nanoparticle size TiO_2 will absorb through the skin. Instead, studies of sun screens containing ultrafine TiO_2 on healthy skin of human volunteers revealed that the particles only penetrate into the outermost layers of the skin (stratum corneum). This suggests that healthy skin is an effective barrier to titanium dioxide. Be aware, however, there are no studies on penetration of TiO_2 on damaged or diseased skin.

Other Hazards of Airbrush Makeup

The air sources for the airbrushes are usually either small compressors or compressed gas cylinders. The compressors do not have the special filters for producing breathable air and

7 www.cfsan.fda.gov/~dms/cos-tan4.html as of 2004. The FDA site still says basically the same thing in 2009, but does not include the numbers of the regulations and quote the wording.

most will be contaminated with small amounts of machine oil mist and carbon monoxide.

Carbon dioxide under pressure is usually the gas used for airbrushes. These gases are released freezing cold and can damage skin. They also increase the carbon dioxide levels in the air which can lead to poor air quality if used long or often.

Air and/or gas from the compressor or the cylinder are used commonly at pressures from 4 to 20 lbs. per square inch (psi) for airbrushing makeup. At the higher pressures, the air pressure will pucker the skin and if used near the eye can blow makeup under the lids and even damage the eye.

Art Materials

Tempera paints, water colors, felt-tip markers, and other art materials are sometimes substituted for cosmetics for face painting or makeup effects in amateur and nonprofessional situations. However, art materials are never suitable for use as cosmetics.

The pigments, dyes, and other ingredients in art materials are not cosmetic grade chemicals and are not safe for use on the skin. Even art materials labeled "non-toxic" are safe only when used for the label-directed artistic purpose. The person responsible for applying the art materials to the clients' skin can be held legally liable for any damages related to this off-label use.

Special Effect Makeups

Putty, wax, beeswax, and Mortician's Wax all can be used to build up a part of the face for theatrical purposes. Collodion can be used to fake age or scars. Natural rubber latex can be made to function in many of these ways, and it also acts as a glue or adhesive, as does spirit gum.

Spirit is an old term applied to alcohol solvents (usually ethyl alcohol). Gum can mean any exudate of a number of plants or trees. Spirit gums today usually are a mixture of natural and synthetic resins in ethyl alcohol. Ideally, the resins should all be identified so users can know if they are likely to have an allergy to one or more of them.

Many people are allergic to these products. One well-known makeup artist told of a case of spirit gum allergy severe enough to require hospital treatment. Another makeup expert avoided an actor's allergy to spirit gum by placing surgical adhesive tape on his face before applying the spirit gum. Collodion allergies are also well known. People who are allergic to one of these products usually can find another that will do.

Spirit gum can be replaced with synthetic resin surgical adhesives in some cases. Removing spirit gum and adhesives by pulling them off the skin can be harmful, as can removing them with acetone or alcohol, which can dry or crack the skin. Some spirit gum removers are mixtures of solvents that even include toxic chlorinated solvents and skin-absorbing methanol. Take care using these products by peeling spirit gum off gently and using as little solvent as possible. Once removed, use oil, emollients, or moisturizers on the skin to counter drying effects.

Nail products. Nail polishes, properly used by consumers, only expose them to small amounts of toxic solvents. Nail salons, on the other hand, should have vented application tables for workers using them all day. Three states, Oregon, Massachusetts, and most recently, New York, have passed laws that require personal protective equipment and ventilation for nail salons. Air quality tests for solvents, formaldehyde, and other chemicals, combined with reports of worker health effects, made the case that these steps are necessary.

Polish removers contain toxic and flammable solvent such as acetone and/or ethyl acetate. The liquid nail products which harden to create long false nails often contain acrylate monomers that harden into plastic. The room where such products are used should have good general ventilation plus the addition of local exhaust tables for the application of the products (example of a local exhaust nail table is in Figure C.1).

Applicators should wear gloves since these products are also associated with transmission of nail fungal infections. These infections are hard to treat and may result in disfigurement of the nails.

Artificial nails must never be used on stage when special effects involving fire, candles, or smoking are done on stage. The fact that long artificial fingernails are a fire hazard was established in a study conducted at Lamar University chemistry lab in Beaumont, Texas.[8]

When in contact with a Bunsen burner flame, 87% of the sample nails ignited in 1 second or less. When a birthday candle was used as the ignition source, 85% of the nails ignited in a second or less.

All of the synthetic nails burned to completion. When victims see their nails on fire, they typically fling a hand, vigorously sending burning drops of melted plastic flying.

When Skin or Eye Trouble Strikes

When skin or eye problems arise, consult an ophthalmologist or dermatologist who can diagnose your problem and tell you

8 Reported by Chemical Health & Safety, Jan./Feb. 2000, p. 45 from a study by: Vanover, W.G., Woods, J.L. and Allen, S.B., in *J. Chem. Educ.*, 1999, 76(11), p. 1521.

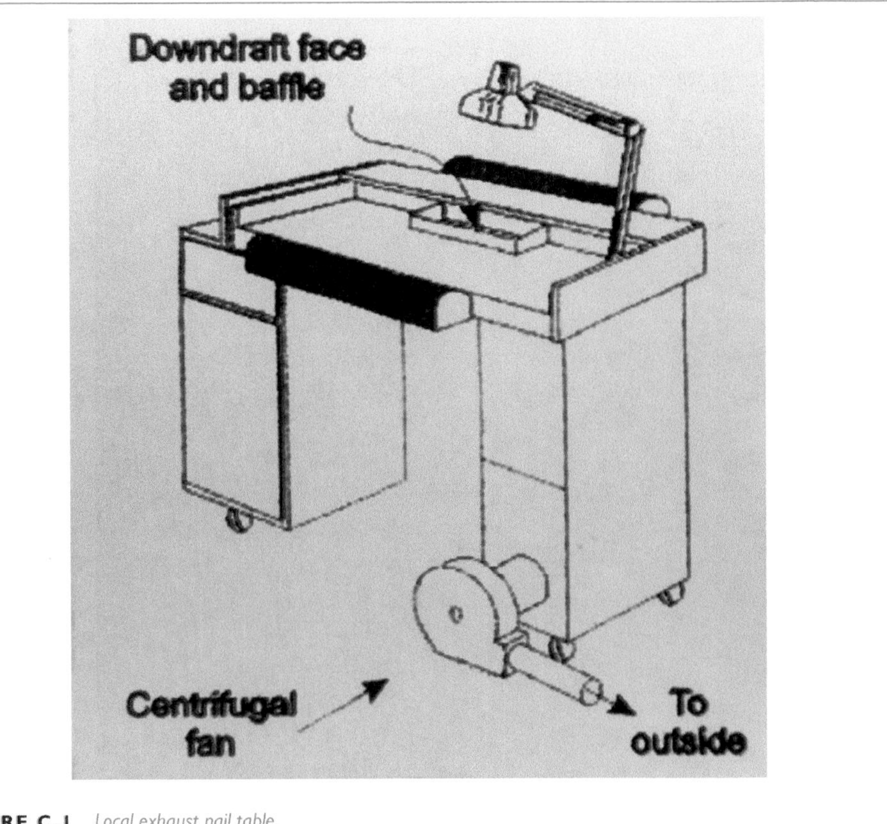

FIGURE C.1 *Local exhaust nail table.*

how to treat it. In general, if your problem is diagnosed as an eye or skin infection, follow the doctor's advice and replace all your cosmetics with new, uncontaminated ones.

If the problem is diagnosed as irritant dermatitis or cosmetic acne, you should identify the offending cosmetic and not use it again until healing is complete. If the doctor determines you are allergic to a particular product or ingredient, there are several steps you can take:

1. Try "hypoallergenic" makeup. The term "hypoallergenic" is unregulated so you are depending on the manufacturer's integrity alone. However, reputable manufacturers honestly try to eliminate those ingredients known to produce allergies in many people.
2. Try unscented makeups or products with a wholly different scent. One person in ten has an allergy to fragrances and you may be one of them.
3. Try a makeup with a different preservative. Preservatives are known to cause allergic dermatitis in some people. Three preservatives recognized as especially hyper-allergenic are Quaternium 15, imidazol idinyl urea, and parabens (both methyl and propyl parabens). Try to avoid them.
4. Try comparing labels of products to which you respond, looking for an ingredient they have in common and avoid it.

General Rules for Makeup Users

1. Use only cosmetic products on your skin. Never use airbrush makeups or tanning products which can be inhaled. Never use paints, dyes, or other non-cosmetic substances on the skin.
2. Purchase only ingredient-labeled cosmetics. Many good professional theatrical brands of makeup are now ingredient-labeled.
3. Use makeups only as directed. Use face makeup only on the face, eye makeup on the eyes, and so on.
4. Eliminate products which contain ingredients known to cause allergies in many people such as natural rubber, or products with toxic ingredients such as solvents.
5. Wash your hands before and after applying makeup.
6. Never lend your makeup to anyone, and never borrow or accept used makeup from anyone.

7. Do not use aerosol sprays or airbrush products unless: a) there is local ventilation in the dressing room or makeup room which can protect both the client and the applicator from inhalation of the ingredients; and b) none of the ingredients in the makeup are deposited on areas of the skin for which they are not FDA-approved.
8. Replace old cosmetics regularly. Do not buy cosmetics which look old or shopworn. Once opened, discard cosmetics after 6 months or sooner. Discard after an eye or skin infection.
9. Avoid creating clouds of face powder or talcum which can be inhaled. Discard old face and bath powders.
10. Moisten brushes or pencils with clean tap water, not with saliva.
11. Seek medical advice and treatment for eye injuries, dermatitis, acne, and other skin and eye conditions.
12. Avoid smoking, eating, or drinking when applying makeup. Do not smoke or stay in dressing rooms where others smoke.
13. When removing spirit gum, latex, etc., avoid prolonged skin contact with solvents like acetone; replace lost skin oils and moisture.

Precautions for Makeup Artists

1. *Ventilation.* Makeup artists are going to spend long hours in the makeup room and need to insist that the ventilation be sufficient for the products used. Most makeup rooms only have inlets in the ceiling for a recirculating ventilation system. Such rooms clearly are not ventilated sufficiently for spray and airbrush products.

    Ideally, makeup rooms should have an exhaust fan or local hood system if sprays are going to be used. The author has seen makeup tables with slot ventilation built around the makeup mirror. At the Santa Fe Opera, the makeup table has a slot vent above the mirror (see Figure C.2); and there are wig room tables with even better slot vents above the mirrors at the Santa Fe Opera (see Figure C.3). In another theater, there were small 2 x 2 square foot spray booths installed for spraying wigs. These kinds of systems should become a standard in the industry.

2. *Monitoring.* Since makeup ingredients are not approved for uses in which inhalation will occur, airbrush makeup should simply not be done. But if the employer insists and the artist is a member of a union, their safety reps should negotiate with management to hire trained industrial hygienists to set up personal monitoring of exposed makeup artists for titanium dioxide (TiO_2) in respirable and nanoparticle sizes using the following standards:

FIGURE C.2 *Slot ventilation system.*

FIGURE C.3 *Slot ventilation system.*

OSHA PEL-TWA total dust, enforceable	= 15 mg/m_3 ACGIH TLV-TWA respirable (<10 microns)	=	1 mg/m_3 NIOSH REL-TWA respirable (<10 microns for TiO_2)	=	2.4 mg/m_3 mg/m_3 NIOSH REL-TWA nanoparticle (< 0.1 microns for TiO_2) =	0.3 mg/m_3 mg/m_3 OSHA recommended limit for carbon nanoparticles	=	0.001 mg/m_3 mg/m_3 (1 ìg/m_3)

(Not enforceable—See OSHA FactSheet on Nanoparticles) OSHA PEL-TWA (Occupational Safety and Health Administration Permissable Exposure Level); ACGIH TLV-TWA (American Conference of Governmental Industrial Hygienists, Inc Time-Weight Average.

We need to work together to demand that monitoring during heavy use of airbrush makeups in the professional setting be done. There currently is no data on this obvious potential hazard.

3. *Safe and Sanitary.* Makeup artists should wash their hands before they start on each client. They should also be observant about the skin condition of their clients and use gloves if open sores, acne, or signs of skin disease are present. Gloves must be changed between clients.
4. *Group Makeup Precautions.* Makeup artists need to insure that their clients' makeup is not shared. Cream sticks and lipsticks can be sliced into pieces and put into small containers and labeled with each client's name. Sponges and applicators should be disposable. Powders can be supplied to each in the smallest possible containers. Eyeliners and mascara should not be shared. The water used to moisten pencils or brushes should be changed for each client. Paper cups can be used to make cleaning water containers unnecessary.
5. *Training.* Makeup artists need training about blood-borne pathogens, in how blood-borne and skin diseases are transmitted, how to dispose of contaminated applicators or sponges, and similar skills. This material is included in cosmetology licensing exams as well. In addition, makeup artists also need OSHA hazard communication

training about the chemicals in makeup, spray products, disinfectants, and other toxic products.

Cosmetics & HAZCOM

HAZCOM, or the OSHA Hazard Communication Standard (29 CFR 1910.1200) requires employers to provide a program for their workers consisting in part of worker training and access to MSDSs on all potentially hazardous products in the workplace.

In a 1994 federal register notice from OSHA clarifying some of the HAZCOM rules (59 FR No. 27, Wed. February 9, 1994, p. 6150) there was the following comment (quote):

> **Cosmetics. OSHA has separated the exemptions applying to cosmetics and placed them in a new subparagraph, but has not changed the substance of the requirements. Cosmetics are exempt when packaged for sale to consumers in a retail establishment, and when brought into the workplace for employee consumption. Otherwise, they are covered by the rule when they contain hazardous chemicals.**

In other words, employees bringing in their own makeup for personal use is not an OSHA issue, but professionals using cosmetics in the workplace as part of their job is. These workers must have training in the hazards and access to the employer's written program and the MSDSs on the cosmetics products they use which contain hazardous chemicals. The definition of hazardous includes all regulated common makeup minerals such as talc, kaolin, and forms of silica; all of the organic chemical solvents such as alcohols, acetone, ethyl acetate, and the like; the propellant gases used in spray cans such as propane and butane; all the inorganic pigments such as those containing chrome, manganese, and cobalt; and more. There are very few cosmetics that contain no chemicals that are considered hazardous under the OSHA definition.

I am especially concerned when makeup products originally formulated for hand application are now being used in airbrush form. In this case, the regulated minerals and pigments, including titanium dioxide which is now listed as a lung carcinogen, are being made airborne and inhaled. FDA does not approve any of the makeup ingredients for inhalation which makes this form of makeup unapproved for use.

The data sheet on theatrical makeup (the HAZCOM 29 CFR 1910.1200) covers this and many other aspects of the hazards of cosmetics and can serve as HAZCOM training material:

Monona Rossol, 3/27/09

from April 2012 ACTS FACTS:

LAWSUIT ALLEGING COSMETIC TALC CAUSED MESOTHELIOMA MAY PROCEED: JUDGE RULES

SOURCE: "Suit Claiming Injury From Alleged Asbestos in Talc May Proceed," by Brendan Pierson, *New York Law Journal*, corrected version, March 19, 2012: www.fda.gov/Cosmetics/ProductandIngredientSafety/SelectedCosmeticIngredients/ucm293184

A lawsuit filed by a woman who alleges she developed mesothelioma from using a cosmetic product tainted with asbestos is not preempted by the federal Food, Drugs and Cosmetics Act because that law's preemption clause, added in 1997, is not retroactive, a Manhattan judge has ruled (*Feinberg v. Colgate-Palmolive Co.*, 190070/11, 2/22/12, Supreme Ct. Justice Sherry Klein Heitler).

The suit, filed by Arlene Feinberg and her husband Jacob Feinberg, alleges that Ms. Feinberg developed mesothelioma from using Colgate-Palmolive's Cashmere Bouquet talcum powder from the 1950s through 1980s. The suit claims the product contained asbestos. The Feinbergs included a charge of "failure to warn," which alleges the company should have included a warning label on the powder. Colgate moved to dismiss on the grounds that the failure to warn claims was preempted by the Food, Drugs and Cosmetics Act, which regulates the labeling of products. In 1997, the FD&C Act was amended to include a clause saying that it preempted state law on the issue of cosmetic labeling, thus protecting manufacturers from failure to warn claims.

Justice Heitler wrote, "Colgate's motion must be denied because it seeks to apply the 1997 Preemption Clause to events that had their genesis more than 45 years before it existed, and which ceased to occur almost 20 years before Congress sought to legislate the labeling of cosmetic products."

COMMENT: A picture of the old pale orange can of talcum is on New York Law's website. I see these cans in prop rental houses for use in period sets and in antique shops. The talc issue was not over in the 1980s when a new container was designed. A study of cosmetic talcs in 1991 found traces of asbestos in six of 15 samples.* We really don't know if it is still a problem today or not.

Recent questions about talc caused the FDA to do a "study" of talc which is on their website. Along with the study, the FDA's limited powers are well defined. In their own words, "cosmetic products and ingredients, with the exception of color additives, do not have to undergo FDA review or approval before they go on the market." And "the law does not require [manufacturers] to share their safety information with FDA." Further, FDA can't act until they have "sound scientific data to show that it is harmful under its intended use." They claim they monitor the industry for potential safety problems, but let's look at how well they monitored talc in this study released in September of 2010.

First, FDA doesn't have asbestos monitoring equipment, so they contracted the tests for the study to another lab. Only four talc suppliers and cosmetic products containing talcs from these suppliers were tested. These four suppliers' mines are ones that have had clean deposits confirmed for many years, but talc is mined all over the world with the largest suppliers being China and India.

Perhaps, if a jury in this lawsuit against Colgate can decide that asbestos fibers in talc caused mesothelioma in this Plaintiff, there will be a course of action for other injured consumers. This is what happened with an industrial talc from RT Vanderbilt used in ceramics. In any case, it looks like we can't rely on the regulators. It is just a shame that people need to die first.

*Blount, Alice M., "Amphibole Content of Cosmetic and Pharmaceutical Talcs," *Environmental Health Perspectives*, Vol. 94, 1991, pp. 225–230.

APPENDIX D
SPECIAL EFFECT CONTACT LENSES

Contributed by: AAV Media LLC

Aimee Surtenich, Executive Editor

Want to look like a vampire? Or show your support of your favorite professional sports team by wearing its logo on your eyes? You can do this and more with decorative special effect contact lenses.

Special effect contacts—including black contact lenses, Halloween contact lenses, and other "crazy" lenses—are soft contact lenses that are available for theatrical and novelty uses.

Just like colored contact lenses, special effect (FX) or crazy contacts can be used whether or not you normally wear eyeglasses or contact lenses, because most types are available both with and without lens powers to correct nearsightedness, farsightedness, and/or astigmatism.

It's important to note that *all* contact lenses, including Plano Halloween contacts and any other special effect contacts, are classified as medical devices by the FDA (Food and Drug Administration) and require a valid contact lens prescription from a licensed eye care practitioner.

Theatrical or novelty lenses are safe to wear—but only when they are properly prescribed and cared for, and purchased from a legitimate source. Bacterial eye infections from contaminated, poorly fitted, or improperly worn special effect contact lenses can occur rapidly, causing a painful corneal ulcer and even blindness.

Putting the finishing touch to your Halloween costume is not worth a sight-threatening eye infection from improper contact lens use (read our Safety Checklist, p. 421).

How Do Special Effect Contacts Work?

Special effect contact lenses have an opaque (non-transparent) tint to completely mask your natural eye color and are available in a wide variety of dramatic colors and designs. The center of the lens, which lies over your pupil, is clear so you can see.

Most novelty or costume contact lenses cover just the colored portion of your eye (iris), but special effect scleral lenses, like all-black, red yellow or white contacts, cover both the iris and the "white" (sclera) of your eyes to create a truly haunting look.

Special Effect Contact Lenses: Trends And Designs

Black sclera contact lenses, white contact lenses, wild eyes, cat eyes—whichever you choose, there's a huge array of Halloween contact lenses to add the ultimate finishing touch to your Halloween costume.

Current trends in theatrical or novelty contact lenses are inspired by movies and cult TV shows. These include the popular black, white, and yellow special effect scleral contact lenses, as worn on the cult TV show *True Blood*; red and amber-colored contacts like those worn in *Twilight*, *New Moon*, and *Breaking Dawn*; and Goth contact lenses in patterns of red, black, white, and yellow which channel *The Exorcist*.

Other movie character special effect lenses include vivid green "Mad Hatter" colored contacts inspired by the movie *Alice in Wonderland*, yellow "alien" contacts as featured in *Avatar*, and even yellow cat eyes like those seen in *Harry Potter*.

Crazy contact lenses remain popular, too. These include zombie, vampire, and other supernatural designs such as spider webs, cat eyes, and werewolves—perfect for adding the "wow" factor to your Halloween or special occasion costume.

If you want even scarier looking contact lenses, there are mesh-look contacts and even neon glow-in-the-dark UV lenses! Special effect contact lenses aren't a recent fad. Morton Greenspoon OD, a pioneer of theatrical lenses, has been providing special effect contact lenses to the film industry since the 1950s.

Dr. Greenspoon has changed Elvis Presley's baby blues to brown for the movie *Flaming Star*, provided Michael Jackson's wolf eyes for the "Thriller" music video, and has received an Academy Award nomination for his work on *Bram Stoker's Dracula*. His most recent film work includes *Pirates of the Caribbean* and the *Twilight Saga*.

But you don't have to walk the red carpet to wear crazy contact lenses. With the array of special effect lenses available today, you too can get into character and portray your favorite Hollywood star.

Do You Need a Prescription?

Yes—while novelty contacts are designed for fun, they still are considered medical devices and cannot be purchased legally in the US without a contact lens prescription.

You must see your eye doctor or have a contact lens exam to have them properly fitted and prescribed, even if you have perfect eyesight and don't need corrective eyewear.

Contact lenses—including special effect lenses—are not a "one-size-fits-all." A poor lens fit can lead to eye infection, corneal ulcer, decreased vision, and even blindness.

Circle Contact Lenses

Circle lenses are a relatively recent phenomenon. Also called "big eye" lenses, they make your eyes look larger than normal to produce a doll-like appearance, inspired by doe-eyed anime cartoon characters. Many companies sell circle contact lenses illegally, which increases the risk of eye health complications. Issues concerning the safety of circle lenses have been well documented in the US media in recent years. Many companies selling circle lenses in the US do so illegally, either without requesting a prescription or selling unapproved lenses—or both.

To help avoid the risk of developing a serious lens-related eye infection, always ensure you are buying contact lenses from a legitimate source.

Where to Buy Theatrical and Special Effect Contacts

By law, your eye doctor must give you a copy of your contact lens prescription if you request it, which means you have the option of buying contact lenses from any eye care professional (ECP), optical chains, and legitimate online retailers.

The cost of contact lenses with special effect designs is comparable to that of more conventional color contact lenses designed to enhance or change your eye color.

Custom hand-painted designs, however, can cost significantly more.

To ensure a safe wearing experience, always buy your special effect contact lenses from an authorized source.

Never buy special effect contacts at any store that doesn't ask you for a valid contact lens prescription.

Don't buy contact lenses from a flea market, street vendor, beauty salon, Halloween store, or similar setting. Such sales are illegal in the US, and for good reasons:

- You might be getting unsafe products that are not FDA-approved for sale in the US. Don't risk your eyes on products that may have been manufactured improperly or don't have sterile packaging.
- Even wearing FDA-approved lenses can be dangerous, if they haven't been specifically fitted to your eyes. Poor-fitting contact lenses can cause serious vision problems, corneal abrasions, and infections. Plus, they probably won't be comfortable to wear!

According to a 2015 consumer survey sponsored by the American Optometric Association (AOA), 26% of Americans who purchased non-corrective color or special effect contact lenses did not have a valid prescription for the lenses from an eye doctor.

Also, a study published recently in the professional journal *Investigative Ophthalmology & Visual Science* found that people wearing cosmetic contact lenses (defined as decorative, color, and non-corrective lenses, often obtained without a prescription) had more than 16 times greater risk of developing an eye infection than people wearing standard corrective contact lenses prescribed by an eye doctor.

Five Must-Knows About Halloween Contact Lenses

- To buy them, you need a prescription from a qualified ECP—even if they're just for looks and aren't correcting your vision.

- Retailers who sell Halloween contacts but don't require a Rx (a Doctor's prescription) are selling them illegally. Don't trust illegal sources! Often they sell non-sterile or expired lenses. They don't care about your eyes—they just want your money.
- As with other contact lenses, you must clean Halloween contacts properly and store them in a clean case. Your ECP can provide instructions.
- Never, ever, ever share them with anyone. This can lead to serious eye problems.
- The most popular costumes that incorporate Halloween contacts are zombies, vampires, and aliens.

Safety Checklist

1. Visit your eye doctor for a contact lens exam, fitting, and prescription (regardless of whether you need vision correction).
2. Buy contact lenses from a licensed ECP or an eyewear retailer that requires you to have a prescription. Never buy contact lenses from an unlicensed source that doesn't require a prescription. Doing so greatly increases your risk of serious eye problems.
3. Always follow your ECP's instructions for wearing and caring for your contact lenses, and visit your eye doctor for follow-up eye exams.
4. Never share your contact lenses! While it may seem like a fun idea to swap special effect lenses with our friends, sharing contacts can spread harmful bacteria and may result in serious eye health problems, including loss of vision.
5. Keep in mind that "crazy" contact lenses generally are designed for daily wear only and are not FDA-approved to be worn overnight.
6. If you experience any eye redness, swelling, or discomfort, immediately remove your contact lenses and contact your eye doctor as soon as possible. This could be the sign of a potentially sight-threatening eye infection.
7. Wear only hypoallergenic, non-toxic makeup. If makeup is used on a child's face, it should be applied and removed by an adult. For removal, use eye makeup remover or cold cream, not soap.
8. Be aware that false eyelashes also can cause eye irritation. Carefully follow the manufacturer's instructions regarding safe application and removal. And read the safety information on eyelash extensions if you're considering those, because they too can irritate eyes.

Protect Yourself and Others from Illegal Contact Lenses

Decorative contact lenses sold without a prescription at convenience stores, flea markets, and online can cause serious eye infections, impaired vision, and even blindness.

In October 2016, the US Immigration and Customs Enforcement (ICE) agency announced that ICE, the FDA and US Customs and Border Protection (CBP) combined efforts to make several hundred seizures totaling around 100,000 pairs of counterfeit, illegal, and unapproved contact lenses. The enforcement actions were conducted under the FDA-led initiative dubbed Operation Double Vision, which is an ongoing effort to protect the health and safety of the American public from illegal contact lenses.

Testing of confiscated illegal lenses revealed many had high levels of bacteria that could cause significant eye infections. Also, the coloring of some decorative contact lenses were made of lead-based materials that could leach directly into the eye.

The agency urged consumers that anyone interested in wearing any type of contact lenses should visit an eye doctor, obtain a prescription, and purchase them from a licensed provider.

"A valid prescription helps ensure consumers get contact lenses that are determined to be safe and effective by the FDA. Without it, people can risk serious eye injuries or loss of eyesight for one night of fun," said George M. Karavetsos, Director, FDA's Office of Criminal Investigations in the ICE press release.

To protect yourself and others, if you see Halloween contacts or other contact lenses being sold without a prescription online or elsewhere, report it to the FDA.

About the Author: Aimee Surtenich has many years of editorial experience in consumer publishing, with an emphasis on the health, pharmaceutical, and beauty fields. Previously she was the executive editor for a website.

INDEX

Note: Page numbers in *italic* refer to figures in the text.

T - #0219 - 271119 - C0 - 279/216/26 [28] - CB - 9781138232587